Roman Alcester Series

Volume 3

ROMAN ALCESTER: NORTHERN EXTRAMURAL AREA

1969–1988 EXCAVATIONS

Roman Alcester Series

Volume 3

ROMAN ALCESTER: NORTHERN EXTRAMURAL AREA

1969–1988 EXCAVATIONS

by Paul Booth and Jeremy Evans

with contributions by
Denise Allen, Peter Cheer, Judson Chesterman, Susan Colledge,
Pam Copson, Stephen Cracknell, John Crossling, Brenda Dickinson,
Edith Evans, Rowan Ferguson, Kay Hartley, Martin Henig,
Glenys Lloyd-Morgan, Mark Maltby, Gerry McDonnell,
Graham Morgan, Quita Mould, Christine Osborne,
Stephanie Ratkai, Wilfred A Seaby, Ann Stirland,
Stephen J Taylor and Margaret Ward

edited by John Chadderton with Joseph Elders and Nicholas Palmer

**CBA Research Report 127
Council for British Archaeology
2001**

Published 2001 by the Council for British Archaeology
Bowes Morrell House, 111 Walmgate, York YO1 9WA

Copyright © Authors and Council for British Archaeology
All rights reserved

British Library Cataloguing in Publication Data
A catalogue for this book is available from the British Library

ISSN 0141 7819

ISBN 1-902771-22-2

Typeset from authors' disks by Archetype IT Ltd, Condicote, Cheltenham
website: www.archetype-it.com

Printed in Great Britain by Henry Ling Ltd., at the Dorset Press, Dorchester, Dorset

Front cover   Trench 1, section drawing (AL 28)

Contents

List of figures ... ix
List of plates ... xiii
List of tables ... xiv
Summary ... xvi
Acknowledgements ... xviii

Introduction *by Paul Booth, John Chadderton, and Jeremy Evans* ... 1
    Site summaries ... 1
    Presentation of the evidence ... 6

1969 and 1972 Baromix excavations (ALC 69 and ALC 72/2) *by Jeremy Evans* ... 7
    Introduction ... 7
    1969 excavations (ALC 69) ... 7
    1972 excavations (ALC 72/2) ... 18
    Baromix 1969 and 1972 phase dates ... 25

1969 and 1972 Baromix finds (ALC 69 and ALC 72/2) ... 27
    Roman coins (ALC 69 and ALC 72/2) *by Wilfred A Seaby* ... 27
    Roman pottery (ALC 69 and ALC 72/2) *by Rowan Ferguson with contributions by Margaret Ward and Jeremy Evans* ... 28
    Glass (ALC 69 and ALC 72/2) *by Denise Allen* ... 67
    Copper alloy (ALC 69 and ALC 72/2) *by Glenys Lloyd-Morgan* ... 70
    Iron and lead (ALC 69 and ALC 72/2) *by Quita Mould* ... 77
    Metalworking slag (ALC 69 and ALC 72/2) *by Gerry McDonnell* ... 83
    Worked bone (ALC 69 and ALC 72/2) *by Glenys Lloyd-Morgan* ... 83
    Stone objects (ALC 69) *by Glenys Lloyd-Morgan* ... 86
    Ceramic object (ALC 69) *by Jeremy Evans* ... 88
    Discussion of the ALC 69 and ALC 72/2 finds *by Jeremy Evans* ... 89

1988 Baromix excavations (AL 28) ... 92
    Excavation summary (AL 28) *by Stephen Cracknell and Jeremy Evans* ... 92
    Roman coin (AL 28) *by Wilfred A Seaby* ... 95
    Roman pottery (AL 28) *by Jeremy Evans and Margaret Ward* ... 96
    Glass (AL 28) *by Glenys Lloyd-Morgan* ... 102
    Copper alloy (AL 28) *by Glenys Lloyd-Morgan* ... 103
    Worked bone (AL 28) *by Glenys Lloyd-Morgan* ... 103
    Discussion of the AL 28 finds *by Jeremy Evans* ... 103

Lloyds Bank excavations (ALB 75) 104
    Excavations (ALB 75) *by Edith Evans and Jeremy Evans* 104
    Discussion (ALB 75) *by Jeremy Evans* 114

Lloyds Bank finds (ALB 75) 116
    Pre-Roman and Roman coins (ALB 75) *by Wilfred A Seaby* 116
    Roman and Saxon pottery (ALB 75) *by Jeremy Evans* 116
    Symbol gem (ALB 75) *by Martin Henig* 121
    Selected copper alloy objects (ALB 75) *by Glenys Lloyd-Morgan* 122
    Human skeletal remains (ALB 75) *by Judson Chesterman and Christine Osborne* 122

Explosion site excavations (AES 76–7) *by Paul Booth* 124
    Introduction 124
    Early occupation (periods 1–4) 127
    Major Roman buildings (periods 5–9) 135
    Late Roman developments (periods 10 and 10A) 160
    Summary of the medieval occupation (periods 11–12) 168
    Summary of the post-medieval and modern developments (periods 13–14) 169

Explosion site finds (AES 76–7) 173
    Roman coins (AES 76–7) *by Wilfred A Seaby and Paul Booth* 173
    Roman pottery (AES 76–7) *by Rowan Ferguson with Brenda Dickinson* 177
    Medieval pottery (AES 76–7) *by Stephanie Ratkai* 232
    Copper alloy (AES 76–7) *by Glenys Lloyd-Morgan* 232
    Lead (AES 76–7) *by Paul Booth* 239
    Iron (AES 76–7) *by Quita Mould* 241
    Jet and shale (AES 76–7) *by Glenys Lloyd-Morgan* 247
    Worked bone (AES 76–7) *by Glenys Lloyd-Morgan* 249
    Glass (AES 76–7) *by Denise Allen* 255
    Metalworking slags and furnace residues (AES 76–7) *by Gerry McDonnell* 259
    Crucibles (AES 76–7) *by Paul Booth* 259
    Stone objects (AES 76–7) *by Paul Booth with John Crossling* 260
    Building stone (AES 76–7) *by Paul Booth with John Crossling* 260
    Roman tile (AES 76–7) *by Peter Cheer and Paul Booth* 262
    Other building materials (AES 76–7) *by Paul Booth* 264
    Faunal remains (AES 76–7) *by Mark Maltby* 265
    Plant remains from the period 2 well (168A) (AES 76–7) *by Susan Colledge* 290
    Charcoal and coal (AES 76–7) *by Paul Booth with Pam Copson* 293

Explosion site discussion (AES 76–7) *by Paul Booth* 294
    Chronological development of the site 294
    Function and economy of the site 298

The northern suburbs and the development of Roman Alcester
by Paul Booth and Jeremy Evans 301
    Origins of the town 301
    Urban topography and the 'fort' 303
    Civil development of the northern suburbs 305
    Social and economic evidence 306

Bibliography 309

Index 318

Microfiche

1969 and 1972 Baromix finds (ALC 69 and ALC 72/2)
    Roman pottery (ALC 69 and ALC 72/2) *by Rowan Ferguson and Jeremy Evans* M1:A5

    Glass catalogue (ALC 69 and ALC 72/2) *by Denise Allen* M1:B13

    Silver and copper alloy catalogue (ALC 69 and ALC 72/2) *by Glenys Lloyd-Morgan* M1:C3

    Iron and lead catalogue (ALC 69 and ALC 72/2) *by Quita Mould* M1:C10

    Iron nails (ALC 69 and ALC 72/2) *by Quita Mould* M1:D1

    Metalworking slag list (ALC 69 and ALC 72/2) *by Gerry McDonnell* M1:D7

    Stone object catalogue (ALC 69 and ALC 72/2) *by Glenys Lloyd-Morgan* M1:D8

    Building stone (ALC 69 and 72/2) *by Jeremy Evans* M1:D10

    Ceramic objects (ALC 69) *by Jeremy Evans* M1:D10

    Fired clay objects (ALC 69) *by Jeremy Evans* M1:D11

    Flints (ALC 69 and 72/2) *by Rowan Ferguson* M1:D11

    Human bone (ALC 72/2) *by Ann Stirland* M1:D11

1988 Baromix excavations (AL 28)
    Detailed structural account (AL 28) *by Stephen Cracknell and Jeremy Evans* M1:D12

    Finds summary tables (AL 28) *by Jeremy Evans* M1:E4

    Roman pottery fabric proportions (AL 28) *by Jeremy Evans* M1:E8

    List of metalworking slag and iron objects (AL 28) *by Jeremy Evans* M1:E9

    Worked stone (AL 28) *by Jeremy Evans* M1:E9

Lloyds Bank excavations (ALB 75)
    Detailed structural account (ALB 75) *by Edith Evans and Jeremy Evans* M1:E10

Lloyds Bank finds (ALB 75)
    Stratified and phased small finds (ALB 75) *by Jeremy Evans* M1:F5

    Post-Roman coins (ALB 75) *by Wilfred A Seaby* M1:F7

    Medieval pottery spot dating evidence (ALB 75) *by Stephanie Ratkai* M1:F7

    Human skeletal remains inventory (ALB 75) *by Judson Chesterman and Christine Osborne* M1:F8

Explosion site excavations (AES 76–7)

    Summary context list (AES 76–7) *by Paul Booth* M1:G3

    Detailed structural account of medieval and post-medieval periods 11–14 (AES 76–7) *by Paul Booth* M1:G13

Explosion site finds (AES 76–7)

    Roman coin catalogue (AES 76–7) *by Wilfred A Seaby* M2:A5

    Roman pottery tables (AES 76–7) *by Rowan Ferguson* M2:B1

    Samian ware catalogue (AES 76–7) *by Brenda Dickinson* M2:C9

    Medieval pottery (AES 76–7) *by Stephanie Ratkai* M2:D7

    Copper alloy catalogue (AES 76–7) *by Glenys Lloyd-Morgan* M2:D13

    Lead object catalogue (AES 76–7) *by Paul Booth* M2:E6

    Iron objects by period (AES 76–7) *by Quita Mould* M2:E8

    Bone object catalogue (AES 76–7) *by Glenys Lloyd-Morgan* M2:E11

    Metallurgical analyses (AES 76–7 *by Gerry McDonnell* M2:F3

    Mortar and plaster (AES 76–7) *by Graham Morgan* M2:F5

    Faunal remains tables (AES 76–7) *by Mark Maltby* M2:F9

List of figures

Introduction

1   Alcester in its Roman regional setting
2   Locations of excavations in Alcester prior to 1989
3   Roman Alcester, main elements

1969 and 1972 Baromix excavations (ALC 69 and ALC 72/2)

4   Location of Baromix excavations (ALC 69, ALC 72/2, and AL 28)
5   Key to plans and sections (ALC 69, ALC 72/2, AL 28, and ALB 75)
6   ALC 69, phases A and B, plans
7   ALC 69, northern section
8   ALC 69, phases C and D, plans
9   ALC 69, phases E and F, plans
10   ALC 69, phases G and H, plans
11   ALC 72/2, phase A, plan
12   ALC 72/2, section 1, west edge of trench
13   ALC 72/2, phase B, plan
14   ALC 72/2, phase C, plan
15   ALC 72/2, phase D, plan
16   ALC 72/2, phase E, plan
17   ALC 72/2, phase F, plan
18   ALC 72/2, phase G, plan
19   Phase sequence diagram (ALC 69 and ALC 72/2)

1969 and 1972 Baromix finds (ALC 69 and ALC 72/2)

20   Proportions of Roman pottery from each phase (ALC 69 and ALC 72/2)
21   Roman pottery, major fabric class proportions by phase (ALC 69)
22   Roman pottery, major fabric class proportions by phase (ALC 72/2)
23   Decorated samian ware (ALC 69), nos 3, 7, 11, 14, 24–5, 28, 35, and 41–2
24   ALC 69, phase A, date distribution of samian ware
25   ALC 69, phase B, date distribution of samian ware
26   ALC 69, phase C, date distribution of samian ware
27   ALC 69, phase D, date distribution of samian ware
28   ALC 69, phase E, date distribution of samian ware
29   ALC 69, phase F, date distribution of samian ware
30   Decorated samian ware (ALC 69), nos 48, 56, and 59
31   ALC 69, phase G, date distribution of samian ware
32   ALC 69, date distribution of all samian ware
33   ALC 69, date distribution of all stamped samian
34   ALC 69, date distribution of all decorated samian
35   Decorated samian ware (ALC 72/2), nos 1, 4, 6, 8, 11, 12–3, 17, 19, 21–2, and 33–4
36   ALC 72/2, phase B, date distribution of samian ware
37   ALC 72/2, phase C, date distribution of samian ware
38   ALC 72/2, phase D, date distribution of samian ware
39   ALC 72/2, phase E, date distribution of samian ware
40   ALC 72/2, phase F, date distribution of samian ware
41   ALC 72/2, phase G, date distribution of samian ware
42   ALC 72/2, date distribution of all samian ware
43   ALC 72/2, date distribution of all decorated samian
44   Functional analysis of vessels by phase (ALC 69 and ALC 72/2)
45   Coarse pottery (ALC 69, phase A), nos 1–29

46	Coarse pottery (ALC 72/2, phases A and B, and ALC 69, phase B), nos 30–45
47	Coarse pottery (ALC 69, phases C and D, and ALC 72/2, phase C), nos 46–67
48	Coarse pottery (ALC 69, phase D), nos 68–90
49	Coarse pottery (ALC 72/2, phases D and E, and ALC 69, phase E), nos 91–115
50	Coarse pottery (ALC 69, phase F), nos 116–146
51	Coarse pottery (ALC 69, phase F, and ALC 72/2, phase F), nos 147–172
52	Coarse pottery (ALC 72/2, phase F, and ALC 69, phase G), nos 173–193
53	Coarse pottery (ALC 69, phases G, unphased and H, and ALC 72/2, phases G and unphased), nos 194–211
54	Coarse pottery (ALC 69, phase H), nos 212–221
55	Coarse pottery (ALC 69, phase H and Unstrat, and ALC 72/2, phase H), nos 222–237
56	Glass vessels (ALC 69), nos 3–12, 17, and 20
57	Glass vessels (ALC 72/2), nos 1, 3–4, and 6
58	Copper alloy (ALC 69), nos 1–3, 7–9, 11, 15–16, 18, 20, and 22–3
59	Copper alloy (ALC 69), nos 25–29
60	Copper alloy (ALC 72/2), nos 1, 3, 6, and 8–10
61	Copper alloy (ALC 72/2), nos 11–16
62	Copper alloy (ALC 72/2), nos 17–18
63	Iron objects (ALC 69), nos 1, 3, and 5
64	Iron object (ALC 69), no 7
65	Lead object (ALC 69), no 1
66	Iron and lead objects (ALC 72/2), nos 2, 7, 9–10
67	Iron object (ALC 72/2), no 11
68	Worked bone (ALC 69), nos 1–9
69	Worked bone (ALC 72/2), nos 1–6
70	Stone object (ALC 69), no 1
71	Stone objects (ALC 69), quernstone no 3 and shale nos 4–5
72	Stone objects (ALC 69), nos 6–7
73	Ceramic lamp (ALC 69), no 1
74	Proportions of finds classes by phase (ALC 69 and ALC 72/2)
75	Comparative proportions of samian ware and glass by phase (ALC 69 and ALC 72/2)

1988 Baromix excavations (AL 28)

76	AL 28, trench 1, section, north side
77	AL 28, trench 2, phases 2.1, 2.2, 2.3, and 2.5, plans
78	AL 28, trench 2, section, north side
79	AL 28, trench 4, sections, north and east sides
80	Decorated samian ware (AL 28), nos 1, 4, 7, and 9
81	AL 28, phases 1.1–1.2, 2.1–2.3, and 4.1–4.3, date distribution of samian ware
82	AL 28, phases 1.3, 2.4–2.5, 3.1–3.2, and 4.4–4.5, date distribution of samian ware
83	AL 28, unstratified contexts, date distribution of samian ware
84	AL 28, date distribution of all samian ware
85	Proportions of major fabric classes from pre-Hadrianic phases (AL 28)
86	Coarse pottery (AL 28), nos 1–29
87	Glass, nos 1–2, copper alloy, no 1, and worked bone, nos 1 and 3 (AL 28)

Lloyds Bank excavation (ALB 75)

88	Location of the Lloyds Bank (ALB 75) and the Explosion site (AES 76–7) excavations
89	ALB 75, phase I, feature plan
90	ALB 75: a) area II, west section; b) burial J; c) section of tank 2
91	ALB 75, phase II, feature plan
92	ALB 75, well 2, timber lining
93	ALB 75: a) phase III, feature plan; b) phases IV–V, feature plan
94	ALB 75, phase VII, feature plan

Lloyds Bank finds (ALB 75)

95	Roman pottery (ALB 75), nos 1–36
96	Roman and Saxon pottery (ALB 75), nos 37–55

97   Intaglio (ALB 75)
98   Copper alloy objects (ALB 75), nos 1–3

Explosion site excavations (AES 76–7)

99   1–5 Bleachfield Street, site layout (AES 76–7)
100   Key to drawing conventions (AES 76–7)
101   Site I, period 1 plan (AES 76–7)
102   Site I, periods 1–6 sections (AES 76–7)
103   Site I, periods 2–4 plan (AES 76–7)
104   Site II trench, all period plans (AES 76–7)
105   Site II trench, north section (AES 76–7)
106   Site I, south section (AES 76–7)
107   Site I, period 5 plan (AES 76–7)
108   Site I, periods 5–9 sections (AES 76–7)
109   Site I, period 6 plan (AES 76–7)
110   Site I, period 7 plan (AES 76–7)
111   Site II, period 7 plan (AES 76–7)
112   Site I, period 8 plan (AES 76–7)
113   Site II west end, periods 8–14 plans (AES 76–7)
114   Site I, period 9 plan (AES 76–7)
115   Site I, period 10 plan (AES 76–7)
116   Site I, periods 10–12 sections (AES 76–7)
117   Site I, period 10A plan (AES 76–7)
118   Site I, period 11 plan (AES 76–7)
119   Site I, period 12 plan (AES 76–7)
120   Site I, period 12 sections. Site II, periods 2–12 sections (AES 76–7)

Explosion site finds (AES 76–7)

121   Coin histograms for all Alcester sites up to 1984 and for the Explosion site
122   Samian ware stamps, nos 1–25, and decorated vessels, nos 26–30 (AES 76–7)
123   Samian ware decorated vessels and other pieces, nos 31–34, mortarium and coarse ware stamps, nos 35–41, and reused pottery, nos 42–55 (AES 76–7)
124   Roman pottery seriation diagram (AES 76–7)
125   Roman pottery, incidence of major fabric groups by period (AES 76–7)
126   Roman pottery (AES 76–7), nos 56–81, period 1
127   Roman pottery (AES 76–7), nos 82–83, period 1, and nos 84–106, period 2
128   Roman pottery (AES 76–7), nos 107–145, period 2
129   Roman pottery (AES 76–7), nos 146–168, period 2, and nos 169–176, period 3
130   Roman pottery (AES 76–7), nos 177–193, period 3, and nos 194–216, period 4
131   Roman pottery (AES 76–7), nos 217–227, period 4, and nos 228–255, period 5
132   Roman pottery (AES 76–7), nos 256–257, period 5, and nos 258–301, period 6
133   Roman pottery (AES 76–7), nos 302–335, period 6
134   Roman pottery (AES 76–7), nos 336–383, period 6, and nos 384–387, period 7
135   Roman pottery (AES 76–7), nos 388–414, period 7, and nos 415–422, period 8
136   Roman pottery (AES 76–7), nos 423–455, period 8, and nos 456–457, period 9
137   Roman pottery (AES 76–7), nos 458–481, period 9
138   Roman pottery (AES 76–7), nos 482–513, period 9
139   Roman pottery (AES 76–7), nos 514–553, period 9
140   Comparison of Roman pottery assemblages in pits 124 and 170: fabrics (AES 76–7)
141   Comparison of Roman pottery assemblages in pits 124 and 170: vessel types (AES 76–7)
142   Roman pottery (AES 76–7), nos 554–586, period 9
143   Roman pottery (AES 76–7), nos 587–615, period 9
144   Roman pottery (AES 76–7), nos 616–653, period 9
145   Roman pottery (AES 76–7), nos 654–688, period 9
146   Roman pottery (AES 76–7), nos 689–735, period 9
147   Roman pottery (AES 76–7), nos 736–746, period 9, and nos 747–775 (period 10)
148   Roman pottery (AES 76–7), nos 776–820, period 10
149   Roman pottery (AES 76–7), nos 821–854, period 10
150   Roman pottery (AES 76–7), nos 855–894, period 10
151   Roman pottery (AES 76–7), nos 895–915, period 10, and nos 916–919, post-Roman

152	Medieval pottery fabrics in stratified contexts (AES 76–7)
153	Medieval pottery (AES 76–7), nos 1–14
154	Copper alloy (AES 76–7), nos 1–24
155	Copper alloy (AES 76–7), nos 26–50
156	Copper alloy (AES 76–7), nos 51–92
157	Lead, nos 109–119, and iron objects, nos 127–139 (AES 76–7)
158	Iron objects (AES 76–7), nos 140–156
159	Iron objects (AES 76–7), nos 157–177
160	Iron objects (AES 76–7), nos 178–187
161	Iron objects and iron nails by period (AES 76–7)
162	Jet, nos 188–194, and shale objects, nos 195–205 (AES 76–7)
163	Bone objects (AES 76–7), nos 206–226
164	Bone objects (AES 76–7), nos 227–247
165	Bone objects, nos 278–284, and glass vessels, nos 285–296 (AES 76–7)
166	Glass vessels and objects, nos 297–231, and crucibles, nos 322–327 (AES 76–7)
167	Stone objects, nos 328–332, stone building materials, nos 333–339, and tile, nos 340–345 (AES 76–7)
168	Ageing values of cattle mandibles from Alcester (AES 76–7, late Roman) and Portchester Castle (Roman)
169	Distal and shaft width indices of cattle metacarpi from Alcester (AES 76–7, late Roman) and Shakenoak Farm, Oxon
170	Scatter diagram of late Roman cattle metacarpi distal epiphyses (AES 76–7)
171	Scatter diagram of late Roman cattle metatarsi distal epiphyses (AES 76–7)
172	Maximum proximal width measurements of cattle metatarsi from Alcester (AES 76–7, late Roman) and Roman Exeter
173	Ageing values of sheep/goat mandibles from Alcester (AES 76–7, late Roman) and Portchester Castle (Roman)
174	Maximum distal width measurements of sheep/goat tibiae from Alcester (AES 76–7, late Roman), Roman Exeter and Shakenoak Farm, Oxon

Explosion site discussion (AES 76–7)

175	Reconstruction plans of building V, periods 5–7, and VI, period 7 (AES 76–7)

The northern suburbs and the development of Roman Alcester

176	The northern suburbs and approximate location of the proposed fort
177	Explosion site (AES 76–7) major pottery fabric classes by phase

List of plates

1969 and 1972 Baromix excavations (ALC 69 and ALC 72/2)

1 Lowest level of excavation showing features of phases A–C (ALC 69)
2 Structure 8, phase E (ALC 69)
3 Final north–south road 40, phase G (ALC 69)
4 Malting kiln 6 and stokehole 5, phase H (ALC 69)
5 West part of site showing features of phases A–C (ALC 72/2)
6 Centre and east part of site, features of phases B and C (ALC72/2)
7 Stone drain 48, phase F (ALC 72/2)
8 West part of site showing features of phase G (ALC 72/2)

1988 Baromix excavations (AL 28)

9 Trench 1, section drawing (AL 28)
10 Trench 2, clay-lined oven 220 (AL 28)

Lloyds Bank excavations (ALB 75)

11 General view of excavations (ALB 75)
12 Well 1, phase I (ALB 75)
13 Well 2, phase II (ALB 75)
14 Burials F and H, phase III (ALB 75)
15 Tank 2, phase VII (ALB 75)

Explosion site excavations (AES 76–7)

16 General view of part of site I and site II, looking east to buildings of 1–5 Bleachfield Street (AES 76–7)
17 Site I, looking west, gravel surface (235), period 4, in foreground and building V, period 5, behind (AES 76–7)
18 Site I, building V, period 5, section of wall (5) with clay floor (44) and later surfaces to left (AES 76–7)
19 Site I, south-east of building V, period 6, wall (155) to right with rubble base of rooms 3 and 4 floors and slot beyond (208) (AES 76–7)
20 Site I, building V, period 6, rubble base of room 2b floor, cut by pit (49), with beam slots (157) to right, and (158) foreground (AES 76–7)
21 Site I, surface (161), period 7, to left, with possible drain and postholes of timber lean-to on south-west side of building VI in foreground. Building V to right (AES 76–7)
22 Site II, building VI, period 7, with surface (20), wall (2), robbed wall (7), slot (23), and tank (19) (AES 76–7)
23 Site II, detail of tank (II 19) in building VI, period 7 (AES 76–7)
24 Site I, timber lean-to on south-west side of building VI, period 7, after excavation, showing postholes (202) and (206) and possible drain (201) (AES 76–7)
25 Site I, section through pit (170), period 9, cut by pit (170A), period 10 (AES 76–7)
26 Site II, crushed stone substructure of building VIA, period 10, with robber trench of wall (II 7) partly excavated behind (AES 76–7)
27 Site I, building II, period 10A, rubble platform on left, with corner post setting in foreground. Medieval wall (10), period 11, to right (AES 76–7)
28 Site I, building I, period 12; white markers indicate position of postholes and bases (AES 76–7)

List of tables

1969 and 1972 Baromix finds (ALC 69 and ALC 72/2)

1   Roman coin list (ALC 69)
2   Roman coin list (ALC 72/2)
3   Occurrence of South Gaulish samian ware (ALC 69)
4   Occurrence of Central Gaulish samian ware (ALC 69)
5   Occurrence of East Gaulish samian ware (ALC 69)
6   Occurrence of South Gaulish samian ware (ALC 72/2)
7   Occurrence of Central Gaulish samian ware (ALC 72/2)
8   Occurrence of East Gaulish samian ware (ALC 72/2)
9   Iron and lead objects (ALC 69)
10   Iron and lead objects (ALC 72/2)

1988 Baromix excavations (AL 28)

11   Samian forms and fabrics, AL 28 phases 1.1–1.2, 2.1–2.3, and 4.1–4.3
12   Samian forms and fabrics, AL 28 phases 1.3, 2.4–2.5, 3.1–3.2, and 4.4–4.5
13   Samian forms and fabrics, AL 28 unstratified contexts
14   Samian forms and fabrics, AL 28 all contexts
15   Functional analysis of vessels from pre-Hadrianic deposits (AL 28)

Lloyds Bank finds (ALB 75)

16   Roman coins (ALB 75)

Explosion site finds (AES 76–7)

17   Roman coins (AES 76–7)
18   Stratified samian ware (AES 76–7, period 1)
19   Stratified samian ware (AES 76–7, period 2)
20   Stratified samian ware (AES 76–7, period 3)
21   Stratified samian ware (AES 76–7, period 4)
22   Stratified samian ware (AES 76–7, period 5)
23   Stratified samian ware (AES 76–7, period 6)
24   Copper alloy by period (AES 76–7)
25   Ironwork by period (AES 76–7)
26   Ironwork by functional category (AES 76–7)
27   Jet and shale objects by period (AES 76–7)
28   Bone objects by period (AES 76–7)
29   Roman tile fabric quantification (AES 76–7)
30   Roman tile types by period (AES 76–7)
31   Roman tile fabrics/types by period (AES 76–7)
32   Roman tile thicknesses (AES 76–7)
33   Number of animal bone fragments identified to species (AES 76–7)
34   Number of unidentified animal bone fragments (AES 76–7)
35   Number of fragments of the major species in Roman contexts (AES 76–7)
36   Cattle fragment numbers identified (AES 76–7)
37   Percentages of cattle fragments in Roman deposits (AES 76–7)
38   Sheep/goat fragment numbers identified (AES 76–7)
39   Percentage of sheep/goat fragments identified (AES 76–7)
40   Pig fragment numbers identified (AES 76–7)
41   Percentage of pig fragments identified (AES 76–7)

42 Incidence of (oyster) shell fragments by period (AES 76–7)
43 Well 168A pollen spectra (AES 76–7)
44 Well 168A seed list (AES 76–7)
45 Incidence of coal by period (AES 76–7)

Microfiche tables (MT)

1969 and 1972 Baromix finds (ALC 69 and ALC 72/2)

MT1	Roman pottery fabric descriptions (ALC 69, ALC 72/2, and AL 28)	M1:A5
MT2	Roman pottery fabric proportions by phase (ALC 69	M1:A14
MT3	Roman pottery fabric proportions by phase (ALC 72/2)	M1:B9

1988 Baromix excavations (AL 28)

MT4	Finds summary, AL 28 Trench 1	M1:E4
MT5	Finds summary, AL 28 Trench 2	M1:E5
MT6	Finds summary, AL 28 Trench 3	M1:E6
MT7	Finds summary, AL 28 Trench 4	M1:E7
MT8	Roman pottery fabric proportions from pre-Hadrianic groups (AL 28)	M1:E8

Lloyds Bank finds (ALB 75)

MT9	Occurrence of finds by phase (ALB 75)	M1:F6

Explosion site finds (AES 76–7)

MT10	Roman pottery fabrics by period (AES 76–7)	M2:B1
MT11	Roman vessel types by major fabric group (AES 76–7)	M2:C5
MT12	Roman vessel types by period (AES 76–7)	M2:C7
MT13	Medieval pottery fabrics (AES 76–7)	M2:D11
MT14	Grouping of mortar and plaster samples (AES 76–7)	M2:F8
MT19	Pearson's *r* correlation coefficients for cattle assemblages in late Roman deposits (AES 76–7)	M2:G3
MT20	Coefficients matrix of cattle assemblages in late Roman deposits (AES 76–7)	M2:G5
MT23	Cattle tooth eruption data (AES 76–7)	M2:G8
MT24	Cattle epiphyseal fusion data – Roman period (AES 76–7)	M2:G8
MT25	Metrical analysis of cattle (AES 76–7)	M2:G9
MT26	Sheep/goat tooth eruption data (AES 76–7)	M2:G10
MT27	Sheep/goat epiphyseal fusion data (AES 76–7)	M2:G10
MT28	Metrical analysis of sheep/goat (AES 76–7)	M2:G11
MT29	Pig tooth eruption data (AES 76–7)	M2:G12
MT30	Pig epiphyseal fusion data (AES 76–7)	M2:G12
MT31	Metrical analysis of domestic fowl (AES 76–7)	M2:G13

Summary

This report presents the results of five excavations on three sites in the northern part of the extramural area which lies to the south of the defended area of the small Roman town of Alcester, Warwickshire. It comprises Volume 3 in the CBA *Roman Alcester Series*, following Volume 1, the Southern Extramural Area (RR 96), and Volume 2, the Defences and Defended Area (RR 106). The excavations took place between 1969 and 1988 in the vicinity of Bleachfield Street; the 'Explosion site' at 1–5 Bleachfield Street and the 'Lloyds Bank site' to the north, and the three excavations at the 'Baromix site' to the south.

These excavations revealed evidence of occupation during the Roman, Saxon, medieval, and post-medieval periods, and in particular of the origins of the Roman town from a postulated fort, strongly indicated by metal objects and ceramics with military associations from the earliest phases. Occupation continued from the early AD 60s throughout the Roman period, the regular, possibly military alignment of the earliest phase of rectilinear timber buildings at the Baromix sites being superseded by differently aligned civilian structures. Large amounts of finds were recovered, including pottery, tile, fired clay, glass, coins, copper alloy, iron, lead, stone objects, worked bone, slag, and building material, along with large faunal and environmental assemblages from the Explosion site. Several Roman burials were discovered within the urban area, mostly of children. The Saxon, medieval, and post-medieval material is also described. The volume concludes with a discussion of the origins of the town and the development of this area in the light of the archaeological work undertaken to date in Alcester.

Übersicht

Diese Arbeit stellt die Ergebnisse von fünf Grabungen auf drei verschiedenen Geländen vor, die in den Jahren 1969–88 im nördlichen Teil des Siedlungsgebiets südlich der Verteidigungslinie der römischen Kleinstadt Alcester, in der Grafschaft von Warwickshire, durchgeführt wurden. Die gröbte Grabung, die sogenannte 'Explosion site' befand sich hinter 1–5 Bleachfield Street, die 'Lloyds Bank site' östlich und die drei Grabungen auf dem Gelände der 'Baromix site' südlich davon.

Der Band ist der dritte Teil der *Roman Alcester Series* der CBA: Während es in Band 1 (RR 96) um die Grabungen im südlichen Teil des Gebiets ging, wurde in Volume 2 (RR 106) über die Verteidigungsanlagen der römischen Stadt berichtet.

Die hier beschriebenen Grabungen zeigten Siedlungsspuren aus der Römerzeit, dem Früh-, Hoch und Spätmittelalter und die Neuzeit auf. Insbesondere lieferten sie neue Erkenntnisse über die Frühentwicklung der römischen Stadt von einem Kastell, das an der 'Baromix site' vermutet wird. Ausschlaggebend dafür sind Metall- und Keramikfunde, die typisch für das Militär sind, ebenso die reguläre Ausrichtung der Holzgebäude (Baracken?) in den frühesten Phasen. Das Gelände wurde ab Anfang der 60er Jahre nach Christus bis zum Ende der Römerzeit in Britannien benutzt. Die frühesten Gebäude wurden durch anders ausgerichtete, wohl zivile Neubauten ersetzt.

Grobe Fundkomplexe wurden geborgen, u.ä. Keramik, Ziegel, verziegelter Lehm, Glas, Münzen, Buntmetall-, Eisen-, Blei- und, Steinobjekte, Schlacke und Baumaterial, und auch grobe Tierknochen und Ecofaktkomplexe aus der 'Explosion site'. Auch einige Bestattungen, meistens Kinder, wurden innerhalb des Stadtgebiets entdeckt. Die mittelalterlichen Befunde und das Fundmaterial wurden auch beschrieben. Im letzten Teil wurde die Bedeutung der Entdeckungen der letzten Jahre diskutiert, besonders was die Wurzeln der römischen Stadt betrifft.

Sommaire

Ce rapport présente les résultats de cinq fouilles sur trois sites dans le nord de la zone extra-muros au sud de la zone protégée de l'agglomération secondaire romaine de Alcester, Warwickshire. Il constitue Tome 3 dans la 'série d'Alcester' de la CBA, suivant Tome 1, 'La zone extra-muros du Sud' (RR 96), et Tome 2, 'Les fortifications et la zone protégée' (RR 106). Les fouilles avaient lieu entre 1969 et 1988 aux environs de Bleachfield Street: l'Explosion site à 1–5 Bleachfield Street et le Lloyds Bank site au nord, et les trois fouilles du Baromix site au sud.

Les fouilles révèlent les traces d'occupation aux époques romaines, médiévales et post-médiévales, et en particulier les origines de la ville romaine autour d'un camp militaire putatif, suggérées par les objets métalliques et céramiques avec les associations militaires. L'occupation continua des années 60 à la fin de l'époque romaine, l'alignement régulier, et peut-être militaire, des bâtiments en bois les plus anciens sur les sites Baromix, étant remplacé par les structures civiles alignées de manière différente.

Un grand assemblage de découvertes a été trouvé: les céramiques, les tuiles et autres objets de terre cuite, les monnaies, les objets de bronze, de fer, de plomb, de verre, de pierre et d'os, les scories métallurgiques et les matériaux à bâtir. De l'Explosion site, il y avait aussi des grands assemblages archéo-botaniques et faunaux. Plusieurs sépultures ont été découvertes à l'intérieur des limites urbaines, la plupart appartenant aux enfants. Les découvertes saxonnes, médiévales et post-médiévales sont aussi décrites. Cet ouvrage conclut en discutant des origines de la ville romaine d'Alcester et du développement de sa zone extra-muros, réunissant toutes les données archéologiques connues à ce jour.

Acknowledgements

Baromix Excavations (ALC 69, ALC 72/2, and AL 28)

A great debt of thanks is due to Rowan Ferguson who prepared the material and many of the preliminary texts for the ALC 69 and ALC 72/2 excavations from Stephen J Taylor's original archive. Steve Cracknell would like to thank Peter Woolerton of Baromix Ltd and John Clegg of Dennison Equipment Ltd for the financing of the AL 28 assessment. The ALC 69 and ALC 72/2 samian, pottery, and small finds drawings are the work of Robin Dalloway and have been remounted by Steve Rigby, who drew the ALC 69 and ALC 72/2 plans, and the AL 28 plans and finds drawings.

Margaret Ward wishes to thank Brenda Dickinson for the samian stamp identifications.

Lloyds Bank (ALB 75)

Edith Evans would like to thank the Manager of the Alcester branch of Lloyds Bank, Mr Mackintosh, and his staff, and also Messrs Peace and Meers of the Premises Department, Birmingham Office, for their kindness and co-operation. Her thanks are also due to all those who helped in the actual work of the excavation, especially Vivienne Metcalf, the finds assistant, and Paul Booth, the site assistant who also gave valuable help during the writing of the report. A great deal of assistance was also given by Dr R G Lamb, then the Field Archaeological Officer for Warwickshire, and Mr Don Sidaway, the secretary of the Alcester Excavation Committee.

Jeremy Evans wishes to acknowledge advice from Paul Booth and Stephanie Ratkai on the Lloyds Bank Roman and Saxon pottery, and A C King for the identification of the Lloyds Bank samian ware from relevant stratified groups. The Lloyds Bank pot drawings are the work of Edith Evans and Steve Rigby, and the small finds drawings are also by Steve Rigby. Judson Chesterman notes the help given by Dr R K Levick (Hon University lecturer and consultant radiologist at Sheffield Children's Hospital) who in 1978 did an X-ray diagnosis of age on the left ilium from Lloyds Bank Burial C.

Explosion site (AES 76–7)

Paul Booth would like to thank Mr David Burden for permission to excavate on the Explosion site, and Dr R G Lamb who was instrumental in organising the work. A debt of thanks must also go to all who took part in the excavation, particularly John Burman, David Symons, and the finds assistant, Sarah Adamson. He is grateful to all the specialist contributors, but particularly to Rowan Ferguson for her work on the pottery and discussion of its significance for dating, and other aspects of the site. Without this, and the work of Bill Seaby, Glenys Lloyd-Morgan, Quita Mould, Mark Maltby, and Denise Allen, the report would be much poorer. Maggi Darling, Kay Hartley, Robin Symonds, and David Williams, among others, kindly helped with different aspects of the pottery report, and Pam Copson and John Crossling assisted with identifications of charcoal and stone types respectively. Quita Mould is most grateful to Jacqui Watson of the Ancient Monuments Laboratory for identifying the minerally preserved organic remains and to Gerry MacDonnell for XRF analysis. Mark Maltby would like to thank Mike Wilkinson for his identification of the fish bones.

None of the above is responsible for any erroneous conclusions which may have been drawn from their findings. Thanks are owed to Helen Maclagan, the County Field Archaeologist, and other colleagues for their help with various aspects of the report, and particularly to Steve Cracknell for detailed discussions of the problems of Alcester. The illustrations were initially prepared by Liz Hooper (small objects), Michelle Draycott (Roman pottery), and Nigel Dodds (medieval pottery). The work of completing and mounting these, and of producing the many remaining figures, graphs, and tables, was done with great forbearance by Andy Isham and Candy Stevens, to whom a particular debt of gratitude is due.

The Lloyds Bank and Baromix reports were edited by Jeremy Evans and the Explosion site report was edited by John Chadderton, who also edited the volume overall. The latter work was taken over and completed by Joseph Elders and Nicholas Palmer. Additional figures and final amendments to the illustrations were completed by Peter Moore, Candy Stevens, and Andy Isham. Helen Maclagan and Nicholas Palmer guided the project through its later stages, and the project staff would like to acknowledge the advice given by Dr Andrew Brown and Ian George of English Heritage. Publication has been made possible by the funding of English Heritage and the co-operation of the Council for British Archaeology.

Introduction
Paul Booth, John Chadderton, and Jeremy Evans

Alcester is the largest and probably the most important Roman settlement in Warwickshire. It is situated in the west of the county at a river crossing and major crossroads, with the next nearest large Roman settlements at Droitwich 20km to the west and Tiddington 13km to the east (Fig 1). It lies on the River Arrow, which is a tributary of the Severn and this probably provided a communications link with the rest of the Severn basin. Comparatively little was known about the layout of the Roman town until the late 1950s when small excavations were undertaken by H V Hughes under the auspices of the University of Birmingham Department of Extramural Studies (Hughes 1960, 1961). This expanded in the 1960s with the discovery of masonry buildings along a Roman street (Fig 3, street A) by Hughes and Tomlinson (both unpublished), and major excavations, mainly to the south of street A, undertaken by C Mahany in advance of a housing development.

The latter excavations have recently been published (Mahany 1994; Cracknell and Mahany 1994) as Volume 1, parts 1 and 2, in the Council for British Archaeology's Roman Alcester series. Following intensive excavations over the last three decades Alcester is now one of the better known Romano-British small towns, and most of the more substantial excavation reports appear in this series. Volume 1 dealt with the so-called 'southern suburbs', ie the extramural area of the town to the south of street A (Figs 2 and 3) in the Birch Abbey area. The second volume concentrated on the major sites recently excavated within the defended area (Cracknell 1996), and this volume (Volume 3), deals with the 'northern suburbs', ie the extramural area of the town to the north of street A. In fact, the use of the word 'suburb' needs some qualification. For the first two centuries of the Roman period the 'suburbs' represented the whole of the town's occupied area, there being virtually no occupation within the area encircled by the later defences, prior to the latter's construction.

This volume presents the results of excavations spread over twenty years in the 'northern suburbs'; two at the rear of 33 Bleachfield Street (close to the Baromix factory site) by S J Taylor (ALC 69 and ALC 72/2), an evaluation from beneath the Baromix factory itself by S Cracknell (AL 28), one at Lloyds Bank (ALB 75) by E Evans, and a major excavation at 1–5 Bleachfield Street (the Explosion site, AES 76–7) by P Booth (Fig 2). These excavations were conducted under varying conditions, and followed differing standards and aims with, for example, only the Explosion site presenting a full range of ecofact evidence. These sites are brought together in this volume as, combined, they provide enough evidence to sketch the development of the 'northern suburbs' and provide strong indications of the origin of the settlement. All the reports were prepared before 1992.

Site summaries

1969 and 1972 Baromix excavations (ALC 69 and ALC 72/2)

These two Baromix sites are taken together as they appear to share their first three phases (A–C). Both sites seem to be first occupied in the early to mid-60s AD, a date as early as any site in the town. Little coherent information can be deduced from the first phase on either site, although phase A on ALC 69 seems to show traces of rectilinear timber buildings aligned approximately north–south and contains items of military metalwork (see Lloyd-Morgan below, ALC 69 copper alloy nos 1–2). There is also some evidence of an approximately north–south road line on the east side of the site, probably the origins of street D (Fig 3). Phase B on both sites is clearly represented by rectilinear timber buildings constructed of small timbers set in a foundation or marking out trench of a type often found on military sites, all aligned approximately north–south. Phase C consists of reconstructions of these buildings on the same alignment using similar construction techniques. This third phase of buildings is sealed by deposits of burnt clay, associated with charred plank remnants on ALC 69, which are phased to the end of phase C on ALC 69 and as phase D on ALC 72/2. This demolition horizon appears to date to early in the Hadrianic era.

Following this, the phasing of the two sites diverges with clear evidence of non-contemporaneity by phase E on ALC 69 and phase F on ALC 72/2, which are given the date ranges of c AD 150/60–170/80 and c AD 150/60–250/70 respectively. Phase E on ALC 72/2 consists of various pits and gullies, aligned approximately north-east to south-west, an alignment closer to those found on the Explosion site to the north (see Booth below). The area appears to have been marginal at this time. On ALC 69 phase D consists of four approximately north–south beam slots which may have defined the wall lines of a timber aisled structure, or may have been part of some other rectilinear timber structure placed on the west side of street D. This phase D structure was succeeded in phase E by a small hut on the west side of the road line, with little evidence of other use of the area. This was followed in phase F by a relaying out of the road, street D, but with no evidence of any associated activity along the road-

Introduction

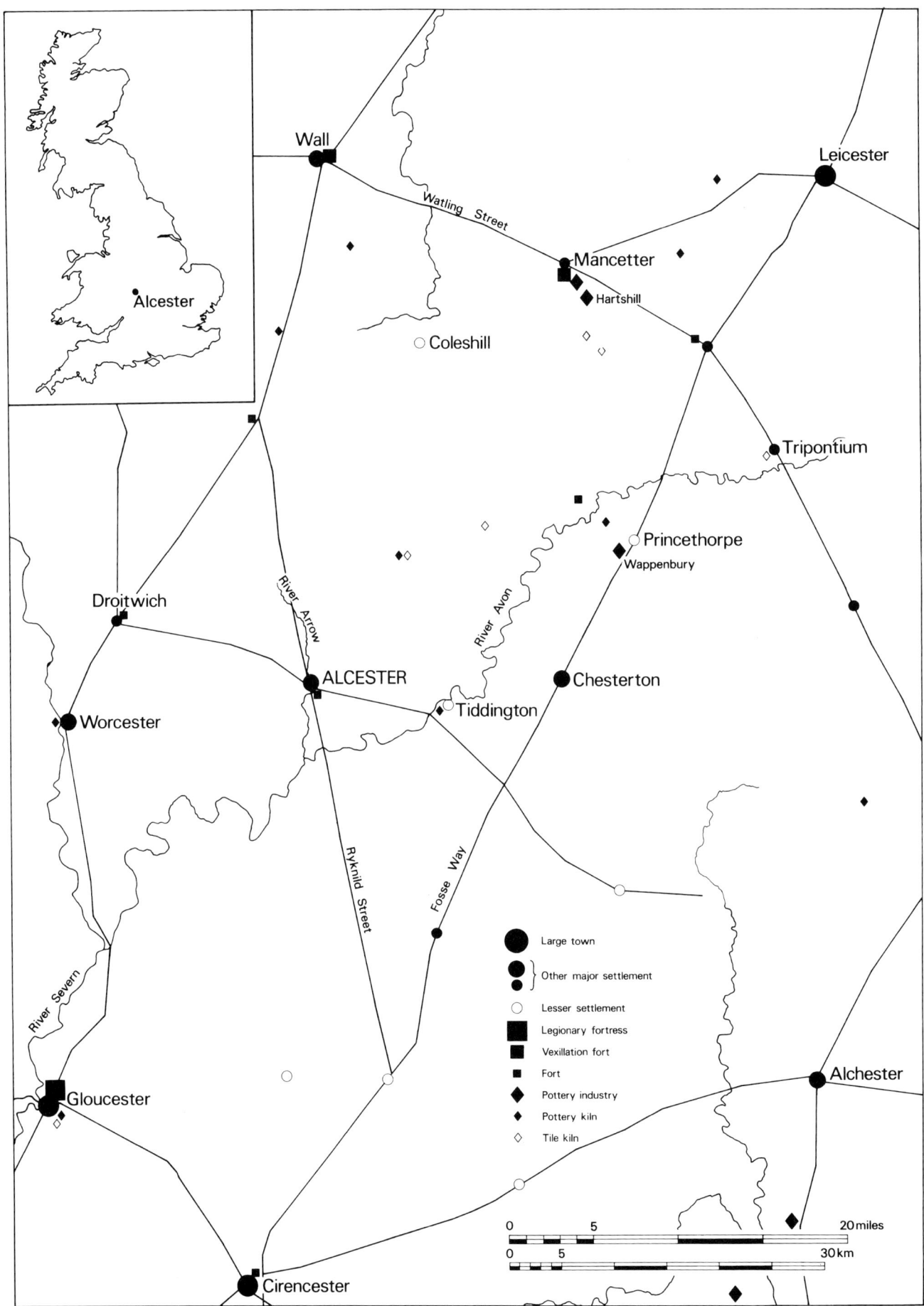

Figure 1   Alcester in its Roman regional setting

side. A similar picture of inactivity is suggested in phase G when the street was resurfaced, but the area remained unused apart from a few pits. On ALC 72/2 in phase F, by contrast there were a few more signs of activity with the construction of a stone lined drain running south from the northwest corner of the trench suggesting activity in the immediate vicinity. In phase G, as at 6 Birch Abbey (Cracknell 1989b, 25–38) and a number of other sites in the vicinity (Fig 2), the site seems to have been covered by gravel surfaces which Booth (1994) has suggested belong to an extensive market area in this quarter of the town (Fig 3), centred on street C. There was also a possible robber trench from a stone structure on the southern edge of the site in this phase. The presence in the finds assemblage of a copper alloy (bronze) tap fitting from medieval deposits (see Lloyd-Morgan below, ALC 72 no 14) also suggests structures of some status in the vicinity in the later Roman period.

The medieval period, phase H, on both sites shows evidence of industrial activity in the form of stone-built ovens, probably malting kilns, perhaps of the 12th/13th century.

1988 Baromix excavations (AL 28)

The AL 28 site consisted of four evaluation trenches excavated within the present Baromix factory in 1988 prior to proposed redevelopment (Figs 2 and 4). Three of the four trenches (1, 2, and 4) showed evidence of pre-Hadrianic activity, with two phases in trench 1, three in trench 2, and two or three in trench 4. The existence of a maximum of three pre-Hadrianic phases including foundation slots aligned approximately north–south, as those on the ALC 69 and 72/2 sites, suggests the presence of a very similar sequence. The clay-lined oven from phase 2.3, would be an unusual feature in a civilian context, and it seems of note that the only copper alloy find from the site was a military pendant (see Lloyd Morgan below, no 1).

The Hadrianic and later deposits from these trenches also seem to show parallels with the ALC 69 and ALC 72/2 sequences, with some 3rd-century activity, but virtually none attributable to the 4th. Trench 1 seems to have contained pits, postholes, and a gravel surface probably of 3rd-century date, whilst in trench 2 various 2nd-century postholes were apparently succeeded by a stone founded structure in the later 2nd century. Trench 3 seems to have had gravel surfaces and some pits in the 2nd–3rd century, whilst trench 4 appears to show traces of 2nd- to 3rd-century post-built structures.

Lloyds Bank excavations (ALB 75)

The Lloyds Bank site was first occupied in the 1st century AD, probably around the middle of the century like the Baromix sites (see above) and the Explosion site (see below). Phase I features, like those on the Explosion site, were laid out on a north-east to south-west axis, in contrast to those on the Baromix sites, and these alignments continued on the site throughout the Roman period. Phase I features seem to have consisted of property boundaries and a well, but no structures were located within the trench. Phase II seems to have consisted of the re-definition of the property boundaries in the later 2nd to early 3rd century and the digging of another well, within which part of the waterlogged timber lining survived. Environmental evidence from this (Osborne *in litt*) suggested an area of waste ground consistent with the interpretation of the enclosed area as a yard.

In the later 3rd to early 4th century (phase III) the boundary lines were renewed again. A small infant cemetery of some sixteen inhumations and a cremation was then placed in the northern half of the site, which suggests the area had become more marginal to the town. In the mid- to later 4th century (phase IV) the boundary ditches seem to have been allowed to silt up, again suggesting little activity here. Unusually for Alcester, however, there is slight evidence of Saxon structural activity on the site in phase V. This was followed by ploughing after which a high level of medieval activity seems to have commenced in the 12th/13th century. This seems to have included some semi-industrial activity with two stone flagged tanks set behind posthole structures which must have fronted onto the Stratford road.

Explosion site excavations (AES 76–7)

The site was occupied throughout the Roman period from about AD 70. The earliest occupation may have belonged to a phase contemporary with, or immediately post-dating, adjacent military activity on the Baromix sites (three items of military metalwork were found). Timber buildings of Flavian to early Hadrianic date were succeeded in the mid-2nd century by a building of stone and timber construction, and a further stone building, at right angles to the first, was added in the mid-3rd century. These were replaced in the later 4th century by timber structures associated with pits. The primary economic focus of the site seems to have been agricultural, with butchery of cattle an important activity. Small-scale metalworking was also carried out. A wide range of artefacts attests a relatively high level of prosperity.

Medieval activity was more restricted, consisting of slight timber structures dating from possibly the later 12th century onwards at the west end of the site. Further east was a possible oven and a series of pits mainly of 13th- to 14th-century date. Post-medieval features consisted of a cobbled surface, a drain, and a 19th-century outbuilding, all related to standing structures.

Introduction

Figure 2   Locations of excavations in Alcester prior to 1989

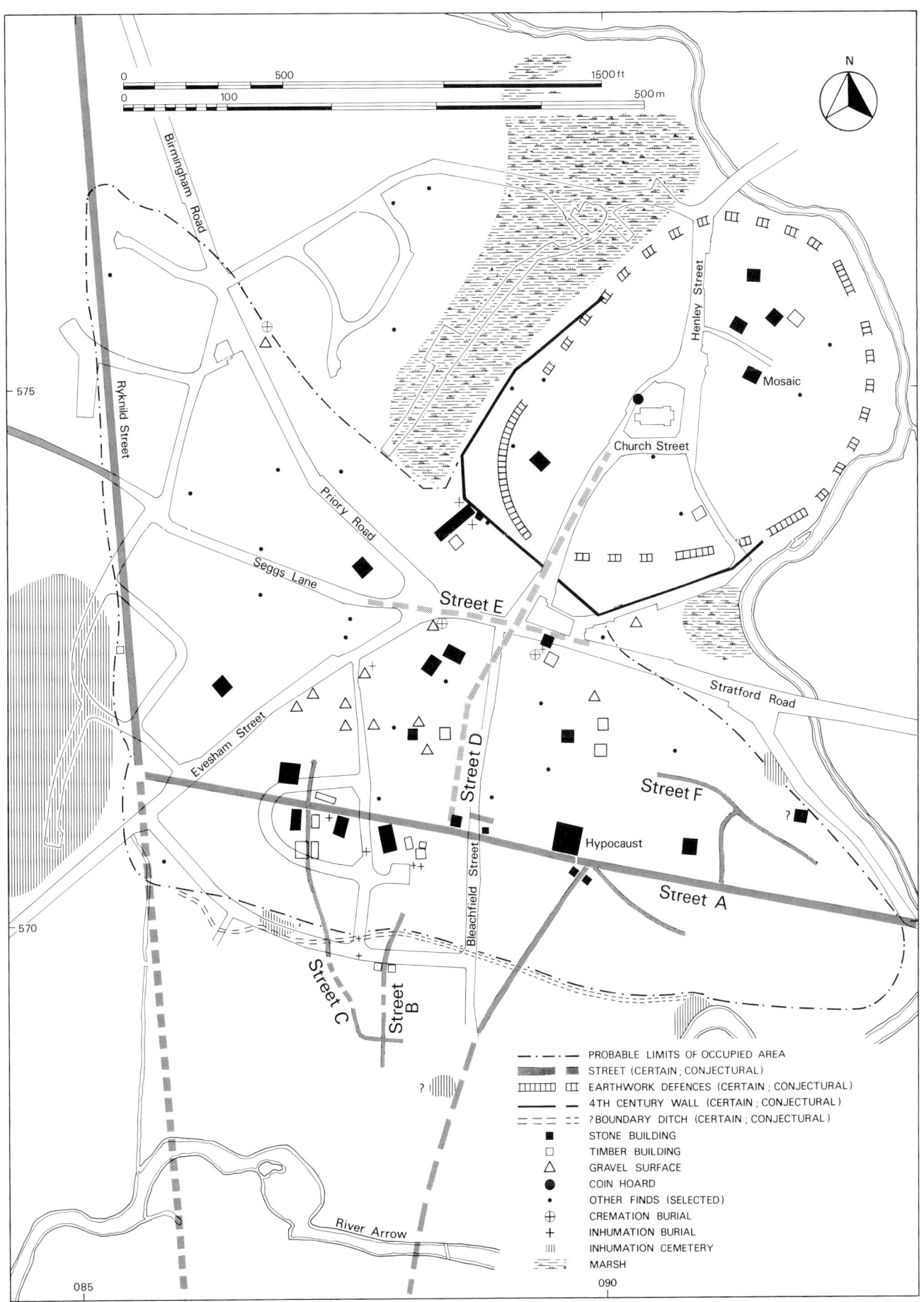

Figure 3   Roman Alcester, main elements

Introduction

Presentation of the evidence

Each of the above excavations is described separately together with their associated specialist finds reports, except ALC 69 and ALC 72/2 which have been grouped together due to their close proximity and similarities. The text dealing with the actual excavations outlines the stratigraphic and structural sequence in varying levels of detail depending on the quality of the surviving records. Some of the data has therefore been summarised, but fuller descriptions of the stratigraphy and the excavations are included either in the microfiche, or can be accessed by visiting the site archive held in the Warwickshire Museum. The evidence for each excavation is discussed in chronological order, from the earliest deposits to the latest, with the archaeological features sub-divided into their various chronological groupings (phases or periods). The phases or periods are illustrated with phase plans identifying the location of the principal features described in the text, and this information is sometimes supplemented with vertical sections to demonstrate various stratigraphic relationships. In the text, context/layer and feature numbers are in **bold** when they are located on a plan, and *italics* when shown on a section. On the plans, where features belonging to later phases cut through an earlier phase, the later features are shown in grey (or cross-hatching for the Explosion site) for clarity. Some of the features recorded on sites ALC 69 and ALC 72/2 were not apparently allocated with a feature number. Where necessary, these features are referred to on the plans and in the text by a letter code (eg un-numbered feature **a**).

It should be noted that the excavations contained within this report were prepared for publication at different times, and were originally not intended for inclusion in a combined volume such as this. As a result, there is a degree of inconsistency in the way various illustrations have been presented. It should be noted in particular that there are some discrepancies between the plan and section conventions used for the Explosion site and those used for the other excavations. The reader's attention is therefore drawn to the two different keys used below (Figs 5 and 100).

As with the stratigraphic and structural texts, some of the specialist finds reports and catalogues have also been condensed. This has been undertaken for reasons of economy of space. Some catalogues, for example, only describe in print those finds that are actually illustrated in the volume. The full versions of these catalogues are reproduced in the microfiche. In some reports a certain amount of methodological and analytical data has also been assigned to the microfiche.

It should be noted that the Baromix and Explosion site pottery reports were completed prior to the publication of the Fulford report (Fulford and Huddlestone 1991) and do not, consequently, fully conform to it.

Note: in these reports terms such as earlier 2nd century and later 2nd century are used to mean the first half of the 2nd century and the last half of the 2nd century respectively.

1969 and 1972 Baromix excavations (ALC 69 and ALC 72/2)

Jeremy Evans

Introduction

The two major Baromix sites (ALC 69 and ALC 72/2) were excavated in 1969 and 1972 by S J Taylor, whilst the third consists of four trial trenches excavated by S Cracknell in 1988 (AL 28, see below) as an assessment prior to proposed development of the Baromix factory site (Figs 2 and 4). The three sites lie to the west of Bleachfield Street and to the north of the major Mahany excavations (Mahany 1994, Fig 3). The sites all lie at around 41m OD on river gravels of the first–second terrace. The 1969 excavation is fairly securely located (Fig 4) and the 1972 main trench seems to have been at the western end of the same site, but no good location plans exist and its location on Fig 4 is hypothetical.

For the ALC 69 and 72/2 sites no site notebooks were available for post-excavation work and this has been done from a partially complete list of contexts, which contained some stratigraphic relationships, together with pencil sketch plans and the main sections. Use has also been made of the excavation photographs for deducing some relationships. As a consequence of this some attributions of features to phase are uncertain and several versions are possible of parts of the sequence, although the number of phases is probably correct, as is the sequence of roads.

Both sites, and AL 28 (see below), display strong similarities in the early Roman period; all seem to exhibit up to three pre-Hadrianic phases, the latest of which is sealed by a burnt clay deposit, probably derived from demolition and clearance of the site. After this the site histories seem to diverge, with Hadrianic–Antonine structures along the western road frontage of street D (ALC 69), but with little activity to the west (ALC 72/2). In the 3rd century, or later, there appears to be some evidence of stone structures set back from the street frontage (ALC 72/2), but no structures at all alongside the street (ALC 69).

Full finds reports are presented for all those finds categories which were retained. However, neither animal bone nor tile was retained from the Taylor excavations, nor were any environmental samples taken.

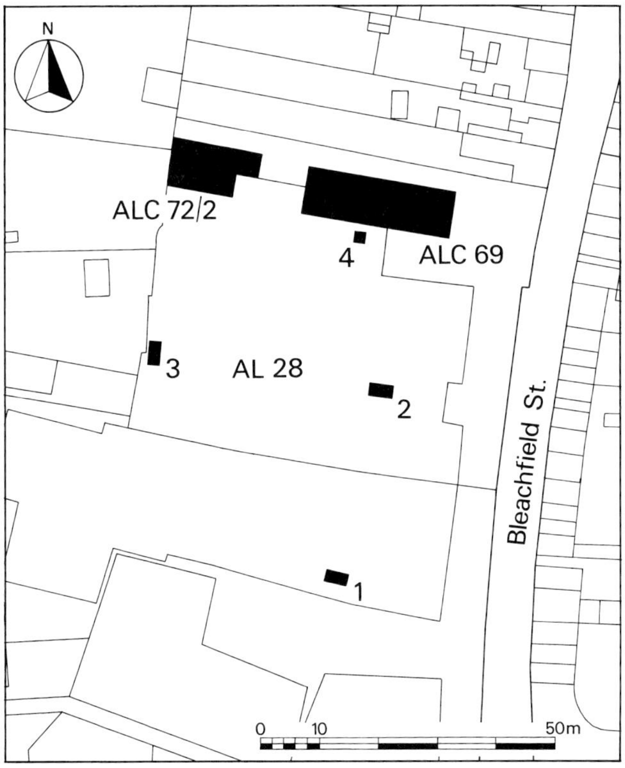

1969 excavations (ALC 69)

Phase A (Fig 6, Plate 1)

It is difficult to make much sense of the features assigned to this phase and, as on the ALC 72/2 site, it seems doubtful that all features of the period were excavated. There are various beam slots assigned to the phase, mostly running north to south. The principal north–south slots would seem to define part of a building, structure 1, the western wall line compris-

Figure 4 Location of Baromix excavations (ALC 69, ALC 72/2, and AL 28)

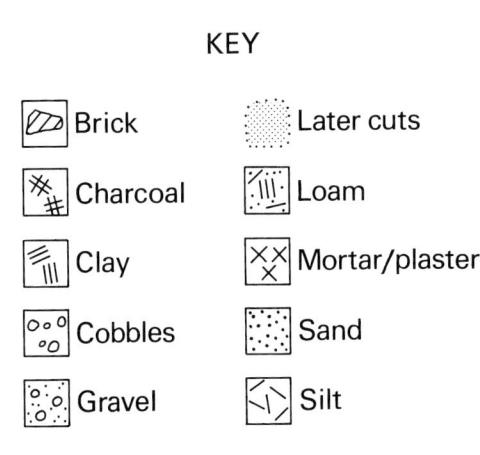

Figure 5 Key to plans and sections (ALC 69, ALC 72/2, AL 28, and ALB 75) (see figs 6–18, 76–9, and 89–95)

Plate 1 Lowest level of excavation showing features of phases A–C (ALC 69)

ing slots (***188***) and (**174**), but whether the gap between these two slots is a real effect is unclear; there is an un-numbered posthole on this alignment, and there are two further postholes (167 and 169) aligned with this which seem to form an east–west cross-wall and may perhaps terminate with the southern of the two postholes (**171**), or may continue east to include posthole 182. The eastern wall of this structure would seem to be defined by the fragmentary slot (**181**), together with postholes (**180**) and (**171**). There is a further slot running north to south around 1.2m to the east of (**181**) (un-numbered feature **a**) shown on plan and this would also seem to be cut by (**166**) of phase B (fig 6), and thus belong to this phase.

Within structure 1 were several enigmatic features which may be of this phase; there seems to have been a circular hearth (**187**) and a square-cut hollow, described as a posthole (**186**). There are also a number of stakeholes which have been assigned to this phase as they appear to be early in the sequence, but do not obviously belong to the succeeding phases. Most are un-numbered, but three (157–9) are identified, and are recorded as cutting an early layer (156). There are also a number of pits of this phase including (*198*) (Fig 7), (119), (165), (**178**), and a posthole (183) (unplanned). After the demolition of the building, or associated with it, is an irregular gully (**179**) which may have been cut by slot (**166**) of phase B, but is recorded as cutting postholes (**171**).

To the east of structure 1 was a wide expanse of cobbling (***163***) which may well be the first of the series of roads that runs north to south across the site. This cobbling seals a soil horizon (126A) which may well have been an old ground surface or subsoil. The latest deposits assigned to this phase, comprise a brown loam deposit (*126/136*, Fig 7) which accumulated over the cobbling, (***163***) and a similar deposit (95/96). There is some intrusive material in (95), but it is sealed by phase C deposits.

Phase B (Fig 6, Plate 1)

This phase clearly succeeds phase A and is sealed by the burnt clay deposits of phase C. Two structures, both aligned north–south would appear to belong to this phase. Structure 2, represented by timber slot (**80**) would seem to represent the north-east corner of a building, the rest of this structure presumably lying beyond the western limits of the excavation. There was a space of 4.8m between structure 2 and structure 3 which appears to have terminated on a similar northern alignment to structure 2, although (**152**) suggests further structural elements to the north. The western wall line of structure 3 is defined by slot (**173**), which joins with east–west slot (**166**), the northern wall of the structure. Slot (**166**) terminates 6.5m east of (**173**) and would seem to turn south as slot (**103/154**) which runs south, parallel to (**173**), to beyond the southern limits of the excavation at this level. Continuing the line of (**166**) was a further east–west slot (**150**) extending 1.9m east from (**166**) and joining up with a north–south slot (**144**), which had a re-cut (**145**). Slot (**144/145**) ran south from (**150**) parallel to (**103/154**) beyond the southern limit of the excavations. Some 1.2m south of (**150**) was a further east–west slot (**172**), running between (**103/154**) and (**144/145**) but joining neither of them. These slots appear in plan to belong together and to be sealed by the burnt clay deposits from the end of phase C. They are clearly of a different phase to slots (**133**) and (**100**) attributed to phase C (which appear to belong together in terms of plan) although the relationships between them are not recorded and their phasing could be transposed.

Running from just to the north of the end of (**144/145**) was a gully (**152**) with a fill containing much stone in a green silty matrix. This may have been a drain rather than a timber slot as there is no clear evidence that (**173**) or (**103/154**) ran to the north of the line of (**166**) and (**150**). To the north of the west end of slot (**150**) was a rectangular pit or posthole (**151**) which may have been related to this building and appears to be sealed by deposits of phase C. East of structure 3 was a pit (**97**) which seems to have been a setting for a rustic ware vessel and a further pit of this period (**79**) occurs in the section (Fig 7) on the eastern edge of the site.

On the west side of structure 3 there is a further slot or gully (**84**) which appears to belong to this phase as it is recorded as being cut by (**83**), which is assigned to phase C. (**84**) runs west south-west from the corner of (**173**) and (**166**) for 0.95m then appears to turn and continue to the north-west. It may be connected with the irregular gully (**81**), which seems to join (**84**) where it turns north-west. The purpose of the two gullies is difficult to guess and their phasing is fairly tenuous, although if not of this phase they are only likely to be of phase A, where they make no more sense in terms of plan.

There is a gully (un-numbered feature **b**), running north–south across the trench some 6.8m from structure 3 and to the east of this is a north–south gravelled strip, (**177**) (Figs 7 and 8). This gravelled strip is assigned to phase C, but its relatively close proximity to the un-numbered gully **b** could well place it as early as phase B, if (**177**) is interpreted as a roadway or path and **b** as an associated drainage gully.

Phase C (Fig 8, pl 1)

This phase succeeds phase B, but with no major accumulations of vertical stratigraphy between phases B and C it has proved difficult to isolate the various elements of the two phases. However, it is reasonably clear from the plan of phases B and C that two phases, at least, are represented.

As noted above in discussing phase B there is a gravelled strip (**177**) running north–south across the site which probably represents the remnants of a road line, with a possible drainage gully (un-numbered feature **b**, Fig 6) to the west. It is difficult to allocate (**177**) to a particular phase. It is truncated to the east by the later roadside ditch (**51/76**) of phase F, and would appear to be earlier than the north–south road (**77**) of phase D and E to the west. While it probably originates in phase B (see above), (**177**) can only be placed in phase C with any degree of certainty. The phase B gully (**b**) alongside the west side of (**177**) is re-cut in this phase (un-numbered feature **c**, Fig 8). Along the western edge of this gully is a north–south timber slot (un-numbered feature **d**) and 3.7m west of this another slot (**143**) (Figs 7 and 8), which runs approximately north–south, but seems to meander to the east as it runs south. These two slots are described here as structure 4 as they seem to be associated. Some 0.9m to the west of (**143**) was a further north–south slot (**100**), recorded on plan in the southern part of the trench, although it is not identified with any certainty on the section (Fig 7) on the north side of the trench.

Running east–west from just beyond slot (**100**) for 2.2m was another slot (**133**) which must be earlier or later than (**144/145**) assigned to phase B. Slots (**133**) and (**100**) cannot be contemporary with (**150**), (**172**), and (**144/145**) described under phase B, but neither do they make any sense by themselves, nor do they seem to fit well into structure 4, although they could be connected with it. The most likely association of (**100**) and (**133**) would seem to be with (**103/154**), and possibly (**166**) and (**173**) (ie the continuing use of the core of structure 3). (**103**) is recorded as appearing rather earlier upon excavation than the other two slots and it could be a re-cut on exactly the same alignment as (**154**) of this phase. It would seem that at least (**103**), and quite probably the entire core of structure 3 remained in use in this phase.

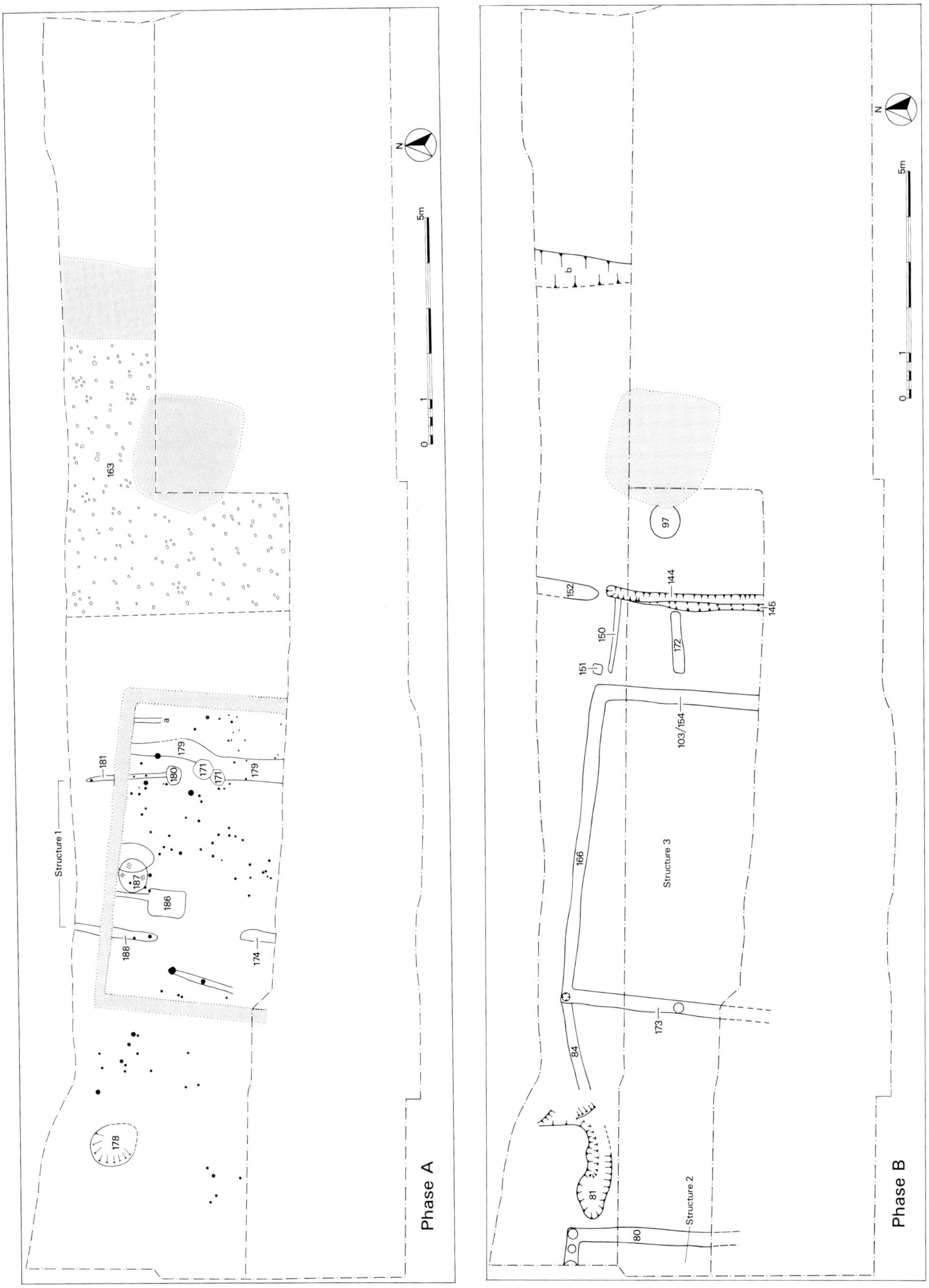

1969 and 1972 Baromix excavations (ALC 69 and ALC 72/2)

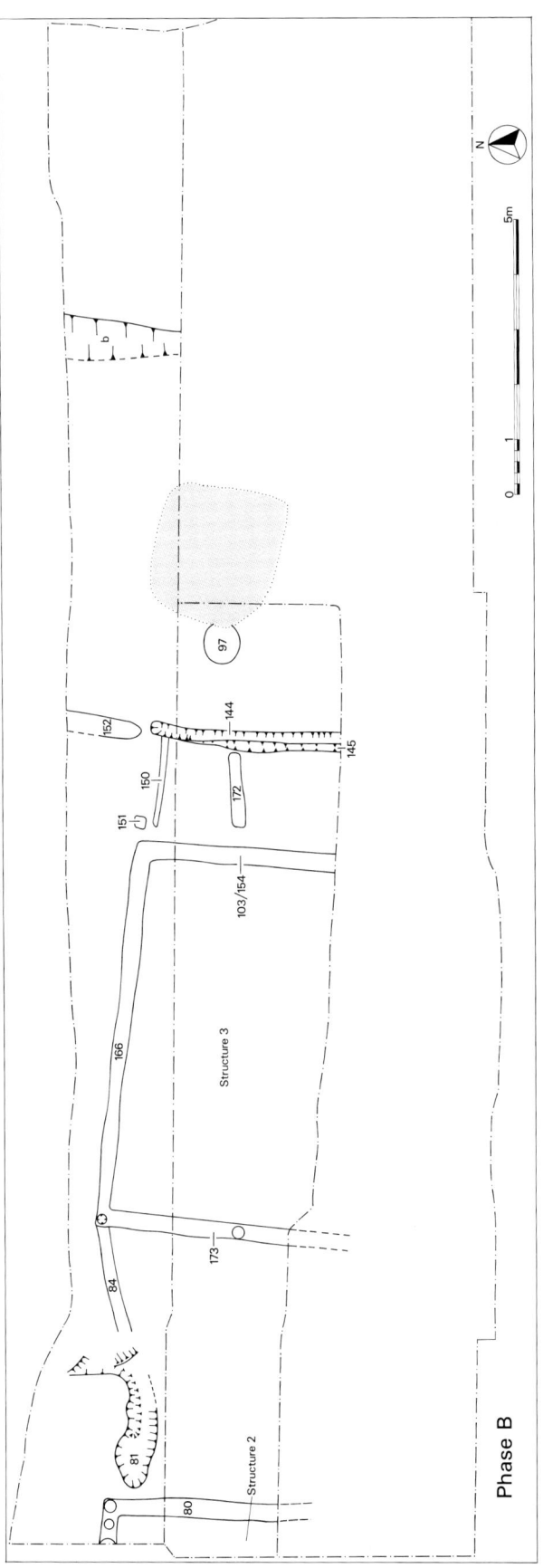

Figure 6   ALC 69, phases A and B, plans

1969 and 1972 Baromix excavations (ALC 69 and ALC 72/2)

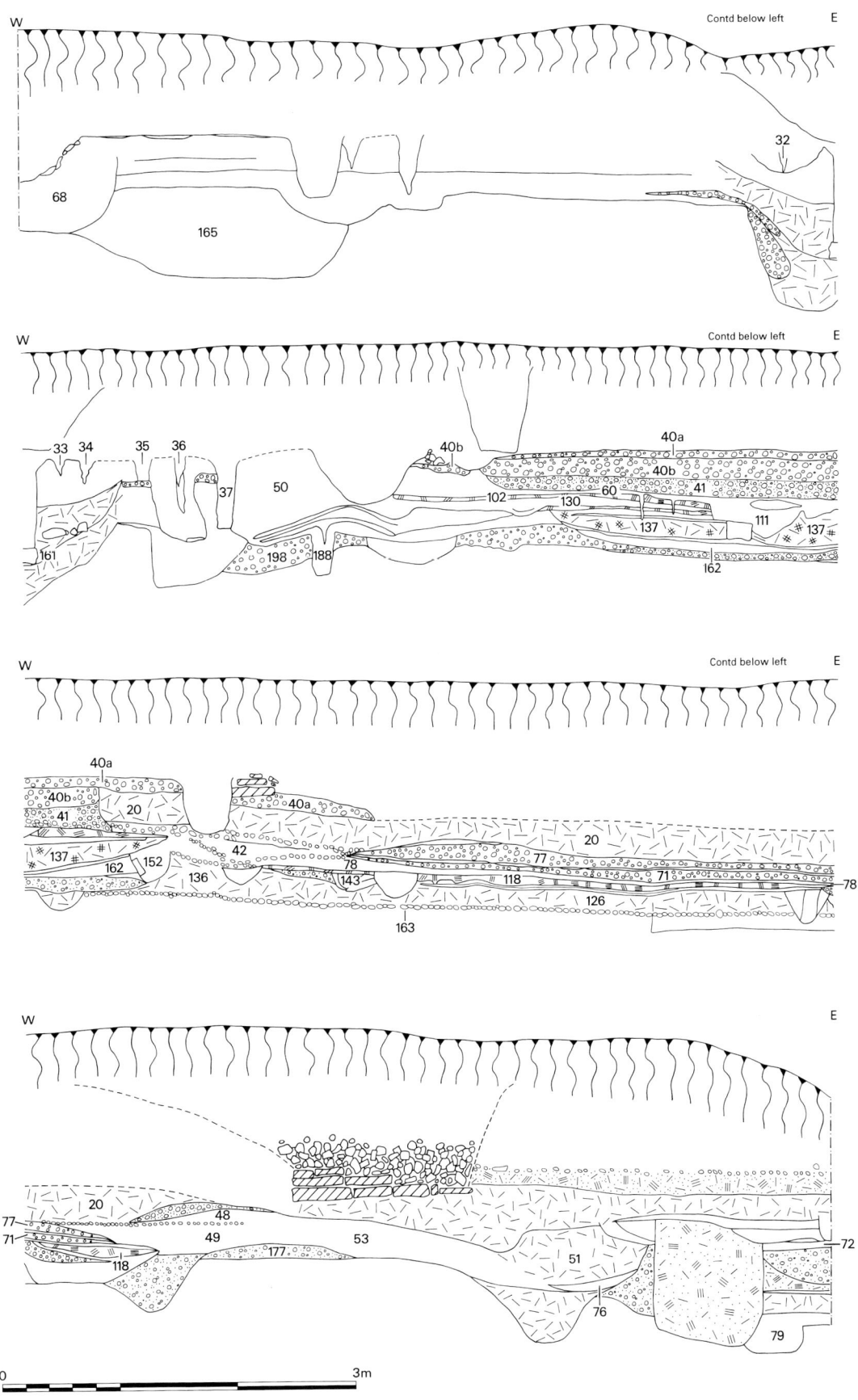

Figure 7   ALC 69, northern section

1969 and 1972 Baromix excavations (ALC 69 and ALC 72/2)

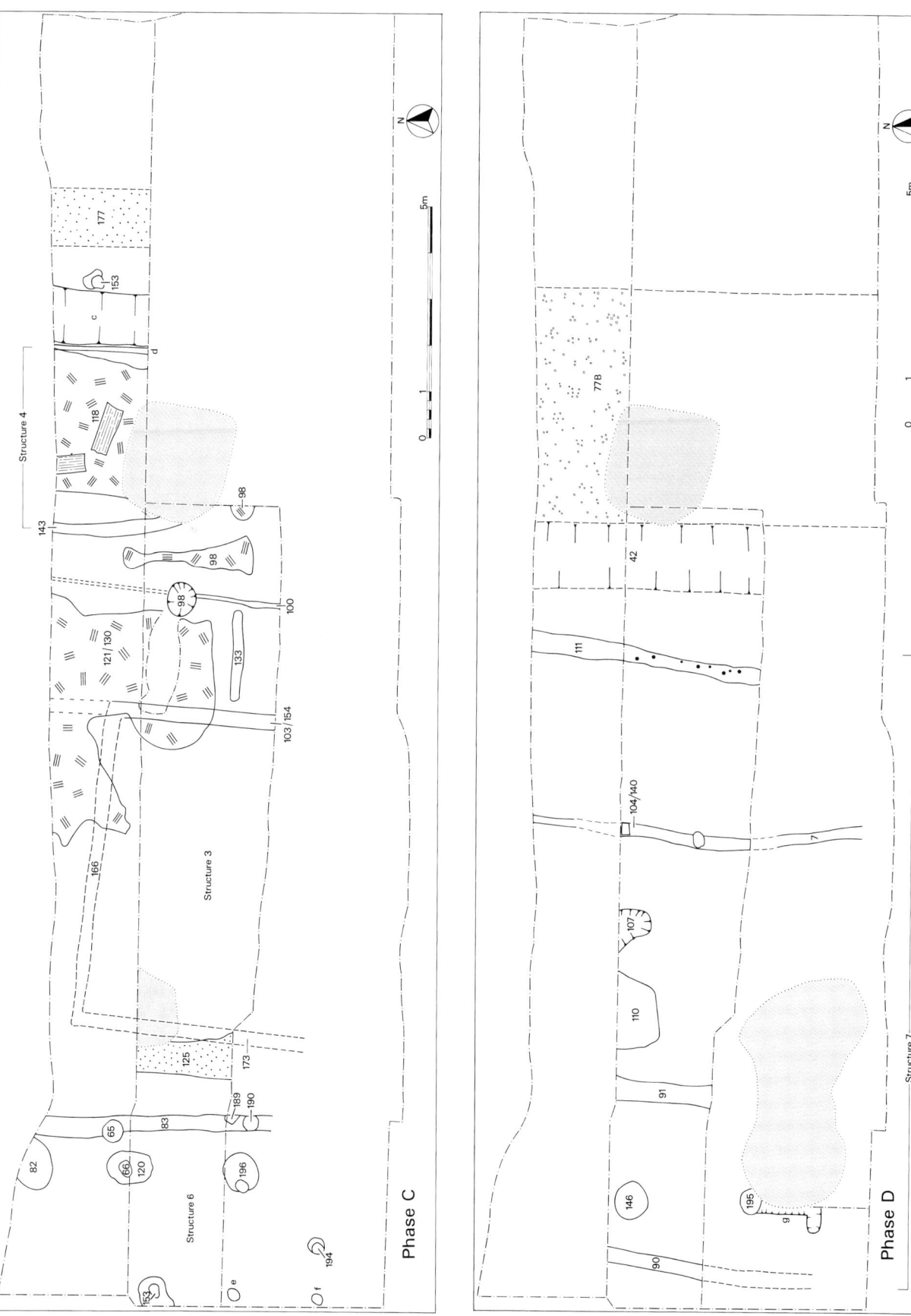

Figure 8   ALC 69, phases C and D, plans

To the west of structure 3 there is a further possible structure which may be of this phase, structure 6. It could, alternatively, belong to phase D, although none of the dating evidence from the features of this structure includes material contemporary with the Hadrianic date of phase D.

Structure 6 is comprised of two north–south rows of postholes fronted by a slot (**83**) also containing various postholes. The westernmost posthole row includes two un-numbered postholes (un-numbered features **e** and **f**), and posthole (**153**); the eastern row comprised (**82**), (**196**) and (**66/89/120**); whilst slot (**83**), contained postholes (**65**), (**189**), and (**190**). Slot (**83**) cuts slot (**84**), which appears to belong to phase B, whilst posthole (**66/89/120**) is sealed by (**44**) of phase D and posthole (**194/195**) is sealed by (192) of phase D. To the east of (**83**) was a north–south strip of gravel, (**125**), which may have been a pathway.

At the end of this phase the site seems to have been deliberately levelled, evidence of this coming from extensive deposits of burnt clay over the eastern half of the site. These deposits (***118***), (***121/130***), and (**98**) included carbonised impressions of burnt planks probably from the superstructure of the buildings.

Phase D (Fig 8)

After the demolition at the end of phase C there seems to have been a general accumulation of silt across the site with deposits (*78*), (106), (***121/130***), and (*46*). These deposits are placed in this phase rather than at the end of phase C as they contain Hadrianic material which is absent from phase C. Cutting (*130*) was quite a large pit (*137*), filled with sand and clay, which would appear to be cut by slot (***111***). After the site had apparently lain open for a little time for the silt accumulation, a new north–south road, (***77B***), seems to have been laid out, around 5.1m wide (Figs 7 and 8), with a shallow ditch (***42***) running along its western margin.

To the west of (***42***) a further building or buildings (structure 7) was constructed, again of posts set in foundation slots. The easternmost north–south slot was (***111***), with evidence of close-set posts within it. Some 3.4m to its west was (***7/104/140***) another north–south slot parallel to (***111***). Some 5.2m west of (***7/104/140***) was a further parallel slot (**91**), with another (**90**), 3.4m west of (**91**). All of these slots could credibly belong to a single structure, either an aisled structure aligned north–south, or one of courtyard form. As with most of the other structures there is no evidence of any floor levels associated with these slots. Slot (**91**) is recorded as cutting a later silt deposit ((87) of phase F), but from the site photographs it would appear to fit much better with the other slots in this phase. Slot (***7/104/140***) seems to have had spaced flat stones placed in it, perhaps post pads for more substantial posts than those in (***111***), which would be consistent with a building of aisled form.

It is possible that the westernmost room/aisle of structure 7 was subdivided by a T-shaped slot, (un-numbered feature **g**) and the posthole (**195**) (it should be noted that this number was also allocated to a post pit of posthole (194) of phase C), which seems to fit reasonably in here in terms of plan, whilst some Hadrianic or later pottery comes from (**195**).

Later in this phase, presumably after the demolition of structure 7, several pits seem to have been cut within it; a small pit (**146**), and two larger ones, (**110**) and (**107**).

Phase E (Fig 9, Plate 2)

This phase directly succeeds phase D with a re-surfacing of road (***77***) (***77A***) and the continued use of the roadside ditch (***42***). There may have been another ditch (***51/76***) to the east of the road, but the dating evidence suggests that this feature is more appropriately placed in phase F. Immediately to the west of (***42***) a post-built hut was constructed. Most of the posts are only recorded on plan, only two (**112**) and (**132**) being numbered. This building (structure 8) seems rather better defined in the site photographs than it appears in plan (Plate 2). It seems to have contained three rooms and to have involved activity which resulted in considerable wear on the earth floor as it was worn down into a large hollow (**108**), up to 0.3m deep. This hollow was backfilled and the area would appear to have been re-floored with a gravel layer, (**101**). There are a few stone blocks on the wall lines, presumably foundations for daub walls. One other feature which might belong to this phase is a pit (**52**) on the west side of the site and also (43/44) described as 'scrappy traces of rubble wall footings' but which were unplanned. The latest feature of this phase would seem to be a silt accumulation (*60*) and (109) over the latest floor level (**101**) of structure 8, presumably after the demolition of structure 8.

Phase F (Fig 9)

This phase seems to succeed phase E after the accumulation of silt (*60*) and consists of the laying out of a new north–south road to the west of (***77***) (phases D and E). The cobbled road surface (***41***) was c 5.9m wide on a make-up of layered stones (61). About 7.5m to the east of the new road is the ditch (***51/76***) which may originally have been cut as the eastern roadside ditch for the earlier road (***77***) (phase E), but the only clear dating evidence from the pottery indicates that this ditch was still open and in the process of silting-up as late as phase F (see discussion below). There is no clear evidence to support its existence earlier than this phase, other than its proximity to (***77***).

There appear to be no other associated structures of this phase, only a few scattered pits, the principal one being (***161***) to the west of the road, although some of the pits on the eastern edge of the site (Fig 10) may also be of this phase rather than phase G.

1969 and 1972 Baromix excavations (ALC 69 and ALC 72/2)

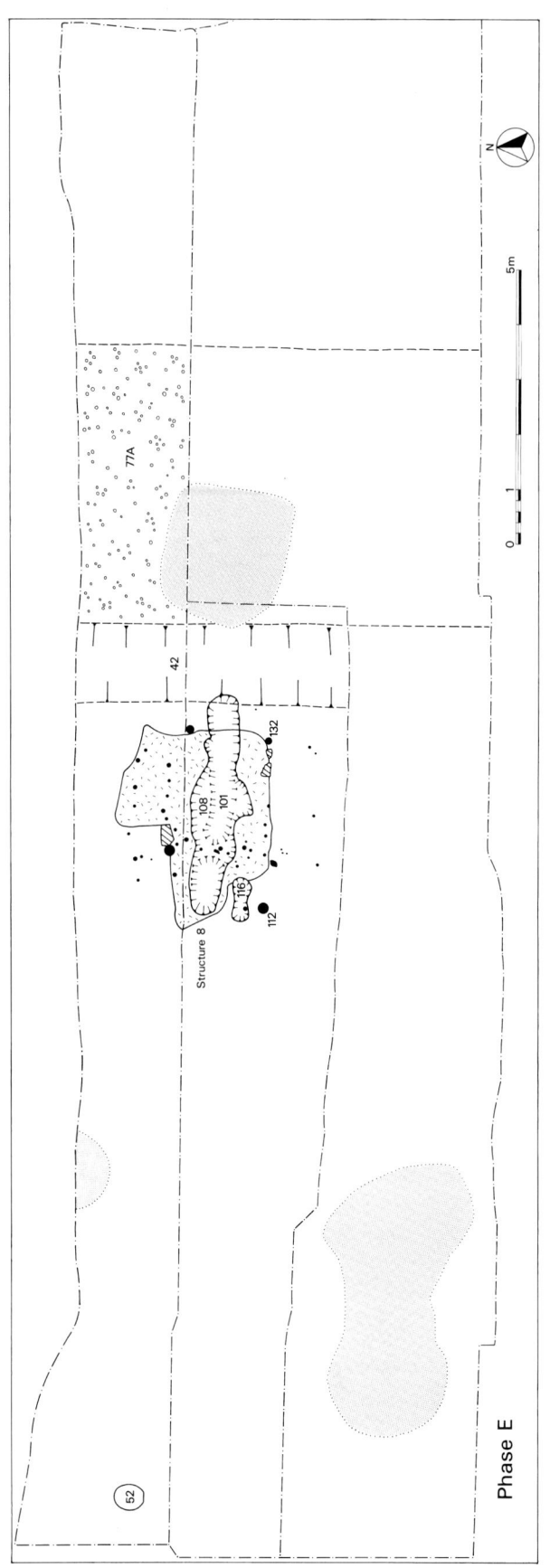
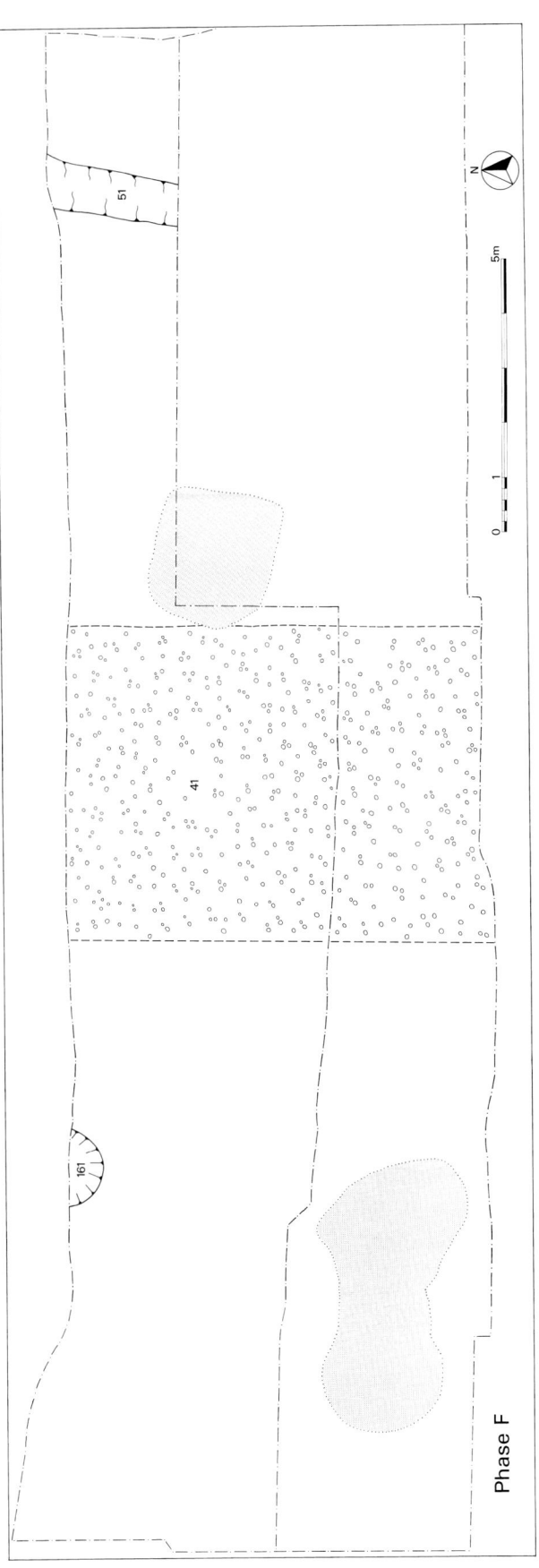

Figure 9   ALC 69, phases E and F, plans

Plate 2   Structure 8, phase E (ALC 69)

Apparently sealing the road surface (*41*) was a silt accumulation (*20*) of some depth.

Phase G (Fig 10, Plate 3)

This is the latest Roman phase on the site and might be sub-divided into two to judge from the section (Fig 7). The principal feature is the laying down of another road surface (*40*) on the same course as the phase F road (*41*), around 8.3m wide (Plate 3).

To the east of the road (*40*) was a complex of pits, (*62*), (*47*), (*58*), (*59*), and (*65B*) which cut the silted-up phase F gully (*51/76*), and these pits were sealed by a silt accumulation (19). To the west of the road were a few pits and postholes, (*68*), (52), and (*92/93*) cutting a silt deposit (*87*), which seems to date from this phase.

Road (*40*), recorded as a single stratigraphic unit appears from Fig 7 to have been resurfaced (*40a*) after a slight silting developed over the surface (*40b*). There is no evidence of any substantial buildings in this latest Roman phase and no foundations or robber trenches are recorded, although the sequence has probably been truncated by medieval agriculture.

Phase H (Fig 10, Plate 4)

This phase includes all medieval activity on the site. This includes a series of pits, gullies and postholes cut into the later Roman silt accumulations of phase F and G. The upper Roman road surface (*40a*) appears to have still remained in use for part of this period as a cambered road, at a higher level than the medieval features on either side (Fig 7 and archive photographs). It was cut, presumably in this phase, by a semicircular gully (**8**), the function of which is unclear, and the eastern side of (*40a*) was cut by a pit (**88**), but otherwise the pits and postholes of this area tended to avoid it. To the east of the road was a zone of pits, (**2**), (**3**), and (**17**), pit (**3**) being apparently associated with a slot (**24**) and a posthole (**38**). Along the eastern edge of the site was a series of postholes, (**10**), (**11**), (**12**), (**13**), (**14**), (**16**), and (**21**) which cannot be interpreted into a structure or structures, but may have been the back of buildings fronting onto the modern line of Bleachfield Street.

To the west of the late Roman road the main structure of this period was a stone lined oven (**6**) fed by a stone flue from a firing pit (**5, 5A**), which was probably a malting kiln (Plate 4). Immediately east of stokehole (**5**) was a posthole (**4**), which may have been associated with it.

North-west of the malting kiln in the north-west corner of the site was a large pit (**23**) and running along the northern margin of the site were several series of small postholes (**26–30**), the (**31**) group, and (*32–37*). These form small groups probably supporting screens or fencing.

There are good pottery groups from pit (**3**) and the malting kiln, all of which seem to be broadly contemporary and probably of 12th/13th-century date.

1969 and 1972 Baromix excavations (ALC 69 and ALC 72/2)

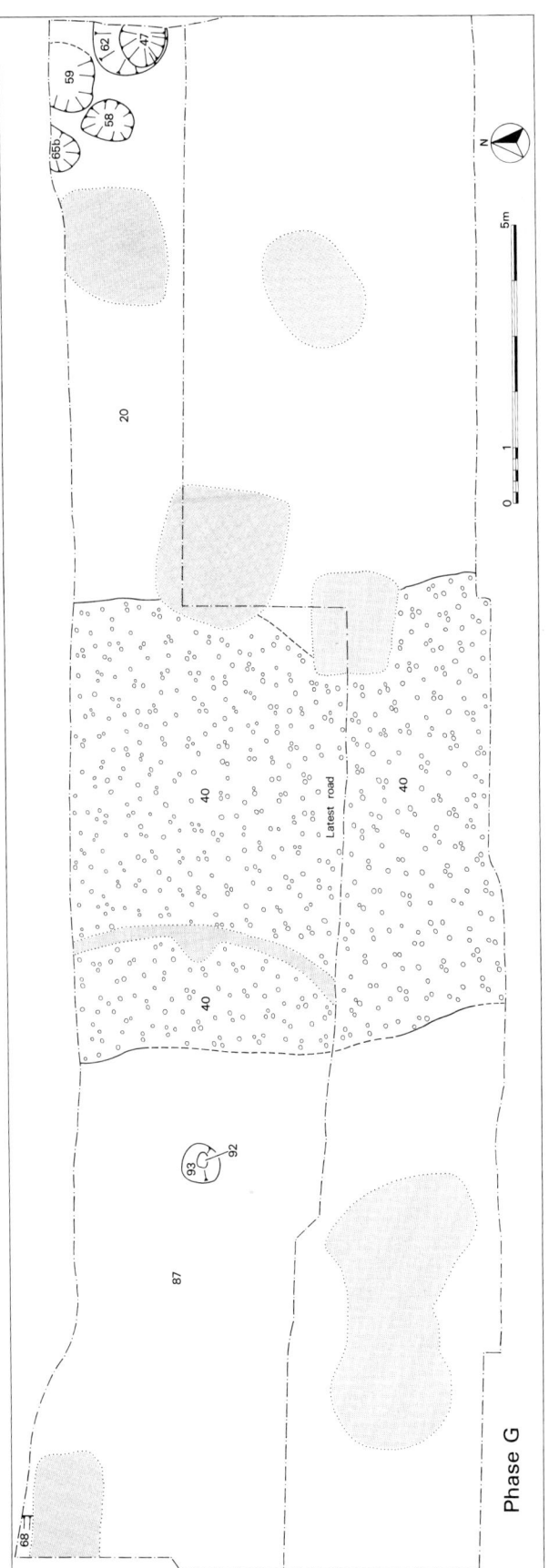
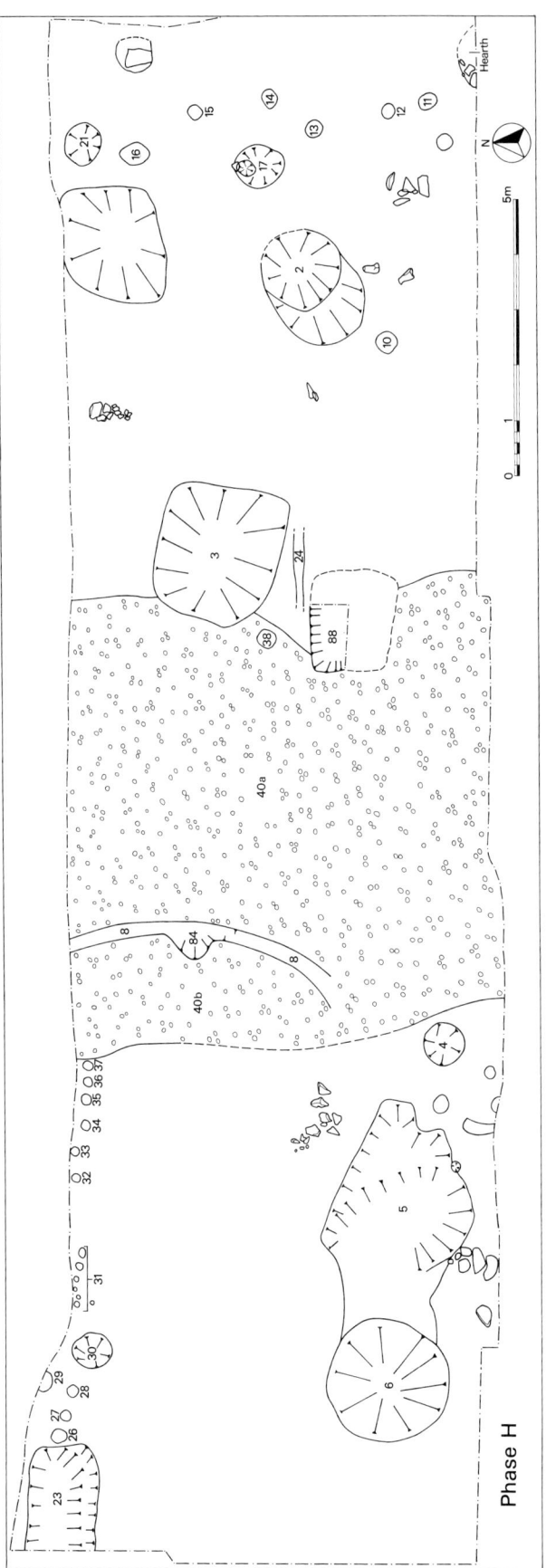

Figure 10   ALC 69, phases G and H, plans

1969 and 1972 Baromix excavations (ALC 69 and ALC 72/2)

Plate 3   Final north-south road 40, phase G (ALC 69)

Plate 4   Malting kiln 6 and stokehole 5, phase H (ALC 69)

1972 excavations (ALC 72/2)

Phase A (Fig 11, Plate 5)

Little can be made of the primary occupation upon the site and it seems probable that it was not fully excavated to natural. It also seems likely that many of the stakeholes, which appeared as voids, were of this period and those which cannot more credibly be assigned to another phase are shown on Fig 11. The only excavated feature of this period was a gully or beam slot, (**72**), in the south-west corner of the site running north-east to south-west and curving slightly. Also possibly of this phase was a yellow sandy layer, (96), in the north-east extension to the trench, and (97), a pit cutting it. The alignment of (**72**), and its relationship to (**88**) (see below phase B), preclude it from belonging with the other features of phase B, whilst material from (96) seems consistent in date with the earliest occupation on the site.

Phase B (Fig 13, Plates 5–6)

In this phase the first substantial building remains can be determined, together with some indication of their plan. The most substantial feature of the phase appears to be (**62**), a deep, square-cut gully entering the area in the north-west, running east-south-east for around 5m and then turning almost 90 degrees to the south and running south out of the south side of the excavated area. The nature and size of the cut and the fact that it runs downhill, the site sloping down from north to south, suggest that this was a drain. This drain is sealed by the phase C cobbling (98) as the section (Fig 12) shows. (The finds from (**62**) are attributed to phase F as its southern part was re-cut then as part of drain (**48**) and the later finds seem to have been mixed with those from (**62**).)

To the east of (**62**) was a series of three north–south timber slots and an un-numbered east–west one (**i**) which runs along their northern ends. These would seem to define the north-western corner of a rectilinear building. The westernmost slot was (**104**), with a series of stakeholes in it, whilst c 1.5m to the east was the next, (**103**). Within this area, towards the northern end, was a pit or posthole, (**122**), sealed by (99), a silt which presumably accumulated after demolition of the structure, and which in turn is sealed by the cobbling (98) of phase C. To the east of (**103**) an un-numbered slot **h**, also recorded as sealed by (99), ran parallel to (**103**) about 0.7m away, the two presumably defining a north–south corridor about 0.8m wide. No further north–south slots were encountered east of the un-numbered slot **h**, suggesting that the eastern room was a minimum of just over 2m wide. The un-numbered slot **i** which runs east–west along the northern end of these slots has been attributed to this phase on the grounds that it seems from the plans that it is early in the sequence and it fits well here in terms of plan.

To the west of (**62**) two parallel east–west slots (**67**), and (**77/78**) have been traced; (**67**), being recorded as sealed by the silt layer (99) discussed above. A north–south slot (**88**) appears to run between (**67**) and (**77/78**) along the western section. This presumably cut the phase A gully (**72**) but no relationship between them is recorded. (It should be noted that the exact location on the plan from which these features are taken is not certain and it is possible that they have been mislocated about 1m south of their true positions, which would put (**67**) in line with (**i**).) Slots (**67**) and (**77/78**) were about 2.6m apart and ran east for at least 2.0m from (**88**). An east wall might be defined by the north–south stake-

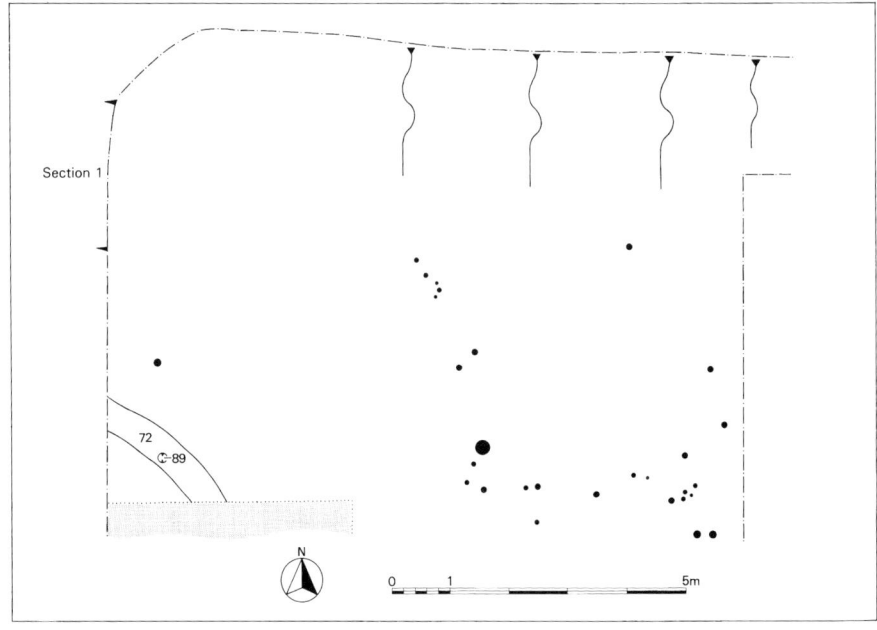

Figure 11   ALC 72/2, phase A, plan

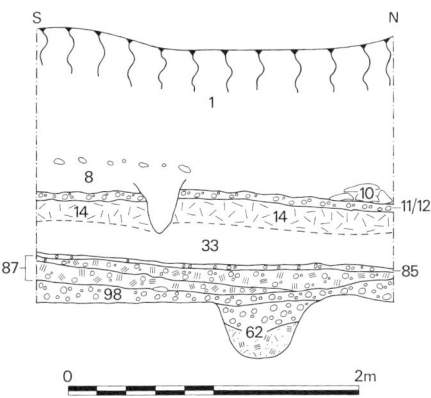

Figure 12   ALC 72/2, section 1, west edge of trench

hole void alignment to the north and east of (**67**), in which case the room so defined would measure *c* 2.6m east–west, making it almost exactly square. These slots are presumably at the north-eastern corner of a rectilinear building aligned north–south or east–west. Presumably after their deliberate demolition, silt deposits, particularly (99), accumulated over the site. One of these (70) contains a sherd of samian which would seem to be intrusive, but it is recorded as being sealed by cobbling (**69**) of phase C so it should belong in this phase.

Phase C (Fig 14, Plates 5–6)

This phase seems to commence with cobbling (*98*) and, perhaps, (**69**) being laid over much of the area, after which a further timber slot building seems to have been constructed. Details of this are less clear than for phase B but two timber slots running north–south and parallel to each other, (**102**) and (**117**), are recorded cutting the cobbling (*98*). Slot (**117**) contains, or appears to contain, a line of stakeholes running up its eastern side, and where the cut finishes to the north, the stakeholes appear to turn west and run on in a westerly direction. It seems that in this area the site was not excavated down to natural, so that this alignment could well have been the northern wall line of the structure. Slot (**102**) terminates at the north somewhat farther south than (**117**), where the plans suggest it was truncated by the later cuts of gullies (**80**) and (**58**). Were there to have been an east–west slot lining up with the north end of (**117**) this would seem to have been truncated by the later gully (**58**). There are various minor pits or postholes which can be attributed to this phase on stratigraphic grounds (**51, 59, 94/95, 110, 111, 114, 115, 112, 119**) of which (**59**) appears to be a small clay-lined oven immediately to the west of (**102**). Also in this area was a shallow pit/scoop (**121**) which may be of this phase as it seems to be fairly early and contains material of a date consistent with this phase. There is also another oven immediately to the east of (**51**) which could be of this phase or perhaps more likely of phase B, but it is not recorded except on the photographs.

Overall this phase would seem to constitute parts of a rectilinear building or buildings, aligned north–south or east–west, of very similar layout to those of phase B.

Phase D (Fig 15)

This phase is somewhat problematic and could well be regarded as part of phase C. The principal features are two superimposed spreads of burnt clay (**52**) and (**53**) in the south-east corner of the site in

Plate 5   West part of site showing features of phases A–C (ALC 72/2)

1969 and 1972 Baromix excavations (ALC 69 and ALC 72/2)

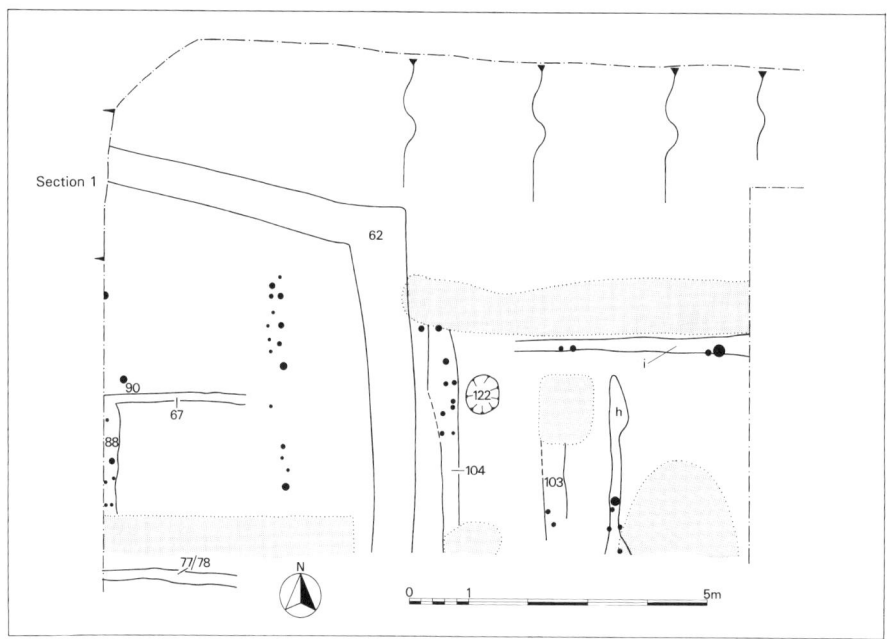

Figure 13   ALC 72/2, phase B, plan

Plate 6   Centre and east part of site, features of phases B and C (ALC 72/2)

the area to the east of, and overlapping, the phase C timber slot (**102**). These are described in the records as a 'burnt clay floor' and could be the flooring for a room to the west of (**102**), although they might equally represent demolition debris. However, these burnt clay deposits are recorded as sealing layer (61/105) a silt accumulation which seals most of the features, including (**102**) and (**117**) of phase C. Also

layer (**53**) contains a little Black-Burnished ware, suggesting a Hadrianic or later date, which none of the preceding deposits contains. It is possible that (**52**) and (**53**) were secondary flooring in this area. Floors might be expected to overlap the timber slots, but they can hardly have been primary floor surfaces unless all the other cut features of phase C precede the construction of the building, and in effect consti-

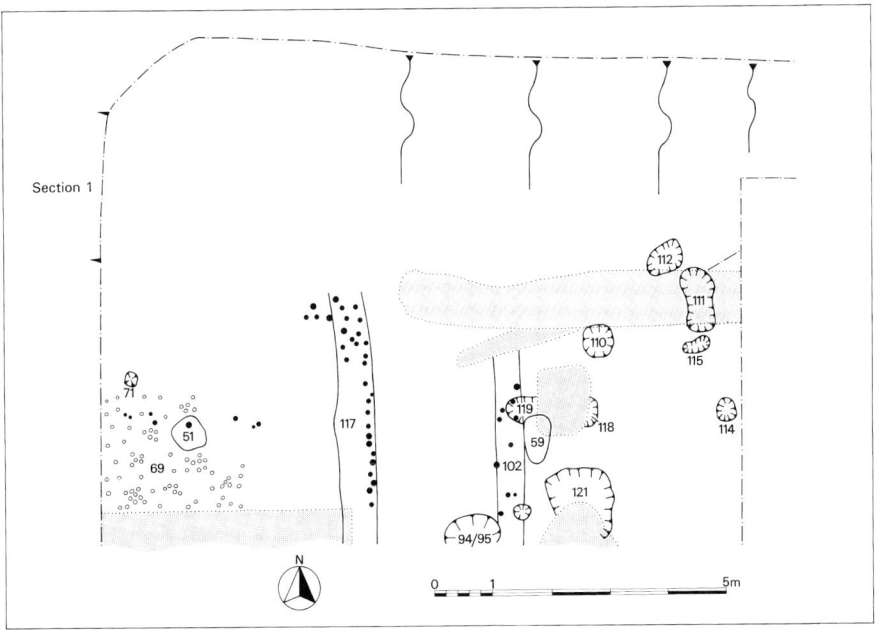

Figure 14 ALC 72/2, phase C, plan

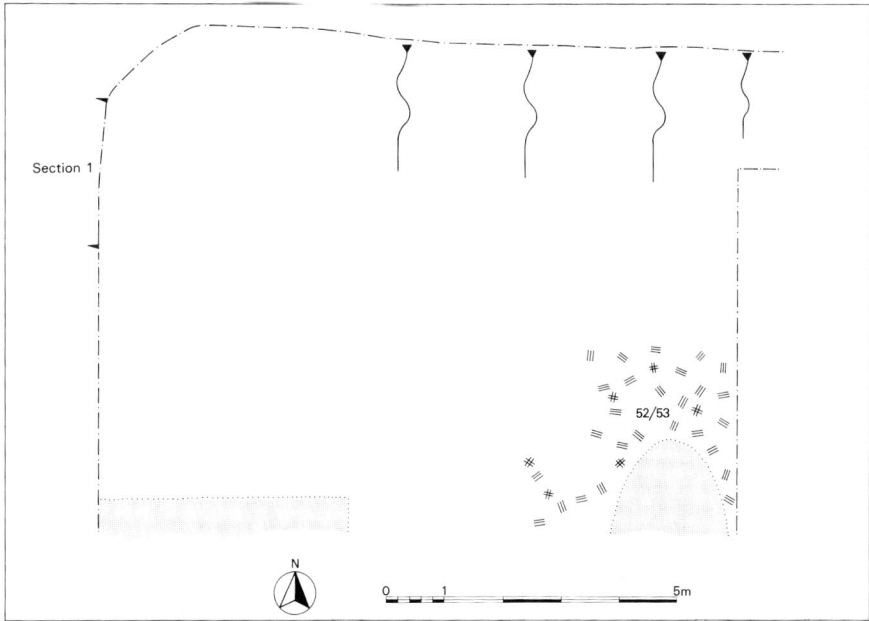

Figure 15 ALC 72/2, phase D, plan

tute a separate phase, along with (*98*), prior to the construction of the building. Overall the sequence of some silting followed by a burnt clay spread seems more credibly interpreted as abandonment of the structures, followed by their deliberate demolition and levelling, with much of the superstructures being burnt.

Phase E (Fig 16)

After phases B and C, with structures of a very similar layout, phase E sees a complete change in the alignments of the site and is clearly of Hadrianic date. The principal features are a shallow gully (**50**), running north-west to south-east across the site, with a second gully or timber slot, (**80**), starting a little to the east of (**50**) and running approximately at right-angles to it. (**50**) is cut by drain (**48**) (phase F), of a similar alignment and appears to cut slot (**117**) (phase C). Gully (**80**) is cut by gully (**58**) of phase F and appears in plan to cut (**102**) of phase C. Both (**80**) and (**50**) contain sherds of Black-Burnished ware (BB1). Gully (**50**), as noted above, has a similar alignment to drain (**48**) of the succeeding phase and may also have performed this

1969 and 1972 Baromix excavations (ALC 69 and ALC 72/2)

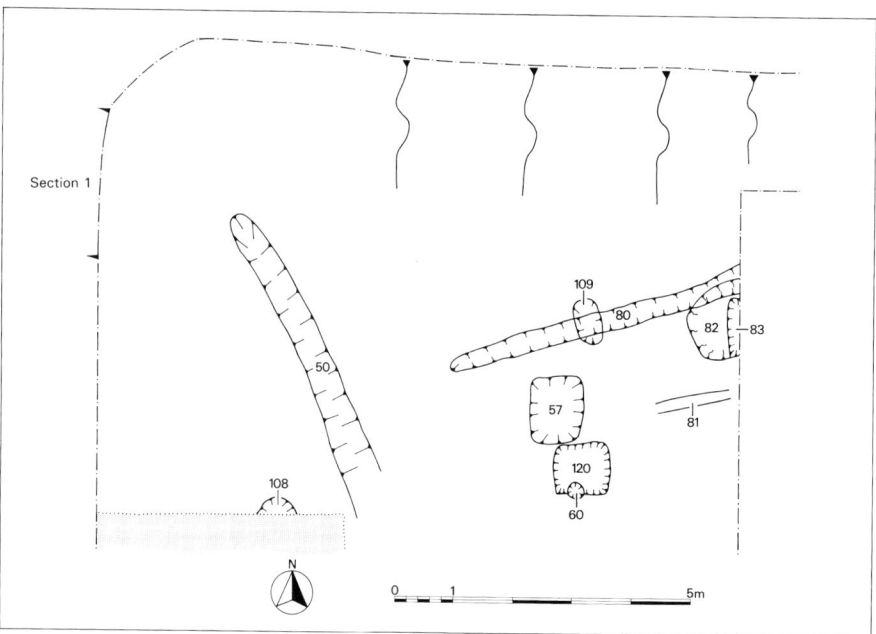

Figure 16 ALC 72/2, phase E, plan

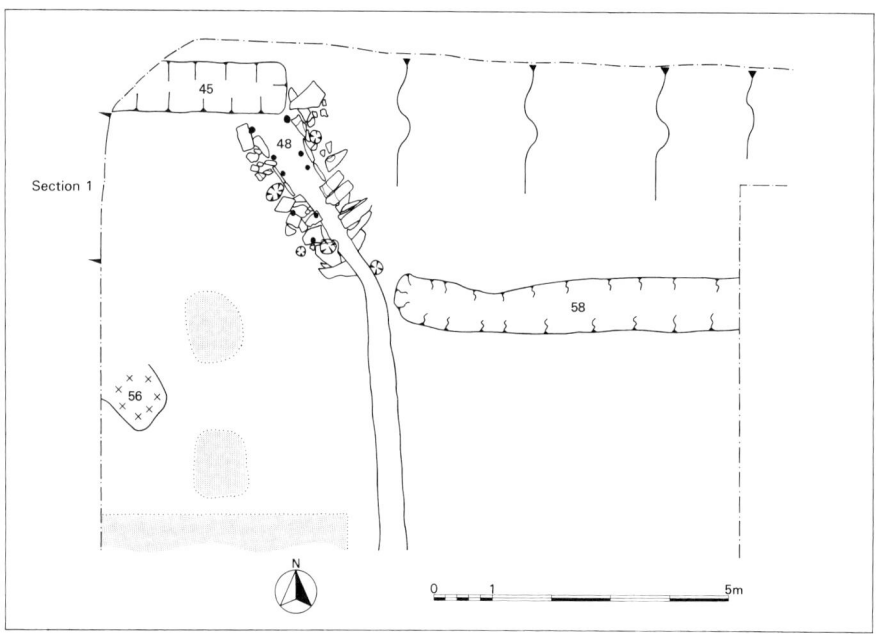

Figure 17 ALC 72/2, phase F, plan

function. Its north end is recorded within the trench but, as will be discussed further below, the northern side of the trench seems to have been badly truncated and it may originally have run further in this direction. Feature (**80**) seems unlikely to be a drain as such but it may perhaps have been a boundary ditch. Running parallel to (**80**) and 1.3m to the south is another stretch of gully or timber slot, (**81**). This is recorded as 'sealed by (61)' (of phase D), but it makes little sense in phase C and the logic of symmetry would suggest that it should be of this phase. Other features of this phase include an area of cobbling (*87*) sealed by a silt accumulation (*86*), and postholes or pits (**82, 83, 57, 120, 60, 108**, and **109**).

The impression given is of an open area used for some minor activity appropriate to the rear of a property, or other peripheral location, and perhaps divided into enclosures by the gullies. It is of note that the alignments of these gullies are similar to those of the property lines on the Explosion site to the north (see below).

At the end of this phase a period of Roman excavation and levelling, truncating previous deposits over the northern half of the site, must be inferred. Virtually no early deposits survive before phase E in this

Plate 7   Stone drain 48, phase F (ALC 72/2)

area, and what there are, appear to be very early in the sequence. As noted above, gully (**50**) may well have originally extended further north. Deposits from phase E and particularly from phase G seal the area, so that the truncation must precede these. Presumably greater activity was envisaged in the area to the north of the site and a levelling out of natural undulations was determined upon.

Phase F (Fig 17, Plate 7)

The principal feature of this phase was a drain, in part stone-lined (**48**/54). This ran north-west to south-east across the northern part of the site and then seems to have turned south and presumably followed the course of the slumped fill over gully (*62*) of phase B. Drain (**48**) was lined in the north with limestone slabs which seem to have been secured by posts and presumably a wattle lining to judge by the rows of stakeholes down each side. The drain had a silt fill, (49). Running east–west up to the north of (**48**) was a deep gully (**45**) which may perhaps have been a continuation of (**48**) turning west, just as (*62*) had done previously. It contained 2nd-century samian ware and was sealed by deposits of phase H. It must therefore belong to this phase or phase E, but seems to fit best in this phase. Also of this phase was an extensive area of cobbling on the west side of the site, (*85*) (which sealed deposits of phase E), and probably an east–west gully, (**58**), on the eastern side of the site. Gully (**58**) cut gully (**80**) (of phase E) and contained 2nd-century material so it presumably belongs in this phase. Its purpose is unclear unless it is a property boundary relating to activity on the street frontage to the east.

Both the cobbling and drain (**48**/54) were sealed by a silt accumulation (*14/33/34*) and (*32*) dated to the 3rd century. Other features which may be of this phase are a mortar spread (**56**) containing 2nd- to 3rd-century material, which succeeds the inferred truncation and was deposited on the

1969 and 1972 Baromix excavations (ALC 69 and ALC 72/2)

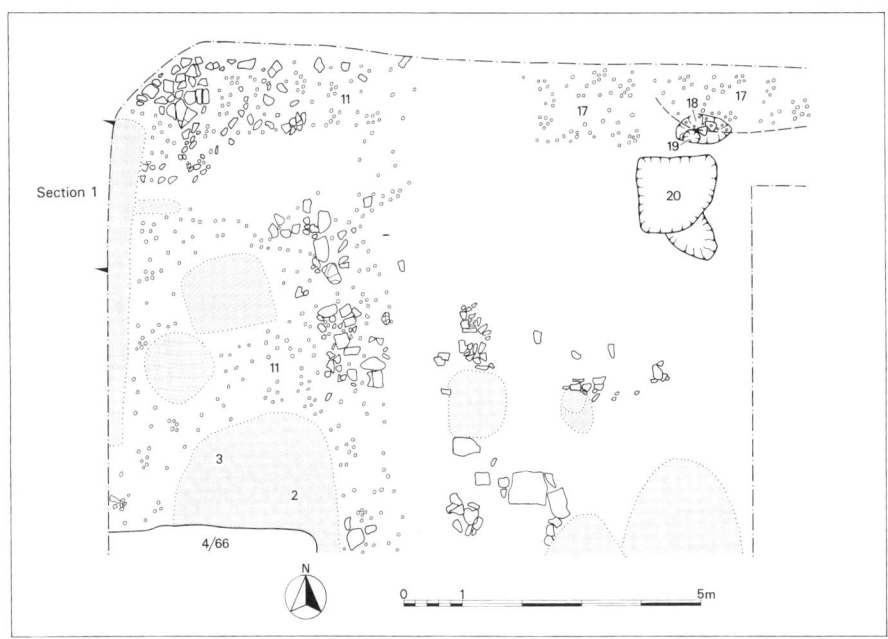

Figure 18   ALC 72/2, phase G, plan

Plate 8   West part of site showing features of phase G (ALC 72/2)

phase C cobbling (**69**), and a shallow irregular area of burnt material (40) which was sealed by (*33*) and contains material of a date consistent with this phase.

Phase G (Fig 18, Plate 8)

The principal features of this phase are extensive areas of cobbling over the western side of the site and on its north. On the west of the site an area of cobbling (13), was succeeded by further extensive cobbling (***11***), whilst other areas of cobbling are represented by (65), and on the north side of the site the upper cobbling is (**17**) overlaying another layer (35). The cobbling (**17**) also seals a posthole (**18**) and probably seals a pit (**20**). Pit (**20**) contains Oxfordshire pottery dated c AD 270–400+.

Other minor features probably of this phase are: (**19**), a posthole cutting the upper cobbling (**17**); (*37*) and (*38/39*), both postholes with material of a date compatible with the phase; and (*10*), an area of sandstone rubble in the north-west of the trench overlying the upper cobbling (*11*).

In the south-west of the trench there is a deep medieval robber trench (**4/66**) which runs 4.0m east from the west section and then turns south. This cuts deposits of phase E and seems likely to represent the robbing out of a later Roman stone wall. This is the latest, and probably the most appropriate phase to which such a putative feature could belong and it may be that there was a stone building of this phase.

Phase H

There appears to have been little activity in the area in the medieval period with only a few pits, the robber trench (**4/66**) (discussed above, phase G) and the flue of a medieval drying/malting kiln (**2**) in a pit (**3**).

Baromix 1969 and 1972 phase dates

Phase A

On ALC 69 this phase contains some Neronian samian but also Flavian material, the latest dating to AD 80–110 (see below, Fig 24). At ALC 72/2 there is only a single samian vessel (see Ward below, Fig 35, no 1) dated *c* AD 55–80. The dating evidence is compatible with both of these adjacent sites commencing at the same time and there are strong reasons from the structural evidence of phases B and C for both of these phases to be exactly contemporary on each site (see above). Overall the samian evidence might seem to suggest occupation from *c* AD 65 to *c* AD 85. On ALC 69 the phase contains two coins of Vespasian (nos 3 and 5) dated to AD 71 and AD 72 respectively.

Phase B

This phase and phase C are marked on both sites by rectilinear buildings aligned roughly north–south, parallel to the road which runs through the ALC 69 site (Fig 2 and 3, street D). These are constructed of timbers set in laying-out/foundation trenches which find parallels on many Flavian military sites, and the copper alloy small finds from both sites include a number of items of military equipment from this phase and phase A. The quantity of early Roman *militaria* amongst the small finds from both sites is relatively great and would tend to suggest the presence of a fort (on undoubted fort sites it may not account for more than 5% of all small finds). Although other reasons may be found for the presence of this type of material on sites (Millett 1990, 60), in this case a fort seems likely, especially when taken with the, admittedly fragmentary, building types. The case seems to be further strengthened by the apparent deliberate demolition and levelling of both sites at the end of phase C on ALC 69 (phase D on ALC 72/2), a phenomenon less likely in a series of privately owned civilian buildings unless they were removed for some coherent succeeding structure, which they were not in this case.

This phase succeeds phase A and therefore would appear to post-date *c* AD 80 and contains one sherd, possibly intrusive, dated *c* AD 100–120 (see Ward ALC 72 no 2). A date range perhaps of *c* AD 85–100 might be suggested.

Phase C (and ALC 72/2, phase D)

This follows phase B on both sites and whilst the ALC 69 samian list is exclusively South Gaulish a number of Les Martres pieces appear on the ALC 72/2 site dated *c* AD 100–20 and *c* AD 100–30. Amongst the coarse pottery BB1 is found in context (117) of phase C on ALC 72/2, but is probably intrusive, and it is notably not found in the demolition debris of phase D. However, five pieces come from the demolition levels at the end of phase C on ALC 69 and some, at least, of these would seem to be securely stratified, suggesting that the demolition may have taken place early in the Hadrianic era. A date range of *c* AD 100 to *c* AD 125 might perhaps be suggested for these phases.

ALC 69, phase D

After the end of phase C there is no longer any reason to suggest that the phases on the two sites should necessarily be equivalent, and, indeed, the evidence tends to suggest otherwise. Consequently the phase dates will be discussed separately for each site. Fig 19 shows the stratigraphic sequence of phases on both sites arranged according to the interpretation of their relative chronology. On ALC 69 phase D contained around 2% of BB1 and samian, the latest being two Central Gaulish pieces dated to *c* AD 120–50 and a date range of *c* AD 125–40/50 might be proposed.

ALC 72/2, phase E

This phase succeeds phase D and contains *c* 4% of BB1 and samian, the latest pieces of which are two (see below, Fig 35, nos 8 and 11) dated *c* AD 140–60 of the early Cinnamus group, and a date range of *c* AD 125–50/60 might be suggested.

ALC 69, phase E

ALC 69 phase E follows phase D and contains *c* 9% of BB1 and a number of pieces of later 2nd-century

1969 and 1972 Baromix excavations (ALC 69 and ALC 72/2)

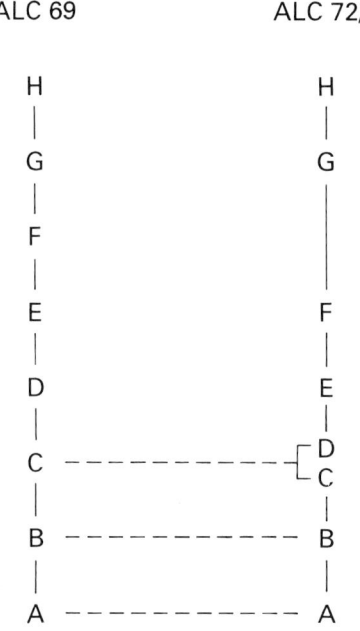

Figure 19 Phase sequence diagram (ALC 69 and ALC 72/2)

samian ware, including nos 30 and 31, dated *c* AD 150–80 and AD 150–200. East Gaulish samian is absent as are Dr 45s and Nene Valley colour-coated ware. Perhaps a date range of *c* AD 150/60–70/80 might be appropriate.

ALC 72/2, phase F

This phase succeeds phase E and contains a good collection of later 2nd-century Central Gaulish samian including two Dr 45s and sherds from twelve East Gaulish vessels, including two flagons dated *c* AD 200–60 (see below, Fig 35, nos 13 and 22). Pink grogged ware (fabric G11; Booth and Green 1989) makes its first appearance, as does Nene Valley colour-coated ware, and BB1 now comprises 22% of the assemblage. The BB1 includes beaded and flanged bowls (Fig 51, no 164) and obtuse lattice decorated jars (Fig 51, no 165), 3rd-century Severn Valley ware forms and Oxfordshire *mortarium*, Young 1977 type M11, *c* AD 180–240 (Fig 52, no 173). Overall a date range of *c* AD 150/60–250/70 might be suggested.

ALC 69, phase F

ALC 69 phase F follows phase E and includes later 2nd-century Central Gaulish samian including a Dr 45 and two pieces of East Gaulish material dated *c* AD 170–220 and *c* AD 160–240. BB1 also rises as a proportion of the assemblage to 12.5%, a lower figure than for ALC 72/2 phase F, and fabric G11 and Nene Valley colour-coated ware first appear in the sequence. However, much of the material in this phase would appear to belong to the 2nd century and is probably residual and there are no BB1 forms datable to the second half of the 3rd century. There are, however, two sherds of wheelmade shell-tempered ware (fabric C11) which does not normally appear before the late 3rd century, although these may be intrusive (contexts (9) and (*51*)), and four sherds of Oxfordshire colour-coated ware come from context (9), which again suggests that material from this context is intrusive. A date range of *c* AD 170/80–230/70 might be suggested.

ALC 72/2, phase G

This phase succeeds phase F. Its pottery includes a sherd of shell-tempered ware (fabric C11) which is unlikely to date before the later 3rd century, an intrusive sherd of medieval material (context (65)), and a BB1 beaded and flanged bowl of later 3rd- to 4th-century date (Fig 53, no 20). There are also four coins of Carausius (see Seaby below, nos 15, 18, 19, and 20) from context (*10*), possibly a small hoard, with another two from unstratified contexts. There is nothing from the phase which need be 4th century and a date range for the phase of *c* AD 250/70–300/10 might be appropriate.

ALC 69, phase G

Much of the pottery from this phase is residual material but sherds of Oxfordshire colour-coated ware (F51) and shell-tempered ware (C11) are present. There is also a BB1 jar of later 3rd- to early 4th-century date (Fig 53, no 197). A later 3rd- to early 4th-century date could be suggested for the phase.

ALC 69 and 72/2, phase H

On both sites phase H contains medieval pottery. On ALC 69 this seems to suggest activity principally of a 12th/13th-century date.

1969 and 1972 Baromix finds (ALC 69 and ALC 72/2)

Roman coins (ALC 69 and ALC 72/2)
Wilfred A Seaby

The coins run from Nero to Arcadius, with at least one each of the coins of those emperors being in very fine condition when lost, suggesting Roman occupation of this area from at least AD 65 to AD 395, although not necessarily continuous. In evidence is the number of recognisable Flavian coins which came to light, no fewer than nine with reasonable certainty out of a total of 38 pieces recovered. One of the Vespasianic specimens, a *dupondius* of AD 72 with the figure of Roma seated left, has on the obverse the legend ending COS III. This type is only quoted by Mattingly and Sydenham (*RIC* II, 77) as a footnote to no 527 and may therefore be considered a rarity. The general absence of *sestertii* and smaller bronze from the 2nd century is surprising, although the *lacuna* of the first half of the 3rd century is very much to be expected. Carausius (AD 287–93) shows up well with six *antoniniani*, but the best preserved pieces are those of the period of Constantine I commencing with a *follis* struck at London in AD 312–3 and following up with one of Constantine II Caesar issued at Lyons in AD 330–1; also one each of the commemorative city types, Urbs Roma and Constantinopolis of much the same period. The Arcadius AE 4 coin has the common VICTORIA AVGGG reverse and was struck at the Arles mint probably about AD 390.

Table 1 Roman coin list (ALC 69)

No	Issuer	Denomination	Date	Mint	Type	Condition	Reference	Context	SF no	Phase
1	Nero	As	54–68	–	Victory advancing l with buckler SPQR; SC	Very fine Decayed	RIC I, 167/ 329	(148)	SF91	D
2	Vespasian	Dup	71	–	COS III SECVRITAS AVGVSTI Securitas seated l in ex SC	Very fine Some decay	RIC II, 72/ 479	(145)	SF122	B
3	Vespasian	As	71	–	COS III FIDES [PVBLICA] Fides l. S-C	Fair/poor	RIC II, 73/ 485	(176)	SF97	A
4	Vespasian	As	71	–	COS III ....[AVG]VSTI. Figure 1	Much decayed	–	(1)	SF4	U/S
5	Vespasian	Dup	72	–	IMP CAESAR VESPASIAN AVG COS III VF ROMA in ex., seated l. on cuirass with wreath & parazonium, circular shield behind; S-C	Some decay	*RIC* II, p 77 n to 527, from description in R It (1896) 161	(178)	SF118	A
6	Vespasian?	Dup?	69–79	–	–	Decayed fragments	–	(137)	SF94	D
7	–	As?	1st/ early 2nd c	–	–	Decayed fragments	–	(177)	SF96	C
8	Trajan	Dup	112–4	–	COS VI FELICITAS AVGVSTI	Very fine Some decay	RIC II, 288/ 626	(148)	SF92	D
9	Gallienus	Ant	253–68	–	–	Very fine Much decay	–	(1)	SF12	U/S
10	Tetricus I	Ant	270–3	–	PAX AVG	Fine Some decay	RIC V pt II, 409/100?	(1)	SF11	U/S
11	Tetricus I?	Ant	270–3	–	Figure standing	Much decayed	–	(6)	SF44	H
12	Tetricus I	Ant, irreg	270–3	–	–	Broken	–	(55)	SF45	H
13	Constantine	Follis	324–8	–	PROVIDENTIAE AVGG	Fine	–	(1)	SF2	U/S
14	Temp Constantine I	AE3	c 333–4	Trier	VRBS ROMA Wolf and twins	Fair+	RIC VII, 218/533	(6)	SF41	H
15	Temp Constantine I	AE3	c 330–1	Trier	CONSTANTINOPOLI Victory on prow	Fine Much decayed	RIC VII, 215/530	(1)	SF3	U/S

Table 2 Roman coin list (ALC 72/2)

No	Issuer	Denomination	Date	Mint	Type	Condition	Reference	Context	SF no	Phase
1	Nero?	As	Mid 1 c	–	S[-C]?	Very worn	–	(98)		C
2	Vespasian	As	69–79		?Rome Female figure l holding cornucopiae?	Poor	–	(98)		C
3	Titus (as Caesar)	As	73	Rome	[VICTORIA] NAVALIS Victory r on prow	Very poor	RIC II, 92/662?	(19)		G
4	Titus or Domitian (as Caesars)	As	72–3	Rome	VICTORIA [NAVALIS]? Victory r on prow, SC	Poor	–	(26)		U/S
5	Vespasian or Titus??	As?	1st c?	–	–	Very poor	–	(61)		D
6	–	As	1st/2nd c	–	–	Very poor	–	(47)		U/S
7	Gallienus	Ant	260–8	Rome	SECVRIT. PERPET Securitas l with sceptre	About fair	RIC V pt I, 155/280?	(1)		U/S
8	Tetricus I	Ant	270–3	–	P] AX AV[G] Pax l	Almost fair/poor	RIC V pt II, 409/100?	(1)		U/S
9	–	Ant?	Late 3c	–	–	Very poor	–	(1)		U/S
10	–	Ant?	Late 3c?	–	–	Very poor	–	(1)		U/S
11	–	AE3?	3rd/4th c?	–	–	Coated with corrosion	–	(1)		U/S
12	–	AE3?	3rd/4th c?	–	–	Thick corrosion	–	(1)		U/S
13	–	AE3?	3rd/4th c?	–	–	Thick corrosion	–	(5)		H
14	–	AE3	3rd/4th c?	–	–	Very poor	–	(15)		U/S
15	Carausius	Ant	291–2	London	CONSE RVAT AVG Sol l holding globe	Poor/fair+	RIC V pt II, 466/29	(10)		G
16	Carausius	Ant	291–2	London	PROVIDENT AVG Providentia l	Almost fair	RIC V pt II, 467/149	(1)		U/S
17	Carausius	Ant	287–93	?	PA[X A]VG. Pax l	Poor	–	(1)		U/S
18	Carausius	Ant	287–92	?	Pax l?	Fine/very poor	–	(10)		G
19	Carausius	Ant	292–3	London	PA[X]AVG Pax l With transverse	Almost fine	RIC V pt II, 474/118	(10)		G
20	Carausius	Ant	292–3	London	P[A]X AVG. PAX l With vertical sceptre	Fine	RIC V pt II, 471/98 var	(11)		G
21	Constantine I	Follis	312–3	London	SIC. Sol l	Almost very fine	RIC VI, 140/281	(1)		U/S
22	Constantine II Caesar	AE3	c 330–1	Lyons	GE. Two standards	Almost fine	RIC VII, 138/254	(1)		U/S
23	Arcadius	AE3/4	388–92	Arles	VICTORIA AV[GGG]	Almost fine	RIC IX, 70/30(e)	(1)		U/S

Roman pottery (ALC 69 and ALC 72/2)
Rowan Ferguson with contributions by Margaret Ward and Jeremy Evans

Introduction
Rowan Ferguson

The exact relationship between these two areas was difficult to ascertain (see discussion of stratigraphy above), but it seems that during the late Neronian and Flavian periods the sites were both occupied by buildings aligned north–south and east–west.

A total of 5102 sherds weighing 98.945kg was found on ALC 69. Of this total, 1188 sherds (23.2%) came from unphased and post-Roman contexts. The 5102 sherds were in 98 different fabrics of which 22 were represented by a single sherd (for fabric descriptions see Table MT1, microfiche M1:A5–A13). On ALC 72/2 the total number of sherds was 1685 and they weighed 38.139kg. Some 575 of these sherds (34.1%) were residual in post-Roman layers or in unphased deposits. There were only 48 fabrics present of which 14 were represented by one sherd.

Fig 20 shows histograms of the proportions of Roman pottery by phase from the ALC 69 and ALC

1969 and 1972 Baromix finds (ALC 69 and ALC 72/2)

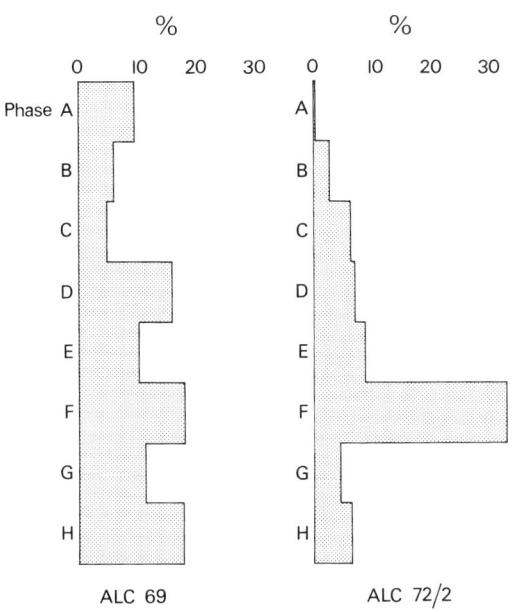

Figure 20 Proportions of Roman pottery from each phase (ALC 69 and ALC 72/2)

72/2 sites. The overall trends are fairly similar with the quantities of pottery gradually rising to a peak in the 3rd century (phase F). However there are marked differences, with the more extensive excavation of phase A deposits on the ALC 69 site being reflected by 9.8% of pottery coming from these, compared with a mere 0.1% from the equivalent deposits on the ALC 72/2 site. The latest phase of rectilinear buildings and the burnt demolition deposits over them (phases C and D at ALC 72/2 and phase C at ALC 69) contain much more pottery on the ALC 72/2 site than on ALC 69, although the reasons for this are not very clear. Phase D on ALC 69 and phase E at ALC 72/2, representing the Hadrianic to early Antonine period, show marked contrasts with 16% of material on ALC 69 and only 9% on ALC 72/2. This seems to adequately reflect the level of activity on them with a possible aisled building at ALC 69, but just property boundaries/gullies on ALC 72/2. Phases E and F on ALC 69 and phase F at ALC 72/2 represent late 2nd- to 3rd-century activity and both add up to around 30% of all the pottery. However, there is little evidence of structural activity on either

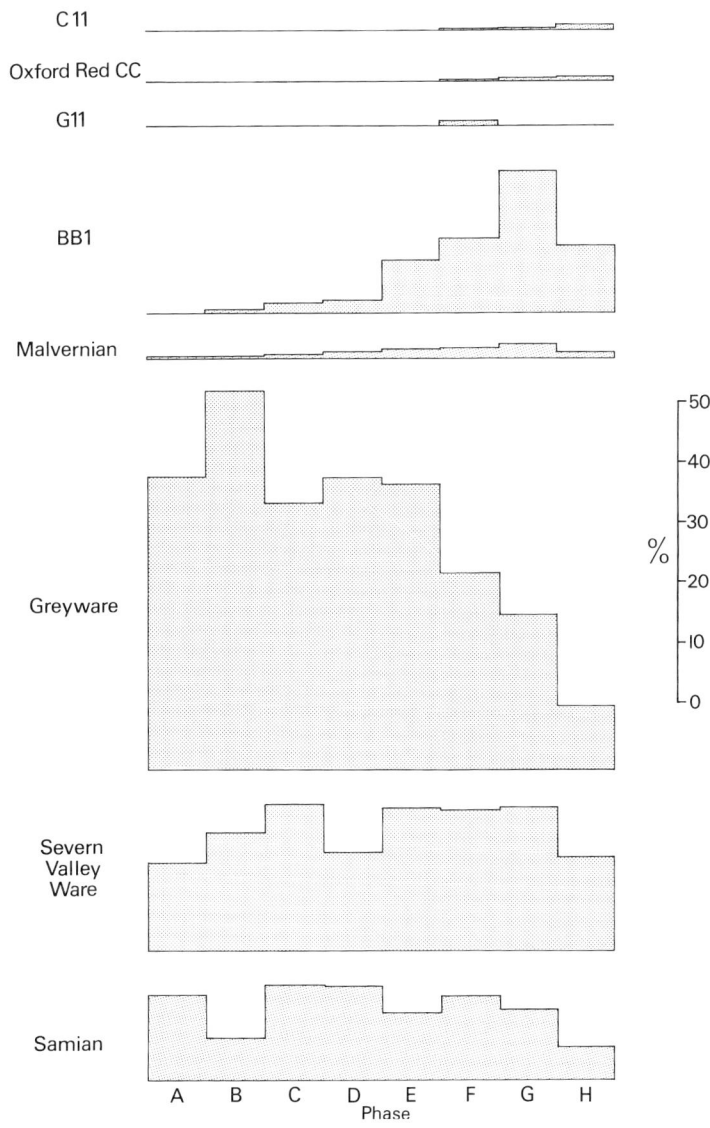

Figure 21 Roman pottery, major fabric class proportions by phase (ALC 69)

1969 and 1972 Baromix finds (ALC 69 and ALC 72/2)

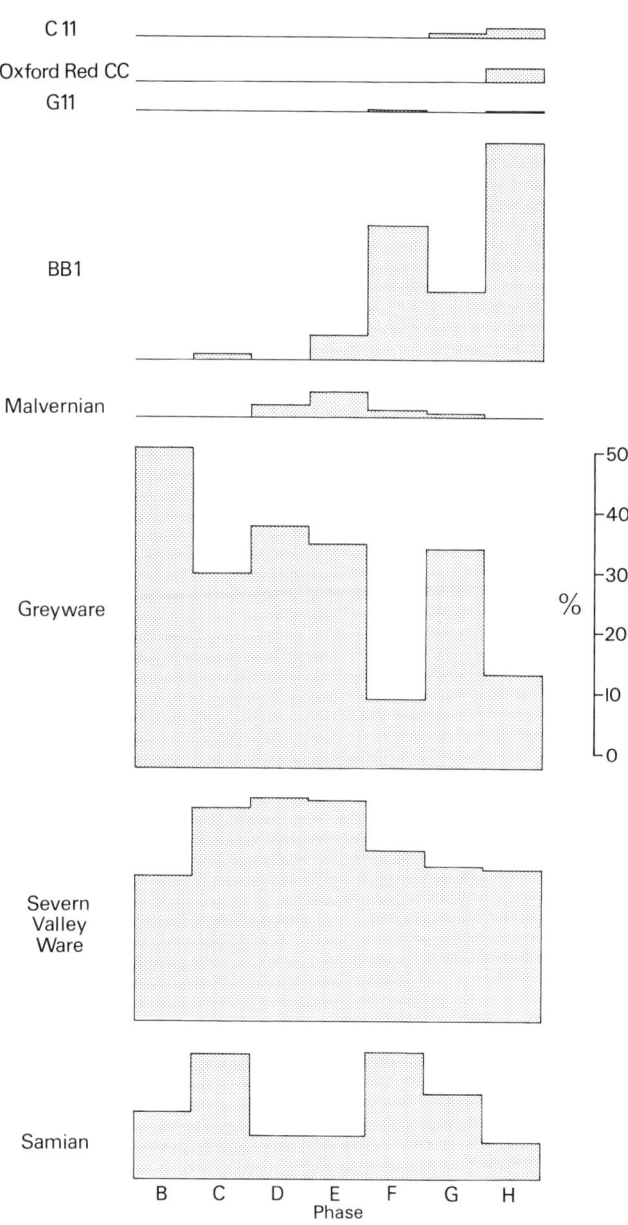

Figure 22   Roman pottery, major fabric class proportions by phase (ALC 72/2)

site. Rather, rubbish seems to have been allowed to accumulate on the sites, which probably suggests activity nearby, either to the south (Cracknell and Mahany 1994), or to the north, with dumps from the walled town and the buildings on the Explosion site (Cracknell 1996; and see Booth below). Both sites show little sign of rubbish accumulation or activity in the 4th century, with much of what pottery there is being residual and these deposits are partly truncated. However, the Roman residual material from post-Roman deposits also shows little material which can be dated to the 4th century. Phase H (medieval) shows much more material on ALC 69 (17.9%), than on ALC 72/2 (6.4%), reflecting greater contemporary activity, much of which cut into the Roman deposits here.

Throughout the Roman period the pottery market in Alcester was dominated by local reduced fabrics, Severn Valley wares, and Black-Burnished ware in varying quantities. The fluctuations in this market will be discussed in detail below. Other coarse wares which were found included Malvernian metamorphic and shell-gritted fabrics. The fine wares represented contact with a wide range of Romano-British and Continental production centres of which Oxfordshire, Mancetter-Hartshill, the Nene Valley, and northern Gaul were perhaps the most significant.

The value of this pottery assemblage in furthering our knowledge of Roman Alcester lies in the probable military connections of the late Neronian to early Flavian activities on the site, the density of 2nd-century occupation and the existence of a large open area during the 3rd to 4th century revealed by excavation both here and at 6 Birch Abbey (Cracknell 1989b).

Figs 21 and 22 show the proportions of the major fabric groups found by phase on each of the sites. Detailed figures for the proportions of each individual fabric by phase are tabulated by sherd count, weight, minimum numbers of rims, and RE in Tables MT2 and MT3 (microfiche M1:A14–B12).

Samian ware (ALC 69 and ALC 72/2)
Margaret Ward

Introduction

The abbreviations SG, CG, and EG are used throughout for South Gaulish, Central Gaulish, and East Gaulish ware; *Déch* refers to Déchelette 1904; *Oswald* to Oswald 1936–7; *Rogers* to Rogers 1974; and *S & S* to Stanfield and Simpson 1958. For other abbreviations and for the terminology employed see Bulmer 1979.

While the archive includes a complete record of all the samian ware recovered from these excavations, the catalogue of vessels for publication has been selected according to significance for dating purposes, for the character of the site, or for intrinsic interest. Each catalogue has been divided by phase and set out by context in order of fabric and form, the plain ware preceding the decorated.

All the stamps with decipherable letters have been listed; all those on plain vessels are basal. Miss Brenda Dickinson of Leeds University kindly provided the information on the stamps in her report, which is incorporated below. These are recorded here in the order: reading, die, potter, pottery of origin, followed by a superscript letter indicating:

a   stamp attested at the pottery in question
b   not attested at the pottery, although the potter is known to have worked here
c   assigned to the pottery on evidence of fabric distribution, etc.

This is followed by notes on the stamp, the dating evidence, and the date proposed for the particular stamp. Plainware stamps have not been drawn, as illustrations will appear in the forthcoming catalogue of stamps at Leeds University.

A quantified summary of the samian from each phase is presented on Tables 3–8 recording forms and fabrics. Maximum numbers of vessels have been calculated, since it was impossible to estimate minimum numbers in larger groups. For the Roman phases, further quantification is represented by histograms and line diagrams illustrating the maximum numbers of vessels according to their date of manufacture. Line diagrams are presented where small numbers of vessels were retrieved from a phase of relevant period; histograms are presented for the larger collections from such phases. All the samian recovered, including plain sherds, has been used to produce the histograms despite the drawbacks in using such imprecisely dated material. The stamped or decorated vessels alone were, in general, too few to be meaningful statistically, and some form of graphical summary was felt to be desirable.

ALC 69

Phase A (Fig 23, nos 3, 7, and 11)

1 SG Dr 18R Stamped LOG[IRNI] Die 5a of Logirnus, La Graufesenque.[a] A stamp noted from Camelon and in the Inchtuthil Gutter, but also from Risstissen (before *c* AD 75). See also no 26 below. *c* AD 70–90. A small fragment. (96)

2 SG Dr 27 External ridge around the footing. Stamped OFBASSI Die 4p of Bassus i, La Graufesenque.[a] Bassus i's activity was almost certainly entirely pre-Flavian, though some of his stamps turn up at Flavian foundations. There is no evidence that this particular stamp was in use later than *c* AD 65; *c* AD 45–65. A nick has been incised on the standing surface of the very worn footring (which may have been hacked off from the vessel). (96)

3 SG Dr 37 Ovolo (probably that used in the style of Memor and Mommo) above a chevron wreath bordered by blurred wavy lines. Below, fragments of decoration include diagonal wavy lines; *c* AD 70–90. Two adjoining fragments. (illus) (96)

4 SG Dr 37 Fragment only of ovolo above a wavy-line border; below, double festoons with a corded outer component include a bird facing right (possibly *Oswald* 2220, blurred); *c* AD 70–90? A small fragment. (96)

5 SG ind (Dr 29?) not closely datable, but probably Neronian or early Flavian. A tiny basal fragment. (136)

6 SG Dr 27 Flavian or Flavian–Trajanic. Part of the surface of the external wall is completely rubbed away and the piece appears to have been sawn down at the carination. (165)

7 SG Dr 29 Upper zone: a neat scroll with a tendril terminating in a small stylised bud and a large, beaded binding. Lower zone: a scroll with tendrils terminating in a slightly blurred leaf and a blurred bifid binding; in the lower interstice a corded medallion containing a bird (*Oswald* 2260C?) is flanked by two 19- or 20-petalled rosettes. The bifid bindings appear similar to those on a Neronian bowl from Asciburgium (Vanderhoefen 1976, Taf 38.269; see also Dannell 1971, Fig 128.23); *c* AD 50–65. Two adjoining sherds. (illus) (167)

8 SG Ritt 1 Pronounced offset at external junction of wall and base. Not closely datable in the pre-Flavian period. A single sherd including part of the rim. (171)

9 CG ind (dish). First-century Lezoux ware. Neronian–early Flavian. A basal sherd, burnt black. (176)

10 SG Dr 18 or 18R Stamped IVSTI Die 12a of Iustus i, La Graufesenque.[b] This potter's output includes decorated ware of Flavian date (both forms 29 and 37), but his occasional use of form Ritt 8 suggests that he began work under Nero. There is no internal dating for this particular stamp; *c* AD 65–90. A small sherd. (178)

11 SG Dr 37 Below and above horizontal wavy lines is a blurred ovolo, used by Memor and Mommo. Below, the upper compartments include a dog (*Oswald* 1923, slightly blurred?) and individual arrowheads, to the right of arrowheads and a composite rosette with two opposing birds (*Oswald* 2232A facing right; that facing left not identified in *Oswald*). The fragments below may represent panelling with corner tendrils and rosettes. For the upper zone, cf Knorr 1919, Taf 59A by Mommo; *Oswald* 2232A was used by potters including Memor; *c* AD 70–90. Six sherds, apparently from the same vessel as a tiny fragment from (165), also phase A. (illus) (178)

12 CG Dr 27g First-century Lezoux ware. Stamped [C]AMPA Die 6a of Campanus i, Lezoux.[c] On this potter see below, no 13. Die 6a was presumably in use in the pre-Flavian period, since it occurs on form 24. The vessel is unlikely to be earlier than the Neronian period (see no 13). Three sherds, adjoining a fragment from (184),

1969 and 1972 Baromix finds (ALC 69 and ALC 72/2)

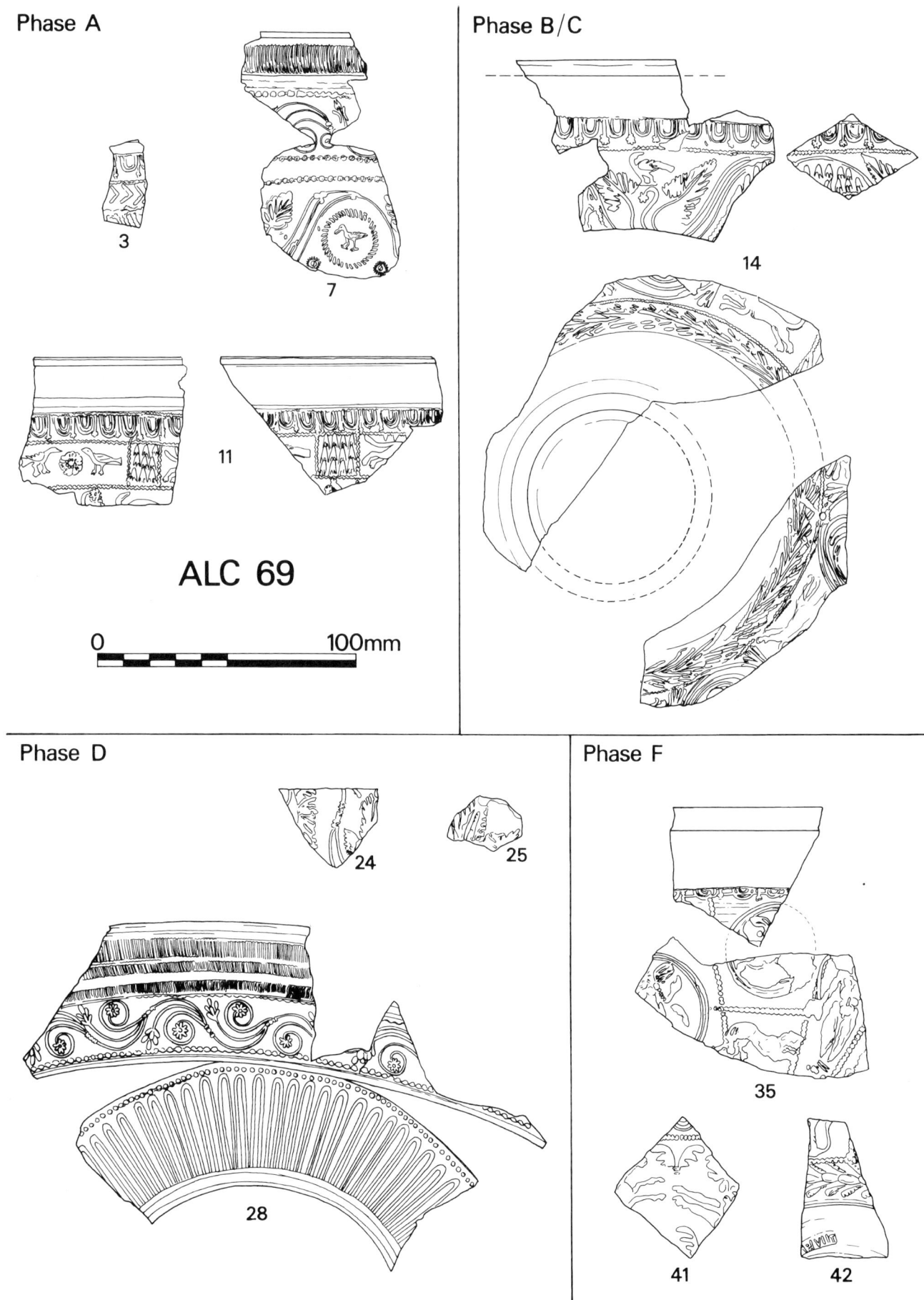

Figure 23 Decorated samian ware (ALC 69), nos 3, 7, 11, 14, 24–5, 28, 35, and 41–2

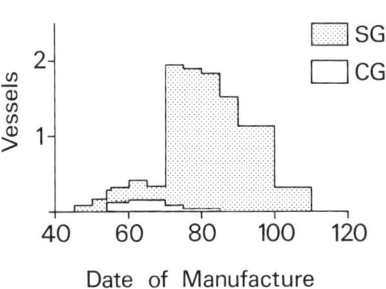

Figure 24 ALC 69, phase A, date distribution of samian ware

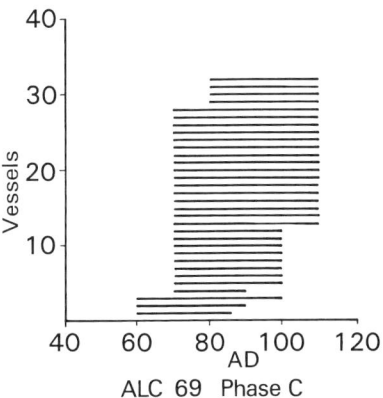

Figure 26 ALC 69, phase C, date distribution of samian ware

also phase A. Worn footring, but incisions inside the base were probably accidental. Two sherds, including that from (184), also phase A, may have been burnt. (185)
13 CG Dr 24 Stamped . . . PANṢ Die uncertain 1 of Campanus i (?), Lezoux.^c There are no other recorded examples of this stamp. The fabric and slip suggest that the potter worked at Lezoux in the 1st century. Probably Neronian: the vessel is unlikely to be earlier since little, if any, 1st-century Lezoux ware reached Britain before that time. See also no 12 above. The worn footring alone has been blackened by burning, from the bottom. (198)

Despite the relatively small size of the sample, a histogram (Fig 24) summarises the samian from phase A contexts according to date of manufacture. The maximum of 58 vessels consisted of 73 sherds. Some 95% of the vessels originated in South Gaul, and the remaining 5% (three vessels) represented contemporary work by Central Gaulish potters at Lezoux in the 1st century. In all, nine vessels (16%) may have been manufactured in the pre-Flavian period. The earliest SG material included a decorated bowl, no 7, and the plain vessels nos 2, 8, and 10 as well as a pre-Flavian dish of form Ritt 1 of which a sherd was found in context 171. The three CG products (nos 9, 12, and 13) are unlikely to have arrived in Britain before the Neronian period. Since 1st-century Lezoux exports were reaching such Scottish sites as Camelon and Strageath in the AD 80s the latest of these three vessels at Alcester could have been produced in the Vespasianic or early Domitianic period at the very latest. Much of the earliest samian ware recovered from this phase will have been manufactured in the Neronian period. Several of the sherds showed signs of wear in use (see nos 2, 6, 12, and 13)

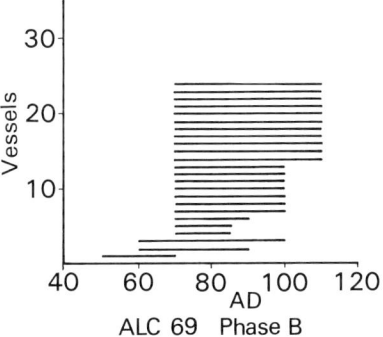

Figure 25 ALC 69, phase B, date distribution of samian ware

and two of these pieces appeared to have been sawn or hacked off for a secondary function. In all, five vessels showed evidence of burning, in addition to the strangely burnt footring of one CG cup, no 13, which may have been blackened by use on or over a fire.

Phase B (Fig 23, no 14)

14 SG Dr 37 Ovolo with large rosette-tipped tongue used by Calvus i (see Atkinson 1914, nos 39–47, etc) above a winding-scroll composition. The upper tendrils terminate in blurred leaves (cf Knorr 1952, Taf 50A OF PATRIC, Dr 29) and a seven-petalled rosette below a goose (*Oswald* 2289). The lower tendrils terminate in an indistinct ?trifid motif beside a blurred dog (not identified in *Oswald*) running left below a set of arrowheads. For similar compositions, cf Knorr 1919, Taf 99A, Dr 30 and Knorr 1912, Taf XX1.9, Dr 37. Complete profile of the vessel, formed by sixteen sherds: one from this context, one from (124), phase C, eleven from (122), phase C, and three from (137), phase D; all were very burnt. Worn footring, with at least two round rivet-holes through the decoration of one of the sherds from phase C. (illus) (151)
15 SG Dr 22 cf Stanfield 1929, Fig 4.17, form 22c. Flavian. Standing surface slightly worn; there is also a worn band around the base at the internal junction with the wall. (166)

Fig 25 displays the range in date of manufacture of the 24 samian vessels (28 sherds) recovered from phase B contexts. All were South Gaulish products, mostly of Flavian origin. The earliest sherd belonged to a pre-Flavian cup of form Ritt 8, found in (173); this may have come from the same vessel as a sherd from phase D (148). Several vessels including nos 14 and 15 had been worn in use. Only one fragment of one decorated bowl, no 14, was found in this phase, while 15 sherds of this vessel were recovered from phases C and D. At some point the bowl had seen repair work, as the sherds from phase C bear witness. In all, six vessels were burnt, including no 14.

Phase C

16 SG Dr 27 Stamped IΛIⱵ by an unidentified potter. Flavian or Flavian–Trajanic. Nine adjoining sherds, all burnt. (118)
17 SG Dr 37 Below the (missing) ovolo, within horizontal wavy lines a wreath of bifid motifs is set above a blurred fragment of a composite grass-plant. Flavian. A small sherd only. (120)
18 SG Dr 37 Extremely battered fragment of decoration: ovolo

1969 and 1972 Baromix finds (ALC 69 and ALC 72/2)

with a trifid-tipped tongue above a blurred horizontal border and a bud-cluster, probably from a stylised tree as used by *amici cognatique Germani*; c AD 80–110. A very small sherd, adjoining another from (106) in phase D. (122)

19 SG Dr 37 Between horizontal wavy lines, an ovolo with a small trifid-tip to the tongue above a chevron wreath. The ovolo is probably that used by Memor and Mommo (see also no 3 above); c AD 70–90. Wall-sherd from the same vessel as a fragment in context (1), phase U/S, and possibly the same vessel as no 21 in phase D. (125)

Fig 26 displays the range in date of manufacture of the 33 samian vessels (32 vessels after cross-joins; 55 sherds) from phase C contexts. All were manufactured in South Gaul, mostly in the Flavian–Trajanic period. Twelve sherds represented the complete profile of a Flavian bowl of which one fragment was found in phase B, and four others in phases C and D (see no 14). As noted above, on the evidence of the sherds from (122), this bowl had seen repair work at some point before its final breakage. Another bowl, no 18, was also represented by a sherd in a phase D context (106). One sherd, no 19, represented a bowl of which a second piece was unstratified; this may have belonged to the same vessel as no 23 in phase D, context (78). In all ten vessels (21 sherds, including twelve from no 14) were burnt. Nine of these vessels were found in contexts (118) and (122), from which all the samian recovered was burnt.

Phase D (Fig 23, nos 24, 25, and 28)

20 SG Dr 18R Fragment only of an illegible stamp. Probably Flavian. (78)

21 SG Dr 37 A wreath of chevrons above a series of diagonal lines (as on no 3 above, but not from the same vessel). Probably c AD 70–90. A small sherd, perhaps from the same vessel as no 19 in phase C. (78)

22 CG Dr 37 Dullish slip on a very pale yellow-pink fabric full of yellow inclusions. Ovolo with rosette-tipped tongue (probably *Rogers* B6) above a neat beadrow (A2). Ovolo B6 was used by Potter X-13; the fabric of this sherd indicates origin at Lezoux. Presumably Hadrianic. (78)

23 SG Dr 15/17 or 15/17R. Flavian. A burnt wall-sherd with a dove-tailed(?) rivet-hole. (106)

24 CG Dr 37 Good quality ware. A fragment of a winding-scroll composition; the tendrils terminate in leaves (*Rogers* H72 inverted, and H58) and a binding (as on S & S plate 85.6). The leaf H72 is known in the styles of Cinnamus and Sacer (cf Dore *et al* 1979, 108, no 19) as well as Attianus, but the use of H58 and this tendril binding might indicate the latter; c AD 125–145, if Attianus (cf Dickinson 1984, 193f, D81). A small sherd. (illus) (106)

25 CG Dr 37 Good quality ware. Probably part of a winding-scroll composition: a fragment of a large leaf in high relief (*Rogers* H20 or H24?). H20 and H24 are recorded for Carantinus II and Cinnamus respectively, but this sherd could be earlier than the Antonine period. Probably c AD 125–150. A small sherd. (illus). (106)

26 SG Dr 18R Stamped LOGIRNI Die 5a of Logirnus, La Graufesenque.[a] For this stamp, see no 1 above; c AD 70–90. Two adjoining sherds, one from (87, phase G) there is a fragment of a graffito below the base. (115)

27 SG Dr 27g Stamped O/([Unidentified. Neronian or early Flavian. A basal sherd. (115)

28 SG Dr 29 Fragment only of basal stamp, reading perhaps M Unidentified. Upper decorative zone: a neat, winding scroll with a five beaded astragalus binding the tendrils which terminate alternately in a nine-petalled rosette and a fairly common bud motif (cf Hermet 1934, plate 13.31). Lower zone filled by straight godroons. Not closely datable in the Neronian or early Flavian periods. Seven adjoining sherds form the complete profile: one may have originated in context (214, unphased). Worn footring. (illus) (115)

29 SG Dr 27 Stamped IWII by an unidentified potter. Probably Flavian. Two small fragments. (140)

Fig 27 illustrates the samian from phase D contexts according to date of manufacture. Of the 107 vessels (maximum; 103 after cross-joins) composed of 142 sherds, 91% originated in South Gaul and 9% in Central Gaul. The SG ware included a fragment of a pre-Flavian cup of form Ritt 8, which may have belonged to the vessel noted in phase B. The large number of pieces representing the cup form Dr 27 should be noted, see Table 3. Here the maximum number of vessels may well be misleading; a minimum number might have been closer to the truth, but this would be little more than guess-work. One of the cups of form 27 from (148) was of such poor quality that it may have been a second. In general the SG material displayed considerable evidence of wear in use; nine footrings had been worn, there was one graffito (no 26) and one sherd bore a rivet-hole (no 23). None of the ten CG vessels was produced later than the Hadrianic to early Antonine period (see nos 24 and 25) and two or three vessels may have originated in the Trajanic–Hadrianic period at Les Martres-de-Veyre. A total of 16 vessels, all South Gaulish, showed signs of burning. Three burnt sherds in context 137 came from one vessel, no 14 above, of which other sherds, all burnt, were found in phases B and C.

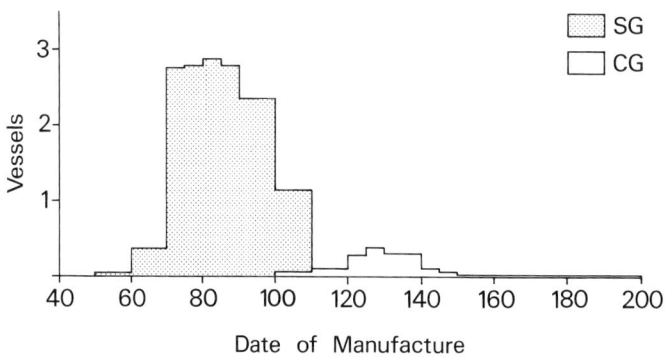

Figure 27   ALC 69, phase D, date distribution of samian ware

1969 and 1972 Baromix finds (ALC 69 and ALC 72/2)

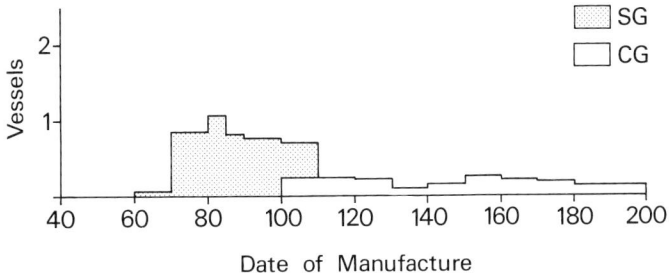

Figure 28   ALC 69, phase E, date distribution of samian ware

Phase E

30 CG Dr 18/31R or 31R Stamped PATERC phallus hIN Die incomplete 1 of Paterclinus, Lezoux.[b] His stamps are noted at Chesterholm and South Shields, and in the Wroxeter Gutter (2). His recorded output includes several examples of forms 31R and 80, and one of the form 27; c AD 150–180. Four sherds; worn on top of the basal kick. (44)
31 CG Dr 37 Ovolo (*Rogers* B105) above horizontal beadrow (A2) and fragment of decoration. Ovolo used by such potters as Albucius and Paternus v (II); c AD 150–200. A small rimsherd. (44)
32 CG Dr 18/31 Stamped COCVRO F Die 1a of Cocuro, Lezoux.[a] This stamp occurs most often on forms 18/31 and 27, but is also known on form 38 and an early variant of form 80. It has been noted in the material from the Antonine fire at Verulamium; c AD 140–170. The form here could indicate a date early within the range. Worn footring; also worn below and above the basal 'kick'. (116)

Again, in spite of the small size of the sample from phase E contexts a histogram (Fig 28) summarises the maximum of 50 vessels (58 sherds) by date of manufacture. The SG ware formed 60% and the CG ware 40% of the total. It may be noted that the absence of any EG samian from phase E may owe more to the small size of the sample than to the dating of the phase. The SG samian was mostly fragmentary; it included three footrings which showed evidence of wear. Much of the CG samian was not closely datable within the Hadrianic–Antonine period. Three vessels, including one dish with a worn footring, are likely to have originated at Les Martres-de-Veyre in the Trajanic–Hadrianic period. Seven vessels were certainly Antonine products, including nos 30–32, of which nos 30 and 31 were dated after c AD 150. One dish, no 30, which was dated by the potter's stamp to the period c AD 150–80, showed internal signs of wear in use. A second stamped dish, no 32, dated c AD 140–70, also displayed evidence of wear; this could have been caused after breakage in some secondary function, perhaps inverted as a spinning-top, for instance. A total of four sherds, all SG products, were burnt.

Phase F (Fig 23, nos 35, 41, and 42)

33 CG Dr 18/31 or 31 Antonine. A wall-sherd with a dove-tailed rivet-hole. (9)
34 CG Dr 45 c AD 170/180–200. Three sherds, presumably from the same vessel: the basal interior has been completely worn away and the underside is worn in a band at the junction with the (worn) footring. (9)
35 CG Dr 37 Ovolo (*Rogers* B52) superimposed on a guide-line. Panels bordered by beadrows (A3) include fragments of cupid (*Oswald* 450) in a double medallion, Pan (*Oswald* 711A blurred?) and a panther (*Oswald* 1518). Style of Secundus; c AD 150–180. Three sherds from the same vessel as four from phase H contexts: three from (88) and one from (22). (illus) (9)
36 CG Dr 18/31 or 31 stamped ꝏT[ITIMꝏ] Die 8a of Titus iii, Lezoux.[b] This stamp was used on form 38. Others appear on forms 18/31R and 31R and in groups of c AD 150–160 and 170, from Alcester and Tác (Hungary) respectively; c AD 145–175. A basal sherd. (20)
37 CG Dr 31R Stamped [ChIIM]IIꝏꝏ Die 3b of Clemens ii, Lezoux.[b] A stamp noted from Catterick and Housesteads. The die is known to have been used, after modification, on form 31R. His decorated ware has stylistic links with Advocisus and Priscus iii; c AD 160–190. A basal sherd. (20)
38 CG Dr 27 Fragment only of stamp]F Hadrianic or early Antonine. Footring worn. (20)
39 CG ind (Dr 27?) Fragment only of stamp]M Hadrianic or early Antonine. A battered basal sherd. (20)
40 CG Dr 37 Ovolo (clearly *Rogers* B143) above horizontal beadrow (A2). Panels, bordered vertically by *Rogers* A9, include the blurred figure of Vulcan (*Oswald* 66) and a fragment of double festoon. For the same decoration with ovolo B144, see Simpson and Rogers 1969, Fig 2.4; the Alcester sherd seems rather to be in Cinnamus's standard style; c AD 150–170. (20)
41 CG Dr 37 Fragment of large ovolo (probably *Rogers* B223) above beadrow (A2) and freestyle decoration including acanthus ornaments (K20 as on Wild 1975, Fig 55.46); the lion facing left is type *Oswald* 1450, and the ?stag facing right may be *Oswald* 1720

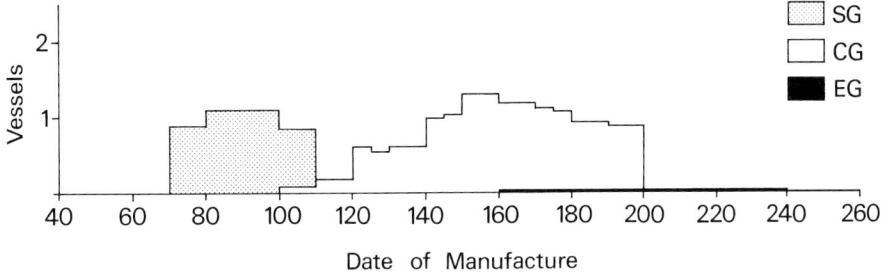

Figure 29   ALC 69, phase F, date distribution of samian ware

1969 and 1972 Baromix finds (ALC 69 and ALC 72/2)

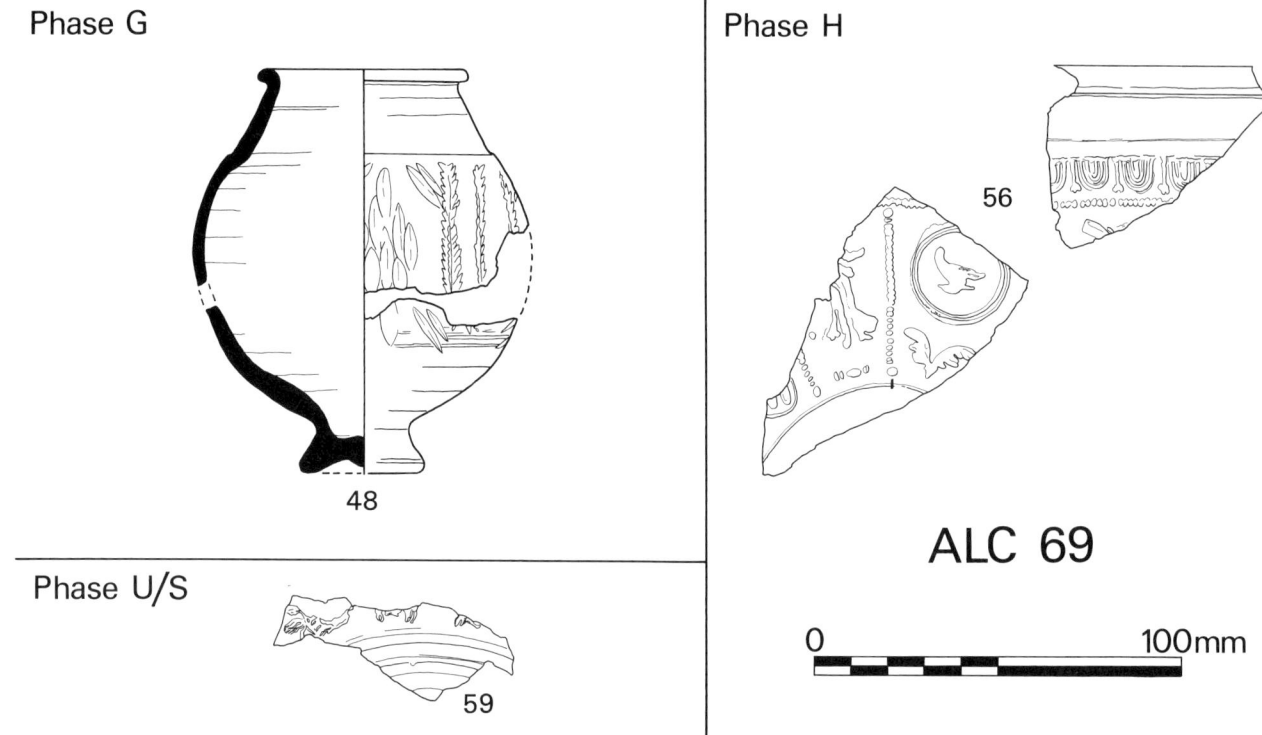

Figure 30 Decorated samian ware (ALC 69), nos 48, 56, and 59

(cf Karnitsch 1959, Taf 78.4). Probably the work of a member of the Cinnamus group including Secundus (see also *S & S* plate 166.4); *c* AD 150–180. (illus) (20)

42 SG Dr 37 Fragment of stylised tree above a basal wreath of leaf-and-bud motifs. Stamped below decoration TIIVh·A[PḥA...] retrograde. Die uncertain 1 of T. Iulius Apla.. The potter's cognomen begins in either Apia... or Apla... The only other example noted of this stamp is on a mould from La Graufesenque, with decoration suggesting a date *c* AD 90–110. (illus) (51a)

43 CG Dr 18/31 Fragment only of stamp]C Unidentified; *c* AD 120–140/150. Footring slightly worn. (51)

44 CG? ind Fragment only of stamp]GE[. Unidentified. Hadrianic to early Antonine? A burnt scrap, adjoining a second; there are signs of wear under the basal kick.(51)

45 CG *Déch* 64 Matt orange slip on pink-buff fabric. Indeterminate fragment of decoration. Probably a Hadrianic product of Lezoux. A small wall sherd, not from the same vessel as no 55. (86)

46 CG Dr 27 Stamped [IOE]NΛḥIS(F) Die 2b (possibly) of Ioenalis i, Les Martres-de-Veyre,[b] Lezoux.[b] This stamp has only been noticed twice before, on forms 18/31 and 27. One of his other stamps occurs in the London Second Fire deposits. The Alcester vessel seems, from its fabric, to have been made at Les Martres-de-Veyre; *c* AD 110–125. Worn footring. (161)

The histogram (Fig 29) summarises the samian ware from phase F contexts by date of manufacture. Of the 118 vessels (maximum) composed of 135 sherds, 32% originated in South Gaul, 66% in Central Gaul and 1% (one vessel) in East Gaul. All 38 SG vessels were manufactured in the Flavian–Trajanic period. Only the bowl no 42, stamped by T Iulius Apla.. was in any way remarkable. Four CG vessels including one stamped cup, no 46, were thought to be products of Les Martres-de-Veyre of Trajanic–Hadrianic date. The histogram (Fig 29) clearly illustrates that, just as the proportion of SG samian is surprisingly high in a late group, so too is the proportion of (presumably residual) early 2nd-century CG ware and of Hadrianic to early Antonine material in particular. This material included five fragmentary stamps, and a small piece of moulded goblet of form *Déch* 64 (all listed above). Products of the Antonine factories of Cinnamus and Secundus represented the latest decorated samian in this phase (see nos 35, 40, and 41). Late 2nd-century forms such as the deep dish Dr 31R, the Walt 79 group, and the *mortarium* Dr

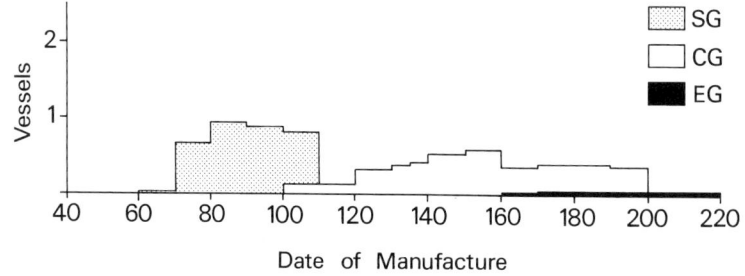

Figure 31 ALC 69, phase G, date distribution of samian ware

45 are noted on Table 4. Amongst these were the dish, no 37, stamped by Clemens ii and dated c AD 160–90, and the *mortarium* no 34, a late Antonine product which had seen considerable wear in use. One sherd from a dish of Antonine manufacture bore a rivet-hole (no 33).

Eleven other CG vessels, four of later 2nd-century origin, showed evidence of wear. There was only one East Gaulish sherd, of indeterminate form, which probably originated at Rheinzabern or Trier in the later 2nd or 3rd century. A total of seven vessels had been burnt; five of them were found in contexts 20 and 51.

Phase G (Fig 30, no 48)

47 CG *Déch* 72 Fragments of 'cut-glass' decoration; c AD 160–200. One sherd, together with two sherds from (2) and two small fragments from (88), both phase H, and one from (1) phase U/S. (19)
48 EG *Déch* 72 Orange-red slip on a good pink fabric with occasional yellow flecks; Rheinzabern ware? Fragments only of 'cut-glass' decoration. Later 2nd or early 3rd century. Eighteen sherds form much of the vessel, including the rim and the footring which is only slightly worn. (illus) (19)
49 CG Dr 33 Stamped PATERNI Die 2b of Paternus iii, Lezoux.[a] This stamp is common on forms 18/31 and 27. It is noted in a group of burnt samian of c AD 140–150 from Castleford (5) and from Camelon. He was associated with Ianuaris ii in the making of decorated ware; c AD 130–160. Slightly worn inside junction of wall and base; a graffito P has been incised below the base within the (very worn) footring. (59)
50 SG ind. Flavian–Trajanic. A small, burnt sherd with a round rivet-hole, broken across. (87)
51 CG Dr 37 Blurred decoration: ovolo (*Rogers* B223) above horizontal border (A2?). Ovolo used by Cinnamus, Secundus, and Casurius; c AD 150–180/190. A small sherd. (87)
52 EG Dr 45 Orange slip on orange-buff fabric. Late 2nd or early 3rd century. A single rim sherd. (87)

Fig 31 summarises the samian ware from phase G contexts by date of manufacture. The maximum of 72 vessels (70 after cross-joins) consisted of 89 sherds, of which eighteen sherds formed one vessel (see no 48). Again the proportion of the earlier samian ware was surprisingly high: 49% was of SG origin, 49% was from Central Gaul and there were only two vessels from East Gaul. The SG sherds were all from Flavian–Trajanic products. They included at least two vessels, in contexts 87 and 40, of which pieces were also found in phase D (no 26) and phase E. Also recovered from (87) was a burnt fragment of a vessel which had seen repair work (no 50). This was one of three burnt SG sherds in this context; they represented the only evidence of burning in phase G. Amongst the CG samian all the early 2nd-century sherds may be presumed to be residual and, with the exception of one stamp date c AD 130–60 (no 49), none of the material pre-dating the Antonine period is included in the catalogue. Three or four vessels showed signs of wear, including no 49; only one of them was dated after c AD 160. The latest moulded ware in this phase was a small sherd manufactured in the range c AD 150–80/90 (no 51). A sherd in context (19), no 47, belonged to a 'cut-glass' beaker of the later Antonine period, of which other fragments were found in phase H and unstratified. The greater part of a second 'cut-glass' beaker was recovered, again from context (19), no 48. This was manufactured in East Gaul, probably at Rheinzabern in the later 2nd or 3rd century; its footring bore slight evidence of wear. Of similar date was the other East Gaulish piece, a rimsherd of the *mortarium* form Dr 45, no 52 above.

Phase H (Fig 30, no 56)

53 CG? ind Hadrianic–Antonine. A tiny chip broken across a round rivet-hole. (10)
54 CG Dr 38 Stamped ALBVCI... Die uncertain, of Albucius ii, Lezoux[b]. The reading of this stamp is not clear, but the lettering suggests that it belongs to Albucius ii. His wares turn up both in Antonine Scotland and on Hadrian's Wall, but are more common in Scotland. The style of his decorated ware shows that he belonged to a group of potters associated with Paternus v; c AD 150–180. Two adjoining sherds: the footring is extremely worn and has had groups of nicks incised on the standing surface. (18)
55 CG *Déch* 64 Dull orange slip on a micaceous buff fabric (see B R Hartley's comments in Webster 1977, 130). The small fragment of decoration displays a small deer (*Déch* 879). Probably Hadrianic. A small fragment. (23a)
56 CG Dr 37 Brown-orange slip on pale micaceous fabric. Ovolo (*Rogers* B18) above beadrow (A2) which also forms the panel borders. The panels include a double medallion containing a blurred bird (*Oswald* 2298?) above an indistinct acanthus (*Rogers* K20 or K22); and the figure of ?Victory (*Oswald* 819A?) above a blurred astragalus. Probably the style of Attianus or an associate; c AD 125–145. Six sherds of a shallow vessel with a dove-tailed rivet-hole through a fragment of the decoration; one sherd was burnt. (illus) (88)

The 79 vessels (76 after cross-joins; 95 sherds) recovered from phase H contexts consisted of 24 SG vessels (30%), 53 CG vessels (67%), and two EG fragments (3%). Only the CG goblet, no 55, of form *Déch* 64 was at all unusual. Several vessels, including no 54, showed considerable signs of use, and two vessels had seen repair work (nos 53 and 56). Sherds of three vessels recovered from phase H certainly belonged to vessels of which pieces were found in phases D, F, and G. A total of six vessels had been burnt.

Unphased and unstratified material (Fig 30, no 59)

57 CG Dr 31 Stamped C.I[Unidentified; c AD 150–200. Footring very worn. (1)
58 CG Dr 31 or 31R c AD 160–200. Rimsherd broken across a rivet-hole (dove-tailed?). (1)
59 EG Dr 37 Dullish brown-red slip on a pink fabric with occasional yellow inclusions; possibly Rheinzabern ware. Fragments only of decoration above a double basal ridge. Later 2nd or early 3rd century. (illus) (1)
60 CG Dr 29 (or 29/37?) Below the moulding at the carination, neat beading is set above a frieze containing a bunch of leaves (*Rogers* L19), probably flanked by animals (cf *S & S*, plate 44.503, Dr 29/37; plate 47.555, Dr 37). The motif L19 is typical of the style of Potter X-13, who used forms 29 and 29/37. The fabric of this small sherd suggests origin at Les Martres-de-Veyre; c AD 110–125. (214)
61 CG Dr 37 A rosette (*Rogers* C280) is set to the left of a gladiator or warrior with out-stretched arm (larger than that on *S & S*, plate 14.178 and probably not *Oswald* 1063). The rosette C280 features in the styles of numerous Les Martres potters and is frequently

1969 and 1972 Baromix finds (ALC 69 and ALC 72/2)

Table 3 Occurrence of South Gaulish samian ware (ALC 69)

Type	Phase									Total
	A	B	C	D	E	F	G	H	U/S	
Ritt 1	1									1
Ritt 8		1								1
Curle 11		1	1		1		1	1		5
15/17	1		1							2
15/17 or 15/17R				2		1		1		4
15/17 or 18							1			1
18	3	1	3	7	3	1	2	1	2	23
18 or 18R	3			3	1	1	2			10
18R	13	6	5	16	2	1	4	1	3	51
18/31R or 18R				1		1	1			3
22		1								1
27	12	4	4	31	8	5	1	8	1	74
33		1			1				1	3
35	1			4	1	2	2		1	11
36	1			1		2	1		3	8
Inkwell								1		1
ind	6	6	12	8	4	16	11	5	3	71
ind encl					1					1
Déch 67			1				1			2
29	5	2		6	5			1	1	20
29 or 37	1									1
30				1					1	2
37	8	1	5	13	4	7	6	4	1	49
Totals	55	24	32	93	30	38	33	23	17	345

noted with such figures as *Oswald* 1063 on bowls of Drusus i (X-3). At any rate, this vessel should have been produced in the range c AD 100–120/130. A small sherd. (214)

Of the 76 vessels (73 after cross-joins; 81 sherds) in this category, 25% originated in South Gaul, 64% were Central Gaulish, and 11% were East Gaulish. Only the five fragments catalogued above were in any way noteworthy.

Summary of samian ware from the ALC 69 excavations

The maximum of 604 vessels was composed of 756 sherds. Some 57% of the total was South Gaulish, 41% was Central Gaulish, and only 2% was East Gaulish. Most of the EG sherds were of Rheinzabern and Trier origin in the later 2nd or 3rd century. The histogram (Fig 32) represents the whole collection; histograms of the stamped and decorated pieces are provided for the sake of comparison (Figs 33 and 34), although there were insufficient stamps to be meaningful statistically. Each of the three histograms reveal the large proportion of SG material in comparison with that of the later Antonine CG samian; the more usual later 2nd-century peak does not clearly stand out from the relatively high level of Trajanic–Hadrianic material. In all, there were 26 stamps with letters or fragments of letters surviving; of these, only 16 were recognisable, and 14 were attributable (to 12 potters). These ranged from the pre-Flavian period in South and Central Gaul (nos 2, 12, and 13) to (only) three dated specifically to the later 2nd century (nos 30, 37, and 54). The two potters represented by two stamps each belonged to the 1st century and were recovered from contexts in phases A and D (nos 1, 26; 12, and 13). Two stamps survived on SG decorated bowls, one below the decoration on form 37 (no 42) and one unidentifiable fragment inside the base of a Dr 29 (no 28). The decorative styles represented on SG bowls included those of Memor and Mommo (on fragments of form 37 in phases A and C), and probably of Calvus i (Dr 37 from phase C contexts). The work of such Trajanic–

Table 4 Occurrence of Central Gaulish samian ware (ALC 69)

Type	Phase									Total
	A	B	C	D	E	F	G	H	U/S	
Curle 15						1				1
15/17 or 15/17R								1		1
18R					1		1		1	3
18R or 18/31R					1			1		2
18 or 18/31					1					1
18/31					1	4				5
18/31 or 18/31R							2			2
18/31R				2	1	6	3	3		15
18/31 or 31					1	6	1		1	9
18/31R or 31R					1	1	1	3		6
31					2	7	1	6	2	18
31/31R						2			3	5
31R						2	2	1	3	8
24	1									1
27	1					3	2			6
33				1	1	4	4	7	3	20
35								1		1
35 or 36				3						3
36					1		2	1	3	7
38						4		2	1	7
44						1				1
45						1			3	4
46 var									1	1
Walt 79						1			2	3
79R						1				1
79 or 80						1				1
80								1		1
79 or Lud Tg									1	1
Lud Tg									1	1
Lud Tx									1	1
ind	1			1	4	23	6	15	13	63
ind encl						1	1			2
Déch 64						1		1		2
Déch 72							1			1
29									1	1
30								2		2
37				3	5	9	8	6	8	39
Totals	3	0	0	10	20	79	35	51	48	246

Table 5 Occurrence of East Gaulish samian ware (ALC 69)

Type	Phase									Total
	A	B	C	D	E	F	G	H	U/S	
31R									2	2
33									1	1
45							1		1	2
ind						1		2	1	4
Déch 72							1			1
37									3	3
Totals	0	0	0	0	0	1	2	2	8	13

1969 and 1972 Baromix finds (ALC 69 and ALC 72/2)

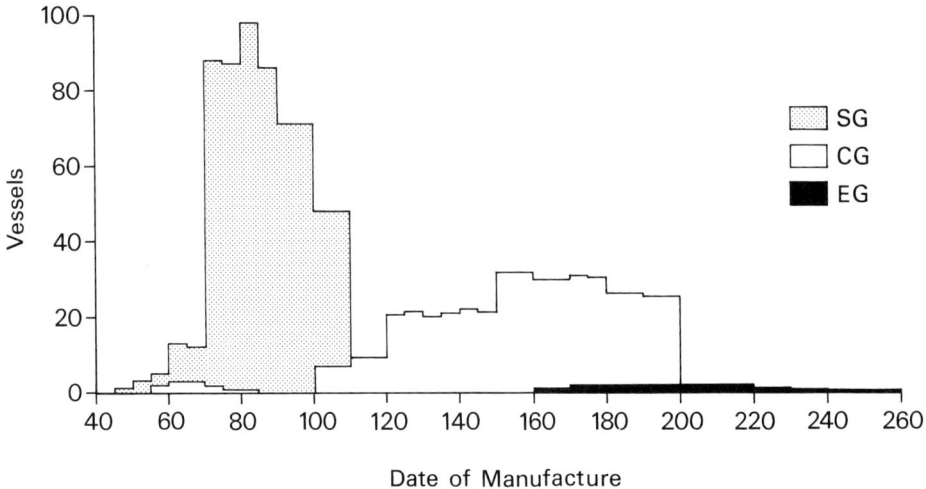

Figure 32 ALC 69, date distribution of all samian ware

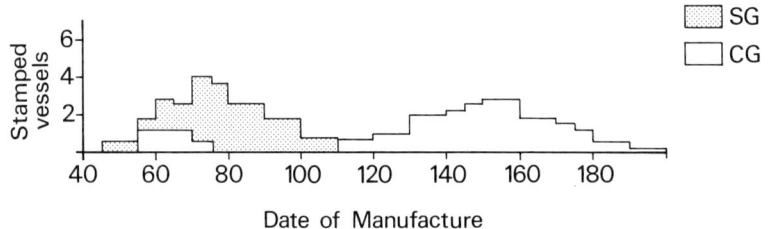

Figure 33 ALC 69, date distribution of all stamped samian ware

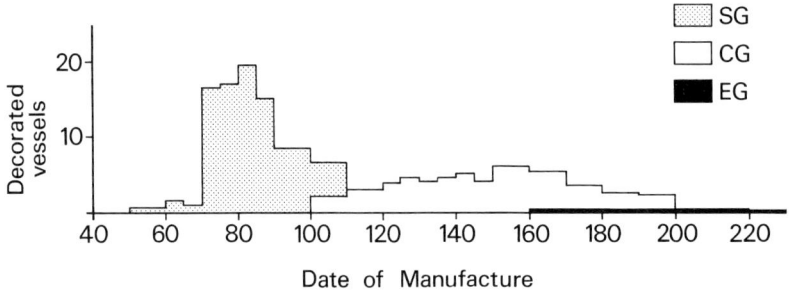

Figure 34 ALC 69, date distribution of all decorated samian ware

Hadrianic CG potters as Igocatus, Drusus i, and X-13 was present in phases D, F, G, and unstratified; the Attianus and early Cinnamus groups were represented in phases D, E, and H; bowls in the 'standard' style of Cinnamus and other later 2nd-century potters were found in phases F, G, and H as well as amongst the unstratified material. The latest CG potters represented were probably Albucius/Paternus (no 31, phase E) and Do(v)eccus (unstratified). Neither of the two fragments of decoration seemingly of EG origin were identifiable (both unstratified, including no 59). Among the more unusual forms, there were two early 2nd-century fragments of form *Déch* 64, a moulded goblet produced by such potters as Libertus and Butrio (see nos 45 and 55), as well as two sherds of form 67 in phases C and G, and two examples of the late form *Déch* 72 with 'cut-glass' decoration (no 47, CG; no 48, EG). The plain samian included sherds of the predominantly pre-Flavian forms Ritt 1 and 8 and Dr 24 (no 13, CG), and one Flavian instance of form 22 (no 15). Apart from the two stamped vessels from 1st-century Lezoux (nos 12 and 13), there was also a fragment from a third vessel (no 9); all were retrieved from phase A. It may be noted that other excavations at Alcester have also produced early Lezoux ware (see below ALC 72/2, phase D).

Although there were no pieces which had been re-used as counters or spindle-whorls in this sample, many vessels showed signs of considerable use (eg nos 2, 6, 34, and 54). There were also two sherds with graffiti incised (nos 26, 58) and six vessels displaying repair-work or attempts at it (nos 14, 23, 50, 53, 56, and 58). The three repaired vessels from the earlier phases were of SG origin; of the CG examples, no 58 was manufactured in the later 2nd century. Sixty vessels (10% of the collection) displayed evidence of burning; the majority was of 1st-century manufacture. Notable among those in phase A was the cup probably from Neronian Lezoux (no 13) whose (worn) footring had been blackened by burning from the bottom upwards.

ALC 72/2

Phase A (Fig 35, no 1)

1 SG Dr 29 Fragment only of leafy decoration below the beading at the carination. Not closely datable in the later Neronian to early Flavian period. A small sherd, representing the only vessel from phase A. (illus) (96)

Phase B (Fig 35, no 4)

2 CG Dr 37 Excellent red gloss on a hard red fabric with dense yellow-white inclusions; probably a Les Martres-de-Veyre product. Ovolo (*Rogers* B28) above a horizontal wavy line (A24). While the ovolo was used by numerous CG potters, the appearance of the ware suggests a Trajanic potter such as X-2 or Drusus i (X-3); the use of the wavy line points to Potter X-2; *c* AD 100–120. One sherd with three adjoining sherds, from the same vessel in context 51 (phase C) and six sherds from context 69 (also phase C). (70)

3 SG Dr 27g Stamp, superimposed to form a cross shape, OFMO[I] Die 9a' of Modestus i, La Graufesenque.[a] This stamp is from a die which, when complete, gave OFMOD. This version appears on forms 24 and Ritt 8. The modified die, although occasionally used on these forms, clearly lasted in use into the Flavian period when, presumably, it had ceased to belong to Modestus. Stamps from the broken die occur at Binchester (2), Caerleon (4), the Nijmegen fortress (8), Ulpia noviomagus (2), and Chester (2). There is also a single example from the pre-Flavian cemeteries at Nijmegen; *c* AD 60–75. Two burnt sherds; footring worn. (106)

4 SG Dr 29 Fragment only of a wreath of leaf-and-bud motifs below the beading at the carination: cf Knorr 1919, Taf 81, VITALIS.A. Not closely datable in the period *c* AD 60–85, but probably Flavian. A small sherd. (illus) (106)

Fig 36 displays the range in date of manufacture of the eight samian vessels, composed of nine sherds, recovered from phase B contexts. As Table 7 indicates, the only Central Gaulish product was a fragment of form 37 which was manufactured in the Trajanic period (see no 2 above). Nine other sherds from the same bowl were found in phase C contexts, and this particular fragment may be intrusive in phase B. The cup, no 3, showed signs of wear in use and its surviving two sherds were burnt.

Phase C

5 CG Dr 27 Stamped [DONN]AVC·F Die 5a of Donnaucus, Les Martres-de-Veyre.[a] Stamps from this die occur at Malton and in the London Second Fire deposits. It was used on form 15/17R, which was not normally made at Les Martres after the Trajanic period; *c* AD 100–120. Five fragments. (69)

Fig 37 displays the range in date of manufacture of the eighteen vessels (34 sherds) recovered from phase C contexts. Of these 72% originated in South Gaul and 28% in Central Gaul. The majority of the thirteen SG vessels may be presumed to have been Flavian or Flavian–Trajanic products. The five CG vessels were manufactured in the Trajanic or Trajanic to early Hadrianic period, possibly all at Les Martres-de-Veyre (see for instance nos 2 and 5 above). One SG sherd may have been burnt.

Phase D (Fig 35, no 6)

6 CG Dr 29/37 (or 37) Below a very faint winding-scroll design, a basal wreath of rosettes (*Rogers* C63 or C80? used in the style of Potter X-13) with indistinct horizontal borders. The very angular lower wall could indicate Dr 29/37, a form favoured by X-13; the fabric could be from Lezoux. At any rate, manufactured in the range *c* AD 110–130. A battered piece; footring worn. (illus) (53)

7 CG Dr 37 Fragment of horizontal beadrow (*Rogers* A2) below a fragment of ovolo? Not closely datable, but probably Hadrianic to early Antonine. (53)

Fig 38 displays the range in date of manufacture of the fifteen vessels (sixteen sherds) recovered from phase D contexts. Some 73% was of South Gaulish origin and 27% was Central Gaulish. None of the sherds which represented the eleven SG vessels of Flavian–Trajanic date was noteworthy. Of the CG ware, one bowl (no 6 above) was manufactured in the Trajanic–Hadrianic period and showed possible evidence of wear in use. Two vessels, including no 7, probably originated in the Hadrianic to early Antonine period. The remaining CG fragment was a rimsherd from a 1st-century product of Lezoux, a cup of form 27, which was found with four residual sherds in (105). One of these four SG fragments represented the only burnt samian ware in this phase. It is interesting to note that of the three samian fragments recovered from the burnt clay floor (53) none displayed obvious signs of burning.

Phase E (Fig 35, nos 8 and 11)

8 CG Dr 37 Purple-red slip on a densely white-flecked fabric, as used by the Quintilianus group. Fragment of panelling bordered vertically by *Rogers* A9; on the right, a boar with a truncated tail (not identified in *Oswald*'s catalogue). Very probably the same vessel as no 11 below, in the style of the early Cinnamus-Cerialis group; *c* AD 140–160? A small sherd. (illus) (60)

9 CG Dr 37 Fragment of horizontal wavy line above a composite ornament (*Rogers* Q42) used by a number of Hadrianic and Antonine potters. This sherd cannot be closely dated, but is probably Hadrianic to early Antonine. A small, battered fragment. (76)

10 CG Dr 37 Dullish, dark orange-red slip on a pink fabric. Below a horizontal wavy line (*Rogers* A24), a basal wreath of eight-petalled rosettes (C63) is superimposed on a faint guide-line, all as used in the style of Potter X-13 (see no 6 above, which is not from the same vessel); *c* AD 110–125, if X-13 at Les Martres-de-Veyre. A small, battered fragment. (86)

11 CG Dr 37 Purple-red slip on a densely white-flecked fabric. Ovolo (*Rogers* B144) above an astragaloid border (A9); below, a fragment of ?tuft. Style of the early Cinnamus-Cerialis group; *c* AD 140–160. A small sherd, very probably from the same vessel as no 8 above. (illus) (120)

Fig 39 displays the range in date of manufacture of the fifteen vessels (fifteen sherds) recovered from phase E contexts. Of these 67% originated in South Gaul and 33% in Central Gaul. The SG ware consisted of residual fragments only, and none of the five CG sherds (four of them decorated fragments of form 37, nos 8–11 above) was manufactured later than the early Antonine period. All were mere fragments, none of which showed signs of use or of burning.

1969 and 1972 Baromix finds (ALC 69 and ALC 72/2)

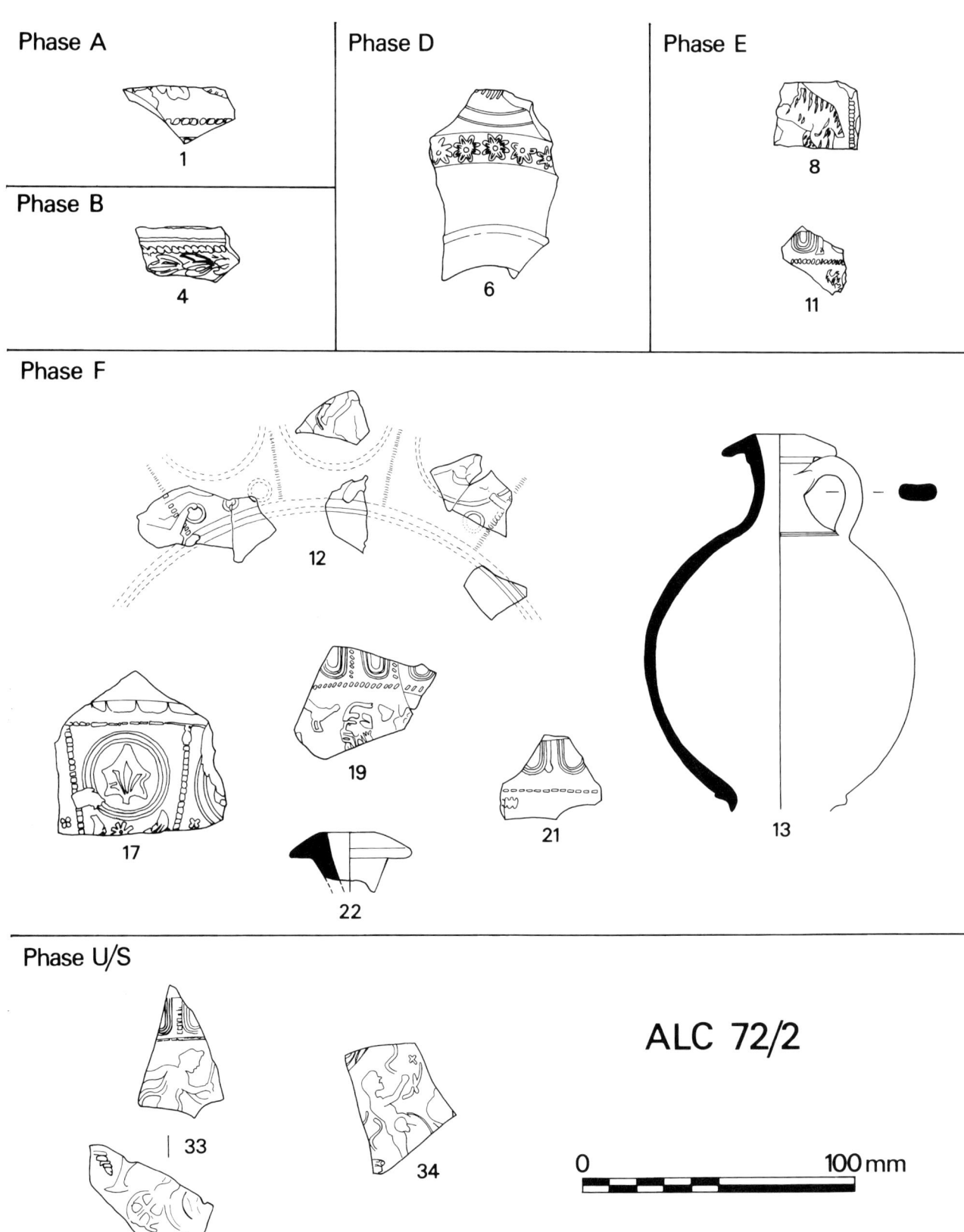

Figure 35 Decorated samian ware (ALC 72/2), nos 1, 4, 6, 8, 11–13, 17, 19, 21–2, and 33–4

1969 and 1972 Baromix finds (ALC 69 and ALC 72/2)

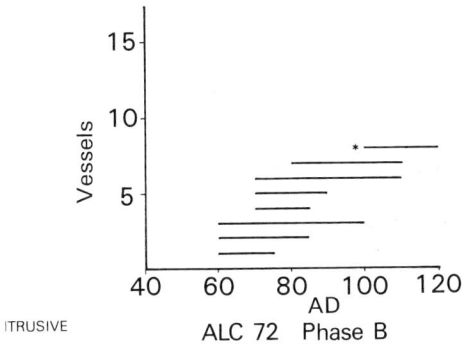

Figure 36 ALC 72/2, phase B, date distribution of samian ware

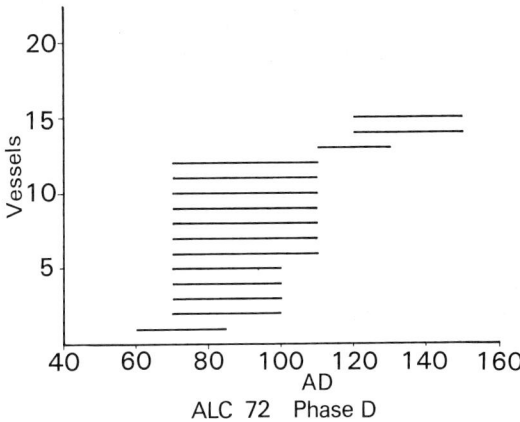

Figure 38 ALC 72/2, phase D, date distribution of samian ware

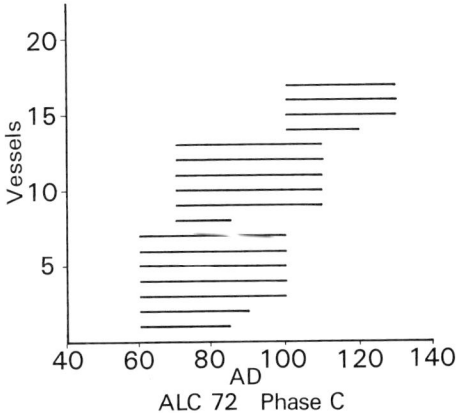

Figure 37 ALC 72/2, phase C, date distribution of samian ware

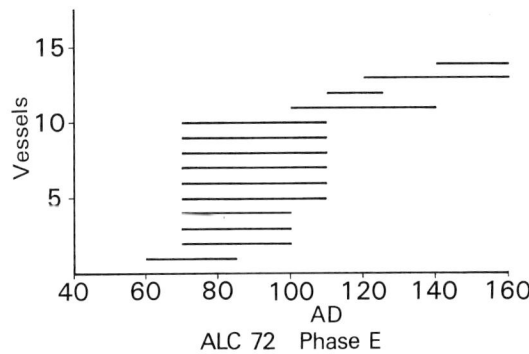

Figure 39 ALC 72/2, phase E, date distribution of samian ware

Phase F (Fig 35, nos 12, 13, 17, 19, 21, and 22)

12 EG Dr 31 Orange-red slip on an orangey fabric; probably Rheinzabern ware. Later 2nd or 3rd century. Two small sherds, including part of the worn footring. (illus) (14)
13 EG flagon A small, single-handled form similar to one from York (Oswald and Pryce 1920, plate LXXXIII.2). Brown-red slip on a brownish buff fabric with occasional white inclusions; probably Trier ware. Interior unslipped below the neck. Three flagons of similar form were recovered in recent excavations at Piercebridge (Ward forthcoming); see also no 22 below. Late 2nd or, probably, 3rd century. Twenty-two sherds form the almost complete profile of the vessel. Some discolouration of the lower interior may be the result of its contents; the vessel seems also slightly burnt in part. (illus) (14)
14 EG(?) ind Good orange-red gloss on a hard, orangey fabric, possibly from East Gaul. Antonine or later. A small fragment only. (18)
15 CG Dr 31 or 31R, *c* AD 150–200. Rim and upper wall very abraded (after breakage?); two angular rivet-holes have been cut through the wall and the vessel has broken through them. Three sherds, two adjoining. (33)
16 EG Walt 79 or 80? Orange ware; possibly a Rheinzabern product. Later 2nd or 3rd century. Two adjoining sherds, possibly from the same vessel as a fragment in context 34, (also phase F). (33)
17 CG Dr 33 Stamped GE[NI]TORF Die 5b of Genitor ii, Lezoux.[a] A stamp noted on Hadrian's Wall and at northern forts evacuated when it was built. It occurs on forms 31R and 79, and so will be mid- to late Antonine, *c* AD 160–190. Worn on top of the base; footring extremely worn. (illus) (34)
18 CG ind *c* AD 150–200. Basal sherd, conceivably reused as a rough counter of diameter 16–18mm. (34)
19 CG Dr 37 Ovolo (*Rogers* B156) above a corded border (A34). Below, a goose (*Oswald* 2239B) and a figure (cupid?) flank a mask of Pan (*Oswald* 1214). Style of Iullinus; *c* AD 160–190. Two adjoining sherds. (illus) (34)
20 CG Dr 37 Very indistinct ovolo (probably *Rogers* B160) and horizontal border above panels bordered by beadrows (A3) with blurred terminals; a small double medallion here encloses a leaf (J86), above leaf-tips and a rosette (C170?). A small four-petalled motif (C274) fills a corner. Style of Do(v)eccus, who used all these motifs in a variety of compositions; messy work on this bowl, including a blob of clay on the medallion; *c* AD 165–200. (34)
21 CG Dr 37 Very battered decoration: ovolo (*Rogers* B106) above a blurred border and a fragment of astragalus (R3?). The appearance of the sherd suggests the work of Paternus v (*S & S* style II), rather than Albucius who also used this ovolo; *c* AD 165–200. (illus) (34)
22 EG flagon. Neck and fragment of the handle of a flagon similar in form to that from York (see no 13 above). Orange slip on a softish orange-buff fabric, possibly with some mica; probably Trier ware. This piece apparently came from a vessel of similar size to no 13 above. Late 2nd or, probably, 3rd century. (illus) (34)
23 CG Dr 18/31 Fragment only of stamp possibly reading]AI[or]IV[; *c* AD 120–140/150. Two adjoining pieces form the complete profile of the vessel; footring very worn. (45)
24 CG ind. Hadrianic–Antonine. A wall-sherd with a dove-tailed rivet-hole, broken across; no trace of the rivet remains. (56)
25 CG Dr 37 Fragments only of the blurred, panelled decoration: borders probably *Rogers* A2, with superimposed astragali (R18?), and small rings as corner motifs. The fragments include a plain festoon or medallion containing a ?cock (*Oswald* 2348?) and a figure with arm raised. Below, a double basal ridge used by such Hadrianic potters as X-6 and Austrus, who also used motif R18; *c* AD 125–140. Ten battered fragments, including footring. (62)

The histogram (Fig 40) summarises the samian from phase F contexts according to date of manufacture, form-

1969 and 1972 Baromix finds (ALC 69 and ALC 72/2)

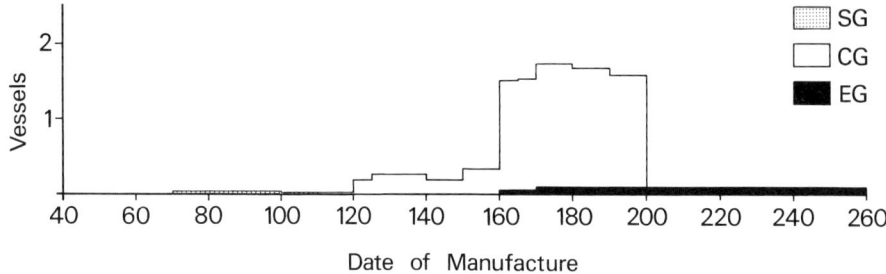

Figure 40   ALC 72/2, phase F, date distribution of samian ware

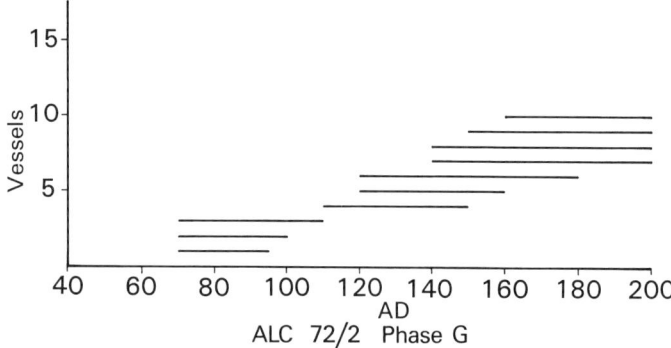

Figure 41   ALC 72/2, phase G, date distribution of samian ware

ing a profile which is fairly typical of a 3rd-century group. Of the 86 vessels (maximum) consisting of 135 sherds, only two fragments were manufactured in South Gaul (2%), while 84% was Central Gaulish and 14% was East Gaulish. As is evident on Table 7 and Fig 40, amongst the CG ware there was a preponderance of later 2nd-century material. The late forms 31R, 79, and 45 were well represented, and the work of the later Antonine potters was identified from both stamps and decoration (see, for instance, nos 17, 19, 20, and 21). The very worn appearance of several footrings, including no 17, suggested that the vessels had experienced considerable life in use following their manufacture in the later 2nd century. Two vessels, nos 17 and 24, had seen repair work, and one piece (no 18) may have been reused as a counter. Most of the EG samian probably originated in Rheinzabern in the late 2nd or 3rd century. On the evidence of their fabric the flagons, nos 13 and 22, are more likely to have been produced at Trier, probably in the 3rd century. While much of the samian in phase F contexts consisted of single small fragments it is perhaps noteworthy that in context (34) the 54 vessels included some rather larger pieces. In context (14) the greater part of the EG flagon, no 13, had survived, along with two late 2nd-century sherds and seven EG pieces dated to the late 2nd or 3rd century. Amongst the samian from this phase only two vessels showed any signs of burning; one sherd was found in the drain (48) and the other was the flagon, no 13, the interior of which also displayed possible traces of its contents.

Phase G

26 CG ind. (cup) Stamped [CATIA̩NI·MN̩ Die 1a of Catianus i,

Table 6   Occurrence of South Gaulish samian ware (ALC 72/2)

Type	Phase									Totals
	A	B	C	D	E	F	G	H	U/S	
15/17R				1						1
18			1		1					2
18 or 18R				2	2					4
18R		1		3	1					5
27		2	5	3	1	1	2			14
35					1					1
ind		2	2	2	3	1				10
29	1	2	2		1					6
37			3				1			4
Totals	1	7	13	11	10	2	3	0	0	47

1969 and 1972 Baromix finds (ALC 69 and ALC 72/2)

Table 7 Occurrence of Central Gaulish samian ware (ALC 72/2)

Type	Phase									Totals
	A	B	C	D	E	F	G	H	U/S	
18/31						1			1	2
18/31 or 31							1	1		2
31						8		1	1	10
31 or 31R						7		1		8
31R						14			3	17
27			1	2		1			1	5
33						9		2	4	15
36						3		1		4
38 or 44								1		1
44						1				1
45						2				2
Walt 79						4		1	1	6
79 or 80								1		1
Walt 80						1				1
ind			2		1	13	3	1	5	25
29/37				1						1
37		1	1	1	3	8	2	2	6	24
Total	0	1	4	4	4	72	6	11	23	125

Table 8 Occurrence of East Gaulish samian ware (ALC 72/2)

Type	Phase									Totals
	A	B	C	D	E	F	G	H	U/S	
Curle 15 variant						1				1
31						1				1
31R						2				2
33								1		1
43 or 45								1		1
79 or 80						1				1
flagon						1				1
ind						4	1	2		7
Total	0	0	0	0	0	10	1	4	0	15

Lezoux.[b] A stamp noted several times on form 80. One of his other stamps occurs in the group of late Antonine samian from the Pudding Pan Rock wreck; c AD 160–200. A small battered fragment, probably from the same vessel as three other sherds (including the worn footring). (35)

Fig 41 displays the range in date of manufacture of the ten vessels (thirteen sherds) recovered from phase G contexts. Three fragments were from South Gaul, six vessels were Central Gaulish, and one was of indeterminate origin, possibly from East Gaul and probably from the Antonine period. There was no evidence of burning.

Phase H

27 CG Dr 31 or 31R Stamped [CAS]VRIVSF or [AS]VRIVSF Die 5b or 5b' of Casurius ii, Lezoux.[b] Stamps from the complete die occur at Birrens (in Antonine I), Cadder (2) and Camelon. It must therefore have been in use in the 150s. A stamp from the broken die occurs in a group of burnt samian of c AD 170 at Tác (Hungary). A range c AD 150–175 is likely, therefore. A small sherd; worn on top of the basal kick, possibly from use. (24)

28 CG Dr 33 Stamped MATERNNIM Die 2a of Maternianus i, Lezoux.[a] Maternianus i's stamps turn up on Hadrian's Wall and in the group of late Antonine samian from Pudding Pan Rock. There is no site dating for this particular stamp; c AD 160–200. Four adjoining pieces form the complete profile of the vessel. Worn bands inside

1969 and 1972 Baromix finds (ALC 69 and ALC 72/2)

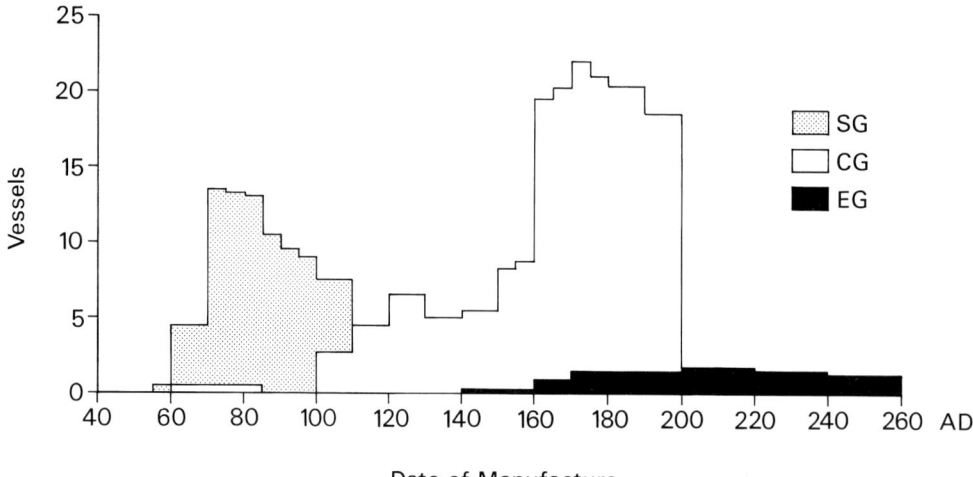

Figure 42   ALC 72/2, date distribution of all samian ware

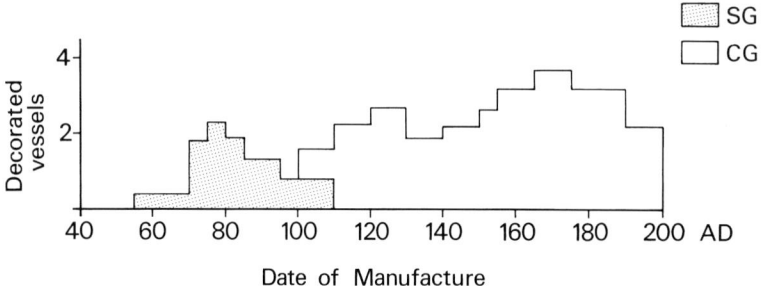

Figure 43   ALC 72/2, date distribution of all decorated samian ware

the junction of wall and base; footring extremely worn, with two nicks and a chip cut out of the standing surface. (24)

The fifteen vessels (twenty sherds) recovered from phase H contexts consisted of eleven CG vessels (73%) and four EG vessels (27%). Only the stamped pieces, nos 27 and 28, were noteworthy. None of the EG fragments was closely datable within the later 2nd- to 3rd-century period. The interior of the single sherd from a *mortarium* of form 43 or 45 was completely worn, and the CG cup, no 28, had been used extensively.

Unphased and unstratified material (Fig 35, nos 33 and 34)

29 CG Dr 38 or 44(?) Stamped [DES]TER F Die 1a of Dester, Lezoux.[a] This stamp occurs at Catterick and South Shields. The die, apparently his only one, was used on forms 31R and (probably) 79, c AD 150–190. A small basal fragment. (1)
30 CG ind c AD 150/160–200. A basal sherd, probably re-used as a counter of which half survives; diameter c 25mm. (1)
31 CG Dr 37 Ovolo (*Rogers* B223) above horizontal beadrow (A2). Probably the style of Cinnamus; c AD 155–175. A battered sherd, possibly re-used as a counter of diameter c 20mm; lines on the internal surface may have been incised accidentally. (1)
32 CG Dr 37 Panels with indistinct borders on which an astragalus is superimposed; to the right, an erotic scene (*Oswald* plate XC, type M) and to the left, a draped figure which may be part of the erotic group, *Oswald* type H; c AD 150–200. A battered sherd of a shallow, thick-walled vessel. (1)
33 CG Dr 37 Blurred ovolo (*Rogers* B164?) and border (A15?); below, the decoration includes a cone motif next to Apollo in a chariot (not identical to *Oswald* 98). Style of Iullinus; c AD 160–190. Two battered sherds. (illus) U/S
34 CG Dr 37 Fragment only of ovolo and border; below, Apollo in a chariot (as no 33) to the right of a fragment of animal running left. Style of Iullinus; c AD 160–190. A very battered sherd, not from the same vessel as no 33. (illus) U/S

The 24 vessels (27 sherds) in this category originated in Central Gaul. All the unstratified pieces, including two possible counters, nos 30 and 31, were manufactured at Lezoux in the second half of the 2nd century.

Summary of the samian ware from the ALC 72/2 excavations

The maximum of 191 vessels was composed of 270 sherds. Some 25% of the total was SG, 66% was CG and 9% was EG. The histogram (Fig 42) representing the whole collection is noteworthy: whereas there is a relatively high level of pre-Flavian material, there is a marked fall-off in the sample of vessels manufactured in the later Domitianic period, followed by a large quantity of Trajanic to early Hadrianic material compared with the samian of early Antonine manufacture. Although there were insufficient stamped or decorated sherds to be meaningful statistically, the histogram representing the decorated samian (Fig 43) displays a relatively small quantity of Flavian material and a high level of Trajanic–Hadrianic material compared with that of Antonine date. There were only eight stamps, of which no 3 was dated *c* AD 60–75. The remainder was CG; two vessels were of earlier 2nd-century date (nos 5 and 23) and five were manufactured after *c* AD 150 (nos 17, 26, 27, 28, and 29). The decorated ware included fragments of form 29 produced in the Neronian to early Flavian period (nos 1 and 4). The earlier 2nd-century potters possibly represented by the decorated vessels included X-13 (two, including one possibly of form 29/37 – no 6), X-2, and Austrus.

There were also fragments of at least one vessel in the early Cinnamus-Cerialis style, and one in Cinnamus' standard style. The later 2nd-century potters represented by decorated sherds were Iullinus (3), Do(v)eccus (1), and Paternus v (1). There were no stamped or decorated sherds of EG origin, but the plain ware from phase F contexts included two flagons of similar form and size which probably were manufactured at Trier in the 3rd century (nos 13 and 22). Other plain sherds included a fragment of form 27 from a 1st century CG workshop; this was recovered from a phase D context where it was obviously residual.

Pieces displaying noteworthy evidence of use included the cup no 28, and perhaps the flagon no 13. Repaired vessels were also noted (nos 15 and 24), and three pieces may have been re-used as counters (nos 18, 30, and 31). Only five pieces (3%) showed likely signs of burning.

Other fine wares (ALC 69 and ALC 72/2)
Rowan Ferguson

White-slipped flagons

This group of fabrics was probably derived from South-West England and was a regular feature of Trajanic–Hadrianic groups in Alcester. It is clear from the assemblages on both Baromix sites, however, that the fabrics were reaching the town from the late Neronian to early Flavian period.

A range of four fabrics was found on ALC 69 of which three were oxidised, fabrics Q11, Q12, and Q25. Fabric Q25 was the only fabric to occur in any sort of quantity and the only one found on ALC 72/2. The fourth slipped fabric, fabric Q22 was reduced and not very common, although it is known from other sites in Alcester and from Tiddington (as were all the oxidised fabrics).

The most commonly found form in these fabrics was the ring-necked flagon of which no 171 illustrates a typical example. These vessels had globular bodies and strap handles, springing from body to the middle of the neck. Several more unusual forms were also found on these sites, such as a narrow-mouthed, double-handled bulbous flask, a plain-necked flagon with a handle springing from the mouth of the vessel and a large jar with a frilled rim.

Imported colour-coats

Colour-coated fabrics were imported to Alcester from the Continent from the Hadrianic period to the 3rd century. The Hadrianic fabrics, which were imported from the Rhineland or possibly South-East England, were found only on ALC 69. There were three of these fabrics; fabrics F37, F38, and F39, of which the first was the most significant. The only vessel type present in these fabrics was a cornice or triangular-rimmed roughcast bag beaker or which vessel no 180 is an example.

The Antonine period saw the introduction of Lezoux Ware and Moselkeramik (F32 and F33) to Britain and this appears in phase F at ALC 72/2 (mid-2nd to 3rd century) and phase F at ALC 69 (late 2nd to 3rd century). These fabrics are present in relatively large quantities during phase F on ALC 72/2 (1.3% which is fairly high for a fine ware of this type). Illustrated vessel no 166 shows a small cup in this fabric. F32, a 3rd-century imported colour-coated fabric, was relatively more important on ALC 72/2 than ALC 69.

As with the *mortarium* fabrics, there seemed to be a concentration of 2nd-century material exclusively on ALC 69 and later fabrics were present in much higher proportions on ALC 72/2.

Romano-British colour-coats

There were only two British colour-coated fabrics present on the Baromix sites in contrast with the much wider range, including several fabrics of probable South-Western origin, on 1–5 Bleachfield Street and at Tiddington. The two present, however, were the most economically successful of this group of fabrics: the Oxfordshire colour-coated and Nene Valley colour-coated wares.

The Nene Valley fabric (F52) appears first on ALC 72/2, phase F (mid-2nd to 3rd century) at 0.19% and on ALC 69, phase F (late 2nd–3rd century) at 1.4% whilst the Oxfordshire colour-coated fabric (F51) appears on the ALC 69 site in phase F (late 2nd–3rd century) but is not found on the ALC 72/2 site except in medieval deposits (phase H) and unstratified material.

The minor role played by these two fabrics did not seem to affect the range of vessel types present, which included beakers, imitation samian forms and *mortaria* in the Oxfordshire fabrics (F51, M71, M23, M43, and W15) and beakers, jars, dishes, and castor boxes in Nene Valley ware (see nos 155 and 224 in the latter fabric).

Despite the fact that the Oxfordshire potters never achieved the same market in Alcester as they did in Tiddington, 12km east, the quantities on the Baromix sites were unusually low reinforcing the idea that the principal period of use of the site was during the 2nd century, well before trade with Oxfordshire reached its peak.

Mica-dusted fabrics

Only one mica-dusted fabric was present on the Baromix sites, this was an oxidised fabric, fabric F22. The origin of this fabric is not known, but it is possible that it came from Gloucester, given the

1969 and 1972 Baromix finds (ALC 69 and ALC 72/2)

well-established trade in flagons and *mortaria* from the south-west.

At ALC 69 the fabric was only found in the Flavian–Trajanic period (phases B and C) where it was definitely in context, it then occurred residually in small amounts in the 3rd-century deposits at ALC 72/2 (phase F). The only identifiable vessel present was the base of a small flagon (no 51), which was decorated with bosses.

Oxfordshire parchment ware

A small amount of this fabric (W15) occurred at ALC 72/2 during the 3rd century (phase F) in the form of the most successful product of those potters, Young's type P24 (Young, 1977), a bowl, which he dates c AD 240–400.

Coarse wares (ALC 69 and ALC 72/2)
Rowan Ferguson

Amphorae

A small percentage of *amphorae* seemed to be part of almost all Roman assemblages from Alcester and, given the concentration of activity in the 1st and 2nd centuries when *amphorae* were still being imported on the Baromix sites, the proportion of *amphorae* (1–3%) was perhaps rather low.

Amphorae fabrics first appeared on the ALC 69 site during the late Neronian to early Flavian period (phase A). The most significant fabric present, A21, was derived from Baetica. On the whole this fabric seemed to have been present on proportions of about 1–3% in both areas.

The illustrated examples of Spanish *amphorae* (ALC 69: Fig 45, no 11 and Fig 52, no 186; ALC 72/2: Fig 47, no 57) are standard Dressel 20 types. One reused sherd was found in this fabric on ALC 69 in an unphased context: the round knob on the base of a Dressel 20 *amphora* had been roughly trimmed to make a concave disc, possibly for use as a pot lid or stopper.

A second *amphora* fabric present in both areas was fabric A22, which was probably Gaulish in origin. This Gaulish fabric is known from both Tiddington (in the form of a Pélichet 47) and other sites in Alcester, but was always secondary in significance to the Spanish fabric A21.

One other *amphora* fabric was found on ALC 69, fabric A31. It seems likely that this fabric was also Spanish (Williams pers comm). This fabric is not known to occur as widely as A21 and A22 in Warwickshire.

Mortaria

Mortaria from a variety of sources were present throughout the Roman period on the Baromix sites. On the whole it seems that the earlier fabrics (Verulamium region, Pas de Calais imports) were more important on ALC 69 and the later (Mancetter-Hartshill and Oxfordshire products) on ALC 72/2.

During the 1st and early 2nd centuries *mortaria* were principally supplied by the potteries of the Verulamium region and Pas de Calais. The Verulamium region exports to Alcester were not limited to *mortaria*, although these were the most numerous of their products found on the majority of sites in the town. A lid, like examples from the kiln at Bricket Wood (Saunders and Havercroft 1977, no 75) was present on ALC 69 and a ring-necked flagon on ALC 72/2, (no 170). Of the *mortaria* only one was stamped (no 63). It has a retrograde stamp of Oastrius who was working in the period AD 60–80. Other *mortaria* manufactured as late as the Antonine period were also present, such as no 79.

Two different fabrics were present from the Pas de Calais and appeared intermittently throughout the Roman period on ALC 69. Another source of *mortaria* during the late 1st to 2nd century was South-West England where kilns were producing oxidised vessels with a white slip. The products of these kilns occurred on ALC 69 only from the Flavian period. Illustrated vessel number 37 shows a common hooked rim type from phase B (ALC 69, 79).

One other *mortarium* from ALC 69 dated to a similar period was from an unidentified source, possibly Wroxeter. The fabric, M33, was oxidised with angular white opaque trituration grits. The example present (no 148 (context (51A), phase F) residual in ALC 69 was probably Trajanic, combining a post-Flavian hooked rim and the scoring of the rim and upper body which Mrs Hartley dates to the Flavian–Trajanic period (Hartley pers comm).

With the beginning of the 2nd century all the above products were available in the Alcester marketplace and the Mancetter-Hartshill potters also began to trade in this area.

Stamps of the potters, Loccius Pro (no 237), Iunius (no 112), and ?Gratinus (no 159) who were working during the 1st half of the 2nd century were found, as well as examples of later 2nd-century to 3rd-century *mortaria*. The later products of the Mancetter kilns, the hammer-headed *mortaria*, were only present on ALC 72/2 (no 233).

The only other vessel type present in the Mancetter-Hartshill fabric was a beaker of which two examples, identical in form but very different in decoration, were found (nos 84 and 85). These beakers both came from the same context (115) on ALC 69. No Mancetter-Hartshill flagons were found in either area.

Around the same time as pottery from Mancetter-Hartshill was first reaching the town, the Oxfordshire potters also began to exploit the Alcester market. The earliest Oxfordshire *mortarium* fabric to reach Alcester was the Oxfordshire white ware (fabric M23; no 235). It was present on ALC 72/2 in larger quantities than on ALC 69. As well as both the simple and more elaborate flanged *mortarium* types (of which the latter were more common), flanged bowls and flagons (no 225) were found in this fabric on ALC 69. Other Oxfordshire *mortaria* to reach these sites, but in much smaller quantities, were those in the white-coated fabric, fabric M43 and the colour-coated fabric, fabric M71.

Severn Valley wares

This group of fabrics formed a major and constant part of pottery assemblages in Alcester throughout the Roman period. Within this general grouping a range of twelve fabrics (differentiated by inclusions), was present on ALC 69 and eight on ALC 72/2. A core of seven fabrics was common to both sites (see the microfiche Tables MT2 and MT3 for quantities of different fabrics present). These fabrics (fabrics O21, O23, O24, O25, O27, O29, and O33) were also the most quantitatively significant on the two sites.

The Severn Valley wares occurred in fairly consistent quantities throughout the use of the Baromix sites. At ALC 69 they represented between 14% and 24% of the assemblages in each phase, and between 24% and 37% of the assemblages at ALC 72/2.

A closer look at the two coarse ware assemblages shows that the relative importance of Severn Valley wares fluctuates in completely different ways on the two areas despite the broad similarity in the proportions the fabric group represent in each case.

Proportions on ALC 69 seem to be very similar to those in other statistically reliable collections such as 1–5 Bleachfield Street (the Explosion site) where Severn Valley wares constituted almost 22% of the total pottery assemblage with a peak in the 3rd century (Booth 1986). A slight 2nd- to 3rd-century peak was also noted at ALC 69 (23%). The picture on ALC 72/2, however, varied from this norm; no 3rd-century peak was present and quantities peaked in phases C–E (Trajanic to early Antonine) at around 36% and then fell to 28% in the later 2nd to 3rd century and 26% in the later 3rd to early 4th century.

The ALC 72/2 pattern of Severn Valley ware use was very different from that at ALC 69 where there was a steady increase from 14% in phase A to *c* 24% in phase C, a level, which after a dip in phase D was maintained throughout the 3rd century. Although the difference in trend cannot be explained, the situation on ALC 72/2 may appear more extreme because of the much lower presence of other coarse wares outside the major fabric groups. On ALC 69 these help to cushion big changes in the relative proportions of the major groups. Another reason may be functional differences between the two areas although these do not show up obviously in the figures (Fig 44). Tankards, which are all in Severn Valley ware, are commoner in the earlier phases at ALC 72/2 than on ALC 69. Otherwise the early phases are dominated by jars. However, there may be a hidden difference in the figures between jars used as cooking pots and those used for storage, the latter more probably being in Severn Valley ware.

The sources of the Severn Valley wares in Alcester are not known, but production in the vicinity of the town has been tentatively suggested (Booth 1986). It is also possible that some material was derived from the Malvern kilns. Many of the forms found in Alcester can be paralleled amongst those manufactured there (Peacock 1967), especially reed-rimmed bowls (eg ALC 69 nos 157 and 204; Peacock 1967, fig 9, no 53), tankards (ALC 69 no 217; Peacock 1967, Fig 4, no 44), small bowls (ALC 72/2 no 176; Webster 1976, Fig 7, no 35), double-lipped, narrow-mouthed jars (ALC 69 no 154; Peacock 1967, Fig 3, no 30) and wide-mouthed jars (ALC 69 nos 218–19; Peacock 1967, Fig 4, no 56). In addition to this the Malvernian metamorphic-tempered fabrics were a typical feature of Roman pottery assemblages from Alcester (see further discussion below) so trade was clearly well-established with this production centre.

The forms present on the Baromix sites represent a range of vessels which may be military inspired in design (such as the carinated bowls, ALC 69 nos 1 and 172, the flat-rimmed bowl, ALC 69 no 44, the beaker ALC 72 no 92, the hemispherical bowl, ALC 69 no 120, and the dish ALC 69 no 6), and can be paralleled in early military assemblages throughout the South-west and West Midlands, (Darling 1977). These forms are mingled with the more typical Severn Valley ware products, a variety of storage jars, tankards, wide-mouthed jars and reeded-rimmed bowls. Some more unusual Severn Valley forms are also present such as jugs (also known in Alcester from Tibbet's Close, Ferguson 1989), flagons, and lids.

Although a wide range of both fabrics and forms was found on the Baromix sites and quantities of the Severn Valley wares remained fairly constant throughout the Roman period, this group of fabrics was never of prime importance in the assemblage and was always second in importance either to the reduced fabric group or to Black-Burnished ware.

Local reduced fabrics

The most significant group of coarse wares on both ALC 69 and ALC 72/2 was this group of reduced fabrics which were probably made locally, possibly within the town itself. Although no kiln site has yet been found it would seem reasonable to assume that a settlement of the size of Roman Alcester would have been able to supply the bulk of its own coarse pottery demand.

A range of 26 of these fabrics were found on ALC 69 where they represented 44–63% during the 1st and 2nd centuries. Quantities then fell in the 3rd century (phase F) as a result of the more significant role played by Black-Burnished ware from the 3rd century and fell further in the 4th century. This pattern was more or less mirrored at ALC 72/2 where the reduced wares were slightly less significant (between 32–53% of the 1st- and 2nd-century assemblage). On both sites there was a peak in the Flavian period (phase B). Only 10 fabrics were present on ALC 72/2, all of which appeared on the other site. The diversity of fabrics on ALC 69 probably explains the increase in the proportion represented by reduced wares on this site in the Flavian period; study of reduced wares from the large 1st- and 2nd-century assemblages present at the Explosion site has shown that a great number of different reduced fabrics were being produced in or around

1969 and 1972 Baromix finds (ALC 69 and ALC 72/2)

Alcester at this time and that it was only in the Hadrianic period that the supply was resolved into a small group of easily distinguished fabrics. This perhaps suggests a degree of experimentation in pottery manufacture in the Flavian period and a proliferation of individual craftspersons who were later organised into a small number of larger workshops. Or it may be that during the Flavian period in Alcester we are seeing the products of transient potters supplying the army who had left Alcester by the Hadrianic period. As is discussed below there were a large number of vessel types in the assemblage which were popular with the army.

There would seem to be no need to search for sources of reduced fabrics much outside Alcester itself and there is little precedent for the marketing of this type of fabric over long distances. There do not seem to be any products of the Wappenbury kilns present, but it is possible that the odd vessel from Tiddington may occur, certainly the small carinated bowl; ALC 72 no 62 is similar in both fabric and form to examples found in the Tiddington kiln deposit, and the rouletted beaker ALC 69 no 133 and the miniature vessels ALC 69 nos 134 and 181 may also have been made there.

Apart from these Tiddington products, three main strands can be defined in the range of vessel types found in the reduced fabrics. The first and most noticeable of these is the range of pyriform jars. These vessels were present in large numbers from the Flavian period until the mid-2nd century. They continued to occur, but residually, throughout the life of the site. To begin with the vessels had a globular profile and were usually decorated with overall rustication from below the shoulder: ALC 69 no 42, (context (97), phase B) although there are also examples where the rustication is confined to vertical strips: ALC 69 no 49 (context (118), phase C). With time, it appears that the profile of these vessels became more elongated and less globular and that the technique of overall rustication was no longer used: ALC 69 no 54 (context (98), phase C). The occasional globular version continued to occur in later phases, however, but with a completely different style of decoration, for example burnished lattice: ALC 69 no 203 (context (201), unphased), or stabbed dots: ALC 72 no 201 (context (19), phase G). This abandoning of the technique of rustication seemed to be the final development of the vessel type and there are examples with horizontal burnished lines, both straight: ALC 69 no 67 (context (148), phase D) and wavy: ALC 69 no 147 (context (51A), phase F) as well as the two variations mentioned above. The pyriform jar in its rusticated form was a common feature of sites throughout the West Midlands, especially those with military connections, such as the Lunt (Hobley 1973 and 1975). It has been suggested that this vessel type may have derived from a Continental form of the early part of the 1st century (Swan 1984).

The second major tradition which can be distinguished amongst the Baromix material is more likely to be indigenous than the pyriform jars, but was also associated with early military sites in the area. This tradition could be described as 'Belgic' and consisted of high-shouldered jars such as ALC 69 no 5 from the earliest group on the site (context (136), phase A) which can be paralleled at Gloucester (Darling, 1977, Fig 6.10, no 7), carinated-necked bowls, for example ALC 69 nos 36 and 205 (context (79), phase B and context (199), unphased; parallels at Kingsholm, Darling 1977, Fig 6.9, no 28) and flat-rimmed carinated bowls, for example ALC 69 no 25 (context (178), phase A) and ALC 72 no 60 (context (107), phase C; parallels at Gloucester, Darling 1977, Fig 6.11, no 9, and Exeter, Fig 6.12, no 15). These forms can also be paralleled at the more northerly sites of the Lunt (Hobley 1969, Fig 12, no 11) and Wall (Gould 1966: Fig 11, nos 29 and 74). Although there is no doubt that these 'Belgic' forms were popular with the army it should also be remembered that kilns in the vicinity at Tiddington, which had no military connections, were also producing in this tradition (Booth 1986).

The third component of the reduced ware assemblages on the Baromix sites was a wide range of dishes, jars, lids, and bowls which could not be ascribed to any particular external influence but contained echoes of both Black-Burnished ware and Severn Valley ware traditions as well as the basic core of forms fundamental to most Romano-British assemblages.

It is clear from the presence of the three main groupings of reduced wares discussed above that the potters who supplied the bulk of the coarse wares available in the Alcester marketplace during the 1st and 2nd centuries were influenced by many diverse traditions as might be expected of craftspersons in such a thriving economic centre.

Black-Burnished ware

As with most Roman centres in the West Midlands, Black-Burnished ware was an important element in the coarse ware assemblages from the Baromix sites from Hadrianic times, but particularly during the 3rd and 4th centuries. In the latter period it was the most significant of all the coarse wares. By the 3rd century (phase F) it had already overtaken the local reduced fabrics in importance at ALC 72/2 and the availability of this product was probably responsible for the decline of the local pottery industries. (This decline is inferred from the steady decrease in the proportion represented by the reduced fabrics in successive periods.) At its peak in phase F at ALC 72/2 and phase G at ALC 69 Black-Burnished ware represented 23.6% of the assemblage on ALC 69 and 22.3% of the assemblage at ALC 72/2. This should be compared with the proportions present at 1–5 Bleachfield Street; 38% in the first half of the 4th century and 35% in the second half, 4th-century activity on this site being much more intensive than on the Baromix sites.

The fabric seems to be the classic Black-Burnished ware from Dorset and the range of vessel types present supports this theory. The vessels present consist of the standard cooking pots, flanged bowls, dishes, and handled dishes; ALC 69 no 121 (context (51), phase F).

Malvernian metamorphic fabrics

This fabric, G44, was a constant factor in the coarse ware assemblages from Alcester. The production site was less than 50km away and pottery may easily have come via Droitwich along the salt ways.

The fabric was found from phase A onwards on ALC 69 and from phase D at ALC 72/2. In pre-Hadrianic deposits less than 1% of the fabric was found in those phases in which it was found, but this increased to between 1% and 2% from the Hadrianic period.

The vessel types present were principally 'tubby cooking pots' such as ALC 69 no 82 (context (78), phase D), and dishes like ALC 69 no 73 (context (148), phase D) but there were also much larger storage jars (see ALC 69 no 202 (context (211), unphased) and ALC 72 no 93 (context (61), phase D), and lids (ALC 69 no 222 (context (22), phase H). The tubby cooking pots were generally decorated with vertical burnished lines, although some had the lattice decoration more commonly found on the dishes. One of the large jars also had a lattice decoration. The similarities between dishes such as ALC 69 no 73 and Black-Burnished ware dishes may be due simply to the influence of the latter industry or possibly to traditions common to both the *Durotriges* and the *Dobunni*, the local Romano-British tribe, as Durotrigian influences can be seen in other pottery industries in this area such as the Severn Valley ware tradition.

There was also a group of five fabrics which may be related to the Malvernian metamorphic family, fabrics also distinguished by particularly coarse tempering. These occur in proportions of less than 1% in both areas from the Flavian period, but represented nearly 10% of the late Neronian to early Flavian assemblage on ALC 69.

Early local fabrics and other oxidised fabrics

Of this group, fabrics W23, E26, E25, E15, E31, E32, and E41 were present on the Baromix sites. These fabrics were principally oxidised and very similar in character to fabrics manufactured at Tiddington, c AD 30–70 (Booth 1986). The only vessel type present, a carinated bowl, is in fabric E15 (ALC 69 no 50 (context (118), phase C), and may well come from Tiddington where vessels identical in fabric and form (one of a range of 'Belgic' types) were being produced.

These fabrics only occurred as about 1% or less of the assemblage and were probably residual by the Flavian period. They had disappeared by Antonine times.

Handmade fabrics

A few sherds of handmade Iron Age style fabrics (fabric group P) occurred on the Baromix sites. A Roman handmade fabric, fabric G43, was also present. These fabrics were always less than 1% of the assemblage. No identifiable forms were present.

Shell-gritted fabrics

Two shell-gritted wares were present on the Baromix sites, fabric C11 and fabric C23. Only the former was of any importance. These fabrics appeared in the later 3rd century and were present in proportions of less than 1% in Roman contexts from phase F on ALC 69 and from phase G on ALC 72/2, with the greatest proportions being just over 1% from the medieval phases (H). This low proportion is probably explained by the lack of 4th-century activity in the area. The slightly higher proportion present in post-Roman contexts may reflect the late 4th century *floruit* of the fabric seen in late contexts on the Gateway site (AL18) (Ferguson, in Cracknell 1996, 20–31).

The fabric was principally present in the form of slack profiled jars loosely based on Black-Burnished ware forms (see vessels ALC 69 no 220, context (23A), phase H). The source of the fabric is thought to be to the east of Alcester, possibly Northamptonshire (Booth 1986).

Fabric G11

This distinctive buff fabric was another regular component in the later 3rd- and 4th-century groups in Alcester. However, it is known to appear in a smaller version of the usual large heavy storage jar in earlier contexts.

The fabric represented less than 1% of the assemblage in phase F, 3rd century, but is absent from phase G. The small quantities of the fabric were, no doubt, due to the low level of 4th-century occupation, the period when this fabric was most common. The fabric was common throughout the Midlands and it originated somewhere near Milton Keynes (Booth and Green 1989).

Discussion

During the late Neronian and Flavian periods in Alcester there seems to have been a proliferation of coarse ware fabrics including a wide range of locally made reduced fabrics, Severn Valley wares, Malvernian metamorphic and related fabrics, local handmade and wheelmade material. These fabrics

1969 and 1972 Baromix finds (ALC 69 and ALC 72/2)

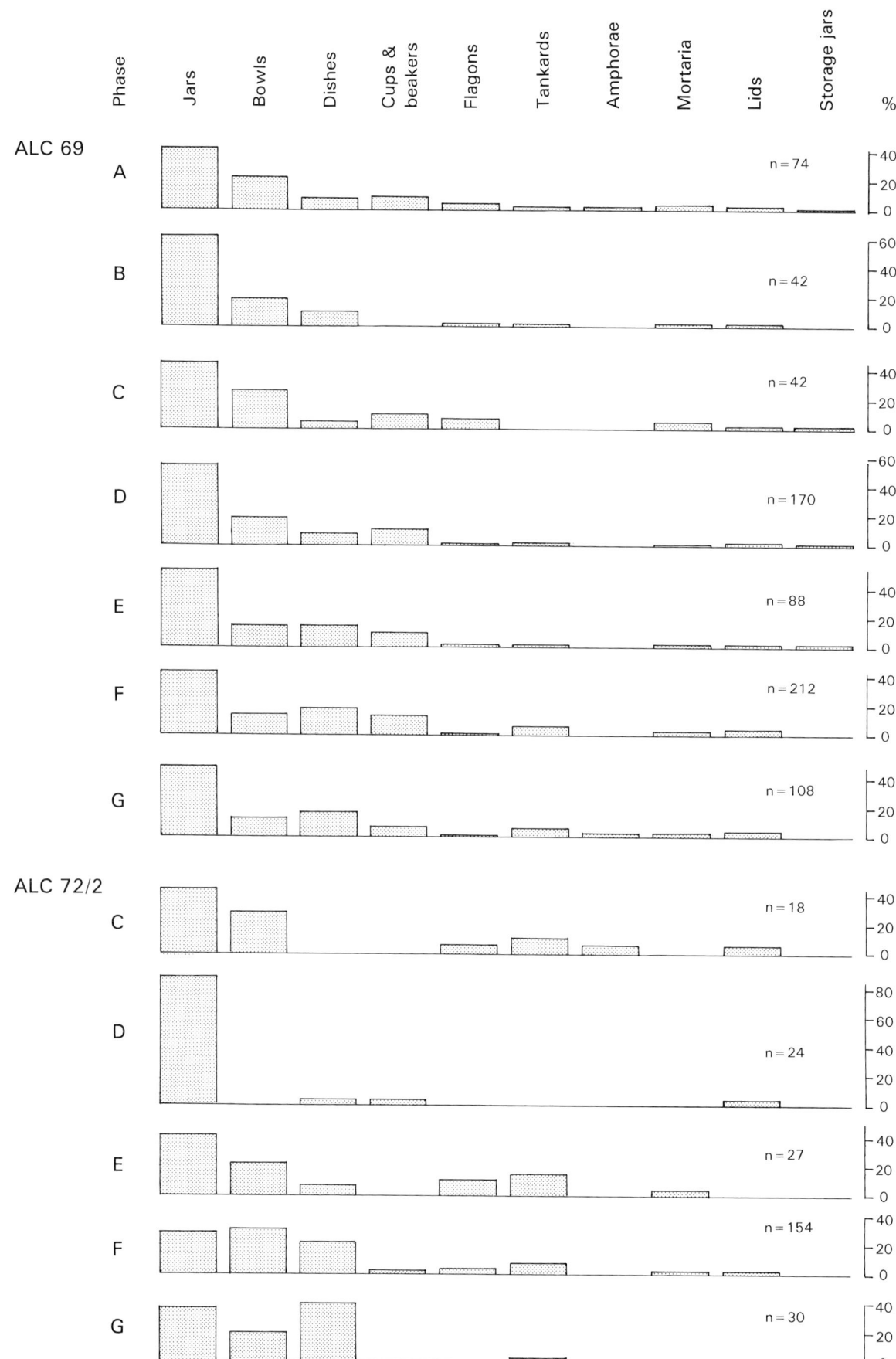

Fig 44 Functional analysis of vessels by phase (ALC 69 and ALC 72/2) (by minimum numbers of rims)

were manufactured in forms which demonstrated a variety of influences of which perhaps the most clearly defined were military and 'Belgic'. Parallels for many of the vessel types occurring in Alcester at this time can be found on early military sites throughout the Midlands and the marketplace seemed to show a steady flow of South-Western influenced traditions.

By the Antonine period the last vestiges of military influence had gone and the market seemed to have settled down with a much smaller core of fabrics available. Many of the smaller local industries were dying away as competition from the Black-Burnished ware potters began.

During the 3rd century, trade with Dorset was well established and the market for Severn Valley wares continued to thrive. Local industries suffered further as these major producers took over. It was during this period that trade with centres to the east of Alcester was established and shell-gritted wares and the coarse buff storage jar fabric, fabric G11, began to appear in these assemblages from the 3rd century (phase F).

Functional analysis of the pottery (ALC 69 and ALC 72/2)
Jeremy Evans

A minimum of 1104 vessels (calculated by rim sherds) was present on ALC 69 and there were 423 from ALC 72/2. These vessels represented the usual range of types found in Alcester and Fig 44 shows how the proportions varied through time. Fig 44 shows a number of chronological trends common to both sites, and also some interesting differences between them. (Unfortunately for most phases the assemblage sizes on the ALC 72/2 site are low and consequently figures for the less frequently occurring classes are not very reliable.) On both sites dishes are rare in the 1st to early 2nd century, but increase in the mid-2nd century and peak in the 3rd century or later (phases F and G). Similarly, tankards are rare in the 1st and earlier 2nd centuries, but rise in the 3rd and 4th at ALC 69, but at ALC 72/2 the peak is earlier in the Hadrianic to early Antonine period (phase E) and there is a high level in phases B and C. The trend in flagons is best observed in the ALC 69 data from a larger number of vessels, but both sites show their decline from a peak in the 1st to early 2nd century to a lower level in the mid- to late 2nd century, with their virtual disappearance by the 3rd. *Mortaria* seem to be a consistent proportion of the assemblages from the beginnings and lids too seem to be consistently present at a low level.

Turning to the major components of the assemblage, jars seem to form a consistent proportion of the assemblage on the ALC 69 site, although there seems to be greater variation at ALC 72/2 and a decline from the mid-2nd century. The bowl figures at ALC 69 fall after the Flavian–Trajanic period (phase C) whereas at ALC 72/2 there is a peak in the later 2nd to 3rd century (phase F). This latter feature is probably a reflection of the peak of samian ware on the site found in this phase (21% by sherd number).

Comparing the sequences from the two sites, generally phases A–C are similar on both and the sites tend to diverge after this. The only notable variations are the high proportions of jars in phase B at ALC 69 and the extraordinarily high proportion from phase D (the demolition horizon equivalent to the end of phase C on ALC 69) at ALC 72/2, whilst tankards seem to be commoner on ALC 72/2 than on ALC 69. The higher proportion of tankards on ALC 72/2 in these phases no doubt correlates with the higher proportion of Severn Valley ware. The high jar proportions from ALC 69 phase B, presumably reflects a concentration of cooking or storage activities on the site in that phase, but material from ALC 72/2 phase D, is unlikely to reflect contemporary activity as such, although it could result from deliberate dumping of stores or dumped levelling material from elsewhere. The latter may be more likely as most of the samian (Fig 38) from this phase is residual.

The sequences from the two sites diverge markedly from the mid-2nd century (phase F at ALC 72/2 and phase E at ALC 69) with a decline in the jar level at ALC 72/2 and a rise in dishes and bowls to between 50% and 60% compared with around 30% at ALC 69. This clearly suggests a tableware-dominated, and presumably higher status assemblage, being the source of the ALC 72/2 material. This is reflected in the 21% (by sherd number) of samian from the latter site and the tentative evidence of a stone building on the site correlates with this.

Turning to more general comparisons, the later phases from these sites may be compared with the sequence from Gas House Lane (Evans, in Cracknell 1996, 58–97) and the site as a whole may be compared with the Explosion site sequence (Ferguson below, Table MT12, M2:C7) although these figures are compiled by RE rather than minimum numbers of rims. It is of note that jar levels on the Explosion site are generally higher than here and bowls much rarer in the early phases. These features suggest a more functional and less Romanised assemblage at that site, especially in its earlier phases. The Explosion site sequence also confirms the general increase of dishes in assemblages as the Roman period progresses, a feature shared with Chichester and Verulamium (Millett 1979, Fig 13), and (excepting the phase A figures) it shares with Chichester and Verulamium a general decline in jar levels with time, if from a rather higher base, like Neatham (Millett and Graham 1986).

Overall of the data under consideration here the ALC 72/2 figures seem to more closely resemble the general trend whilst the ALC 69 ones seem to reflect a more basic functional assemblage. However, the ALC 69 sequence undoubtedly contains much residual material by phase F, with c 33% of grey wares, nearly all of which must have been residual (compare Gas House Lane, Evans, in Cracknell 1996, 58–97) which probably masks changes.

1969 and 1972 Baromix finds (ALC 69 and ALC 72/2)

Summary catalogue of illustrated vessels (ALC 69 and ALC 72/2)
Rowan Ferguson

ALC 69 Phase A (Fig 45, nos 1–29)

The group from layer 136 and the vessel from 198 were associated with late Neronian samian (see Ward above) and military bronzes (see Lloyd-Morgan below). All the illustrated vessels further underline the late Neronian–Flavian date of this phase. The assemblage as a whole compares interestingly with those of similar date from early military sites to the south-west and west of Alcester. On the whole it is closest to material from the pre-fortress levels at Gloucester (Darling 1977, Fig 6.10). Almost every illustrated vessel can be paralleled in the group shown by Miss Darling. The preponderance of native forms at both sites shows that competent pottery industries were already well established before contact with the military began. As Gloucester and Alcester were both within the territory of the *Dobunni* (Booth 1986), the similarity in their native pottery industries is not surprising. Although kilns have yet to be found in the immediate vicinity of Alcester, kilns at nearby Tiddington (about 12km east of the town) were producing material in the same tradition as the vessels illustrated here.

One of the illustrated vessels, no 4, was sprinkled on both interior and exterior with spots of glaze. It has been suggested to me (S Ratkai pers comm) that the most likely way for the pot to have acquired this 'glaze' is through bits of burning ash falling on the surface during firing. This could have occurred either during manufacture or disuse of the pot.

Other pots in what appeared to be local fabrics were the two flagons, nos 3 and 10. These are not native forms and the continental/military connections they hint at are underlined by parallels at Wroxeter (Darling 1977, Fig 6.6, no 2), Usk (no 3, cf Darling 1977, Fig 6.2, no 6), and Kingsholm (no 10, cf Darling 1977, Fig 6.8, no 13). This last vessel, a thin-walled ring-necked flagon was made in fabric R32, an organically tempered grey ware which continued to occur in Alcester throughout the 1st and 2nd centuries and possibly even later, for example at 1–5 Bleachfield Street, the Explosion site (see Ferguson below).

Trade with other local centres was represented in the assemblage as a whole by the presence of Malvernian metamorphic and related fabrics. Imported fabrics were also found in this period including samian, a Spanish amphora fabric, the Pas de Calais *mortaria*, and the Verulamium Region *mortarium* fabric, which generally appears in Alcester in the form of *mortaria* but in this instance occurs as a small, flat lid (no 8). This range of imports suggests that trading links were already well established even at this early stage in the town's development.

		Context
1	Severn Valley ware (O28) carinated bowl	136
2	Severn Valley ware (O21) storage jar	136
3	Large flagon (O61) cf Darling 1977, Fig 6.6, no 2	136
4	Small jar (O14) with fuel ash glaze spots	136
5	High-shouldered jar (R32)	136
6	Severn Valley ware (O27) dish	136
7	Jar (R41)	136
8	White ware lid (M11)	136
9	Severn Valley ware (O21) tankard	136
10	Ring-necked flagon (R32)	198
11	Spanish *amphora* (A21)	163
12	Severn Valley ware jar (O21)	96
13	Small jar (R12)	96
14	Carinated bowl (R14)	96
15	Small jar (R57)	96
16	Carinated bowl (O51)	96
17	Small jar (R41)	96
18	Small jar (R15)	96
19	Small jar (R44)	96
20	Flanged bowl (R44)	96
21	Pyriform jar (R32)	176
22	Small bowl	176
23	Cup-necked flagon (F41)	138 + 136
24	Jar (R01)	182
25	Flanged bowl (R15)	178
26	Pyriform jar (R52)	95
27	Malvernian dish (G44)	95
28	Pyriform jar (R15)	119
29	Lid-seated handled jar (O81)	119A

ALC 72/2 Phase A (Fig 46)

30	Jar (R32)	72

ALC 69 Phase B (Fig 46)

31	Jar (R01)	142
32	Severn Valley ware jar (O21)	79
33	Pyriform jar (R01)	79
34	Jar (R32)	79
35	Dish (R32)	79
36	Carinated bowl (R41)	79
37	White slipped *mortarium* (M44)	79
38	Pyriform jar (R41)	170
39	Pyriform jar (R01)	170
40	Malvernian jar (G44)	170
41	?Tankard/carinated bowl (R01)	170
42	Pyriform jar (R22)	97
43	Pyriform jar (R32)	97
44	Severn Valley ware carinated bowl (O27)	97

ALC 72/2 Phase B (Fig 46)

45	Carinated bowl (R32)	62 + 104

ALC 69 Phase C (Fig 47)

46	Large Severn Valley flagon (O21)	196
47	Pas de Calais *mortarium* (M12)	196
48	Jar (R42)	194
49	Pyriform jar (R32)	118
50	Carinated bowl (E15)	118
51	Mica-dusted flagon (F22)	149

1969 and 1972 Baromix finds (ALC 69 and ALC 72/2)

ALC 69   Phase A

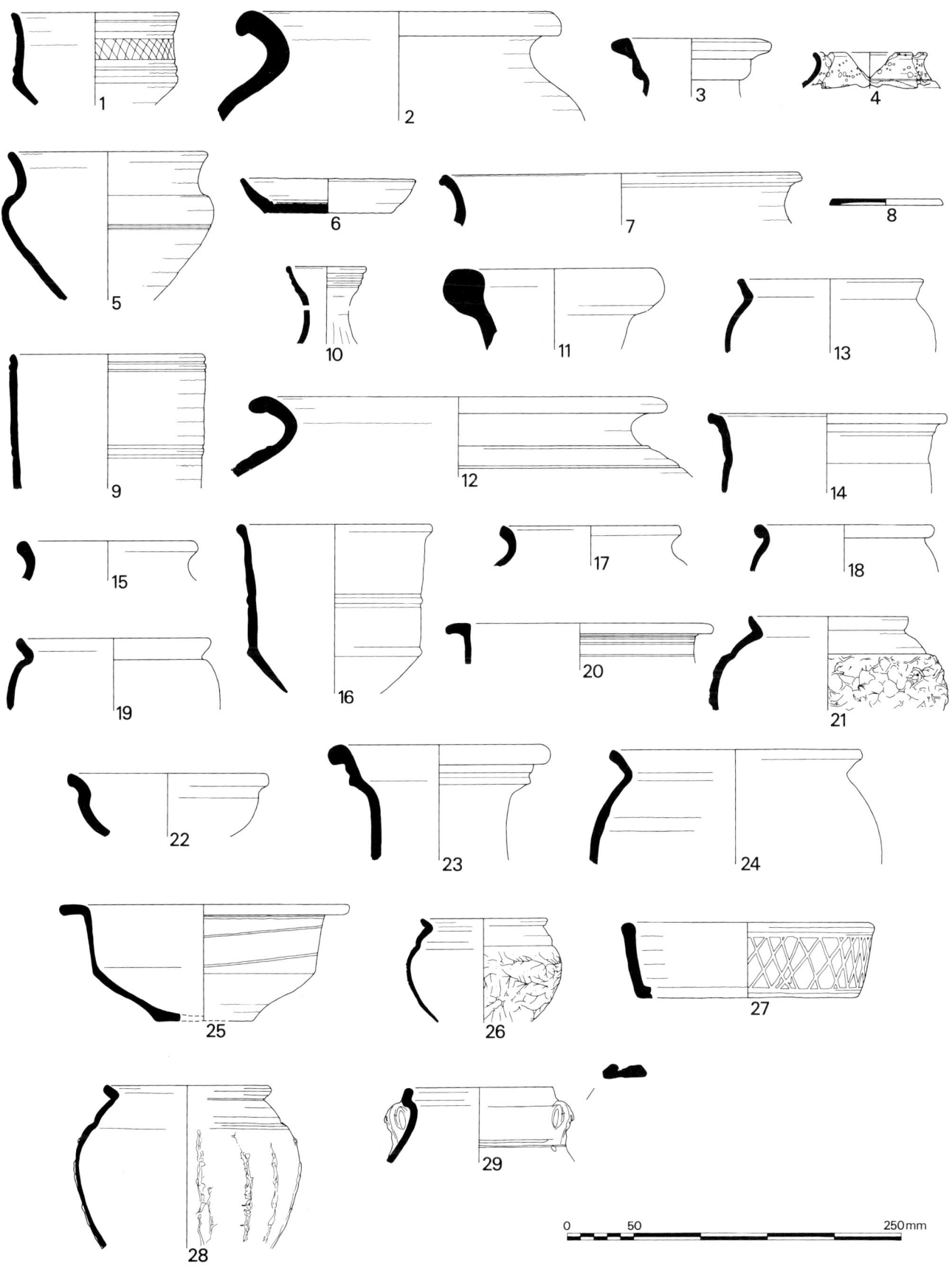

Figure 45   Coarse pottery (ALC 69, phase A), nos 1–29

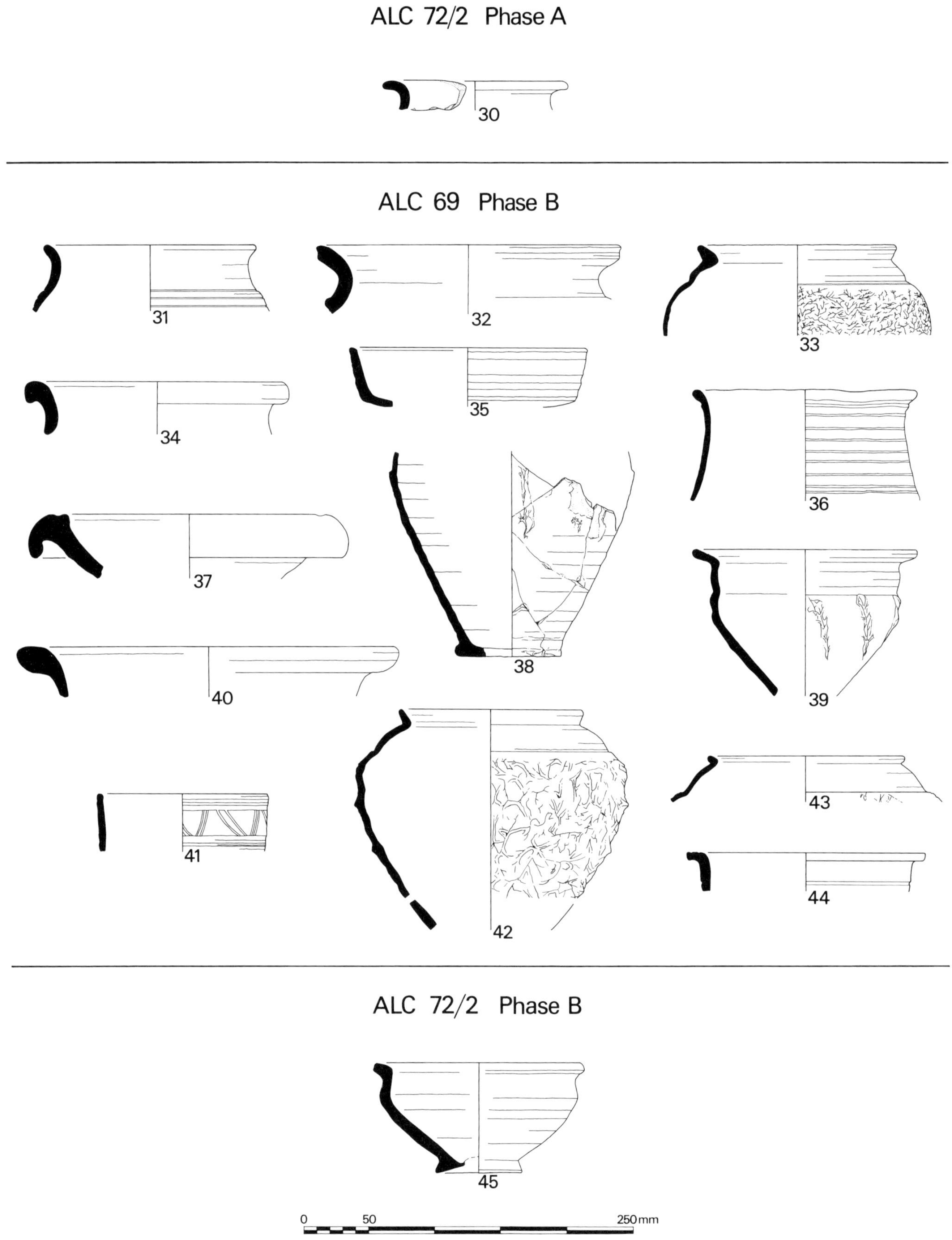

1969 and 1972 Baromix finds (ALC 69 and ALC 72/2)

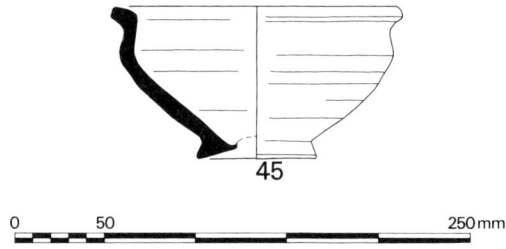

Figure 46   Coarse pottery (ALC 72/2, phases A and B, and ALC 69, phase B), nos 30–45

1969 and 1972 Baromix finds (ALC 69 and ALC 72/2)

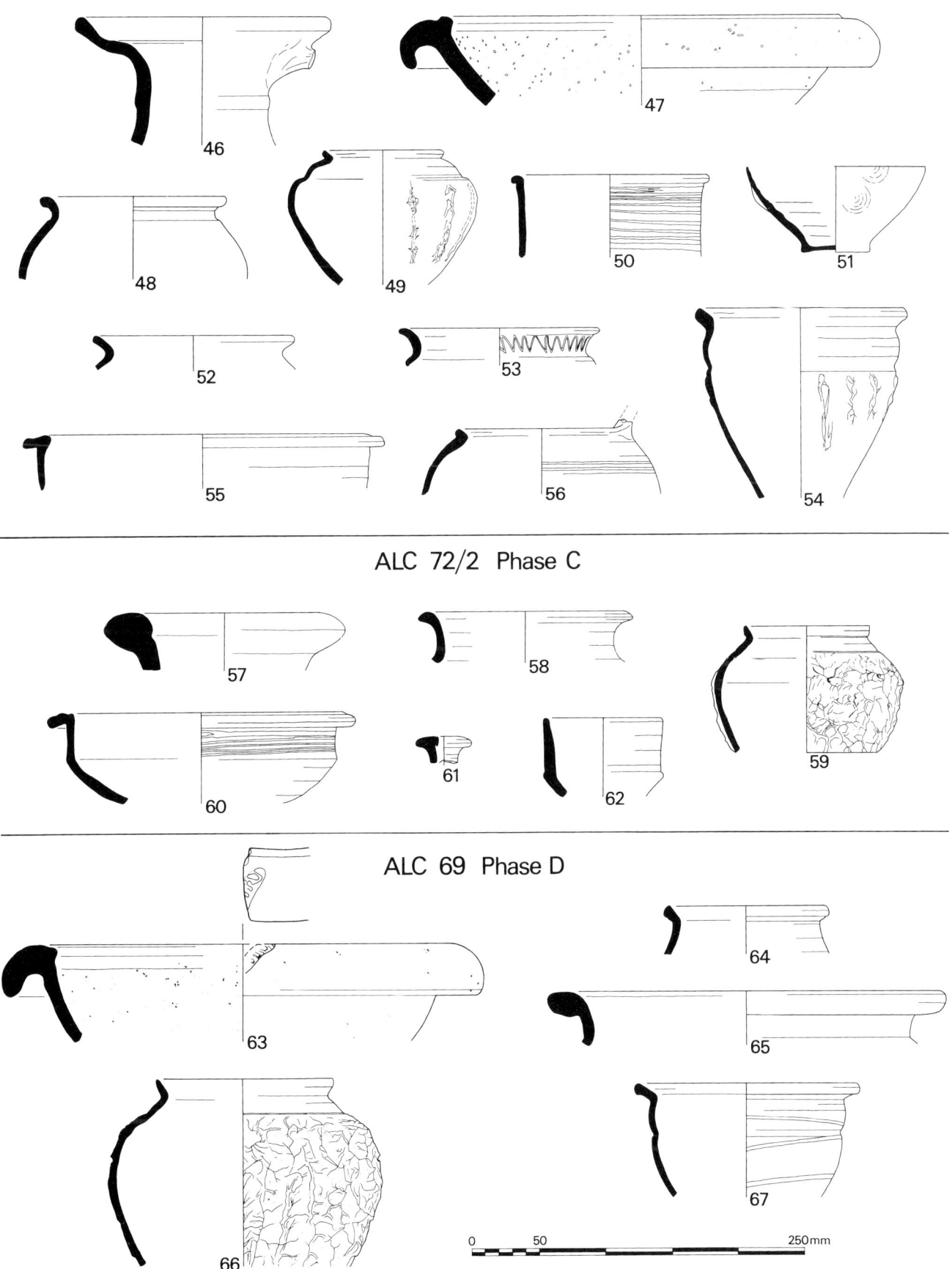

Figure 47   Coarse pottery (ALC 69, phases C and D, and ALC 72/2, phase C), nos 46–67

1969 and 1972 Baromix finds (ALC 69 and ALC 72/2)

Figure 48   Coarse pottery (ALC 69, phase D), nos 68–90

1969 and 1972 Baromix finds (ALC 69 and ALC 72/2)

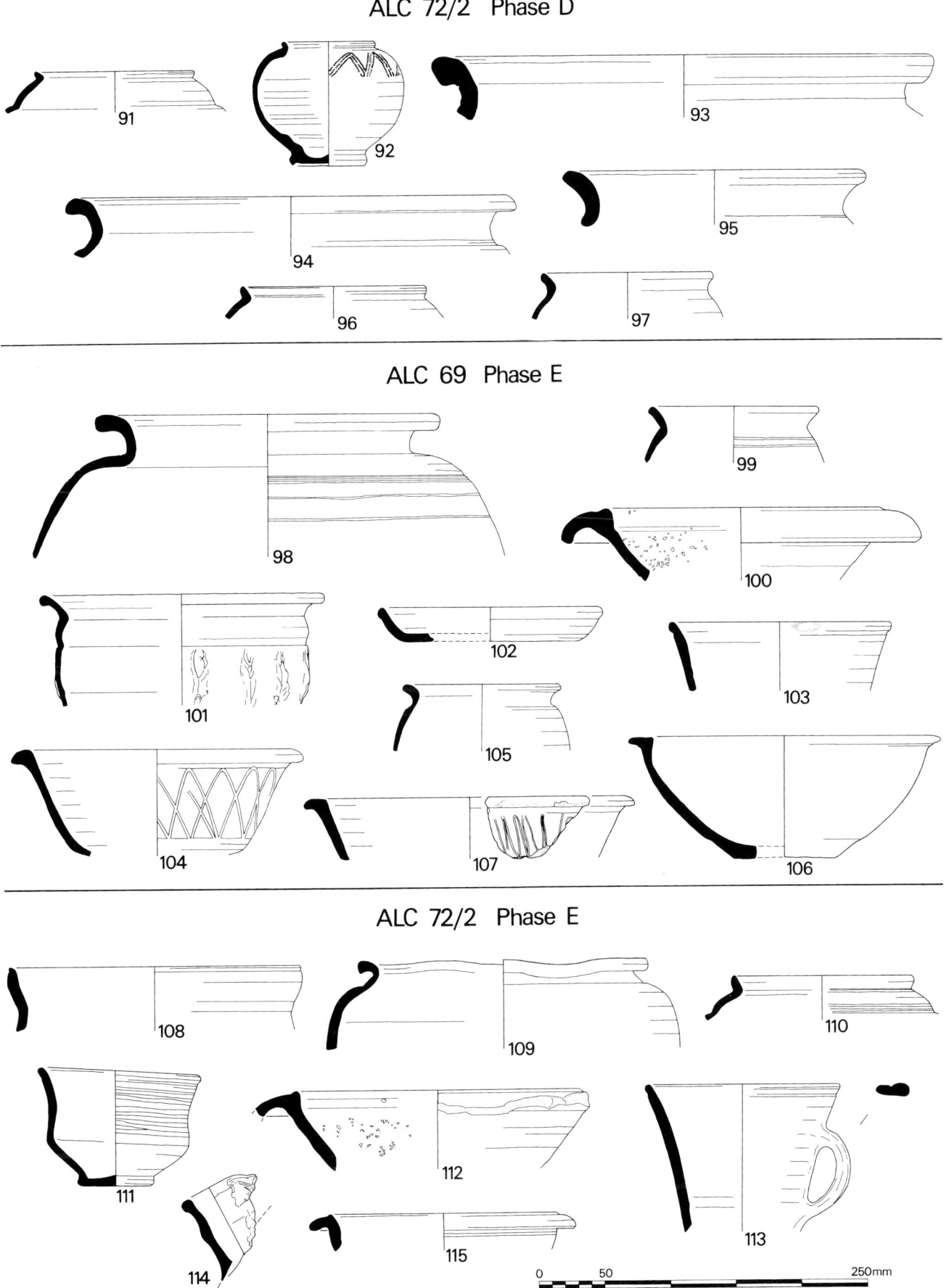

Figure 49   Coarse pottery (ALC 72/2, phases D and E, and ALC 69, phase E), nos 91–115

1969 and 1972 Baromix finds (ALC 69 and ALC 72/2)

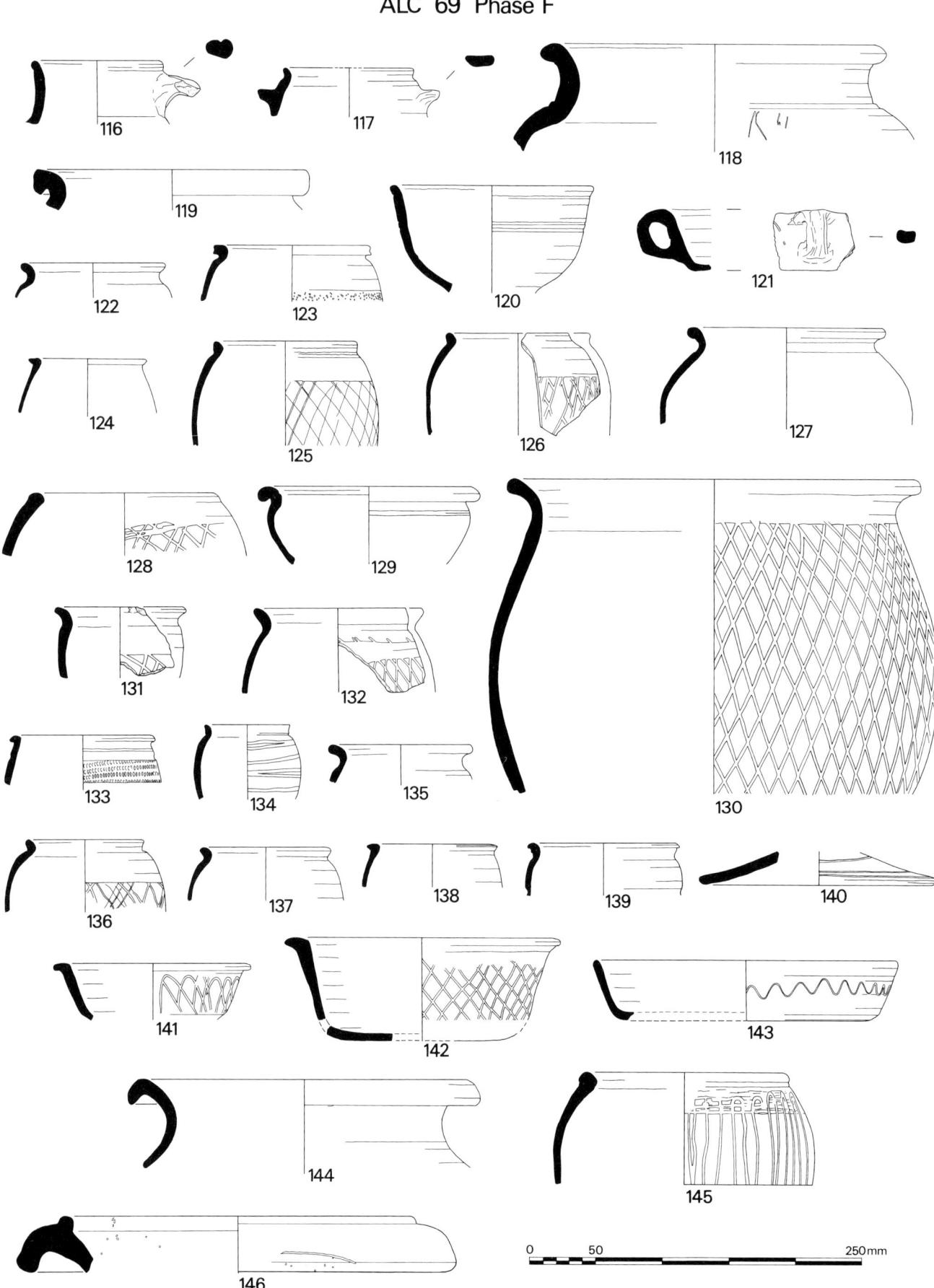

Figure 50   Coarse pottery (ALC 69, phase F), nos 116–146

1969 and 1972 Baromix finds (ALC 69 and ALC 72/2)

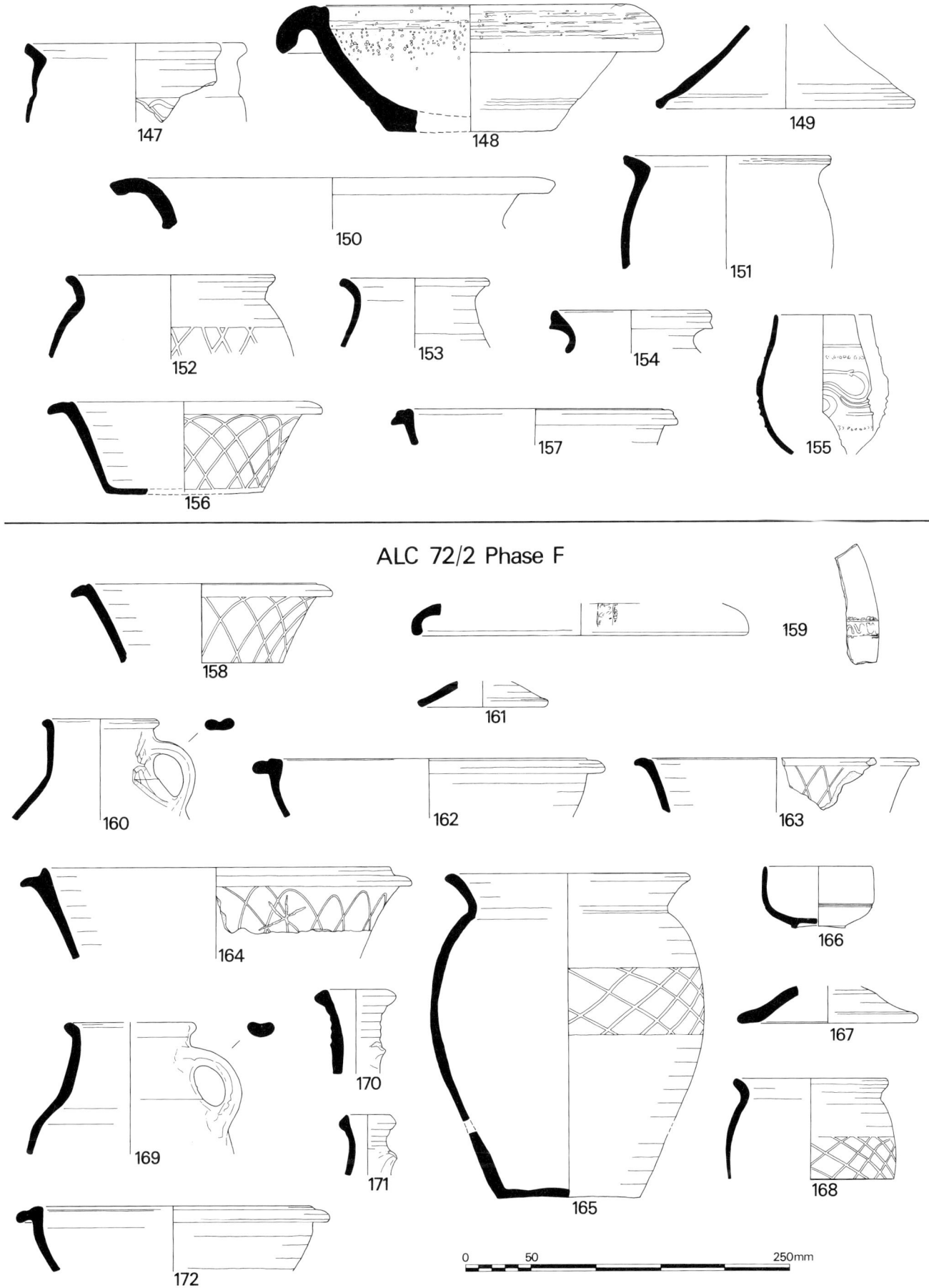

Figure 51   Coarse pottery (ALC 69, phase F, and ALC 72/2, phase F), nos 147–172

1969 and 1972 Baromix finds (ALC 69 and ALC 72/2)

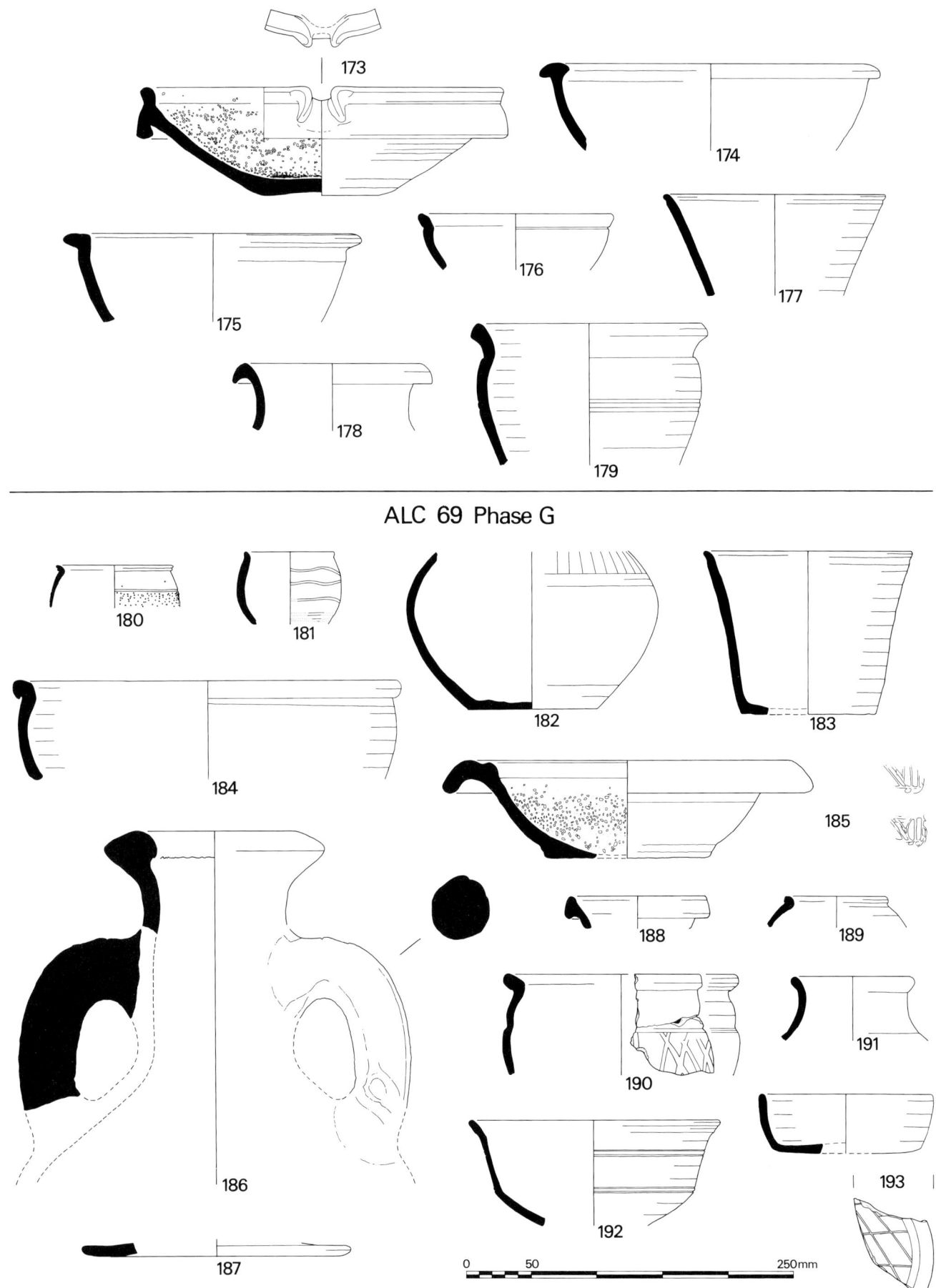

Figure 52   Coarse pottery (ALC 69, phase F, and ALC 72/2, phase G), nos 173–193

1969 and 1972 Baromix finds (ALC 69 and ALC 72/2)

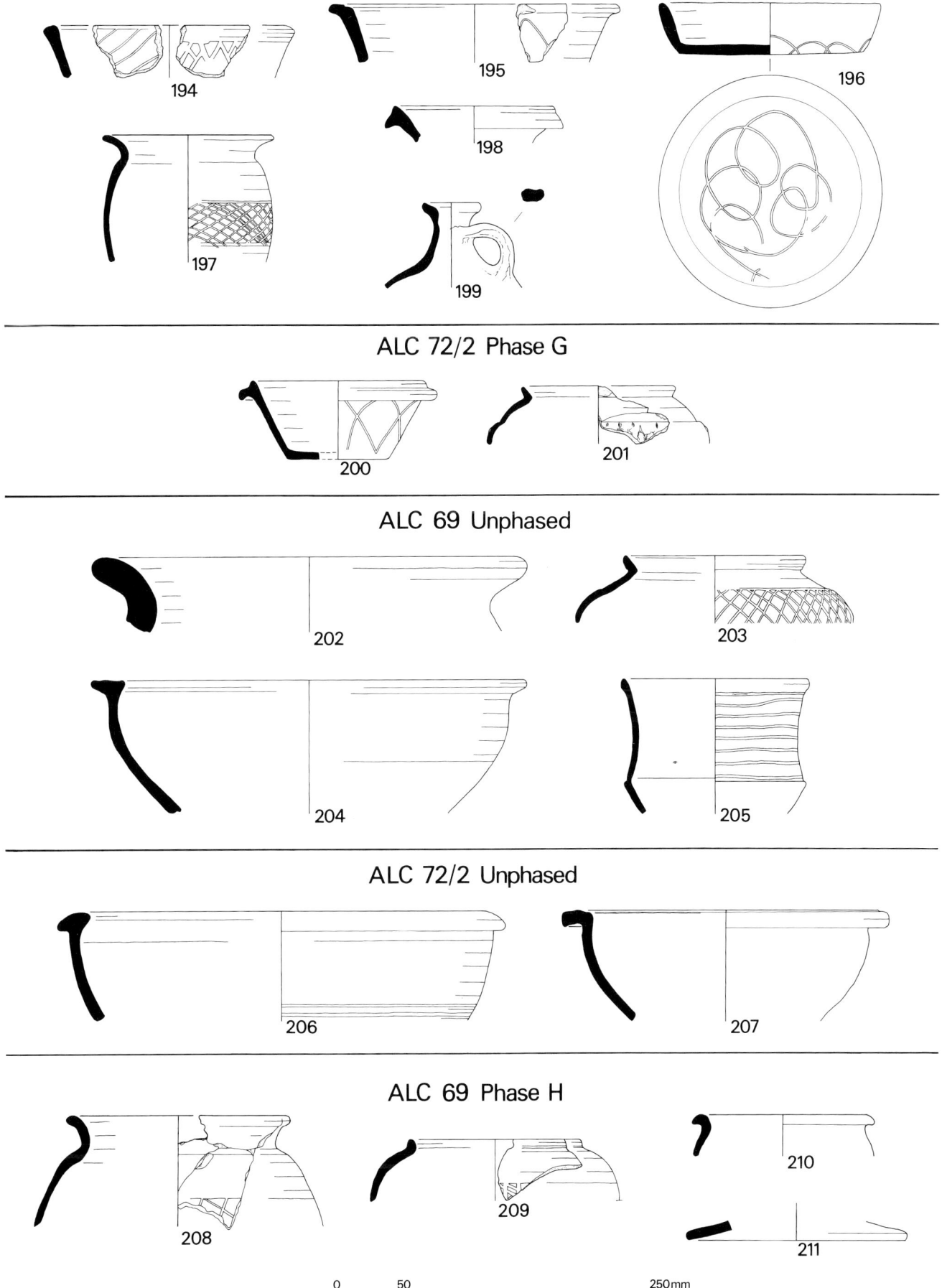

Figure 53 Coarse pottery (ALC 69, phases G, unphased and H, and ALC 72/2, phases G and unphased), nos 194–211

1969 and 1972 Baromix finds (ALC 69 and ALC 72/2)

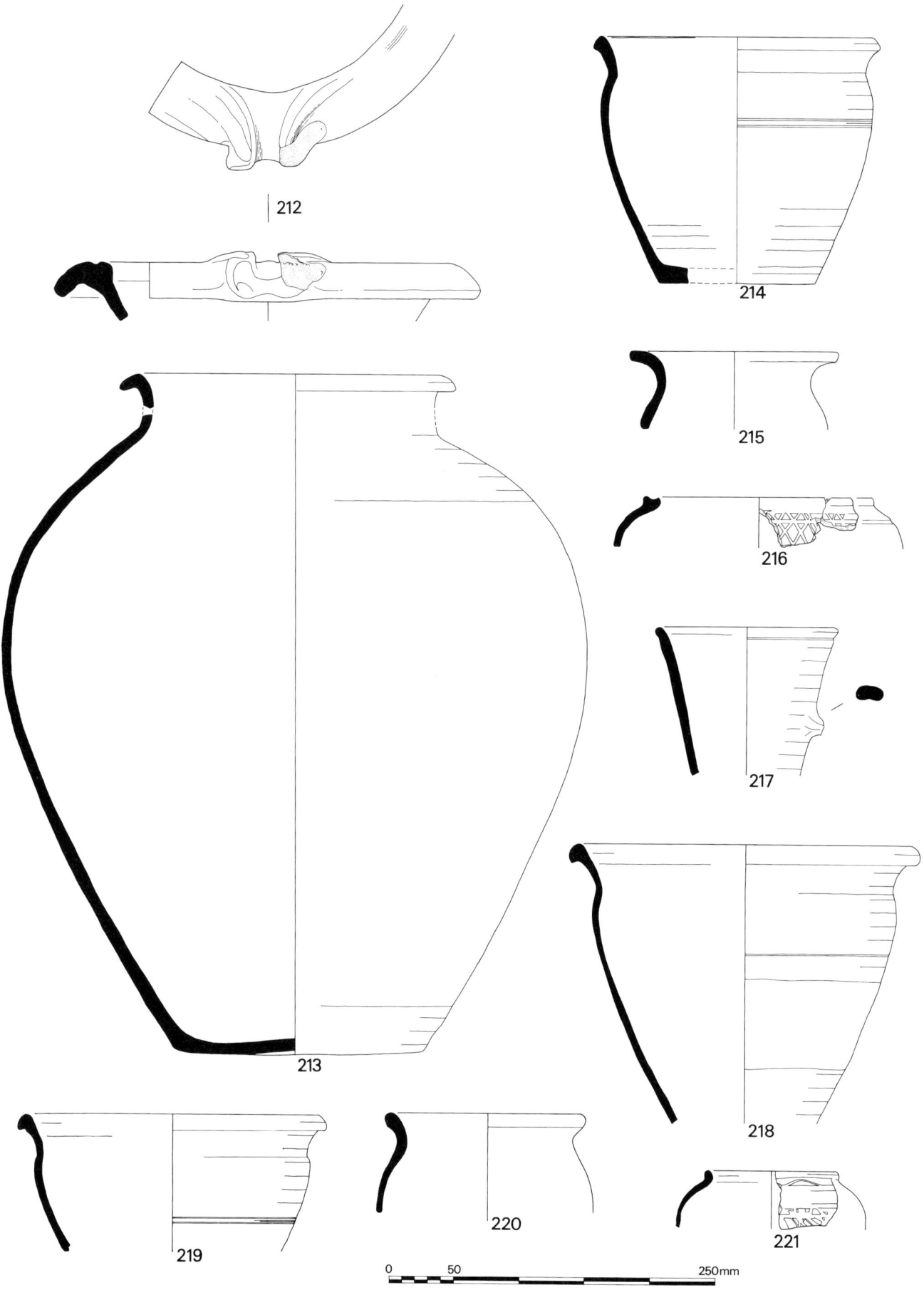

Figure 54   Coarse pottery (ALC 69, phase H), nos 212–221

1969 and 1972 Baromix finds (ALC 69 and ALC 72/2)

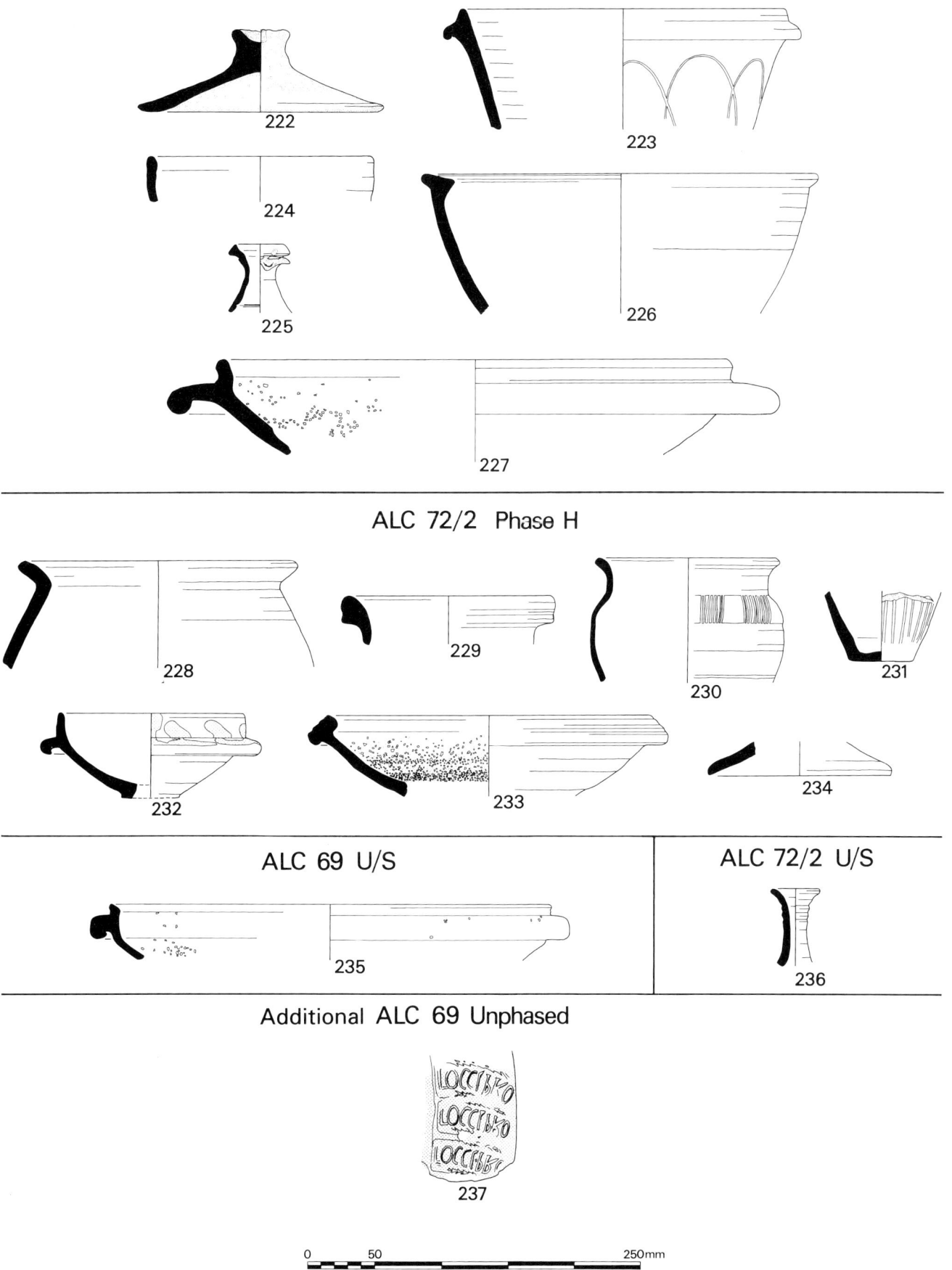

Figure 55   Coarse pottery (ALC 69, phase H and Unstrat, and ALC 72/2, phase H), nos 222–237

1969 and 1972 Baromix finds (ALC 69 and ALC 72/2)

52 Severn Valley ware jar (O25)		125
53 BB1 cooking pot (B11)		125
54 Pyriform jar (R01)		98
55 Severn Valley ware bowl (O23)		66
56 Globular jar (R32)		133

ALC 72/2 Phase C (Fig 47)

57 Spanish *amphora* (A21)		98
58 Severn Valley jar (O21)		98
59 Pyriform jar (R15)		118
60 Carinated bowl (R15)		107
61 Flagon (R01)		102
62 Miniature carinated vessel (R41?)		121

ALC 69 Phase D (Figs 47–48)

63 Verulamium region *mortarium* (M21)		121
64 Butt beaker (R32)		121
65 Jar (G24)		121
66 Pyriform jar (R41)		148
67 Pyriform jar (R01)		148
68 White-slipped jar (Q12)		148
69 Severn Valley ware jar (O24)		148
70 Jar (R01)		148
71 Jar (R41)		148
72 Severn Valley ware tankard (O21)		148
73 Malvernian dish (G44)		148
74 BB1 flanged bowl (B11)		148
75 Verulamium region lid (W11)		148
76 Jar (R32)		106
77 Jar (R32)		106
78 Globular jar (R15)		106
79 Verulamium region *mortarium* (M21)		106
80 Severn Valley ware jar (O21)		78
81 Severn Valley ware jar (O21)		78
82 Malvernian cooking pot (G44)		78
83 BB1 dish (B11)		78–77
84 Mancetter-Hartshill beaker (W12)		115
85 Mancetter-Hartshill beaker (W12)		115
86 Small bowl – Severn Valley ware (O23)		115
87 BB1 cooking pot (B11)		110
88 White-slipped two handled flask (Q25)		46
89 Severn Valley ware tankard (O25)		46
90 Carinated bowl (R32)		90 + 86

ALC 72/2 Phase D (Fig 49)

91 Pyriform jar (R15)		61
92 Severn Valley ware beaker (O23)		61
93 Malvernian jar (G44)		61
94 Severn Valley ware jar (O21)		61
95 Severn Valley ware jar (O21)		105
96 Jar (R32)		105
97 Jar (R01)		105

ALC 69 Phase E (Fig 49)

98 Jar (R52)		77
99 Jar (R41)		77
100 Mancetter-Hartshill *mortarium* (M22)		48
101 Pyriform jar (R01)		101
102 Dish (R32)		108
103 Tankard (R32)		44
104 BB1 flanged bowl (B11)		44
105 Severn Valley ware beaker (O23)		44
106 Severn Valley ware bowl (O24)		43 + 43a
107 BB1 flanged bowl (B11)		43

ALC 72/2 Phase E (Fig 49)

108 Severn Valley ware ?carinated bowl (O23)		82–83
109 Severn Valley ware jar (O21)		82–83
110 Pyriform jar (R15)		82–83
111 Carinated bowl (O51)		120
112 Mancetter *mortarium* (M22)		50
113 Severn Valley ware tankard (O24)		50
114 White-slipped strainer spout (Q25), cf Marsh 1978, type 46		76
115 Severn Valley ware bowl (O24)		76

ALC 69 Phase F (Fig 50–51)

116 Severn Valley ware jug (O27)		51
117 BB1 two-handed jar (B11)		51
118 Severn Valley ware storage jar with graffito (O21)		51
119 Fabric G44 storage jar (G44)		51
120 Severn Valley ware hemispherical bowl (O24)		51
121 BB1 handled dish (B11)		51
122 Small beaker (R01)		51
123 Cornice-rimmed beaker (F42)		51
124 Triangular-rimmed beaker (F42)		51
125 Large beaker (F42)		51
126 Large beaker (F42)		51
127 Jar (R01)		161
128 Malvernian cooking pot (G44)		161
129 Necked bowl (R32)		161
130 Malvernian jar (G44)		20
131 BB1 beaker (B11)		20
132 Jar (R01)		20
133 Rough rouletted beaker (R32)		20
134 Miniature beaker (R42)		20
135 Beaker (F42)		20
136 Beaker (F42)		20
137 Beaker (F42)		20
138 Beaker (F42)		20
139 Beaker (F42)		20
140 Lid (R01)		20
141 BB1 flanged bowl (B11)		20
142 BB1 flanged bowl (B11)		20
143 Dish (B11)		20
144 Severn Valley ware jar (O21)		86
145 Malvernian cooking pot (G44)		86
146 Mancetter-Hartshill *mortarium* (M22)		61
147 Pyriform jar (R01)		51a
148 Oxidised *mortarium* (M33)		51a
149 Lid (R21)		51a
150 Severn Valley ware jar (O24)		9
151 Malvernian jar (G44)		9
152 Jar (R15)		9
153 Severn Valley ware jar (O24)		9
154 Severn Valley ware jar (O23)		9
155 Nene Valley CC beaker (F52)		9
156 BB1 flanged bowl (B11)		9
157 Severn Valley ware bowl (O21)		9

ALC 72/2 Phase F (Fig 51–52)

158 BB1 flanged bowl (B11)		49

1969 and 1972 Baromix finds (ALC 69 and ALC 72/2)

159	Mancetter *mortarium* flange (M22) stamped by Gratinus	49
160	Severn Valley ware jug (O24)	48
161	Lid (R01)	48
162	Severn Valley ware bowl (O21)	48
163	BB1 bowl (B11)	48
164	BB1 flanged bowl (B11) with graffito	14
165	Cooking pot (R01)	14
166	Central Gaulish cup (F32)	14
167	Lid (R42)	56
168	BB1 cooking pot (B11)	62
169	Severn Valley ware jug (O21)	62
170	Verulamium Region flagon (W11)	62
171	White-slipped flagon (Q25)	62
172	Severn Valley ware bowl (O24)	40
173	Oxfordshire white ware *mortarium* Young (1977) type M10/11, AD 180–240 (M23)	34
174	Severn Valley ware bowl (O24)	34
175	Severn Valley ware bowl (O21)	34
176	Severn Valley ware bowl (O21)	34
177	Severn Valley ware tankard (O21)	34
178	Severn Valley ware narrow-mouthed jar (O21)	34
179	Severn Valley ware wide-mouthed jar (O27)	33

ALC 69 Phase G (Fig 52–53)

180	Roughcast beaker (F37)	52
181	Miniature beaker (R32)	93
182	Severn Valley ware jar (O21)	68
183	Tankard (R01)	68
184	Bowl (R42)	68
185	Mancetter-Hartshill *mortarium* (M22)	68
186	Spanish Dressel 20 *amphora* (A21)	87
187	Severn Valley ware lid (O24)	87
188	Narrow-mouthed jar (R32)	87
189	Pyriform jar (R01)	76
190	Severn Valley ware beaker (O23)	65
191	Severn Valley ware narrow-mouthed jar (O27)	40
192	Severn Valley ware carinated bowl (O21)	40
193	Dish (R41)	40
194	Malvernian dish (G44)	40
195	BB1 flanged bowl (B11)	40
196	BB1 dish (B11)	19
197	BB1 cooking pot (B11)	19
198	Severn Valley ware narrow-mouthed jar (O27)	19
199	Severn Valley ware flagon (O24)	59

ALC 72/2 Phase G (Fig 53)

200	Black-Burnished ware bowl (B11)	39
201	Pyriform jar (R32)	19

ALC 69 unphased (Fig 53)

202	Malvernian jar (G44)	211
203	Pyriform jar (R32)	201
204	Severn Valley ware reeded-rimmed bowl (O24)	94
205	Carinated bowl (R32)	199

ALC 72/2 unphased (Fig 53)

206	Severn Valley ware bowl (O21)	43
207	Severn Valley ware bowl (O21)	43

ALC 69 Phase H (Fig 53–55)

208	BB1 cooking pot (B11)	88
209	Globular jar (R81)	88
210	Jar (R15)	88
211	Severn Valley ware lid (O23)	88
212	Verulamium Region *mortarium* (M21)	88
213	Severn Valley ware jar (O24)	4
214	Severn Valley ware wide-mouthed jar (O24)	4
215	Shell-gritted jar (C11)	23a
216	Jar with drop-stop (R32)	23a
217	Severn Valley ware tankard (O25)	23a
218	Severn Valley ware wide-mouthed jar (O23)	22
219	Severn Valley ware wide-mouthed jar (O23)	22
220	Shell-gritted jar (C11)	22
221	Globular jar (R21)	22
222	Malvernian lid (G44)	22
223	BB1 flanged bowl (B11)	22
224	Nene Valley dish (F52)	25
225	Oxfordshire white ware flagon (W13)	25
226	Severn Valley ware bowl (O24)	23
227	Oxfordshire white ware *mortarium* Young (1977) type M18, AD 240–300 (M23)	3

ALC 72/2 Phase H (Fig 55)

228	Malvernian jar (G44)	24
229	Narrow-mouthed jar (R15)	24
230	Jar (R68)	24
231	Jar (C44)	24
232	Flanged bowl (W15)	24
233	Mancetter-Hartshill *mortarium* (M22)	24
234	Lid (R01)	24

ALC 69 unstratified (Fig 55)

235	Oxfordshire white ware *mortarium* Young's (1977) type M22, AD 240–400 (M23)	1

ALC 72/2 unstratified (Fig 55)

236	Severn Valley ware flagon (O23)	1

Additional ALC 69 unphased (Fig 55)

237	Stamped mortarium flange of Loccius Pro.. (M22)	–

Glass (ALC 69 and ALC 72/2)
Denise Allen

Only three fragments of the bright monochrome glass favoured for finer tableware during the 1st century were found (two blue, one brown; ALC 72/2 no 7, ALC 69 SF 108, 165, and ALC 69, 88 (the last two are not included in the catalogue)), and only one of the colourless metal which tended to replace this from the Flavian period onwards (ALC 72/2 no 3). The collection also includes one piece of window glass, six beads and one fragment of probable post-medieval date (ALC 69 SF 6, 1 (not included in catalogue)). All

1969 and 1972 Baromix finds (ALC 69 and ALC 72/2)

the glass is in very fragmentary condition, and only a few vessel forms can be identified with certainty.

The rotary-ground rim and thick rib of ALC 69 no 6 makes it easily recognisable as part of a pillar-moulded bowl. This vessel type was extremely common throughout the empire during the 1st century AD, particularly the variety made of blue-green glass. Manufacture probably ceased at some time within the Flavian period, but the sturdy shape enabled survival of several examples until the end of the 1st century and beyond. Manufacturing techniques have been discussed with reference to a complete blue-green specimen from a Flavian burial at Thornborough, Bucks (Price 1975, 18–20, no 1, group 3, Fig 10:1).

ALC 69 nos 8, 17, and 20 and ALC 72/2 no 4 are all from bowls whose rims have been finished by folding into a tube. This technique was used throughout the Roman period for a variety of vessel forms, and it is therefore difficult to be certain of those represented here. However, ALC 72 no 4, is most likely to be part of a cylindrical-bodied vessel of a type popular during the later 1st and earlier 2nd centuries (Isings 1957, 56–60, form 44a-b). Several examples have been found in contexts of between AD 60 and 100 at Richborough (Radford 1932, 85–6, no 63, plate XV; Henderson 1949, 158, nos 369 and 372, plate BXVIII), and another example was found with Neronian samian at Long Melford, Suffolk (Avent and Howlett 1980, 246, Fig 41). ALC 69 nos 18, 17, and 2 quite possibly come from one vessel, irregularities in the rim of the bowl accounting for their slight variations in profile. The form is probably a fairly shallow bowl or plate, sometimes occurring with a very large rim diameter, which seems to belong to the later 2nd and earlier 3rd centuries. Several fragmentary examples came from a context dated AD 160–230 at the legionary bath-house at Caerleon (National Museum of Wales), and another came from a context of similar date at Exeter (Charlesworth 1979, 227–9, Fig 71: 42).

ALC 72 no 3, one of the few colourless pieces from the site, comes from the body of some form of carinated beaker. The exact type cannot be determined from this tiny fragment, but it almost certainly dates to somewhere between the Flavian period and the early 3rd century.

A few more items of tableware are represented by ALC 69 nos 7, 9, and 18 and ALC 72 no 7. ALC 69 nos 7 and 18 and ALC 72 no 7 are likely to belong to a group of jugs and jars popular during the years c AD 50–130. The jars have globular ribbed bodies and hollow tubular rims; the jugs may have globular or conical bodies, often ribbed, long cylindrical necks and flat, angular, ribbed handles. They were made somewhere in the Seine–Rhine region of north-western Europe, and occur in bright monochrome colours as well as blue-green glass. They have been discussed at length by Harden (1962, 238–40, Fig 7, plate XLIIIa) and Price (1977, 156–8, no 2, Fig 27: 2, plate 7; 1980, 66, nos 9, 10, and 11, Figs 15–16).

The remaining identifiable vessel fragments come from blue-green bottles of a type which was extremely common during the 1st and 2nd centuries AD. These have cylindrical or prismatic mould-blown bodies, cylindrical necks, and angular, multi-ribbed handles, and were traded and transported for their contents rather than as tableware. The moulded trade-marks on the bases of the prismatic vessels occur in great variety. Charlesworth has discussed in particular the combination of diagonal cross and square of circle (1966, 33–4, Fig 11 and 12), but the vertical cross which occurs on ALC 69 no 11, here is not quite as common.

Six beads are catalogued here, of which four (ALC 69 nos 4, 5, and 12, and ALC 72 no 1) are of the 'melon' variety, common on 1st-century sites in Britain and elsewhere, becoming much rarer in 2nd-century contexts. ALC 69 no 16 and ALC 72 no 6 cannot be closely dated.

One fragment of window glass is included in the collection, of the 'matt-glossy' type, made by casting in a shallow tray of stone or wood. This manufacturing technique continued until c AD 300, when cylinder-blown window-glass was introduced (Boon 1966, 41f).

Most of the glass catalogued and discussed here would fit comfortably into a date bracket of the later 1st to earlier 3rd centuries AD. The predominance of blue-green glass and scarcity of both brightly coloured and colourless glass, suggest that very fine tableware was a rarity on the site. The relatively high frequency of bottle glass is usual on British sites, and most of the identifiable fragments of tableware also belong to fairly common forms.

Catalogue of illustrated glass

(Complete glass catalogue in microfiche M1:B13–C2)

ALC 69 (Fig 56)

Some 41 fragments of Roman vessel glass, four of window glass and four glass beads were recovered from the site.

Phase A

3 Base fragment of a cylindrical bottle of blue-green glass; flaking whitish iridescent weathering. Base slightly concave. Diam of body c 210mm. (193, phase A)

4 Fragment comprising about half a melon bead of blue faience, with patches of turquoise surface glaze surviving in score marks. D-sectioned body, divided into segments by deep vertical lines. Height 15mm. Diam 18mm. (198, phase A)

Phase B

5 Small fragment of a melon bead of blue faience; very worn. Shape as no 4 above. Height 11mm (SF 66, 84, phase B)

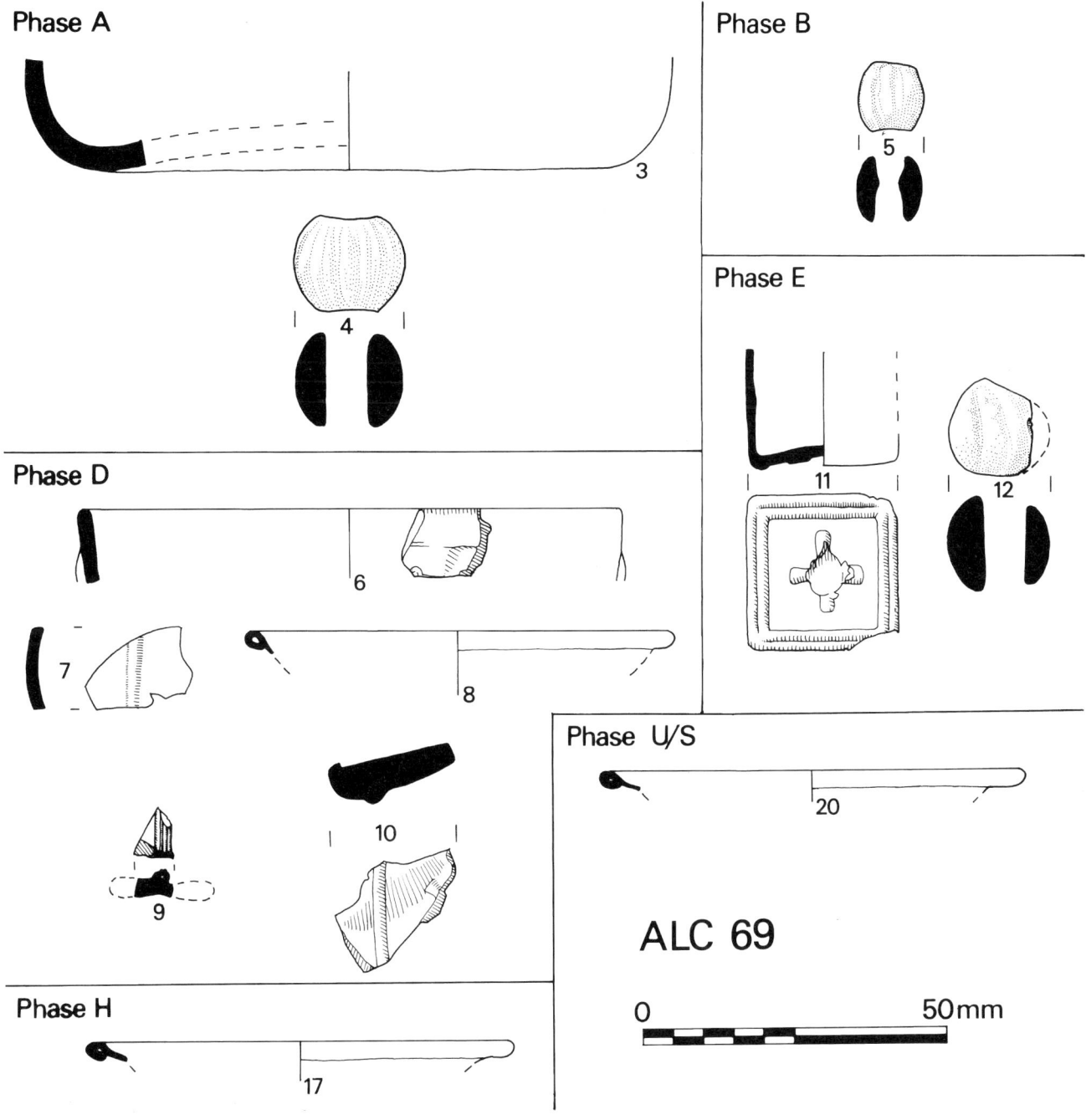

Figure 56   Glass vessels (ALC 69), nos 3–12, 17, and 20

Phase D

6 Rim fragment of a pillar-moulded bowl of blue-green glass; some flaking iridescence. Cast in a ribbed mould, rim and inside surfaces rotary-polished. Part of one rib extant. Diam of rim *c* 180mm. (SF 104, 148, phase D)

7 Body fragment probably of a jar or jug of blue-green glass; bulbous or globular profile, with part of one optic-blown rib. (195, phase D)

8 Rim fragment of a plate or shallow bowl of blue-green glass; surfaces dulled. Rim folded outward and downward forming hollow tube. See nos 17 and 20 below. Diam *c* 140mm. (SF 79, 78, phase D)

9 Small fragment of a handle of bubbly blue-green glass. Apparently flattened cross-section with pronounced central rib. (SF 112, 140, phase D)

10 Base fragment of a prismatic bottle of blue-green glass; flaking whitish iridescent weathering. Blown into a square-sectioned body mould; slightly distorted, perhaps by fire; extant basal design comprising single (?)square surrounding a central motif. (SF 105, 146, phase D)

Phase E

11 Base of a square bottle of blue-green glass; flaking whitish iridescent weathering. Blown into a square-sectioned body mould; design in relief on base comprising a central cross, partly obscured by a pontil mark, surrounded by a single square. Width of sides 50mm. (SF 59, 43, phase E)

12 Fragment of a melon bead of blue faience. Shape as no 4 above

1969 and 1972 Baromix finds (ALC 69 and ALC 72/2)

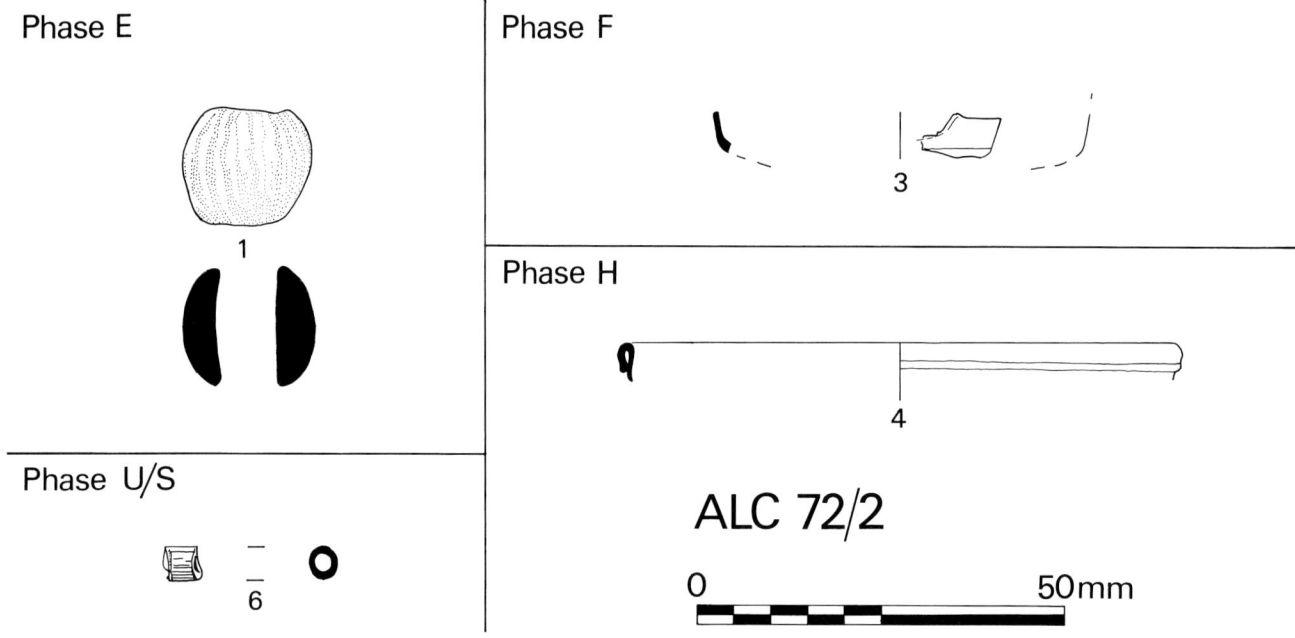

Figure 57   Glass vessels (ALC 72/2), nos 1, 3–4, and 6

but roughly made, score marks widely spaced and on a diagonal. Height *c* 15mm. (SF 27, 60, phase E)

Phase H

17 Rim fragment of a plate or shallow bowl of blue-green glass; tubular rim folded outward and downward. ?Same vessel as no 8 above. See also no 20. Diam *c* 140mm. (23a, phase H)

Unphased

20 Rim fragment of a plate or shallow bowl of blue-green glass; tubular rim folded inward and downward then outward and downward. (?)Same vessel as nos 8 and 17 above. Diam 100mm. (SF 61, 1, U/S)

ALC 72/2 (Fig 57)

Twelve objects and fragments of Roman glass were recovered from the site.

Phase E

1 Fragment comprising about half a melon bead of blue faience with patches of pale turquoise glaze surviving in score marks. D-sectioned body. Height 16mm. Diam 18mm. (SF 36, 87, phase E)

Phase F

3 Body fragment of a bowl or beaker of colourless glass; part of carination with rotary-ground outer surface extant. Diam of body *c* 100mm. (SF 39, 48, phase F)

Phase H

4 Rim fragment of a bowl of blue-green glass. Rim folded outward and downward, then turned in slightly. Diam *c* 150mm. (SF 34, 24, phase H)

Unphased

6 Fragment of a tubular bead of streaky blue glass. Outer surfaces flattened slightly to give polygonal cross-section, roughly cylindrical longitudinal perforation. Diam *c* 5mm. (SF 33, 1, U/S)

Copper alloy (ALC 69 and ALC 72/2)
Glenys Lloyd-Morgan

Although the number of metal objects from these various sites is statistically small, it is clear from the group of military bronzes found during excavations at ALC 69 (nos 1, 2, and 3), with an outlier in ALC 72/2 (no 1), that there was a military presence during the 1st century. If the small bell, ALC 69 no 11, is included in the count as at Wanborough, then cavalry rather than infantry can be suggested.

As at Tiddington the brooches are the most numerous single type of artefact, accounting for about 15% of the total collection, and again they are all 1st to 2nd century in date.

Among the most extraordinary items which have come out of Roman Warwickshire, the copper alloy (bronze) finger-shaped fitting ALC 72 no 14 can surely claim precedence. Only one parallel has so far been discovered, and that suggests it was some form of tap or fitting for the water supply, but unfortunately no firm date can be given.

The fragments of vessel handles from a 1st-century Campanian basin, ALC 72 nos 2 and 13 suggest that traders had followed the military to Alcester with some commercial success.

Catalogue of illustrated copper alloy objects

(Complete copper alloy and silver catalogue in microfiche M1:C3–C9)

ALC 69 (Figs 58–59)

Phase A

1 Connector loop for horse trappings, with the undersection now mostly lost. There is some slight engraved detail below the moulded loop. Length 67.2mm. Max width 13.3mm. The closest parallel is on a four-way fitting found at Newstead, in the roadway outside the west gate (Curle 1911, 302, plate LXXIV, no 6). Other examples are listed by Webster including one from Gloucester (1958, 80, no 100, Fig 5), Walbrook, London (Webster 1958, 85, no 153, Fig 6), Sea Mills, Bristol (Webster 1958, 89, no 180, Fig 7), Verulamium (Webster 1958, 91, no 202, Fig 7), and Wroxeter (Webster 1958, 98, no 262, Fig 8). A further example comes from excavations at Longthorpe 1967–73, occupied between AD 44/48 – *c* AD 62 (Frere and St Joseph 1974, 56, 58, no 58, Fig 30). (SF 98, 136, phase A)
2 Probably part of a connector loop for horse trappings, of the type noted above. Only one decorated arm with the holes for two rivets survives. Length 41.6mm. Width 12.3mm. (SF 113, 198, phase A)
3 Looped section of a belt fitting, for use with a 'T'-shaped hook on a sword belt. Incomplete. Present length 43mm. Max width 18.6mm. Hawkes and Hull illustrate an example with a brief description of its use on the sword belt (1947, 339, plate CIII, no 4), see also the reconstruction drawing in H Russell Robinson (1975, colour plate I). For other parallels cf Webster (1958, 91, no 21, Fig 7) for a piece from Waddon Hill, Dorset, and Curle for examples found at Newstead (1911, 300, plate LXXIII, no 5, from pit LXXVIII, also p 134, with various horse trappings; and plate LXXVI, no 14). (SF 114, 198, phase A)

Phase D

7 Polden Hill type *fibula*, rather corroded and with only slight traces of decoration towards the outer ends of the wings. Length *c* 74mm. This is one of the more common examples found at Tiddington, both plain and ornamented. Other examples have been noted from Castell Collen and dated later 1st to 2nd century AD (Boon 1973, 19, Fig 3, no 7); London (Wheeler 1930, 94, Fig 27, no 21) and Verulamium from a context dated AD 115–130 (Frere 1972, 116, Fig 29, no 10). (SF 86, 106, phase D)
8 Small scoop from a toilet set, made of sheet metal with the edges folded in to produce a stronger, waisted shaft. Length *c* 41mm. An example from Fishbourne comes from first period levels dated AD 43–75. Another from Gadebridge Park Villa is part of a set with nail cleaner and tweezers (Neal 1974a, 40, Fig 62, no 184). Note also the piece from Coleshill no GH 1979 SF 629. (SF 75, 130, phase D)
9 Drop handle with split pins for attachment still *in situ*, for use on a small casket or toilet box. The centre part of the grip has a diamond-shaped cross-section. A little distorted. Max depth 21.5mm. Max width 56mm. Compare the examples from Exeter (Bidwell 1979, 238, Fig 73, no 28 dated either AD 60/65–75 or AD 75–80; and no 29 dated late Antonine to 3rd century); another piece from Balkerne Lane, Colchester was from a context dated *c* AD 250–400 (Crummy 1983, 82, Fig 85, no 2134). (SF 95, 148, phase D)

1969 and 1972 Baromix finds (ALC 69 and ALC 72/2)

11 Fragment of a hemispherical item, probably a bell? Height 17.6mm. Diam was *c* 41mm. Compare the smaller example from Hod Hill (Brailsford 1962, 2, no A33, Fig 2) and from Wanborough, Wilts. (Anderson and Wacher 1980, 123, Fig 4, no 2). (SF 88, 106, phase D)

Phase F

15 The upper half of a trumpet brooch, probably Collingwood's group Riii, Hull's 'Chester' type. Present length 32.4mm. Cf Hull's comments in Dudley (1967, 42, no 108, Fig 17), though in proportion to other finds of brooches from Chester, it may not be quite so common as he seems to imply. Compare also the examples from Wroxeter (Bushe-Fox 1913, 26, Fig 10, no 8, 'from a deposit dated AD 110–130') and Richborough (Bushe-Fox 1949, 115–6, plate XXIX, no 41). There are two examples from Tiddington nos SF M1 and SF M20. (SF 29, 20, phase F)
16 Curved fragment with mouldings on the upper curved surface, perhaps part of the bow of a trumpet brooch type Riii? Length 29mm. Compare a similar fragment from South Shields (Allason-Jones and Miket 1984, 98, no 3.34, and Fig). (SF 26, 20, phase F)
18 *Ligula* with disc-shaped end and much of the shaft lost. Present length 38mm. Compare the examples from Gadebridge Park (Neal 1974a, 143, nos 200–203, 206–208, Fig 63) and Chichester (Down 1981, 169, Fig 8.32, no 46). There are further pieces from Tiddington no SF M28, SF M672, TD 80 SF 37, TR 82 SF 185, Coleshill GH 1978 SF 66 and the Explosion site (see below, no 28). (SF 53, 20, phase F)

Phase G

20 *Fibula*, Camulodunum type IV. The ends of the spring covers are closed by discs which are pierced to hold the axial bar. There are nine coils to the spring and the chord survives, though most of the pin is lost. There is a little hatched decoration on the ridge which extends for a short length down the upper part of the bow. The brooch is broken across the bow but is virtually complete. Length *c* 56mm. Cf Hawkes and Hull (1947, 311, plate XCI, no 42, also no 43) where a date of AD 50–65 for the type is suggested. Compare also an example from Hales, Staffs described by Hull as 'pre-Flavian' (Goodyear 1968, 114, no 2, Fig 4). A more elaborate example is noted at Verulamium coming from a context dated AD 75–95 with redeposited Boudiccan burnt daub (Frere 1984, 23, no 24, Fig 6). (SF 63, 93, phase G)
22 Pin with baluster-shaped head, the shaft is a little bent, and the tip is lost. Present length 94mm. Diam head 6mm. Compare the example from Woodeaton (Kirk 1949, 18, no 39, Fig 4, no 7); and Leicester (Kenyon 1948, 262, Fig 89, no 2 with p 42; one example is dated *c* AD 220; two come from a context dated AD 200–250). There are also pieces from Piddington Roman villa, Northants 1979 SF 41; Tiddington TR 82 SF 61; and Coleshill, Warks. GH 1978 SF 1001. (SF 60, 40, phase G)
23 Shaft of a (?)medical implement broken at both ends. Part of a panel with a decorative spiral incision can still be made out, despite the eroded surface. Present length 48mm. (SF 76, 87, phase G)

Phase H

25 Dressmaker's pin, compare SF 8, no 29. Length 25mm. (SF 14, 16, phase H)
26 Implement tapering to a point at one end, the other flattening out but now broken and its original function indeterminate. Present length 118mm. (SF 24, 22, phase H)

1969 and 1972 Baromix finds (ALC 69 and ALC 72/2)

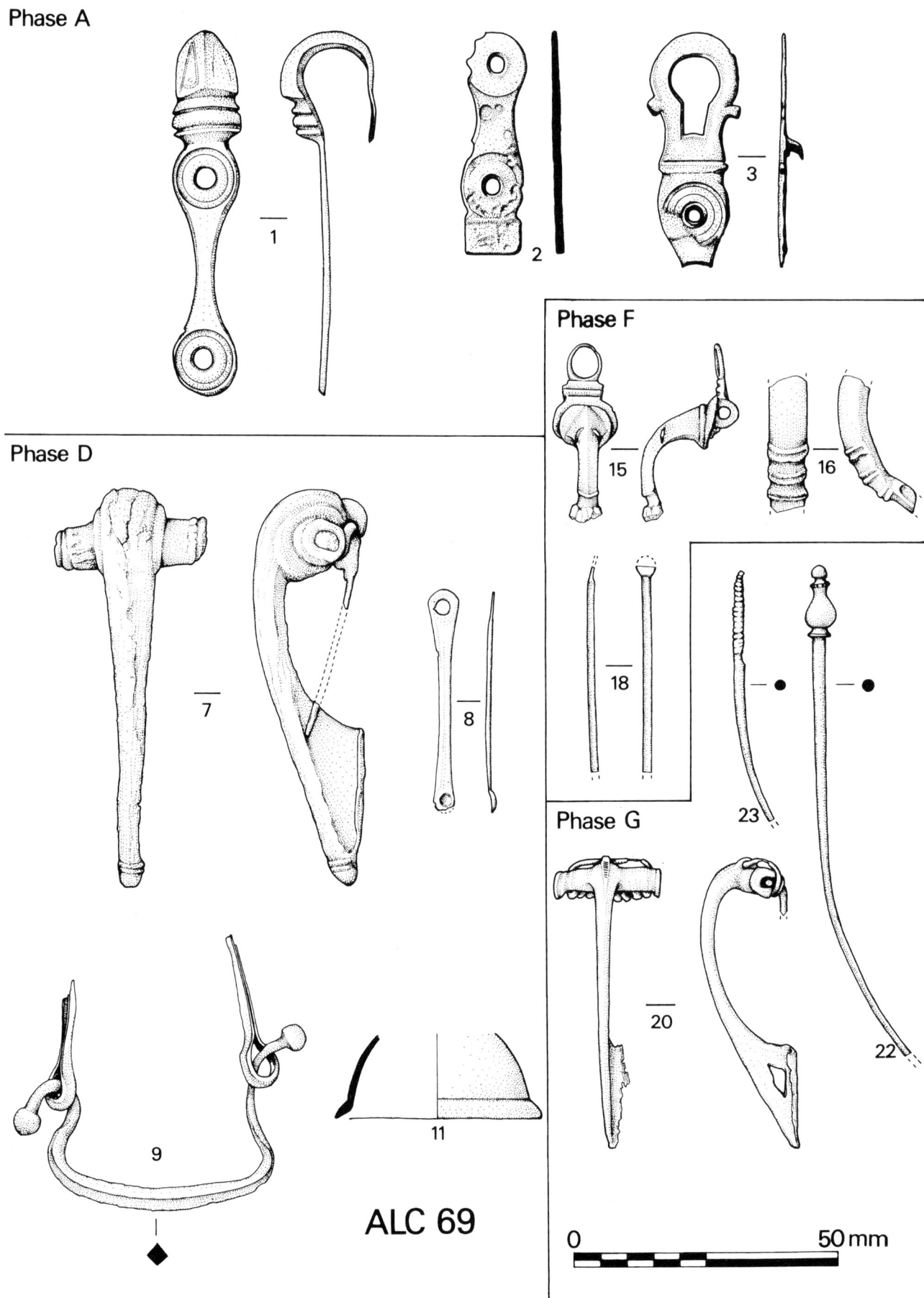

Figure 58   Copper alloy (ALC 69), nos 1–3, 7–9, 11, 15–16, 18, 20, and 22–3

Unphased (U/S)

27 Hook terminal of a bracelet made of three stout wires twisted together. Present length 25mm. Cross-section 5mm × 6mm. Note the complete example from Butt Road, Colchester from a context dated *c* AD 320–450 (Crummy 1983, 38, no 1628, Fig 41); and examples from Nettleton, Wilts (Wedlake 1982, 259, no 3b, Fig 113, no 4) and Catsgore, Somerset (Leech 1982, 113, Fig 79, no 3, 4, 5, and 6). There are also further pieces from Tiddington TD 81 SF 498, SF 719, SF 971; and Coleshill GH 78 SF 90, GH 79 SF 558. (SF 15, 1, U/S)

28 Penannular bracelet with rounded 'D'-shaped cross-section, tapering to thin pointed strap-like terminals. Undecorated. Overall dimensions 62mm × 55mm. Max cross-section 5mm × 4.3mm. (SF 1, 1, U/S)

29 Dressmaker's pin, post-medieval. Length *c* 25mm. (SF 8, 1, U/S)

ALC 72/2 (Fig 60, nos 1, 3, 6, 8, 9 and 10; Fig 61, nos 2, 11–16; Fig 62, nos 17–18)

Phase B

1 Harness connector loop for horse trappings, a little damaged. Length 43.7mm. Max width 17.5mm. For parallels cf ALC 69 no 1 above. (SF 1, 75, phase B)

2 Fragment of the animal head terminal from a bowl handle, as SF 13, catalogue no 13 below, but not part of it, though it may well have been from the other handle of the same bowl. The head was broken off during excavation. Rather corroded. Present length 29mm. (SF 7, 70, phase B)

Phase D

3 T-shaped *fibula* with hinged pin, now bent and heavily corroded. The catch plate and foot are damaged. Length *c* 55mm. Compare the example from Richborough where a 1st-century date is suggested (Bushe-Fox 1928, 41, no 2, plate XVI). (SF 4, 61, phase D)

Phase E

6 Crude irregular ring with eroded surface. Diam 22mm. Depth 2.9mm. (SF 15, 83, phase E)

Phase F

8 Spoon with fiddle-shaped bowl and offset handle. The bowl is damaged and the end of the handle is now lost. Present length 77mm. Width bowl *c* 21.3mm. Strong (1966) notes that the fiddle-shaped bowl came in during the 2nd century, was especially popular in the 3rd century and continued into the 4th (1966, 177–8, Fig 36c). Compare the example from Balkerne Lane, Colchester (Crummy 1983, 69, no 2016, Fig 73, from a drain dated *c* AD 250–300). (SF 3, 33, phase F)

9 Wire flattening out at one end, now a little distorted and corroded. Present length 39mm. (SF 11, 62, phase F)

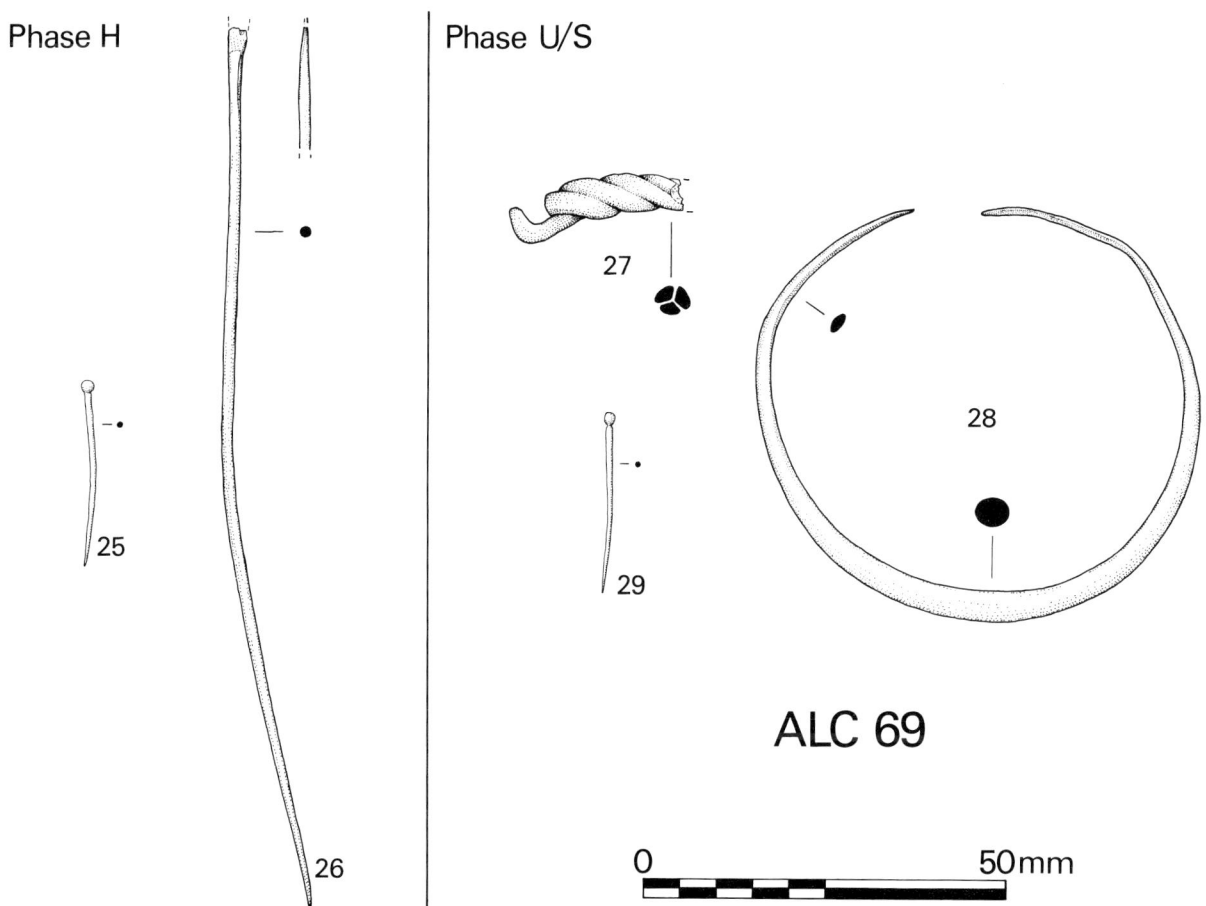

Figure 59   Copper alloy (ALC 69), nos 25–29

1969 and 1972 Baromix finds (ALC 69 and ALC 72/2)

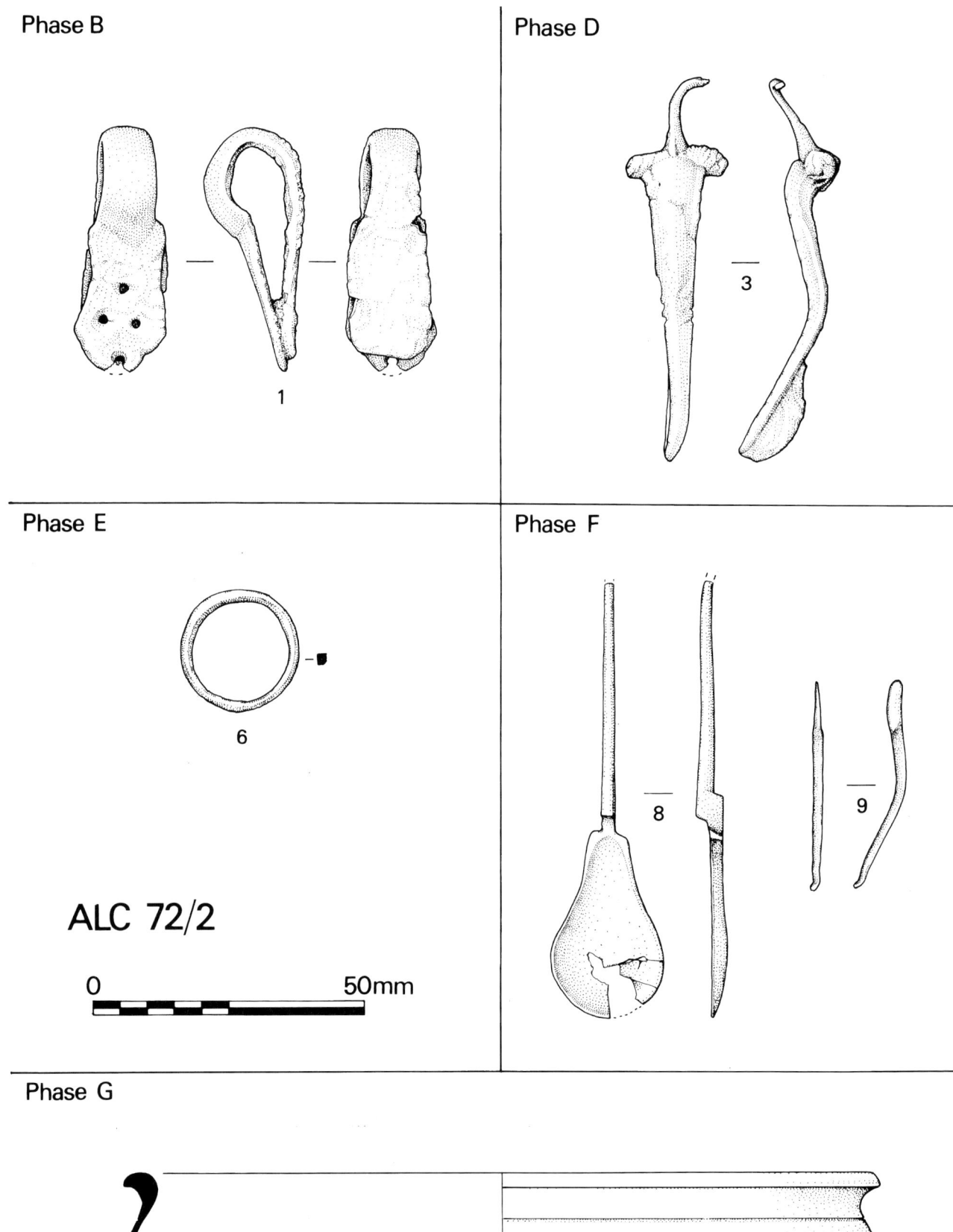

Figure 60   Copper alloy (ALC 72/2), nos 1, 3, 6, and 8–10

1969 and 1972 Baromix finds (ALC 69 and ALC 72/2)

Phase H

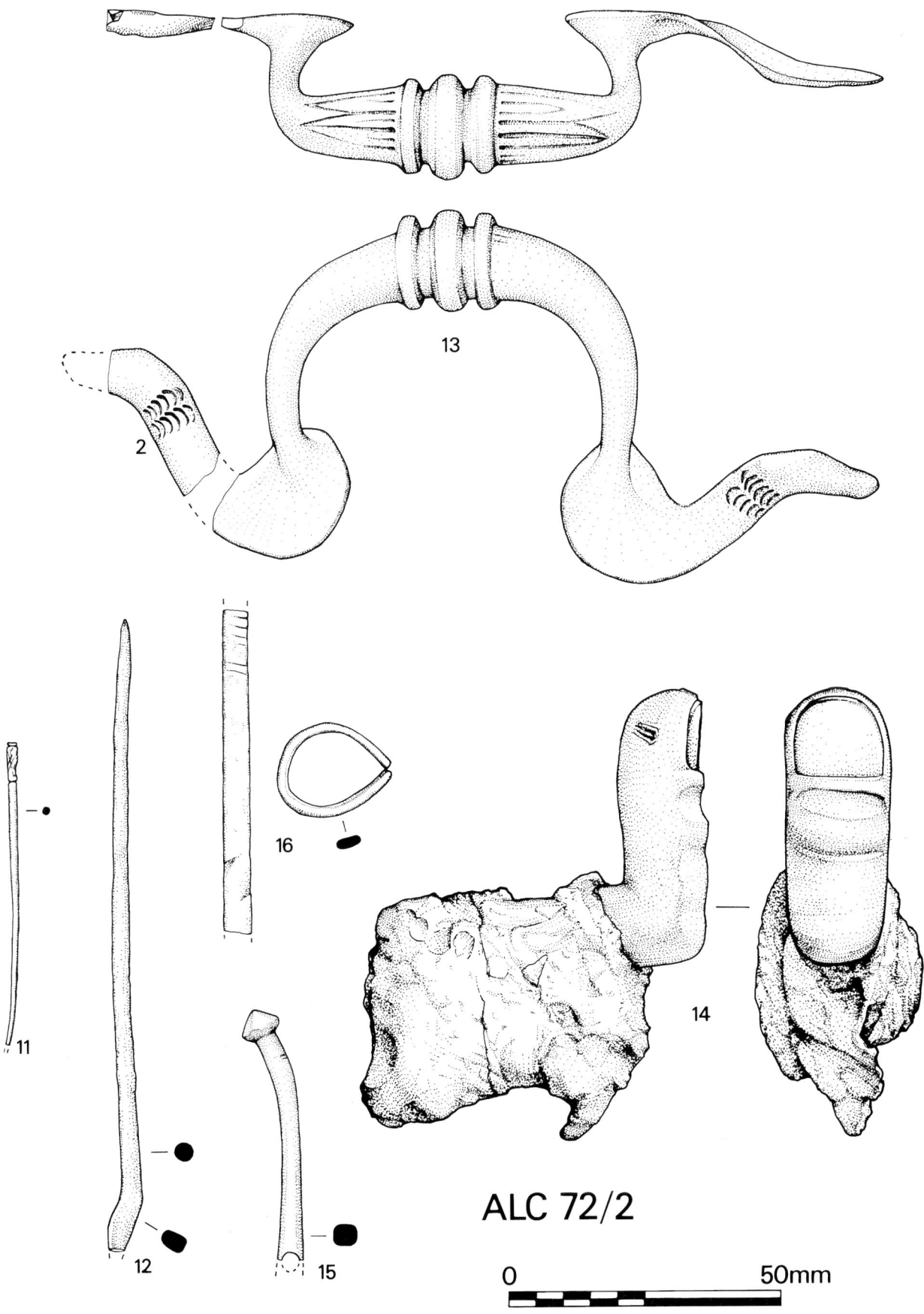

Figure 61   Copper alloy (ALC 72/2), nos 11–16

1969 and 1972 Baromix finds (ALC 69 and ALC 72/2)

Phase U/S

ALC 72/2

0   50mm

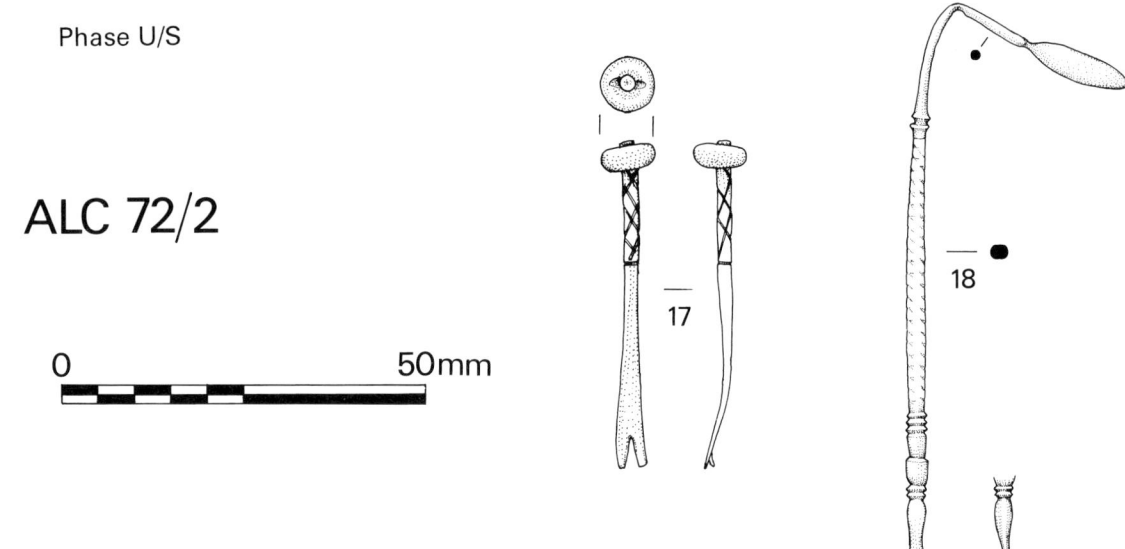

Figure 62 Copper alloy (ALC 72/2), nos 17–18

Phase G

10 Fragment of vessel rim, probably a *patera*, with the flange spreading out towards a possible handle. Length 107mm. Depth 19.5mm. Original diameter *c* 125mm. (SF 6, 11, phase G)

Phase H

11 Pin, the head is decorated with a panel of light cross-hatching. The shaft is bent, the tip lost and there is some surface erosion. Present length 53.3mm. Max diam head 2.1mm. Compare the example from Campsfield, Kidlington, Oxon. (Hunter and Kirk 1954, 52, no 2, Fig 25, no 11) and Caerleon (Wheeler and Wheeler 1928, 169, plate XXXIII, no 1). There is also an attractive series from Tiddington nos SF M737, SF M689, SF M693, and TD 81 SF 941. (SF 2, 4, phase H)

12 Handle, possibly from a spoon, with offset bowl, badly preserved. Present length 111mm. (SF 5, 24, phase H)

13 Handle from a large basin, with three central mouldings and the ends terminating in animal heads, one of which is incomplete. Present width 122mm. Present depth *c* 65mm. Den Boesterd, in her discussion of the bowls with 'omega-shaped handles ending in dog's heads wearing collars' suggests a 1st-century date and an origin in the workshops of Campania (1956, 52–3, no 172, plate VII, diam basin 391mm, said to be from the Rhine near Doorwerth; no 173, diam basin 337mm from the river Waal near de Winseling, Nijmegen; no 179–181, 53 are further examples of handles, no 181 coming from the Hunerberg at Nijmegen). Mutz illustrates the two complete bowls from Nijmegen with detailed plates and construction drawings (Mutz 1972, 90–91, plate 222–225, is den Boesterd no 173; Mutz 1972, 92–3, plate 226–230 is den Boesterd no 172; Mutz 1972, 90–91, plate 218–221 is from a princely grave at Marwedel, Kreis Lüchow-Dannenburg, now in the Museumverein für das Furstentum Lüneburg, Lüneburg, Germany). An example from Zohar, Bratislava district of Slovakia, comes from a grave dated to the first half of the 2nd century AD (Kraskovská 1978, 24–25, plate XV, no 3, Fig 8, no 4, Grave 5, item no 3). Examples from Britain include one from Broxtowe, Nottingham (Webster 1958, 70, Fig 3, no 11, unfortunately illustrated upside down) and Long Wyre Street, Colchester from a context dated AD 49/55–*c* 75 (Crummy 1983, 73, no 2046, Fig 76). (SF 13, 25, phase H)

14 Solid cast finger-shaped fitting, consisting of the nail and top two joints. At a right angled bend, the fitting becomes angular in cross-section and is set into an iron framework and completely encased in a lead block, or solder. Length of finger from nail to second joint 48.8mm. Max width 20.7mm. Overall height *c* 67mm. Zadoks-Josephus *et al* note a similar solid cast copper alloy (bronze) finger on top of a tap fitting from Tienakker near Wijchen lake, Netherlands, 1971 or earlier. But the first two phalanges are supported, in this example, by a vertical rod with circular cross-section. Both support and the base of the flexed finger rest on a disc on top of a pipe pierced by two large facing holes. The overall height is 149mm and the height of the finger 56mm (Zadoks-Josephus 1973, 111, no 197, with plate. Acc no 5.1971.1). (SF 16, 46, phase H)

15 Fragment of fitting or utensil (? a steelyard) consisting of a tapered rod with cone-shaped terminal, broken across a circular drilled hole. A little bent. Present length *c* 47mm. Max cross-section 3.9mm × 5.1mm. (SF 9, 28, phase H)

16 Strip with rectangular cross-section, curved or bent for use as a fitting? Length *c* 63mm. Cross-section 1.6mm × 3.2mm. (SF 8, 4, phase H)

Unphased (U/S)

17 Nail cleaner with disc-shaped bone head. The upper section of the shaft is decorated with a panel of incised diagonal lines, and the tip is a little worn and bent. Length 43.5mm. Diam head 8mm. Compare the examples from Woodeaton (Kirk 1949, 25, no 1, Fig 6, no 5); Cirencester (Wacher and McWhirr 1982, 103, Fig 30, no 71); Nettleton (Wedlake 1982, 219, Fig 94, no 8, 11, also no 7, without the bone disc-shaped head, said to come from 3rd- to 4th-century levels), and the Explosion site (see below, no 26). There is also an unpublished example from 1968–9 excavations at Malton, Yorks. (SF 10, U/S)

18 Probe with a decorated handle, now a little worn. The other end, now lost was probably an elongated oval spoon. Now a little bent. Present length 103mm. Compare the examples from South Shields (Allason-Jones and Miket 1984, 170, no 3.451 and fig with further parallels); Chichester (Down 1978, 302, Fig 10.37, no 87), and an unpublished example from, Malton, Yorks 1968–9, find no 102. Künzl (1983) in his survey of medical instruments from Roman burials notes further dated examples (1983, 73, Abb 46, no 4 from cremation grave no 14 found at Belginum/Wederath (Rheinland Pfalz) now in the Rheinisches Landesmuseum, Trier and dated late 1st to early 2nd century; no 107, Abb 85, no 5, Grave 17, Luzzi (Cosenza) Italy, late 1st century). (SF 10, U/S)

Iron and lead (ALC 69 and ALC 72/2)
Quita Mould

The two excavations have been dealt with separately, each with a summary of the objects found by phase followed by a catalogue of selected items (a full catalogue can be found in microfiche M1:C10–C14). The catalogues are arranged by phase. In the summaries all objects described are of iron unless stated otherwise.

The iron objects were examined with the help of radiographs; a small number have been mechanically cleaned by Barbara Clayton of the Shakespeare Birthplace Trust Conservation Laboratory.

The timber nails have been classified according to the typology proposed by Manning (Manning in Frere 1972, 186; Manning 1976, 41–2). The nails are listed in microfiche M1:D1–D6. All measurements are given in millimetres (mm). Clenched objects have been given two measurements of length.

ALC 69 (Figs 63–65)

Summary

Phase A: late Neronian to early Flavian

A large structural fragment of lead sheet (no 1, illus) was found in a pit (178) probably dating to the 1st century. The sheet had been wrapped around a square sectioned ?post and secured at each end by iron nails.

Phase C: Flavian–Trajanic

A deposit of burnt clay (118) of late 1st- to early 2nd-century date contained heavily encrusted fragments of a key stem (no 2), a ferrule/socket (no 1, illus) which could have been broken from any hafted implement, and a spadeshoe blade (no 3, illus).

Phase D

Layer 148, belonging to the early 2nd century, contained a fragment of strip and a broken handle strap (no 4). A *stylus* of Manning Class IV (Manning 1976, 34–5) with a decorative inlaid band of non-ferrous metal was found in a general layer (no 5, illus) thought to date to the 2nd century.

Phase F

A lead cramp (no 2) came from the fill of a feature cutting the roadside ditch and believed to be of the same date (51a). Four fragments of slag occurred amongst material to the west side of the road (context (9), microfiche M1:D7), whilst around 30 hobnails (microfiche M1:D3) encrusted with minerally preserved remains of the leather shoe sole came from a deposit below (45).

A fragment of lead waste (no 4) was found in a pit (161). A fragment of lead, possibly a window frame (no 3) came from layer (86).

Phase G

An arm of an angled binding with a decorative terminal was found in a silty layer (87) near the road probably belonging to the 3rd century, and a complete spadeshoe (no 7) was recovered from context (19).

Phase H: medieval

A small ring (no 8) came from a ?rubbish pit (4) likely to be of similar date. A general layer (22) of medieval date contained a joiner's dog (microfiche M1:C11) and a spatulate-headed implement likely to be a simple *stylus* of Roman origin (no 10). A second joiner's dog (microfiche M1:C11) and a fragment of key stem (no 9) were found in the fill (6) of the stokehole of a drying oven.

Table 9 Iron and lead objects (ALC 69)

Material	Function	Quantity
Iron	Binding, angled	2
	Ferrule	1
	Handle strap	1
	Hobnail	30
	Joiner's dog	2
	Key stem	2
	Ring	2
	Slag fragment	4
	Spadeshoe	2
	Strip	1
	Stylus	2
	Timber nail, type Ib	65
	Timber nail, type II	2
	Timber nail shank	47
Lead	Buckle	1
	Came	1
	Cramp	1
	Sheet	2
	Sheet, nailed	1
	Waste	1

1969 and 1972 Baromix finds (ALC 69 and ALC 72/2)

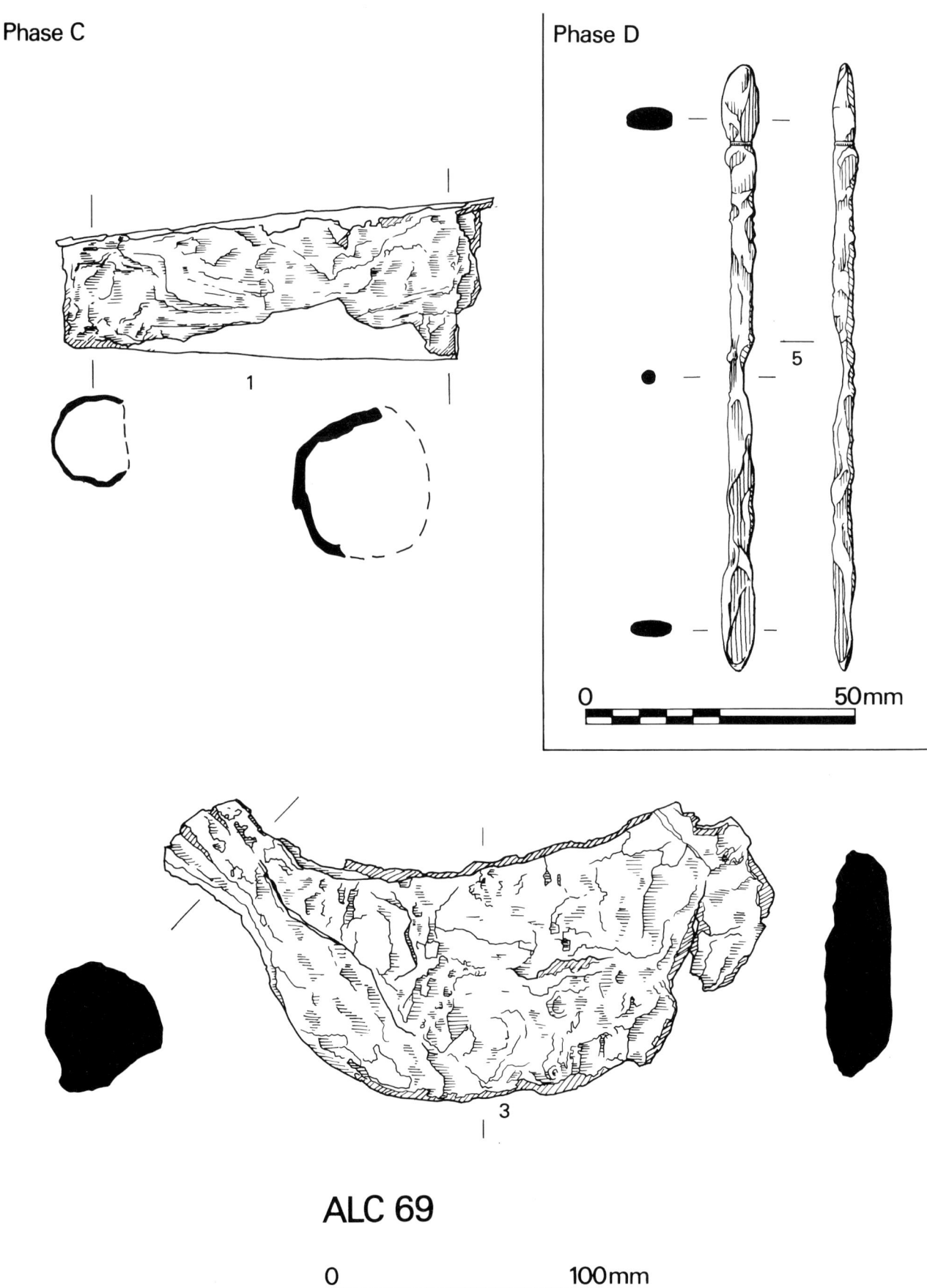

Figure 63   Iron objects (ALC 69), nos 1, 3, and 5

Phase G

ALC 69

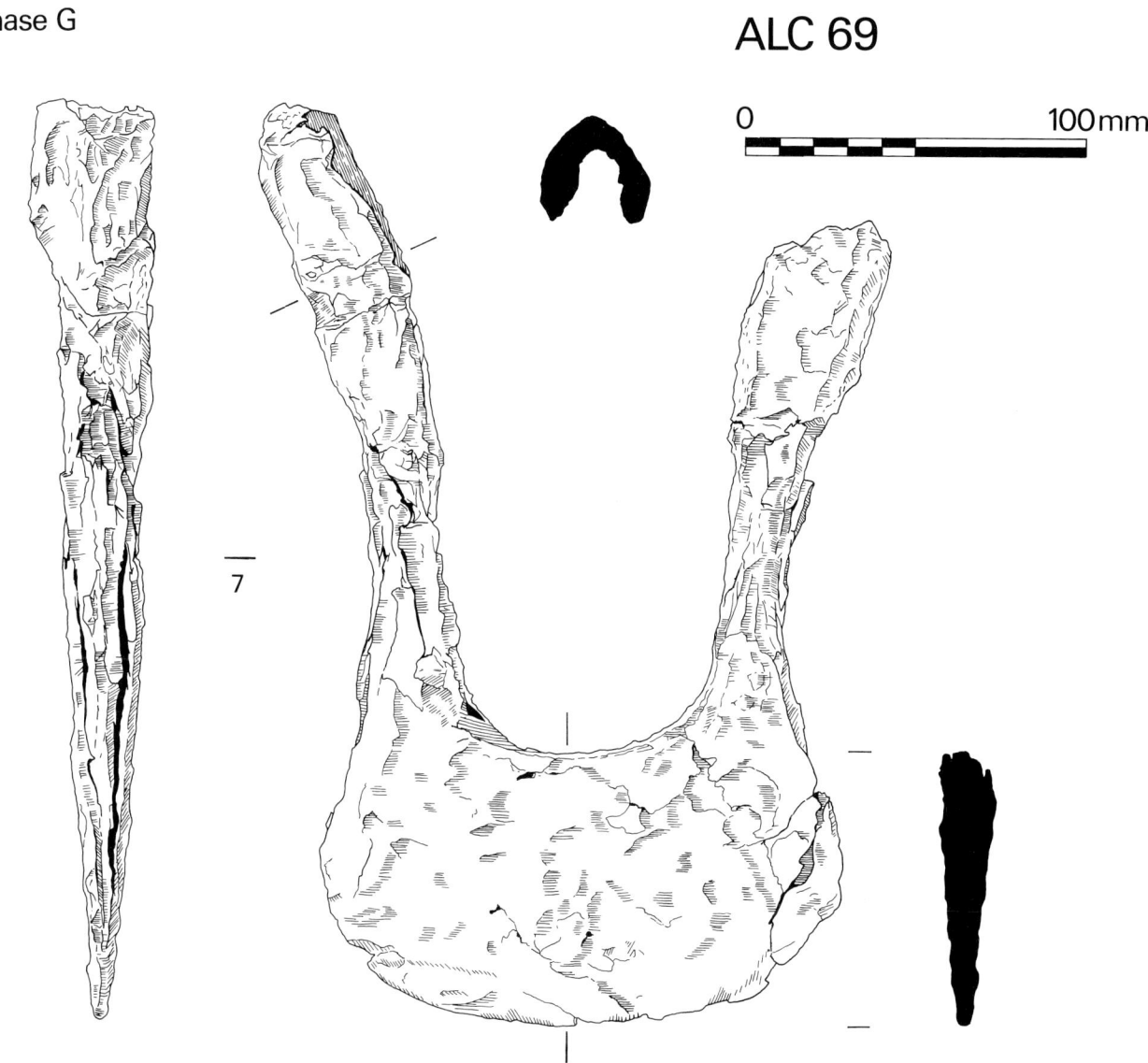

Figure 64   Iron object (ALC 69), no 7

Unphased (U/S)

A broken ring (no 12) and the arm of an angled binding (no 11) were found in topsoil, along with a lead (?pewter) buckle (no 5) and fragments of lead sheet (nos 6 and 7).

Catalogue of illustrated iron and lead objects (ALC 69)

(For complete ALC 69 iron and lead object catalogue see microfiche M1:C10–C12)

Iron

1 Iron ferrule. Fragment of conical ferrule or broken socket, very heavily encrusted. Measured from x-ray length 75mm, diam *c* 20mm. (ALC 69, SF 82.1, 118, phase C)
3 Iron spadeshoe. Large crescent-shaped blade fractured at each end, with the beginnings of an upturned tang at one end. Heavily encrusted and very little metal remaining visible in radiograph. Probably a fragment of spadeshoe blade. Length 113mm, max width 40mm. (ALC 69, SF 85, 118, phase C)
5 Iron *stylus* with slender round sectioned stem with a small wedge-sectioned eraser with a single transverse moulding apparently with a decorative non-ferrous inlaid collar below. The stem tapers to a gently pointed tip with no distinction between the stem and point. Manning Class IV (1976, 34). Length 111mm, diam 6mm. (ALC 69, 115, phase D)
7 Large spadeshoe with curved blade and outward flaring, grooved arms with U-shaped section. Type Ib of Manning's classification (Rees 1979, 322–26). Similar to an example from Braughing, Herts (Rees 1979, 368, Fig 109). Complete. Flaking, fragmentary. Measured from x-ray: length *c* 266mm; blade width 153mm; blade depth 77mm. (ALC 69, SF 93, 19, phase G)

The ALC 69 nails are listed in microfiche M1: D1–D5.

Lead

1 Lead sheet of square/rectangular shape folded to form a hollow square- sectioned tube having been wrapped around a square-

1969 and 1972 Baromix finds (ALC 69 and ALC 72/2)

sectioned slightly tapering object. Both ends are open and were secured through a pair of nail holes, the wider end having iron corrosion products from the nails *in situ*. The wider end has the edges bent over at the back where the sheet casing was abutted to the object to which it was nailed. Hammer blows are present on the upper surface. Structural. Length 220mm, max diam 56mm, max width 95mm, sheet thickness 1mm. (ALC 69, SF 117, 178, phase A)

ALC 72/2 (Figs 66–67)

Summary

Phase B: Flavian

A strap fragment (no 1) and a curved nail shank from context (93) occurred in contexts of this phase.

Phase C: Flavian–Trajanic

The narrow knife blade (no 2), found in a feature below context (105) cutting natural, is of a known type and comparable with an example from Housesteads (Manning 1976, Fig 21, 126).

Phase D: 2nd century

Two fragments of strip (no 3), the latter possibly part of a handle, along with fragments of thick strap (no 4) came from context (105), a silt accumulation over the demolished phase C buildings.

Phase F: later 2nd/3rd century

The barb-spring padlock key (no 7) occurred within the fill of a stone-lined drain (48); there were also fragments from a probable knife blade (no 8).

Contexts 14 and 33, the silt layers below the phase G cobbled surface 11, contained a fragment of lead waste slag (SF 26, microfiche M1:D7), and a small quantity of type Ib timber nails and shank fragments (SF 26, microfiche M1:D6), as well as a group of about 200 hobnails (SF 18, microfiche M1:D6) encrusted with minerally preserved leather from the surrounding shoe sole.

Phase G: 3rd century

A small carpenter's flat chisel (no 10) was found in a ?3rd-century posthole (38). A small drift (no 9) used by a smith to enlarge a hole in hot metal, was found in a 2nd/3rd-century posthole (19).

A fragment of nailed lead sheet (no 21) was found on the cobbled surface (11) dated to the late 3rd century.

Table 10   Iron and lead objects (ALC 72/2)

Material	Function	Quantity
Iron	Blade, knife	2
	Blade, knife/strap	1
	Chisel, flat	1
	Drift	1
	Hobnail	200
	Key padlock	1
	Strap	2
	Strip	2
	Timber nail type Ib	3
	Timber nail shank	3
Lead	Sheet, nailed	1
	Strip	1

Phase H: medieval

The robber trench (4) of a substantial Roman building contained a knife blade of common Roman form (no 11).

A rectangular-sectioned shank fragment occurred in the medieval oven/drying kiln (2).

Catalogue of illustrated iron objects (ALC 72/2)

(For complete ALC 72/2 iron and lead object catalogue see microfiche M1:C13–C14)

Iron

2 Iron knife blade. Slender blade with straight back and edge, broken before the tip. The short square-sectioned tang is set midway between the back and edge. Fairly common Roman type comparable with an example from Housesteads (Manning 1976, Fig 21, 126). Fractured, encrusted heavily. Length 137mm; max width 16mm; tang length 34mm. (ALC 72/2, SF 20, 114, phase C)
7 Iron barb-spring padlock key with a square-sectioned stem with a rolled loop terminal and remains of a square pierced bit. A common key type found in both Roman and medieval contexts. Roman examples occur on various sites such as Verulamium (Manning in Frere 1972, Fig 68, 80–81) where the two examples were dated to AD 310–15 and AD 280–90, respectively. Almost complete. Flaking. Length 127mm; bow diam 12mm; bit width 13mm. (ALC 72/2, SF 22, 48, phase F)
9 Iron drift. Heavy square-sectioned shank with remains of a badly flaked head, expanding in width to a pronounced shoulder before tapering sharply to a fine, pointed tip. Almost complete. Flaking. Length 103mm; max width 20mm. (ALC 72/2, SF 17, 19, phase G)
10 Iron chisel. Round-sectioned stem with a flat head tapering gradually to a wedge sectioned, narrow chisel blade. Similar to chisels found at Niederbieber and Pompeii (Gaitzch 1980, tafel 45,

1969 and 1972 Baromix finds (ALC 69 and ALC 72/2)

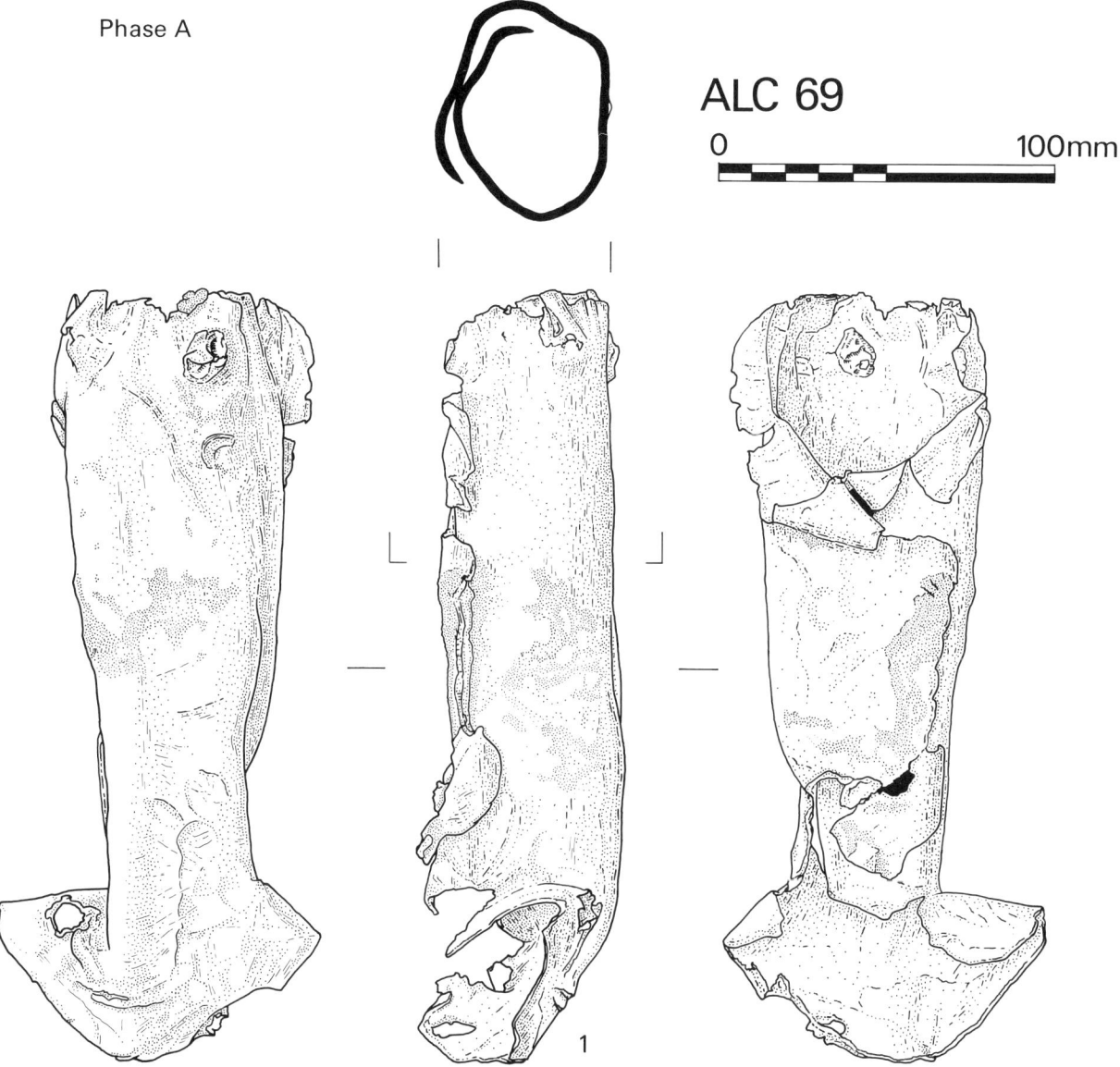

Figure 65   Lead object (ALC 69), no 1

210–211; tafel 18, 94). Complete, flaking. Length 110mm; diam 10mm; chisel blade width 7mm. (ALC 72/2, SF 25, 38, phase G)

11 Badly flaked remains of a small knife blade with convex back and edge, with a rectangular-sectioned tang positioned midway between the two. The back drops to meet the edge at a gently pointed tip. The back is not distinctly thickened in the radiograph. Commonest form of Roman knife, general purpose (Manning 1976, Type I, 37). Flaking. Length 113mm; tang length 25mm; blade width 34mm. (ALC 72/2, SF 27, 4, phase H)

One other iron object (SF 28) now missing is recorded from 114, phase C, described as a 'hinge' in the small finds list.

The ALC 72/2 nails are listed in microfiche M1:D6.

Discussion

The majority of the metalwork represents structural fittings, principally timber nails and shank fragments, with joiner's dogs, fragments of binding, and nailed lead sheet. No objects with military associations could be recognised amongst the material, with the possible exception of a heavily encrusted fragment of ferrule or socket (ALC 69 no 1) which may have been broken from a spear originally. The objects found suggest a rural, domestic assemblage. Craft tools are represented by a smith's drift (ALC 72 no 9) and a carpenter's flat chisel (ALC 72 no 10); domestic utensils by knives (ALC 72 nos 2, 8, and 11), keys (eg ALC 72 no 7) and a handle strap (ALC 69 no 4). Some agricultural activity is indicated by a crescent-shaped blade fragment (ALC 69 no 3), which may be broken from a heavily encrusted spadeshoe, and a complete spadeshoe (ALC 69 no 7). Other finds include a *stylus* with decorative inlay (ALC 69 no 5), and weights. Leather footwear with nailed soles is attested by several groups of hobnails.

1969 and 1972 Baromix finds (ALC 69 and ALC 72/2)

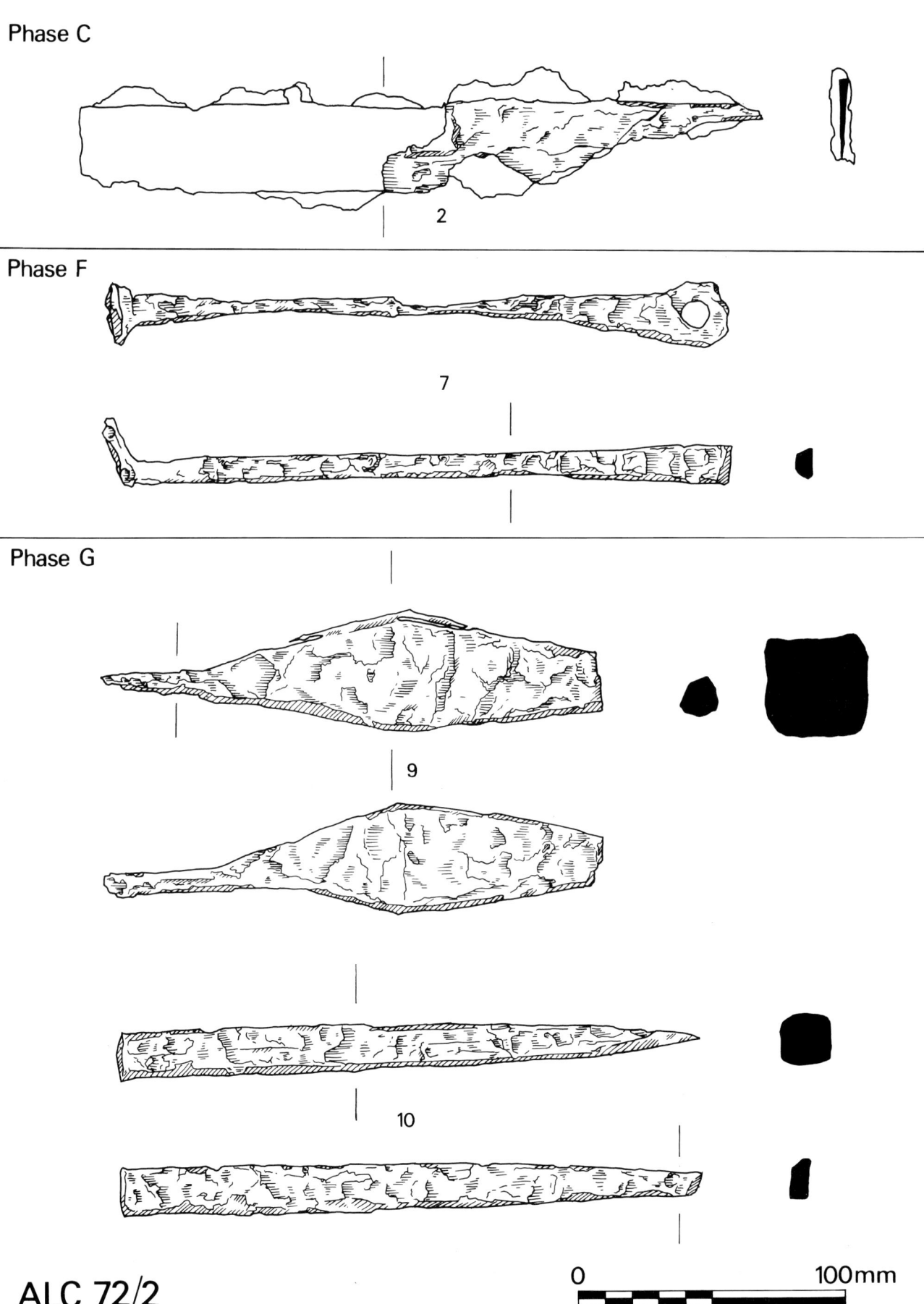

Figure 66   Iron and lead objects (ALC 72/2), nos 2, 7, and 9–10

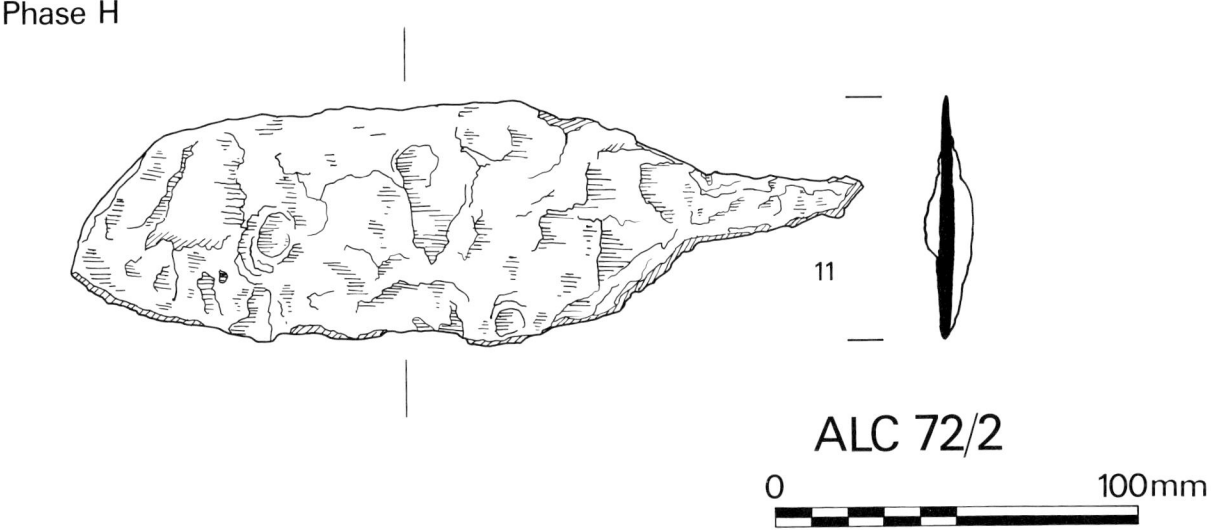

Figure 67   Iron object (ALC 72/2), no 11

Metalworking slag (ALC 69 and ALC 72/2)
Gerry McDonnell

All the slag found on the sites was smithing slag and included several fragments of smithing hearth bottoms. Although it is possible that smithing of a temporary nature took place on the site it is more likely that the slag was incorporated into cobbled road or yard surfaces. The occurrences of slag on the two sites are listed in microfiche M1:D7.

Worked bone (ALC 69 and ALC 72/2)
Glenys Lloyd-Morgan

As in many other sites where the worked bone has been fully recorded, the pins tend to account for over half the total finds, whether they are complete or survive as fragments. Although the number of pins from these excavations is small, the most popular forms, according to Crummy's typology (1979), cover the whole of the Roman period. The unfinished state of ALC 72/2 no 3, suggests that some pins, and probably other items too, were being made locally, though a few pieces such as the unusual ALC 72/2 no 5, may well have come from elsewhere. The needles and bodkins are undatable, though it is curious that there are no copper alloy examples with which they might have been compared.

If the die, ALC 69 no 8, was carelessly made without regard to the marrow cavity, as Crummy suggests for a parallel example from Colchester (Crummy 1983, 96, no 2501), the counter sunk holes of ALC 72/2 no 1, are even more curious. It would seem highly likely that it had been weighted in some way, though in its present state practical experiment shows that over a series of throws no one side is more favoured than the others.

The late medieval comb fragment, ALC 69 no 9, suggests not only the well documented continuity of the site, but also highlights the lack of similar items which were made of wood both in the Roman and medieval periods.

Catalogue

ALC 69

1 Shaft of pin or needle. Present length 52mm. (ALC 69, SF 43, 6, phase E)

2 Shaft of pin or needle, surface rather eroded in places. Present length 43.7mm. (ALC 69, SF 31, 49, phase E)

3 Shaft of pin, the head broken off just above a lightly incised collar. The lower part of the shaft and tip are also lost. Present length 36mm. (ALC 69, SF 77, 86, phase F)

4 Pin with elongated conical head and slight collar underneath, the lower part of the shaft and tip are missing. Present length 47mm, Diam head 3mm. (ALC 69, SF 77, 86, phase F)

Crummy pin type 2 with date range c AD 50–200/250 (1979, 160–1, Fig 1, no 2). Compare the example from Leicester found in a context with 2nd-century samian and a *mortarium* stamp (Hebditch and Mellor 1973, 49 and 25, Fig 21, no 36); and South Shields (Miket 1983, 136, Fig 81, no 15, from layer 31 with a 4th-century date); and an unpublished example from Tiddington, no TD 81 SF 805. See also the Explosion site below, no 213.

5 Fragment of die with side numbered 2 as the only complete surviving face, and part only of sides numbered 6, 3, and 4. The edges are bevelled. The piece has suffered some fire damage. Size of complete face 13.6mm × 12.2mm. Surviving depth 5.3mm. (ALC 69, SF 102, 161, phase F)

Compare a parallel fragment from Lion Walk, Colchester, where, like ours 'no attempt has been made to avoid the marrow cavity' during manufacture (Crummy 1983, 96, no 2501, Fig 102, dated c AD 150–?200).

6 Pin with low conical head, as Crummy type 1, cf ALC 72/2, SF 45, no 2 below (or is this a crudely fashioned tip?) incomplete. Present length 42.6mm. Max diam shaft 3.2mm. (ALC 69, SF 25, 22, phase H)

7 Needle with small circular eye near conical head, lower part of shaft lost. Present length 49mm. (ALC 69, 88, phase H)

Compare the examples from South Shields (Allason-Jones and Miket, 1984, 67, nos 2.275; 2.277; 2.281; 2.282, and Figs).

8 Pin with subspherical head; tip and part of shaft lost. Length 50.4mm. Diam head 7.5–8.3mm. (ALC 69, SF 13, 1, phase U/S)

Crummy pin type 3 with date range c AD 200– late 4th/early 5th century (1979, 161, Fig 1, nos 3 and 4). An example from Wadham

1969 and 1972 Baromix finds (ALC 69 and ALC 72/2)

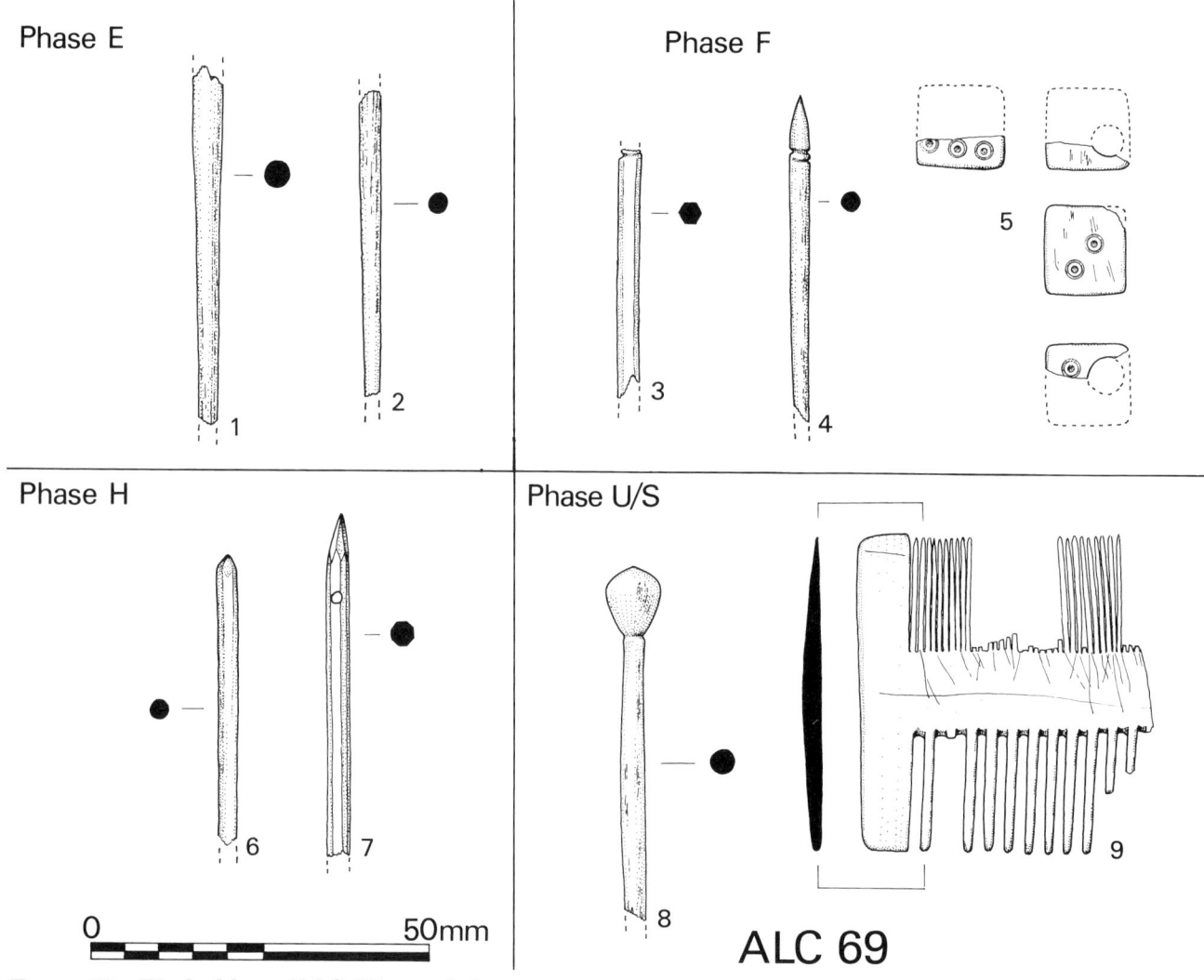

Figure 68   Worked bone (ALC 69), nos 1–9

House, Dorchester, Dorset, was dated early 4th century (Draper and Chaplin 1982, 24, Fig 12, no 5), and further pieces from Shakenoak, Oxon came from late 4th-century deposits (Brodribb *et al* 1973, 142, nos 122, 123, 124, Fig 72). Finds from Tiddington include nos SF M602, SF M722, SF M723, SF M937, SF M938, SF M939, TD80 SF 5, TD81 SF 880.

9 Double-sided comb cut from a single sheet of bone. Incomplete and sections of teeth missing. The coarser teeth are 3.5 to the centimetre, the finer number *c* 11 to the centimetre. Present length 42.4mm. Depth 45.7mm. (ALC 69, SF 5, 1, phase U/S)

Combs of this type remain popular throughout the medieval and later periods, and there are close parallels amongst finds of Roman combs, though these tend to be of wood. Compare the examples from Northampton (Williams 1979, 310, no WB44, Fig 137, described as ivory, from House 4, phase 6 D(i), later part of the 15th century); Exeter (Allen 1984, 351, Fig 195, no B 12, dated late 16th/early 17th century; no B 13 *c* AD 1670–1700; no B 14, dated *c* AD 1740–60); and from Southampton (Platt and Coleman-Smith 1975, 274, no 1939, Fig 248, dated AD 1375–1425; 274, no 1944, Fig 249, dated early 16th century; 274, no 1946, Fig 249, dated *c* AD 1630–40; p 274, no 1947, Fig 249, dated AD 1630–40).

ALC 72/2

1 Worn die with countersunk hole between sides numbered 1 and 6. The numbers are indicated by dot-and-circle patterns. 15mm × 13mm × 11.5mm. (ALC 72/2, SF 44, 33, phase F)

No traces remain of any plugging in the hole, and no parallel examples have come to light so far. For the more usual solid bone dice, compare the finds from London (Jones 1980, 93, no 489, Fig 54 from a context dated not later than AD 125); and Dover (Philp 1981, 167, no 220, Fig 41, from a context dated AD 130/140–155).

2 Bone pin with low conical head, the tip and part of the shaft lost. Length 43.6mm. Max diam shaft 4.2–4.7mm. (ALC 72/2, SF 45, 2, phase H)

Crummy pin type 1 with date range AD 70–200/250 (1979, 159–160, Fig 1, no 1). Compare other examples from York dated not later than late 2nd or early 3rd century (MacGregor 1976, 12, 23, nos 128, 129, Fig 9); and Dover (Philp 1981, 157, nos 148–151, Fig 36, pp 150–1, no 148, from period III contexts dated AD 190–200 to AD 208). See also the Explosion site below, no 206.

3 Pin with head incomplete or damaged during manufacture. The tip and shaft are smooth but a little angular in cross-section. Length 57.8mm. Cross-section head 6mm × 4.5mm. (ALC 72/2, SF 40, 22, phase H)

4 Pin with roughly spherical head, in two pieces but complete. Length 57.3mm. Diam head 5.5mm. (ALC 72/2, SF 46, 1, phase U/S)

Crummy type 3. Cf ALC 69, SF 13, no 8 above, and the Explosion site below, no 216 for discussion and bibliography.

5 Pin with irregular biconical head. The upper section is plain and separated from the lower part by a collar. The elongated lower section is decorated with diagonal incisions, and below this is a further collar marking the division between the head and the shaft. The tip and lower part of the shaft is lost. Present length 71mm. Max diam head 6.7mm × 8.5mm. (ALC 72/2, SF 46, 1, phase U/S)

Compare the example from South Shields (Allason-Jones and Miket 1984, 82, no 2.497 and fig).

1969 and 1972 Baromix finds (ALC 69 and ALC 72/2)

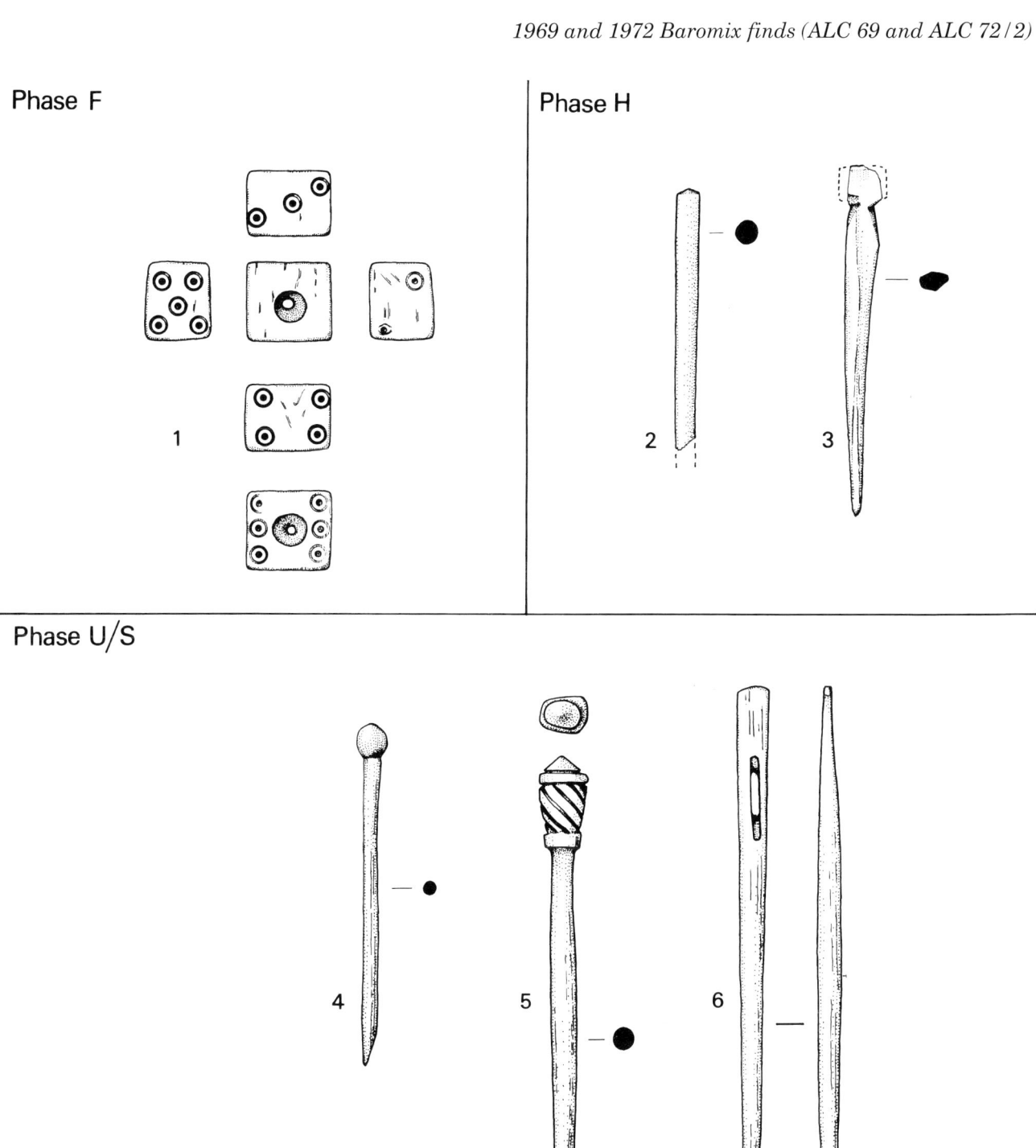

Figure 69 Worked bone (ALC 72/2), nos 1–6

1969 and 1972 Baromix finds (ALC 69 and ALC 72/2)

Phase C

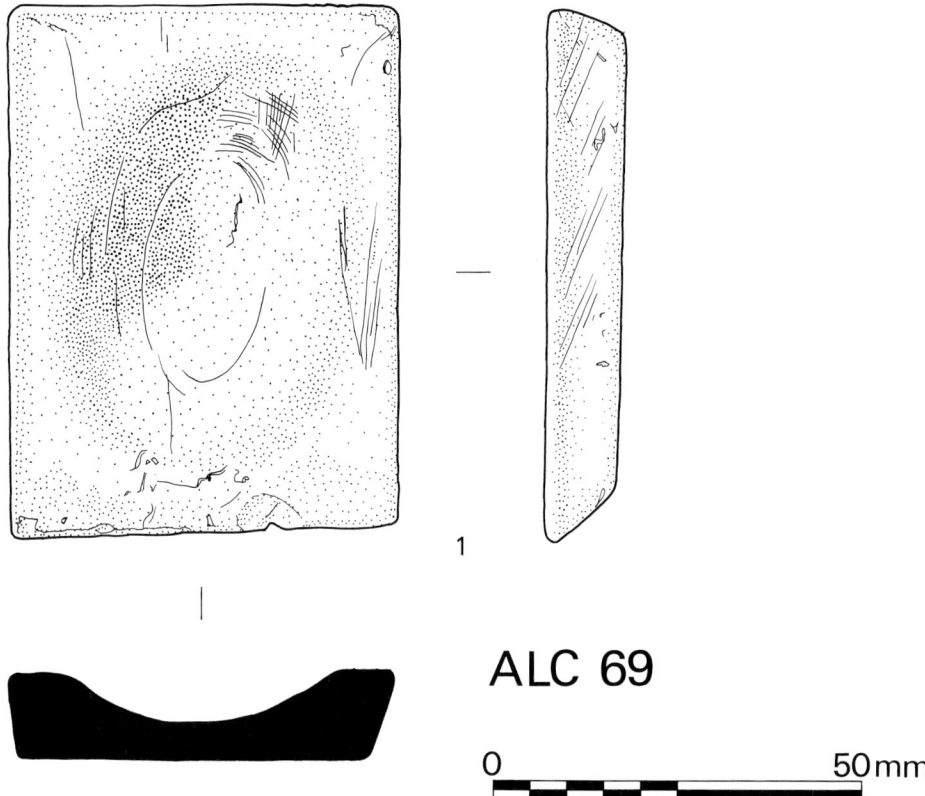

Figure 70 Stone object (ALC 69), no 1

6 Needle with rectangular eye, complete. Length 124mm. (ALC 72/2, SF 42, 1, phase U/S)
Compare the examples from South Shields (Allason-Jones and Miket 1984, 65, no 2.268, 2.269; 67, nos 2.270, 2.271, 2.272 and figs); Ilchester (Cox 1982, 130, no 42, 131, no 44 and figs); and Balkerne Lane, Colchester (Crummy 1983, 67, Fig 70, no 1982 from a pit dated *c* AD 150–250).

Stone objects (ALC 69)
Glenys Lloyd-Morgan with a contribution by Jeremy Evans

Some of these items can be classed as luxury objects. The fragments of shale bracelet are a not uncommon form of personal decoration, though not easy to date closely due to the simplicity or lack of decoration in many cases.

Although stone palettes can be used for grinding and mixing up cosmetics, they are also used in the making of medicines either by trained doctors or others with skill in such crafts. The presence of the copper alloy probe, ALC 72 no 18, suggests a medical use, as does the depth of wear on the palette, ALC 69 no 1, despite the thin line that separated the mixing of salves and unguents for medical or cosmetic use in antiquity.

The overall impression from this small group of items (only from ALC 69), is of a certain degree of wealth and of a standard of living which might be anticipated in a larger town, rather than a simple market centre.

Catalogue of illustrated stone objects (ALC 69)
(for complete ALC 69 stone object catalogue see microfiche M1:D8–D9)

ALC 69 (Figs 70–72)

Phase C

1 Palette of a fine grained grey stone, more trapezoidal than rectangular in outline. There are bevelled edges to the unused surface, the other side has an oval depression worn away by much use. 54mm × *c* 70.0mm, depth 10.2–12mm. (ALC 69, 118, phase C)

A list of palettes from Roman Britain was compiled by Dobson and Jarrett, and includes one from Binchester made of Purbeck Marble (1958, 121–123). One of polished marble from Rushmore (Cranbourne Chase) noted on 123, is described as having a thin copper alloy plating 0.022 inches (0.6mm) thick, most of it being worn off. This was probably the remains of the box into which it was once set. For a complete example probably from Andernach, Kr. Mayen see Menzel (1966, 78, no 187, Taf 62, Rheinisches Landesmuseum, Trier, inv no 06,56). This has a stone palette set into the top of a decorated copper alloy salve box, and can be slid out for use. There is also a narrow cylindrical case attached to one of the long sides of the box, presumably for small toilet implements.

More recent finds of palettes from Britain include one of 'metamorphosed mudstone' from Verulamium from a context dated AD 115–130, now broken and incomplete (Frere 1972, 156, no 229, Fig 58). From Colchester, one of onyx marble from Lion Walk came from a context *c* AD 100–350 (Crummy 1983, 57, no 1865, Fig 62), and one of greenstone, found in Balkerne Lane was dated *c* AD 75/80 (Crummy 1983, 57, no 1867, Fig 62). This new example from Alcester is almost certainly in a Blue Lias Limestone of the Lower Lias, Lower Jurassic and could well be of local origin. The nearest known quarries of similar rocks are at Temple Grafton (John Crossling pers comm).

1969 and 1972 Baromix finds (ALC 69 and ALC 72/2)

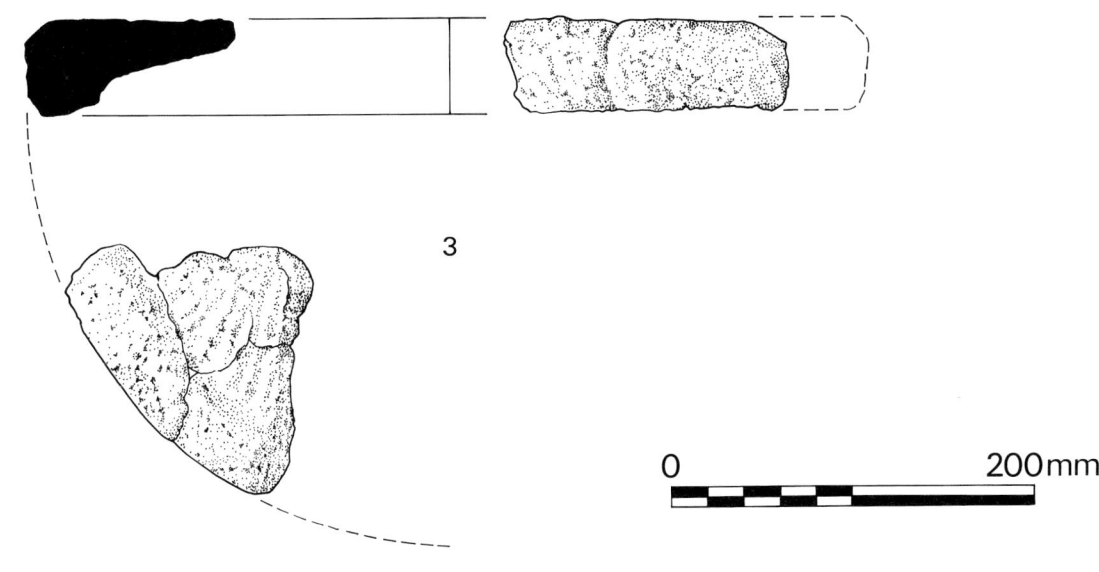

ALC 69

Figure 71 Stone objects (ALC 69), quernstone, no 3, and shale, nos 4–5

1969 and 1972 Baromix finds (ALC 69 and ALC 72/2)

Phase H

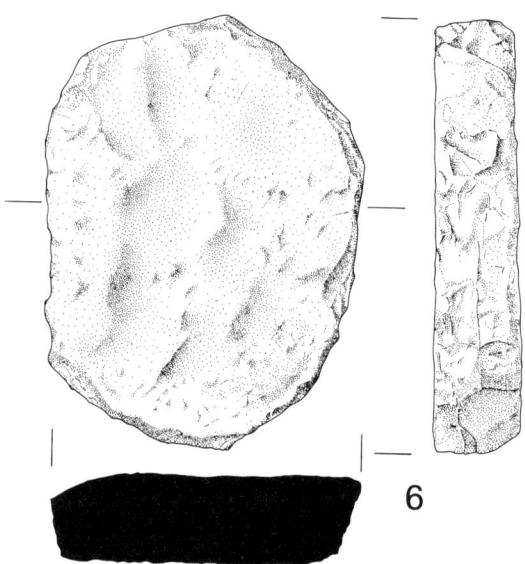
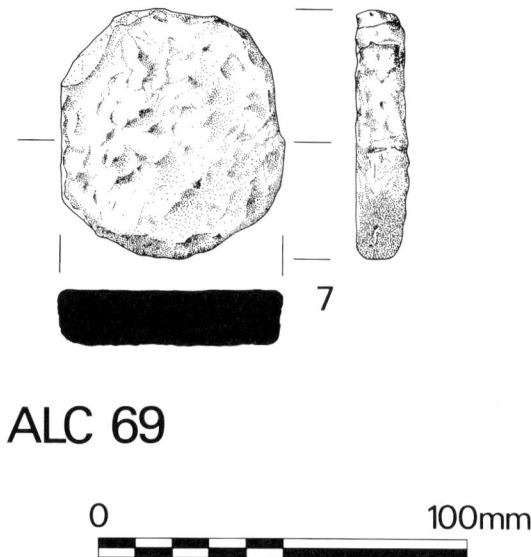

Figure 72 Stone objects (ALC 69), nos 6–7

3 Around 10% of the circumference of the upper stone of a Continental lava quernstone fragment. The fragment is much abraded and broken and no evidence of tooling around the edges remains. The grinding surface is gently angled and cut in harps, cf Curwen 1937, Fig 40. (JE) Diameter *c* 500mm, Height 40mm at circumference. (ALC 69, SF 87, 89, phase C)

Phase G

4 Shale bracelet fragment, plain with sub-circular cross-section. Present length *c* 58mm, depth 5.7mm, Diam when complete *c* 67mm. (ALC 69, SF 115a, 19, phase G)

J Crossling (pers comm) identified it as of Bituminous shale of the Kimmeridge clay. Compare the examples from Silchester (Lawson 1975, 250, Fig 4, no 26 a–d; p 252, Fig 4, no 27, a–i); Chester (Lloyd-Morgan 1981b, 42, no 8, Fig 1B; 44, no 10, 13); York (Macgregor, A, 1976, 6, 21, cat nos 3, 4, and Fig 5) and South Shields, where a date range of mid-2nd to early 4th century is suggested for the type (Allason-Jones and Miket 1984, 313, no 7.121, 7.123 figs on 315, further parallels are also noted).

5 Shale bracelet fragment which would originally have had a rounded 'D'-shaped cross-section, but has split in an uneven horizontal fashion. It was originally decorated along the widest part to the outer side with a grooved pattern, of which little can now be made out. Present length *c* 89mm, max depth 8.5mm, diam when complete *c* 95mm. (ALC 69, SF 115b, 19, phase G)

J Crossling (pers comm) identified it as of Bituminous shale of the Kimmeridge clay. Compare the examples from Silchester (Lawson 1976, 254, Fig 5, no 41b, no 42a, b, c); another from Chichester was found in a context dated Flavian to early 2nd century (Down and Rule 1971, 45, no 5, Fig 3.16, no 5). A piece from Canterbury was found in the upper fill of a well shaft on the Rosemary Lane Car Park site with samian dated AD 150–180 (Bennett *et al* 1982, 181, Fig 94, no 96); and a further fragment from Cirencester was found in the same context as a coin of Hadrian and other 1st- to 2nd-century material (Wacher and McWhirr 1982, 103, Fig 30, no 74).

Phase H

6 Roughly shaped pale grey limestone oval disc, perhaps of White Lias from the Langport Beds (J Crossling pers comm), perhaps a pot lid. (JE). Length 114mm, Width 84mm, Thickness 23mm. (ALC 69, SF 51, 6, phase G)

7 Roughly shaped circular pale grey limestone disc, perhaps of White Lias from the Langport Beds (J Crossling pers comm), perhaps a large counter or pot lid. (JE). Diameter 63mm, Thickness 13mm. (ALC 69, SF 46, 3, phase G)

The building stone is listed in microfiche M1:D10.

Ceramic object (ALC 69)
Jeremy Evans

1 A handmade lamp in a buff fabric with some fairly coarse sand temper, exterior hand-burnished, interior burnt. For another open lamp also in a crude handmade fabric see Adkins and Adkins (1983). (ALC 69, SF 100, 51A, phase F)

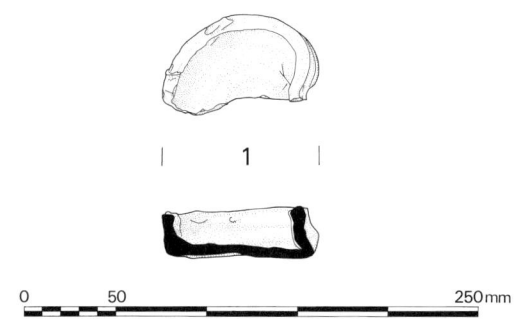

Figure 73 Ceramic lamp (ALC 69), no 1

All the ceramic objects are listed by Jeremy Evans in microfiche M1:D10. Fired clay objects by Jeremy Evans is in microfiche M1:D11. Flints by Rowan Ferguson is in microfiche M1:D11. Human bone by Ann Stirland is in microfiche M1:D11.

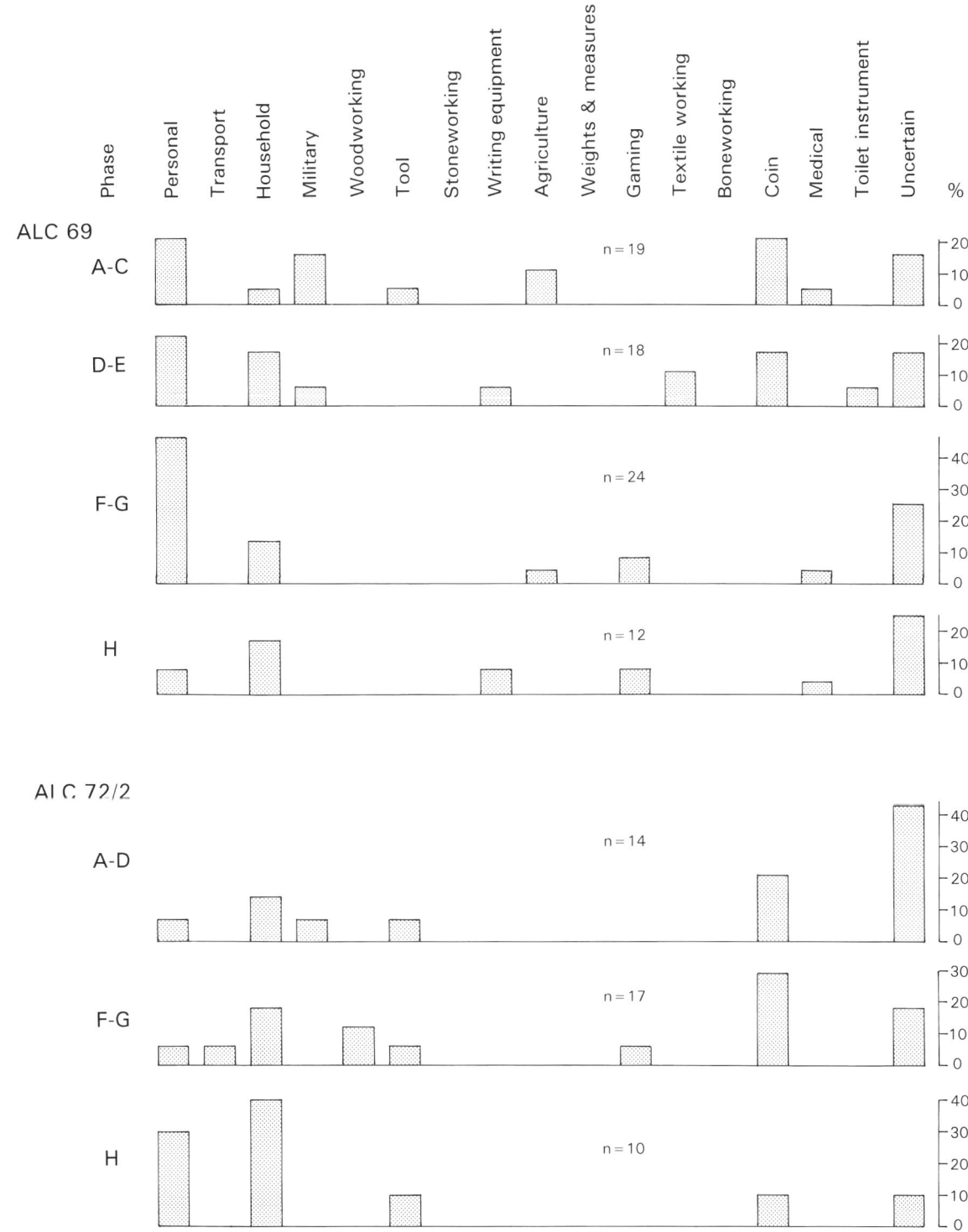

Figure 74 Proportions of finds classes by phase (ALC 72/2 and ALC 69)

Discussion of the ALC 69 and ALC 72/2 finds
Jeremy Evans

Summaries of individual finds classes are made above, but a general overview of the small finds assemblage will be attempted here in relation to the early Baromix sites. Fig 74 shows the percentages of finds classes by phase group from ALC 69 and ALC 72/2. There are too few finds to make these very reliable but some features do stand out. Sixteen percent of the finds from the early phases at ALC 69 and 7% of those from ALC 72/2 are *militaria*. This is a very high proportion, the fort at Segontium in comparison (Casey *et al* 1993) not producing more than 5% normally from any phase, and it strongly suggests that these early phases are military. As noted above (Ferguson) the pottery from the early phases has military parallels elsewhere and the strong samian ware supply also tends to strengthen the suggestion of a military link. Similarly the functional analysis is not inconsistent with military origins, lacking the very high early jar levels in the pattern observed by Millett (1979) at Neatham, Chichester and Verulamium (see Evans above in Ferguson). None of these cases is absolutely convincing by itself; military finds have been made before in contexts reasonably regarded as civilian (Millett 1990, 60), but the number of items of *militaria*, taken with the other hints, does, on balance, suggest the presence of a fort. The number of coins further suggests this. In civilian contexts it would seem unusual to find coins representing 21% of small finds in the Flavian-Trajanic period as they do here on both sites. Indeed this is the highest representation of coins at ALC 69 relative to other finds, whilst on ALC 72/2 the 3rd-century group (which perhaps contains a small dispersed hoard of Carausius?) only amounts to 29% of all small finds. In comparison Flavian coinage is absent from the Lloyds Bank site discussed below and is not found before period 4 at the Explosion site (see Seaby and Booth below), and is not particularly common there. The ratios of pre-Hadrianic coinage to coins from Hadrian to AD 259 highlight the strong early coin loss on the Baromix sites (14:2), a ratio of 7.0:1, compared with 0.5:1 at Lloyds Bank (see Seaby below) and 0.6:1 at the Explosion site (see Seaby and Booth). The highest other figures from the town are 2.2:1 from Mahany sites D and G, and 2.0:1 from the site at 6 Birch Abbey, all areas which are likely to have been immediately adjacent to, or on the edge of, the putative fort.

This evidence for the existence of a fort is in turn strengthened by the structural sequence, with linear buildings aligned north–south, a foundation slot construction with common Flavian military parallels, and apparently contemporary sequences on both sites.

After phase C on ALC 69 and phase D on ALC 72/2 the civilian archaeology produces a rather varied finds assemblage. On ALC 69 phase D (the aisled building?) produces clay loom weights, presumably from textile manufacture and this is reflected on Fig 74, whilst in phase E there is evidence of the construction or demolition of a bath building somewhere in the vicinity with finds of tufa. Chronologically this would seem to tie in with the construction of the first stone building on the Explosion site (period 5; see Booth below) to the north. In phases F and G the road to the defended area on ALC 69 had no flanking buildings, the finds being dominated by personal items, brooches, pins, and so on, perhaps lost in passing, although there are few coins, in contrast with ALC 72/2. Also found in phase G was the only window glass from the site, presumably residual or rubbish scattered from nearby.

On ALC 72/2 coins, woodworking tools and household fittings are more common finds in phases F and G, possibly associated with a stone building on the site in phase G. In phase H a limestone *tessera* from a tessellated floor somewhere in the vicinity occurs residually as does the almost unique copper alloy (bronze) tap fitting (see Fig 61 and Lloyd-Morgan above, no 14).

Samian ware relative to the glassware

Fig 75 shows the proportions of samian ware, and glassware, by phase quantified by sherd count. The quantity of samian ware from the site is proportionately quite high and on both sites there seems to be a slight pattern of fairly high levels in the 1st to early

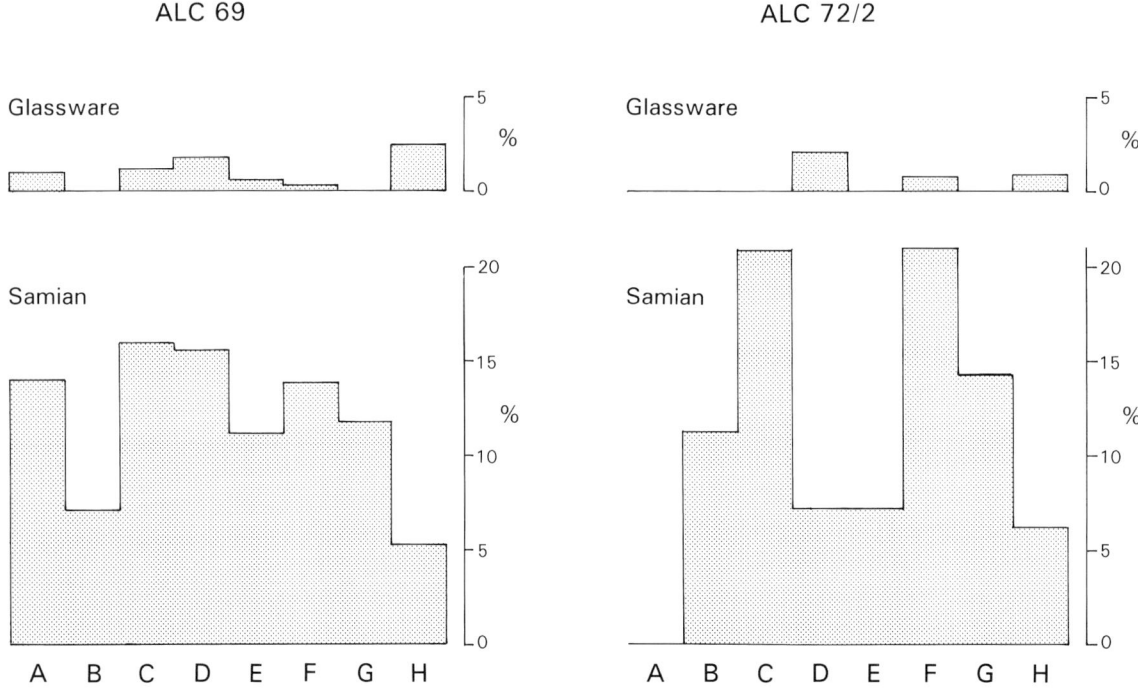

Figure 75 Comparative proportions of samian ware and glass by phase (ALC 69 and ALC 72/2) (by sherd count)

2nd century with a fall in the Hadrianic to early Antonine period and a peak in the later 2nd to 3rd century (phase F), with the expected falls in the later 3rd century and amongst residual material of phase H. There is no great pattern to the glassware finds, but they do seem to be commoner on ALC 69 in phases A–D and fall off thereafter, whilst glassware is generally commoner on this site than on ALC 72/2. On both ALC 69 and ALC 72/2 the greatest quantity of glassware appears in phase D (late Trajanic/early Hadrianic on ALC 72/2 and Hadrianic on ALC 69). The higher proportions of glassware on the ALC 69 site may reflect the evidence of the functional analysis (see Allen above) of a greater proportion of tablewares on this site in the 1st to mid-2nd century. The proportions of samian ware in the assemblages at both sites are quite high when compared with other sites in the town and elsewhere. At the neighbouring Explosion site (see Ferguson, below) samian ware never exceeded 8% of the assemblage by sherd count and at the fort of Segontium, Gwynedd (King and Millett 1993) it generally accounted for around 10% of the assemblage by sherd count. The Baromix figures can also be contrasted with those from another small town, Neatham, Hants, where samian levels never exceeded 5% of the groups by sherd number (Millett and Graham 1986, fig 52; although in fairness the availability of coarse pottery from very local kilns may depress levels here). The proportions of samian ware at the Baromix sites by sherd weight is of course much lower, as generally tends to be the case.

The high samian proportions in the early phases are consistent with the efficient supply seen on military sites. The slight peak on ALC 69 in phase F is a little deceptive, as a reasonable proportion of this material is residual South Gaulish material, but that on ALC 72/2 appears to be contemporary and seems to suggest higher status activity occurring nearby to the site.

1988 Baromix excavations (AL 28)

Excavation summary
Stephen Cracknell and Jeremy Evans

Four trenches were laid out within the Baromix factory (Figs 2 and 4, Plate 9) in December 1988 to evaluate the site prior to proposed development (Cracknell 1989a). Three of these, trenches 1, 2, and 4 were on an east–west axis roughly at right angles to the Roman street (street D, Fig 3) and one, trench 3, was set back from the frontage on a roughly north–south axis. The site sits upon a slight ridge of sand and gravel of the second quaternary river terrace.

Trenches 1–3 measured approximately 4m by 2m, and trench 4 was c 1.6m square. The trenches were sufficiently separated and small enough for it to prove impossible to produce a single phasing scheme for all of them, so each is phased separately. Only a summary of the excavations is reproduced here. A detailed structural account can be found in microfiche M1:D12–E3. Dating evidence was also rather scarce. All Roman small finds from the trenches are reported here, but only the pottery from the pre-Hadrianic phases is fully discussed. Too little animal bone was recovered for it to be usefully reported on. A summary table of all stratified finds is provided in microfiche (Tables MT4–MT7, microfiche M1:E4–7).

Plate 9   Trench 1, section drawing (AL 28)

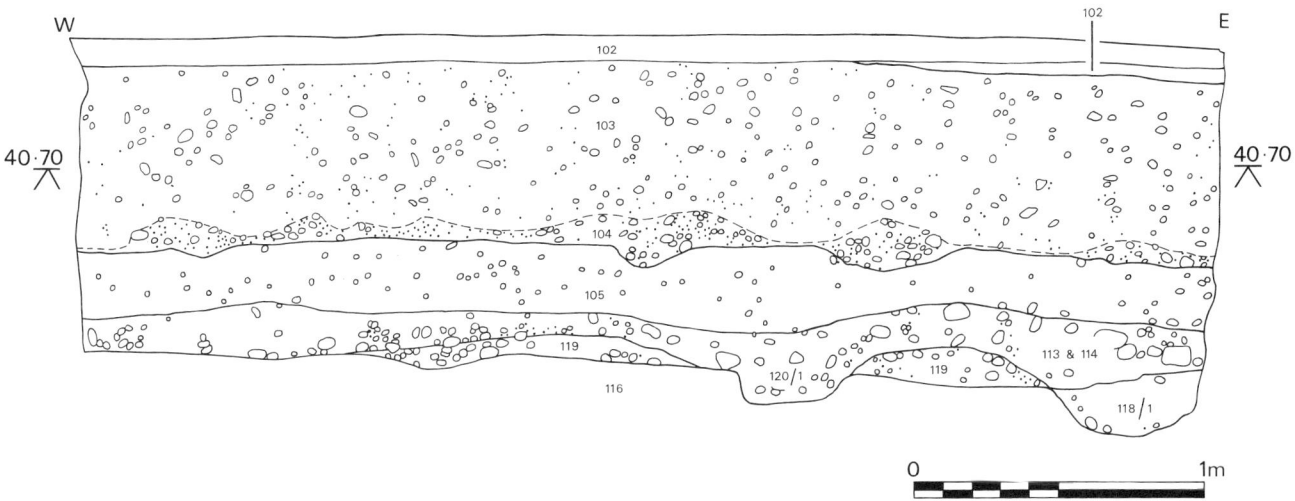

Figure 76 AL 28, trench 1, section, north side

Trench 1 (Fig 76, Plate 9)

The first phase contains pottery consistent with a pre-Hadrianic date and included a number of postholes, a north to south gully (*118*) and a north-west to south-east one (*120*). This was sealed in phase 1.2 by a sandy-silt deposit (*113/114*) probably dumped from elsewhere, also apparently of pre-Hadrianic date. Phase 1.3 opened with a clay dump, some of it apparently burnt, which was cut by a series of pits and postholes and its pottery seems to suggest it spanned from the Hadrianic period to the early 3rd century. Phase 1.4 succeeds this and consisted of a gravel surface surrounding one of the phase 1.3 post pipes which remained *in situ*.

Trench 2 (Figs 77–78, Plate 10)

The first phase in trench 2 consisted of a gully (**224**) aligned roughly north to south and a pit/posthole (**227**) (Figs 77a and 78). This was succeeded in phase 2.2, apparently of Flavian–Trajanic date, by a truncated beam slot (**222**) aligned approximately east–west with a ditch (**223**) running parallel just to its north (Figs 77b and 78). This in turn was suc-

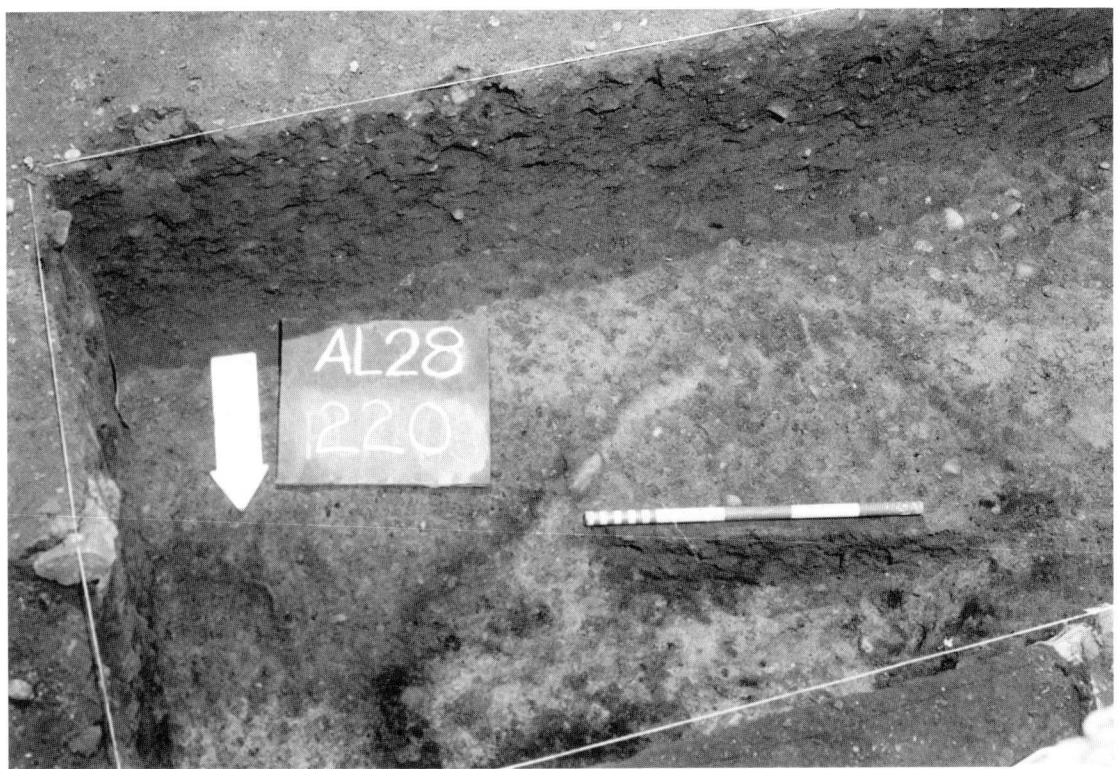

Plate 10 Trench 2, clay-lined oven 220 (AL 28)

1988 Baromix excavations (AL 28)

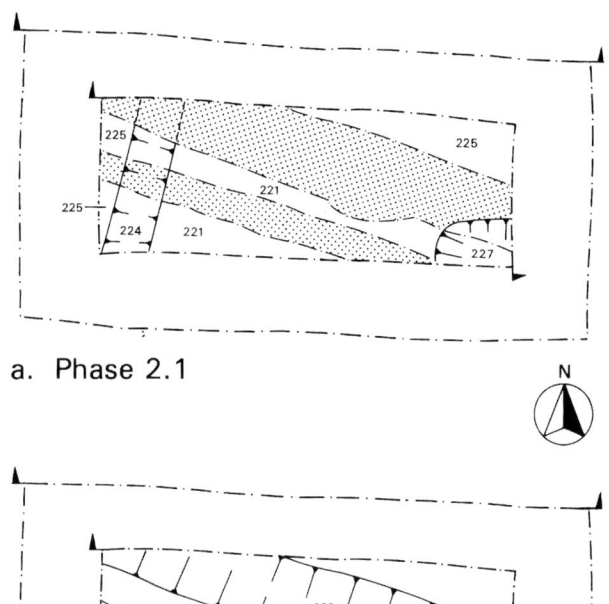

a. Phase 2.1

b. Phase 2.2

c. Phase 2.3

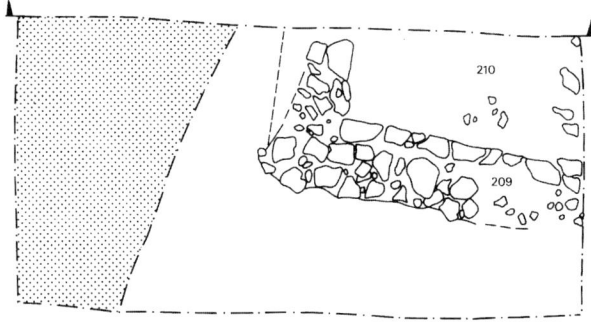

d. Phase 2.5

 Later cuts

Figure 77   AL 28, trench 2, phases 2.1, 2.2, 2.3, and 2.5, plans

ceeded in phase 2.3 by a clay-lined oven (**220**), aligned approximately east to west with a stakehole to the east dug into the fill of ditch **223** and containing material consistent with a Flavian–Trajanic date (Fig 77c, Plate 10). These features were sealed by a levelling dump in phase 2.4, which was in turn cut by stone-packed postholes of Hadrianic–Antonine date. Following this the corner of a stone-founded building was constructed (phase 2.5), the corner of which was present in the north-east end of the trench (Fig 77d). This building was also aligned roughly north to south and east to west and must have been located close to the north–south street identified in ALC 69 (street D, Fig 3). It presumably dated to the later 2nd or 3rd century, containing no dating evidence later than that from phase 2.4. After this phase the site stratigraphy had been truncated and the only later feature was a north-east to south-west ditch *212* cutting across the west end of the trench containing 14th/15th-century ceramics.

Trench 3

The first phase in trench 3 is represented by a large irregular pit, 311. This was succeeded (phase 3.2) by a clay dump, which was possibly a floor level. Phase 3.2 was followed by an east–west gully, (310), containing BB1 consistent with a Hadrianic–Antonine date (phase 3.3). After this a gravel surface (306) was laid down. This was cut by a north–south gully (305) along the west side of the trench and by a pit (308). At this point the sequence was truncated by later disturbances.

Trench 4 (Fig 79)

The first phase in trench 4 was represented by a pit (*424*) which was succeeded by a clay layer, possibly a floor-level, cut by a posthole. This in turn was sealed by a clay deposit (*421*) cut by stone-packed postholes (phase 4.4). Phase 4.5 consisted of a dump layer (*413*) with the edge of a mortar floor in the south-east corner of the trench and a number of postholes. It contained samian dating to the later 2nd century. This was succeeded by a further dump layer (*415*) cut by a row of stone-packed postholes running roughly north to south (phase 4.6). After this the sequence was truncated.

Discussion

The sequences from the AL 28 trenches suggest that up to three phases of pre-Hadrianic activity were present on the site with features aligned approximately north to south and east to west, like those on the ALC 69 and ALC 72/2 sites to the north. These and the oven, a type of feature less common on civil sites, and the find of military metalwork (see

1988 Baromix excavations (AL 28)

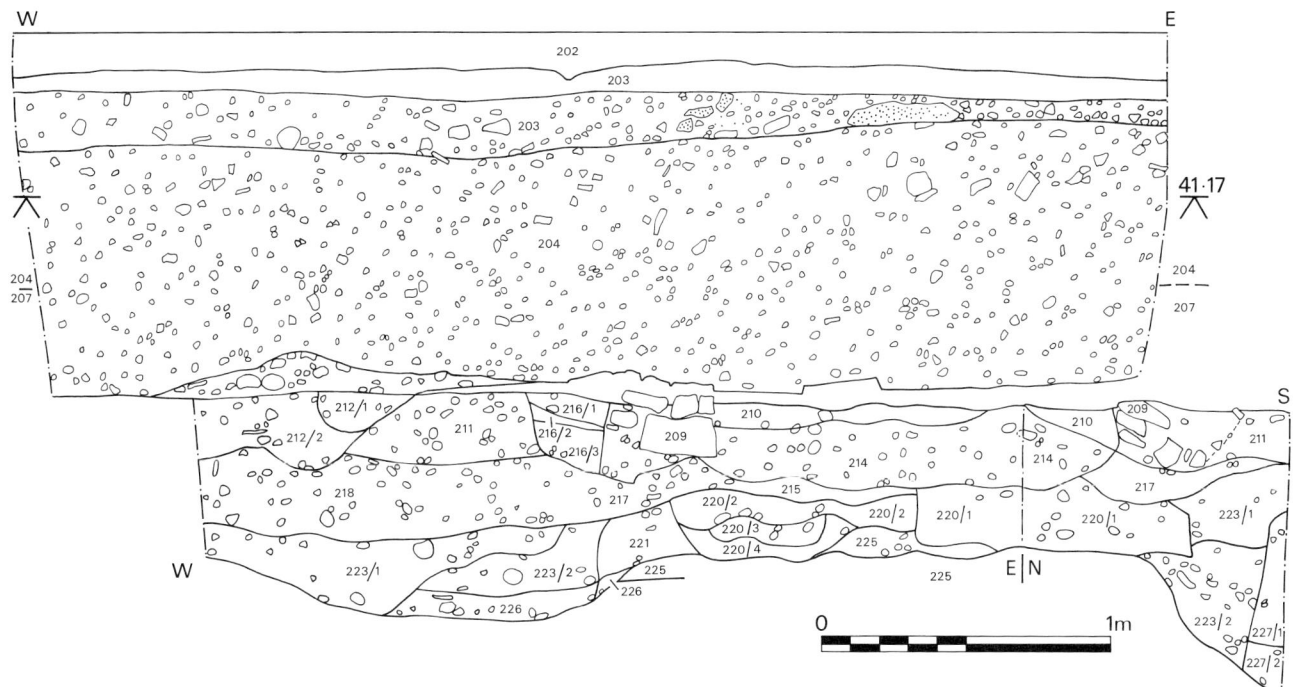

Figure 78   AL 28, trench 2, section, north side

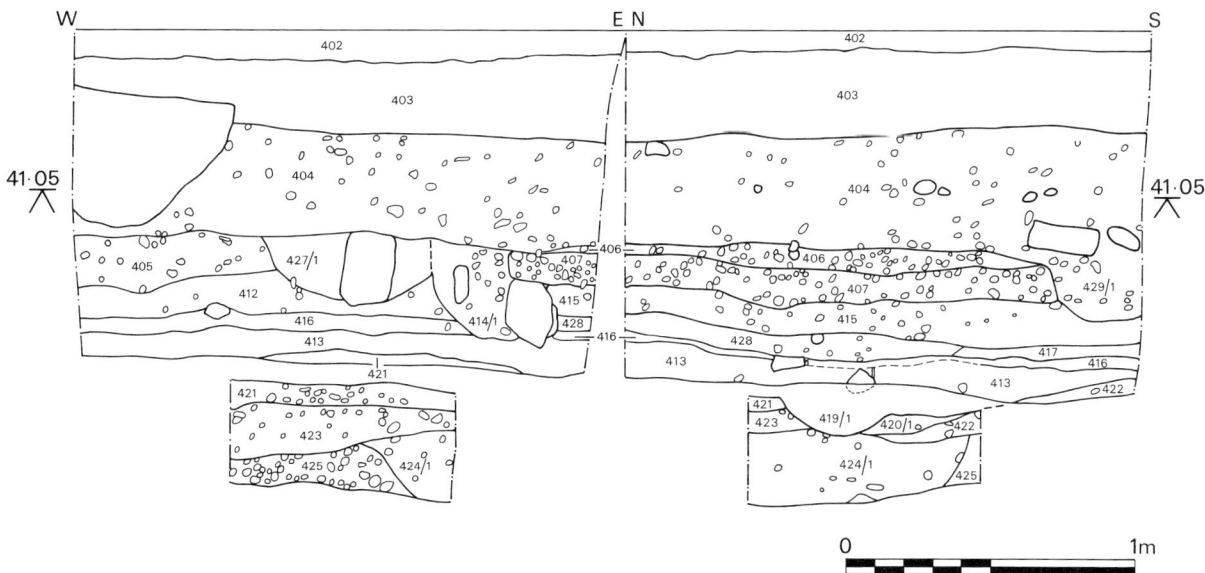

Figure 79   AL 28, trench 4, sections, north and east sides

Lloyd-Morgan below) all suggest a similar archaeology here to that found on the ALC 69 and ALC 72/2 sites. The Hadrianic and later phases also suggest similarities with the ALC 69 sequence with 2nd-century timber buildings, succeeded at one point by a masonry-founded structure probably of the later 2nd–3rd centuries, but with no clear evidence of 4th-century activity. Although the truncation of the stratigraphy undoubtedly partly explains the latter phenomenon, the lack of pits and foundation trenches of that date is notable and the pottery collection does not include any quantity of residual material of that date, as might have been expected if it had been present.

Roman coin (AL 28)
Wilfred A Seaby

1 Vespasian (AD 69–79) *As* (AD 72–3), Rome mint, *Obv* IMP. CAESAR VESPASIAN. AUG. IIII, Laureate head right, *Rev* Eagle on globe, head right, S-C. *RIC* II, p 77, 528(b). (SF 4, 211, phase 2.4)

1988 Baromix excavations (AL 28)

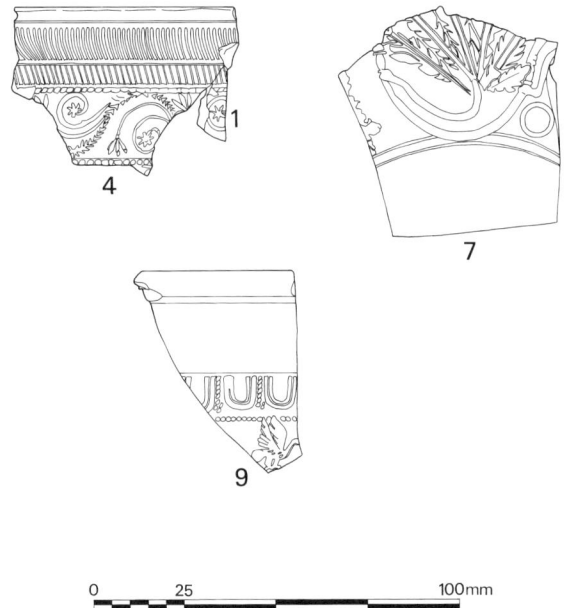

Figure 80   Decorated samian ware (AL 28), nos 1, 4, 7, and 9 (1:2)

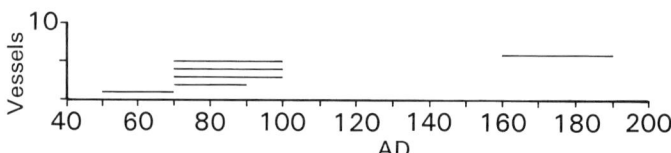

Figure 81   AL 28, phases 1.1–1.2, 2.1–2.3, and 4.1–4.3

The somewhat worn condition might suggest loss about the end of the 1st century.

Roman pottery (AL 28)
Jeremy Evans and Margaret Ward

Introduction

Some 1540 sherds of Roman pottery were excavated from the AL 28 trenches, 391 sherds of which were from pre-Hadrianic contexts. The material from the pre-Hadrianic, possibly military, contexts was fully recorded using the Warwickshire Museum fabric series and coding system, as comparatively little material from groups of this date has been published from the town. Later material has only been examined to provide dating evidence, and only key pieces and those of intrinsic interest are illustrated. The full site samian list has, however, been catalogued in order to provide as much information as possible about the early occupation. The fabric types are described in Table MT1, microfiche M1:A5–A13).

Samian ware (AL 28)
Margaret Ward

The archive includes a complete record of all the samian ware recovered from this excavation. The catalogue here has been selected according to stratigraphic value, intrinsic interest, or relevance to the subject of survival. Vessels are listed in order of phase, context, form, and fabric. The abbreviations SG, CG, and EG are used to denote South Gaulish, Central Gaulish, and East Gaulish origin; ind denotes a sherd of indeterminate form. For terminology, see Bulmer 1979.

A quantified summary of the samian from each phase is provided in tables recording forms and fabrics, and in line-diagrams summarising the chronological spread of the material (Figs 81–83). The collection is also summarised on Fig 84, a histogram illustrating all the vessels from the site according to their date of manufacture. All the samian from the site has been used to produce this histogram, as it was felt that some form of graphic representation was desirable, despite the drawbacks of using such imprecisely dated material. Maximum numbers of vessels have been given, for experience has shown that estimation of minimum numbers of vessels based on small fragments is little more than guesswork

Catalogue (Fig 80)

Phases 1.1–1.2, 2.1–2.3, and 4.1–4.3

1 SG Dr 29 In the upper zone a winding scroll was neatly moulded, with terminals composed of seven-petalled rosettes and

Table 11 Samian forms and fabrics,
AL 28 phases 1.1–1.2, 2.1–2.3, and 4.1–4.3
(maximum number of vessels)

Fabric	31	27	35 or 36	29	37	Total
SG	–	1	1	2	1	5
CG	1	–	–	–	–	1
Total	1	1	1	2	1	6

trifid motifs. The leafy element of the scroll consists of a series of linked festoons, used in a similar arrangement on bowls in the OFBASSICOEL style (see Knorr 1952, Taf 10E). Neronian. The single tiny fragment from (114) is unburnt; it adjoins a large rimsherd from (111/1), no 4 below, which appears burnt. (illus) (114)

2 SG Dr 29 Upper zone: diagonal wavy lines enclosed blurred arrowheads (cf Karnitsch 1959, Taf 3.2). Lower zone: one panel included here in the corner a fragment of a scroll motif with a rosette terminal; the panel to the right probably contained a saltire including another set of arrowheads. Probably c AD 70–85 (cf Knorr 1952, Taf 23.A OFFELICIS). A small fragment only. (220/2)

3 CG Dr 31 Stamped, almost certainly [M]ALL[EDO•F] Die 2a of Malledo, a stamp attested at Lezoux. Miss B M Dickinson has kindly noted that site dating for Malledo is slight, but this stamp and one from a different die occur at Wallsend. This evidence, combined with his use of forms such as 31R, 79, 80 (all stamped with 2a), and Ludowici Tx, suggests a mid- to late Antonine range. c AD 160–190. (223/1)

Phases 1.3, 2.4–2.5, 3.1–3.2, and 4.4–4.5

4 SG Dr 29 A rimsherd with decoration; Neronian. Apparently burnt, this piece adjoins a tiny, unburnt fragment from (114) (no 1 above, with which it is illustrated). (111/1)

5 SG Dr 27g A fragment of the basal stamp survives, reading perhaps IVI[Possibly the work of an illiterate potter of the Flavian–Trajanic period. The footring is worn, the upper wall has been sawn away, and a hole has been cut through the stamp. (111/2)

6 CG Dr 30 A rather orange rimsherd with rouletted decoration. Probably a product of Central Gaul (where the rouletted bowls of this sort were often in an orange ware) and perhaps Hadrianic to early Antonine in manufacture. (111/2)

7 CG Dr 37, with an orange-red slip. Part of a large winding scroll: for the large leaf, see *Rogers* H24. The blurred binding is probably the astragalus *Rogers* R14. There is also a fragment of an unidentifiable leaf at the bottom left of the sherd. The style appears to be that of Cinnamus rather than one of the Hadrianic potters, and may belong to the period c AD 140–160 or 170. (illus) (211)

8 CG Dr 37 The fabric indicates origin at Les Martres-de-Veyre. Above a basal beadrow lies a fragment only of a wreath (*Rogers* G370 or similar). c AD 100–130. A small, battered fragment. (305/1)

Phases 1.4, 2.6

CG Curle 11 rimsherd; Trajanic–Hadrianic. (104)
Two SG ind fragments; Flavian–Trajanic. (212/2)

Unstratified material

9 CG Dr 37 Ovolo with a beaded, rosette-tipped tongue (*Rogers* B22?) above a neat beadrow (*Rogers* A2). Below flies a bird, apparently Oswald 2318 although Oswald lists this as East Gaulish. Ovolo B22 was used by Acaunissa. This sherd was probably manufactured c AD 125–150. (illus) (304)

Summary of the samian collection (AL 28)

The collection of 66 sherds consisted of mere fragments with few distinctive features. Consequently, the maximum number of vessels (64) may be taken to be an over-estimate. Of this, the South Gaulish vessels formed 57.8%, the Central Gaulish vessels formed only 40.6%, and the single East Gaulish sherd 1.6%. Only one vessel was certainly of pre-Flavian origin (see no 1 above), although two other sherds from contexts (111/1) and (309) could be dated only loosely as Neronian–Flavian. Most of the remaining SG sherds could not be dated more precisely than to the Flavian–Trajanic period. These included the stamped cup, no 5 above, which had been sawn down for reuse in some secondary function; it appears that the stamp had also been cut through. Of the CG vessels, four (15%) probably originated at Les Martres-de-Veyre in the Trajanic–Hadrianic period; none of these four was found in the earliest contexts on the site. However, from a context presumed to be Flavian–Trajanic, (223/1), came an intrusive stamped dish, no 3, which was certainly a product of the Antonine era. In a later context, one decorated piece

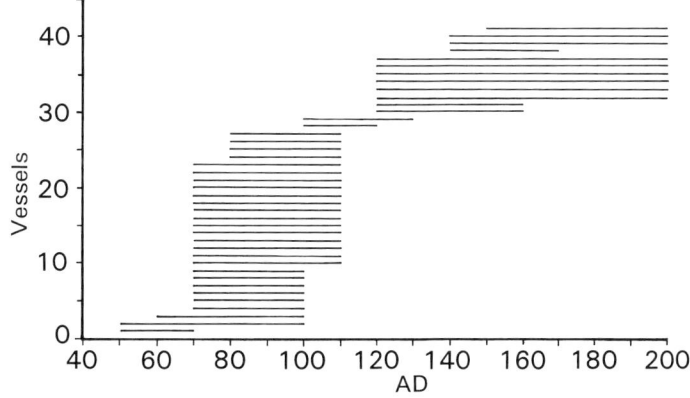

Figure 82 AL 28, phases 1.3, 2.4–2.5, 3.1–3.2, and 4.4–4.5, date distribution of samian ware

1988 Baromix excavations (AL 28)

Table 12 Samian forms and fabrics, AL 28 phases 1.3, 2.4–2.5, 3.1–3.2, and 4.4–4.5
(maximum number of vessels)

Fabric	18	18R	18R or 18/31R	18/31R or 31R	27	33	ind	30	37	67	Total
SG	1	2	1	–	9	–	9	–	4	1	27
CG	1	–	–	1	–	1	7	1	3	–	14
Total	2	2	1	1	9	1	16	1	7	1	41

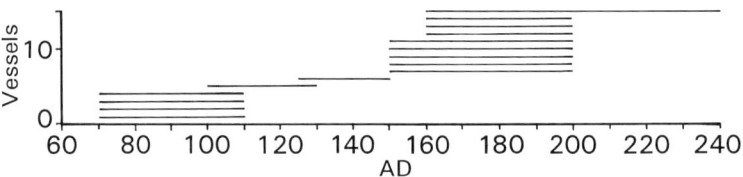

Figure 83 AL 28, unstratified contexts, date distribution of samian ware

Table 13 Samian forms and fabrics, AL 28 unstratified contexts
(maximum number of vessels)

Fabric	C11	31R	33	35	36	Lud Tx	encl	ind	37	Total
SG	–	–	–	1	–	–	1	2	–	4
CG	1	2	1	–	1	1	–	3	1	10
EG	–	–	–	–	–	–	–	1	–	1
Total	1	2	1	1	1	1	1	6	1	15

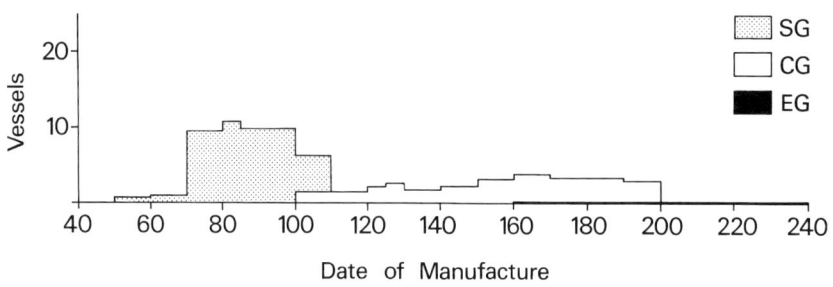

Figure 84 AL 28, date distribution of all samian ware (maximum 64 vessels)

Table 14 Samian forms and fabrics, AL 28 all contexts (maximum number of vessels)

Fabric	C11	18	18R	18R or 18/31R	18/31R or 31R	31	31R	27	33	35	35 or 36	36	Lud Tx	encl	ind	67	29	30	37	Total
SG	–	1	2	1	–	–	–	10	–	1	1	–	–	1	13	1	2	–	4	37
CG	2	1	–	–	1	1	2	–	2	–	–	1	1	–	10	–	–	1	4	26
EG	–	–	–	–	–	–	–	–	–	–	–	–	–	–	1	–	–	–	–	1
Total	2	2	2	1	1	1	2	10	2	1	1	1	1	1	24	1	2	1	8	64

was probably produced in the mid-2nd century by Cinnamus or an associate (no 7). Only five vessels were noted in this collection as certainly originating after c AD 160; of these, four were unstratified. These included, in (207), the one small fragment which was probably an East Gaulish product (possibly a *mortarium*) in the later 2nd or 3rd century. Seven sherds, all of Flavian–Trajanic origin and forming 11% of the total, were burnt.

Other fine ware and coarse ware fabrics (AL 28)
Jeremy Evans

Fig 85 shows a histogram of the major fabric classes from the pre-Hadrianic phases, which may be compared with Figs 21 and 22 from the other Baromix sites, and Table MT8 (microfiche M1:E8) gives the detailed fabric quantification (by sherd count,

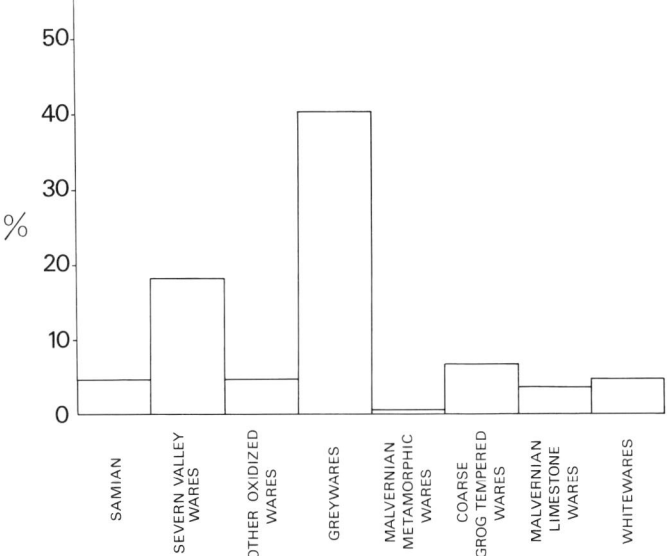

Figure 85   Proportions of major fabric classes from pre-Hadrianic phases (AL 28)

weight, minimum numbers of rims, and RE) for the group. As is the case on the other Baromix sites grey wares provide over 50% of the assemblage at this date, with quite a high proportion of rustic wares amongst these, some 8% of sherds from the grey ware group being recorded as bearing rusticated decoration. Four main fabrics make up the bulk of this section of the assemblage, R21, R31, R32, and R93. R21 is a coarse sand-tempered rustic ware fabric with some organics, visually identical to material from the Tiddington kiln site, although material from other sources may be included in the group. R31 is a handmade reduced organically tempered storage jar fabric commonly found on 1st- and 2nd-century sites in Alcester and Tiddington and recovered in small quantities as far as Hereford (V Buteux and J Evans pers comm). R32 is a similar organically tempered grey ware, possibly from the same source, mainly exemplified in a range of small jars. R93 is a fabric group isolated on this site (the contents of which might previously have been assigned to the R1/R41 sand-tempered groups) consisting of a well-burnished sandy blackware, often with oxidised margins, present in a range of carinated dish and bowl forms.

Amphorae are not well represented in the group, c 2% by sherd count, all being Dressel 20 bodysherds. Calcareously tempered fabrics are represented by c 3% of the Malvernian Paleozoic Limestone-tempered ware, of mid- to late 1st-century date, and have also been noted at the Lloyds Bank site (see below). Non-samian fine wares are only represented by a single sherd of F31, Lyons ware, a fabric often found on military sites and not previously recorded in Alcester.

Samian ware is not well represented at 4.6% by sherd numbers and 1.1% by weight, a marked contrast with similar deposits on the other Baromix sites (Figs 21 and 22).

Heavily gritted fabrics make up around 7% of the assemblage, of which only 0.5% is in Malvernian metamorphic-tempered ware, considerably less than of the Paleozoic Limestone-tempered fabric, and a similar level to that on the other Baromix phases of this date. The commonest fabric in this group is G27, an abundantly grog-tempered handmade storage jar fabric, at around 3% of the assemblage and much of the remainder of the gritted wares is in G42, another grog-tempered fabric. G27 is not common in later Alcester deposits and probably does not extend in use much beyond the end of the 1st century.

Oxidised wares make up around 32% of the assemblage, the vast majority of which comprise Severn Valley wares, principally fabric O21/O36 with common–abundant organic tempering voids. This is the common early Severn Valley ware at Alcester, but ceases to be a significant part of the Severn Valley ware assemblage by the 3rd century (Evans forthcoming), and probably has a fairly local origin. The principal non-Severn Valley oxidised ware is fabric O51, a sandy oxidised fabric visually identical to products from the Tiddington kilns, and this is probably its origin. Only a single vessel form is represented, a reeded-rimmed carinated bowl (no 7 below).

White slipped flagon fabrics make up 1.4% of the group, a reasonable representation, with three fabrics, Q11, Q14, and Q18, being present. There are small quantities of Verulamium region white ware (W11) and Mancetter-Hartshill white ware (W12), and two other white wares W21 and W24, the latter being the most frequently represented.

The fabric proportions from this group are very comparable with those from the two other Baromix sites (see Ferguson above). Both have similar levels of *amphorae*, although calcareously tempered fabrics are a little commoner on the AL 28 site and the wheelmade grog-tempered E fabrics are present on Baromix 1 and 2, but not on AL 28. The larger ALC 69 and ALC 72/2 collections have a wider range of fine wares, with mica-dusted and colour-coated vessels, although these do not include the Lyons ware found on AL 28. The heavily gritted fabrics, group G, are commoner on AL 28, at around 7%, compared with around 2% on ALC 69 and ALC 72/2, in a similar range of fabric types. The higher proportion of these possibly relates to functional variations in the groups with relatively more storage jars in the AL 28 group. Oxidised wares at 25% form a similar proportion of the group to the ALC 72/2 site and a rather higher proportion than on ALC 69. As on those sites, the predominant fabric amongst the Severn Valley wares is O21/O36 and there is a consistent, if fairly low representation of the possible Tiddington oxidised ware, O51, on all three sites. The proportion of reduced wares is similar to that on ALC 69 phases A–E and phase A on ALC 72/2 and the principal fabrics are also similar, with R32 being the commonest fabric on ALC 69 and ALC 72/2. On ALC 69 and ALC 72/2 this tends to be followed by R01 rather than R21 on AL 28, but this difference is more apparent than real, both fabrics being visually very similar and the difference in assignment is likely to be the result of work by different recorders. On both sites these fabrics are mainly represented by waisted rustic ware jars of the type mainly restricted to Warwickshire (Evans 1994).

The presence of reeded-rimmed carinated bowls and Lyons ware in the small AL 28 collection both tend to suggest military connections for the assemblage, as do the collections from ALC 69 and ALC 72/2 (see Ferguson above).

Functional analysis

Table 15 shows the functional composition of the group. Interestingly it is dominated by bowls, mainly samian ware and carinated vessels in fabric R93, with around 40% of jars. Cups and beakers at c 9% are also well represented, but there are no tankards, unusually compared with later groups, whilst dishes are also surprisingly absent.

The predominance of bowls and the fairly high proportion of cups/beakers is unusual in a group of this date when, even in urban assemblages (Millett 1979), the predominant Iron Age type, the jar, usually represents over 50% of assemblages. Such a pattern, however, is reasonably typical of military assemblages (cf Evans 1993 and Evans 2001) and may be found in sophisticated urban contexts. Table 15 may be compared with the contemporary groups from phases A–C on the other Baromix sites (Fig 44) with which it has many similarities. All three sites have low proportions of tankards in this period compared with cups and beakers in contrast to the usual position in the 2nd and 3rd centuries in Alcester, and the proportion of dishes is low on all the sites compared with later periods. The level of bowls on the AL 28 site is high when compared with the other two sites and the level of jars is in the lower part of the range found on ALC 69 and ALC 72/2, which itself is low when compared with the Explosion site (Ferguson, below).

Catalogue of illustrated vessels (Fig 86, nos 1–29)

From pre-Hadrianic contexts

1 A waisted-necked reduced rustic ware jar with squarish, everted rim, burnished bands on rim and neck (fabric R93). Later 1st to early 2nd century (115, phase 1.1)
2 Bead-rimmed jar in Malvernian Paleozoic Limestone-tempered ware (fabric C22), mid- to late 1st century AD (115, phase 1.1)
3 Slightly bead-rimmed carinated (?) beaker/ small jar (fabric R93) (115, phase 1.1)
4 Small fine white ware everted rimmed jar, rim and exterior burnished (fabric W21) (117, phase 1.1)
5 Carinated dish (fabric R93), interior and exterior burnished, cf Wall, Gould 1966, Fig 12, no 54, Neronian. (118, phase 1.1)
6 A bead-rimmed jar in Malvernian Paleozoic limestone ware (fabric C22), mid- to late 1st century (Jane Evans pers comm) (114, phase 1.2)
7 An everted rimmed jar with ovoid rim (fabric R21) (114, phase 1.2)
8 A reeded-rimmed carinated bowl rim (fabric O51), Flavian–Trajanic (113, phase 1.2)
9 A rather vertical rimmed jar (fabric R01), possibly an early globular rustic ware jar rim (113, phase 1.2)
10 A rounded everted grey ware jar rim (fabric R52) (113, phase 1.2)
11 An S-bend medium-mouthed necked jar (fabric R32) (114, phase 1.2)
12 A slightly bead-rimmed carinated(?) beaker/small jar (fabric R93) (114, phase 1.2)
13 Medium-mouthed necked jar with everted, almost horizontal rim (fabric R32). Rim and exterior burnished (113, phase 1.2)
14 Everted jar rim, burnished on top (fabric R93) (113, phase 1.2)
15 Carinated dish (fabric R93), interior and exterior burnished, cf Wall, Gould 1966, Fig 12, no 54, Neronian (114, Ph1.2)
16 Carinated bowl (fabric R93), interior and exterior burnished (114, phase 1.2)
17 Carinated dish (fabric R93), interior and exterior burnished, cf Wall, Gould 1966, Fig 12, no 54, Neronian (114, Ph1.2)
18 Wide-mouthed everted rimmed storage jar with slight internal groove (fabric R93) (223, phase 2.2)
19 Bowl rim with grooved top, cf Darling 1977, Fig 6.11, no 8, (fabric O13) (223, phase 2.2)
20 Bowl (?) rim (fabric R32) (223, phase 2.2)
21 A cordoned rimmed lid rim (fabric R93) (223, phase 2.2)
22 Everted jar rim (fabric R32), burnished (220, phase 2.3)
23 A jar base in a reduced fabric (R81) burnished with a zone of well cut grooves over which is an applied decoration of ring and dot in barbotine (cf Evans 1990, motif D). The vessel is rather large for a ring and dot beaker although none of the poppyhead beakers illustrated by Tyers (1978) has barbotine ring decoration. The grey ware examples are generally a little later than the white ware and oxidised ones, perhaps c AD 60–80 (421, phase 4.3)
24 A grey ware lid with grooved rim (fabric R21) (419, phase 4.4)

Table 15 Functional analysis of vessels from pre-Hadrianic deposits (AL 28)

Storage jars	Jars	Bowls	Dishes	Cups and beakers	Tankards	Lids	Mortaria	Amphorae
3%	38%	44%	0%	9%	–	6%	–	–

n = 34 (n = the total minimum number of rims)

1988 Baromix excavations (AL 28)

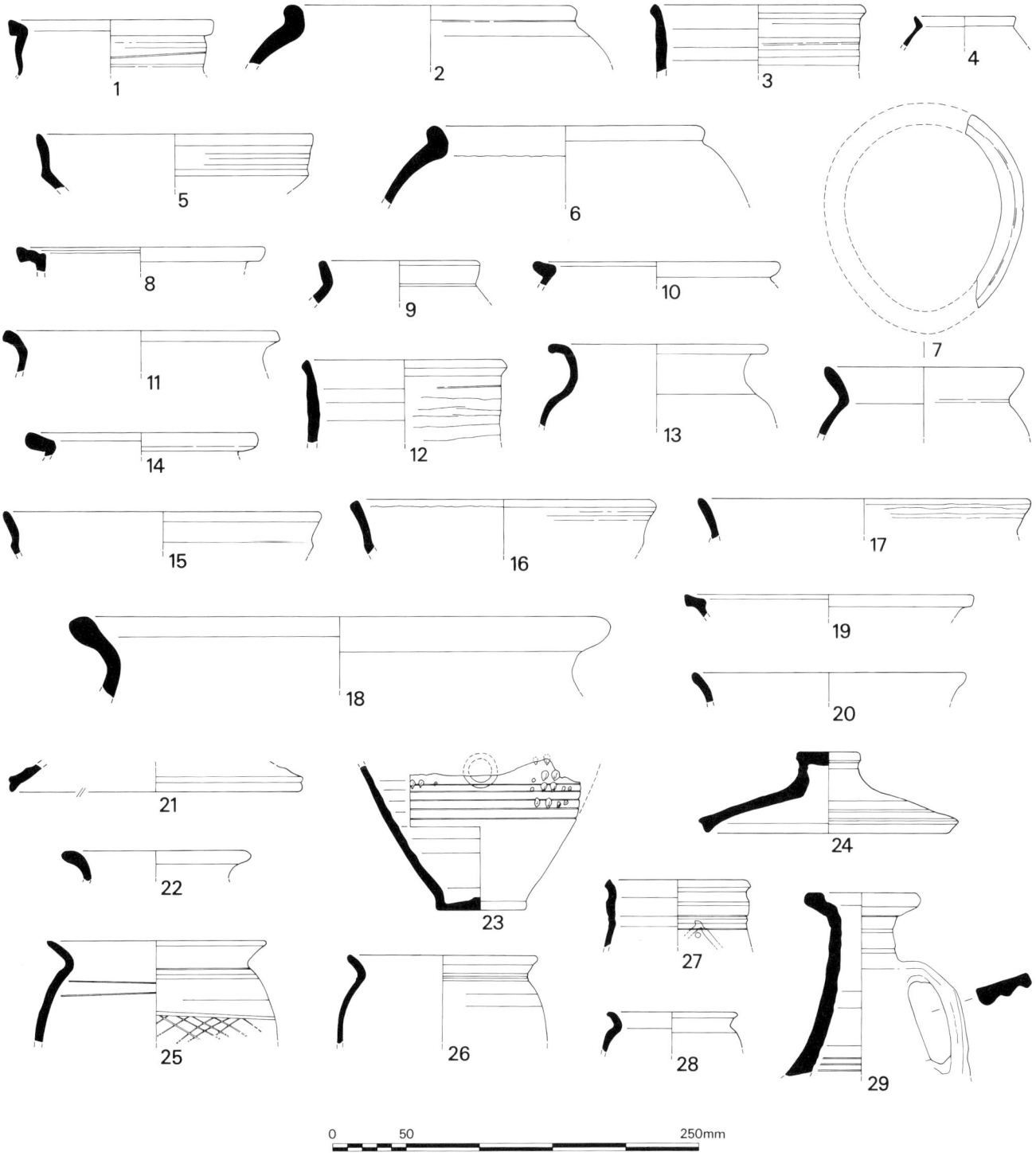

Figure 86 Coarse pottery (AL 28), nos 1–29

Other illustrated vessels

25 A BB1 jar with obtuse lattice decoration, cf Gillam 1976, no 9, mid- to late 3rd century (109, phase 1.3)

26 A local(?) grey ware everted rimmed jar copying Hadrianic–Antonine BB1 vessels (211, phase 2.4)

27 A white ware bowl copying Dr 29/30 with an orange iron-rich slip painted decoration. Oxfordshire white ware (fabric W13), Young 1977, type W53, late 1st to early 2nd century. (211, phase 2.4)

28 A BB1 miniature jar rim, cf Gillam 1976, no 17, later 2nd century (215, 2.4)

29 An internally ledged complete flagon neck with triple-ribbed strap handle (fabric W11) Verulamium region white ware. The breaks show clearly that the rim and neck have been thrown sepa-

1988 Baromix excavations (AL 28)

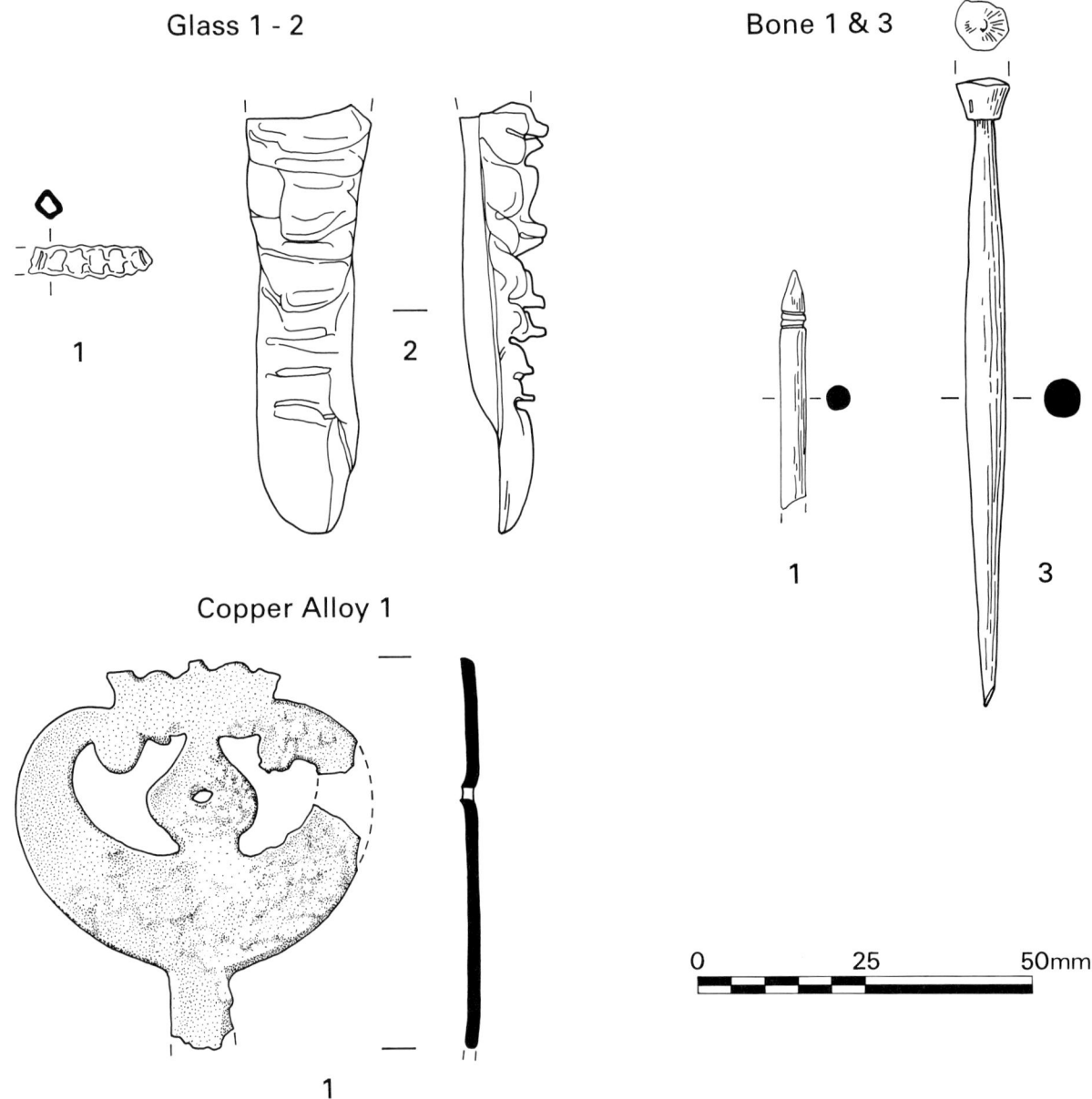

Figure 87 Glass, nos 1–2; copper alloy, no 1; and worked bone, nos 1 and 3 (AL 28)

rately and then luted onto the body. The type appears absent from London, Tyers 1983 (308, phase 3.4)

Glass (AL 28)
Glenys Lloyd-Morgan

(Fig 87, nos 1–2)

1 Small segmented blue glass bead, with around seven surviving segments, now in two adjoining pieces. Length 18.4mm, max diam 4.6mm × 3.9mm. (illus) (SF 1, 208, phase U/S)

Guido notes that the overall date range for the type is from the 2nd to 4th centuries AD (1978, 91–3, Fig 1, schedule of finds on 201–4). In her discussion of the beads from Catsgore, Somerset, she states that they were rare in the earlier Roman period and mostly belong to the 3rd and 4th centuries (in Leech 1982, 134, Fig 93, no 15). A further example from Shakenoak, Oxon, is described as coming from a 'late Roman context' (Brodribb *et al* 1978, 93, no 298, Fig 39). An unpublished, incomplete piece was found at the Grimstock Hill Temple, Coleshill, Warwickshire, GH 1978, SF 54.

2 Fragment of the lower part of the handle of a conical or bulbous jug of blue green glass with a long neck (Isings forms 52b and 55), including a fragment of the side of the vessel to which it is still attached, and decorated with a pincered rail of teeth. Length 61.6mm, max width 19.2mm. (illus) (SF 3, 405, phase 4.6)

Compare the similar fragments from the *canabae legionis* at Nijmegen (Isings 1980, 302, no 226, Fig 12, no 9); and from Verulamium, where a date range of AD 55–150 was suggested, though the piece came from a slightly later context dated AD 160–200 (Charlesworth in Frere 1984, 163, no 198, Fig 66, no 92, see p 162 for dating); and Canterbury where the date range for fragments of this type is given as *c* AD 60–150 (Frere *et al* 1987, 227, no 39, fig 90).

3 One blue-green glass vessel body fragment. (211, phase 2.4)

Copper alloy (AL 28)
Glenys Lloyd-Morgan

(Fig 87, no 1)

1 Openwork military pendant or fitting of pelta-shaped design with central ivy leaf motif, pierced in the centre for attachment to a backing or strap(?). The upper flange with narrow rectangular cross-section, possibly for suspension, is broken. The lower section is not quite symmetrical. Present height 55.4mm, max width c 53mm, thickness c 2.2mm. (SF 6, 111/3, phase 1.3)

The piece may be related to the simple lunular pendants with small leaf-pendant suspended from the centre of the lower, concave, edge, as for instance noted by Bishop (1987, 118, Fig 6) and the complete piece with a suggested 1st-century date from Richborough (Cunliffe 1968, 97, plate XXXIX, no 146). Compare also the pelta-shaped plaques and fittings from the German *Limes* area noted by Oldenstein (1976, 178–184, Taf 53–54), and the related unprovenanced piece from Richborough (Cunliffe 1968, 96, plate XXXVIII, no 31). Compare the slightly larger lunular fitting from Alcester, Birch Abbey 1965 (Lloyd-Morgan in Cracknell and Mahany 1994, no 146) which has a rectangular cross-sectioned shaft in one piece with the crescent-shaped head.

Worked bone (AL 28)
Glenys Lloyd-Morgan

(Fig 87, nos 1 and 3)

1 Incomplete bone pin, being the upper section only, with a narrow conical head with two to three grooves beneath it in the form of a narrow spiral. The tip and most of the shaft is missing. Length 34.1mm, max diam 3.4mm. (illus) (SF 5, 211, phase 2.4)

The pin can be classed as Crummy type 2 with a date range of AD 50–200/250 (1979, 160–161, Fig 1, no 2). One example from Quinton, Northants came from a context dated Claudio-Neronian, c AD 50–60 (Friendship-Taylor 1979, 153, no 549, Fig 70, for the phasing see p 5). Another from Silchester came from a Hadrianic–Antonine context (Fulford 1984, 115, Fig 38, no 4). Examples from Warwickshire include pieces from Tiddington nos TD 81, SF 805; SF M715; SF M716 and SF M721. Other examples from Alcester are from Baromix ALC 69, Lloyd-Morgan no 3 above; the Explosion site, Lloyd-Morgan, nos 213–215 below; and from the Birch Abbey 1964–6 site (Lloyd-Morgan in Cracknell and Mahany 1994, nos 12–18).

2 Tapering lower section of the shaft of a pin or needle, the tip head is now lost. Length 50.3mm. (SF 2, 208, phase U/S)

3 Complete bone pin with head in the form of an inverted truncated cone with a slightly domed upper section. The shaft swells out towards the centre section. Length 91.2mm, max diam head 7mm × 7.4mm. (illus) (404, phase U/S)

Crummy type 3 pin (1979, 161, Fig 1, nos 3 and 4 with date range c AD 200 to late 4th/early 5th century). Compare the example from Balkerne Lane, Colchester 1973–6 (Crummy 1983, 22, Fig 19, no 300), also Tiddington TD 81 SF 880, SF M602 and SF M939.

4 Bone needle, incomplete, broken across lower end of the eye. The point may have been re-sharpened. Length 62.1mm, upper cross-section 3.5mm × 3.1mm. (304A, phase U/S)

Compare the piece from Tiddington, SF M724

Discussion of the AL 28 finds
Jeremy Evans

Overall the impression given by the AL 28 pottery assemblage is of a group with possible military associations from a very similar set of sources to the ALC 69 and ALC 72/2 groups. It seems to have been a fairly functional group, with comparatively little in the way of samian ware and finewares, but has the features of an early military or sophisticated civilian assemblage, with less than 50% of jars in the group. The non-ceramic finds from the site also tend to confirm its military associations: the only copper alloy small find is a military piece (see Lloyd-Morgan above) and the only coin is one of Vespasian which tends to strengthen its military associations (see Evans above).

Lloyds Bank excavations (ALB 75)

Excavations (ALB 75)
Edith Evans and Jeremy Evans

Introduction

Excavations were carried out in the garden of Lloyds Bank, Alcester at the corner of Stratford Road and Bleachfield Street (SP089572) in advance of work on a new car park (Fig 88, Plate 11). The work was carried out between 1 October and 23 December 1975 and was financed by Lloyds Bank and Warwickshire Museum.

The site lies just outside the line of the Roman defences. This closeness to the defended area of the town and the fact that the site is above the normal levels of flooding recorded in modern times raised the possibility that occupation might continue into the 5th century. It was therefore decided to excavate on the east side of the garden, which it was hoped would be beyond any medieval buildings flanking Bleachfield Street. A further objective was to ascertain, if possible, whether the road postulated by Hughes (1960), on the line of Seggs Lane and Swan Street (street E) continued across this area. An area of 4m × 10m was therefore opened adjacent to the east wall of the garden, and later extended towards the north and west, the topsoil in these extensions being removed by machine. A total area of some 268 sq m was excavated to the undisturbed subsoil. After the excavation a watching brief was held on the Bleachfield frontage during the construction of the car park, but this only produced a few modern pits.

Excavation was made difficult by the very dry summer and autumn of 1975, which made it impossible to recognise the medieval features until they cut through the Roman layers. Only after several weeks' heavy rain did it become clear from the sections that they had originated at a higher level.

The excavated area lies on the river gravels of the first–second terrace. At the east and south ends the Roman layers were immediately above the gravels, but at the north and west ends the gravels were overlaid by clay into which the archaeological features were cut.

The archaeological material consists of a series of mainly linear features of Roman date, mostly at the east side, and a number of medieval features which

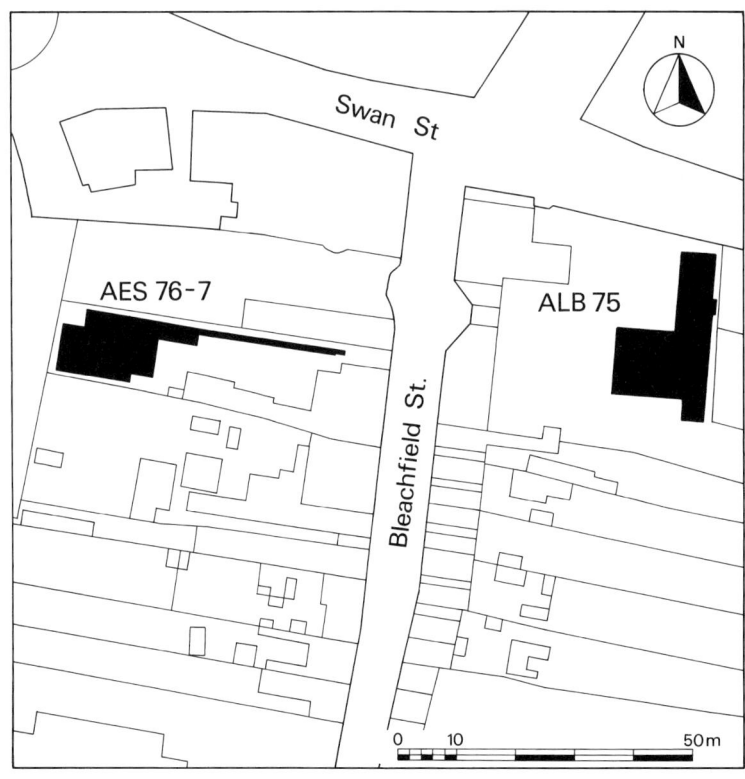

Figure 88   Location of the Lloyds Bank (ALB 75) and the Explosion site (AES 76–7) excavations

Plate 11   General view of excavations (ALB 75)

are mainly concentrated at the west side. The whole of the excavated area had been badly disturbed in modern times, especially at the eastern edge where a strip averaging rather over a metre in width had been removed by a series of 19th-century pits.

Only a summary of the excavations is given here. A detailed structural account can be found in the microfiche (M1:E10–F4). Given the circumstances under which the site was excavated it is not intended that this account report fully upon the finds assemblage (summary lists of finds from phased features are given in microfiche (M1:F5–F6), but only upon those pieces which are of intrinsic interest or which provide dating evidence for the main sequence. Finds providing dating evidence all come from cut features (all of which are phased), finds from the horizontal stratigraphy being contaminated by cuts of later features not observed until a later stage. The original excavation report, together with the site notebooks, plan archive, and finds are deposited in the Warwickshire Museum.

In the report each feature type is given its own number sequence (eg Ditch 1). Fills in the finds section and in the detailed description on microfiche are further referenced by an area code (Area I or II, as on the plans), an original feature number and an original fill number in brackets (eg II 5 (4b)).

Phase I (Fig 89, Plate 12)

This primary phase saw the laying out of boundaries which remained in use throughout the Roman period and beyond. A property line was defined by the end of a beam slot (**Beam Slot 1**) and **Postholes 1** and '**a**' which continue this alignment. Probably intersecting with this, at approximately 90 degrees, is a wide shallow gully (**Gully 1**).

Other features of this phase are **Gully 2**, which runs approximately parallel to **Beam Slot 1** about 7m to its south-west and, perhaps, **Posthole** '**b**' and **Pit 5**. To the north of **Beam Slot 1** a well (**Well 1**) seems to have been used briefly (Plate 12). The phase probably dates to the Neronian–Flavian or Flavian–Trajanic eras.

Phase II (Figs 91 and 92, Plate 13)

This phase, which is not closely dated but probably belongs in the later 2nd to early 3rd century, saw the reconstruction of the northern boundary with the digging of a wall trench (**Wall 1**) on the north side of **Beam Slot 1**. The line of the phase I **Gully 1** seems to have been replaced by **Beam Slot 5** running up to **Wall 1** at approximate right angles. Immediately on the south side of **Wall 1** a well (**Well 2**) was sunk. It was impossible to examine the whole of the well pit as it extended dangerously close to the modern garden wall, but it appeared to be oval in shape with the long axis east–west. At the bottom it was almost square in plan and cut to fit the timber lining almost exactly. The whole pit was 2.15m deep from the lower Roman ground level, of which 1.05m was above the surviving part of the wood lined shaft. This upper part of the pit was filled with mottled green clay. The

Lloyds Bank excavations (ALB 75)

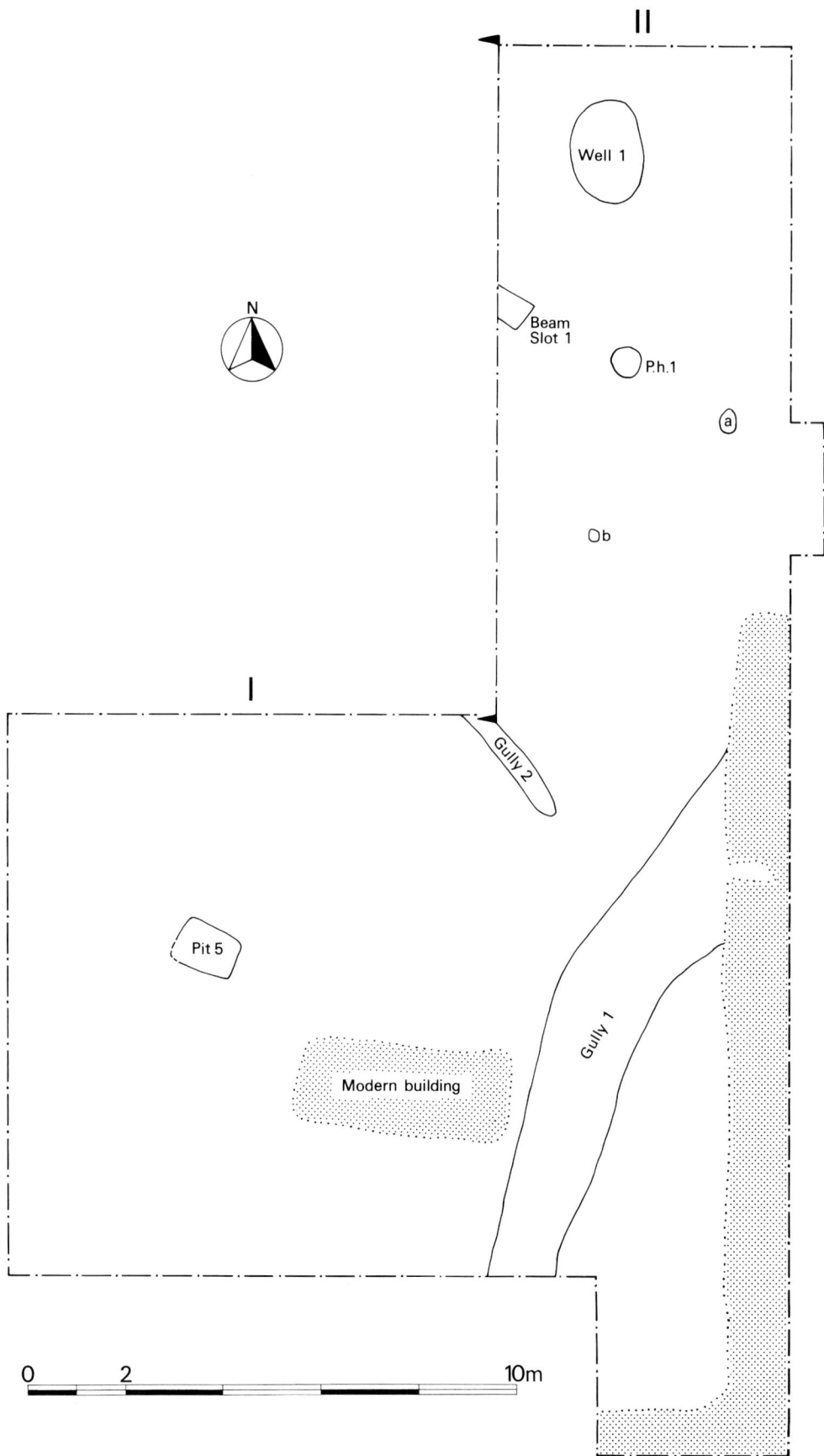

Figure 89   ALB 75, phase I, feature plan

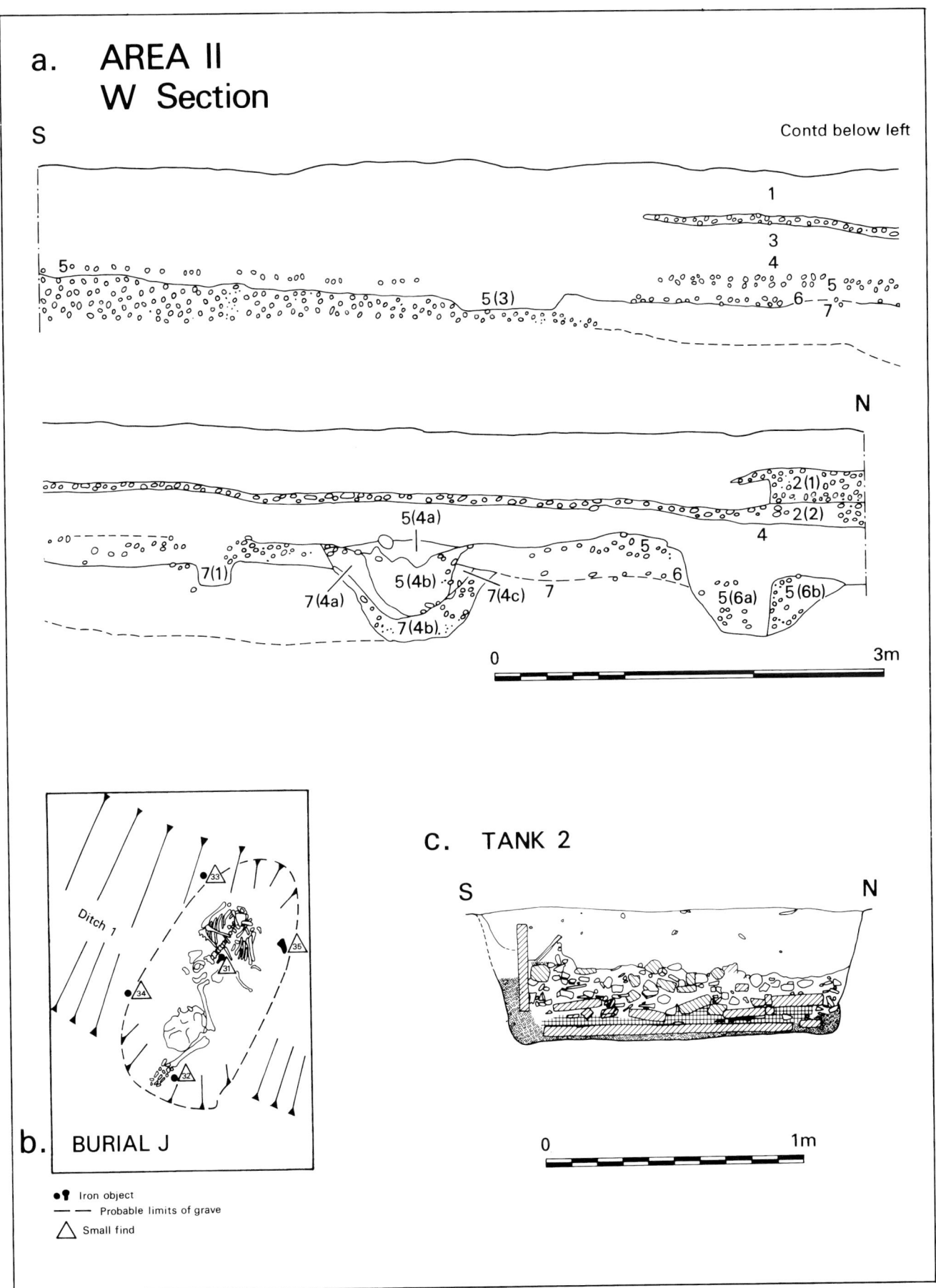

Figure 90 ALB 75: a) area II west section; b) Burial J; c) section of Tank 2

Lloyds Bank excavations (ALB 75)

Plate 12   Well 1, phase I (ALB 75)

timber lining of the shaft survived from just above the water table at the time of excavation (Fig 92 and pl 13). It framed a square of the interior measuring 2 by 2 Roman feet, and the shaft was filled with dark grey, silty clay-loam. Outside the lining, the pit was filled with green clay and gravel.

Three layers of the timber survived more or less intact with the remains of a fourth above. The lining was prefabricated, being made up of oak planks with a roughly wedge-shaped cross-section, and slots cut through from the thicker side for about half the width of the plank. They were assembled in sets of four, so that the slots of the east and west timbers always faced upwards with the north and south timbers fitting down into them. Each set was assembled separately with no connection with those above and below, and appeared to have been wedged into place by large pebbles, especially at the corners. Outside the horizontal timbers, and also apparently for the purpose of keeping them firmly in place, was a set of vertical timbers, one at the north side, one in the north-east side, and three each at the east and south sides. There were none at the west side, but another had fallen in from the south-western corner under the box of horizontal timbers. This fallen timber, the one at the north side, and the northernmost example on the east side, were planks with their bottom ends cut to a point; the other six were just rough pieces of wood hardly shaped at all. These vertical timbers were set at the bottom of the pit and firmed up by packing them around with gravel. They were apparently in place before the horizontal timbers, on the evidence of the fallen upright which could never have been able to fall flat in the bottom if even the lowest set of timbers had been in place, but they could not have been left to stand on their own, as the others would also have fallen in. In addition, if the vertical timbers had represented an earlier lining it would have been easier to pull them out before laying the horizontals, so tightly do the two sets fit together. As

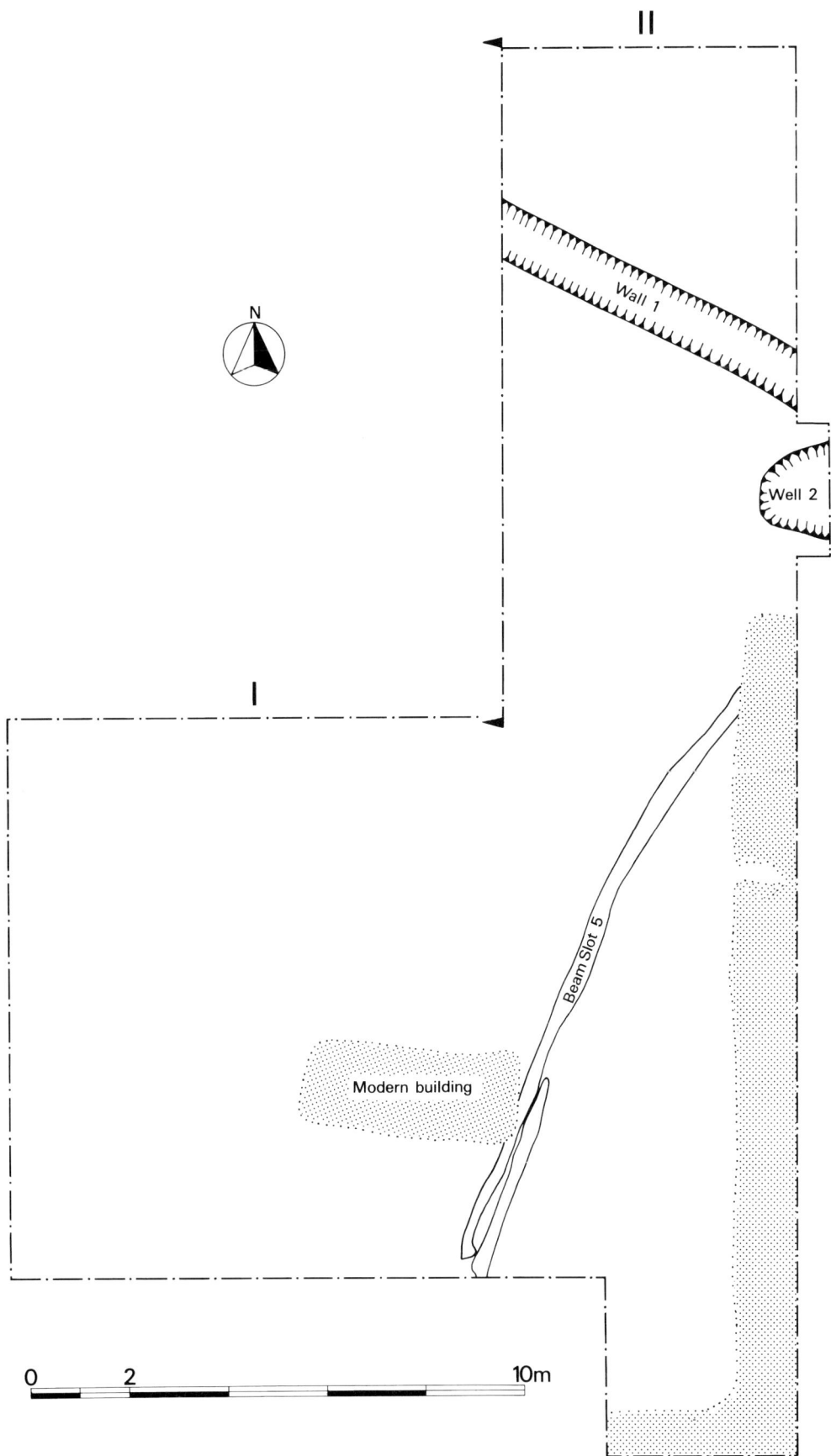

Figure 91   ALB 75, phase II, feature plan

Lloyds Bank excavations (ALB 75)

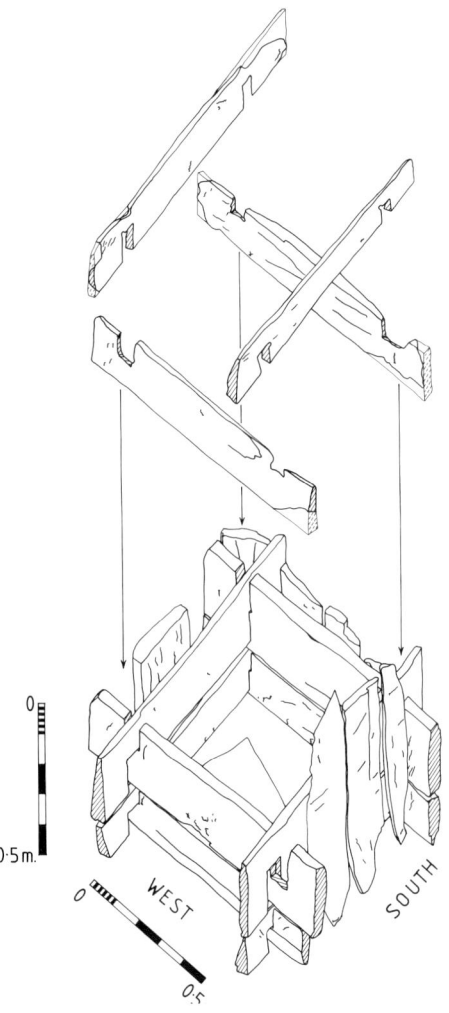

Figure 92   ALB 75, Well 2, timber lining

the bottom of the pit is only just large enough to contain the timbers, it seems probable that the lining was assembled by a man standing in the middle of the pit, building it around him. After the well went out of use, the timbers were presumably robbed down to the water level and the pit filled with clay.

An attempt was made to date the well timbers dendrochronologically, but without success.

Phase III (Fig 93a, Plate 14)

This phase comprises the resurfacing of the area within the property boundaries with gravel and cobbles. Subsequently the line of **Wall 1** was re-cut, probably for another fence line, but this was replaced by **Wall 2** and the line of **Wall 1** was re-cut as a ditch (**Ditch 1**). The line of the phase I **Gully 1** was also refurbished, a little to the east, with the cutting of **Beam Slot 4**.

After **Ditch 1** had silted up for some time two of a series of infant burials were dug into the silting, whilst others were scattered to its south in area II (Plate 14, Burials F and H). This small cemetery amounted to some sixteen inhumation burials and a cremation, Burial A, was in a Severn Valley ware jar (see below, no 33). Another, **Burial J**, contained the remains of two individuals, the principal one probably being a child, aged three–five years, who had been decapitated (Fig 90b).

The re-cutting of **Wall 1** did not precede the late 3rd century, whilst the primary silting of **Ditch 1** contained material with a late 3rd to early 4th-century date range. The silting of **Ditch 1** would

Plate 13   Well 2, phase II (ALB 75)

Plate 14   Burials F and H, phase III (ALB 75)

seem to be in the early 4th century and the cemetery ought, therefore, to commence at this time. Late 3rd- to 4th-century material also comes from **Wall 2** and 4th-century material from **Beam Slot 4**.

Phase IV (Fig 93b)

This phase covers the re-cutting and silting up of **Ditch 1** dating to around the mid-4th century and the accumulation of a deposit over the hollow caused by settlement in the fill of **Well 2** in the late 4th century.

Phase V (Fig 93b)

There is only one feature to this phase, **Beam Slot 2**. **Beam Slot 2** runs parallel and just to the west of **Beam Slot 4** and would seem to be a continuation of this property boundary. **Beam Slot 2** included a collection of Roman pottery of mixed date and a single Saxon style jar rim (see below, no 49): a 6th- or 7th-century date is therefore likely for it.

Phase VI

There is evidence of ploughing over the site in the post-Roman period.

Phase VII (Figs 90c and 94, Plate 15)

Activity in the high medieval period seems to have commenced on the site in the 12th–13th century. A tentative sequence of three structures may be defined, with two stone flagged tanks (Fig 90c, Plate 15, Tank 2) associated with the first, which is dated to

Lloyds Bank excavations (ALB 75)

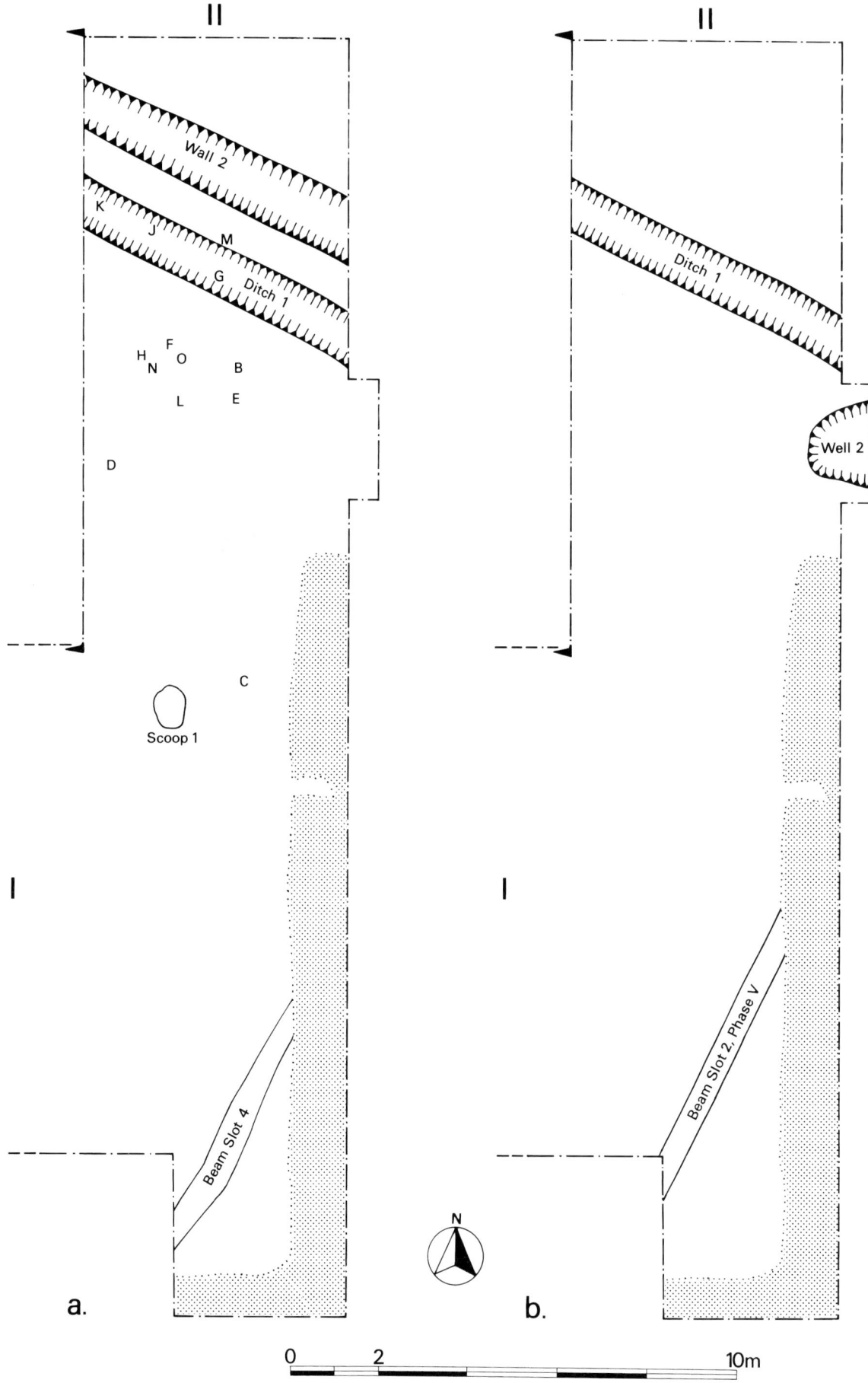

Figure 93   ALB 75: a) phase III, feature plan (A–O are graves); b) phases IV–V, feature plan

Lloyds Bank excavations (ALB 75)

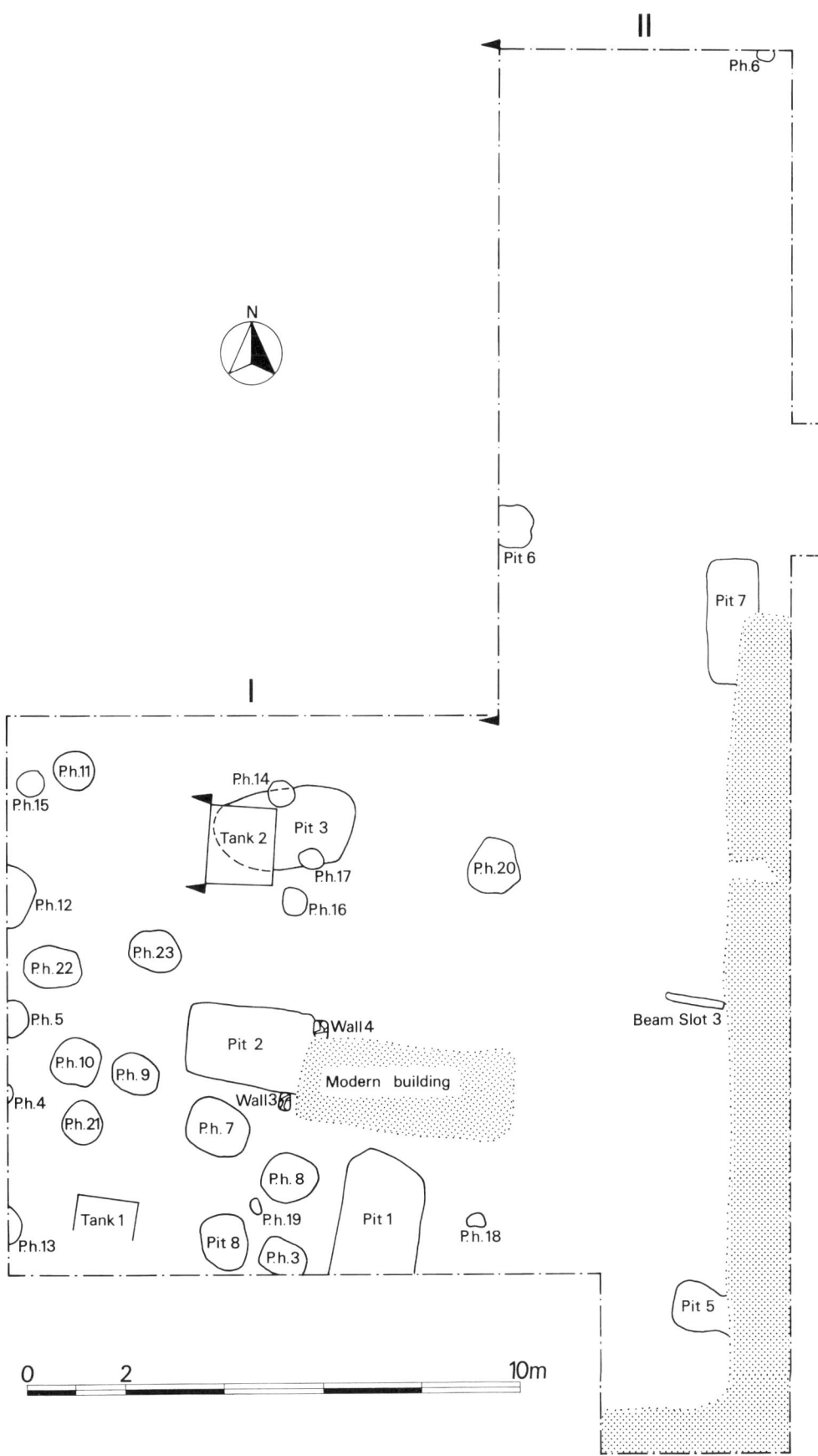

Figure 94   ALB 75, phase VII, feature plan

Lloyds Bank excavations (ALB 75)

Plate 15   Tank 2, phase VII (ALB 75)

the 12th–13th century. These presumably suggest some kind of industrial activity was taking place on the site. The second building phase also seems to date to the 12th–13th century, with the third being perhaps of 13th- to 14th-century date. After this little activity apart from pitting seems to have taken place, presumably with the structures being on the street frontage of Bleachfield Street and the present site being tenement plots.

Discussion
Jeremy Evans

The layout and function of the Lloyds Bank site seems to have remained very much the same from its initial occupation in the 1st century AD throughout the Roman period. Despite its location towards the periphery of the known extent of the town (Figs 2 and 3) the site seems to have originated shortly after the Roman occupation commenced, either in the Neronian or Flavian periods. The principal features of the site would seem to be two property boundaries, one running north-west to south-east at the north end, and the other running south-west to north-east across the south-east corner. The northern boundary seems to have slowly crept northwards, encroaching 4m by the late 3rd century, whilst the eastern one seems to have meandered about the same line until the 6th or 7th century. There is no evidence that the area enclosed by these boundaries was ever more than a yard or other open space, as the preliminary environmental assessment of the insect fauna from **Well 2** suggests for the early to mid-3rd century (P Osborne *in litt*).

In the 4th century the area seems to have been partly used as a small cemetery for infants; this could be regarded as reflecting its marginal location, but infant burials do not seem to have been subject to the same restrictions as those of adults during the Roman period, as the more than 30 neonate or infant burials from within the interior of the fort at Malton, North Yorks, show (Corder 1930). The decapitated burial (Burial J, Figs 90b and 93a) is of note. Clarke (1979, table 40) suggests decapitated burials are a minority rite practised throughout southern Britain, of rural origin, spreading to urban centres in the later 4th century. The cemetery would seem to date to the early to mid-4th century and little activity seems to have taken place on the site within the Roman period after this date. However, the alignment of the phase V **Beam Slot 2** (Fig 93b) suggests that, despite the infant cemetery, the property boundaries were still respected at this time.

The alignment of the property boundaries suggests that they were determined by the road line north from Birch Abbey (Fig 3, street D) and the putative continuation of the Salt Way (street E) intersecting street D. The dating of phase I on the site must suggest that one, or both of these, was laid out in the 1st century.

It is of interest that the eastern boundary on the site, possibly relating to a frontage on the Salt Way (street E), was still being respected in the Saxon period. This is the first evidence of Saxon structural activity from the town. The only other evidence of Saxon occupation so far comes from a sherd of pottery from the Gas House Lane excavations (Ratkai in Cracknell 1996, 97–99) in the defended area and a 7th-century silver bracelet fragment from Bleachfield Street (Savile 1986, 23). The area around the intersection of streets D and E would be a classic location for a *wic* settlement, just outside the late Roman defended area.

After the Saxon occupation, the site would seem to have been ploughland before a sequence of medieval structures occupied the site. Details of these are not clear, but the two associated stone-flagged tanks suggest some industrial activity was taking place in the 12th–13th century.

Lloyds Bank finds (ALB 75)

Pre-Roman and Roman coins (ALB 75)
Wilfred A Seaby

Pre-Roman

1 Copper core of counterfeit coin (?). Early British. Allen's British QB (*c* 40–25 BC perhaps later). Uninscribed uniface stater, probably originally gold-plated but no trace of this now showing. *Convex obv*: blank. *Concave rev*: triple-tailed horse to right; wheel below; pellets, and other symbols in field. Wt 3.75g. Mack 1975, 44, plate IV, no 59 and Van Arsdell 1989, 115, no 216–1 show the gold prototype. (SF 33)

Note: The question of plated coins used as currency, especially in respect of the very high percentage found in Belgic and other Celtic settlements is a vexed one. Whether they were forgeries and tolerated in the main *oppida* or made specifically for market use, as the moulds for blanks from which such coins were struck found at Bagendon, St Albans, Colchester, Silchester, Hengistbury, and elsewhere would seem to suggest, has yet to be determined. Also their exact relationship with the 'official' gold, silver, and potin coins is another matter to be resolved. See, however, D Allen in his contribution on coins of the *Dobunni* (1961), which is chiefly concerned with the methods of production; also J R Collis (1971). Van Arsdell (1989, 31–2) considers all such plated coins as forgeries.

Roman

The Roman coins (2–15) are listed in Table 16. (The post-Roman coins are listed in microfiche M1:F7)

Roman and Saxon pottery (ALB 75)
Jeremy Evans

Phase I (Fig 95, nos 1–11)

Well 1 II 5 (6c)

1 An oxidised butt-beaker rim

Also an everted grey ware jar rim, probably 1st or 2nd century and bodysherds from organically tempered grey ware storage jars (Warwickshire Museum fabric R31), rusticated grey ware bodysherds and Severn Valley ware bodysherds, many organically tempered (Warwickshire Museum fabric O21).

The collection is not large, but there is no BB1 nor any material which needs to be later than the 1st century AD.

Beam Slot 1 II 7 (1)

This contains little material, but includes a grey rusticated bodysherd, a white-slipped oxidised flagon bodysherd, a chip of South Gaulish samian ware (identified by A C King), and two bodysherds with coarse grog temper, of Savernake ware (Booth pers comm confirms the identification).

There is too little material for secure dating, but the material present is not inconsistent with a 1st-century date.

Posthole 1 II 7 (5)

This contains a gritty everted jar rim and an Oolitic limestone-tempered storage jar rim, cross-joining with I 6 (2), together with sherds of Warwickshire Museum fabrics R31, Severn Valley ware, a white ware rouletted bodysherd, probably from a butt-beaker, and a chip of South Gaulish samian (identified by A C King).

This material is not inconsistent with a 1st-century date.

Gully 2 I 4 (23)

This contained a rusticated grey ware bodysherd, two sherds of Severn Valley ware and grey ware, and a buff jar bodysherd with orange-painted linear decoration – not a Mancetter or Oxfordshire product, but probably in the early fine ware tradition (cf Rushden (Woods and Hastings 1984), and Cherry Hinton (Evans 1990)).

None of the material is incompatible with a 1st-century date.

Gully 1 I 5 (26)

2 A Severn Valley ware beaker, cf Webster 1977, nos 59–60, 1st to 2nd century, Warwickshire Museum fabric O21.
3 A slightly carinated jar with thickened rim in a coarsely sand-tempered, wheelmade fabric.
4 A white ware butt-beaker.
5 A Severn Valley ware beaker, cf Webster 1977, nos 38–9, 1st to 2nd century.

Also various sherds of Severn Valley ware, much organically tempered, and fabric R31 storage jar bodysherds. The lack of BB1 and the material present would all seem to suggest a 1st-century date.

Table 16 Roman coins (ALB 75)

No	Ruler	Type	Date	Inscription	Mint	Reference	Context	SF no	Phase
Regular issues									
2	Faustina Junior	Dup	c 145–75	*Rev* Juno.	Rome	*RIC* III (M Aurelius) 1647		SF 7	
3	Gallienus	Ant	260–8 sole reign	*Rev* DIANAE CONS AVG. Antelope	Rome	*RIC* V, Pt I, 181	PostH 9	SF 40	VII
4	Constantine I	Follis	330–5	Urbs Roma/Wolf and twins				SF 1	
5	Constans (as Caesar)	AE 3	335–7	GLORIA EXERCITVS. One standard	Treveri	*LRBC* I, 90.	Tank 2	SF 42	VII
6	Constans (as Augustus)	AE 3	341–6	*Rev* Two Victories	Treveri	*RIC* VIII, p 152/196		SF 2	
7	Constantius II	Cent	353–4	*Rev* FEL. TEMP. REPARATIO Virtus spearing fallen horseman	Arelate	*RIC* VIII, p 219/215	Rubbish pit in top of well 2	SF 16	
8	Constantius II	Cent	?	*Rev* FEL. TEMP.REPARATIO	?Rome SM R	As no 7	PostH 13	SF 23	VII
9	Valentinian I	AE 3	c 367–75	*Rev* SECVRITAS REIPVBLICAE Victory		*RIC* IX p 121/24(a)?	Upper surface	SF 29	
10	Valens	AE 3	367–75	Same type	Lugdunum	*RIC* IX, p 46/21(a)		SF 4	
11	Valens	AE 3	367–75	1s Officina. Same type	Siscia	*LRBC* II. 1417; *RIC* IX, p 147/15(b) but ? mint marks		SF 6	
Contemporary imitations									
12	Barbarous Radiate		–	Head on obverse difficult to identify	–			SF 9	
13	Constantius I	Small barbarous copy of AE 3	–	*Obv* Helmeted bust of Constantinopolis left *Rev* Victory on prow.	–			SF 18	
14	House of Valentinian	Small barbarous copy of AE 3	–	*Rev* SECVRITAS REIPVBLICAE. Victory left.	–			SF 9	
15	House of Valentinian	Minim.very small barbarous copy	–	*Obv* Inscription largely illegible. Tiny diademed head of Emperor to right *Rev* Victory to left with wreath and palm.	–		Upper surface	SF 32	

Lloyds Bank finds (ALB 75)

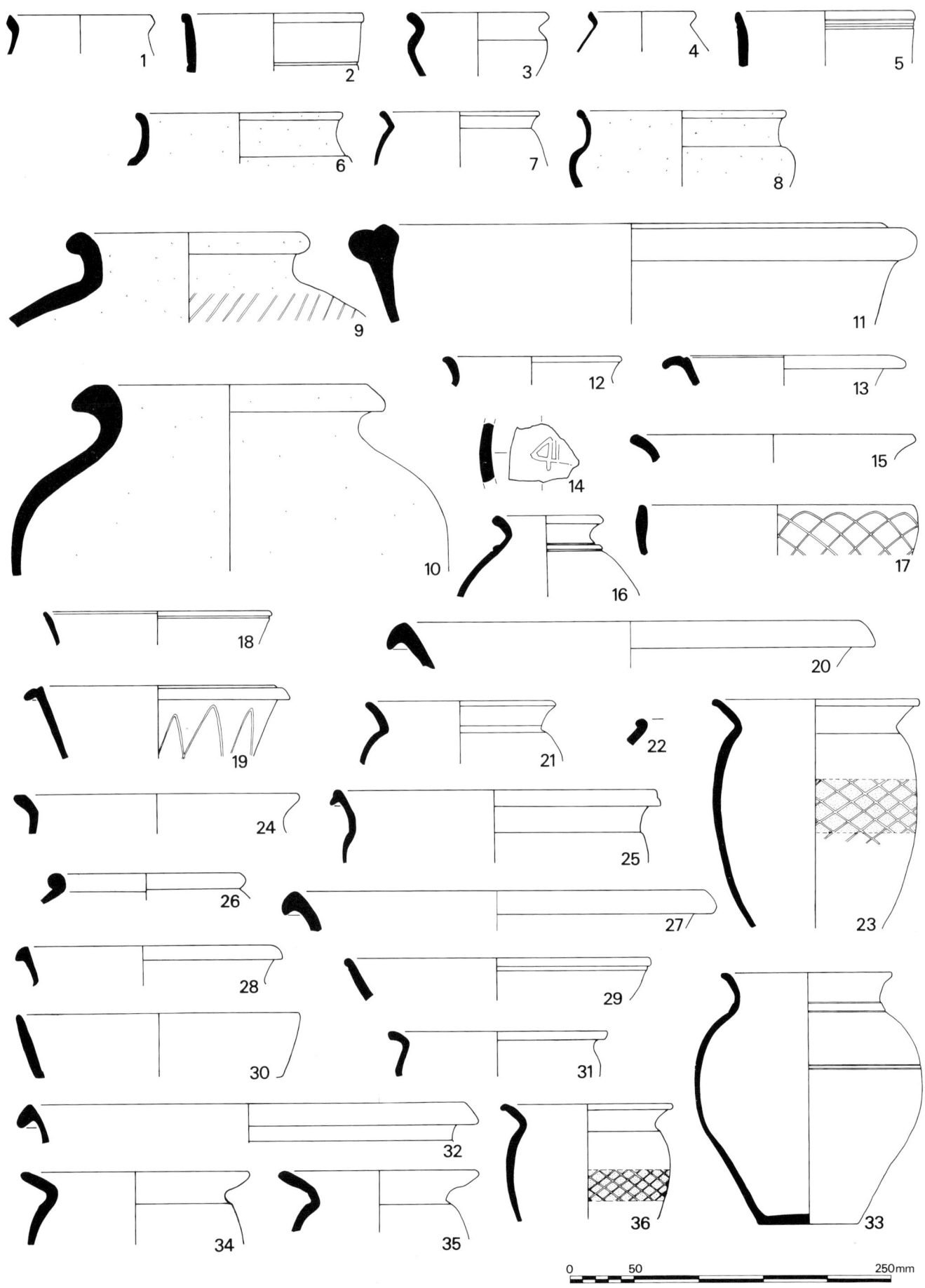

Figure 95   Roman pottery (ALB 75), nos 1–36

Pit 5 I 5 (27)

This contains various Severn Valley ware sherds, an oxidised flagon bodysherd with white slip, a sherd of Warwickshire Museum fabric R31, and a South Gaulish samian cup footring (identified by A C King). The material is not incompatible with a 1st-century date, although most of the other pits on the site are medieval and stratigraphically this one could be, although it precedes Posthole 23.

Hollow I 6 (2)

6 Medium-necked jar, fabric R31.
7 Everted rimmed jar in sandy grey ware.
8 Medium-necked jar, fabric R31.
9 Storage jar, fabric R31.
10 Storage jar, fabric R31.
11 Paleozoic Limestone-tempered Malvernian, wide-mouthed jar/bowl (sherds from the same vessel in Posthole 1), paralleled at Beckford, mid- to late 1st century AD (Jane Evans pers comm).

Also a Severn Valley ware constricted necked jar with rising rim, cf Webster 1977, no 1, 1st–4th century, bodysherds of a jar-beaker in a burnished sandy grey ware with vertical-combed decoration, two rouletted oxidised sherds, possibly from a butt-beaker, Severn Valley ware, and fabric R31 bodysherds.

A 1st-century date range would seem appropriate for all of the material.

Phase II (Fig 95, nos 12–17)

Wall 1 – upper fill II 7 (*4b*)

12 BB1 jar, Hadrianic–Antonine.
13 BB1 flanged bowl with flange rising above bead, late 2nd to early 3rd century.
14 A *graffito* on a grog-tempered handmade storage jar bodysherd.

Also a BB1 obtuse lattice decorated bodysherd, a sandy grey ware butt-beaker rim, many grey ware, rusticated grey ware and organically tempered Severn Valley ware bodysherds. The samian ware includes a South Gaulish Dr 15/17 of mid-1st-century date; an early Dr 27 fragment a Martres-de-Veyre bodysherd, Trajanic; and a single Central Gaulish bodysherd, Hadrianic or later (identified by A C King).

The illustrated pieces suggest a late 2nd- to early 3rd-century date.

Wall 1 – primary fill II 7 (*4c*)

15 An everted rimmed Malvernian metamorphic ware storage jar.

Also a South Gaulish Dr 18/31 of late 1st- to early 2nd-century date (identified by A C King).

Well 2 II 7 (7)

16 A constricted necked Severn Valley ware jar with rising rim, cf Webster 1977, no 1, 1st– 4th century.
17 BB1 simple-rimmed dish with intersecting-arc decoration, later 2nd century or later.

Phase III (Fig 95, nos 18–33)

Beam Slot 4

18 Severn Valley ware tankard rimsherd with wide, splaying mouth, cf Webster 1977, no 44, 4th century.

Also, amongst a collection of fabric R31 storage jar bodysherds and Severn Valley ware bodysherds, was a Nene Valley black colour-coated beaker bodysherd in the oxidised fabric, probably 3rd century.

The rather meagre evidence would tend to suggest a 4th-century date.

Wall 1 II 7 (*4a*)

19 BB1 flanged bowl, late 3rd to mid-4th century. Cross-joins II 5 (*4a*).

Also various BB1 bodysherds including ones with obtuse lattice decoration and a collection of apparently 1st-century residual material.

Ditch 1 II 5 (*4c*)

20 A wide-mouthed jar in Severn Valley ware, cf Webster 1977, no 27, late 3rd to 4th century.
21 A BB1 jar with everted rim, 3rd century.
22 A Malvernian metamorphic-tempered bead-rimmed jar, 1st to early 2nd century.

Also a BB1 flanged bowl with grooved rim, early to mid-3rd century.

A late 3rd- or late 3rd- to early 4th-century date range seems appropriate.

II 5 (4b)

23 A BB1 jar with obtuse lattice decoration, late 3rd to early 4th century. Cross-joins II 5 (*4a*).
24 An everted rimmed jar in Southern Shell-Tempered ware, late 3rd to early 4th century.
25 A wide-mouthed Severn Valley ware jar, 3rd to 4th century.
26 A bead-rimmed jar in sandy grey ware.
27 A wide-mouthed Severn Valley ware jar, cf Webster 1977, no 27, late 3rd to 4th century.
28 A wide-mouthed Severn Valley ware jar, cf Webster 1977, nos 28 and 30, late 3rd to 4th century.
29 An Oxfordshire colour-coated bowl, form C45, AD 270–400+ (Young 1977).

The material would seem to fit an early 4th-century date range.

Lloyds Bank finds (ALB 75)

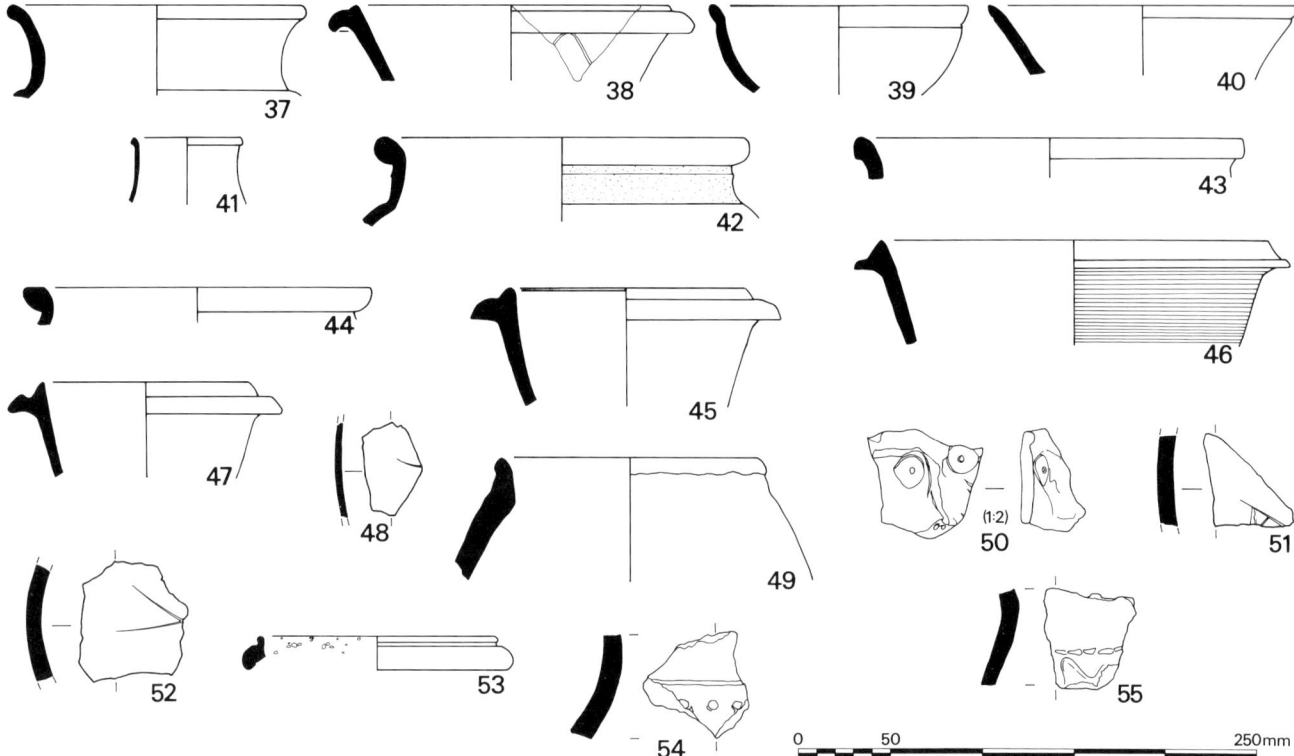

Figure 96   Roman and Saxon pottery (ALB 75), nos 37–55

Wall 2 II 5 (6)

30 BB1 dish.
31 Grey ware jar with everted rim.
32 A Severn Valley ware wide-mouthed jar, cf Webster 1976, no 27, late 3rd to 4th century.

Also a BB1 flanged bowl rim, late 3rd to 4th century, bodysherds of wheelmade Shell-Tempered ware, late 3rd century onwards, and a variety of residual 2nd- to 3rd-century material. A late 3rd- to 4th-century date range seems appropriate.

Burial A

33 Constricted necked Severn Valley ware jar with rising rim, cf Webster 1977, no 1, 1st–4th century.

I 5 (18)

This contains various residual 1st- to 2nd-century bodysherds and an Oxfordshire red colour-coated bowl, form C50, AD 325–400+ (Young 1977).

Phase IV (Fig 95, nos 34–36 and Fig 96, nos 37–48)

Ditch 1 II 5 (4a)

34 BB1 jar, mid-4th century.
35 BB1 jar, mid-4th century.
36 BB1 jar, mid-4th century.

37 A Severn Valley ware constricted necked jar with rising rim, cf Webster 1977, no 1, 1st–4th century.
38 BB1 flanged bowl, late 3rd to 4th century.
39 A Severn Valley ware bowl, cf Webster 1977, nos 34–5, 2nd–4th century.
40 A Severn Valley ware tankard, cf Webster 1977, no 44, 4th century.
41 A Nene Valley ware funnel-necked beaker, later 3rd–4th century.

The material from this group seems to suggest fairly conclusively a mid-4th-century date.

Well 2 settlement deposit II 5 (2)

42 A shouldered bead-rimmed jar in sandy grey ware.
43 A Harrold Southern Shell-Tempered ware hooked jar rim, *c* AD 340+ (Plouviez 1976).
44 A Nene Valley colour-coated jar rim, cf Howe *et al* 1980, type 75, 4th century.
45 A flanged bowl in Nene Valley colour-coated ware, Howe *et al* (1980) type 79.
46 A Harrold Southern Shell-Tempered ware flanged bowl, exterior rilled, mid- to late 4th century.
47 A flanged bowl in Nene Valley colour-coated ware, Howe *et al* (1980) type 79, 4th century.
48 A bodysherd of a handmade jar in a sandy grey ware with the edge of a graffito cut *post cocturam*, exterior sooted.

Also a BB1 simple-rimmed dish, a battered Nene Valley flanged bowl rim, a flanged bowl rim in a coarse sandy black fabric, and a Harrold Southern Shell-Tempered ware jar rim as no 43. Other finds; coin no 7 dated AD 353–4 (see Seaby above)

The contents of this group are very similar to those from the Gateway Supermarket site, area B, and Gas

House Lane, phase D, in the defended area (Cracknell 1996), and would seem to date it to the last decade or so of the 4th century.

Phase V (Fig 96, no 49)

49 A Saxon rimsherd.

Also a mixture of 1st- to 4th-century Roman material.
Date, presumably 6th or 7th century.

Other pottery of intrinsic interest (Fig 96, nos 50–55)

50 Face mask from a Severn Valley ware vessel, form unclear (Warwickshire Museum fabric O27) with applied pellet eyes and stamped pupils and nostrils. (Topsoil I 3)
51 Graffito cut *post cocturam* on a storage jar bodysherd (fabric R31), a symbol, probably a bisected triangle. This form of symbol seems common at Alcester (cf Evans *et al* 1994). (I 5)
52 Graffito on a handmade gritty storage jar bodysherd, probably 'X', a number, or more likely an illiterate mark of ownership or apotropaic symbol. (I 4)
53 A miniature mortarium in Oxfordshire white *mortarium* fabric, form similar to Young's (1977) M17.5, dated AD 240–300. (I 5 (8))
54 A shoulder sherd from a shell-tempered jar with grooved shoulder and a line of impressed dot decoration. Traces of internal carbonised deposits near rim and exterior sooted. (I 3)
55 A shoulder sherd from a shell-tempered handmade jar with dashed grooved shoulder and wavy line decoration below, exterior sooted. Decoration is unusual on Roman shell-tempered fabrics. (I 2 (2))

Unfortunately a full report on the samian could not be commissioned, principally owing to the lack of samian experts who could produce a report within the necessary timespan. However it is of note that the collection, though not large, includes several Dr 15/17s suggesting that it may commence as early as those from the Baromix sites at the southern end of Bleachfield Street. This is not inconsistent with the presence of several butt-beakers from the site and the presence of Savernake ware.

Despite a coin list of similar length to those from the Baromix sites, Flavian coinage is absent from the site.

A summary list of the medieval pottery spot dating evidence for the phase VII features can be found in microfiche M1:F7–F8.

Symbol gem (ALB 75)
Martin Henig

Intaglio (Fig 97)

Nicolo Onyx (light blue upper surface on a translucent brown ground). Flat, oval with bevelled edge (Henig 1978, 35, Fig 1, F4) 13mm × 11mm (11mm × 9mm excluding bevelling), thickness 3mm. Traces of

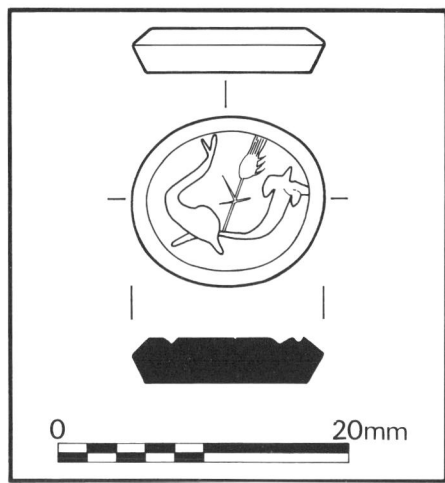

Figure 97 Intaglio (ALB 75)

iron on the back of the stone, show that the ring was of that material. (Context I 4 (8), Pit 1, phase VIID)

The device is a dolphin, with a cornucopia apparently projecting from its snout. An ear of wheat sprouts from the point of juncture. Previously published in Henig 1978, 316 and plate XXXII, no App 203.

Comparanda

A green prase in Munich depicts a dolphin with a cornucopia but here a steering oar replaces the cereal. A sardonyx in Berlin and a nicolo in Hanover each portray a dolphin approaching a cornucopia; in the field, a steering oar, club, and poppy, another traditional Roman crop. A nicolo from Alesia and a sardonyx from Lattes each portray a dolphin with a corn-ear. These stones are all dated to the 1st century AD. A sealing from the public record office of Cyrene, destroyed early in the 2nd century AD depicts a dolphin, cornucopia, and horse's head (Brandt 1972, 44 and pl 211, no 2363; Furtwängler 1896, 296 and pl 58, no 8081; Zazoff 1975, 250 and pl 182, no 1323; Guiraud 1988, 186, nos 866–867, pl LVII and Maddoli 1963, 135, and Fig 47, no 1003).

Discussion

Although the meaning of some symbols used on gems is quite specific – the horn of plenty and the wheat represent abundance and prosperity – others are more ambiguous. In art the dolphin is sometimes an allusion to the journey of the soul after death to the Blessed Isles although it also has other meanings such as naval prowess and speed. Dolphins were regarded as friendly and beneficent creatures to mankind. I have suggested that in a British context an intaglio from Waddon Hill, Dorset (Henig 1978, 105 and plate XIII, no 408) which shows a Capricorn, palm, globe, prow, and dolphin might have been understood as a reference to the victory of *Legio II*

Lloyds Bank finds (ALB 75)

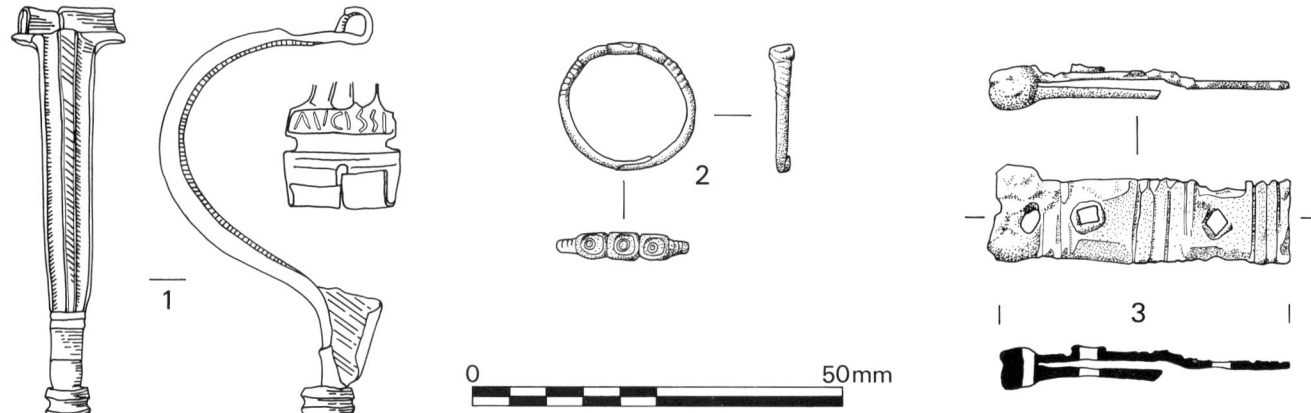

Figure 98   Copper alloy objects (ALB 75), nos 1–3

Augusta and another gem from Caerleon may have similar 'local' significance.

Note also a green prase from the earliest deposit in the drain of the Legionary Baths at Caerleon. Beneath the Greek inscription *XAPA* ('Joy') we see the clasped hands of Concord, a parrot (sacred to Bacchus) upon a cornucopia, a capricorn (incidentally the emblem of *legio II Augusta* stationed at Caerleon), and a dolphin (Zienkiewicz 1986, 129–30, plate V) though I read the inscription differently and the animal above the dolphin is almost certainly a capricorn not a hippocamp as stated by Zienkiewicz.

Certainly such symbolism was employed by Octavian in the 1st century BC: a cornelian in Florence which depicts his portrait together with a dolphin and corn-ear is interpreted by Vollenweider as a reference to the Naval victory of Naulochus (36 BC) when Agrippa finally deprived Sextus Pompey of the rich corn-lands of Sicily (Vollenweider 1972, 95, plate 151, 16; Vollenweider 1974, 212 ff). Dolphins are also shown on gems which allude to Actium in 31 BC (eg Neverov 1971, 88 and plate 71).

The Alcester gem was probably cut in the 1st century AD. Apart from the parallels cited above, all assigned to the 1st century, small lightish-coloured onyx intaglios frequently with a pale ground were very popular in this period (eg Henig, 1978, 233, plate XXXVII, no 381). It is quite possible it was intended as a reminder of the more recent prowess of the legions which had crossed the stream of Ocean to Britain in AD 43. Even if not, the symbols shown are all auspicious ones with wide appeal as emblems of prosperity.

Selected copper alloy objects (ALB 75)
Glenys Lloyd-Morgan

(Fig 98, nos 1–3)

1 Aucissa brooch, with 'AVCISSA' stamped at the head. The raised central rib along the bow is hatched, and there is light moulding to the edge. The pin and swivel are lost, and part of the hinge section is broken. There is some slight surface wear. Length 54.5mm. (ALB 75, SF 36, I, 4)

Mackreth notes that the date range for this type runs from the conquest to c AD 60 (Bennett *et al* 1982, 172, no 5, Fig 88). Compare also the inscribed example from Richborough, though the detail on this is different to that on the Alcester piece (Cunliffe 1968, 84, plate XXX, no 42). Our example was originally noted by Booth (1980, Fig 8, no 1). Other examples from Warwickshire include two from Coleshill, nos GH 1978 93 and GH 1979 595.

2 Finger-ring, the bezel is in the form of three adjoining discs, each with a raised ring to produce a central disc-shaped field, and an outer ring-shaped one, all filled with enamel of white colour. The slightly worn shoulders are hatched with six or seven vertical lines. The back of the ring is split diagonally. Bezel height 34mm, length c 12mm, external hoop diameter 18.6mm × 16.8mm, internal hoop diameter 16mm × 14mm. (ALB 75, SF 5, II, U/S)

Compare the ring from Nor'nour with a single disc-shaped bezel. White coloured enamel survives in the inner disc-shaped field; the outer ring-shaped field was also originally enamelled. The piece was dated to around the 2nd century AD (Dudley 1967, 22, Fig 8, no 13). Note also the ring from Jewry Wall, Leicester which has hatched decoration on the shoulders and two oval settings, now empty, as a bezel. From a context dated AD 125–130 (Kenyon 1948, 252, Fig 83, no 12, see chronological table on p 42 for dating). It is curious to note that there is no reference to finger rings with enamelled bezels in Henry's magisterial survey (1933, reprinted 1983); nor any example related to the Alcester example in Bateson (1981, 55–56, Fig 8B).

3 Buckle plate with the corroded iron swivel still *in situ*, but the pin and buckle hoop now lost. There are two holes with square cross-section for the nails or rivets to attach the plate to the strap. The outer face of the plate has chip-carved decoration to give the effect of transverse mouldings between plain rectangular panels with bevelling at the edges. The buckle plate is not completely regular in outline. Length 40.4mm, max width 11.4mm, max depth 4.7mm. (ALB 75, SF 10, II, 4)

Compare the related decoration on an ornamental bar from Exeter, found in a context dated late 13th to early 14th century (Allan 1984, 345, 348, Fig 193, no 194).

Human skeletal remains (ALB 75)
Judson Chesterman and Christine Osborne

The human skeletal remains in this group are generally in a good state of preservation. With the exception of Burial A which is a cremation, all are inhumations. The fourteen burials appear to represent at least seventeen individuals, although the presence of two of the latter (one of those in Burial C and that in Burial M) is indicated by very few bones which may belong to one of the other skeletons. (Four fragments of possibly human bone found in Burial D and not associated with the main skeleton have not been included in this count.) However, none of the skeletons was complete. This would not appear to be poor excavation techniques (for example, although there is an absence of pelvic bones and femora in Burial B, the tibiae, fibulae and some metatarsals are present. One might expect the smaller bones of the foot to be missed, but not the larger thigh bones), the preservation is good, and there is little sign of weathering. It is possible that the burials were reinterred, and in such a manner that various bones were lost.

Age

The cremation (Burial A) is that of an adult. A narrower age range could not be determined given the fragmentary nature of the material. The term 'adult' is based upon the evidence of a fully fused epiphysis on the iliac crest of a fragment of pelvis and fused epiphyseal rings on the vertebral body fragments. All the inhumations are of immature individuals. The ageing of immature skeletons is generally considered less problematical than the ageing of adults where it is only possible to assign a broad age range. The age ranges given to immature individuals are much narrower. They are based primarily on tooth development and eruption, longbone lengths and epiphyseal fusion. Within this group all the immature skeletons fall into the broad category of neonate (birth ± six months) except for the two individuals in Burial J (Fig 90b) of which one is a child aged three to five years whilst the other can only be said to be immature, and the skeleton in Burial K which is that of an infant of nine months ± three months. The list below shows the ages of all the skeletons in this group.

Burial	Age
A	adult
B	neonate (birth ± two months)
C1, 2, and 3	all fall into the category of neonate, but the relative sizes of the bones suggest that two may be foetal. A third is aged birth ± two months
D	neonate
E	neonate (birth ± two months)
F	neonate (birth ± two months)
G	neonate (birth ± two months)
H	neonate (birth ± two months)
J1	child (three to five years)
J2	immature
K	infant (nine months ± three months)
L	neonate (six months ± three months – probably at the younger end of the scale)
M	neonate (possibly late foetal)
N	neonate
O	neonate

Sex

It was not possible to sex the adult individual from Burial A. The sexing of immature skeletons should not be attempted as the characteristics of sexual dimorphism only develop during puberty. It is certainly not possible to sex individuals of the ages of the inhumations in this group.

Pathology

The only pathology was noted in the main skeleton from Burial J where cribra orbitalia occurs in both eye sockets (this is a pitting in the roof of the socket). Though not fully understood it is though to be related to dietary deficiency.

A detailed inventory of the skeletal remains is given in microfiche M1:F8–G2.

Explosion site excavations (AES 76–7)   *Paul Booth*

Introduction

This site, on the west side of Bleachfield Street, in the centre of the Roman town of Alcester (Figs 2 and 88), became available for excavation after an explosion had severely damaged existing storage premises. (The name 'Explosion site' has been retained as a convenient means of distinguishing this from the considerable number of other sites excavated in Bleachfield Street). The damaged structures were outbuildings belonging to the houses on the street frontage, which were in origin of 17th-century date (Plate 16). All the buildings were due to be demolished and the site redeveloped. Permission was granted by Mr David Burden, the owner, to excavate in advance of the redevelopment. Finance was provided by the Department of the Environment (now the Historic Buildings and Monuments Commission for England, English Heritage), and the excavation was administered by the Warwickshire Museum, at which all the finds and excavation records are held.

Demolition of the buildings on the site did not take place until after the excavation was completed. Consequently the area available for examination was quite limited. The end of the site nearest the street (to the east) had been much built on in recent times and it was considered that this area would be archaeologically less profitable, at least from a Roman point of view, than the garden area further west. Any attempt to excavate the whole area would have involved removing the spoil heap and filling in the excavated half of the site before embarking on the second stage. It was never likely that time and finance would permit this. It was in the western part of the site, therefore, that the initial effort was concentrated, between mid-August and late December 1976. A trial trench 8m × 1m was cut by hand adjacent to the north boundary wall of the property in order to locate the top of the Roman deposits (Fig 99). On the basis of this an area of 17m × 11m was excavated to a depth of 0.75m–1m by JCB, and thereafter by hand. Virtually all the remaining space was used for spoil disposal, but when excavation resumed in March 1977 the excavated area was extended in an attempt to solve various problems, particularly concerning building VI and the relationship of the site to a possible Roman road. Site II was therefore added to the east side of site I. It consisted of an area 7m × 3m with a trench 25m × 1m running eastwards from it towards Bleachfield Street, a machine being again employed to remove the topsoil. Site II context numbers are distinguished in the text (but not on the plans) by the prefix II.

In addition to the excavations a survey of the house standing in front of the site was carried out, though the outbuildings were not surveyed. This work was done under the guidance of Mr N A D Molyneux of Birmingham City Museum.

The main feature of the archaeology of the site was deep and complicated stratigraphy, which meant that the progress of excavation was slow. Consequently the excavated area was not completely bottomed. However, the depth of excavation was such that where the subsoil was not reached the surviving deposits should be below the level of any disturbance which redevelopment might cause.

In site I excavation was halted at the level of a major period 4 gravel surface (**235**), except where this was sealed by the clay floor of building V (**44**), which was only partly cleared off. In one small area (**235**) was removed in an attempt to define an early pit underneath it (see below). In site II the main level reached was again a gravel surface (II **20**), somewhat later in date than (**235**) and equivalent to (**161**) in site I (period 7). East of building VI, however, all features in the trench were completely excavated to subsoil. The character of the features in the site II trench was different from that of the rest of the site. In the following account these features are described after the other developments in each period. Features at the west end of site II, however, were often closely related to those in site I and where appropriate (eg in period 7) are described together with them.

Not all contexts/features are referred to in the following account of the excavation; a full list of the contexts, with their period numbers and summary descriptions, can be found in microfiche M1:G3–G12. Subdivisions of contexts/features, both in plan and section, are indicated by a letter suffix.

In addition to the numerical sequences of contexts and periods of occupation of the site a further sequence of Roman numerals was used to distinguish the series of excavated structures, and in one of these, building V, room numbers were also assigned (see Fig 175).

The periods of the site identified as post-Roman (periods 11–14) are only summarised here. Detailed descriptions of the archaeology associated with these periods can be found in microfiche M1:G13–M2:A4.

Chronology and dating

The Roman and later activity on the site was divided into 14 periods: Roman (periods 1–10), medieval (periods 11–12) and post-medieval and modern (periods 13–14). Contexts were assigned to individual periods on the basis of their stratigraphic relationships and dating, the latter being based largely on the pottery evidence (see below). The lack of a direct stratigraphic link between sites I and II before

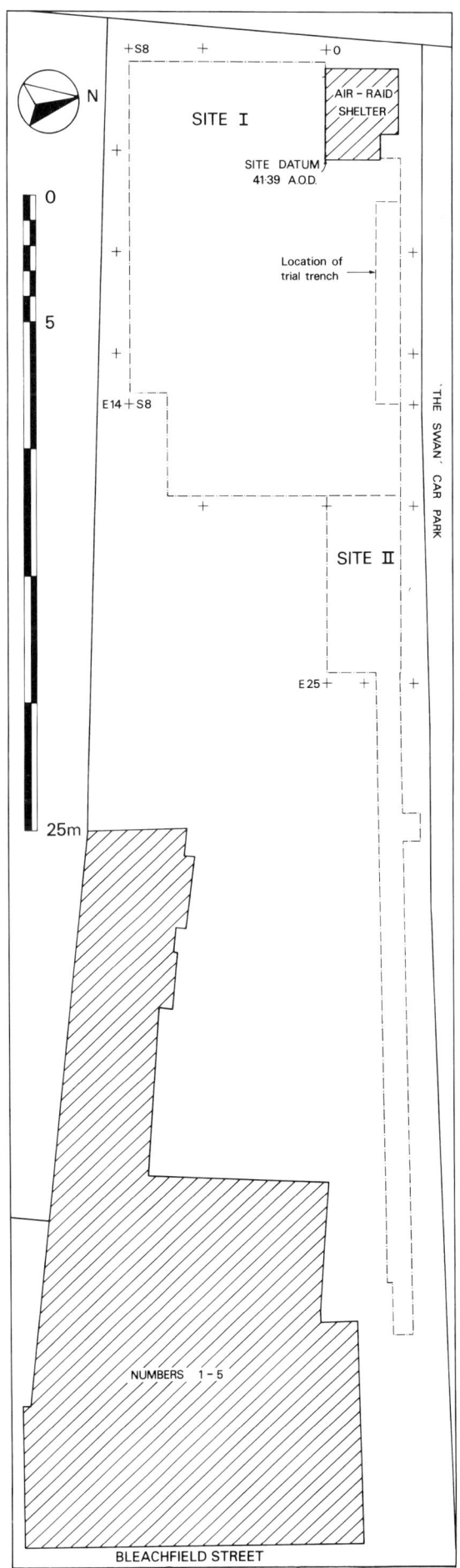

period 7 created problems of assessing the contemporaneity of deposits in the two parts of the site before this period. The chronology presented below is based primarily on the sequence from site I. Contexts in the site II trench, dating from period 2 onwards, were assigned to various periods on the basis of their relative stratigraphy and the restricted quantity of dating material which they contained. The ascription of these contexts to specific periods is therefore less secure than for site I.

The dating of the Roman periods was partly based on coin evidence but relied principally on the pottery, while the medieval deposits were dated solely by pottery. For periods 1–6 samian ware was an important dating tool. Thereafter both coarse and fine wares were used, but with less precision. Of these, the various Oxfordshire products were of particular importance (the dating given below follows, with some reservations, that of Young 1977). The date-ranges assigned to each period were therefore defined with varying degrees of precision. Even when exact dates are given, these can only be regarded as a 'best guess' based on the available evidence. When beginning or end dates for a period are expressed in terms of a range (eg AD 125/140–140/150) the earlier date in each case indicates a *terminus post quem*. For the 1st- and 2nd-century periods the earlier date was usually preferred, but the range is given to demonstrate that the preferred date is not the only possibility. From the mid-3rd century onwards the later date of each range was preferred. In those cases where no range is indicated this is because the *terminus post quem* (usually based on pottery evidence) seems to be the latest possible date for the event in question, though this cannot be regarded as beyond dispute.

The length of the periods of activity on the site was variable. This reflects the possible nature of such activity. In some cases intense building activity, leaving extensive traces in the archaeological record, would have been confined to a short period (eg periods 6 and 7). In others, relatively lengthy periods of occupation, in which there were few structural developments, might involve only a few features and small amounts of dating material (eg period 5).

Topography and geology (Figs 2 and 3)

The site, like much of the rest of the Roman settlement of Alcester, lies on gravels of the first–second terrace to the west of the river Arrow, some 280m distant (Williams and Whittaker 1974, 65). At an elevation of *c* 41.80m OD on the modern ground surface at the western end of the site, it is one of the higher points in the southern part of the town (the site datum was at 41.39m above Ordnance Datum). The ground falls away to the east (the drop from west to east within the site was just over 2m) and to the north.

Figure 99 1–5 Bleachfield Street, site layout (AES 76–7)

Explosion site excavations (AES 76–7)

Plate 16   General view of part of site I and site II, looking east to buildings of 1–5 Bleachfield Street (AES 76–7)

Here the dip caused by the existence of a probable former watercourse approximately on the line of the present Swan Street separates the whole of the southern part of the Roman and later settlements from the gravel island on which the Roman defended area and the nucleus of the later medieval settlement were sited. To the south, Bleachfield Street slopes down slightly towards the floodplain of the river, and the ground rises only marginally to the west.

Soils

The subsoil throughout the site was sandy gravel, with occasional patches of clayey gravel, though alluvial clay was encountered within 50m to the east, in excavations carried out in 1975 at Lloyds Bank. The gravel was encountered at levels from c 39.84 to c 39.35m OD (from west to east). In the side of well (168) the gravel was exactly 2m thick and overlaid a layer of sand at least 0.5m deep. It is not known if this was a widespread deposit.

Soils on the site were not always described in detail, but were fairly uniform, most being sandy loams. Distinct sands, gravels, and clays were noted. Many layers were of very mixed composition, the mixing a result of human agency, and the most common additives stone, pebbles, small lumps of clay, charcoal, and so on. These were described in some detail on the site record cards (in archive), as was the colour of each layer, a Munsell soil colour chart being used.

The uniformity of many of the soils presented a major problem, especially where several similar layers were superimposed without the intervention of differentiated deposits. It was frequently quite impossible to establish exactly where pits and postholes had been cut through such deposits since their fill was often identical to the surfaces through which they were cut. This was particularly a problem in the north-east corner of site I, but was encountered elsewhere. Interpretation was thus complicated by the difficulties of trying to decide where a pit had been cut from when it was only identified at the point at which it disturbed a gravel or some other distinct surface. This point should be born in mind throughout the account of the site.

Archaeological background

Some previous archaeological excavation has been undertaken in the immediately adjacent areas, but this was on a small scale and none of it has been published. The most significant of these sites is the one excavated by H V Hughes and R J Horsfall (Hughes' site S) in the garden of the Dog and Partridge public house immediately to the south of the Explosion site. Very little is known of this excavation (Hughes 1960, 32), but surviving finds include an extremely good group of Hadrianic pottery from a pit. The relationship of this, and any other features, to those excavated at the Explosion site is unknown.

Early occupation (periods 1–4)

Activity of periods 1–3 was encountered only in two limited areas of the site, since in general the earliest layers were not examined (see above). These areas were at the eastern end of the site II trench and in the middle of site I. In character the two areas were rather different, though the scope for interpretation offered by each was limited because of the small areas involved. The earliest features in the site II trench may have been rather later in date than those in site I and it is possible that none of the site II features predated the 2nd century. They were assigned to period 2, but it is likely that most were of period 3 or later. The ascription of these and later features to specific periods can at best be regarded as tentative. For discussion of the specific site II trench dating problems see period 2 (below).

Period 4 was the first period to be widely encountered in site I, where excavation halted at the level of a widespread gravel surface (*235*).

Period 1 (AD 70–80/85): Early pits and gullies
(Figs 101 and 102)

Evidence for period 1 in site I was confined to a small area adjacent to the period 5 building V, to the east of which the underlying pebbled surface (*235*) had subsided suggesting that there was an early pit underneath. The edge of this pit had been cut by a large late 3rd-century (period 9) pit (*124*), in the side of which burnt layers, thought to be in the fill of the early pit, were visible.

It was realised that there would not be sufficient time to excavate the early layers in site I, so it was decided to examine this pit (*266*) in an attempt to date the earliest occupation. (*266*) had a maximum diameter of c 3.75m and was c 0.5m deep, though the fill had settled and in the middle of the pit was at most 0.25m deep. It was this sinkage which accounted for the depression in the layers above, despite apparent attempts to fill it with patches of pebbles.

Many different layers were identified in the fill of the pit. These seemed to fall into three groups, (*266S–V*), (*266N–R*), and (*266A–M*), though there was no indication that the deposits accumulated

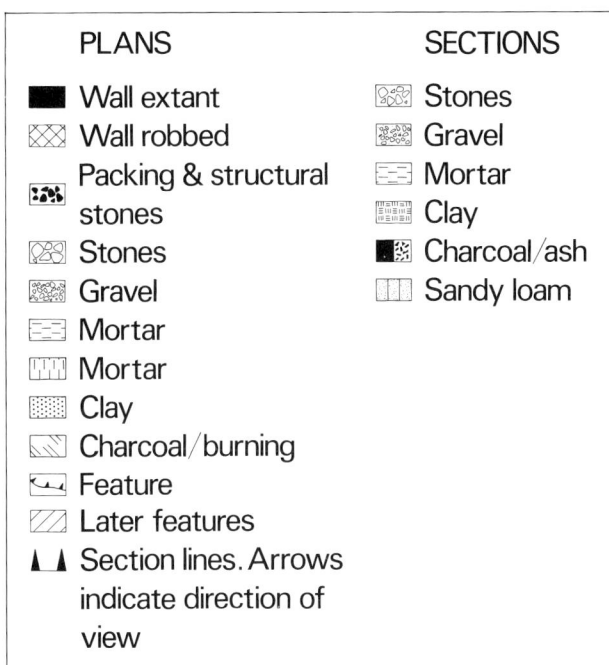

Figure 100 Key to drawing conventions (AES 76–7) (Figs 101–120)

over a long period. The interpretation of (*266*) as a pit is not certain. It appears rather too wide and shallow to have been a convenient receptacle for rubbish; its precise function remains unknown. It was sealed by a sandy loam layer (*292*). To the south-east of (*266*) were two smaller pits; (*268*), a shallow ill-defined depression in the gravel subsoil, partially cut away by (*267*), a larger pit, part of which had also been removed by (*124*). South-west of (*266*) was another ill-defined feature (*270*), disturbed on its south side by the (*247*) complex (see below), but enough remained to suggest that it was a gully or beam slot running on the same north-west/south-east alignment as most of the other features of the site.

Pit (*267*) contained a quantity of roof tiles (fragments of one *imbrex* and several *tegulae* being represented) and this in conjunction with the slot (*270*) suggests that there was a building of some sort close by, if not actually on this part of the site.

The dating for period 1 is quite consistent (Roman pottery, below, illustrated vessel nos 56–83). The samian ware (Table 18 below) includes several pre-Flavian pieces, but also material attributable to the early Flavian, the latest individually dated piece being a stamp (no 9) dated AD 65–85. While this material only gives a *terminus post quem* the combined evidence of this and the subsequent phase suggests a date range for period 1 of c AD 70 to c AD 80/85. Pit (*266*) contained a reasonable group of samian ware almost all of Flavian date, including a Dr 37 with decoration typical of Germanus dated c AD 70–85, and a stamped *mortarium* of Q Valerius Veranius (no 61), not closely dated but falling within the period c AD 70–100.

Explosion site excavations (AES 76–7)

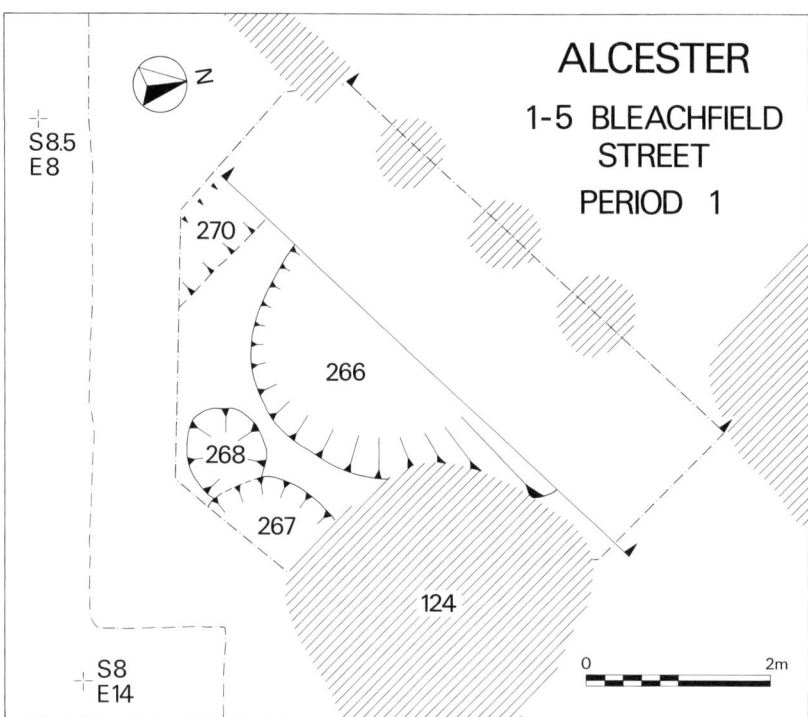

Figure 101   Site I, period 1 plan (AES 76–7) (for location see Fig 103)

Period 2 (AD 80/85–125/140): possible timber buildings and well

Site I (Figs 102 and 103)

Period 2 deposits were again limited in extent. Confined to the hollow in (**266**), immediately above the period 1 layer (*292*), were layers (*290*) and (*291*), both clay surfaces, the lower of which was burnt. Like the deposits above them, these may simply have been layers intended to fill in the hollow caused by the settling of the pit fill. Alternatively they may have been floor surfaces, which originally extended beyond the confines of the pit, but had been worn away where they were not protected by the hollow of the fill settling. A clay layer (**256**), located some 2m south-west of the deposits in question, may indicate a possible extension of such surfaces (see below, period 3).

The clay layers were sealed by a thin (up to 0.04m), but pronounced charcoal layer (*281*). Associated with this were layers of burnt clay and ash. The burning above (*290*) and (*291*) strongly suggests the destruction of a timber building and may possibly represent burning *in situ* rather than a dump of material from elsewhere. Closely associated with the charcoal layer were patches of clay and several pieces of daub, some with wattle impressions, indicating the presence of walls. There seems little reason to doubt that the building would have been roofed with tile, since tile, possibly from this building, was found in the earlier feature (*267*) and also in association with the daub fragments.

Dating evidence for these early features was not plentiful (pottery vessels nos 84–134), but the samian ware (Table 19 below) suggests a date range of Flavian–Trajanic, with two layers containing slightly later material: (*279*) included a samian sherd with a Trajanic or early Hadrianic date, and a few sherds of Black-Burnished ware in the layer would be consistent with this, but (*293*) included a sherd of a Central Gaulish Dr 30, dated Hadrianic or early Antonine. If this piece is not intrusive then the latest date for this phase must be at the very least *c* AD 125, and possibly as late as *c* AD 140, though the heavy preponderance of earlier material argues in favour of an earlier date. Considerable numbers of cross-joining sherds from period 1 and 2 contexts suggested that the earliest period 2 activity perhaps involved some disturbance of period 1 features.

One other feature assigned to this period was the well (**168A**). This was situated beneath the north end of the later building V and was at most 2.90m deep with a diameter at the head of 1.20m or possibly a little less. A later (period 10) pit (**168**) had been cut through building V and exactly into the top of the well shaft, obscuring its original appearance and relationships to adjacent strata. Nevertheless its position and contents (pottery vessels nos 146–167, Table 19) made it clear that the well was probably at the latest of early 2nd-century date and must have been filled in before the construction of building V over the top of it in period 5. It was not possible to be certain if the well had been cut through (**235**) or sealed by it. Consequently it could have belonged with the period 2 structures above (**266**), or with the (**247**) complex (period 3), or even have post-dated both, though the dating evidence strongly suggests that it is most likely to have been of period 2.

For the most part the well was cut through natural gravel, but the bottom 0.50m cut into sand beneath the gravel. The sides of the shaft in the sand were tapered,

Explosion site excavations (AES 76–7)

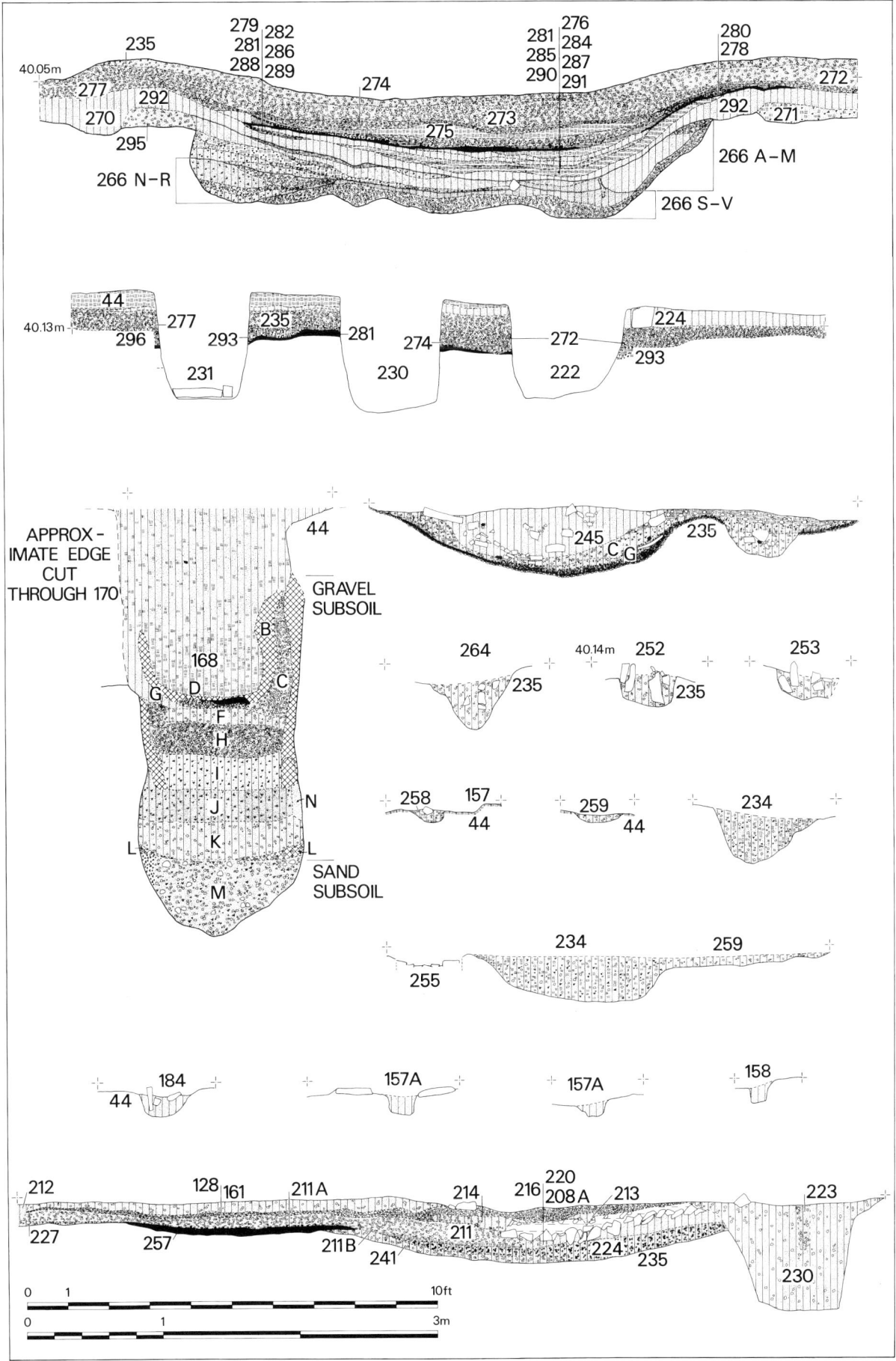

Figure 102   Site I, periods 1–6 sections (AES 76–7)

Explosion site excavations (AES 76–7)

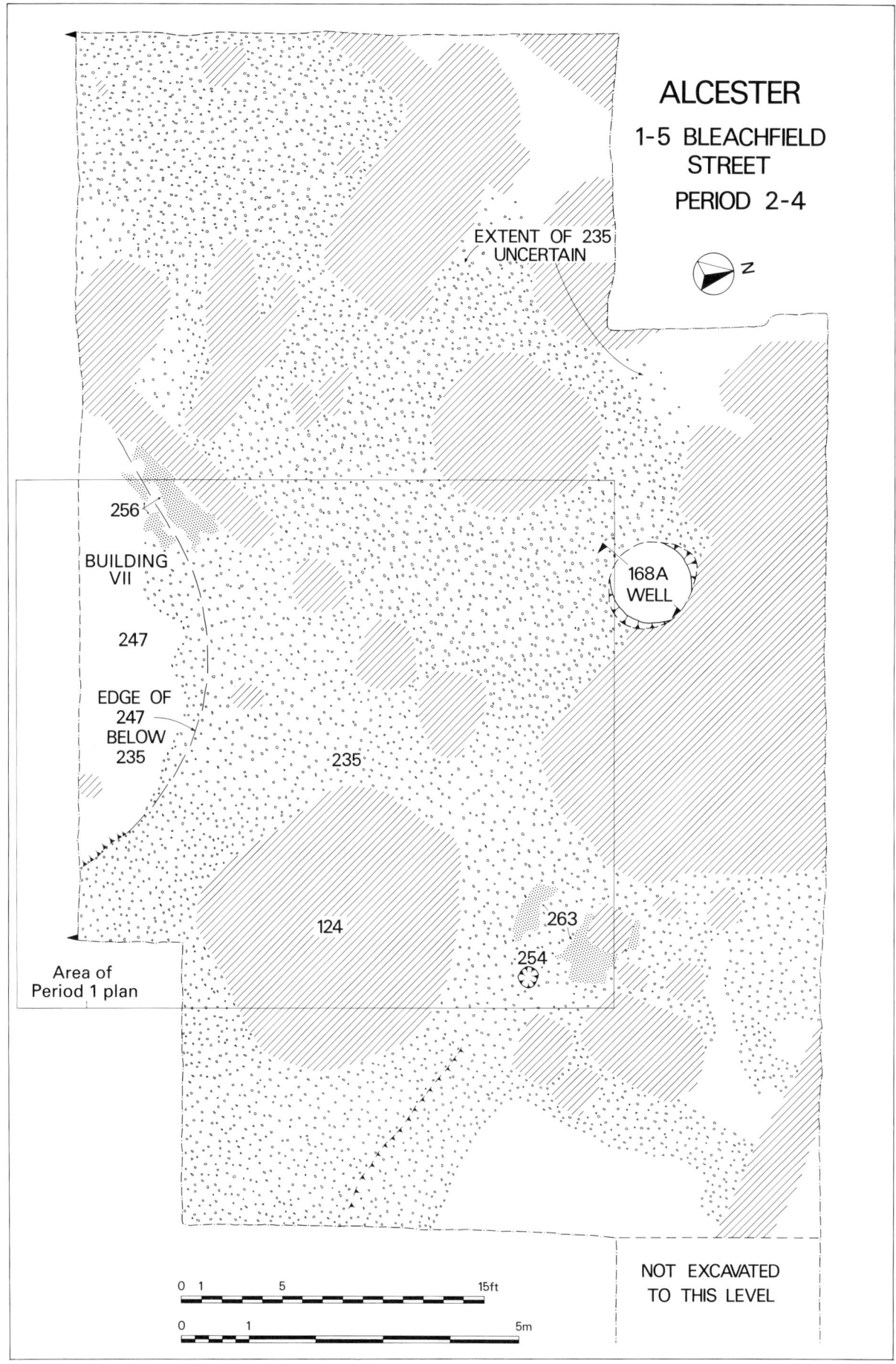

Figure 103 Site I, periods 2–4 plan (AES 76–7)

forming a bowl shape. The bottom part of the shaft seems to have been filled fairly quickly to a depth of 0.55m with mixed dirty sand and gravel. On top of this, organic matter accumulated, particularly against the sides of the shaft where the layer was up to c 0.15m thick. The layers above this presumably belonged to the deliberate backfilling of the well and consisted of grey mud with pebbles, and cleaner sand and gravel. The well shaft had had a clay lining, and there was evidence for some sort of organic lining inside this, in the form of a gap and a dark vertical stain up to 0.12m wide between the fill and the clay lining. This could have formed when the fill settled and moved away from the edges of the shaft, but this seems unlikely. The nature of the organic lining is unknown. For the bottom 1m of the well there was no evidence for any lining other than the clay, which became more sandy with increasing depth until it ceased to be distinguishable some 0.40m above the bottom. Samples taken from the organic deposit in the well produced pollen and macroscopic plant remains indicative of an environment of cultivated and waste ground (see below).

Site II (Figs 104, 105, and 120)

A 17m length from the eastern end of the trench was excavated down to the gravel subsoil. Most of the deposits in this part of the site had been truncated by post-medieval activity. Of the features which survived below this level very few were later than 2nd century in date. All those producing finds contained homogeneous groups of coarse wares broadly of later 1st- to early 2nd-century date, notable for high proportions of storage jar sherds. Fine wares were almost totally absent except for samian ware which provided the only relatively precise dating. While some contexts contained 1st-century (including pre-Flavian) pieces, Antonine sherds occurred sufficiently consistently, even in some of the stratigraphically earliest features, to suggest that most if not all of the features were of this date. The pottery in these features did not show any chronological development, so that although there was a complex stratigraphic sequence, providing a relative chronology, none of the features within the sequence could be precisely dated. The consistency of the assemblages, however, suggests that this area of the site saw intensive activity over a relatively limited space of time, perhaps mainly in the period c AD 130–180, but that much of the material deposited in features of this date was already residual.

The stratigraphically primary features in site II were a series of rather irregular pits and hollows of variable size and profile, (II **76**), (II **71**), (II **75**), (II **62**), (II **53**), and (II **73**) (from west to east), the major exception being (II **53**), which was attributed to the subsequent period (period 3). Of these features, (II **75**), a shallow, roughly circular depression c 0.90m across, may have been earlier than the rest and (II **74**), which cut it, could possibly have been part of the same feature as the primary gully (II **71**), c 0.90m wide and aligned roughly east–west.

Period 3 (AD 125/140–140/150): gravel layers and structure (building VII)

Site I (Figs 103 and 106)

The complex of early deposits was sealed by two or three gravel surfaces (**235**), (272) and (273). The uppermost of these (**235**), at which the bulk of the excavation in site I halted, was assigned to period 4. (**235**) and (273) were disturbed on the south side of the site in the area to the east of building V by what was called building VII, but consisted principally of feature (**247**), which was, unfortunately, imperfectly understood at the time of excavation.

As first exposed this feature projected about 1.50m northwards from the south baulk of the site and was in all about 6.50m east–west. Its original edge, below (**235**) (see below) lay up to c 1.85m north of the south baulk. The main part of (**247**) was sealed by material belonging to period 6 (the enlargement of building V), and period 7 (**211** and **161**). Marginally, however, (**247**) was sealed by (**235**), which made it clear that it was stratigraphically (as well as on the basis of the finds) an early feature, though directly sealed by deposits of much later date. This point was not at first appreciated, and understanding of (**247**) was not aided by the fact that (**235**) was not generally removed over the site. The fill of (**247**) was made up of a series of thin deposits (to a maximum depth of c 0.18m) which gave the impression of being fairly loose, rather than any hard packed or trampled surface, and at the edges of the feature the deposits were very disturbed, which considerably complicated their interpretation. It did seem, however, that on the eastern side (**247**) had a reasonably defined edge where the loose material of (**247**) peeled away from pebbles beneath (**235**) in such a way as to suggest a curving slot at the edge of (**247**). This feature was not always well defined, since most of (**235**) was not removed to expose the slot. Adjacent to building V, (**235**) was worn away, revealing some of the deposits beneath including part of a clay surface (**256**) which was presumably associated with the deposits identified above (**266**). This surface had been cut by a slot-like line, which may be equivalent to the edge of (**247**) found further east. This assumed edge of the feature is indicated on the plan (Fig 103).

Feature (**247**) contained a fairly large group of pottery suggesting a date in the first half of the 2nd century (pottery vessels nos 173–192), with samian of Trajanic date (Table 20).

The function of (**247**) is quite uncertain. The feature was presumably defined by some kind of timber structure, either a wall or fence, in the slot identified. If it was circular the projected diameter of the feature would have been a little over 7m. The evidence might suggest a circular timber building, though an unroofed enclosure is also possible. This structure was clearly out of use by the time (**235**) was laid, or at least the wall or fence had been removed, since the pebbles lay over where it had been.

The fact that the top of (**247**) was apparently

Explosion site excavations (AES 76–7)

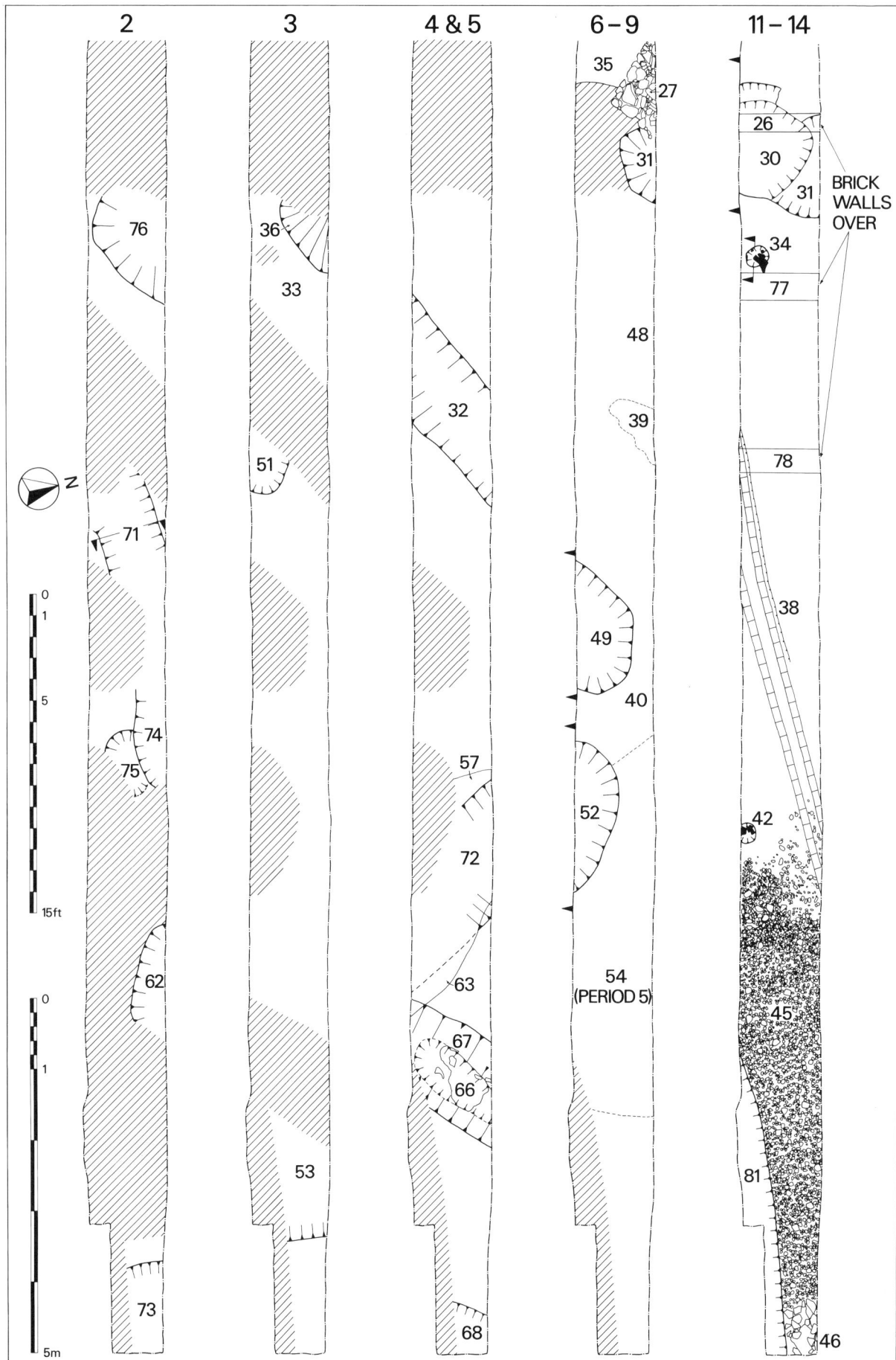

Figure 104 Site II trench, all period plans (AES 76–7)

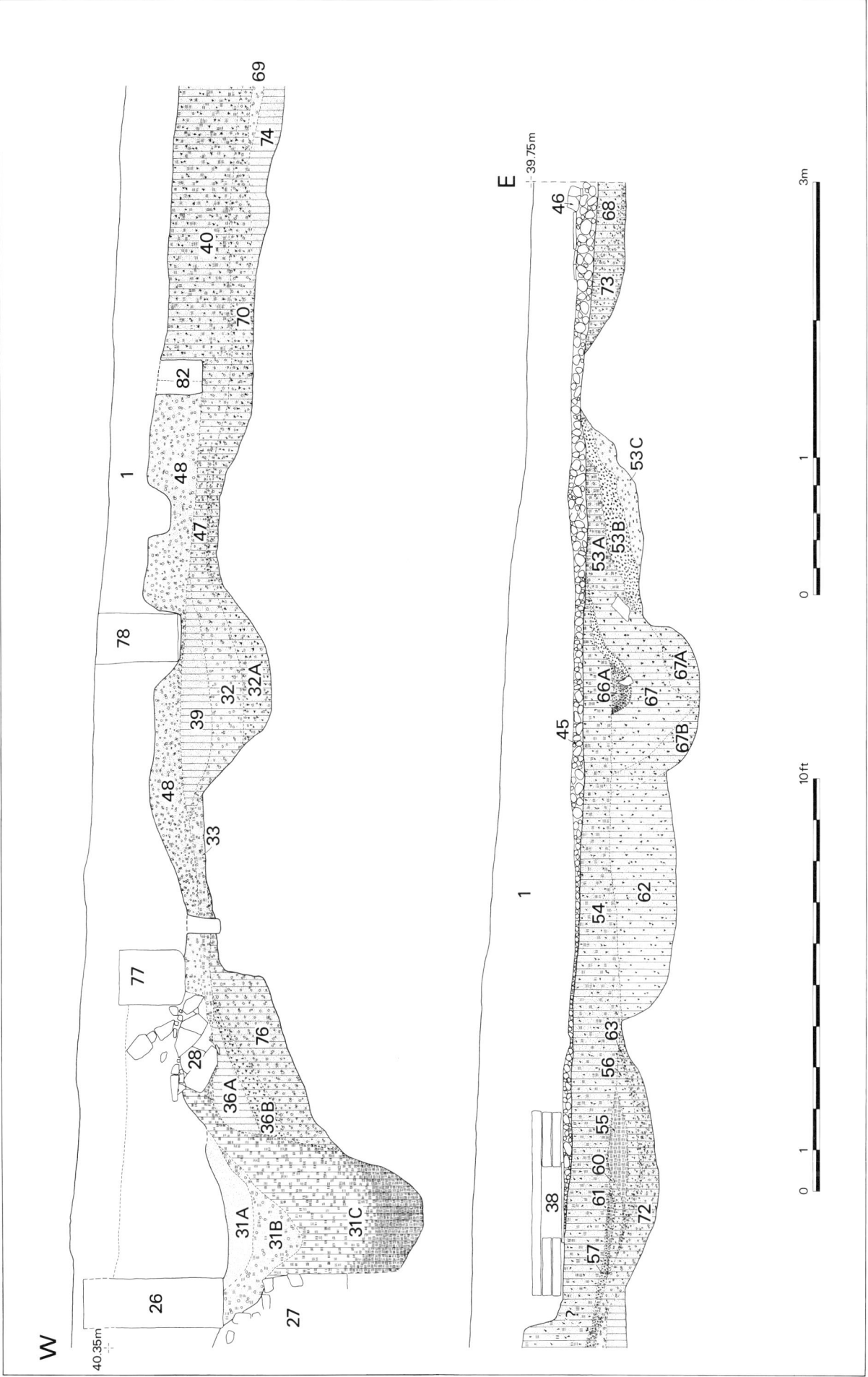

Figure 105 Site II trench, north section (AES 76–7)

Explosion site excavations (AES 76–7)

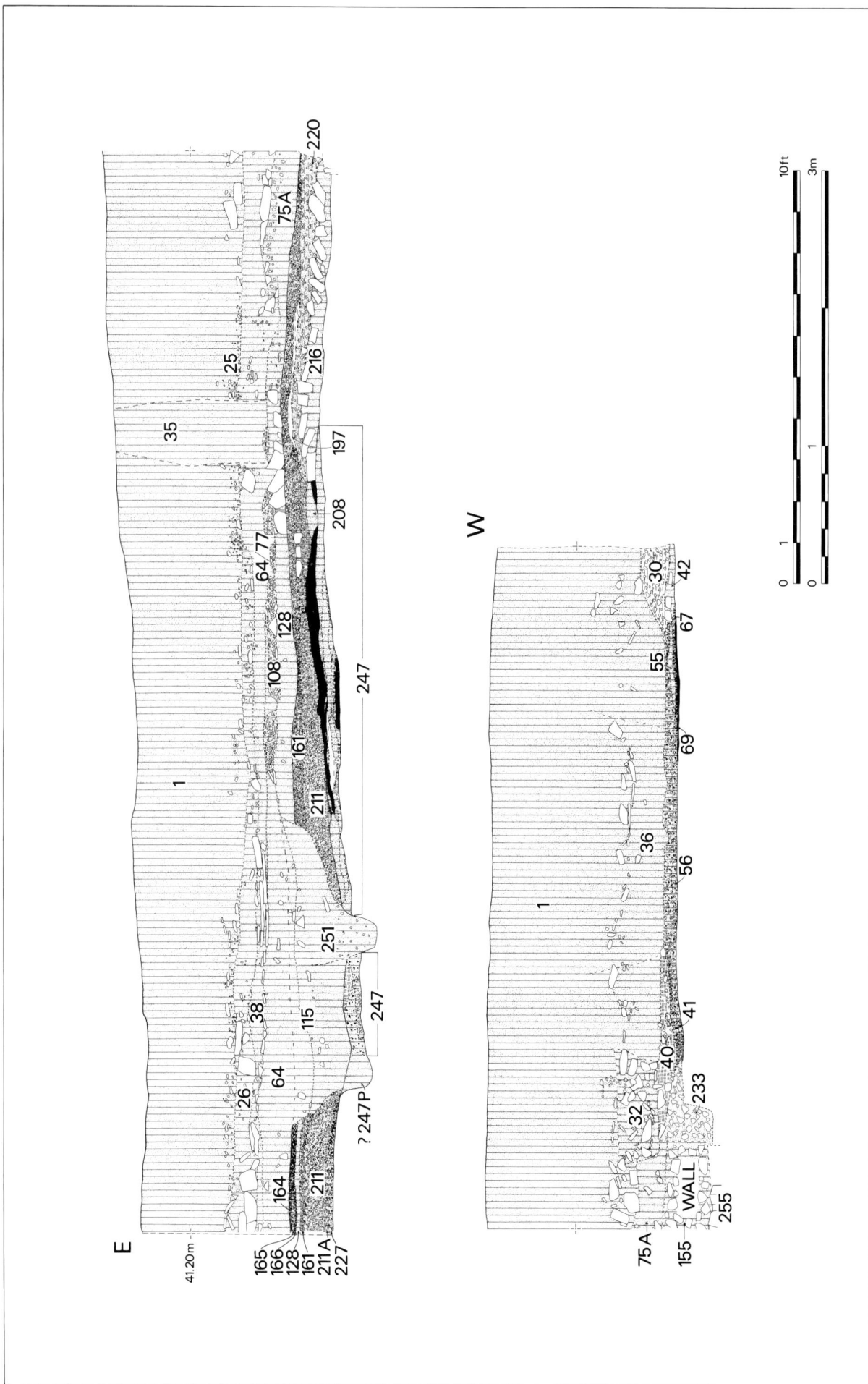

Figure 106 Site I, south section (AES 76–7)

exposed for some considerable time before being covered by deposits related to the secondary and later phases of building V is surprising. It may be that (*247*) was sealed by layers, including the gravel surface (*235*), which were later truncated by building activity or worn away. The evidence for assigning (*247*) and the gravel surfaces (*272*) and (*273*) to the same period rests on their identical stratigraphical relationship to (*235*). It is quite possible that (*272*), (*273*) and (*247*) were all contemporary.

Site II (Figs 104, 105, and 120)

A group of features at the east end of the site II trench was ascribed to period 3. Of these the earliest may have been (II *53*), which had three layers of fill. This possible pit, though stratigraphically primary, may have post-dated the other early features described under period 2. Its fill contained a sherd of Antonine samian which, if not intrusive, may mean that the feature should be assigned to period 4.

The features in this part of the site which were stratigraphically secondary and therefore assigned to period 3 include one upper fill or re-cut of a primary context, (II *36*) over (II *76*). This feature cannot be precisely categorised. The other feature in this group was a shallow pit (II *51*) cutting the gully (II *71*). The latest activity in this period was represented by layer (II *70*) and (II *33*), which was cut by features assigned to period 4.

Period 4 (AD 140/150–150/170): yard surfaces and layers predating construction of building V

Site I (Figs 102, 103, and 106, Plate 17)

Layer (*235*) was a major pebbled surface which extended over much of the site (Plate 17), and it appears to have marked a fairly important stage in the development of the area. (*235*) was not a universal layer; it did not cover all of (*247*) (see above) and there were curious and unexplained breaks in the pebbles in the north-eastern part of site I. Some of these demonstrated the north-east/south-west alignment common to most of the Roman features on the site, and they presumably related to building, or other activity in the north-eastern part of site I predating the period 7 building VI, but time did not permit examination of any of these anomalies in the gravel surface.

To the east of the period 5 building V layers (*224*), (*244*), and (*257*), consisting of dark grey-brown sandy loam with charcoal, lay immediately on top of (*235*). (*224*) in particular, which seemed to have accumulated in the hollow caused by the settling of layers above the fill of (*266*), had a useful pottery group (pottery vessels nos 194–206, Table 21), including Hadrianic samian ware and coarse wares of equivalent date. (*257*) contained a coin of Domitian. These layers also sealed a gravel layer (*241*) which probably represented a localised repair to (*235*). The original westward extent of these layers is unknown, but (*224*) extended beneath the floor (*44*) of building V (most of which was not removed).

Close to the northern limit of (*224*) was a small irregular posthole (*254*) c 0.15m in diameter, which was cut through (*235*) and was partly overlaid by the period 5 features (*245*) and (*208*). The function of this apparently isolated feature is not clear, but it does not fall into any meaningful pattern in relation to the other features which occurred in this part of the site in period 5, so its ascription to period 4 seems reasonable.

Site II (Figs 104 and 105)

At the eastern end of the site II trench the period 3 layer (II *70*) was cut by (II *32A*), stratigraphically a third phase feature, the first stage of a north-east/south-west ditch c 1.20m across and perhaps originally c 0.50m deep. Approximately parallel to (II *32A*) and about 5.5–6.0m to the east was a deeper and steeper-sided ditch (II *67*) c 1.45m wide and c 0.80m deep, of U-shaped profile. This and (II *32A*), in approximately equivalent stratigraphical positions, may have been contemporary. While it is difficult to project alignments from an excavation trench only 1m wide, (II *67*) and (II *32A*) do not appear to have been precisely parallel, so their contemporaneity cannot be certain. The alignment of both ditches was comparable to that of building V in site I.

Both (II *32A*) and (II *67*) had later fills, which were (II *32*) and (II *67–67A*) respectively, the original fill of (II *67*) possibly being represented by (II *67B*). The upper fill of (II *67*) was cut by a small gully (II *66*) which had a series of fills of burnt material (assigned to period 5).

The dating evidence for period 4 derives very largely from the contents of layer (*224*), underlying the period 5 building (pottery vessels nos 194–227, Table 21). None of the samian in this layer was considered to date after c AD 140 and none of the other contexts in this phase in site I contained later material. In site II, however, the evidence was less definite, demonstrating the difficulty of correlating the site I and II sequences. Features such as (II *68*) and (II *66*), which on other criteria might have been assigned to this period, contained Antonine samian ware and were thus assumed to be of period 5.

Major Roman buildings (periods 5–9)

Period 5 (AD 150/170–240): construction and use of building V

Site I (Figs 102, 107, and 108, Plates 17–18)

The next major development of the site after surfacing with pebbles was the construction of building V, a complete contrast to earlier structures.

Explosion site excavations (AES 76–7)

Plate 17 Site I, looking west, gravel surface (235), period 4, in foreground and building V, period 5, behind (AES 76–7) (2m scales)

Building V followed the north-east/south-west alignment of most of the Roman features on the site. In its initial form the building was fairly simple, but demonstrated an interesting range of construction techniques. At this time the excavated portion of the building probably consisted of two rooms (it is possible that there was an extension on the east side of the building, see below and Fig 175). The more south-westerly of these (room 1) had stone walls. These were wall (**5**) to the west, and wall (**255**) to the east. Wall (**5**) appears to have served building V throughout its life without being replaced. Of (**255**) only the foundations remained. The foundations of (**5**) were not examined since blocks of the superstructure remained *in situ*, but there is no reason to suppose that they differed markedly from those of (**255**).

The foundation of (**255**) was cut through (**235**) and layers beneath to a depth of approximately 0.60m. The trench, varying in width from *c* 0.50–0.70m, was filled with sandstone rubble, apparently in several layers. The top of (**255**) was examined, which showed that the rubble, although of varied shape, had been fairly carefully pitched, starting at the north end and working southwards.

The foundation of wall (**5**) was more uniform in width, from *c* 0.70–0.75m. On top of this foundation was the wall itself, of roughly squared sandstone blocks of varying size. In wall (**5**) a maximum of three courses survived, to a height of about 0.35m. The wall was double faced and the blocks were mortared. The core was filled with tightly packed rubble and mortar.

The original height of the wall is not known, but it is possible that it had stood only a little, if at all, higher than it survived. Although the construction could have been carried up to eaves level, it is quite likely that the walls were sills carrying a timber superstructure either fastened into the stonework, or more likely, resting on horizontal beams laid on top of the masonry. Both walls had butt ends to the north, and the walling of the northerly room appears to have been continued entirely in timber (though no evidence exists for the west side).

The timber structure of this room (room 2) rested on large blocks of sandstone up to 0.60m × 0.42m and 0.75m × 0.30m, and *c* 0.20m high, which were probably closely laid. These were best preserved along the north side of the building where an almost continuous line existed from the north east corner up to the point where it was disturbed by a series of late pits (**168**), (**24**) and (**122**). Two very large blocks, one on

Plate 18 Site I, building V, period 5, section of wall (5) with clay floor (44) and later surfaces to left (AES 76–7) (0.15m scale)

top of the other, found in pit (**122**) were probably redeposited, but could perhaps have come from the original north-west corner of the building, which would have required particularly strong support.

On the east side of the building one block was found in place between the later postholes (**230**) and (**231**) and another (not on plan), which had clearly belonged to the same series from the side of the building, between postholes (**230**) and (**222**). The stone blocks presumably carried timbers on which the superstructure was based; these could have been vertical or horizontal. The purpose of the blocks would have been to give support to the timbers, but particularly to raise them above ground level so that their bottoms would not rot.

The floor of building V was put down after the line of the walls had been laid out. The floor (**44**) consisted of red clay with some patches of greenish-grey clay in the easterly part of room 1. The clay was laid up against the stones of wall (**5**), and between the sandstone blocks outlining the northerly room so that it lapped round them.

There were several slots in the clay floor, and it was not always easy to determine to which period of building V they related. Two short lengths appeared to belong to the first phase of the building. The first of these (**258**) was in line with the change of construction techniques in the east and west walls, and although it was only short it seems most reasonable to assume that it represented some kind of timber partition between rooms 1 and 2. Both ends of the slot were disturbed by later features. The only other feature which seems likely to have been associated with the primary phase of the building was a short length of slot or gully (**171**) in room 2. This was sealed by the period 6 rubble (**141**), but how it fits into the scheme of building V in any phase is not clear.

There is some evidence that there was an extension on the east side of building V in its primary phase, the predecessor of the rooms (3/4) which certainly existed in period 6. The eastern wall of these rooms, represented by the slot (**208**), while confirmed as a period 6 structure, appeared to have earlier origins. This is suggested by the position of the rubble making up the floor of the period 6 room 4. Whereas the corresponding rubble of room 3 was laid up to the west edge of the timber contained in slot (**208**), the edge of the rubble in room 4 (**216**) was in line with the outer (east) edge of the slot (see Fig 109). Furthermore there was evidence for a slot beneath the period 6 rubble, confirming that (**208**) had originally extended the full length of the east side of building V,

Explosion site excavations (AES 76–7)

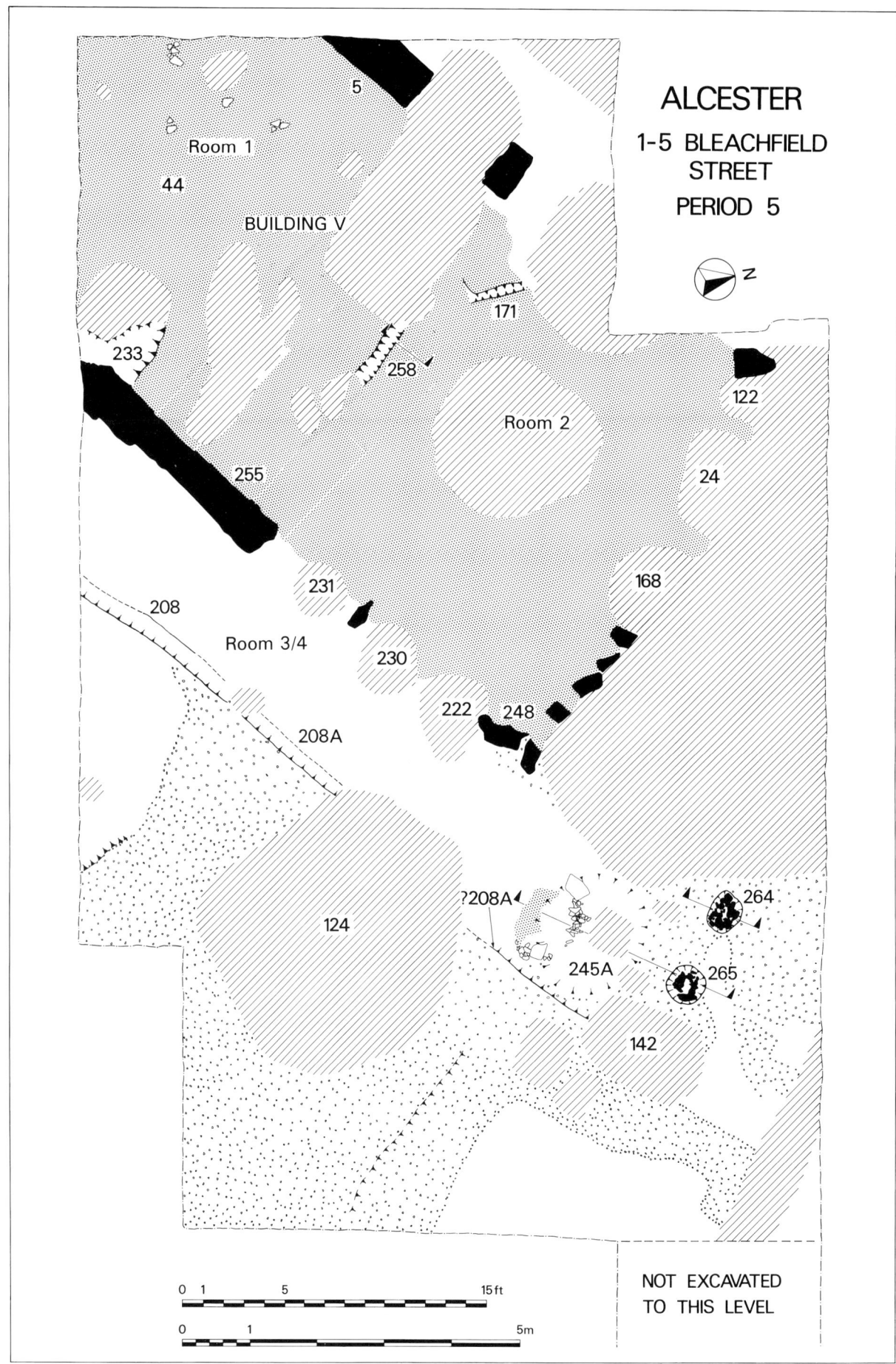

Figure 107   Site I, period 5 plan (AES 76–7)

Explosion site excavations (AES 76–7)

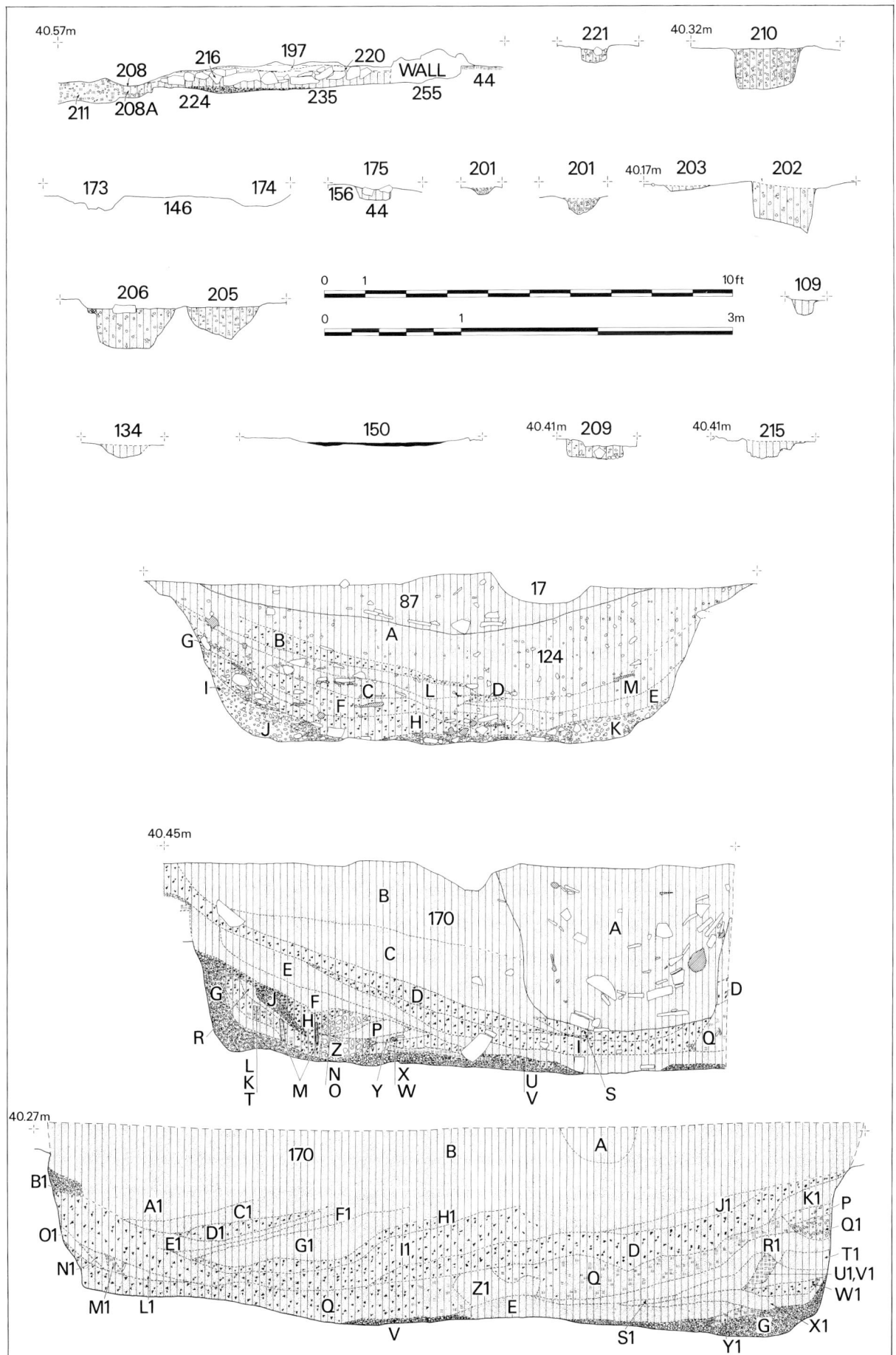

Figure 108   Site I, periods 5–9 sections (AES 76–7)

presumably during period 5. The slot lay some 1.60–1.80m from wall (*255*) and its northward continuation. It may have extended even further north than room 2, since a clear edge on approximately the right alignment was observed in the make-up material for the (period 7) gravel surface (*161*), between the later pits (*124*) and (*142*).

It is suggested that in its original form the building had a long narrow room or rooms (it is not known if the partitions in use in period 6 existed at this time) extending the whole length of the eastern side of the building and probably a little beyond. It seems quite likely that the north end of this room could have been marked by two postholes (*264*) and (*265*), the predecessors of two more (*252*) and (*253*) which probably related to the period 6 state of building V. (*265*) was round and (*264*) was irregular in outline, but both were about 0.55m across and had well preserved stone packing. This showed that (*265*) had held a timber c 0.10m × 0.16m, and although the packing of (*264*) was less regular the post it held would probably have been of a similar size. Since these posts projected well beyond the line of the north wall of room 2 they may have been the only survivors of a row of posts which ran along the north side of the building. Such posts could have supported a portico or veranda which would have been about 4m deep.

The one stratigraphical objection to the scheme outlined above is the question of the relationship between the slot (*208*) and the supposed make-up layers relating to the (period 7) major gravel surface (*161*) to the east of it. It has been mentioned already that the potential northern continuation of the slot was seen as a clearly defined edge in layers underlying (*161*), and elsewhere (*208*) had consistently the same relationship to these layers. However, (*161*) was assigned to period 7, so if the layers in question are considered to have been make-up layers they should therefore have immediately preceded the gravel surface, which would make it difficult to establish their existence, and that of (*208*), prior to period 6. The most likely explanation of this problem is that the process of accumulation of deposits to the east of the timber slot was in fact a gradual one which commenced relatively soon after the timber was in place. There was some evidence to support this suggestion. A patch of clay (297), lying on the west side of slot (*208*) was comparable to material forming the lowest part of the make-up layers (*211*) on the east side of (*208*). (297) was sealed by the period 6 rubble and mortar floor of room 3, and so must have been of period 5, suggesting that the process of accumulation of surfaces against (*208*) had already begun at this time.

Within the area defined by the slot (*208*) and postholes was a shallow, pit-like feature. In this phase a succession of layers, of clay and sandy loam (*245*) accumulated in the centre of a hollow in the pebbles, presumably caused by sinkage of the fill of the early pit (*266*). They contained pottery of early 2nd-century date, with perhaps some earlier residual material. These deposits were disturbed by a later cutting (*245*) in the top of the feature (see below, period 6).

The date of the primary phase of building V is not certain. A small quantity of pottery was recovered from the clay floor itself (pottery vessels nos 243–246, Table 22); this included a good proportion of rusticated and other coarse wares which should be of the first half of the 2nd century, and also several sherds of a Les Martres-de-Veyre Dr 37 (no 29) dated c AD 110–125, which was riveted and had therefore probably been in use for some time. Most of the material had obviously been trampled into the clay in small fragments, the samian bowl being almost the only exception. It could have been dropped rather later than the other fragments. Other samian ware included a fragment of Hadrianic or Antonine date. If it is accepted that there were timber rooms on the east side of building V in this period the dating evidence is augmented by the material from the period 4 layer (*224*), which was overlaid by slot (*208*) and therefore provided a *terminus post quem* for the building. It contained Hadrianic samian and coarse wares, as also did the pit (*245*) (pottery vessels nos 248–257, Table 22).

On this evidence the construction of building V can hardly have taken place much after the middle of the 2nd century at the latest. The evidence for the commencement date of the following period, however, is also clear and period 5 must have extended well into the 3rd century. There was a marked lack of later 2nd-century features (particularly in site I) which could be assigned to the continuation of period 5. It must therefore be assumed that building V was in use without major alteration for a considerable length of time and moreover that it and the associated yard area were kept free of rubbish.

Site II (Figs 104 and 105)

At the eastern end of the trench (II *68*), an upper fill or re-cut of a stratigraphically primary context (II *73*), was assigned to this period on the basis of a sherd of Antonine samian in its fill. If this sherd was intrusive, as is possible and was certainly the case with a medieval sherd from the same context, this feature might have belonged to period 3.

Further west, running between and approximately at right angles to the period 4 ditches (II *32A*) and (II *67*) was a third ditch or gully (II *72*), of comparably shallow profile to (II *32A*) and, like it, cutting layer (II *70*). There were two groups of fills, the lower consisting of (II *63*), (II *56*), and (II *55*), with a possible re-cut on the west side filled by (II *60*), (II *61*), and (II *57*). The lower of these two groups of fills overlaid (II *67*) suggesting that (II *72*) was the later of the two ditches, though the relationship was uncertain. A later re-cut of (II *67*), (II *66*), was also assigned to this period. It was a small gully with a relatively steep, rounded profile. Its fills contained much burnt material, and one side of the gully was very hard-packed. It is possible that some industrial function took place here, but what this might have been is unknown.

At the east end of the site II trench most of the -

features just described were overlaid by a general layer (II *54*). The layer contained a pottery assemblage identical to those of the underlying features and was probably of Antonine date (pottery vessels nos 228–242, table 22). It may therefore have accumulated at a time when there were few deposits in site I. The precise relationship of (II *54*) to (II *40*) and (II *47*) to the west remains unclear, but it is possible that (II *47*) represented a deposit analogous to layer (II *54*).

Period 6 (AD 240–250/260): expansion of building V

Site I (Figs 102, 106, 108–9, and 175, pls 19–20)

Period 6 saw a major but, in part, fairly short-lived reworking of building V, in which the core of the building was retained but was expanded on the west side. The postulated rooms on the east side of the building were replaced by a more substantial construction.

Room 1 of building V remained substantially unaltered from the previous period, apart from the apparent reconstruction of the east wall (**255**) (see below). While there were no features in this room which could be confidently assigned to period 6, since disturbance of the floor surfaces was very extensive and direct dating evidence was lacking, there were several which will be discussed here, although they could have belonged to period 5 as easily as period 6 (they are less likely to have been of period 7).

In the extreme south-west corner of the excavated area there was a small complex of layers, the first of which was an area of very dark burnt material with much charcoal (**69**) which was cut down a couple of centimetres into the period 5 clay floor (**44**), and appeared to represent a hearth. The shape of the cutting was irregular but it had probably been intended to be roughly circular, c 0.90m across; its southern side lay beneath the south baulk of the site.

Closely associated with the apparent hearth was a hard surface of compacted sand or mortar (**68**) which probably post-dated the hearth, but could have been cut by it. This surface was in turn sealed by layers (**65**) and (**67**) over the hearth area. Layer (**67**), and a patch of very gravelly mortar (**66**), were cut by a small irregular hole (94), which was itself cut by a medieval posthole (31). All these deposits (apart from the medieval posthole) appeared to be fairly close to each other in date. Further north in room 1 a small posthole (**184**), c 0.35–0.40m across, cut through a compacted layer (182) overlying the period 5 clay floor (**44**).

East of (**184**) was an oval pit or trough (**234**) c 1.30m long × 0.68m maximum width and c 0.25m deep, cut through the clay floor (**44**) and the pebbles beneath, with a gully (**259**) about 1.40m long and at most c 0.35m wide leading into it from the west. The gully was partly cut through a clay surface over (**44**) so it was not a primary feature after (**44**). Though both slightly irregular, these features were basically parallel to the partition dividing the two main rooms of building V.

The function of these features is unknown. The fill of (**234**) contained mixed material, including burnt stone, pebbles, lumps of clay, and some ash, presumably rubbish. (**259**), however, had been carefully constructed with a slope from its west end down into (**234**), the overall drop being about 0.14m – a gradient of 1 in 10. This suggests that (**259**) may have served as a drain for some liquid accumulating in (**234**), but what this might have been is unknown.

Of more significance was the rebuilding of wall (**255**). All the superstructure blocks were removed and in places, where the top of the foundation was not properly level, gravel was laid over it. A new foundation (**155**), identical to the previous one, was then laid on top of the gravel, with the rubble pitched from south to north, so that laying commenced from the north end. This foundation was very similar in character to, and on the same level as, the rubble (**216**) of the floor of rooms 3 and 4 (see below) which makes it clear that this was a secondary layer of foundation material; had it been a part of the original structure it would have stood well above the contemporary ground level at the time of the initial construction.

The only difference between (**155**) and its predecessor was that a stub wall or buttress approximately 0.70m square projected from the west side of (**155**). This feature (**116**) could have been a later addition to (**155**). No superstructure blocks remained in place on (**155**) and (**116**); they had been removed when this part of the site was levelled in the late Roman period.

The northerly room of building V was completely refashioned at the same time as the extensions were made. A beam slot (**157**) extended right across the line between the ends of walls (**255**) and (**5**), separating rooms 1 and 2. From this another slot (**158**) ran at right angles to the north-east, dividing the former north room (room 2) into two, room 2a to the north-west and room 2b to the south-east. A new stone wall was constructed to the west of wall (**5**). Of this a small portion of robber trench (**88**) in the extreme north-west corner of the site was all that survived, indicating wall foundations at least 0.90m wide, ie more substantial than the earlier walls and probably implying that this was an external wall. There was space for a passage (room 5) just over 1m wide between (**88**) and wall (**5**). Much of this passage south of the partition was obliterated by the late Roman pit (**4**) and the nature of its flooring is not known.

Building V was also remodelled on the east side, in timber, perhaps partly reusing the structure whose presence was postulated in period 5. Here the period 5 sleeper beam (**208**) was either partly reused or replaced by another timber in an identical position parallel to wall (**255**). In this period, however, (**208**) did not extend as far north as in period 5. It now ran only as far as a slot at right angles to it (**221**), which marked the north wall of a room at least 4m long (room 3).

Explosion site excavations (AES 76–7)

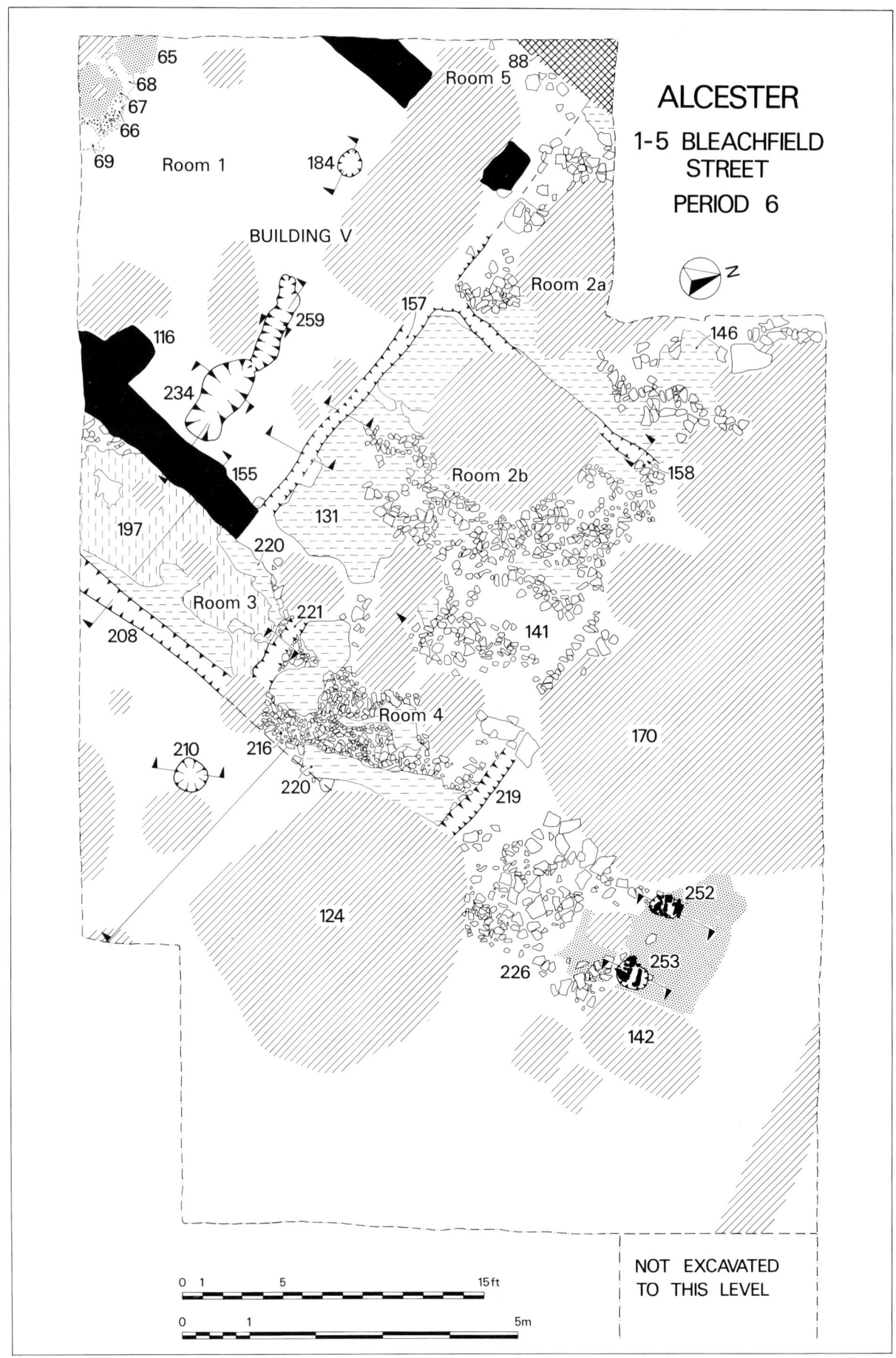

Figure 109   Site I, period 6 plan (AES 76–7)

Plate 19   Site I, south-east of building V, period 6, wall (155) to right with rubble base of rooms 3 and 4 floors and slot beyond (208) (AES 76–7) (2m scales)

The end of the northerly room (room 4) was defined by a further slot (**219**). This was in line with the original north wall of building V (room 2) and gave a room just over 3.2m long. It is not known if either of the slots (**221**) or (**219**) had existed in period 5.

The flooring of all the rooms, except for 1 and 5 as mentioned above, was identical. Indeed this was the main evidence for the contemporaneity of this phase of rooms 3 and 4 with the reworking of the rest of building V. The flooring consisted of carefully laid sandstone and lias rubble set around the timbers, which were presumably already in place. Over this rubble was poured a mix of mortar and pebbles ((**131**) in room 2, (**220**) in rooms 3 and 4) which, where it survived undisturbed, was thick and very hard.

The position of the floor material (see also above, period 5) highlights the problem of the structure of the rooms on the east side of building V. It has already been mentioned that the beam slot (**208**) appeared in this phase to terminate at the north-east corner of room 3, rather than running the whole length of the eastern side of the building, as it apparently had in period 5. In room 4 the line of the slot (**208A**) was well and truly sealed by the rubble and mortar floor. It is noticeable that at this point room 4 had sunk into a hollow, which probably developed as material filling the underlying period 1 pit (**266**) became compressed. It is suggested that this settlement caused the original period 5 structure to become unstable, and that at the time of the period 6 refurbishment the slot was not retained in use beyond the corner of room 3. In room 4 (and in the porch to the north, see below) the timber in (**208**) was probably left in position (which explains why its edge remained well-defined even at a late stage in period 6) and the period 6 floor was laid right over it. There is little indication of exactly how the superstructure of room 4 was supported at this time, but it may have had a horizontal timber on its eastern side. This is suggested by the poorly defined layer (**214**) which overlaid the edge of the floor of room 4 and might have resulted from the removal of a timber in this position.

It is notable that (*214*), while apparently overlaid by the period 7 gravel surface (**161**), clearly sealed the putative make-up layer (*211*), supporting the suggestion (above, period 5) that there was a time lapse between the deposition of (*211*) and (*161*). The suggestion also receives support from the presence of a possible posthole (**210**) to the east of building V. This feature was clearly cut through layer (*211*), but equally clearly did not cut the overlying surface

Explosion site excavations (AES 76–7)

Plate 20   Site I, building V, period 6, rubble base of room 2b floor, cut by pit (49), with beam slots (157) to right, and (158) foreground (AES 76–7) (1m scales)

(**161**). Even if it had only been in use for a short time (as an isolated feature with no really diagnostic characteristics its function was uncertain) it must indicate that the deposition of (**161**) did not follow (**211**) immediately.

To the north of room 4 there were deposits which may have been connected with this phase of building V. The first of these was (**232**), a mixed layer containing clay, crushed sandstone, and large quantities of mortar which, from its position and contents, was perhaps connected with the reconstruction of building V in period 6, serving as a dump or as a preparation area for the materials required in the rebuilding. It was sealed by a deposit containing many blocks of stone (**226**). Though these had been disturbed, the surviving stones gave the impression of having been part of a surface. The majority of them were flat, and many appeared to have been worn. The shape and condition of the stones made it clear that they had never been intended, unlike (**141**) and (**216**), to have a mortar surface above. Nevertheless they had presumably been intended to form a surface roughly comparable to those within the extended building V. As with layers further south, the main problem of (**226**) was its relationship to the period 7 gravel surface (**161**), but in general it seems clear

that the edge of (**161**) respected the structure of which (**226**) was presumably the floor, and that (**226**) was associated with building V before the demolition of the extensions on the east side.

Immediately to the north-east of (**226**) was a series of features overlying or cutting the period 4 gravel surface (**235**). Of these, the postholes (**265**) and (**264**), and the first phase of pit (**245**) are thought to have belonged to period 5.

In its second phase (**245**) was re-cut and backfilled with large quantities of stone and broken tile, and other finds included coins of Nero (no 1) and Faustina Junior (no 9), which gives a *terminus post quem* of AD 161–175 for this stage of activity. North of (**245**) the period 5 postholes were sealed by a layer of red clay with pebbles and larger cobbles (263). A further pair of postholes (**252**) and (**253**) was cut through this layer to the south of the first pair. They lay immediately adjacent to the north edge of (**245**). Both were oval, with a maximum dimension of c 0.50m, ie slightly smaller than the first pair. Again stone packing was *in situ*. In (**252**), the westerly of the pair, the post could have been at least 0.10m × 0.12m, and in (**253**) perhaps as much as 0.10m × 0.20m, though in both cases a size of post identical to those in (**264**) and (**265**) (ie c 0.10m ×

0.16m) is likely. In all four postholes the greater dimension of the timber was from east to west.

It seems certain that (*252*) and (*253*) replaced the period 5 posts in forming the north end of the range of rooms along the eastern side of building V. The straight edge of the period 7 surface (*161*) between (*124*) and (*142*) suggests that there was a structure still standing west of this edge which precluded (*161*) being laid there. (*226*) was presumably the floor of this structure and (*252*) and (*253*) supports for its front. These features may have represented a porch giving access to rooms 3 and 4. Since, however, on the evidence of (*161*), room 3 was certainly and room 4 probably demolished by the time this surface was laid, and yet, on the same evidence of (*161*), the 'porch' was still standing, this interpretation seems unlikely. An alternative explanation is that there was a veranda or portico along the whole of the north side of building V, which was later completely removed by pit (*170*) and other disturbances, apart from the small surviving portion between (*170*) and (*142*). This veranda could have remained in existence after rooms 3 and 4 had gone out of use.

The proposed sequence can be summarised as follows:

Period 5
1 (*245*) represented the initial levelling up of this part of the pebbled surface (*235*) which had slumped into an earlier pit.

Period 6
2 (*232*) (the building dump) accumulated.
3 (*245*) was re-cut and filled with building debris.
4 (*226*) was laid, possibly just post-dating postholes (*252*) and (*253*), the packing of which may have been sealed by (*226*).

Period 7
5 (*161*) was laid up alongside the structure which was still standing though rooms 3 and 4 had been demolished.
6 This part of building V went out of use, and (*226*) was cut by (*262*), part of the timber structure associated with building VI, and a pebbled surface (*225*) was laid subsequent to this.

At a later stage in period 6 there was more activity on the east side of building V. The floor of room 3 was resurfaced in period 6 with a mortar distinct from that used in the construction of the enlarged building. This mortar (*197*) was lighter in colour than the previous surface (*220*), and contained no pebbles.

Outside building V the gravel surface (*235*) may have continued for a time to serve as a yard surface, but the principal deposit east of building V was a uniform grey-brown layer (*227*) which sealed (*235*) and the early surfaces over it and was overlaid by the make-up layers for the period 7 gravel surface (*161*). (*227*) itself contained a large pottery group, including considerable quantities of rusticated ware.

The accumulated dating evidence for this period (pottery vessels nos 258–383, Table 22) derived largely from layers associated with or outside building V, although some other construction deposits (eg (*232*) and (*226*)) themselves also produced useful dating material. This included a small Black-Burnished ware cooking pot (no 263) set in the rubble (*141*) of room 2a. This vessel is unlikely to have been earlier than mid-3rd century in date and is also unlikely to been inserted into the floor after its construction. The remaining evidence was quite consistent with this (see below for detailed discussion). While layers such as (*227*) contained large quantities of pottery of mid-2nd-century character, all the contexts in this period included material which could not, on present evidence (eg Young 1977) have dated before c AD 240 at the earliest. This pottery, though in small quantities, occurred so consistently that it could not have been intrusive.

Site II (Figs 104 and 105)

Few features in site II could be assigned to this period. Layer (II *39*), overlying the earlier ditch (II *32*) and layer (II *47*), was perhaps of period 6. The other feature which probably belonged to this period was a pit (II *31*), lying at the west end of the group of early Roman deposits in the site II trench immediately east of the end of the period 7 building VI. The evidence for this pit was partly obscured by a medieval re-cut (II *31A*) and by a further medieval pit (II *30*) which cut the southern side of (II *31*). The relationship of (II *31*) to other contexts was less certain, except that it appears to have been partly overlaid or cut by one of the walls (II *27*) of building VI, which would mean that it must have predated period 7. The pottery in (II *31*), admittedly limited in quantity, was comparable with material from the other features in the east end of the trench, perhaps suggesting a 2nd-century date, but on stratigraphic grounds ascription to period 6 was slightly preferred.

Period 7 (AD 250/260–270): gravel surfaces and buildings V and VI

Site I (Figs 106, 108, and 110–111, pls 21–24)

This was a period of intensive building and other activity, all of which probably took place within a short timespan.

Gravel surface

The major development at the beginning of period 7 was the deposition of a gravel surface (*161*). This surface was located over most of the eastern part of site I, and also extensively in site II, where excavation in the main part of the site was halted at this level (II *20*). It is not known whether the surface originally extended further east than the end of building VI. It may have done, but all later deposits in this part of the site had been completely removed.

(*161*)/(II **20**) was distinguished from all other gravel surfaces on the site by having a very thick make-up layer beneath it, in places up to 0.20m thick and on average about 0.15m. This layer (*211*) consisted almost entirely of clean orange sand and gravel, with occasional patches of red clay, particularly on the west edge of the deposit. In the north-eastern part of site I the make-up layer for (*161*) was generally much more clayey than elsewhere and was numbered (228). Parts of the make-up layers were probably deposited in period 6 at the latest (see above, periods 5 and 6).

Building V

The laying of (*161*) in site I was preceded by the demolition of room 3 and probably of room 4 of building V. The timber in slot (*208*), forming the east wall of room 3, was removed and the slot was carefully packed with selected rubble and large cobbles. Sand and gravel had already been laid right up to the edge of rooms 3 and 4 and north of pit (*124*) the straight edge of the sand and gravel make-up was continued in the area of rubble (*226*) (see above), but it is less clear what happened beyond (*142*). (*161*) may have extended further west, the isolated patch beside wall (*13*) being separated from the main area by a shallow, approximately rectilinear cutting.

The evidence for the demolition of room 4 was not as clear as that for room 3. Room 4 seems to have received rather different treatment since its floor surface was only lightly covered with gravel (*161*), but this did apparently overlie (*214*), the feature which it is postulated related to the removal of the east wall of room 4. It is therefore likely that both rooms 3 and 4 were demolished at the same time.

The porch or veranda along the north side of building V may have lasted rather longer. It seems certain to have survived into the early part of period 7 since it was clearly respected by the western edge of (*161*). It cannot, however, have remained in use throughout the period since its floor (*226*) was cut by one of the postholes (*262*) of the timber structure which was built against the south wall of building VI and was also assigned to period 7.

As a result of the demolition of rooms 3 and 4 the east wall of rooms 1 and 2 of building V became an external wall, and it was probably at this time that it was reconstructed to allow for this. The new structure was carried on three posts (*222*), (*230*) and (*231*). The pits for these posts were quite large: (*231*), the southerly one, was slightly smaller than the other two, being some 0.70m in diameter, whereas (*230*) was 0.85m across and (*232*) c 0.95m. All were 0.55–0.60m deep. The pits were cut through the rubble and mortar floors of the period 6 rebuilding, and therefore probably belonged to period 7, though they could have been later. The posts themselves may have been dug out at some late stage, and the post pits were filled with a variety of rubbish, including a few fragments of painted plaster. The stumps of the posts had, however, rotted *in situ*. Those in (*230*) and (*222*) were circular and 0.19m in diameter. (*231*) was rather different in that it had flat lias slabs at the bottom of the hole – presumably for the post to rest on. However, the picture had been complicated by the apparent reuse of the pit (and just possibly the post itself) for building III (period 10). The hole had some stone packing at the top, but this most probably related to the building III post. The original post was probably of the same order of size as those in (*222*) and (*230*).

Within building V there were problems of close dating. Features which may have existed in this period have been shown on the plan (Figs 110–112). In room 1 the period 6 posthole (*184*) was very carefully packed with thin blocks of stone set edgeways into the hole and with their upper edges flush with the top. Over this, and identified elsewhere in room 1, was laid a floor (*74*) comprised of mixed rubble, mainly sandstone, and some tile, fairly small pieces being employed. Fragmentary as this floor was, it did appear to have been laid with regard to the partition (*157*) dividing rooms 1 and 2, the stones forming lines roughly parallel to the partition.

A further patch of stonework (*84*) was of similar character (and probably similar date) to (*74*), and an adjacent patch of decayed mortar (*83*) might also have been of period 7 date. At the east end of room 1 there was what appeared to be a dump of material (*120*) against wall (*155*). This was very mixed indeed, and contained a large quantity of small sandstone fragments, clay, mortar, and wall-plaster, some of it painted. There was, indeed, more plaster in this deposit than from the rest of sites I and II combined. This plaster and other rubbish may have derived from the remodelling of the interior of building V contemporary with the demolition of rooms 3 and 4. (*120*) was sealed by several of the stone slabs of (*140*). These were laid on both sides of the beam slot (*157*) at its east end, (north of (*157*)) they sealed the period 6 mortar floor (*131*)) and it is clear that the beam was still in place. The slabs were well worn, and also well laid: clean sand had been used to level some of the blocks on top of (*120*). They might have been part of a general floor layer, but it seems more likely that they were just laid in this one place, which was presumably an entrance through the partition and susceptible to wear.

In room 2 there were no identifiable floor surfaces post-dating the major period 6 rebuilding. However, in room 2a there was slight evidence for three parallel slots post-dating the period 6 work. Of these only very short lengths of the two western ones (*174*) and (*180*) remained, although they seemed to be reasonably well defined. The easternmost slot (*173*) survived to a length of c 1.70m. The function of these slots is unclear, but being close together they could have held timber supports for a construction of some kind within the building. The Black-Burnished pot (no 263) already mentioned above was set between slots (*173*) and (*174*) and may possibly have been

Explosion site excavations (AES 76–7)

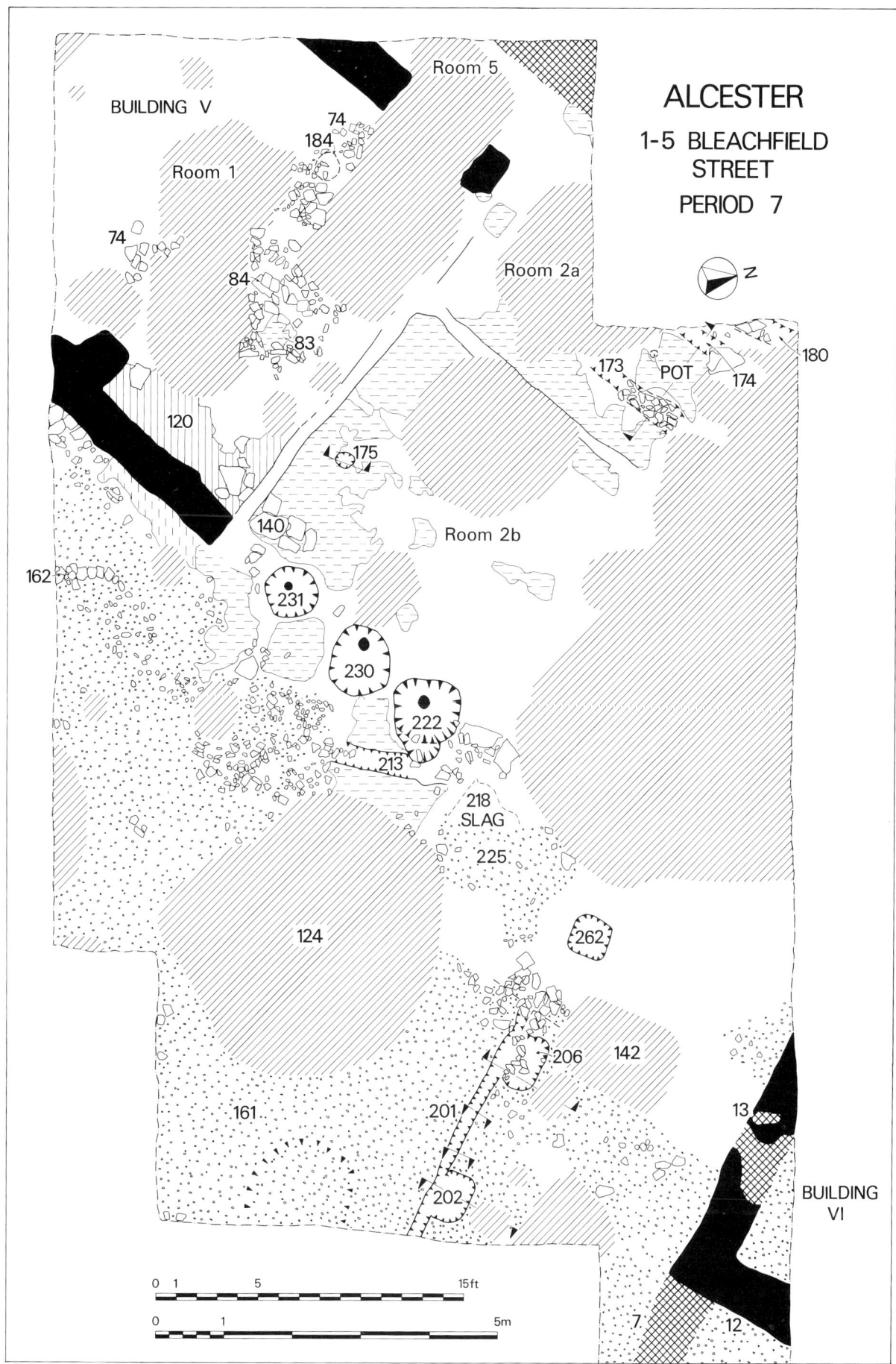

Figure 110 Site I, period 7 plan (AES 76–7)

Explosion site excavations (AES 76–7)

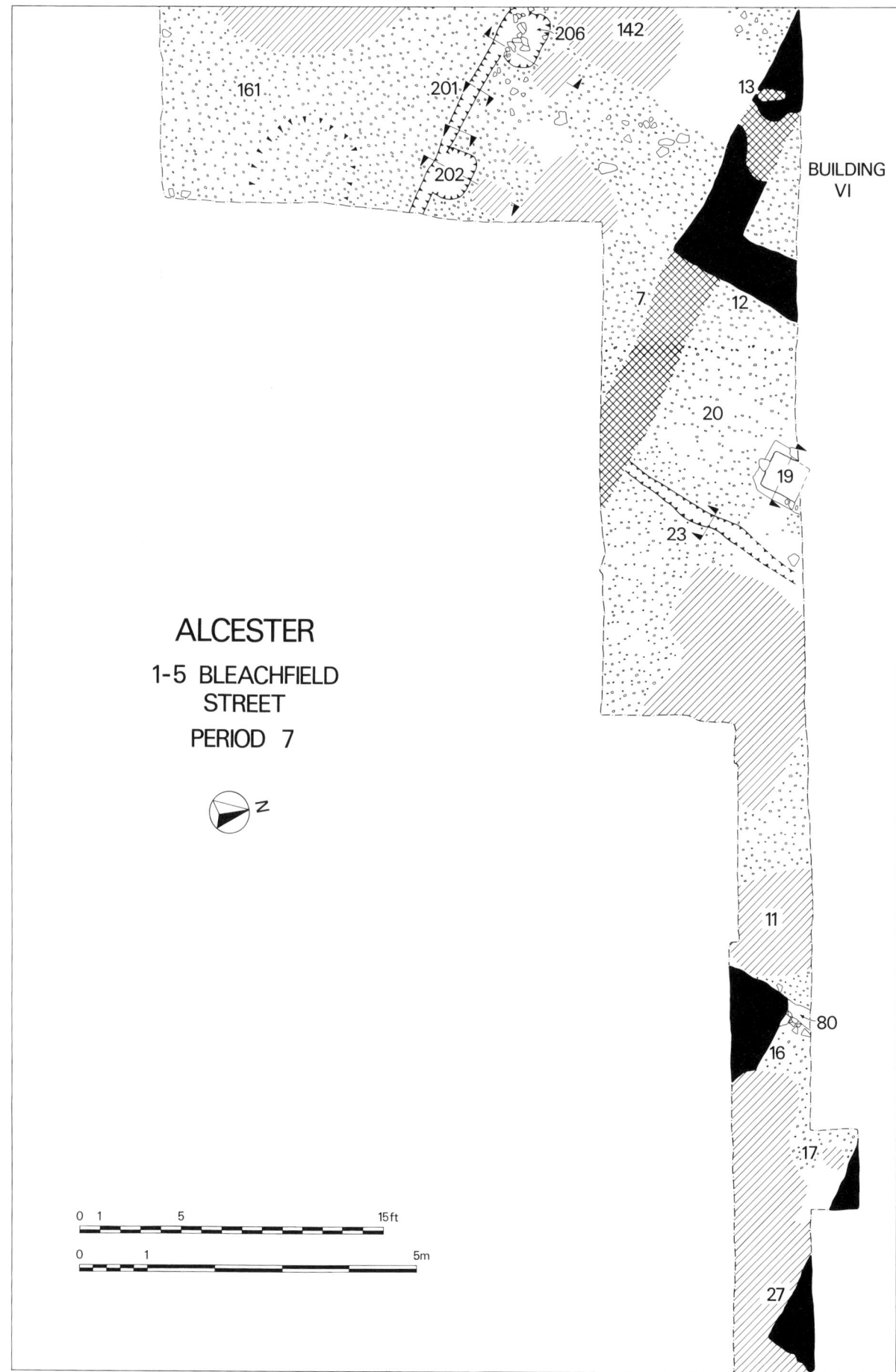

Figure 111   Site II, period 7 plan (AES 76–7)

Plate 21 Site I, surface (161), period 7, to left, with possible drain and postholes of timber lean-to on south-west side of building VI in foreground. Building V to right (AES 76–7) (2m scales)

connected with this activity. In room 2b there were a couple of small holes cut in the rubble surface, (*175*) and (160), which may have been postholes.

Building VI

The other major event of period 7 was the construction of building VI. This took place after the gravel surface (*161*) had been laid, though it is uncertain how much time elapsed between these two operations.

Building VI was found primarily in site II, but parts of it (wall (**13**) and a timber structure) were encountered in site I. Only a small part of the plan of building VI was recovered. The rest must have been to the north of the excavated area, beneath the car park of the Swan Inn, and may still survive there, though the surface of the car park is rather lower than that of the Explosion site.

Wall foundations still survived in places, with perhaps the lowest coursed stones of the walls (albeit small ones) still *in situ* in site II (II **12**). These small flat stones occurred some 0.15m below the level of (*161*), which might suggest that (*161*) was laid subsequent to the construction of the walls, but in site II, the south side of construction/robber trench (II **7**), cut a small pit or posthole which in turn cut (*161*), suggesting that the construction of the wall must have been after the deposition of the gravel.

Building VI consisted at its east end of a pair of parallel walls some 1.80m apart and about 4m long running approximately north-west/south-east, though only the west end of the southern (II **16**), and the east end of the northern (II **27**) were found. At the west end of the south wall, and probably connecting the two, were flat lias blocks (II **80**) which seemed to form a threshold.

It is assumed that the southerly wall had a return to the south at its western end, linking with the easterly extension of wall (II **7**) in the main part of site II, though even this cannot be certain (for a reconstruction plan of the building, see Fig 175). Wall (II **7**), with its continuation into site I (**13**), was probably the major wall of the building. A short length of wall (II **12**) ran at right angles to it, to the north. Although structurally subsequent, being butted up against wall (II **7**), it must have been contemporary in terms of the use of the building. The walls were on average some 0.70–0.80m thick. The depth of the roughly

Explosion site excavations (AES 76–7)

Plate 22 Site II, building VI, period 7, with surface (20), wall (2), robbed wall (7), slot (23), and tank (19) (AES 76–7) (2m scale)

pitched stone foundations was c 0.60m. The foundation stones appeared to have been pressed into the side of the construction trench. The foundation was of mixed sandstone and lias; the coursed stone which survived was all sandstone. Within the building there were no floor surfaces other than the pebbles of (*161*) and (II **20**).

Associated with the stone structure were features suggesting timber buildings. These could have been contemporary with the initial construction of building VI, or they could have been later. To the north of wall (II **7**), and parallel to wall (II **12**) (and about 3m from it), was a shallow and rather irregular slot some 0.20m wide (II **23**). This could have been an internal partition within building VI, or could (if, as is just possible, this area was not roofed) have represented a lean-to building against wall (**12**). In the latter case the slot could have served either as the emplacement for a horizontal timber on which the structure was based, or else (since it was rather irregular) as an eaves drip from such a structure based on timbers lying on the gravel surface. The fill of the gully did contain two pieces of daub, which was otherwise scarce in contexts post-dating period 2. These could possibly have derived from a light wall adjacent to the gully.

Within this 'lean-to' structure, or partitioned area, was a small tank (II **19**) which was cut into the pebbled floor and probably belonged to the initial phase of the structure. Internally the tank measured 0.50m × 0.55m and was c 0.40m deep. It was constructed of selected sandstone and lias rubble, with smooth internal faces, and the whole was grouted with clay, all the gaps being carefully filled with this material. The bottom was of clay, and the tops of the sides were finished with clay. The top stood some 0.06–0.08m proud of the pebbled surface. No real clue to the function of the tank was given by its contents since it had been filled with rubbish, including a quantity of slag. It had presumably been intended to hold liquid of some sort, probably water.

South of wall (II **7**) and I (**13**), and parallel to it, were three alignments of features only identified where they cut the gravel surface (*161*). From south to north they comprised a slot (**201**); postholes or post pits (**202**) and (**206**); and postholes (**203**), (**204**) and (**205**) (see period 8). (**201**) seemed to be clearly later than (**206**) and probably later than (**202**), and (**203**) appeared to be later than all these features. It is likely that (**203**) and (**205**) were related and probably contemporary, but it cannot

Plate 23   Site II, detail of tank (II 19) in building VI, period 7 (AES 76–7) (0.15m scale)

be certain that this was so, and their relationship to (**204**) is unknown. The most likely explanation is that (**202**) and (**206**) were primary and that (**262**), to the west, was related to them. All three were of similar dimensions, rectilinear in shape, and had approximately vertical sides. The spacing from centre to centre ((**202**)–(**206**) 2.20m, (**206**)–(**262**) 2.10m) also suggests that these features should be seen together. They are most likely to have supported a timber lean-to structure against the south wall of building VI, whereas the later slot (**201**) is interpreted as a drain running in front of the structure, constructed after its initial erection and hence cutting the edges of the post pits (**202**) and (**206**).

'Yard' area

After the deposition of (**161**) there were very few features within the 'yard' area between buildings V and VI which were assigned to period 7.

A small stone feature (**162**) was constructed over (**161**) at the south edge of the site and adjacent to building V, but its nature and function are completely unknown. North of this was a slot-like feature (**213**) also adjacent to building V. It was aligned almost exactly north–south (a most unusual orientation on this site), and situated in what had been room 4 of building V, running diagonally across it and probably post-dating its destruction. It is difficult to see what function this feature, whether gully or beam slot, could have fulfilled. The lie of the ground at this point might suggest some sort of drain, carrying water away from the north-east corner of building V, but there is no definite evidence for this, or any other, suggestion.

Site II (Figs 104, 105, and 120)

In the eastern part of the site II trench there was evidence for a layer (II **48**) of clean orange gravel up to c 0.38m thick, which may have been analogous with the make-up (**211**) for layer (**161**). This layer contained no finds. It was sealed and cut by post-medieval features, as a result of which it was largely removed in the machine excavation of the upper deposits of the trench. At its western end it was cut by a sandstone filled feature (II **28**), possibly a shallow wall foundation and perhaps of late Roman date. (II **48**) had an Antonine *terminus post quem* provided by the layers beneath, the latest of which, (II **39**), is assigned to period 5 or perhaps more likely to period 6, but its precise date is very uncertain. (II **48**) is

Explosion site excavations (AES 76–7)

Plate 24 Site I, timber lean-to on south-west side of building VI, period 7, after excavation, showing postholes (202) and (206) and possible drain (201) (AES 76–7) (2m scale)

assigned to period 7 primarily on the basis of its possible equivalence to the make-up layer (*211*), but is possible that it was an entirely post-Roman feature (see period 13 below).

Among the stratigraphically latest Roman features in the eastern part of the site II trench were two pits, (II *49*) and (II *52*), which lay partly beneath the south baulk. They were similar in character with steeply sloping sides and rounded bottoms. While these features might have been approximately contemporary, only (II *49*) could be assigned to period 7 with any degree of certainty.

The dating evidence for period 7 was limited in quantity (pottery vessels nos 384–414). Definition of the chronological range of the period depended primarily on the evidence from the preceding and succeeding phases.

Period 8 (AD 270–280/290): gravel surfaces, buildings IV, V, and VI

This period covered a fairly short span of time from after the construction of building VI to the later part of the 3rd century (for dating see pottery vessels 415–455).

Explosion site excavations (AES 76–7)

Site I (Figs 106, 108, and 112)

Building V

There were few layers within building V which could be confidently assigned to this period. In room 1 a fragment of a good quality mortar floor (*73*) survived between pit (*4*) and the area damaged by (*3*). It overlaid the period 7 stone surface (*74*), but it is possible that it represented only a limited patching of this surface (otherwise more of (*73*) might have been expected to have survived), which otherwise remained in use. In the extreme south-west corner of the site a hard, compact layer (*55*) overlaid the period 6 layers, and north and north-east of this were (*52*) and (*63*), both of which partly sealed (*62*).

In rooms 2a and 2b a series of mixed, dirty layers related to the continued use of the rooms, but did not constitute proper floor surfaces. These included (*130*) and (*138*) and related layers (147), (148), and (149).

The main developments on the site in this period seem to have taken place outside building V. It is not known how long the pebble surface (*161*) was kept clean and in use as a surface. After it ceased to be used an extensive layer of sandy loam with many pebbles, up to 0.15m thick, (*128*) accumulated over it. This contained a useful group of pottery (pottery vessels nos 415–441) including several sherds of an Oxfordshire colour-coated beaker with a *terminus post quem* of at least AD 270.

Building IV

The features which constituted building IV rested immediately on top of layer (*128*) at the extreme south of the site, immediately east of building V. Running under the south baulk of the site was a distinct but irregular area of crushed mortar and sandstone fragments up to 0.10m thick (*108*).

This was presumed to be the front of a more extensive platform of this material, roughly at right angles to building V and separated from it by a gap of about 1m. Running through the spread was a rough slot (*109*), probably at least 2m long, but the east end had been disturbed by later features. The platform projected about 0.60m in front of this slot, and had at its north-west corner a well-defined 'cut out' which may have indicated the position of a vertical post. The projecting part of the platform appeared not to have extended very far eastwards, at most 1.20m beyond the possible post position.

Although the evidence is extremely tenuous it is possible to postulate the presence of a timber building at right angles to building V, with its front wall perhaps constructed on a timber resting in slot (*109*), and with a porch projecting northwards from its north-west corner supported by upright timbers. There was little close dating evidence for this structure, except insofar as the contents of the underlying layer (*128*) provided a *terminus post quem*. The building may have been roughly contemporary with a series of gravel surfaces (*164–166*), but the date of the building relative to these surfaces cannot be considered certain. There was no indication of a long time lag between the laying of the three gravel surfaces (*164–166*), unless the lower ones had been kept very clean prior to the deposition of the upper one (*164*), which seems unlikely. As with (*108*), the contents of (*128*) and the surfaces themselves gave a *terminus post quem*, and the latest contents of the period 9 pit (*124*), which cut all these layers, provided a *terminus ante quem*.

The gravel surfaces did not extend right up to the east wall of building V. The reason for this is not known, but it may have had something to do with the remains of rooms 3 and 4 of building V. The north edge of (*164*) was well-defined and ran parallel to wall (*13*) of building VI at a distance of some 3.5–3.8m. There seems little doubt that the pebbles were laid up to the south edge and around the south-western corner of the period 7 timber structure ((*202*), (*206*), and (*262*)) leaning against the south wall of building VI. The structure was clearly still in use at this time.

Building VI

Building VI appears to have undergone some alterations during period 8. A few centimetres north of each of the postholes (*202*) and (*206*) was another; (*203*) north of (*202*) and (*205*) north of (*206*). These features were smaller and less regular than their counterparts to the south, though still approximately rectangular. While there appeared on the basis of shape and position to be a connection between these features and (*202*) and (*206*), they may not have been exactly contemporary. Between (*203*) and (*205*) was a smaller hole (*204*), but none of these features contained any packing for posts, or any other indication of function.

Posts set in (*203*) and (*205*) (and possibly (*204*)) might have represented a late phase of the lean-to building initially set on (*202*), (*206*), and (*262*). If this was so, this phase must have fallen within the latter part of period 8, since the period 8 surfaces (*164–6*) respected the original, southerly line of the structure. It is perhaps more likely that the features were internal.

Site II (Figs 104, 105, and 113)

No surfaces which might have served as floors at this time were identified inside the lean-to building. Any floors were presumably of earth, which escaped detection as a result of the extensive disturbances in this part of the site. Within building VI, north of wall (*13*) and (II **7**), there was likewise no evidence of any floor levels or structural features later than the main period 7 gravel surface (*161*) and (II **20**), the only

Explosion site excavations (AES 76–7)

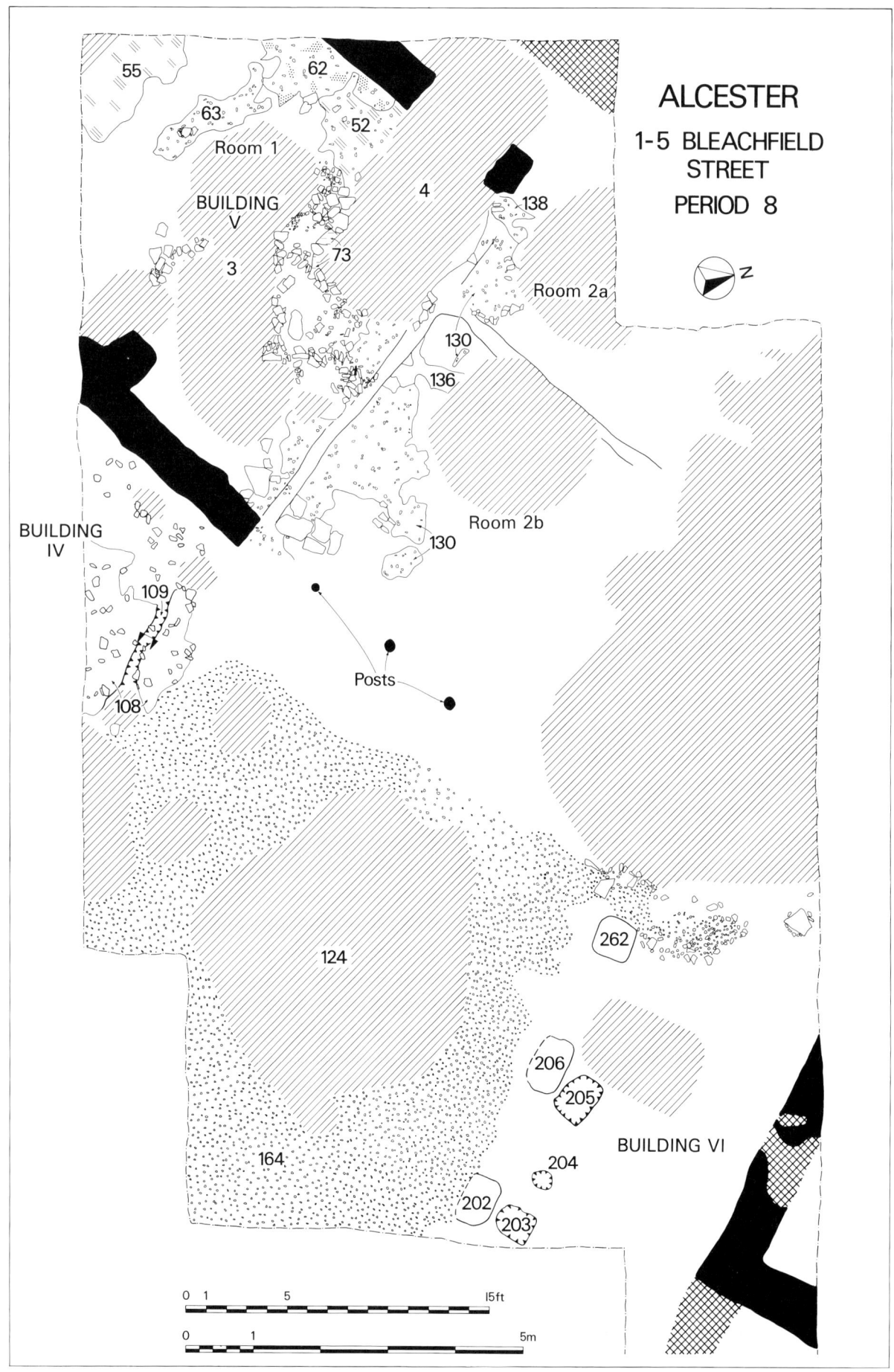

Figure 112 Site I, period 8 plan (AES 76–7)

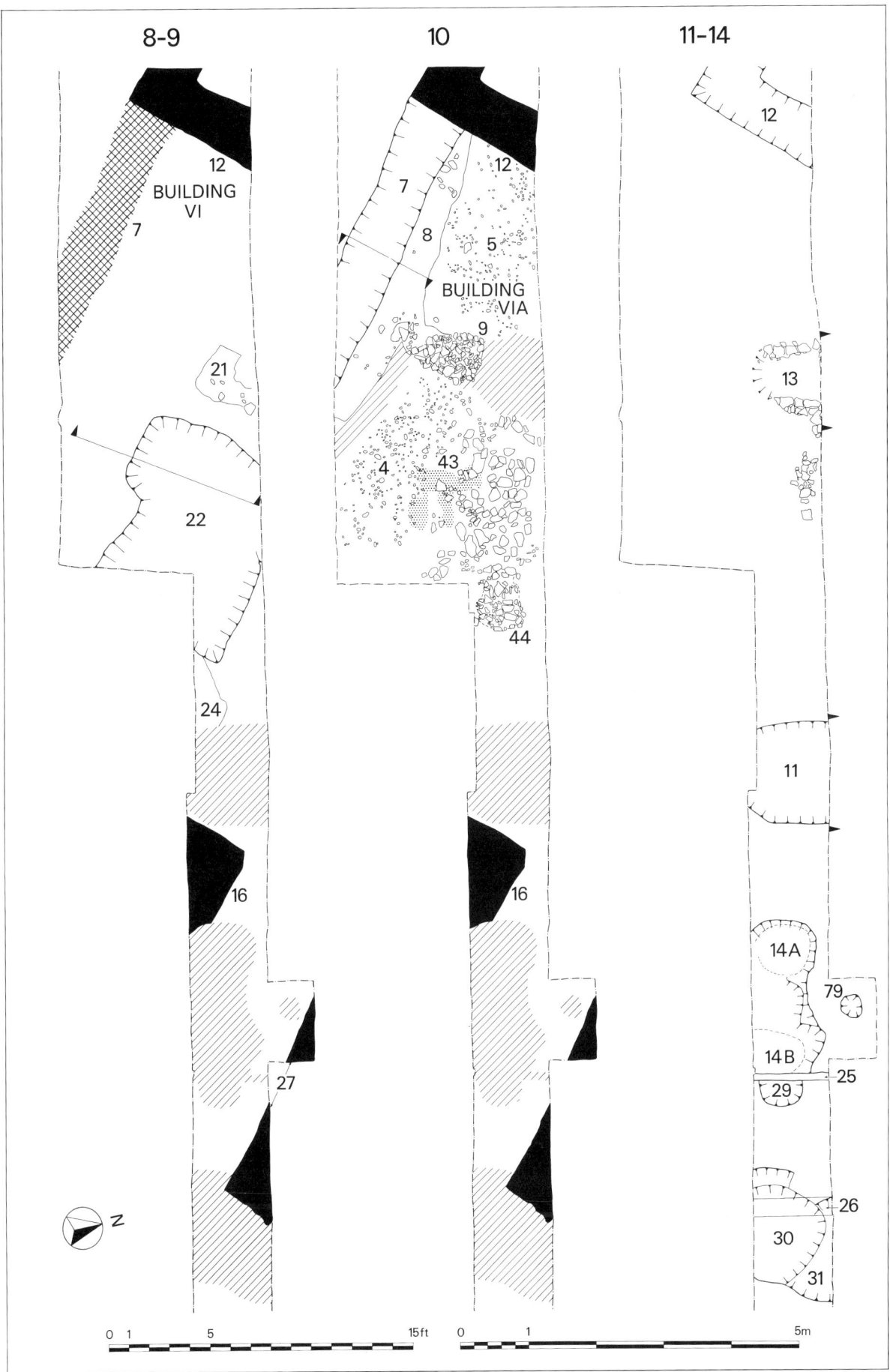

Figure 113 Site II west end, periods 8–14 plans (AES 76–7)

Explosion site excavations (AES 76–7)

exception being a patch of burnt material c 0.02–0.04m thick (II **24**) lying close to the west end of wall (II **16**) and cut by a medieval pit (II *11*).

A single feature in the eastern part of the site II trench was tentatively ascribed to period 8. This was the suggested pit (II **40**), of which very little survived within the trench after the removal (by machine) of topsoil and post-medieval deposits. The feature was located immediately to the east of the enigmatic gravel layer (II **48**) assigned to period 7, which it was thought to cut, and it also appeared to cut (II **54**) and (II **49**), The pit was post-dated by pit (II **52**), the latest Roman feature in this part of the site.

Period 9 (AD 280/290–340/350): late use of buildings V and VI and pits

Site I (Figs 106, 108, and 114, Plate 25)

Building V

Late developments in building V were very difficult to date. In room 1 there were fragmentary remains of a variety of floor surfaces, some of which may have belonged to this period, but many of which were probably earlier. In various parts of room 1 there were five surfaces which were fairly certainly floors of some kind, and at least another five which could have been floors. Processes of wear and disturbance in the Roman period had already made many of these surfaces fragmentary, and medieval activity magnified the problem. The earliest medieval features were cut well into the Roman deposits, and the floor of building I was cut for the most part right down to the earliest Roman floor level (the clay surface (**44**)). As a result of all this disturbance it was not possible to relate surfaces in one part of the room to those on the opposite side.

The floor surfaces which did survive were concentrated in the south-west corner of the site against wall (**5**). The earliest probable period 9 surface was a sandy clay floor (**43**). This layer was most important in containing a coin of Licinius I (No 60) dated AD 312, in good condition, which provided a *terminus post quem* for this surface and the ones above it. (**43**) and some still-exposed parts of period 8 surfaces were sealed by an extensive spread of very pebbly sand incorporating burnt material (**50**). This may have been a badly decayed mortar floor. Four layers intervened between layer (**50**) and the spread which marked the destruction of building V. Of these, two were probably floor surfaces, (**40**) and (47).

In the extreme south-west corner the latest feature, (**42**), was a line of stones at right angles to the stone walls, consisting of flat blocks more or less in line, cut through the superimposed surfaces almost down to the first clay floor (**44**). If this was another wall it was different in character from the earlier ones, having no foundations. It may have been a more limited feature, its position suggesting perhaps a stone replacement for the earlier hearth, though there were no clear traces of burning.

The period 7 stones (**140**) seem to have remained in use up to the end of the life of the building. By this time they were worn smooth and had been almost completely covered over with accumulating dirt when what appeared to be the final constructional features in building V were built. The main feature was a band of dirty red clay (**72**) running the width of building V between the ends of walls (**5**) and (**155**). The exact significance of this layer is not known, but it sealed the position of the sleeper beam in slot (**157**) which must have been out of use by this time. Other patches of clay (not on plan), perhaps originally connected with (**72**), occurred between pits (**4**) and (**78**) and further north in room 2 in the area of the parallel timber slots (**173**), (**174**), and (**180**), sealing one of them. There were two groups of stone associated with the clay, the rough clusters (**114**) and (**183**) around which the clay was set. These seem to have been post bases – groups of stone rammed into holes dug to accommodate them. The two clusters were about 1m apart, and were equidistant from walls (**5**) and (**155**).

The removal of the timber in (**157**), and the infilling of the resulting void, would have taken place while building V was still in use, the partition between rooms 1 and 2 now being carried on vertical posts set on the bases (**114**) and (**183**). It is not clear if the partition (**158**) between rooms 2a and 2b remained in use at this time, but the balance of evidence suggests that it did not. In room 2b there was one apparently late feature, a concentration of burnt deposits (**150**) suggesting a hearth close to the east wall of the room. There was no indication of the function of the hearth, nor that it was enclosed in any way. This latter point is slightly surprising in view of its proximity to the wall of building V and this may indicate that the hearth was in use after the building had been demolished, but there is no other evidence for this suggestion.

Pits (Figs 108 and 114)

Outside building V there was activity of various kinds in the yard. One of the first developments in period 9 was the cutting of a large pit (*124*) in the yard in front of buildings IV and V. This feature had two phases, the second of which, while distinctly later than the first, probably still belonged to period 9. The pit was cut from just above the latest period 8 gravel surface (*164*). It was irregular in shape, at most c 3.90m across and about 1.05m deep. The sides were quite steeply sloped and the bottom was flat. The fill of the pit contained a quantity of rubbish, including a large and important pottery group dating probably to the last quarter of the 3rd century (pottery vessels nos 456–537). There was support for this date from two coins which, although in poor condition, were probably radiates likely to date after c AD 270 (nos 54 and 55). The contents gave no indication of the function of the pit; considering its position it

Explosion site excavations (AES 76–7)

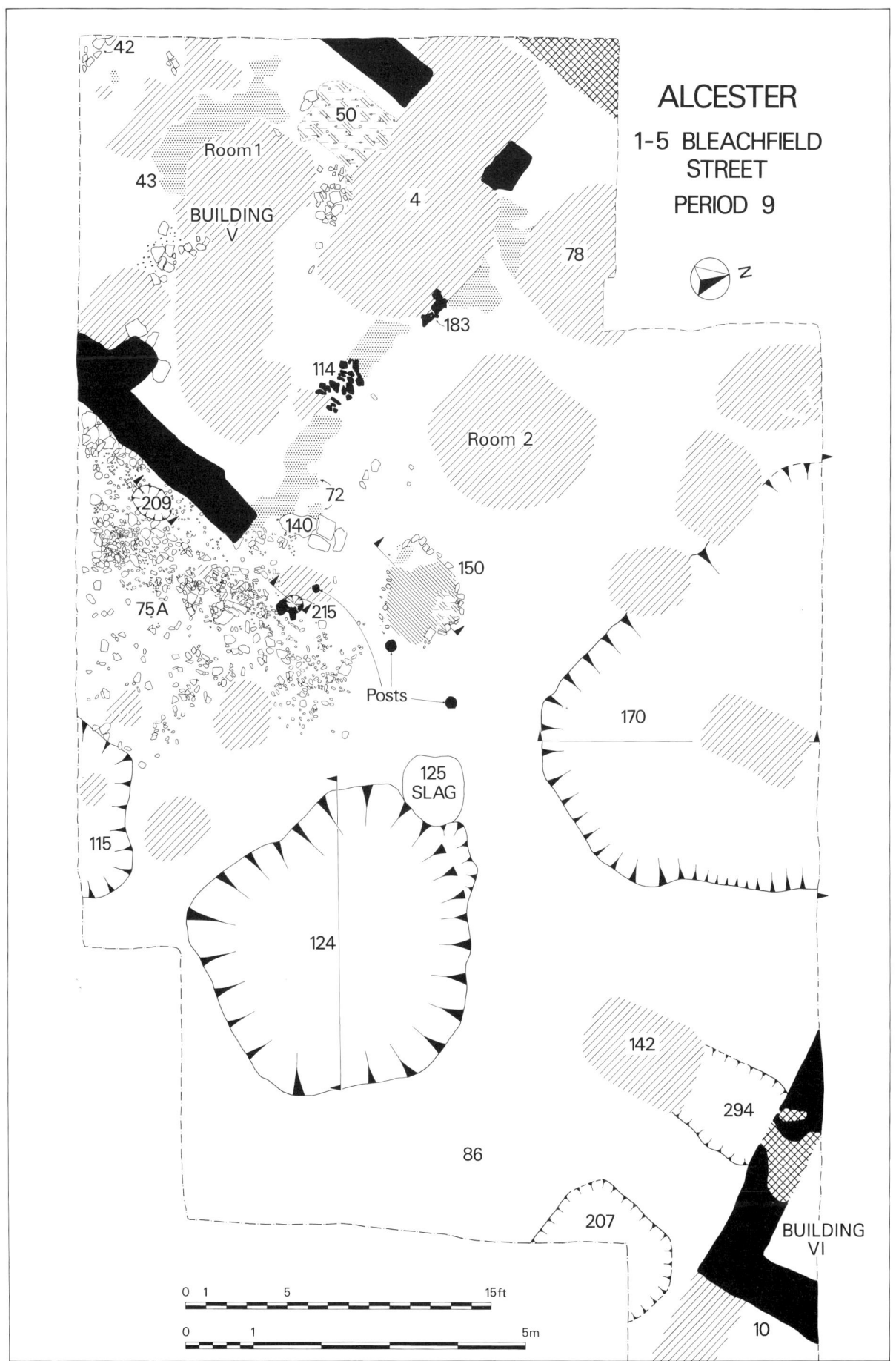

Figure 114   Site I, period 9 plan (AES 76–7)

may have been simply for the purpose of extracting gravel for use nearby with the minimum possible effort. Alternatively it may always have been intended as a rubbish pit.

The upper fill of the pit (*124A*) was clearly of slightly later date. The distinctive feature of its pottery assemblage was the presence of flanged Black-Burnished ware bowls, and also of a moderate quantity of shell-gritted ware, neither of which were found in the lower fills of the pit. (*124A*) probably represented a later re-cut of the pit – a two-stage filling operation seems less likely since the pit would have constituted a considerable hazard if left open in the yard area for any length of time.

Pit (*124*) cut through a concentrated patch of iron smithing slag (**125**) to the west of it, and the fill of the pit included parts of several small copper alloy working crucibles. This indicates that there was metalworking in progress in this or the immediately preceding periods, and, if the position of the slag dump is significant, this may have been carried on in the open air. The location of another slag concentration (**218**) immediately to the north of (**125**) is apparently coincidental since this layer was assigned to period 7, but the juxtaposition of the two deposits may, however, indicate continuity of metalworking over a considerable period of time in this part of the site.

Also assigned to period 9 was another large pit (*170*) which occupied much of the north side of site I (Plate 25). Its contents (pottery vessels nos 549–615) were similar to those of (*124*), though with reasonable quantities of shell-gritted ware, suggesting perhaps a slightly later date, at least for its fill (for a more extended discussion of the differences between the two pits see the pottery report below).

Pit (*170*) was at least 5.90m east–west. Its northerly part lay beneath the north baulk of the site, from which it projected up to 4m southwards. Its maximum depth was *c* 1.45m and the sides, while slightly sloping, were more nearly vertical than those of (*124*), particularly on the east. A noticeable feature was the way in which the pit was cut immediately outside the north wall of building V (the postulated northern veranda having gone out of use by period 8 at the latest). This suggests that the building was still standing (and probably in use) at the time when the pit was dug; later pits showed no such respect for the position of building V.

As with pit (*124*) there was some evidence for more than one phase of activity. There seems to have been a distinction between the relatively jumbled and complex deposits around the edge of the pit, and the more uniform accumulations in its centre. On the south side of the pit there was evidence of some sort of lining. Unfortunately, owing to the way the pit was excavated, this was seen more clearly in section than in plan. The lining was not a primary feature. After the pit had been excavated and an initial slip of gravel from the side had occurred (*170G, V,* and *W*) a series of fill layers (*170K, Q, R, T, U, X, Y,* and *Z*) seems to have accumulated to a depth of *c* 0.20m before a substantial lining was put in place. The evidence for this consisted of a cutting some 0.23m wide, with narrow vertical bands of clay packing (*170M*) on each side. This suggests the presence of a vertical timber, to which a less substantial fence or revetment could have been attached, though there was no evidence as to whether such a structure was attached to the inside or outside of the post, which was nearly 0.50m from the edge of the pit. The post was not dug to a great depth, and it must have always been fairly loose, supported only by the fill of the pit. The post leaned slightly back towards the edge of the pit. This may have been intentional, since any lining inclining inwards would have collapsed quickly.

The lining itself was observed as a partly carbonised linear mark along the south side of the pit. There is no definite indication that the lining or revetment occurred on any side other than the south, though lumps of clay (*170V1*) and possibly (*170M1*) appeared at each end of the east–west section in positions roughly equivalent to that occupied by (*170M*) and may have performed a similar function.

It is uncertain how long the lining remained in use. Fill layers which may have accumulated after its insertion (*170N–P*) were up to *c* 0.20m thick. The lining then seems to have been removed, and a band of clean sand and gravel (*170J*) slipped across the slot which the post had occupied. Later fill layers may have belonged to a rather different phase of activity, possibly a re-cut, as in pit (*124*). They certainly post-dated the removal of the lining.

The function of the pit is uncertain. Its enormous size suggests that it was more than an ordinary rubbish pit or even gravel quarry. The position of the pit might imply some direct connection with building V, and in view of its proximity it is tentatively suggested that (*170*) represented an abandoned attempt at the construction of a cellar or semi-subterranean chamber attached to the building. What function the 'lining' fulfilled is not clear. It could have been inserted after the change of plan merely to help protect the north wall of building V from erosion at its base. It seems unlikely that the post seen in the north–south section was part of the cellar construction, since deposits had already accumulated in the pit, suggesting that it may already have been in use for rubbish disposal when the 'lining' was cut through it.

The dating evidence from this pit has already been mentioned (see above). An outstanding small find from the pit was part of a fine Negro's head lamp, of Antonine date from central Gaul (Fig 123, no 33).

On the south side of the site, building IV was cut by an irregular pit (**115**) most of which lay beneath the south baulk of site I. It was presumably cut after building IV had gone out of use. The fill of (**115**) included two coins of the House of Constantine fused together. Their diameters suggested a date in the second or third decades of the 4th century. West of (**115**) the crushed stone base of building IV (**108**) was sealed by a rough cobbled and rubble spread (**75A**). Beneath (**75A**) and adjacent to wall (**155**) was an

Plate 25   Site I, section through pit (170), period 9, cut by pit (170A), period 10 (AES 76–7) (2m scales)

oval, straight-sided posthole (**209**) c 0.50m × 0.35m. The associations of this feature are uncertain.

To the east of pit (**170**) the timber structure built against the south side of building VI was probably out of use by period 9 and may have been demolished, as the features which comprised the structure were all sealed by a substantial layer (**86**) (see below). Within the area occupied by this structure were several features, most of which were assigned to period 8 (see above). Probably of period 9, however, was the largest of these (**207**), a roughly square pit, probably c 1.20m across (its eastern edge lay beneath the east baulk of site I). The gap in (**161**) between (**142**) and wall (**13**) may indicate the position of a further pit (**294**) of similar size and perhaps of similar date to (**207**).

The removal of the timber structure against wall (**13**)/(II **7**) may not have been the only alteration to building VI at this time. Indeed there was some suggestion (see below) that part of the south wall of the building may have been demolished. The central area of the building was disturbed by a pair of intercutting pits (II **22**A) and (II **22**B), both roughly rectilinear and fairly shallow, at most 0.40–0.50m deep. The fact that there were two pits was not immediately recognised, and they were excavated as one, the contents not differentiated. However, the group of pottery contained in them was very homogeneous, suggesting that the pits were close to one another in date. Their general appearance was reminiscent of (**207**), with the roughly rectilinear plan distinct from that of other period 9 pits such as (**115**), (**124**), and (**170**).

*Layer (**86**)/(II **10**)*

Period 9 also saw the accumulation of a substantial sandy loam layer up to 0.25–0.30m thick (**86**) over the eastern part of site I, continuing into site II, where it was layer (II **10**). This layer sealed the gravel surface (**164**), apparently sealed the large pit (**124**) and certainly overlaid other features in the north-eastern part of site I, including those relating to the lean-to structure on the south side of building VI. (II **10**) covered the whole of the area of building VI between walls (II **12**) and (II **7**), sealing the period 7 gravel surface (**161**)/(II **20**), if this had not already been covered by less well-defined deposits. It also overlaid the period 9 pits (II **22**).

The dating evidence for the layer was fairly consistent (pottery vessels nos 628–729), though there were differences in the pottery between (**86**) and (II **10**). The pottery was closely comparable to that contained

Explosion site excavations (AES 76–7)

in pits (*124*) and (II *22*), but included a high proportion of residual material as well as some late 3rd- to 4th-century types, particularly in (II **10**). The coin evidence, however, made it clear that the layer was probably forming up to the mid-4th century. (**86**) contained a worn coin of AD 310–312, and (II 10) produced a coin dated AD 337–341 (although the latter coin was found at the extreme east end of site II in a position where its stratification cannot be regarded as certain).

The similarity of (II **10**) to (**86**), even within the confines of building VI, raises the question of how the layer was formed. It is perhaps possible that at this time the central part of building VI was open in some way which allowed (II **10**) to accumulate in parallel with (**86**) in the adjacent yard area. How this could have happened is uncertain, but it is possible that wall (II **7**) went out of use and was at least partly demolished, if not taken down to ground level, in period 9. This suggestion would help explain the similarities between (II **10**) on the north side and (**86**) on the south, and is supported by the location of a possible structure overlying the wall line in the following period (see below). The western end of building VI was presumably still in use at this time, and is thought to have continued in use in period 10 (see below).

Site II (Figs 104, 113, and 120)

At the east end of the site II trench was a pit (II *52*), *c* 2.10m east–west and *c* 1.90m deep. It appeared to cut both the period 5 (Antonine) layer (II *54*) and the period 8 pit (II *40*). The most distinctive feature of (II *52*) was the fact that it contained in its primary fill a quantity of roofing 'slates' of a granular limestone (as opposed to the more usual lias or oolite). Although there were occasional fragments of stone roofing material in contexts of 2nd-century date they occurred mainly in period 9 and 10 contexts and seem to have been used principally on late Roman buildings. Apart from the slender stratigraphic evidence the presence of the 'slates' is the only indicator of a late Roman date for the pit, since all the pottery found in it was (with one exception) of 2nd-century date. Pit (II *52*), like (II *68*) (see above) contained a single 13th- to 14th-century sherd in its fill. Both these features had been truncated and were sealed directly by post-medieval deposits. There was otherwise nothing in their character to suggest a medieval date and the medieval sherds are presumed to be intrusive.

Late Roman developments (periods 10 and 10A)

Period 10

This period saw a complete change in the character of the site. Building V was demolished and part of building VI was out of use. Both were replaced in part by a series of timber buildings (III and II) with associated features, principally pits. The later of the sequence of timber structures (building II) and a late gravel surface (*2*) possibly associated with it are assigned for convenience of depiction on plan to period 10A.

Site I (Figs 106, 115, and 116, pls 25–26)

Building V

The building had been in use throughout period 9. A late floor surface had a *terminus post quem* of *c* AD 312, with five successive deposits post-dating it. When the building finally ceased to be occupied is not clear, but this need not have been much after *c* AD 350 (a *terminus ante quem* was provided by the contents of pit (*4*)). Once the building became disused its east wall (*155*) was demolished down to the top of the foundation material, though the west wall of room 1 (*5*) was left standing. The extreme west wall (*88*) was completely robbed, including the foundations, but the date of this robbing is not known. In room 1 of building V a destruction layer (*6*), containing many fragments of lias roof slates, covered all the late floor surfaces (where it survived post-Roman disturbance). In room 2 there were no distinctive destruction/demolition deposits.

Building VI and associated features (Fig 113)

It is not known exactly when building VI was abandoned. There is some evidence that parts may have remained in use after the central area had been standing derelict (and perhaps been demolished) for some time (see period 9 above). Wall (II **7**) was robbed up to its junction with wall (II **12**), where the foundations and in places the lowest coursed stonework remained *in situ*. This suggests that the west end of building VI remained in use for a time after the complete removal of part of the east end, but this activity itself seems to have post-dated a phase of rather insubstantial timber buildings which may have overlain the line of wall (II **7**). Despite the difference in the degree of robbing it is likely that the final robbing of wall (II **7**) was also of medieval date, since two medieval sherds came from the robber trench.

Building VIA

Within the central area of building VI there were several features above the build up of layer (II **10**) which appeared to belong to this late Roman period, though their interpretation in structural terms was not as clear as in the case of the buildings which replaced building V.

The evidence consisted of areas of rough pebbling, and patches of stone. There were two separate patches of very worn pebbles (II **4**) and (II **5**). These had probably never been well laid surfaces, but the density of pebbles was sufficiently high to indicate

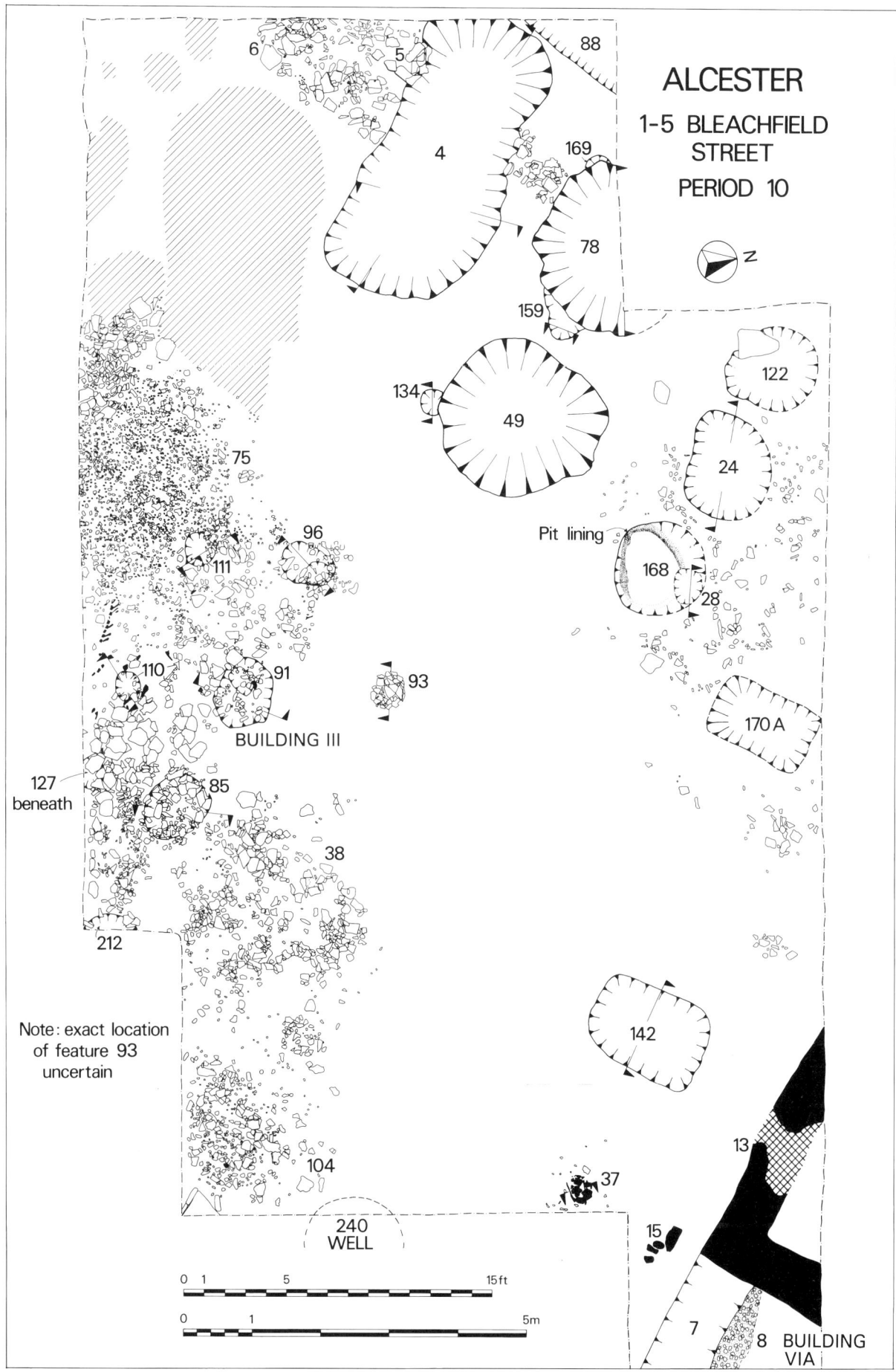

Figure 115 Site I, period 10 plan (AES 76–7)

Explosion site excavations (AES 76–7)

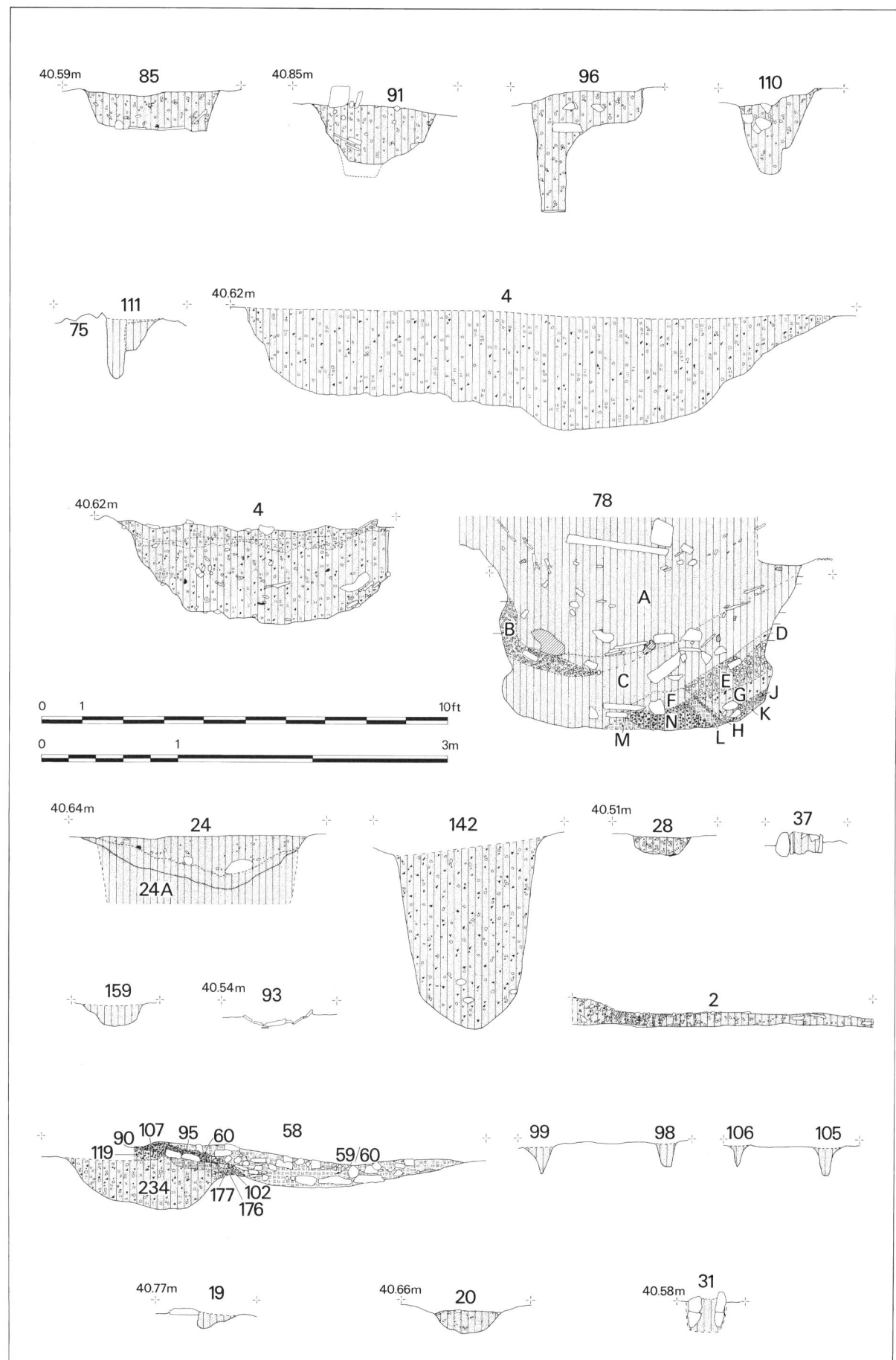

Figure 116 Site I, periods 10–12 sections (AES 76–7)

Explosion site excavations (AES 76–7)

Plate 26 Site II, crushed stone substructure of building VIA, period 10, with robber trench of wall (II 7) partly excavated behind (AES 76–7) (2m scales)

an attempt at surfacing. Separating the patches of pebbling were areas of sandstone rubble. In the north-east part of site II this took the form of a fairly well defined and compacted platform (II 6) composed of irregular sandstone blocks and also crushed stone.

Related to the rubble platform were two linear arrangements of identical material. The first of these (II **9**), probably originally linked directly to (II 6) but disturbed by a medieval feature (II *13*), was a well-defined but rather irregular band of rubble varying from 0.50–0.70m in width, running roughly north–south and surviving to a maximum length of c 1.20m. This was connected at right angles to a much longer feature (II **8**) which was on a line similar to, but slightly convergent with, the earlier wall (II **7**) of building VI (Plate 26). It seems almost certain that (II **8**) was once of uniform width and owed its final form to disturbance caused by the proposed medieval robbing of the foundations of wall (II **7**), having originally overlaid the remains of the wall. The south edge of (II **8**) coincided exactly with the north edge of the robber trench, which suggested that the robber trench had cut through it. If this was so the stone robbers can only have been removing foundation material and the lowest course of the wall, the rest having already been removed and covered by the crushed stone layer (II **8**), if not by the period 9 layer (II **10**). It seems most unlikely that (II **8**) would have lain against wall (II **7**) while the latter was still standing, but this remains a possibility. In this case the wall could have been removed and its foundations robbed from behind (II **8**).

The interpretation of these features is uncertain but it seems most likely that they served a structural function, perhaps supporting timber buildings. It is possible that (II **8**) and (II **9**) formed areas of foundation for timber structures and that the rubble spread (II **6**) was also a part of this scheme. The plan and form of the structure is not clear and it is uncertain how elements based on (II **8**), (II **9**), and (II **6**) related to one another. It is possible that the timber structure leaned against wall (II **12**), since this wall was almost certainly still standing at this time. The area of crushed stone (II **6**) resembled a building platform (cf building IV in site I) and could have supported a timber-framed structure with a wooden floor. By contrast the structure(s) suggested by (II **8**) and (II **9**) may have had floors of earth. Whether these structures would have been subsidiary to a 'main' one based on (II **6**) is unknown.

No other features in this area could be linked with these rather tenuous structures, with the possible exception of two stone packed postholes, (II **15**) and I (**37**). These both occurred at the same level as the

Explosion site excavations (AES 76–7)

other late site II features and could have represented some extension of the structure to the south. The fact that they imply a completely different construction technique from the other features of building VIA may indicate that they were not associated with it. Since they were almost in line with the south-east corner of building VI (after the removal of wall (II **7**)) it is possible that they related to this structure.

The date of the construction and period of use of building VIA is quite unknown, though it was presumably within the second half of the 4th century. One sherd of medieval pottery was recovered from the pebbled area (II **4**), but this was on and not in the surface, and could well have arrived there long after the building fell out of use. In general the pottery content of the medieval features was quite unambiguous. There was no other evidence to suggest a medieval date for building VIA, and the limited evidence for alignment suggests that it fell into the Roman rather than the medieval pattern.

In site I the edge of a rubble area (**104**) was found in the extreme south-east corner, but no assessment of its precise nature could be made. The maximum depth of the deposit was c 0.50m, and it consisted largely of lias roofing stone, with one large flat block (at least 0.50m in length) incorporated. The spread had a fairly clearly defined western edge parallel to the east side of building V, which suggested that this may have been a structural feature rather than a random deposit. It is possible that the rubble formed part of the base of another timber building. It may have been analogous to layer (**38**), also composed of lias fragments, which perhaps formed part of the period 10 building III. The exact date of feature (**104**) is not known. It fits into the relative chronology in that it post-dated the period 9 layer (**86**) and was sealed by the pebbles (**2**), which formed the latest major Roman surface in any part of the site.

Building III

East of building V a smooth spread of sandy loam (*64/77*) built up over the period 8 building IV. This layer was in turn partly covered by a rough patch of pebbling (**75**). The east wall of building V had certainly been removed by this time since the pebbles were spread over the foundation of the wall (***155***). This area of pebbling may have formed part of the floor of building III, though it did not extend significantly into the building.

The evidence for building III consisted primarily of two series of postholes, four large ones (**96**), (**91**), (**85**), and (**212**), and two or three smaller ones to the south (***111***), (***110***), and (**127**), all cutting layer (*64/77*). The alignment of the postholes was exactly at right angles to building V.

The large postholes of the northerly row differed somewhat in character, but all had substantial pits, c 0.80–0.95m across. (**212**) was not examined in detail because of its position beneath the east baulk of the site. (**85**) was only 0.25–0.30m deep with no stone packing surviving, but with a couple of flat lias blocks in the bottom of the hole. (**91**) and (**96**) were deeper. Both had stone packing and some evidence for two phases of use in that the packing stones did not line up with the original post positions. The spacing of the posts was quite regular: their centres were on average about 2.00m apart. Their size is uncertain, but they could have been c 0.20–0.25m across.

South of this line were three smaller postholes. Two of these, (***110***) and (***111***), formed a line parallel to the main series. The third (**127**) was slightly off this line and close to (***110***), but seems to have been stratigraphically equivalent to the other two. All three holes contained stone packing around posts which were probably c 0.12–0.15m across, and again there was some evidence from (***110***) of two phases.

There was little evidence for a floor within the building apart from the pebbles at (and outside) its extreme west end (there is no indication that building III extended further west than (**96**)). In its original form the floor of the building (if any) probably rested directly on layer (*64/77*) or perhaps in part on (**75**). Above (*64/77*) was a layer of limestone roof slate fragments (**38**), probably derived from the demolition of building V, which overlaid the post pits but not the positions of the posts themselves. In the case of (**91**), however, the stones of (**38**) sealed the position of the primary post socket in the base of the pit. This suggests that (**38**) was not a primary component of building III, and that it had been laid after the remodelling or reconstruction of the building which involved the use of the secondary post positions in the post pits. (**127**) was, however, completely sealed by (**38**), so if it belonged to building III at all it must have been in use only in its primary phase. (**38**) may either have formed a floor surface in its own right or have supported a timber floor. Curiously, it extended well north of the edge of building III. It may therefore have been laid during the reconstruction process (which presumably involved the replacement of some if not all of the major structural timbers of the building) before the north wall was put in place, since it must have run beneath this wall.

The precise date of building III is not known. Material from (*64/77*) provided a *terminus post quem*, but none of it was closely datable (pottery vessels nos 792–4). The fact that the building underwent two phases, apparently of identical construction, could be taken to suggest a fairly long period of use, the main vertical posts being replaced only when they became rotten, though there could have been other reasons which necessitated reconstruction of the building. The building was presumably demolished before the construction of building II.

Late pits (Figs 115 and 116)

North and west of building III (and II) was a series of late Roman pits. There were eight pits which fell into four groups according to size, shape and position.

Group 1: a large single rectangular pit (4).
Group 2: two large roughly circular pits (78) and (49).
Group 3: three smaller irregular sub-circular pits (168), (24) and (122).
Group 4: two rectangular pits (170A) and (142).

Groups 1–3 were all cut through building V, presumably post-dating it, and were all aligned parallel to its former layout. It seems almost certain that they related to buildings II and III which perpetuated the line of building V. The group 4 pits, by contrast, were aligned as building VI – not quite at right angles to building V.

Group 1: Pit (*4*)

This roughly rectangular pit was 4.25m × 1.90m with the long axis north-west/south-east. At most it was about 0.80m deep. All sides sloped, but the long sides were more nearly vertical than the ends, of which the west end was particularly sloping. The pit was sited in what had been building V, cutting the final destruction layer and completely removing part of wall (5). The bottom of the pit was stepped down slightly so that the deepest point lay between the ends of the bisected wall. The layers within it were not readily differentiated, but tip lines were located by feel indicating that filling had taken place from the east end of the pit, suggesting perhaps a connection with buildings II and III. The function of the pit is quite unknown. It might have been important, in order to justify cutting through a stone wall, though even this cannot be certain. There was no medieval pottery in the fill of the pit, which combined with the argument of alignment makes it certain that it was of late Roman date. The primary fill included two complete Black-Burnished vessels, a cooking pot, and a dish (nos 900 and 908). These were of roughly mid-4th-century date, but other pottery in the pit was dated after AD 350 (pottery vessels nos 875–915).

Group 2: Pits (**49**) and (**78**)

Pit (**49**) was not completely excavated and only the south half of (**78**) was emptied since the rest lay beneath the air raid shelter which stood in the north-west corner of the site. Despite the partial nature of the evidence the similarities of the two pits were very apparent. Both were roughly circular in plan, 2.25m (**49**) and 2.30m (**78**) in diameter, and both *c* 1.50m deep, with rather irregular sides which were probably originally vertical. In both cases the sides of the pit were lined with a pale sandy clay, though this was not immediately recognised. There was a suggestion that (**78**) may have had an organic lining inside the clay one, and (**78**) was remarkable in producing an entire pot in shell-gritted ware (no 866) and a very large quantity of dumped waste from butchering of animal carcasses. (**78**) also appeared to have been used as a cesspit, much of the fill having a characteristic greenish tinge. In neither case was there any indication of the original function of the pits apart from what might be deduced from the presence of linings. There was no trace of clay lining at the bottom of the pits; the clay was presumably intended to hold the sides in place. It was clear from the section of (**78**) that slumping of the gravel subsoil occurred once parts of the lining had fallen out of place.

It is possible that some sort of timber structure was associated with both pits. On each side of (**78**) was a small cutting, (**159**) on the east side and (**169**) on the west. While it is possible that these were both earlier features cut by (**78**) they could have held vertical posts at the edges of (**78**). Alternatively the two holes could have been cut to take the ends of a horizontal timber across the top of the pit. A similar cut (**134**) was found on the south side of (**49**). No corresponding feature appeared on the north side, but this area had been disturbed and all traces of a shallow cutting could have been obliterated. It is not known if the two pits were open at the same time, or if one was superseded by the other, but at least approximate contemporaneity seems certain.

Group 3: Pits (**168**), (**24**), and (**122**)

This group consisted of three irregular pits in line parallel to (**49**) and (**78**) and north of them. From east to west they were (**168**), (**24**), and (**122**). All were cut through the position of the original north wall of building V and also the fill of pit (**170**), which increased the difficulties of identification and excavation. All three pits were smaller than those of group 2. (**168**) and (**24**) were roughly 1.40m across. The size of (**122**) was less certain: its edges where it cut (**170**) were not precisely located, and it is possible that there were further contemporary pits in the extreme north-west corner of the site.

Pit (**168**) was cut exactly into the top of the period 2 well (**168A**). It is possible that the fill of (**168A**) had settled and even that the clay floor (**44**) of building V had slumped at this point, indicating a soft spot to the later pit diggers. In its re-cut form the pit was *c* 1.50m deep. It seemed to have been lined, probably with organic material (cf (**49**)) which appeared in plan as a dark line enclosing an oval shape. The lining could have been of basket work, though it is possible that a barrel was employed, in which case the pit could have been used for storage of a wide range of products.

Pit (**24**) appeared to have been much the same size as (**168**), though perhaps rather shallower (it was not completely excavated). There were two distinct phases to (**24**). The first, (**24A**), was a vertical-sided cut in the style of the other pits. This part of the pit produced no evidence of a lining, and had been used as a rubbish pit, producing several large sherds. The upper fill contained large quantities of stone including a large number of roof slate fragments. There is no indication as to when this upper filling took place, though a date within the late Roman period seems likely as no medieval pottery was recovered from the pit.

Definition of the north side of pit (**122**), where it cut (**170**), was not possible. The east, south, and west sides were initially vertical, but from the south-west corner

Explosion site excavations (AES 76–7)

the sides tended to slope in. The maximum depth was not more than *c* 1m. In the south-west corner of the pit were two very large blocks of sandstone one on top of the other. These may have been part of the supports for the timbers of building V room 2 but were presumably not in their original position here, though probably close to it (see above, period 5). The upper fill of (**122**) contained a number of stones, particularly roofing material. In this respect it was comparable to (**24A**).

What dating evidence there was for these pits (pottery vessels nos 821–838) suggested a mid- to late 4th-century context, although the only fixed date was provided by a coin of Crispus of *c* AD 321 in (*168*) (no 67). As with (**78**) and (**49**) there was no evidence as to whether the pits were open singly or all together.

Group 4: Pits (**142**) and (**170A**)

These pits were aligned, unlike those of groups 1–3, on building VI rather than building V. Both were rectangular, (**170A**) was *c* 1.60m × 0.80–0.90m, and perhaps 1.40m deep (Plate 25), while (**142**) was 1.80m × 1.00–1.20m and of a very similar depth. (**170A**) contained a large amount of stone in its fill, while (**142**) was relatively free of stone. The function and date of these pits was not certain, though their size and shape and evidence for some fill layers with a characteristic green tinge rather suggested that they may have been cesspits. The pottery (pottery vessels nos 867–8, 870–4) suggested a 4th-century date, and the fill of (**170**) provided an early to mid-4th century *terminus post quem* for the cutting of (**170A**).

Period 10A

Site I

A late structure, building II, and associated features were assigned to a secondary phase of period 10 on the basis of both relative and absolute chronology and for the purposes of distinguishing building II from the underlying building III on plan. It is possible that some of the late Roman pits (above) could also have been of this very late phase, the exact date of which is uncertain, but which must have fallen in the last quarter of the 4th century at the earliest.

Building II (Figs 106 and 117, Plate 27)

This building, probably the latest Roman structure on the site, was positioned exactly on top of building III, and its construction may have followed the demolition of building III almost immediately. The technique employed in this building was that of the rubble platform, but with much less crushed stone than in the case of the building VIA construction. The limestone floor of building III, (**38**), was sealed by a spread of sandstone rubble (**26**) which, while disturbed at its west end, had a very clearly defined north side. The nature of the rubble composing this north side was such that it could not have rested there unsupported. It must have been held in place by a horizontal timber. The rubble was not held together by crushed stone, but consisted entirely of loose pieces – producing a very rough, though level, surface. At the north-west corner of the platform several larger blocks were disposed in such a way as to suggest that they might have held a vertical post in position, though there was no posthole as such to suggest that a timber had been firmly bedded in the ground.

The edge of (**26**) may have been held in place by a sleeper beam on which the superstructure rested. However, this would have rendered the rubble platform structurally superfluous, since the object of constructing a timber building on a platform was presumably to raise the timber frame above ground level to prevent it rotting in the damp earth.

It is suggested that the entire structure rested on the rubble platform, with the timber frame for the walls set directly on the wooden floor, which in turn lay on joists positioned on the rubble platform. If the superstructure had consisted of a weatherboarded type construction, the lowest boards could have extended below the level of the joists to protect their ends, and in doing so could have held the edge of the rubble platform in place. It is clear that the corner post stood in line with the north wall and not in advance of it. It is possible that, as the long axis of the building was probably north-west/south-east, the gable ends of the building were the only exceptions to the rule of not allowing timbers to come into contact with the ground. Since the corner posts of the gable ends were structurally the most important parts of the building they required extra stability. To rest posts some 0.20m across (as the corner one seems to have been) directly on the floor of the building would have been to impose excessive strain on it. The whole building would have been given added stability by projecting the posts forward at the end of the building, though it is surprising that the one identified was not dug into the ground. Presumably this was not considered necessary.

The date of building II, as with the other late structures, is not known. The only coin recovered from the rubble raft of the building was of Salonina (AD 260–68, no 16).

There were several features which appeared to be associated with the later buildings as they all appeared at the same overall level as buildings II and III, followed the same alignment, and in many cases cut building V.

At the extreme east end of the site a band of gravel (**2**) intruded into the excavated area. This lay above the area of rubble (**104**) already discussed. Its extent was fairly clearly defined to the west, and it lay at right angles to the line of buildings II and III. Within this surface was a well (**240**), roughly lined with sandstone. The edge of the well shaft only extended *c* 0.10–0.15m into the site, but after the main part of the excavation was completed the top of the well was cleared sufficiently to leave the form and function of the feature in no doubt. The gravel was laid right up to the edge of the stonework and thus

Explosion site excavations (AES 76–7)

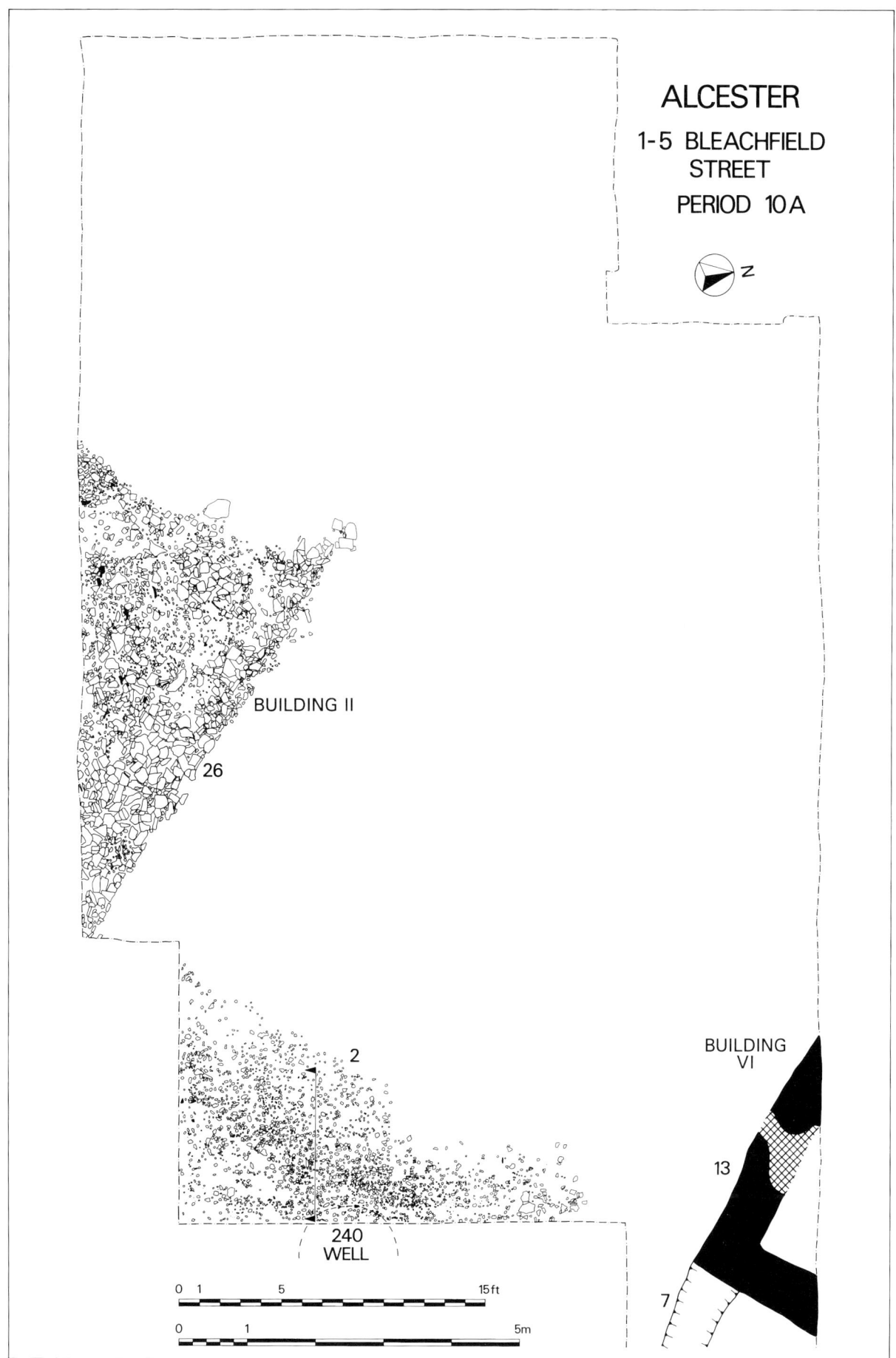

Figure 117   Site I, period 10A plan (AES 76–7)

Explosion site excavations (AES 76–7)

Plate 27 Site I, building II, period 10A, rubble platform on left, with corner post setting in foreground. Medieval wall (10), period 11, to right (AES 76–7) (2m scale)

probably post-dated it. The dating evidence for the gravel spread was ambiguous. Four small medieval sherds were recovered from the top of the surface. Strictly speaking they provide a *terminus ante quem* of the 13th–14th centuries. The evidence of alignment and association, however, strongly suggests that the surface dated from the latest Roman occupation of the site, and it contained a good group of late Roman pottery (pottery vessels nos 766–784). It is probable that (**2**) formed part of a late Roman yard surface.

Summary of the medieval occupation (periods 11–12)

Periods 11–12 (Figs 104, 105, 113, 116, 118, 119, and 120, pls 27–28)

(For a detailed description of periods 11–12, see microfiche M1:G13–M2:A2)

Medieval features occurred principally in the southwest corner of site I, and in the central part and western half of site II. There seems to have been very little accumulation of deposits between the late Roman layers and the earliest medieval activity which, on the basis of a small number of sherds of Stamford and St Neots type wares, may have occurred in the 11th century. There is, however, little evidence to suggest activity before the later 12th century.

In several places medieval layers overlaid Roman ones directly and some late Roman surfaces may have been in use in the medieval period. The gravel layer (**2**) had medieval sherds on its surface, and it is possible that the well (**240**) which it surrounded was still used at this time. Only in the north-eastern part of site I was there evidence for the accumulation of a substantial sandy loam layer (**12**) which was at least partly of medieval date. This was very difficult to identify precisely in plan or section since it covered much the same area as the period 9 layer (**86**) which it closely resembled in character. In parts of the site, where period 10 activity was sparse, (**12**) sealed (**86**) directly. It is quite possible that in origin (**12**) was a period 10 layer of late Roman date only later contaminated by medieval material, on the basis of which it was assigned to period 11.

Many of the medieval features on the site were unrelated to each other or to widespread surfaces. It was thus not possible to establish a relative chronology for these features. The only place on the site where a rela-

Plate 28 Site I, building I, period 12; white markers indicate position of postholes and bases (AES 76–7) (2m scale)

tive chronology was established was in site I where building I overlaid earlier features. A few medieval features contained datable pottery, on the basis of which two periods of activity were distinguished: a later 12th- to 13th-century phase, with perhaps a few earlier features (period 11), and a principally late 13th- to 14th-century one (period 12). Building I was assigned to the latter and layers and features underlying it to the earlier period, whether or not they contained datable material. The major component of building I was the clay floor (*3*). The floor was 6.45m long east–west and at its maximum 2.50m wide, though the average width was nearer 2.20m.

Summary of the post-medieval and modern developments (periods 13–14)

Periods 13 and 14 (Figs 104–6, 113, and 119)

(For a detailed description of periods 13–14, see microfiche M2:A2–A4)

Significant post-medieval and modern features were absent from site I, although the site II trench suffered from considerable post-medieval disturbance, particularly in the eastern half of the trench where all layers later than the late Antonine period had probably been removed.

In the central part of the trench were four parallel brick walls (II *26*), (II *77*), and (II *78*) aligned north–south, presumably from a former outbuilding constructed against the east–west brick boundary wall of the site which lay at this point some 1.10m north of the trench.

It is likely that most of the post-medieval features in the site II trench were of 17th century date.

Explosion site excavations (AES 76–7)

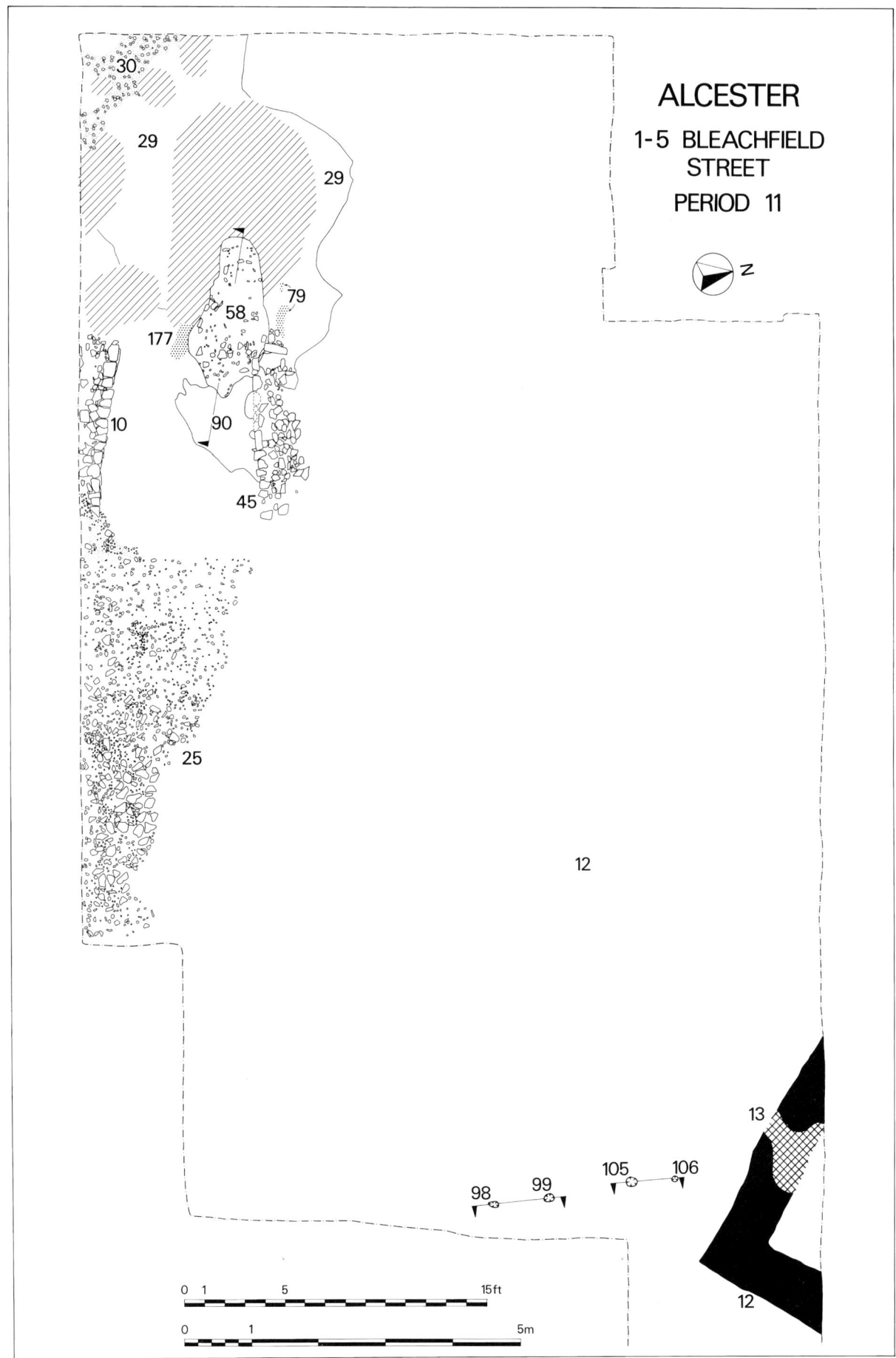

Figure 118   Site I, period 11 plan (AES 76–7)

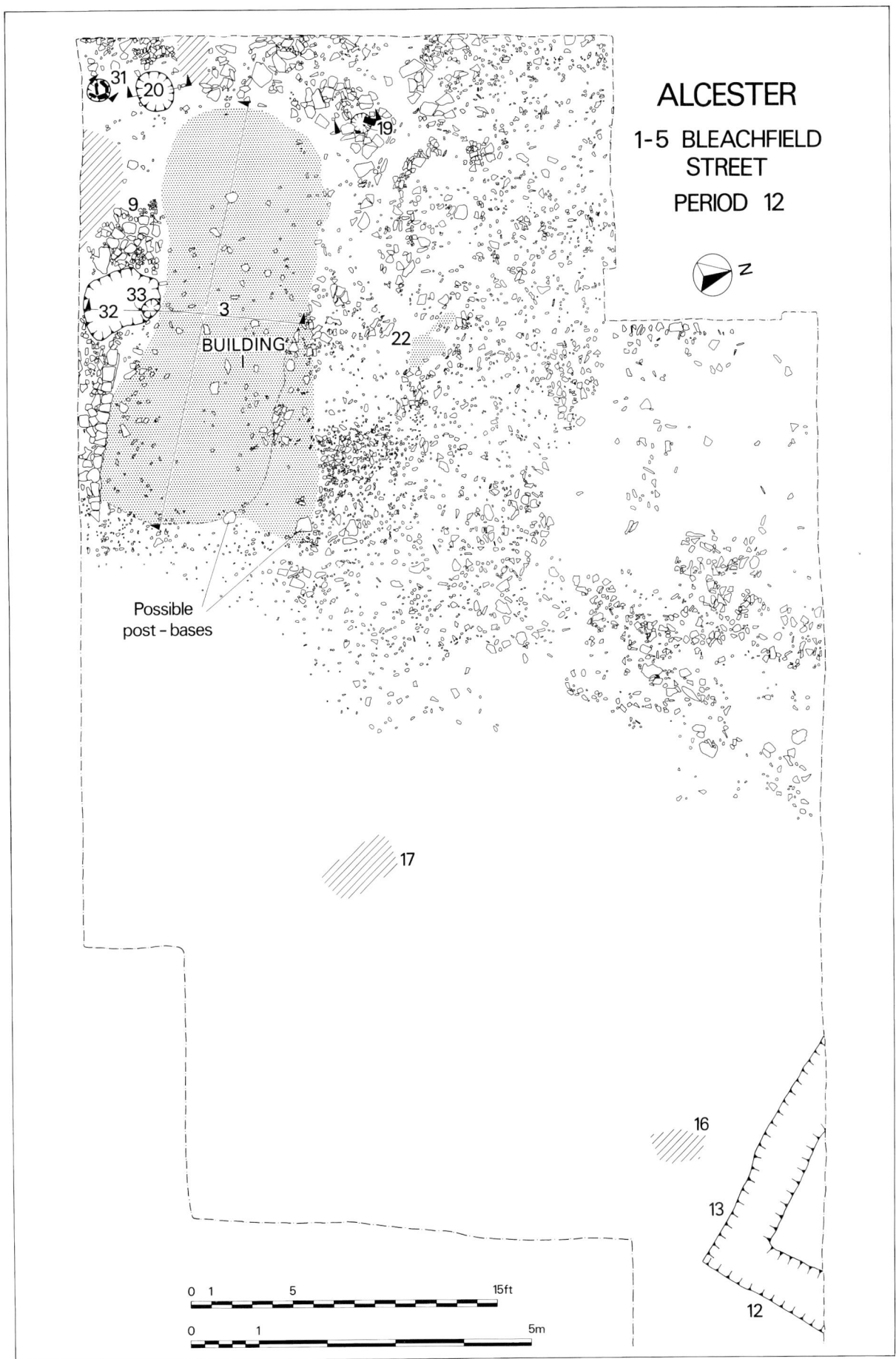

Figure 119   Site I, period 12 plan (AES 76–7)

Explosion site excavations (AES 76–7)

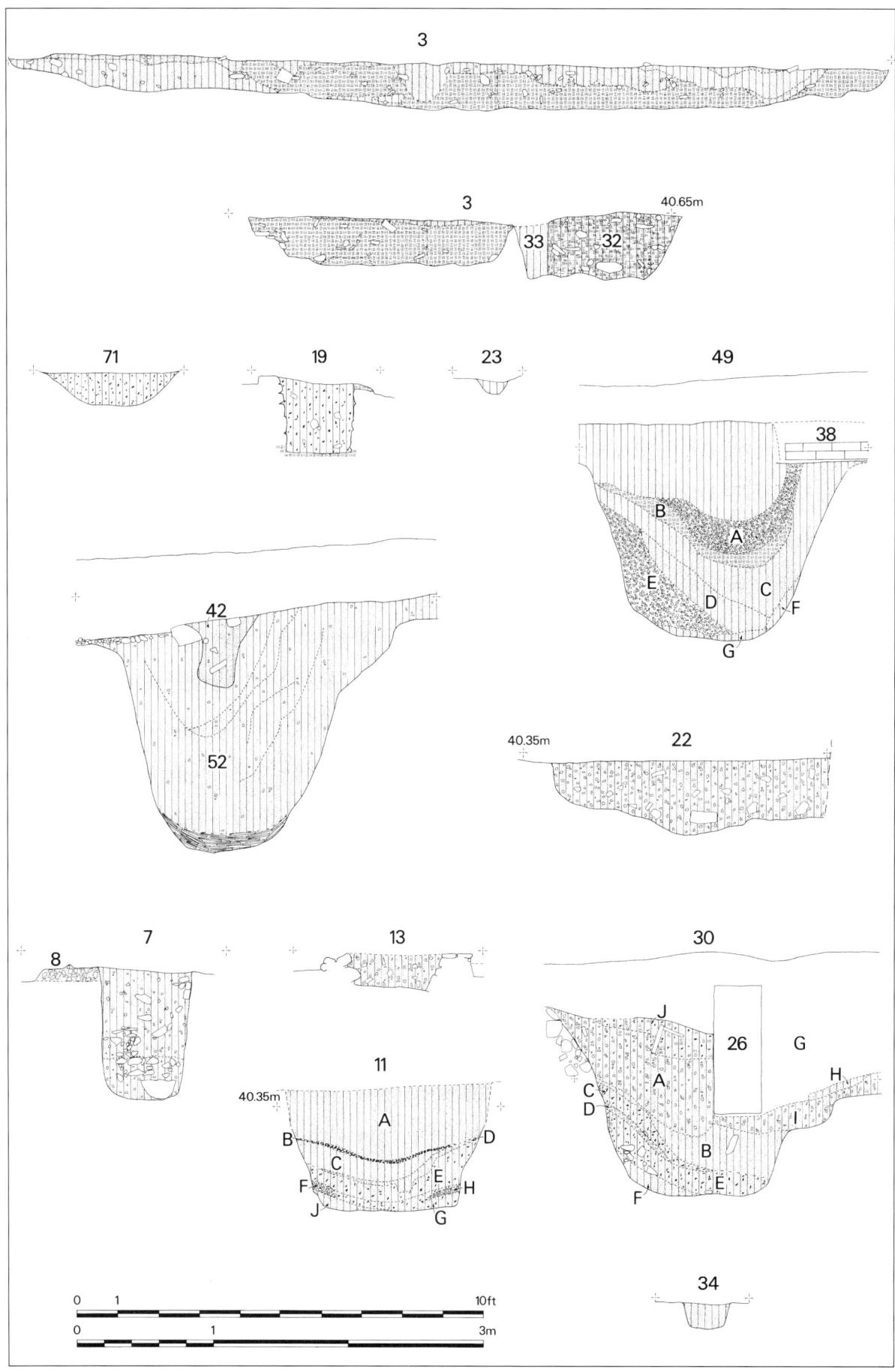

Figure 120 Site I, period 12 sections (top two). Site II, periods 2–12 sections (AES 76–7)

Explosion site finds (AES 76–7)

The site produced a very large quantity of finds of all materials, many of which were considered to merit being reported on in detail. In the catalogues which follow entries are followed by the site small find number (prefixed SF), the context number, and the period number of the context in which the object occurred. Separate numbering sequences are used for coins (1–103), illustrated Roman pottery (1–919), illustrated medieval pottery (1–14), and metalwork and other finds (1–339).

Many of the following reports have been edited for the printed page for reasons of economy of space. This is indicated where relevant. The sections of the reports that have been edited out, or the full versions of the reports, have been reproduced in the microfiche.

Roman coins (AES 76–7)
Wilfred A Seaby and Paul Booth

The coins were identified by W A Seaby of the Warwickshire Museum. His detailed identifications can be found in microfiche M2:A5–A13, but are presented in more summary form below (Table 17). The excavations recovered 103 Roman coins, a remarkable quantity for such a small area in a site of this type. Of these coins, however, 72 were from post-Roman contexts, and even if the 18 coins from site I layer (12) are excluded from this total this still leaves over 50% of the coins from post-Roman deposits. (Layer (12) is assigned to period 11 on the basis of a few medieval sherds within it, but is really a continuation of the period 9 general layer (86).) Very few of the remaining coins occurred in 'contemporary' contexts. Coins were thus of little value for dating the site, but where significant for the chronology they are referred to in the stratigraphic account.

The coins were plotted as a histogram (Fig 121) using the periods defined by Reece (1972, 271), incorporating imitation issues. The resulting histogram can be compared with one showing overall coin losses from Roman Alcester. This is based on 1527 identified Roman coins, from both collections and excavations, and includes all the coins known to the Warwickshire Museum up to 1984 (excluding hoards).

While there are basic similarities between the two histograms there are also differences, which may in part reflect the small size of the Explosion site sample, but may also indicate ways in which the pattern of coin loss at this site differed from the norm prevailing throughout the settlement. The most striking difference is in the proportion of 3rd-century as

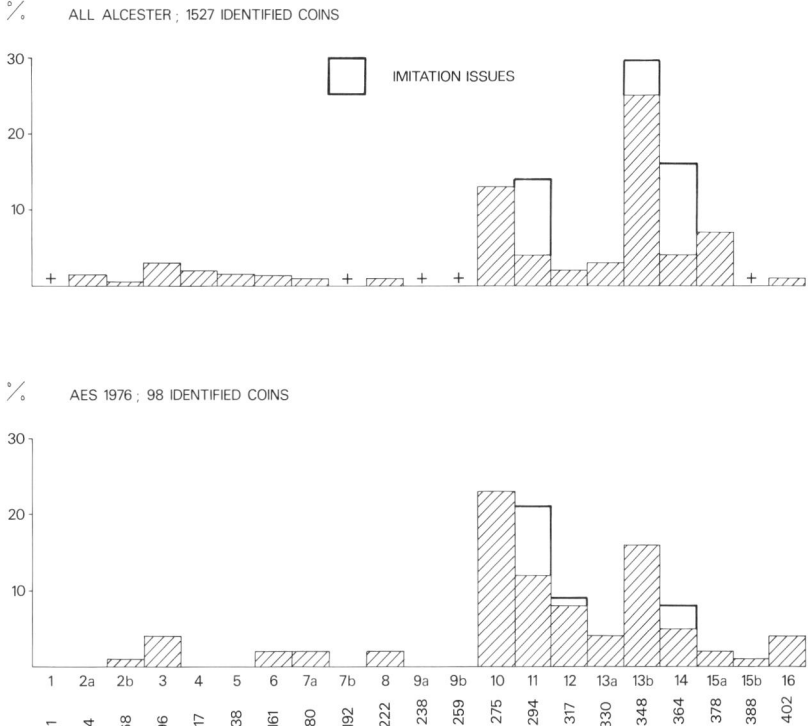

Figure 121 Coin histograms for all Alcester sites up to 1984 and for the Explosion site (periods after Reece 1972)

Explosion site finds (AES 76-7)

Table 17 Roman coins (AES 76–7) (in approximate chronological order of issue)

No	Emperor	Denomination	Approx date	RIC reference	Context	SF no	Period
1	Nero	Dupondius	63–68	I p 164/286	I (245)	470	6
2	Vespasian	Denarius	70–72	II p 19/39	I (124)	342	9
3	Vespasian	As	69–70	?	II (52)	520	?9
4	Titus (as Caesar)	As	69	II p 107/784	I (235)	495	4
5	Domitian	Dupondius	81–96	?	I (257)	471	4
6	Antoninus Pius	Sestertius	140–144	III p 113/651a	II (22)	473	9
7	Antoninus Pius	Sestertius	157–158	III p 147/981	II (10)	464	9
8	Faustina Junior (under M. Avrelivs)	Sestertius	161–175	III p 344/1628	I (86)	290	9
9	Faustina Junior (under M. Avrelivs)	Sestertius	161–175	III p 345/1645	I (245)	472	6
10	?	?Dupondius	C1	?	I (185)	398	5
11	Septimus Severus	Denarius	194–195	IV pt 1 p 97/53	I (86)	321	9
12	Septimus Severus	Denarius	197–198	IV pt 1 p 103/105	I (124)	348	9
13	Gallienus	?Denarius	260–268	V pt 1 p 161/348	I (12)	218	11
14	Gallienus	Antoninianus	260–268	?	I (1)	12	14
15	Salonina	Antoninianus	260–268	V pt 1 p 193/12?	I (12)	123	11
16	Salonina	Antoninianus	260–268	V pt 1 p 194/32	I (26)	182	10
17	Claudius II	Antoninianus	268–270	V pt 1 p 213/18	I (12)	296	11
18	Claudius II	Antoninianus	268–270	V pt 1 p 218/100	I (1)	60	4
19	Claudius II	Antoninianus	268–270	V pt 1 p 226/181	I (1)	69	14
20	Claudius II	Antoninianus	268–270	V pt 1 p 226/177	I (86)	29	19
21	Claudius II (post)	Antoninianus	?c 270	cf V pt 1 p 233/261	I (12)	219	11
22	Claudius II (post)	Antoninianus	?c 270	cf V pt 1 p 233/261	I (1)	20	14
23	Claudius II (post)	Antoninianus	?c 270	?	I (1)	49	14
24	Claudius II (post)	Antoninianus	?c 270	V pt 1 p 234/266	I (2)	111	10
25	?Victorinus	Antoninianus	268–270	V pt II p 391/47?	I (1)	43	14
26	?Victorinus	Antoninianus	268–270	V pt II p 394/81?	I (87)	282	10
27	Tetricus I	Antoninianus	270–273	V pt II p 407/65?	I (1)	24	14
28	Tetricus I	Antoninianus	270–273	V pt II p 408/77	I (86)	320	9
29	Tetricus I	Antoninianus	270–273	V pt II p 409/100	I (2)	206	11
30	Tetricus I	Antoninianus	270–273	V pt II p 409/101	I (2)	158	10
31	Tetricus I	Antoninianus	270–273	V pt II p 411/148	I (12)	108	11
32	Tetricus I	Antoninianus	270–273	?	I (12)	251	11
33	Tetricus I	Antoninianus	270–273	?	?II U/S	679	14
34	Tetricus I	Antoninianus	270–273	?	?II U/S	680	14
35	Tacitus	Antoninianus	275–276	cf V pt 1 p 332/69	I (1)	121	14
36	Carausius	Antoninianus	287–293	V pt II p 472/101	I (12)	273	11
37	Carausius	Antoninianus	287–293	V pt II p 472/101	I (12)	208	11
38	Carausius	Antoninianus	287–293	V pt II p 473/108	I (87)	265	10
39	Carausius	Antoninianus	287–293	V pt II p 474/121	I (1)	25	14
40	Carausius	Antoninianus	287–293	V pt II p 490/305	I (1)	44	14

Explosion site finds (AES 76-7)

Table 17 (*cont.*) **Roman coins (AES 76–7)** (in approximate chronological order of issue)

No	Emperor	Denomination	Approx date	RIC reference	Context	SF no	Period
41	Carausius	Antoninianus	287–293	V pt II p 490/305	I (2)	114	10
42	Carausius	Antoninianus	287–293	V pt II p 490/305	I (12)	203	11
43	Carausius	Antoninianus	287–293	?V pt II p 491/310	I (12)	256	11
44	Carausius	Antoninianus	287–293	cf V pt II p 497/388	I (1)	9	14
45	Carausius	Antoninianus	287–293	V pt II p 543/1014	I (1)	81	14
46	Carausius	Antoninianus	287–293	?	I (12)	244	11
47	Allectus	Antoninianus	293–297	V pt II p 561/28	I (12)	207	11
48	?	Antoninianus	?later C3		I (12)	301	11
49	?	Barbarous radiate	?later C3		I (12)	175	11
50	?	Barbarous radiate	?later C3		I (12)	246	11
51	?	Barbarous radiate	?later C3		I (2)	144	10
52	?	Barbarous radiate	?later C3		I (1)	72	14
53	?	?	?later C3		I (1)	103	14
54	?	?Barbarous radiate	?later C3		I (124F)	389	9
55	?	?	?later C3		I (124)	349	9
56	?	?	?later C3/C4		U/S	681	14
57	?	?	?later C3/C4		I (164)	380	8
58	Maximianus	Follis	303–305	VI p 200/582b	I (1)	85	14
59	Maximianus	Follis (reduced)	309	VI p 226/845a	I (7)	91	14
60	Licinius I	Follis (reduced)	312	VI p 136/209c	I (43)	215	9
61	Constantine I	Follis (reduced)	310	VI p 133/121a	I (29)	186	11
62	?Constantine I	Follis (reduced)	?310–312	cf VI p 136/185–7?	I (86)	306	9
63	Constantine I	Follis (reduced)	310–313	VI p 227/870	I (1)	1	14
64	Constantine I	Follis (reduced)	310–313	VI p 227/873	I (1)	104	14
65	Constantine I	Follis (reduced)	?310–313	?	I (29)	188	11
66	?Diocletian	Barbarous follis	?early C4		I (1)	112	14
67	Crispus (as Caesar)	Follis/AE3	321	VII p 110/211	I ?(168)	378	10
68	Constantine I	Follis/AE3	323	VII p 134/199	I (18)	110	12
69	?	Follis} (2 fused)	?310–330	?	I (115)	400	9
70	?	Follis}			I (115)	400	9
71	Constantius II (as Caesar)	AE3	332–333	VII p 217/540	II (12)	429	12
72	?	AE3	332–333	VII p 217/542	I (1)	26	14
73	Constantine I	AE3	335–337	?VII p 218/549	I (12)	232	11
74	Delmatius	AE3	335–337	VII p 142/288	I (1)	55	14
75	?	AE3	330–340	?	II (30)	508	11
76	?	AE3	335–340	?	I (1)	78	14
77	Constantine II	AE3	337–340	?VIII p 143/59?	I (1)	15	14
78	Helena (post)	AE3	337–341	VIII p 143/63	I (1)	38	14
79	Constans	AE3	337–340	VIII p 355/103	II (10)	419	9
80	Constans	AE3	337–350	?	II (1)	434	14

175

Explosion site finds (AES 76-7)

Table 17 (*cont.*) Roman coins (AES 76–7) (in approximate chronological order of issue)

No	Emperor	Denomination	Approx date	RIC reference	Context	SF no	Period
81	Constans	AE3	341–346	?	I (1)	62	14
82	Constantius or Constans	AE3	342–343	VIII p 180/36 or 37	I (1)	56	14
83	Constans	AE3	347–348	VIII p 151/185	I (1)	22	14
84	Constans	AE3	347–348	VIII p 152/195	I (1)	23	14
85	Constans	AE3	347–348	VIII p 152/195	I (1)	86	14
86	Constans	AE3	347–348	VIII p 209/86	I (1)	21	14
87	Constantius II	AE3	348–350	VIII p 154/233	I (1)	88	14
88	Constans	AE2	348–350	VIII p 182/86	I (1)	18	14
89	Magnentius	AE2	351–352	VIII p 122/25?	II (12)	424	12
90	Constantius II	AE3 imitation	350–364	?	II (11)	430	12
91	?	AE4 barbarous	350–364		I (1)	34	14
92	?	AE4 barbarous	350–364		I (1)	90	14
93	?	AE4 barbarous	350–364		I (12)	300	11
94	?	AE4 barbarous	350–364		I (1)	51	14
95	Valentinian I	AE3	367–375	IX p 66/17a	I (1)	89	14
96	Valens	AE3	375–378	IX p 66/19a	I (1)	33	14
97	Gratian	AE3	378–383	IX p 48/30a	I (1)	84	14
98	Arcadius	AE3	388–392	IX p 52/44d	I (12)	171	11
99	Theodosius I	AE3	388–392	IX p 52/44c	I (1)	13	14
100	Honorius	AE4	392–395	IX p 70/30g	I (1)	45	14
101	Honorius	AE4	392–395	IX p 70/30g?	I (1)	50	14
102	?	?AE3	? C4		II (10)	445	9
103	?	?	? C4		I (12)	242	11

against 4th-century coin losses, the former being much more frequent at the Explosion site than in the general Alcester histogram, for reasons which are not clear. Nevertheless, the contrast in the two histograms between the percentage of coins of AD 259–294 and those of AD 330–402 (a ratio used by Reece (1980a, 120) as an indicator of the difference between the major towns/cities of Roman Britain and other settlement types) is not so marked as to indicate that the Explosion site was radically different from the rest of Alcester. A comparison of the ratios of coin losses of these two periods for both histograms with data derived from Mann and Reece (1983, 66, Fig 67) shows both the Explosion site and Alcester as a whole falling on the periphery of the group of major settlements. This may suggest that Alcester had some of the characteristics of these sites and some similarities with the 'small settlements'. This conclusion would seem to be consistent with what is known of the status of the town from other evidence, suggesting that it was a major local centre.

The majority of the coins at the Explosion site (88.2%) were of late 3rd- to 4th-century date, a figure which may be slightly inflated as a result of the very restricted excavation of the earliest deposits on the site. Coins of Reece's period 12 were unusually well-represented, but thereafter, as has already been mentioned, 4th-century coin losses were generally below the average for Alcester. The reduced coin loss after the mid-4th century, but particularly in period 15a, may possibly reflect a temporary period of reduced activity on the site after the demolition of building V and perhaps also of part of building VI. A strong late Roman presence, indicated by evidence of timber buildings and associated pits, is borne out by the occurrence of coins of the House of Theodosius, albeit unstratified, at a level above the Alcester average.

The breakdown of identifiable 4th-century coins by mint demonstrates, as would be expected (Fulford 1978, 78), a predominance of western mints, particularly Trier, Lyons, and Arles (in that order of importance). After AD 348 there are very few coins with identifiable mintmarks. There was only a single coin (from Siscia) not from a western European source.

Roman pottery (AES 76–7)
Rowan Ferguson with a contribution by Brenda Dickinson

Introduction

A total of 24,694 sherds weighing 347.519kg was found on the site. Of this total 5376 sherds (21.8%) came from post-Roman contexts. The Warwickshire Museum Roman pottery recording system was used to quantify and describe the material. This involved assigning the sherds to one of thirteen major, general fabric categories:

S   samian ware
F   fine (mica-dusted, colour-coated, etc) wares
A   *amphora* fabrics
M   *mortarium* fabrics
W   white wares
Q   white-slipped wares
P   handmade (usually prehistoric) fabrics
E   early 'Belgic type' (usually wheelmade) fabrics
O   oxidised coarse wares
R   reduced coarse wares
B   Black-Burnished ware
C   calcite/shell-tempered wares
G   coarse-gritted (storage jar, etc) fabrics

These broad major groupings were further subdivided on criteria of inclusion types and other characteristics at increasingly precise levels. This work was done using a binocular microscope at 20× magnification. Coarse wares such as the reduced fabrics were only identified by principal inclusion type (eg fabric R30 = all reduced fabrics with organic inclusions), but the Severn Valley wares and many of the fine wares, which could be identified to a particular source (eg the Oxfordshire colour-coated fabric F51), were defined more precisely. Roman material from post-Roman contexts was mostly identified only to the broadest groupings but, where possible, further microscopic identification was applied to the fine wares. Vessel, rim, base, handle, spout, and decorative types were recorded uniformly in line with other sites in the county. This system was designed to give maximum information in the time available for the project.

Quantification was by sherd count, weight, an estimate of the minimum number of vessels based on a rim count, and EVEs (estimated vessel equivalents, based on rim percentages). The discussion below draws mainly on the data for number of sherds and EVEs. The occurrence of all fabrics by period is expressed in these terms in Table MT10 (microfiche M2:B1–C4); this also gives the percentages which these figures constitute of the relevant period totals. Table MT10 also provides a summary description of each fabric; the fabric reference collection is held by the Warwickshire Museum, where it can be consulted.

This report draws extensively on as yet unpublished data derived from the study of the Roman pottery from a number of sites in the county, of which Tiddington and Wasperton are the largest groups, but which also include important material from other sites in Alcester itself. To avoid tedious repetition no references are given for statements in the text which draw on this data unless the work is actually in press.

Fabrics (Table MT10, microfiche M2:B1)

Samian ware (1133 sherds, 4.6%; 21.04 EVEs, 6.4%)

Samian ware was an important component of the Roman pottery assemblage. The date range extended from Neronian to 3rd century and all the main suppliers were represented. South Gaulish samian was better represented here than at neighbouring sites like Tiddington where such material was rare (despite the existence of extensive 1st-century occupation). Central Gaulish sources, including Les Martres-de-Veyre, were also well represented and East Gaulish vessels indicate the import of samian to the site probably well into the 3rd century.

The potters' stamps and selected other pieces are discussed below, and stratified samian ware groups up to period 6 are tabulated in the relevant period by period discussion of the pottery groups. The full samian catalogue is in microfiche (M2:C9–D7).

Fine wares: mica-dusted fabrics (18 sherds, 0.1%; 0.28 EVEs, 0.0%)

These fabrics occur in Flavian–Hadrianic contexts in Alcester. At the Explosion site they were present throughout this period and then recurred residually in later large groups (ie in periods 6 and 9 and the post-Roman period). They never exceeded 0.4% of the assemblage. Three separate mica-dusted fabrics were identified on the site (F22, F23, and F24). No source is known for them, although F24 and the early occurrences of F22 were unusually fine and may have derived from a Continental source.

Mica-dusted vessel types

Only two vessel types, both in fabric F23, were identifiable from rim sherds. These were illustrated vessels nos 573 and 574 (an imitation Dr 38 and a lid respectively). The very fine body sherds of F22 found in periods 1 and 2 were probably from a small beaker.

Fine wares: colour-coated fabrics (1268 sherds, 5.1%; 21.9 EVEs, 6.4%)

The colour-coated fabrics found at the Explosion site can be divided into imports and Romano-British material. The Romano-British fabrics were present in greater quantities. Of these the Nene Valley and Oxfordshire colour-coated wares were the only ones to represent more than 1% of the assemblage at any

Explosion site finds (AES 76-7)

time. Nene Valley ware (fabric F52) first appeared on the site in period 2 (early 2nd century), in which context it was intrusive, and it did not appear properly until period 5. It then continued to be present until the end of the Roman period. At the end of the 4th century it formed almost 3% of the period 10 group. It remained at about that level in the post-Roman deposits, rising to almost 9% in topsoil.

The Oxfordshire colour-coated fabric (F51) was present from period 6 in the mid-3rd century in quantities similar to Nene Valley ware until period 10 when it made up almost 6% of the assemblage. Following the same pattern as Nene Valley ware, it was present in the greatest quantities in topsoil (13.6%).

Other Romano-British colour-coated fabrics present in very small quantities (usually one or two sherds) included New Forest ware (fabric F55) amongst a couple of unattributed fabrics. This is the only recorded instance of New Forest products in Warwickshire, Alcester lying well beyond the normal range of distribution of this industry.

The possible imports consisted of three dark slipped fabrics (F36–F38) used for the manufacture of cornice-rimmed, roughcast beakers and found in Alcester during the Hadrianic period, and Rhenish and Central Gaulish fabrics. There is some dispute as to whether the Hadrianic fabrics derive from the Continent (Anderson 1980, 28–34, North Gaulish fabrics 1 and 2) or south-east England (Symonds pers comm). At the Explosion site they only occurred in contexts from periods 6–10, in which they must have been residual, and only as less than 1% of the assemblage.

In an archive report on the Rhenish and Central Gaulish material Robin Symonds says:

'. . . about 31% of the vessels are probably from Lezoux, about 28% are probably from Trier, and about 40% are not clearly identifiable. It is also worth noting that although the East and Central Gaulish vessels seem to be found side by side regardless of the stratigraphy, there is at least a general trend that the Trier vessels are more prevalent in the upper layers, while the Lezoux vessels are found more in the lower layers, which correlates with the general dates of the industries.'

Sherds falling within the general Rhenish and Central Gaulish category were assigned to one of two fabrics, F32 for Central Gaulish products and F33 for Trier vessels, even though, as indicated above, these sources did not necessarily account for all the vessels in this category. Attribution of sherds to these specific sources must therefore be regarded with caution.

Colour-coated vessel types

There was a good range of vessel types overall, dating from the late 2nd/early 3rd century to the late 4th century. The most common type in these fabrics was the beaker. All the unattributed Romano-British material seemed to be from beakers, for example no 283. There was a wide range of different beaker types from the Nene Valley and Oxfordshire potteries, such as the hunt cup no 481 from the Nene Valley, and the pentice-moulded (no 919) and barbotine decorated beakers (eg nos 766 and 767) from Oxfordshire. The possibly imported Hadrianic fabrics are only known to occur as beakers with roughcast decoration. Amongst the Rhenish and Central Gaulish ware there was a fine example of an indented beaker (no 476) and a barbotine decorated vessel (no 477). There were also Central Gaulish cups, nos 522 and 523, paralleled at the Baromix site, and handled cup sherds (cf Greene 1978a, 24–25, no 8) including no 521.

Other vessel types included a flagon, no 400, a Castor Box lid, no 917, and straight-sided bowls and dishes in Nene Valley ware, several imitation Dr 18/31 bowls (nos 749, 768–9, 814, and 858) in the Oxfordshire fabric and a handled bowl, no 880. Several of the Oxfordshire vessels, including the latter piece, can be dated to the last half of the 4th century. There were also occasional jar types in Nene Valley and Oxfordshire fabrics.

Amphora fabrics (555 sherds, 2.2%; 1.39 EVEs, 0.4%)

Amphora fabrics constituted 2.2% of the total number of sherds from the site and made up over 10% of the assemblage during periods 1 to 3. The most important component of this group derived from Spain. Two Spanish fabrics were identified but only one of these was particularly significant (fabric A21). It was probably residual after about the early 3rd century, but continued to be present as less than 1% of the assemblage into post-Roman times. The Spanish fabrics represented 67.8% of the total number of *amphora* sherds in the collection.

From period 6 Gaulish *amphora* fabrics appeared in the assemblage. The more important of the two fabrics present was fabric A22, a southern Gaulish product. It was also the second most significant of all the *amphora* fabrics (11% of all *amphora* sherds) and was probably in context until the end of the 3rd century (about period 9). Although it did not appear at this site before the late 2nd century it is known from other sites in the town, for example Baromix, earlier in the century. The other possible Gaulish fabric (A24) is thought to have a northern origin (M Darling pers comm). Only one sherd is known from Warwickshire so far.

The only remaining fabric to occur on the site in any quantity was an eastern Mediterranean fabric (A42) of probable Rhodian origin (Peacock and Williams 1986, 102). It represented 7.6% of all *amphora* sherds and first appeared in the later 3rd century. It then continued to be present as most important *amphora* fabric in the later part of the occupation of the site. All of this material must have been residual as the date range for the Rhodian fabric is late 1st to early 2nd century. It is also known from Tiddington. There was one sherd of a later, possibly eastern Mediterranean fabric (A41), a micaceous oxidised fabric with a buff exterior surface from a thin walled, ridged vessel. Parallels at Caistor-by-Norwich are thought to be 3rd century in date (M Darling pers comm) so it is likely that this piece too was residual. As yet there are no other incidences from Warwickshire.

During the late 1st and early 2nd centuries *amphorae* (or perhaps large flagons) were also reaching Alcester from the Brockley Hill kilns (fabric A11). A further source of *amphorae* at this time was Campania. Three sherds of fabric A23 are from this source (D Williams pers comm; Peacock and Williams 1986, 87). The fabric has not been identified at other local sites but *mortaria* in a very similar fabric are known from both Tiddington and Alcester (see below).

Amphora vessel types

The most commonly found *amphora* type from this collection was the globular Dressel 20. The rim types present date to the late 1st to early 2nd centuries. This was the only vessel type from which rim sherds were present. The Gaulish sherds were probably from the thin-walled, flat-bottomed form Pelichet 47 (Peacock and Williams 1986, Class 27). Some of the sherds show the ribbing which was occasionally found on the shoulder of this type. The Rhodian wine *amphora* (*ibid*, Class 9) sherds were from conical vessels with rod handles. Two of the Campanian (fabric A23) sherds were of a bifid handle from a Dressel 2–4 type (*ibid*, Class 10). A body sherd in this fabric was probably of the same type.

Mortarium fabrics (288 sherds, 1.2%; 10.12 EVEs, 3%)

Until the mid-2nd century the *mortaria* found on this site came from north-east Gaul, possibly Italy, and the Verulamium region. Of these, one of the north-east Gaulish fabrics (M12) was most important. This was the fabric used by Quintus Valerius Veranius, a Flavian potter (Hartley 1977); the illustrated vessel no 61 was stamped by him. (One of his stamps is also known from Tiddington.) The second perhaps Gaulish fabric (M11), was less numerous and no stamped examples have been found. Both fabrics occur at Alcester, Tiddington, and Wasperton.

The possibly Italian fabric M13 is also known to occur in very small quantities at Tiddington and Wasperton. *Amphora* sherds in a very similar fabric (A23) were also found on the site (see above). This fabric, together with M12 and Verulamium region material, appeared in period 1. The imported fabrics were found in periods 1 to 3 where they were probably in context. The Verulamium region material was perhaps still in context as far as the middle of the 2nd century (period 4), but probably not later, occurrences in periods 5, 9, and 11 being residual.

Other *mortaria* which must have been supplied to Alcester during the 2nd century derived from south-west England. Illustrated vessel no 284 in fabric M44 probably dated to the mid-2nd century; it is unlikely, therefore, to have been in context in period 6, its only appearance on the site. The other south-western fabric, M42, was found only in topsoil. Both of these fabrics are known from other sites in the town but are not common further east in Warwickshire. Other assemblages from Alcester, particularly that from the Baromix factory in Bleachfield Street, suggest strong links with the south-west during the early stages of the town's development (see below), and the occurrence of these fabrics in Alcester may be seen as part of this picture.

The most important *mortaria* industries, as far as the Alcester market was concerned, were the north Warwickshire kilns at Mancetter-Hartshill and the Oxfordshire potteries. Mancetter-Hartshill products appeared in the mid-2nd century and steadily increased in quantity throughout the Roman period. However, the most significant source of *mortaria* from the mid-3rd century onwards was undoubtedly Oxfordshire, producing 70% of all *mortarium* sherds from the site. Over two-thirds of these sherds were in the white fabric (M23) which was first found in the mid-3rd century (period 6). The remaining third was largely Oxfordshire colour-coated ware (M71) with a few examples of the white-coated ware (M43). The white-coated ware appeared from the 4th century onwards while the colour-coated fabric came mainly from late 4th-century and post-Roman contexts.

Mortarium vessel types

The range of *mortarium* types shows a marked bias towards 3rd- and 4th-century types. The early hook-rimmed forms were all in the imported fabrics, or from the Verulamium region or the south-west. Although the products of the Mancetter-Hartshill potteries occurred on the site from the mid-2nd century only two sherds were conclusively dated to before AD 160. These are the stamped vessels nos 37 and 38. The former, stamped by Braruco, is dated AD 110–50. There was one example of a collared *mortarium*, illustrated vessel no 485, which was probably AD 170–230 in date. All other Mancetter-Hartshill vessel types which can be identified are 3rd century or later. None of the Oxfordshire *mortaria* predated AD 240. The types present were M17, M19, M20, M21, M22, M22/23, C97, C98, and C100 (Young 1977). The most numerous of these were M17 and M22. It is known from other sites in the town that plenty of 2nd-century *mortaria* reached Alcester from the Mancetter-Hartshill kilns, but a picture is beginning to emerge of trading links with Oxfordshire becoming important in the 3rd century.

White ware fabrics (476 sherds, 1.9%; 7.78 EVEs, 2.3%)

This group is made up of two categories. The larger of the two consisted of those fabrics which were also

Explosion site finds (AES 76-7)

used in the manufacture of *mortaria*. Products of all the major British *mortarium* production centres have been identified on the site. Verulamium region material (fabric W11) was present into the post-Roman period but never represented more than 0.5% of the assemblage. Mancetter-Hartshill (fabric W12) and Oxfordshire products (fabric W13) typically represent 0.5%–2.5% each of the assemblage but may be slightly more or less. The two centres seem to have had a much more equal share of the market for vessels other than *mortaria*. The only imported white ware in this group was possibly from north-east Gaul (W42), similar to the *mortarium* fabric used by Quintus Valerius Veranius (M12). It only occurred in period 6 by which time it must have been residual.

The other category of white ware in this general grouping consists of those fabrics which were not used in the manufacture of *mortaria*. This category can be subdivided into a further two groups. The first consists of fine white wares of unknown source which occur, as here, in very small quantities on sites throughout Alcester: two fabrics (W21 and W22) are represented here. The second sub-group contained those slightly coarser fabrics which could be identified to source: Nene Valley white ware of which there was one sherd in period 8; Oxfordshire parchment ware and Oxfordshire Burnt white ware. These latter two can be up to 0.4% of the later Roman assemblage. Parchment ware has been found at most Roman settlements in the county and is known from other excavations in Alcester. This is the first incidence of Burnt white ware in Warwickshire.

White ware vessel types

The most common vessel types in these fabrics were flagons and jars. There were also bowls, beakers, and a lid. The most unusual vessel was the perforated base from a possible candlestick (illustrated vessel no 575).

The Verulamium region products were all flagons apart from a possible small flask (illustrated vessel no 789) which occurred residually in period 10. Beakers only occurred in Mancetter-Hartshill fabric W12. Other vessels from these kilns were ring- and cup-necked flagons and flanged bowls. The widest range of forms was in the Oxfordshire fabric and included flagons, jars, hemispherical and flanged bowls, a lid, and a candlestick.

The only identifiable vessels in the fine white fabrics were a small shallow bowl and a narrow version of what may be a Dr 37 (no 229). The parchment ware bowl (no 760) and Burnt white ware jar (no 771) were standard forms from the rather narrow repertoire of these potters.

White-slipped flagon fabrics (184 sherds, 0.7%; 3.49 EVEs, 1.0%)

Eleven different fabrics were identified within this broad group of white-coated, oxidised wares. Only five of these were present in any quantity (Q11, Q12, Q13, Q24, and Q25). The group was present from the Flavian period until post-Roman times. After the beginning of the 3rd century it dropped to less than 1% of the assemblage. This supports the evidence already accrued from other sites in the town for the use of these fabrics in the late 1st and 2nd centuries, with the material becoming residual during the 3rd century.

White-slipped flagon vessel types

The fabrics occurred almost exclusively in the form of ring-necked flagons with ribbed handles (eg no 85) which were similar to examples from Gloucester (Rawes 1982, 42–7, nos 119–125 and 128), although the fabrics are not identical (J Timby pers comm). It seems possible that these fabrics were made fairly locally, but formed part of the Severn Valley ware tradition. The parallels from Gloucester are Flavian in date whilst similar vessels are known from Wroxeter in a Hadrianic context. Ring-necked flagons in these fabrics represented a much higher proportion of the total number of vessels than at Tiddington (where flagons as a class were never more than 0.8%), or Wasperton (0.1%). Other vessels occurring in these fabrics were a butt beaker, a possible carinated bowl, a bowl of uncertain type, and what may be a lid.

Handmade fabrics (8 sherds, 0.0%; 0.4 EVEs, 0.1%)

Very little handmade material was found on the site. This is consistent with the evidence from previous excavations in the town, in which small amounts of handmade material occur occasionally in Roman deposits (eg Booth 1989, 29, no 4). The fabrics seem to be related to Iron Age material found at sites such as Tiddington and Wasperton, but as none of these fabrics contains diagnostic inclusions it would be impossible to assign them to the same source with any certainty, and it seems probable that all such simple fabrics were made locally according to demand. They are unlikely to have been in context after the early 2nd century and it is possible that they represent entirely residual, Iron Age material.

Handmade vessel types

As at other sites in the county the forms were simple bucket and barrel-shaped jars.

Oxidised fabrics (except Severn Valley wares) (268 sherds, 1.1%; 4.43 EVEs, 1.3%)

Oxidised fabrics not originating from the Severn Valley region were regularly present in Alcester, albeit in small quantities, throughout the Roman period.

They are likely to have been the products of local potters (eg fabric O51, known to have been produced at Tiddington) and were probably residual after the mid-2nd century. At the Explosion site they were best represented during period 1 (6%). From the mid-2nd century these fabrics generally made up less than 1% of the assemblage.

Oxidised vessel types

The most common form used by these potters, as with contemporary grey wares, was the everted rim pyriform jar. There were also occasional examples of narrow- and medium-mouthed jars and a small straight-sided tankard (illustrated vessel no 110), a form known from the Tiddington kilns (Booth 1986, 29).

Oxidised fabrics: Severn Valley wares (6546 sherds, 26.5%; 63.78 EVEs, 18.7%)

Seven different Severn Valley ware fabrics were identified of which the most important were O21, O23, O24, O25, and O27. No source has yet been discovered for any of these fabrics although many of the vessel types can be paralleled at Malvern and Droitwich. Severn Valley ware formed part of the assemblage from period 1 (in which it constituted 10%) until the end of the Roman period (almost 35%) and persisted at between 16% and 35% of the post-Roman groups. It was most important in the 3rd and 4th centuries when, together with Black-Burnished ware, it dominated the coarse ware collection. The Severn Valley ware fabric present in the greatest quantity was fabric O21 which was proportionately more significant before the end of the 3rd century than the other Severn Valley wares (50% of the fabric came from contexts dating to before the middle of the 3rd century whilst only about 27% of the other fabrics were concentrated in the same period). By the early 4th century O21 and the other Severn Valley fabrics occurred in equal proportions.

Severn Valley ware vessel types

The repertoire of the Severn Valley ware potters included a range of different jar types, jugs, beakers, flanged bowls, necked bowls, tankards, strainers, and lids (cf Webster 1976). All of these types are present on the site and there was a great variety of rim types within them.

Some of the vessel types were derived from Belgic prototypes, for example the carinated bowls such as nos 196 and 214. This latter is very similar to a vessel from Malvern kiln IV (Webster 1976, no 60) which is thought to be of 2nd-century date. Loosely similar forms, but not in Severn Valley ware, have been found in a possible production waste deposit at Tiddington, which has been assigned a pre-Flavian date. Another 'Belgic' form, also paralleled at Tiddington, was the squat, high-shouldered jar (eg illustrated vessels nos 154 and 247). Neither type was especially numerous (carinated bowls formed only 1.9% of all Severn Valley ware vessels), and they were probably residual after the later 2nd century. Shallow dishes, such as illustrated vessel no 626, made up 1.1% of the group and occurred exclusively in fabric O21. They are thought to have derived ultimately from another Belgic type, Camulodunum 16 (Webster 1976, 35–36).

A further native-derived form used by the Severn Valley potters was the tankard, which can be traced to a Durotrigan ancestry (Webster 1976, 41). This occurred during the 1st and early 2nd centuries in a straight-sided version (eg no 89). With time the tankard developed a more flared profile. The latter type was more common on this site than the earlier version as a result of the increased importance of Severn Valley ware itself in the 3rd and 4th centuries. Tankards were an important part of the Severn Valley ware assemblage (18.5%), second only to the general jar category.

Jars amounted to 57.5% of all the Severn Valley ware types. Narrow- or medium-mouthed jars were a constant feature of Severn Valley ware groups in Alcester throughout the Roman period. They were often decorated with grooves, cordons, and burnishing on the neck and shoulder. They represented 42.8% of all the Severn Valley ware vessels. No clear chronological evolution of these types could be discerned. Storage jar body sherds were also present in all periods, but the vessel type was only really frequent and represented by rim sherds in the larger groups such as period 9, by which time, however, most of these vessels may have been residual. Overall, storage jars made up 5.0% of the Severn Valley ware vessels. They were most common in fabric O21 (eg no 159).

From the 3rd century, wide-mouthed jars and rounded flanged bowls made up an important part of this group (wide-mouthed jars 9.6%, bowls 10.5%). The flanges of the bowls were often reeded and most of the types found in Alcester can be paralleled at Malvern kilns 2 and 3 and Wroxeter (Webster 1976, nos 53 and 56). There are also parallels for such vessels at Droitwich (eg Gelling 1959, Fig 7, nos 13 and 14). These two later types were concentrated in fabrics O23, O24, and O25.

Other, less common forms were beakers, flagons (eg nos 301 and 404), and jugs (nos 97 and 677), which are known from other sites in Alcester, but only the jugs can be traced (to Great Buckmans Farm, Malvern), whilst the kiln source or date of the beakers and flagons remains uncertain. Carinated bowls also occurred in small quantities and lids were found occasionally. No source or date has been identified for the latter but examples are known from Gloucester (Webster 1976, 37) and Droitwich, where the type occurs in a 4th-century context (Gelling 1959, Fig 9, no 10). Strainers occurred (nos 66, 401, and possibly 847) in fabric O21, one of which (no 66) was from a period 1 context and combined a

Explosion site finds (AES 76-7)

carinated pre-Flavian profile with a triangular everted rim similar to those found on the locally manufactured pyriform jars during the Flavian and Hadrianic periods.

Reduced fabrics (7404 sherds, 30%; 97.13 EVEs, 28.5%)

These fabrics constituted the single most numerically important group of coarse wares on the site. Until the late 3rd century they appeared to represent between 55%–65% of the assemblage. After this point they declined to 31% or less. This confirms the pattern of pottery supply to Alcester hitherto only guessed at from relatively small groups of excavated material. This slump is best illustrated by comparing the two largest groups from the site: the period 6 assemblage (3862 sherds) of which 64.3% were reduced fabrics, and the period 9 assemblage (7098 sherds) where the same fabric group made up only 12.6%. The fall in the quantities of reduced coarse wares was matched by the rise in Severn Valley and Black-Burnished wares which took their place in the assemblage.

Most of these fabrics may have been of local origin but only one has so far been identified to source: fabric R21, which is known to have been made at Tiddington kiln 2 but may have been produced at other sites as well. Fifty percent of the fabric was found in contexts dating to before the mid-2nd century. Of the other grey wares present only four occurred in large numbers (R01, R30, R40, and R50). Of these R30 and R50 were present in greater quantity slightly earlier than the other two. Thirty percent of the former was found in contexts dating no later than the mid-2nd century, whilst the same proportion of the latter took until the end of the 2nd century to accumulate.

Smaller amounts of fabrics R60, R70, and R80 were also found. R70 was a fabric distinguished by very coarse inclusions. It cannot be isolated within a particular date bracket. The association of the very fine grey ware, R80, with 'London type' decoration at sites such as Tiddington suggests that this fabric was probably out of production by the end of the 2nd century if not earlier.

Reduced fabric vessel types

All of the different grey ware fabrics used the same basic repertoire of forms which were themselves derived from a variety of sources. The earliest vessel types were those which could be assigned to a 'Belgic' tradition, such as squat, high-shouldered jars (like nos 141 and 79) and carinated bowls (eg nos 86 and 92).

Although a wide variety of types occurred in grey ware fabrics the great majority of these vessels were jars (83.1%). All other types were relatively unimportant. Of the lesser types bowls (5.0%), lids (4.3%), beakers (2.9%), and carinated bowls (2.4%) were the principal forms. Tankards and dishes were also found, and a single example of a handled jug or flagon.

The most common grey ware form was the everted rim pyriform jar, usually found with rusticated decoration. This form is thought to have derived from the Rhineland (F H Thompson 1958, 30–32). It was in use in Warwickshire from the Flavian period until the late 2nd to early 3rd centuries. It was a major vessel type at Tiddington kiln 2 (in fabric R21) and was the principal form produced in two of the three Lapworth kilns. It was common in fabric R21 at the Explosion site (68.9% of all vessels in this fabric) and occurred as a significant proportion of the output of most of the grey ware fabrics, but particularly of R19, R15, and R01, in all of which it exceeded 45% of all vessels). In south Warwickshire the type seems to have developed from a globular profile with overall rusticated decoration (eg no 57) to a more open, conical shape with rusticated strips (eg no 321). This type was present as an ever increasing proportion of the assemblage from 17%, in the early Flavian period, to around 55% in the second half of the 2nd century. It declined steeply to 6% by the end of the Roman period.

Many of the other vessel types used by the local potters were very similar to Severn Valley ware forms, such as storage jars (eg nos 62 and 235), tankards (eg nos 622 and 623), and bowls (eg no 155). Many of the grey ware bowls, however, were copies of straight-sided Black-Burnished ware types (eg nos 779 and 897), though curving-sided forms were slightly more common. Other imitations of Black-Burnished ware forms were dishes and 'cooking pot' style jars (see nos 748 and 777). Their dates are likely to be similar to those of their Severn Valley or Black-Burnished ware prototypes.

Another vessel type which was made in all of the major grey ware fabrics was the globular jar (eg nos 431 and 651). Some examples were found with vertical burnished lines, giving the form a marked similarity to the Malvernian 'tubby cooking pot' type. This may point to its derivation and indicate a 2nd-century date for the type consistent with its low occurrence after period 6.

Fabric R70 was used almost exclusively for the manufacture of storage jars whose forms remained very much the same throughout the Roman period. The repertoire of the potters making fabric R80, however, consisted of vessels such as poppyhead beakers and small bowls often decorated with 'London type' motifs.

Black-Burnished ware (5742 sherds, 23.2%; 83.6 EVEs, 24.5%)

Fabric B11 is equated with Gillam's 'BB1' and as such needs no further description (see also Farrar 1973, 69–78 and Williams 1977). There is no reason to query Gillam's date of AD 120 (Gillam 1976, 57) for the fabric's appearance in this area and we see it first on the Explosion site in period 2. By the late 3rd century it formed 11% of the assemblage (calculated in numbers of sherds) and reached 36% in the 4th century. This is consistent with the pattern observed on other sites in the town with Black-Burnished ware becoming of greater importance than the local reduced fabrics which made up a high proportion of the coarse ware assemblage until the beginning of the 3rd century.

Black-Burnished ware vessel types

All the standard vessel types were represented here. Cooking pots were the most numerous of these, except in period 7 when bowls formed 8.3% of the total number of vessels from this period and cooking pots only 6%. Otherwise Black-Burnished ware cooking pots started in period 2 as 0.1% of the total assemblage and by period 9 had reached 14.7%. Bowls ranged between 0.1%–10.7% and dishes between 0.1%–8.9%. Fragments of handled beakers, 'fish dishes', and lids also occurred, and a large body sherd with overall burnish may have been from a flagon.

Shell-gritted wares (269 sherds, 1.0%; 7.53% EVEs, 2.2%)

These fabrics first appeared in the late 3rd century but did not make up more than 1% of the assemblage until the mid-4th. They were at their most important in the immediately post-Roman period, period 11 (3.3%), the assemblage which is likely to have represented the situation at the very end of the Roman occupation (see discussion of post-Roman deposits below). Shell-gritted wares consisted almost entirely of fabric C11. This fabric was a constant feature of late groups from Alcester but never achieved the same numerical significance as at Tiddington. This may have been because Tiddington lay closer to the source of fabric C11 which is thought to have possibly been made in Northamptonshire.

Shell-gritted vessel types

Although examples of shell-gritted ware dishes and bowls are known from Warwickshire (eg at Tiddington) only jars were found at the Explosion site. These were generally cooking pots (eg no 866) and storage jars (nos 612 and 613), often decorated with a combination of incised wavy and straight lines. Some rilled sherds were also found, and one jar had deeply incised lines across the top of the rim.

Coarse-gritted fabrics: pink grogged ware (G11) (32 sherds, 0.1%; 0.12 eves 0.0%)

This fabric and its suggested south-east Midlands derivation have been discussed in detail elsewhere (Booth and Green 1989). At the Explosion site it constituted 0.1% of the total number of sherds. One sherd appeared in the second half of the 3rd century but the remainder of the material was concentrated in later periods. This bears out all other evidence for the fabric in Alcester; it was principally a late 3rd- to 4th-century ware but occasionally occurred earlier in the 3rd century. It was a regular component of later Roman assemblages in Warwickshire.

Pink grogged ware vessel types

The most common vessel type in this fabric known in Warwickshire is a large, narrow-mouthed storage jar with a heavy rim, burnishing over the rim and shoulder and an incised wavy line on the shoulder (Booth and Green 1989, 79, Fig 1). This is the form represented here; there was no conclusive evidence for the other (less common) vessel types in the same fabric (a smaller storage jar and an open bowl) found at other sites in the county.

Coarse-gritted fabrics: Malvernian metamorphic fabric (G44) (228 sherds, 0.9%; 4.47 eves, 1.3%)

The Malvernian metamorphic fabrics (Peacock 1967) formed a small but consistent presence in Roman assemblages from Alcester. At this site material was present in every period (except the very small group from period 5) until medieval times. It formed between 0.1% and 1.8% of the assemblage and was most significant in periods 1, 2, and 8. Trade with Malvern via Droitwich along the saltways was probably a regular part of the economy of Roman Alcester.

Malvernian metamorphic vessel types

Vessels in Malvernian fabrics represented 1.3% of the total from the site. Some 45% of these vessels were baggy storage jars or cooking pots similar to Black-Burnished ware vessels. Almost as many were simple lids and the remainder were of Peacock's 'tubby cooking pot' type. One unusual omission from the assemblage was the shallow dish (Peacock 1967, Fig 1, nos 15–17) a type which is known from other sites in the town and elsewhere in Warwickshire.

Discussion of fabrics

Three of the major fabric groups were the principal contributors to pottery supply to the site. Reduced (grey) wares were most common, particularly up to the mid-3rd century, and amounted to 30% of all the pottery. Oxidised wares, consisting almost entirely of Severn Valley fabrics, totalled 27.7% of the pottery. Present throughout the Roman period, they increased considerably in importance in the mid-3rd century before declining slightly in the second half of the 4th century. The other main fabric was Black-Burnished ware, which comprised 23.3% of all the pottery and was particularly prominent from the late 3rd century onwards. Other coarse ware fabric groups, shell-tempered, and coarse-gritted wares, were poorly represented. There were a few sherds in a handmade Iron Age tradition (apart from the Malvern ware sherds which made up most of the 'coarse-gritted' fabric group), but early wheelmade 'Belgic type' fabrics were completely absent on this site, emphasising the unimportance of this native tradition at Alcester. Sherds in these fabrics have been found in very small quantities on other sites in the town, but are nowhere sufficient to demonstrate extensive settlement before the arrival of the army and the establishment of Roman occupation (see below).

Samian ware totalled 4.6% of the pottery and other fine ware fabrics amounted to a further 6.1%. The fabrics used for 'specialist' vessel types such as *amphorae*, flagons, and *mortaria* together also totalled 6.1%. *Amphorae*, with 2.2% of the total pottery, were better represented here than in any other recently studied Warwickshire assemblage, but *mortaria*, only 1.1%, were relatively poorly represented (though they did amount to 2.9% of the total EVEs). The total of 'fine and specialist' wares was thus 16.8% (19.5% in terms of EVEs). The proportion which this component of the assemblage comprises in relation to the remaining coarse wares shows marked variation from site to site. The Alcester figure contrasts with those for rural sites such as Crewe Farm and Wasperton (3.4% and 4.8% respectively), and larger settlements such as Stretton-on-Fosse and particularly Tiddington (8% and 7.9% – the Tiddington figure is for all the pottery from the settlement, that from the 1981 excavation alone (see below) was 10.5%). The Explosion site representation of fine and specialist wares was more closely comparable with that from other major settlements in the county such as Tripontium (17.7%) and Chesterton (23.6%). These figures are clearly related in part to the economic status of the sites in question, reflecting their importance as local market centres.

Vessel types

Vessel types, like the fabrics, were defined with varying degrees of precision. Major vessel type categories (*amphorae*, flagons, jars, beakers, cups, tankards, carinated bowls, bowls, dishes, *mortaria*, lids, and miscellaneous) were used to define broad functional classes of vessels without regard to nuances of typology. Subdivision of these classes was on the basis of shape, and the detailed recording of rim forms allowed further refinement of the typology where necessary. Vessel types are quantified in tabular form in relation to the major fabric groups and by period in Tables MT11 and MT12 (microfiche M2:C5–C8).

Jars, as usual, were the dominant main vessel type, amounting to 51.3% of all the vessels (all figures are expressed as percentages of the total of EVEs (340.12) from the site). This figure compares quite closely with that from the 1981 excavations at Tiddington (55.4%), a site with a similar date range to the Explosion site. Bowls were the next most important major type (16.2%), followed by dishes (9.1%), beakers (6.1%), tankards (4.9%), flagons (3.5%), and *mortaria* (3.1%). Other types were insignificant in percentage terms.

Jars were most common in reduced (grey ware) fabrics; 83.1% of all reduced vessels were jars, 23.8% of all the vessels from the site. They were the exclusive vessel type in shell-tempered fabrics, and were an important component (62.7%) of coarse-gritted fabric production. They were also common in oxidised fabrics (58.1%) and in the cooking pot form were 40.3% of all the Black-Burnished ware. The most characteristic jar type was the shouldered 'pyriform' jar with an angled everted rim, which dominated assemblages up to the middle of the 3rd century at which point it was clearly residual. Thereafter the general category of medium-mouthed jars became more important until replaced by the cooking pot as the principal jar type at the end of the 3rd century, reflecting the importance of Black-Burnished ware at that time. Wide-mouthed jars, never particularly common, were most common in the later 3rd- to mid-4th-century phases. They occurred almost entirely in Severn Valley wares. Narrow-mouthed jars, in contrast, although most common in Severn Valley fabrics, also occurred in grey wares and were found throughout the Roman period in roughly consistent quantities.

Bowls were divided almost equally between curving- and straight-sided types. The majority of the latter were in Black-Burnished ware, with a small number of grey ware and a few colour-coated (Nene Valley ware) examples. Consequently the type was most common from the mid-3rd century onwards and hardly occurred at all before the mid-2nd. Curving-sided bowls were found in a wider range of fabrics. Many were in samian ware since the type includes bowls of forms Dr 31, 37, and 38, and fine ware copies of the same types (mainly in Oxfordshire colour-coated ware) were also common. Curving-sided bowls also occurred frequently in oxidised fabrics, particularly in Severn Valley wares, and in white wares, but were rare in reduced fabrics.

Dishes were also divided between curving- and straight-sided types. Despite the fact that the former were entirely in samian ware (forms such as Dr 18) they occurred mainly from the later 3rd century onwards. Straight-sided dishes were found in small quantities in fine and oxidised and reduced fabrics, but the large majority were in Black-Burnished ware. While present in the late 1st/early 2nd century, therefore, the type only became common in the later 3rd and occurred most frequently in post-Roman contexts.

Beakers made up 6.4% of the total assemblage. They were found in a wide range of fabrics, of which fine wares accounted for 55%. 'Jar beakers', ie those vessels of jar-like form but small enough perhaps to have functionally distinct from other jars, made up most of the remainder of the type. Such vessels occurred in white, oxidised, and reduced coarse wares and Black-Burnished ware, with the samian form Déchelette 72 also included in this type. Jar beakers occurred from period 1 onwards, but other beaker types were only represented (eg in Nene Valley, Oxfordshire, and Rhenish wares) from period 9. Beakers as a whole were therefore more common at this time than earlier, and actually amounted to 10.5% of vessels in topsoil. Butt beakers were rare and were recorded in very small amounts in oxidised, reduced, and white-slipped wares. There was also part of a fine white ware butt beaker, possibly an import, in a period 3 context.

Tankards, like beakers, were found from period 1 onwards, but were most common in the later 3rd to mid-4th century. This reflected the peak occurrence of Severn Valley ware, in which most tankards were made. Grey ware examples were also found and the type included the Black-Burnished ware handled jar, on the grounds that this form had the same function as the tankard. Such vessels amounted to 3.3% of all examples of the type.

The other drinking vessel type, the cup, was found almost entirely in samian ware, with hemispherical and carinated examples in Rhenish ware and a single campanulate form (no 248) in a fine oxidised fabric. The type was never common, totalling only 1.4% of all vessels from the site. Only the occasional fine ware occurrences would not have been residual after period 6.

Flagons, another vessel type relevant to drinking practises, were relatively numerous at the Explosion site. They occurred in a range of fabrics of which white wares were most common. Flagons accounted for over half the white ware vessels on the site. White-slipped fabrics were also important for flagons, 26.7% of which were in these fabrics. Ninety percent of all white-slipped vessels were of this type. Oxidised coarse ware flagons were also surprisingly common (almost 25%) and fine wares, particularly Oxfordshire and Nene Valley colour-coated wares, were also used for flagons. The range of fabrics used for flagons meant that the type occurred throughout the Roman period, in white-slipped and oxidised fabrics earlier and fine wares later. White ware flagons seem to have been used all through the period.

Types specific to particular fabric groups, such as *amphorae* and *mortaria*, have been discussed above and require no further comment except to add that 7.7% of the latter were in samian ware. Little can be said about the less common vessel types. Lids were found primarily in grey wares and the Malvernian fabric G44 and seem to have persisted right through the Roman period. Carinated bowls, only 1.1% of the assemblage, were also mainly in grey wares, with fewer oxidised (including Severn Valley ware) examples and occasional instances in white and white-slipped fabrics and samian ware. Miscellaneous types consisted largely of strainers in Severn Valley ware and Castor boxes in Nene Valley ware. The only other miscellaneous types were possible miniature vessels, all in Severn Valley fabrics.

Illustrated samian ware
Brenda Dickinson

The complete samian ware catalogue (in context order) is in microfiche M2:C9–D7.

Potters' stamps (Fig 122)

Notes: (1) stamp recorded at the pottery in question; (2) other stamps of the same potter, but not this particular one, recorded at the pottery in question; (3) assigned to the pottery on distribution, fabric, and so on.

1 Bio 4a, 27(?) BIOŁCIT La Graufesenque (2). Although Bio's stamps sometimes occur at Flavian foundations, his activity is almost certainly pre-Flavian. His work occurs in the Boudiccan burning at Colchester and his forms include 24, Ritt.5 (once) and Ritt.8. This stamp occurs at Carlisle, Chester, and Valkenburg ZH (Per III/IV). *c* AD 50–65. (SF 537, 266L, period 1)
2 Canpanus 1a, 31 CANPANI: retrograde Lezoux (3). This could well be a stamp of Campanus ii, with Canpani for Campani. However, it can be dated independently through the forms on which it appears and its occurrence at Chesterholm and Malton. *c* AD 155–195. (SF 496, 170, period 9)
3 Clemens ii 2a, 38, or 44? [CL]EM[ENTI] Lezoux (1). A stamp of a potter who was associated with Priscus iii in the making of decorated moulds. It occurs at South Shields and on forms 31R and Ludowici Tg. *c* AD 160–190. (SF 340, 124, period 9)
4 Conatius 3a, 32, etc. [CON]ATIVSF Rheinzabern (1). Conatius is datable chiefly through his use of the later Rheinzabern forms. This particular stamp occurs on forms 31R, 32, 32, and Ludowici Tb and Tz. *c* AD 180–260. (170 and 12, period 9).
5 Dagodubnus ii 1a, 33 DAGODBVN[VSF] Rheinzabern (1). Dagodubnus specialised in form 33 and only used one die. This stamp occurs at sites in Britain reoccupied *c* AD 160. The form of his cups suggests a 2nd-century date rather than later, and his range is probably *c* AD 160–200. (SF 459, II 10, period 9)
6 Decmanus i 1a, 79, or Ludowici Tg DECM[ANIM] Lezoux (3). This potter has so far only been recorded on forms 79 and 79R, suggesting a date *c* AD 160–200. (SF 345, 124, period 9)
7 Donatus iii 1b, 32, etc. DON[ATVSF] Rheinzabern (1). The original die (1b) was broken and the beginning of the frame acquired a swallow-tail, as here. Donatus is dated by his forms, which, for this stamp, include 31R, 32, 40, and Ludowici Tc. *c* AD 180–260. (SF 329, 86, period 9)
8 Fuscus ii 4a, 15/17R or 18R OFFVSCI La Graufesenque (2). Used only on dishes, mainly the rouletted variety, this stamp has been noted at Flavian foundations, including the Saalburg. His work in general is common at sites founded under Domitian. *c* AD 80–110. (SF 427, 86, period 9, and SF 279, 12)
9 Iucundus ii 5f, 15/17, or 18 [OF.IV]CVN La Graufesenque (2). This stamp has been recorded at Verulamium (period II) and at Flavian foundations, including the Nijmegen fortress. *c* AD 65–85. (270, period 1)
10 Iulius Numidus 4a, 79R, or Ludowici TgR (burnt) [NVMID]IMA Lezoux (2). His work occurs at sites in northern Britain reoccupied *c* AD 160. It has also been recorded at the Brougham cemetery. This particular stamp has been noted at Benwell. *c* AD 160–200. (SF 385, 124C, period 9)
11 Martius iv 1b, Ludowici Tx MARTIM Lezoux (1). The record for this stamp includes sites in northern Britain reoccupied *c* AD 160 and the Brougham cemetery. It was used mainly on form 33,

Explosion site finds (AES 76-7)

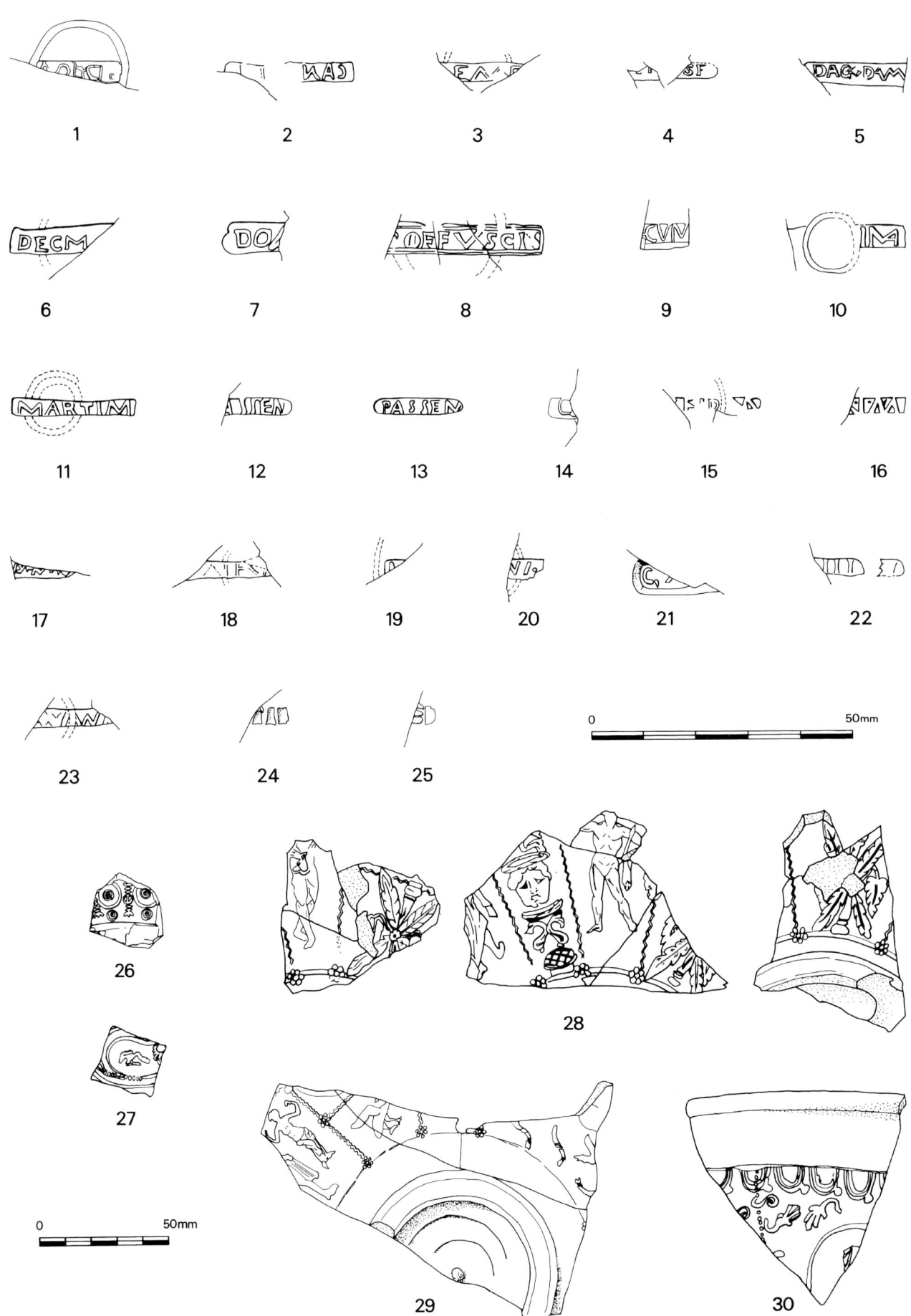

Figure 122   Samian ware stamps, nos 1–25, and decorated vessels, nos 26–30 (AES 76–7)

but has also been noted on form 80. *c* AD 160–190. (SF 511, 170, period 9, with fragments in 12 and 87)
12 and **13** Pass(i)enus 13 33a, 15/17, or 18; 18 PASSEIV[La Graufesenque (2). One of his later stamps, recorded at Aldborough, Chester, and York, but also at the Ubbergen site at Nijmegen. *c* AD 60–70. (SF 669, 270 and 279, period 2; SF 529, 275, period 2)
14 Quintus v 5a (almost certainly this), 31R Q[VINTIM] Lezoux (1). A stamp of the later Lezoux Quintus, recorded at Pudding Pan Rock and at forts on Hadrian's Wall reoccupied *c* AD 160. The forms include 79 and 79R. *c* AD 165–200. (SF 668, 170C, period 9)
15 Sacero 1a, 31 [SAC]EROM Lezoux (3). This potter probably only used one die. The stamp appears on the rim of a decorated bowl, probably with an ovolo used by Albucius ii or Paternus v, and has been noted, burnt, in the material from the Wroxeter forum, where it presumably belongs to the destruction deposit. His forms include 18/31R, 27, and 38. *c* AD 145–175. (SF 554, II 10, period 9)
16 Sacrillus 3a, 30, or 37 rim [SACRIh]h·I·M Lezoux (1). Sacrillus' most common stamp, recorded at Pudding Pan Rock and used on forms 31R, 79, 79R, and 80. *c* AD 160–200. (SF 552, II 10, period 9)
17 Tabus-Virtus i 1a, 15/17, or 18 TABI.VIRIVTI bottom of the letters only surviving) La Graufesenque (3). Perhaps an association of the better-known Virtus, at the end of his career, with an otherwise unknown potter (Tabus?). The stamp occurs at Flavian foundations, including some founded under Domitian (Butzbach, the Saalburg, and Wilderspool). *c* AD 75–100. (SF 553, 285, period 2)
18 Illiterate [ΛΙΙ]/\ΙΙ/\ [– –, probably this, on form 33, etc. Les Martres-de-Veyre (3). Another stamp, almost certainly from the same die, is in Chesters Museum, and presumably comes from Hadrian's Wall. Trajanic or Hadrianic. (SF 371, 86A, period 9).

Unidentified

19 { or } on form 15/17R or 18R (slightly burnt) La Graufesenque (3). This may belong to a dish of form 18R also in (245F). Flavian? (SF 551, 245F, period 5)
20]VI· or ·IΛ [on form 18/31R or 31R Les Martres-de-Veyre (3). Perhaps from a broken die, reused, to judge by the end of the frame. Late Hadrianic or early Antonine. (SF 518, 218, period 7).
21 C\·⋎ on form 33 Lezoux (3). Hadrianic or early Antonine. (SF 426, II 10, period 9)
22]III.../I on form 31, probably illiterate Lezoux (3). Mid- to late Antonine. (SF 287, 86, period 9)
23]RIΛNI[on form 33 Lezoux (3). Antonine. (SF 351, 124, period 9)
24 IA[or LA[on form 33 Lezoux (3). Antonine. (SF 512, 170, period 9)
25]Я on form 33, Lezoux (3). Antonine. (SF 670, II 10, period 9)

Selected decorated samian (Figs 122 and 123)

Notes: D. Figure-type in Dechelette 1904; O. Figure-type in Oswald 1936–7

26 Form 29, South Gaulish, a fragment from the lower zone. The roundels and bow-shaped motifs used in the dividers were used at La Graufesenque on bowls stamped by Primus iii. The roundels are on a bowl from the Cirencester fort ditch (*c* AD 55–65) and the other motif, used in its normal way as a scroll-tie, is on bowls from London (Museum of London) and Vindonissa (Knorr 1952, Taf 51B). The circles enclosing the roundels, and the roundels themselves, were probably inscribed in the mould freehand. *c* AD 55–65. (II 49, period 7)
27 Form 29, South Gaulish. Lower zone, with a winding scroll with a Nile goose and a heart-shaped leaf with a looped border. No precise parallel has been found for the leaf, but both motifs were used at La Graufesenque in the Neronian and early Flavian periods. This piece probably falls within the range *c* AD 60–75. (270, period 1)
28 Form 37, Central Gaulish. A panelled bowl with: a) captive

Explosion site finds (AES 76-7)

(D.643), b) Leaf-cross (Rogers L6), c) (not necessarily the next panel) philosopher (D.523), d) composite column (Rogers Q1), e) Perseus (D.146), f) as b). All these details, the zigzag borders, and seven-beaded rosettes were used at Les Martres-de-Veyre by Igocatus (X-4). (See Stanfield and Simpson 1958, pls 17, 218, 222 and 19, 238, 240.) *c* AD 100–120. (224, 226, 232, and 245B, period 4, etc)
29 Form 37, Central Gaulish. Riveted bowl, with panels: a) Perseus (D.145) and Venus (D.175), b) (upper half) festoon, (lower half) crane (no precise parallel, but closest to O.2196), c) no decoration surviving, d) cornucopiae (Rogers U282) and a crane (as in b). All the figure types, wavy-line borders, and seven-beaded rosettes (Rogers C280) were used at Les Martres-de-Veyre by mould-makers for Medetus and Ranto. *c* AD 110–125. (44, period 5)
30 Form 37, Central Gaulish. The ovolo (Rogers B263), leaf (Rogers J144), small S-motif, and untidy beads were all used at Les Martres-de-Veyre by Cettus, one of the Hadrianic–Antonine group of potters there. All these details are on a bowl at Les Martres with the end of a cursive signature]ttus retrograde (Terrisse 1968, plate XX 526). The motif in the single medallion is perhaps the boar's head, as on the Les Martres bowl. For Cettus' date, see Hartley (1972, 34). *c* AD 135–160. (II 31D, period 6)
31 Form 37, Central Gaulish. Several joining fragments from a bowl in the style of Iullinus ii of Lezoux. The panels contain: a) double medallion with trophy (Rogers Q43) and cups (Rogers T36), b) Hercules (D.444) over an acanthus leaf (Rogers K7), c) warrior and suppliant (D.150) over dolphin (smaller than O.2408). All the details except for the Hercules and trophy appear on stamped bowls of Iullinus, the ovolo (Rogers B153), cups, dots in the background, and warrior with suppliant at Corbridge (Stanfield and Simpson 1958, plate 126, 13), the acanthus and dolphin at Lezoux (Coll. Rambert). *c* AD 160–190. (115, 124, and 128, period 8, etc)
32 Form 37, Central Gaulish. The details are all recognisably from Lezoux, but they are all about 10% smaller than usual. This suggests that someone made poinçons by taking impressions from moulds. In this instance, moulds from more than one potter seem to have been used. The ovolo (Rogers B164), double medallion, and seated Apollo (D.57) all come from Iullinus ii. The stylised tree is from Rogers Q42, but has lost the leaves terminating the top tendrils. This was used by Hadrianic and Antonine potters but not, apparently, by Iullinus. There is no parallel for the dog. This is perhaps unlikely to be a practice pot by an apprentice. Alternatively, the details may have been pirated by one of the workmen. This small bowl is certainly Antonine in date and, in view of the connections, presumably belongs to the period *c* AD 160–190. (22, period 12)

Miscellaneous pieces (Fig 123)

33 Lamp in the form of a Negro's head. Central Gaulish. Compare the example from London (Oswald and Pryce 1920, plate LXXXV, no 7). The upper part of the lamp was broken in antiquity and the broken sides were smoothed off to allow reuse. ?Antonine. (170, period 9)
34 Form 18/31, East Gaulish. The profile and fabric suggest origin at Chemery-Faulquemont. Trajanic–Hadrianic. (224, period 4)

Mortarium and other stamps (Fig 123)
(incorporating comments by Kay Hartley)

Mortarium **stamps**

35 Fabric M12. Q Valerius Veranius. The probable source of this piece is possibly north-east Gaul and the date range *c* AD 70–100 (Hartley 1977). See vessel no 61. (266I and 266O, period 1)
36 Fabric M23. Trademark, probably Oxford, *c* AD 100–140, but a

Explosion site finds (AES 76-7)

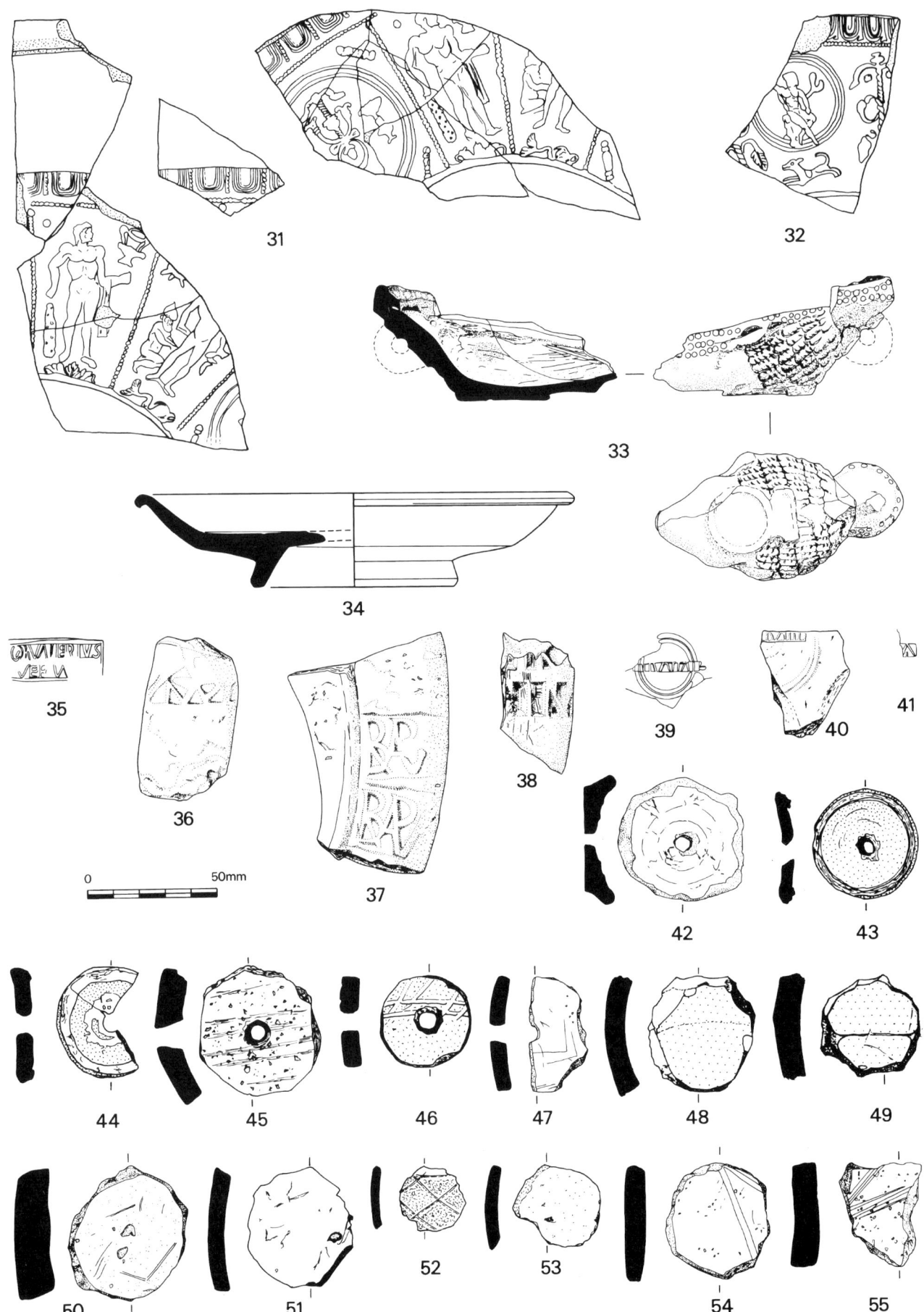

Figure 123 Samian ware decorated vessels and other pieces, nos 31–34, mortarium and coarse ware stamps, nos 35–41, and reused pottery, nos 42–55 (AES 76–7)

date of AD 90 would not be too early for the rim on which this stamp occurs. (SF 550, 245, period 6)

37 Fabric M22. Braruco or Brapuco. Midlands, *c* AD 110–150. Note that this date is rather earlier than that of AD 130–170 proposed by Hartley 1971, no 69. (SF 489, 216, period 6)

38 Fabric ?M22. Broken, deeply impressed stamp. The reading and orientation are uncertain. Midlands, perhaps West Midlands, *c* AD 100–160. (SF 515, 227, period 6)

Other pottery stamps (Fig 123)

39 Fabric F51 (Oxfordshire colour-coated ware). (SF 183, 26, period 10)
40 Fabric F51 (Oxfordshire colour-coated ware). (SF 543, 78, period 10)
41 Fabric F51 (Oxfordshire colour-coated ware). (SF 404, 12, period 11)

All these illiterate stamps belong to the common group which use vertical and diagonal lines (Young 1977, 179–81).

Reused pottery objects

There seems to have been no particular significance in the selection of specific fabrics for reuse, though it is possible that some of the trimmed sherds may have been intended as gaming pieces, in which case the use of sherds in contrasting colours such as red (samian ware) and black (Black-Burnished ware) may have been a conscious choice. The occurrence of spindle whorls and possible counters/gaming pieces primarily in later Roman contexts probably reflected more on the size of finds groups of that date than their period of use. However pieces such as no 43, in a fabric unlikely to have been in circulation before the early 2nd century, may have been in roughly contemporary deposits.

Spindle whorls (Fig 123)

42 Fabric W13. (SF 557, 1, period 14)
43 ?Fabric F37. (SF 501, 44, period 5)
44 Fabric F52. (SF 545, 124A, period 9)
45 Fabric R30. (SF 401)
46 Fabric R30. (SF 497, 230, period 7)
47 Fabric B11. (SF 675, 124F, period 9)

Trimmed sherds/counters (Fig 123)

48 Fabric S (samian ware). (SF 555, 170, period 9)
49 Fabric S (samian ware). (SF 556, II 35, period 6)
50 Fabric A21. (SF 673, 252, period 6)
51 Fabric O20. (SF 548, 124G, period 9)
52 Fabric B11. (SF 546, 124, period 9)
53 Fabric B11. (SF 547, 124, period 9)
54 Fabric B11. (SF 674, 78, period 10)

Graffito (Fig 123)

55 Fabric R30. Part of a possible incised ownership or contents/measure mark on a shoulder sherd of a storage jar. Comparable marks were common elsewhere in Alcester, particularly in the 1960s excavations by C Mahany (*RIB II*, 8, 2503.34–7, 40, 47–9, 57, 68–9, 89, 91; Cracknell and Mahany 1994, Fig 57, 1, 4–6, 8–9, 12–13; Fig 58, 30–32, Fig 59, 38), and also occurred at Tiddington, principally in late 1st- to 2nd-century contexts. (SF 676 (279) period 2)

See also illustrated vessel no 918, with a simple incised + on the shoulder.

Pottery groups (Figs 126–151)

Within each period important groups have been selected for individual discussion. The provenance and fabric of the illustrated coarse ware vessels is indicated at the head of the discussion of each period. The samian ware dating evidence for each of periods 1–6 is tabulated at the appropriate point in the discussion (Tables 18–23). Fig 124 is a seriation diagram which summarises the developing trends in pottery supply. Fig 125 presents the same material in a different way, showing the different major fabric groups as proportions of the assemblage in each period.

Early occupation (periods 1–4)

This phase of the site's occupation was characterised by the predominance of local grey wares, especially in the form of the everted rim pyriform jar with rusticated decoration. Regional supply routes came mainly from the west bringing the products of the Malvernian kilns and those of the Severn Valley ware potters. By the middle of the 2nd century, trade was also established with the north Warwickshire *mortarium* kilns at Mancetter-Hartshill.

Long distance trade with the south-east brought *mortaria* from the Verulamium region and may also have been the route by which samian ware, *mortaria* from north-east Gaul (and perhaps Italy), and *amphorae* from Italy and Spain reached the town. Other national contacts at a slightly later date brought a gradually increasing quantity of Black-Burnished ware from south-west England.

The regional pattern of pottery supply may have been in part a development of the situation during the Iron Age. In the late middle Iron Age, Alcester was already receiving pottery from Malvern (Ferguson 1989, 18) and there is some possible evidence at the end of the Iron Age for thriving localised pottery industries, for example at Tiddington, making a range of 'Belgic' forms. This material is, however, scarce in early Roman assemblages from Alcester, though it does occur, as on the Baromix site in Bleachfield Street. The source of this pottery, whether Tiddington or more local, is unknown. Limited evidence for Iron Age occupation has been found at Meeting Lane in the north-east part of the town. No 'Belgic' centre of settlement has been identified yet but its traces may be seen residually in some early groups from the town. This would suggest the existence of a small settlement which expanded

Explosion site finds (AES 76-7)

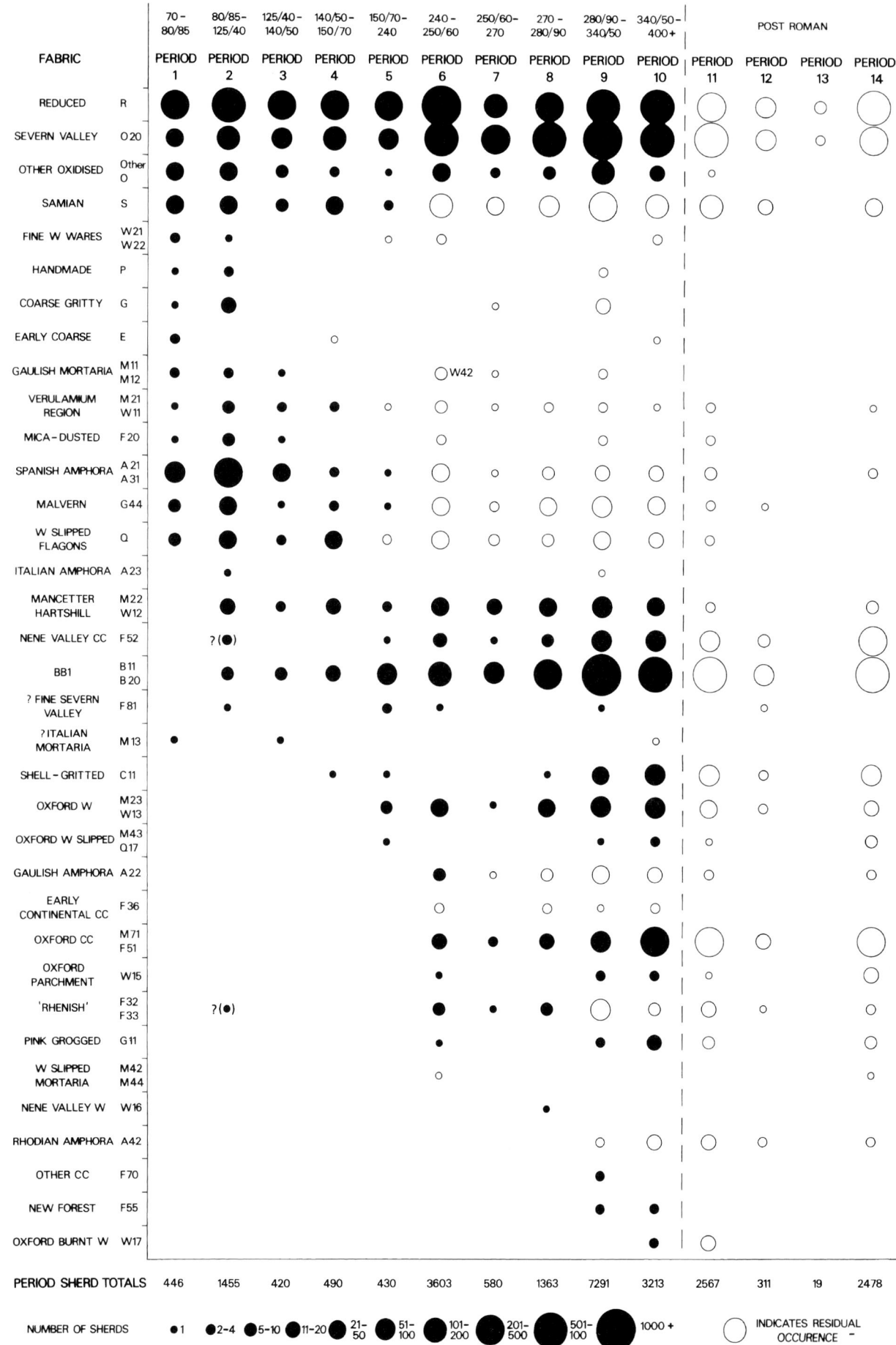

Figure 124 Roman pottery seriation diagram (AES 76–7)

Explosion site finds (AES 76-7)

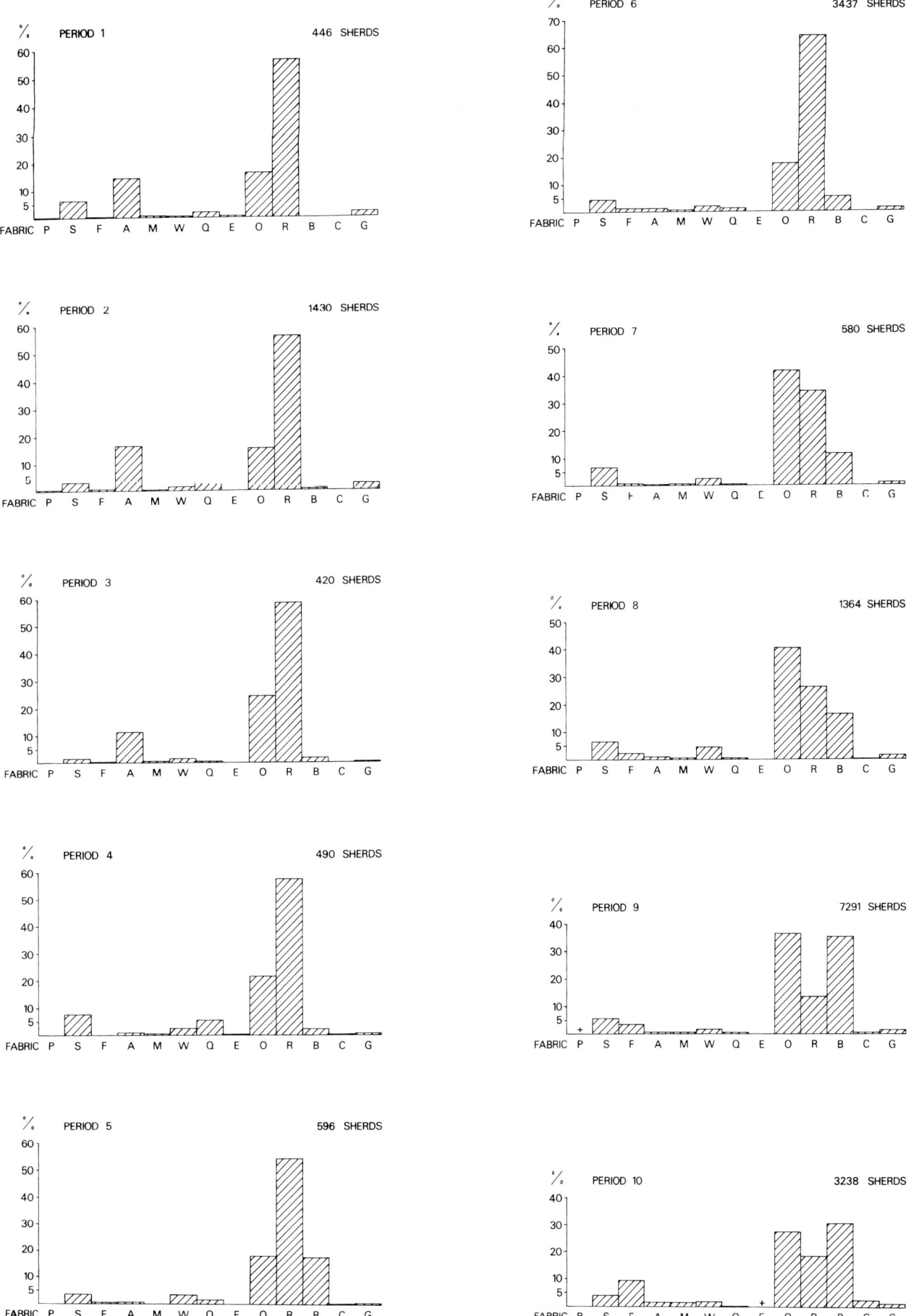

Figure 125 Roman pottery, incidence of major fabric groups by period (AES 76–7)

Explosion site finds (AES 76-7)

after the arrival of the Roman military establishment. The local ceramic traditions associated with such a site, however, were of little importance in determining the character of the early Roman pottery assemblages at the Explosion site.

In common with other West Midlands sites Alcester's 1st- and 2nd-century assemblages clearly show the military influence of the earliest Roman occupation. Perhaps the most striking example of this is the widespread prevalence of the rusticated jar. Another aspect of the early assemblages which would have catered to military tastes was the swift development of the trade in *mortaria* and *amphorae*; by the end of the 1st century Alcester was already receiving *mortaria* from the north-east Gaulish kilns, the Verulamium region, and possibly Italy and *amphorae* from Italy and Spain. Possibly imported mica-dusted ware, a fine ware often associated with the military (eg Greene 1979, 129), was found from the earliest phases of occupation at the Explosion site. Mica-dusted wares were later produced to meet military demand at sites such as Holt and Gloucester.

The late Neronian to early Flavian assemblage from the Baromix site (see above), less than 100m south of the Explosion site excavations, contained military bronzes and showed distinct affinities with military groups from Gloucester (cf Darling 1977, 64–67 and 85–93). It is therefore not surprising that the almost contemporary groups from the Explosion site should have exhibited some of the same characteristics. These characteristics largely determined the ceramic character of the early occupation of the site.

Period 1 ?AD 70–80/85 (446 sherds, 1.8%; 8.55 EVEs, 2.5%)

Illustrated vessels 56–83: 56–59, (266S); 60, (266L); 61–62, (266I); 63, (266K); 64, (266F); 65–72, (266A); 73–74, (266); 75–76, (292); 77–81, (267); 82–83, (270) (Figs 126–127)
Catalogue: 56–58, R30; 59, R15; 60, R30; 61, M12; 62, R30; 63, R30; 64, O81; 65, O21; 66, O21; 67, R30; 68, R30; 69, R01; 70, R30; 71, R30; 72, R01; 73, O24; 74, R40; 75, O51; 76, R01; 77, A21; 78, O32; 79, R50; 80, R50; 81, G44; 82, ?P11; 83, ?R01

The assemblage from this period is dated to the Flavian period both by the samian it contained and the presence of a *mortarium* (no 61) made by Q Valerius Veranius, a Flavian potter from north-east Gaul (Hartley 1977). Despite this some Neronian samian was also present and a few coarse ware vessels of 'Belgic' type (eg nos 65 from (266A) and 79 from (267)), though whether these vessels were also of pre-Flavian date is less certain.

Military involvement in the development of Alcester had already begun during the pre-Flavian period but in this phase there was still some evidence for earlier local traditions. These included a handmade vessel (no 82) which is very similar to Iron Age types, and Malvernian sherds including part of a very large storage vessel (no 85). All these sherds, however, only totalled 2.2% of the group.

The Romanising influence was well developed and the single most important aspect of this period was the dominance of possibly locally made grey wares (57%) and in particular the rusticated jars made in these fabrics. Examples of the earlier form of this vessel included nos 57 and 60 from layers within pit (266). A particularly striking reduced ware vessel was no 83, a well-made ?beaker perhaps originally with a pedestal base. This was in a very fine black fabric and had neat, lightly combed decoration on the surface. Its source and date are unknown.

Oxidised wares were also significant (16.6%) and included a high-shouldered jar (no 64) in a fine non-local fabric. *Amphorae* (eg no 77) were particularly well-represented in this period (14.6%) and other purely Roman types included *mortaria* and ring-necked flagons.

Pit (266) (illustrated vessels 56–74)

This was the single most important group from period 1. There were many joining sherds between the different layers within and those overlying the pit. The assemblage was homogeneous in date and was of a domestic character containing many sherds of a large storage jar (no 62), the greater part of a Dressel 20 *amphora*, and most of a *mortarium* (no 61). Other vessels were mainly jars (of angled everted rim type) or jar beakers of which nos 64 and 72 were good examples. The latter, with barbotine dots, is paralleled at Kingsholm (Darling 1977, 185 and 187, Fig 6.8, no 4) in an early military assemblage and is also paralleled in form and decoration (but not fabric) in a similar context at Cirencester (Rigby 1982, 166–68, no 59). There was also a tankard (no 74), an imitation of the Severn Valley ware 'Durotrigan' type, in a local reduced fabric, and a strainer (no 66). The group is typical of the early Flavian period in Alcester.

Period 2 AD 80/85–125/140 (1430 sherds, 5.8%; 22.50 EVEs, 6.6%)

Illustrated vessels 84–167: 84, (291); 85–86, (281); 87–88, (286); 89–94, (285); 95–102, (276); 103–105, (278); 106, (275); 107–134, (279); 135–143, (250); 144–145, (293); 146–154, (168A); 155–159, (168B); 160–165, (168J); 166–167, (II 76B) (Figs 127–129)
Catalogue: 84, R30; 85, Q11; 86, R01; 87, R50; 88, Q21; 89, O21; 90, R50; 91, R01; 92, R01; 93, R30; 94, R70; 95, A21; 96, O70; 97, O24; 98, R40; 99, R01; 100, R50; 101, R30; 102, G44; 103, R50; 104, O41; 105, O21; 106, R50; 107, O51; 108, O13; 109, O51; 110, O13; 111, O25; 112, O81; 113, O23; 114, R15; 115, R01; 116, R01; 117, R40; 118, R01; 119, R40; 120, R01; 121, R01; 122, R30; 123, R50; 124, R01; 125, R01; 126, R40; 127, R30; 128, R01; 129, R01; 130, R21; 131, R01; 132, R50; 133, B11; 134, B11; 135, O51; 136, O21; 137, R30; 138, R30; 139, R21; 140–142, R30; 143–145, R01; 146, M12; 147, W12; 148, O24; 149, R30; 150, R40; 151, R01; 152, R60; 153, R40; 154, R01; 155, O24; 156–158, R30; 159, O21; 160–164, R30; 165, G44; 166, R01; 167, R30

The relative importance of the different fabric groups remained much the same as in the previous period. There were still occasional examples of 'Belgic' vessel types, (eg nos 86 and 141, the former

Explosion site finds (AES 76-7)

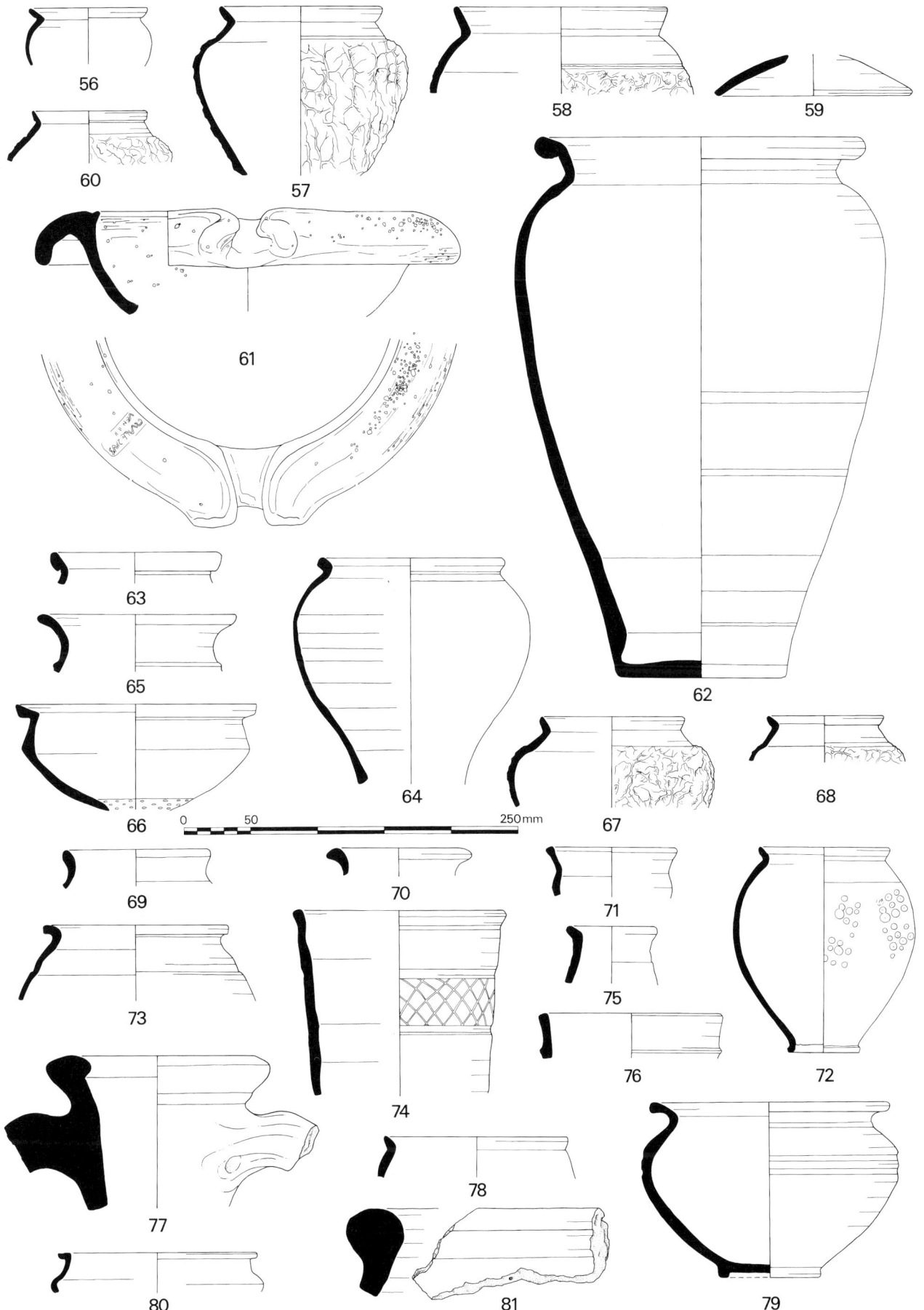

Figure 126   Roman pottery (AES 76–7), nos 56–81, period 1

Explosion site finds (AES 76-7)

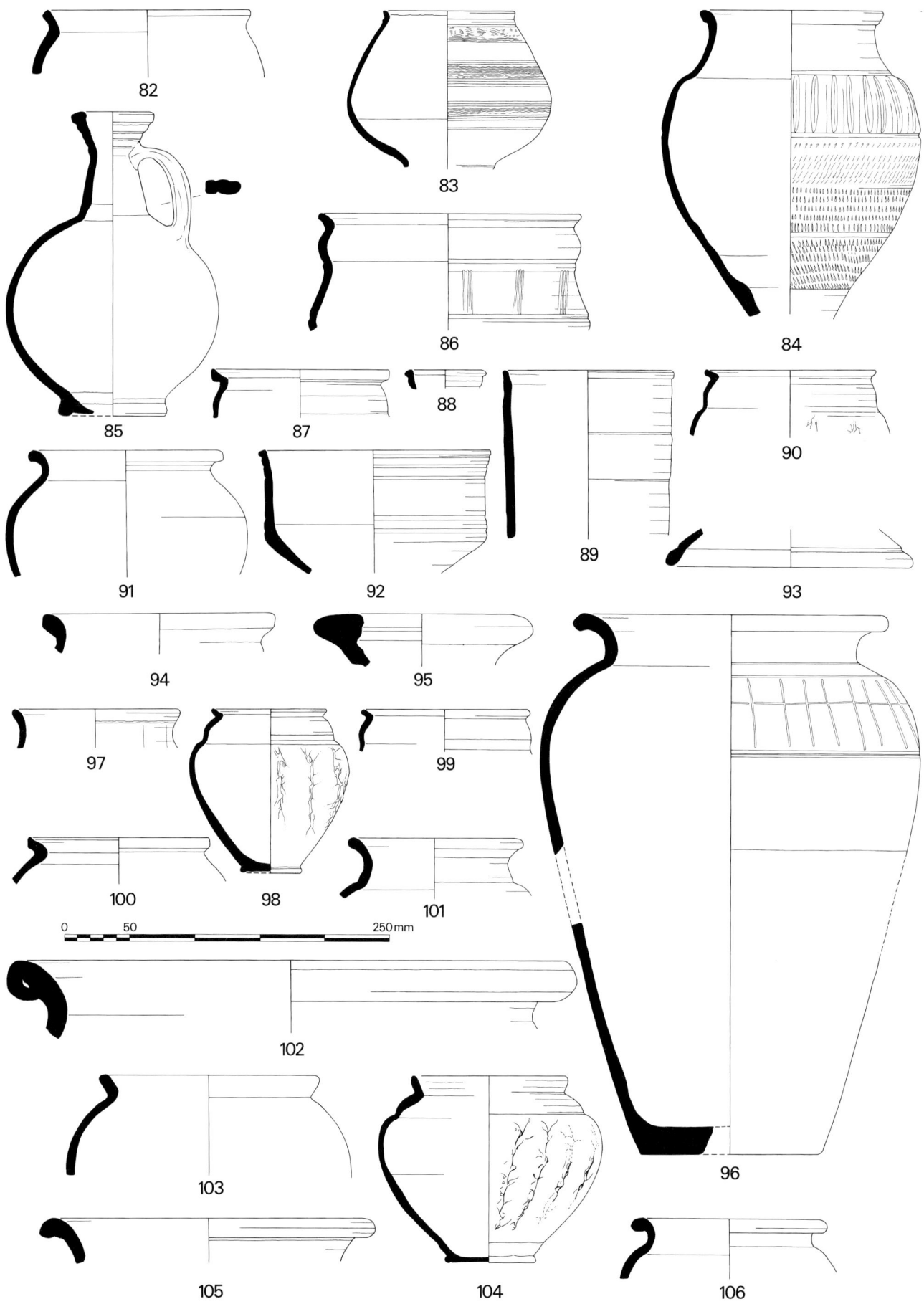

Figure 127   Roman pottery (AES 76–7), nos 82–83, period 1, and nos 84–106, period 2

Table 18 Stratified samian ware (AES 76–7, period 1)

Content	Source	Form	Date	Comments
266A	SG	15/17–18 (2)	?Flavian	
266A	SG	18 (3)	?Flavian	
266A	SG	27	?Flavian	
266A	SG	37	AD70–85	lattice decoration & ovolo of Germanusi
266A	SG	37	?Flavian	
266F	SG	27	Flavian	
266I	SG	15/17–18	Flavian	
266I	SG	18	Flavian	
266L	SG	?27	AD 50–65	stamp no 1
266L	SG	16	Neronian	
266L	SG	18	Neronian	
266O	SG	18	l Ner–e Fl	
266O	SG	?	1st C	
268	SG	27	Ner–e Fl	
268	SG	15/17–18	1st C	
270	SG	15/17–18	AD 60–70	stamp no 12
270	SG	15/17–18	AD 65–85	stamp no 9
270	SG	29	AD 60–75	
270	SG	15/17	Ner–e Fl	
292	SG	15/17	Ner–e Fl	
292	SG	15/17–18	Ner–e Fl	
292	SG	29	Ner–e Fl	straight gadroons

perhaps derived from forms such as Thompson's type D2-1 (1982, 319–321)), but the jars were generally of Romanised types, such as the Severn Valley ware products and rusticated jars. Malvernian material was still a regular part of the assemblage and some of the grey ware jars may have been derived from Malvernian vessel types (eg no 126). Jars in all fabrics constituted *c* 75% of all the vessels in this period. The most notable example was no 84 in fabric R30, with vertical indentations on the shoulder and rouletting on the rest of the body.

It was during this period that Black-Burnished ware began to reach Alcester in small amounts and it is possible that it was contact with the Dorset potters that also prompted the appearance of the flanged bowl in the local reduced fabrics (eg no 145). However this type may alternatively have developed independently, perhaps from reeded rim types (eg Darling 1977, 91 and 93, Fig 6.11, nos 6–11). A further change in the local fabrics was the decoration of angled everted rim jars with rustication arranged in strips rather than overall (eg nos 98 and 104).

Trade with the Verulamium region potters began to be established although *mortaria* were the only manifestation of this. Some white ware flagons possibly came from north-east Gaul but this vessel type was mainly manufactured in oxidised, white-slipped fabrics (eg no 85) as in the previous period.

Possible building destruction layer (279) (illustrated vessels nos 107–134)

This was the largest group of material from period 2. It is typical of the period 2 assemblage in that it was made up largely of grey wares with small amounts of Severn Valley ware, local oxidised fabrics, two of the oxidised white-slipped fabrics, and *mortaria* and flagons from north-east Gaul. The range of forms and the presence of Black-Burnished ware suggests, however, that it was probably one of the later groups in the period. The samian dating for this context is Trajanic to early Hadrianic. The illustrated vessels show a representative selection of rusticated jars from this period. These show greater variety of rim form than in earlier times and the change of decoration style from overall rustication to vertical strips. Vessel no 120 shows the incised wavy lines which were occasionally used instead of rustication; other examples are known from the Baromix site and they

Explosion site finds (AES 76-7)

Table 19 Stratified samian ware (AES 76–7, period 2)

Context	Source	Form	Date	Comments
168A	SG	15/17–18	Flavian	
168A	SG	18 (2)	Flavian	1 burnt
168A	SG	27	Flavian	
168A	M de V	18/31	Trajanic	
168I	SG	15/17–18	Neronian	
168I	SG	29	l Neronian	
168I	SG	27	Ner–e Fl	
168J	SG	18	Flavian	
168J	SG	18 or 18R	Flavian	possibly same as previous
168K	SG	?17	?Pre-Fl	
168K	SG	30	Ner–e Fl	
168K	SG	?37	Fl–e Tr	
250	SG	18 or 18/31	Fl or Fl–Tr	
250	SG	27 (2)	Fl or Fl–Tr	
250	SG	Cup	Fl or Fl–Tr	
250	SG	Curle 11	Fl–Tr	variant form. Riveted
275	SG	18	AD 60–70	stamp no 13
276	SG	?Ritt 12	Ner or Fl	or Curle 11
276	SG	18	Flavian	
276	SG	42	Flavian	
276	M de V	27	Trajanic	
278	SG	?	?Flavian	
279	SG	15/17–18	AD 60–70	stamp no 12
279	SG	15/17–18	l Ner–e Fl	
279	SG	15/17R–18R	l Ner–e Fl	
279	SG	18 (4)	l Ner–e Fl	
279	SG	?27	l Ner–e Fl	
279	SG	29	l Ner–e Fl	
279	M de V	27 (2)	Tr–e Had	
279	?	37	?	
285	SG	15/17	Flavian	
285	SG	27	Flavian	
285	SG	15/17–18	AD 75–100	stamp no 17
285	SG	29	AD 70–85	footring burnt
286	SG	Cup	Ner–e Fl	
291	SG	29	?pre Fl	
291	SG	18	Ner–e Fl	
293	CG	30	Had–e Ant	?intrusive
II 76	SG	Curle 11	Flavian	
II 76	M de V	18/31	Tr–e Had	

Explosion site finds (AES 76-7)

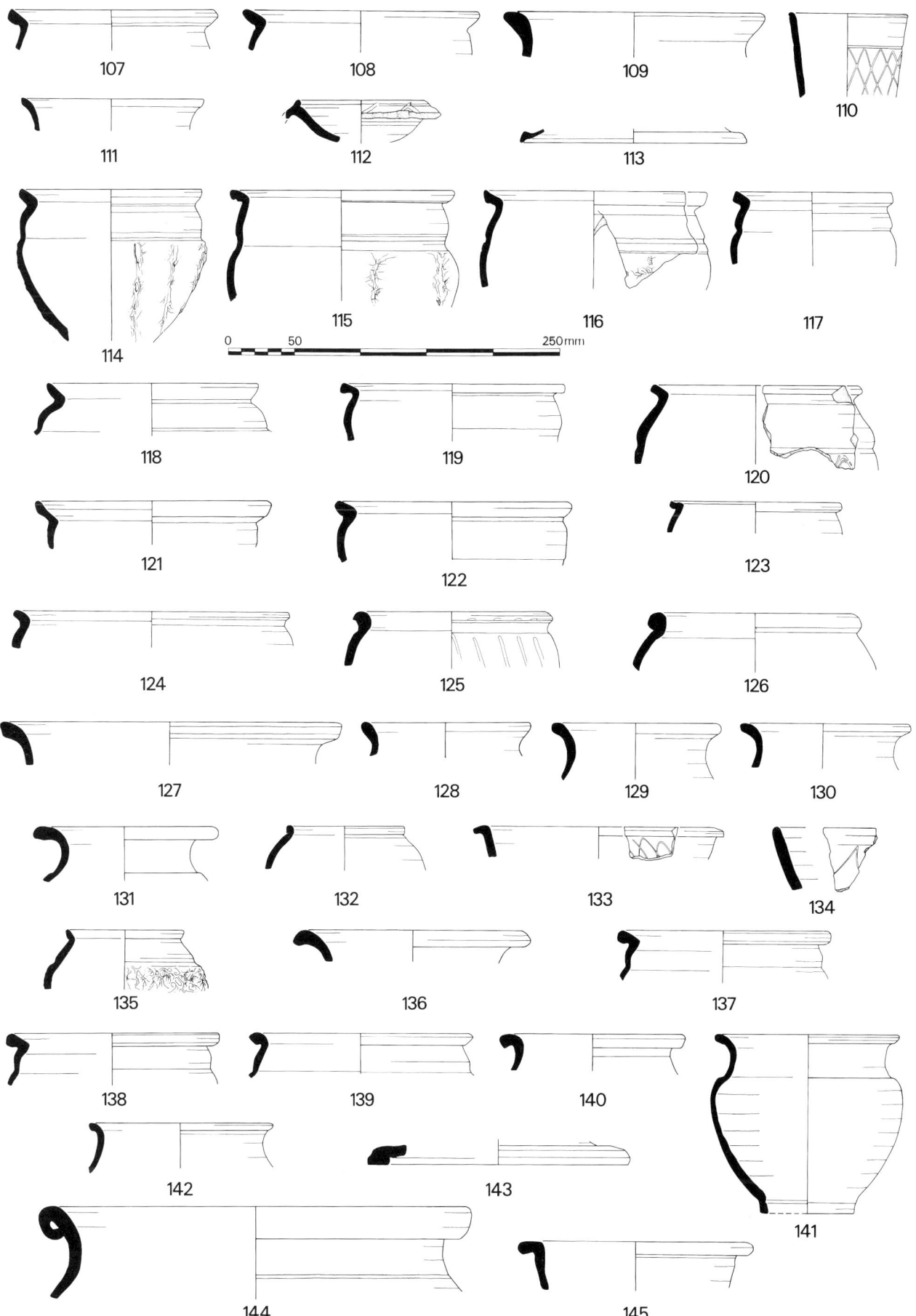

Figure 128   Roman pottery (AES 76–7), nos 107–145, period 2

Explosion site finds (AES 76-7)

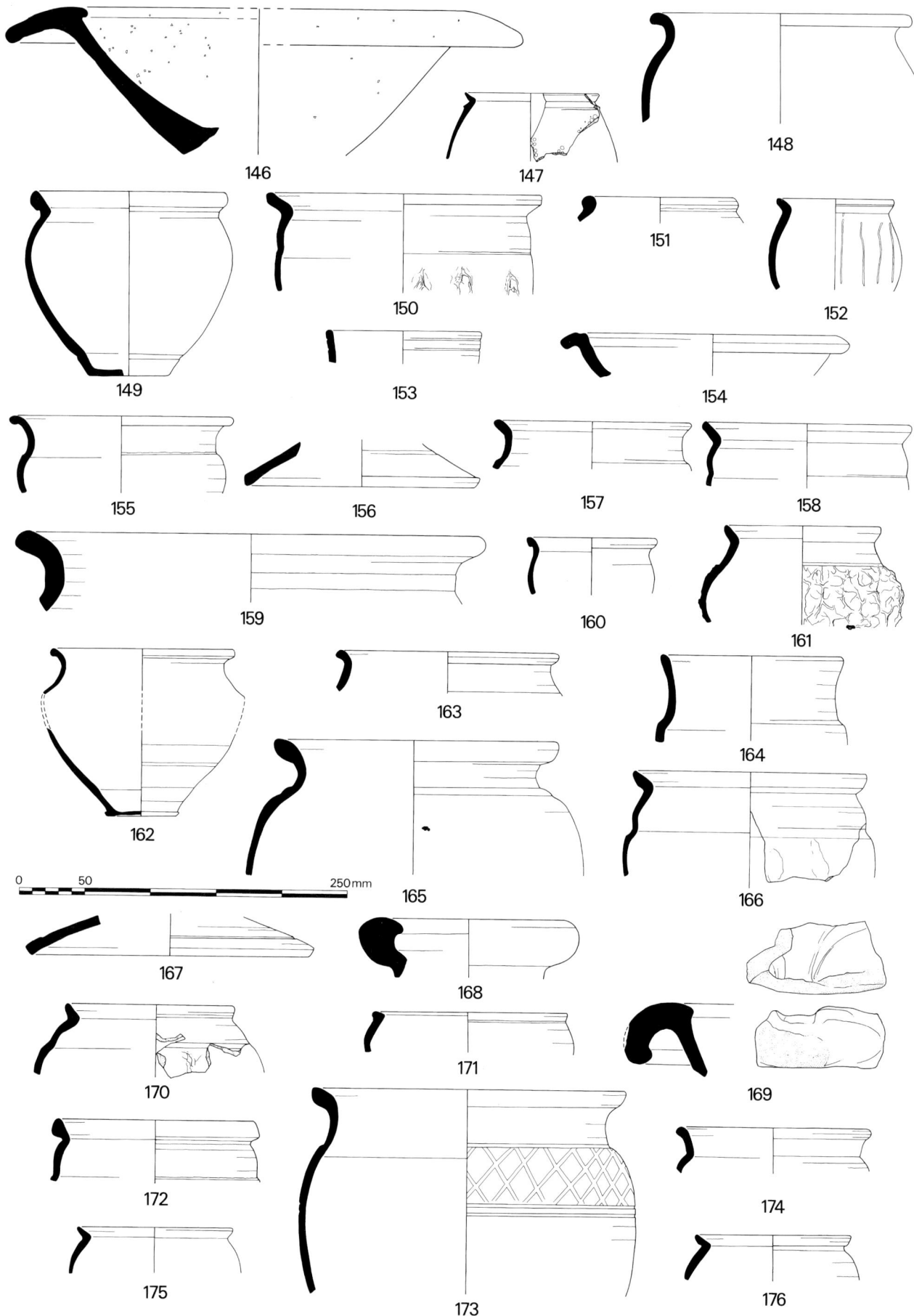

Figure 129 Roman pottery (AES 76–7), nos 146–168, period 2, and nos 169–176, period 3

also occurred at Tiddington. There were also examples of vessels in local oxidised fabrics (nos 108–112). The small tankard no 110 was very similar to types made at Tiddington.

The range of Severn Valley ware forms was limited and two of the less common vessels have been illustrated. The first of these is a lid (no 113) which is different from the types figured by Webster and must be earlier than the 3rd- to 4th-century date he assigns to them (Webster 1976, 37). The second vessel, a segmental bowl (no 112) with white painted decoration on the rim probably of early 2nd-century date, was not certainly a Severn Valley product.

Well (168A) (illustrated vessels nos 146–165)

This group consisted of much larger sherds than were found in (279), which would be consistent with the disposal of rubbish in the well after it fell out of use. Many of these large sherds were of *amphorae*. There were also two large storage jars (nos 159 and 165). Vessels such as the high-shouldered jar no 162 and the carinated bowl no 164 were of an early type. These two, the rusticated jar no 161, and the small jar with rather crude vertical burnished lines, no 152, can be contrasted with the later rusticated jars (eg nos 150 and 158). Distinctive vessels included the north-east Gaulish *mortarium* no 146 and a white ware, cornice-rimmed beaker with orange barbotine dot decoration (no 147) which possibly came from Mancetter-Hartshill. If so it is likely to have dated after *c* AD 100 and was probably one of the later sherds of this group.

The well contained no Black-Burnished ware. A single small sherd of Nene Valley colour-coated ware, in the upper fill, is likely to have been intrusive from the 4th-century pit which cut the well. Material from the lowest fills of the well (nos 160–165) could have been of 1st-century date. Even the upper fills, if the absence of Black-Burnished ware can be regarded as significant, are unlikely to have dated after *c* AD 120. The latest samian sherd was of a Dr 18/31 from Les Martres-de-Veyre of Trajanic date.

Period 3 AD 125/140–140/150 (420 sherds, 1.7%; 5.81 EVEs, 1.7%)

Illustrated vessels 168–193: 168–172, (273); 173–192, (247); 193, (II 51A) (Figs 129–130)
Catalogue: 168, A21; 169, M13; 170, R30; 171, R40; 172, R40; 173, O28; 174, O21; 175, R21; 176, RO1; 177, R50; 178, R30; 179, R30; 180, R21; 181, R21; 182, RO1; 183, R30; 184, R40; 185, R30; 186, R60; 187, R21; 188, R30; 189, R21; 190, R21; 191, R40; 192, G44; 193, B20

The assemblage remained much the same as in the previous period. The fabrics were dominated by the grey wares (58.3%), though oxidised wares increased in importance to 24.3% of the group. *Amphorae* were still well-represented and all the other fabric groups, including samian, were of minimal significance. Rusticated jars were the principal vessel type, and jars of all types amounted to almost 80% of the vessels in this period.

Possible circular floor (247) (illustrated vessels nos 173–192)

This group seems to be of early Hadrianic character. It contained very little Black-Burnished ware and was made up largely of a range of grey wares. Rusticated jars were still the main vessel type represented although there were other types such as a butt beaker, a flanged bowl, a shallow dish, and a lid (nos 186, 189, 190, and 191 respectively). The flanged bowl form was perhaps derived from a Black-Burnished ware prototype as was the cooking pot style jar, no 183. Vessel no 192 is a typical Malvernian 'tubby cooking pot' and the grey ware jar, no 182, must surely support the theory that these vessels, too, were imitated by local potters.

The group also contained Severn Valley wares, a Dressel 20 *amphora* sherd, Verulamium region and Mancetter-Hartshill white wares, and a white-slipped flagon fabric.

Table 20 Stratified samian ware
(AES 76–7, period 3)

Context	Source	Form	Date	Comments
247	SG	15/17 (2)	Flavian	1 burnt
247	SG	37	AD 90–110	?Mercato(r) i
247	M de V	?37	AD 100–120	?Ioenalis i
273	SG	18–18/31	Flavian	
II 53	CG	37	Antonine	

Period 4 AD 140/150–150/170 (490 sherds, 2.0%; 7.24 EVEs, 2.1%)

Illustrated vessels 194–227: 194–206, (224); 207, (244); 208, (257); 209, (241); 210–215, (II 67); 216–217, (II 32A); 218–219, (II 32); 220–222, (II 37); 223–224, (II 56); 225–227, (II 47) (Figs 130–131)
Catalogue: 194, W11; 195, O24; 196, O24; 197, O21; 198, R40; 199, R01; 200, R21; 201, R40; 202, R40; 203, R50; 204, R40; 205, B11; 206, B11; 207, Q25; 208, O21; 209, O21; 210, Q25; 211, R30; 212, R30; 213, R40; 214, O21; 215, R30; 216, O21; 217, O25; 218, R01; 219, R40; 220, RO1; 221, O21; 222, R40; 223, R40; 224, R19; 225–227, R30

The samian from this period was Hadrianic and there were no coarse wares which would definitely indicate a later date. A fractional increase in the importance of Black-Burnished ware, however, perhaps corroborates the stratigraphic evidence that these features were later than the period 3 deposits. Problems in dating may have been caused by the apparent lack of stylistic development in the grey wares (see above). Fabric supply remained much as before with local reduced wares relatively most important and Severn

Explosion site finds (AES 76-7)

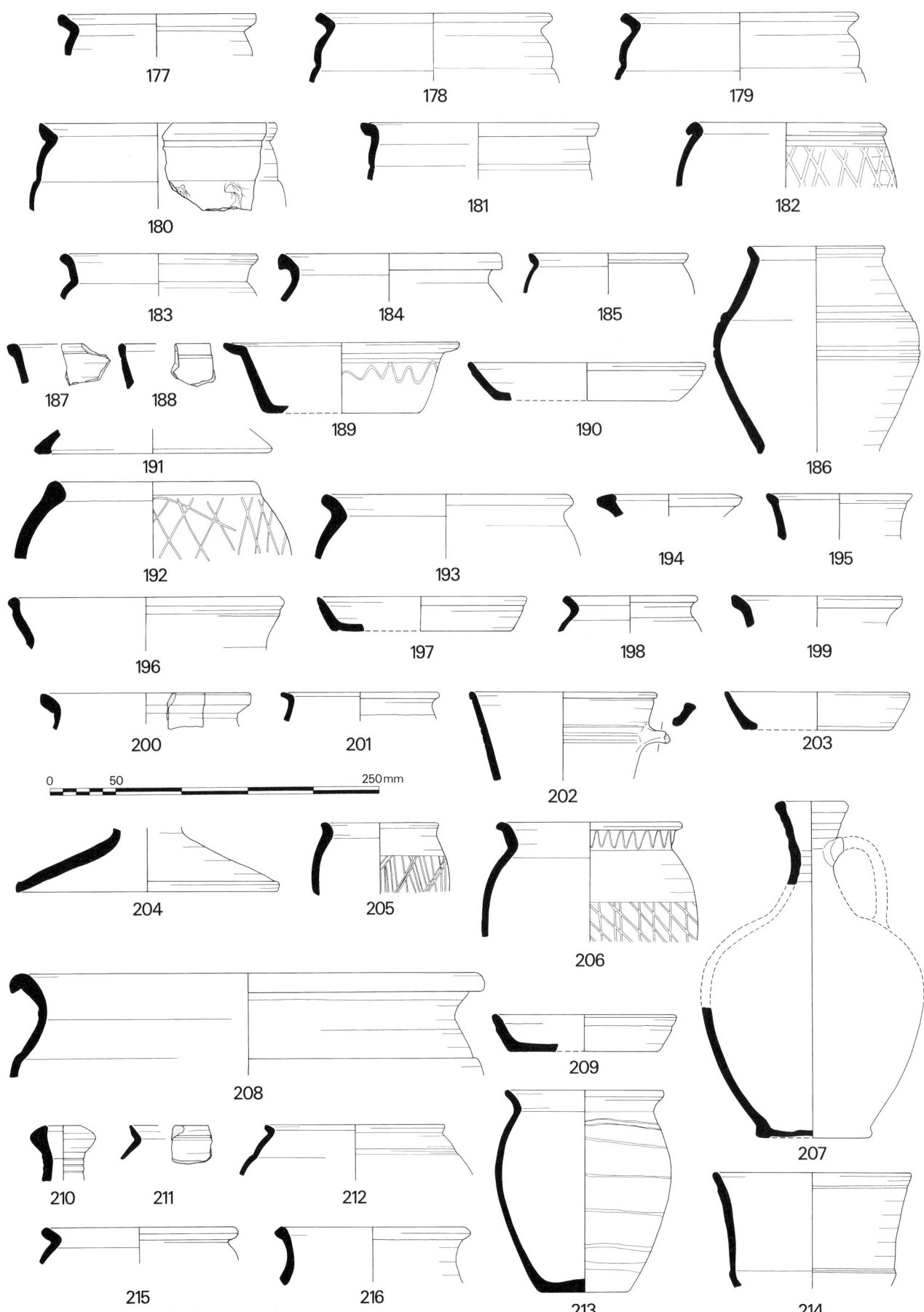

Figure 130 Roman pottery (AES 76–7), nos 177–193, period 3, and nos 194–216, period 4

Explosion site finds (AES 76-7)

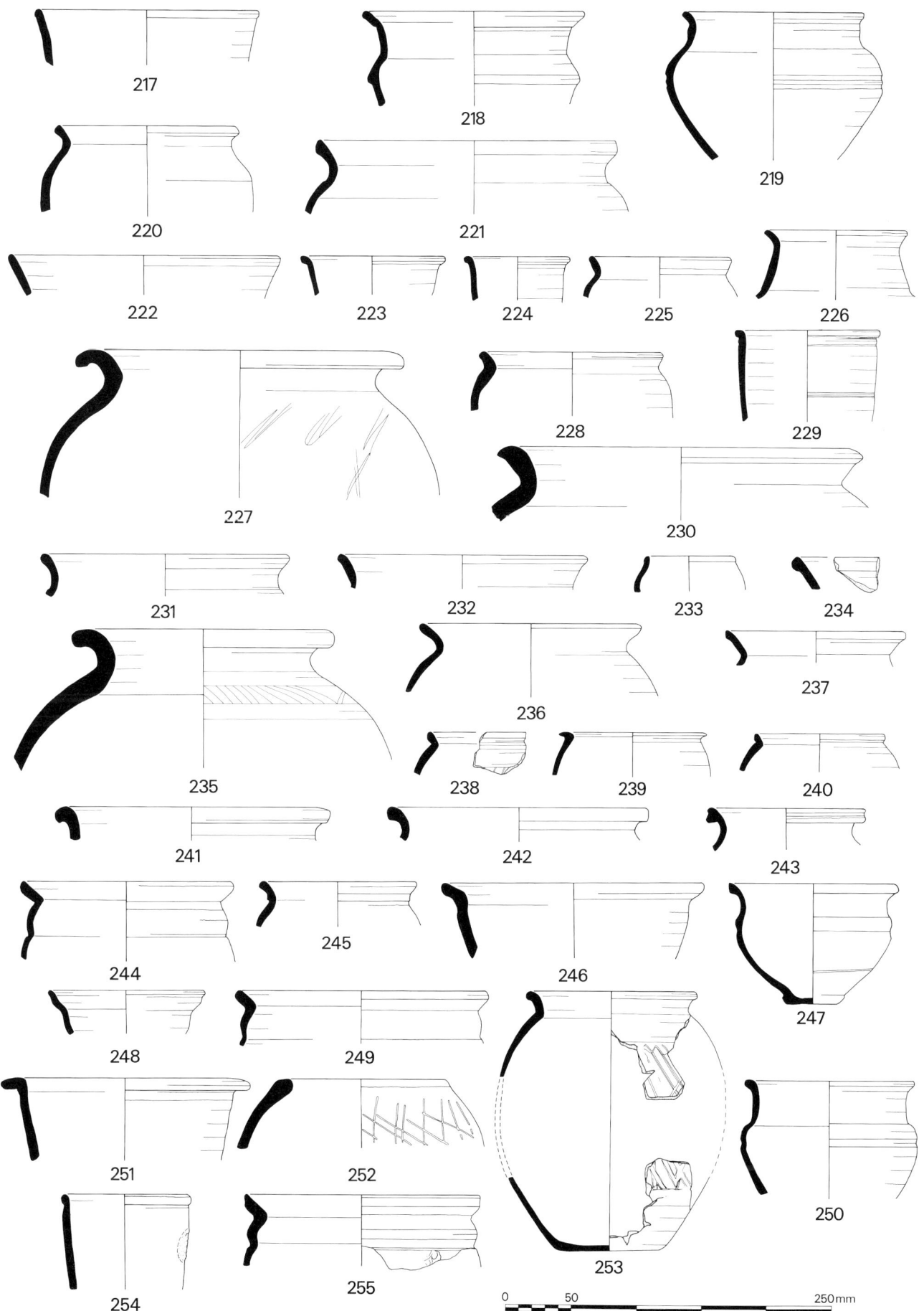

Figure 131   Roman pottery (AES 76–7), nos 217–227, period 4, and nos 228–255, period 5

201

Explosion site finds (AES 76-7)

Valley wares, Malvernian fabrics, Spanish *amphorae*, white-slipped flagons, *mortaria* and flagons from the Verulamium region and Mancetter-Hartshill being constant features of the assemblage.

The small size of the group means that an apparent sudden drop in the proportion of jars in this period (only 39% of the total vessels) may not have been significant. Both bowls and dishes correspondingly increased in importance, and flagons were also well-represented, but these figures have to be regarded with caution.

Layer (224) (illustrated vessels nos 194–206)

This was one of the latest groups in this period and was sealed by a period 5 layer, the floor of building V (44). The material had accumulated in a hollow in the yard surface (235) which covered most of the site at this time. The yard itself yielded very little pottery and must have been kept fairly clean. The material from (224) was not at all worn suggesting that it is unlikely to have been the sweepings from (235). The group may therefore have consisted of material redeposited to level out the yard surface. The material was of fairly consistent early to mid-2nd-century date and included several sherds of Hadrianic samian. Dishes occurred in both Severn Valley ware (no 197) and grey wares (203), and the grey wares also included a flaring-sided tankard (no 202). The Black-Burnished ware cooking pots were typical of this period.

Late 2nd and 3rd centuries (periods 5–8)

The absence of any uncontaminated late Antonine groups from the site made it difficult to be certain whether the local grey ware industries showed any stylistic developments which could be isolated to this period. From the evidence of groups such as (227) it would seem that the styles were indistinguishable from those used earlier in the century. It was only after the mid-3rd century that the proportion of the assemblage formed by these fabrics began to decline.

Regional contacts were expanded by the beginnings of trade with Oxfordshire around AD 240. Otherwise the pattern remained much the same as during the early occupation of the site with contacts with the Severn Valley and Malvernian potters to the west and Mancetter-Hartshill to the north-east. The volume of trade in Severn Valley wares increased after the early 3rd century as the importance of the local reduced fabrics dropped. On a national scale, the developments were quantitative with increased amounts of Nene Valley colour-coated ware and Black-Burnished ware arriving at the site.

From the end of the 2nd century the only *mortaria*

Table 21 Stratified samian ware (AES 76–7, period 4)

Context	Source	Form	Date	Comments
224	SG	?	1st C	
224	M de V	27	Tr–Had	
224	M de V	36 (2)	Tr–Had	
224	M de V	37	AD 100–120	Igocatus; Fig 122, no 28
224	M de V	37	AD 120–140	Drusus ii
224	M de V	Curle 11	Tr–Had	
224	CG	18/31	Hadrianic	
224	CG	18/31–31 (3)	Hadrianic	
224	CG	27	Hadrianic	
224	CG	36	Hadrianic	riveted
224	CG	Curle 15	Hadrianic	
224	EG	18/31	Tr–Had	?Chémery-Faulquemont
235	SG	18	Flavian	
241	M de V	18/31	Tr–e Had	
241	M de V	Curle 11	Tr–e Had	?same vessel as above
II 32	SG	27	e Ner	
II 47	SG	37	AD 70–90	
II 67 & 67A	SG	15/17–18	Flavian	
II 67 & 67A	SG	27	Flavian	
II 67 & 67A	SG	30 or 37	Flavian	

being brought into Alcester were from Mancetter-Hartshill and Oxfordshire as Verulamium region, Gaulish and possibly Italian vessels were no longer widely available. Rhodian and Italian *amphorae* were also residual after the late 2nd century, while Spanish vessels may have continued to be traded until the mid-3rd.

The period saw a gradual change in pottery supply, from a situation where over half of the pottery was made locally, to one in which the marketplace was dominated by industries from outside the town, some of which, like the Black-Burnished ware and Oxfordshire industries, were operating on a large scale. Almost all of Alcester's trading contacts apart from those with north Warwickshire were to the south and west of the town.

Period 5 AD 150/170–?240 (596 sherds, 2.4%; 6.84 EVEs, 2.0%)

Illustrated vessels 228–257: 228–242, (II 54); 243–246, (44); 247, (264); 248–253, (245F); 254–257, (245B) (Figs 131–132)
Catalogue: 228, ?B20; 229, W21; 230, O21; 231, O24; 232, O25; 233, O23; 234, O23; 235, R30; 236, ?R40; 237, R40; 238, R40; 239, RO1; 240, R30; 241, R50; 242, R40; 243, O24; 244, R30; 245, R40; 246, RO1; 247, O23; 248, O81; 249, R01; 250, R50; 251, R50; 252, G44; 253, B11; 254, O22; 255, R30; 256, R40; 257, R01

The relatively small size of this assemblage made it difficult to determine the significance of the apparent changes in the pottery supply at this time. Much of the pottery in this period was from a pit (245). This feature contained a large number of (fairly small) sherds of Black-Burnished ware, which was consequently abnormally highly represented at 16.8% of the period sherd total. This anomalous figure cannot be taken as representative of the true importance of Black-Burnished ware at this time. Despite the exaggerated representation of Black-Burnished ware, grey wares remained remarkably constant at 54.2% of the group. Oxidised wares decreased in significance, but probably only in compensation for the high representation of Black-Burnished ware.

Samian from the floor of building V (44) was of Hadrianic date but had been in use for some time and repaired. None of the associated coarse ware vessels (nos 243–246) was closely datable. Sherds of no 247, a small, wide-mouthed jar in Severn Valley ware, came from several contexts, one of which was a posthole (264) of this period. The pottery from pit (245) (nos 248–257) comprised material consistent with a date in the first half of the 2nd century, including an oxidised ware copy of Dr 27 (no 248), a Malvernian jar (no 252), and a Black-Burnished ware cooking pot (no 253). The absence of later material is difficult to explain, but may indicate that building V and its environs were kept clean and free of rubbish. This must particularly have been the case if the duration of this period was as long as is suggested.

Layer (II 54) (illustrated vessels nos 228–242)

This layer produced one of the largest pottery groups from site II (166 sherds). It has been mentioned already that many of the groups from the east end of the site II trench were similar in composition, despite the fact that the features from which they derived spanned several periods in the development of the site. The group from (II 54), a layer overlying a series of pits and gullies, was no exception to this. A prominent characteristic of all these groups was the high representation of the Severn Valley fabric O21, which here comprised almost 20% of the total sherds. Grey wares constituted exactly 50% of the group, and samian and Black-Burnished wares were reasonably represented. As in other groups in this part of the site storage jar sherds were unusually common, occurring in fabrics O21 (eg no 230) and R30 (eg no 235). Apart from these the only vessel of note was a fine white ware bowl (no 229). Much of the rest of the group consisted of jars and beakers in reduced fabrics. Dating depended on the Black-Burnished ware and particularly on the samian. The latter contained six Antonine sherds and a date in the later 2nd century seems very likely for this context.

Period 6 AD 240–250/260 (3437 sherds, 13.9%; 32.77 EVEs, 9.6%)

Illustrated vessels 258–383: 258–259, (155); 260, (234); 261, (208); 262, (157); 263, (141); 264–270, (232); 271–278, (226); 279–282, (263); 283–298, (245); 299–383, (227) (Figs 132–134)
Catalogue: 258, R30; 259, M23; 260, ?R30; 261–263, B11; 264, R50; 265, R01; 266, R40; 267, R50; 268, R40; 269, R01; 270, B11; 271, O23; 272, O23; 273, R40; 274, R15; 275, R01; 276, R80; 277, B11; 278, B11; 279, W12; 280–282, R01; 283, F53; 284, M44; 285, O25; 286, 023; 287, O24; 288, O23; 289, R40; 290, R30; 291, R30; 292, R01; 293, R40; 294, R30; 295, R30; 296–298, B11; 299, W12; 300, W13; 301, O21; 302, O24; 303, O23; 304, 051, 305, O21; 306, 081; 307, O21; 308, O23; 309, O21; 310, O28; 311, O21; 312, O25; 313, O21; 314, O25; 315, R40; 316, R30; 317, R21; 318, R30; 319, R01; 320, R01; 321, R40; 322, R19; 323, R30; 324–326, R01; 327, R21; 328, O51; 329, R40; 330, R01; 331, R50; 332, R40; 333, R01; 334, R40; 335, R01; 336, R40; 337, R01; 338, R21; 339–345, R01; 346, R40; 347, R30; 348, R01; 349, R40; 350, R01; 351, R40; 352, R01; 353, R40; 354, R01; 355, R01; 356, ?R40; 357–359, R40; 360, R01; 361, R19; 362, R01; 363, R01; 364, R50; 365–367, R40; 368, R01; 369, R01; 370, R30; 371, R30; 372, R40; 373, R01; 374, R01; 375, R40; 376, R01; 377–380, B11; 381–383, G44

In this period grey wares reached their peak, amounting to 65.6% of the assemblage. Oxidised wares totalled 17.9% and Black-Burnished ware comprised 5.1% of the group, a significant advance on its earlier levels (apart from the unreliable figure in period 5). Samian ware made up 4.2% of the group, and all other major fabric types were relatively insignificant. Jars amounted to almost 70% of all the vessels and the shouldered type with angled everted rim was still over half of these. Bowls amounted to 10.5% of the assemblage; other main vessel types were only slightly represented, except for lids, which at 4.5% were much more common than was usual,

Explosion site finds (AES 76-7)

Table 22 Stratified samian ware (AES 76–7, period 5)

Context	Source	Form	Date	Comments
44	M de V	37	AD 110–125	Fig 122, no 28
44	CG	?	Had or Ant	
233	SG	27	Flavian	
245B	SG	?	1st C	
245F	SG	15/17R or 18R	?Flavian	?same as above
245F	M de V	33	1st h 2nd C	
245F	M de V	36	1st h 2nd C	
245F	CG	Curle 11	Hadrianic	
II 66	SG	27	Fl or Fl–Tr	
II 66	CG	18/31R	Mid-Antonine	
II 68	CG	31	Antonine	
II 72	?EG	?32	?l 2nd–3rd C	
II 54	SG	18	Flavian	
II 54	SG	?36	Flavian	
II 54	SG	37	Flavian	
II 54	CG	18/31R	Antonine	
II 54	CG	33 (2)	Antonine	
II 54	CG	35 or 36	Antonine	
II 54	CG	38	Antonine	
II 54	CG	Dish/bowl	Antonine	

perhaps mirroring the importance of jars at this time.

The pottery assemblage from this period exemplifies one of the main problems of interpreting pottery supply in Alcester. The groups present contained large quantities of material which could easily have been assigned to the first half of the 2nd century. However, there was a small but consistent element of later vessels which could by no means be explained away as intrusive. This later material consisted in particular of Oxfordshire products, both white wares and the colour-coated fabric (F51). The latter indicates that at least some of the activity in this period was post c AD 240 (Young 1977, 123–124). As discussed above it seems unlikely that any Oxfordshire products reached the town before the mid-3rd century. In addition to the Oxfordshire material there was also a fragment of a Nene Valley ware scale beaker which was at least early 3rd century in date (Howe *et al* 1980, 7–8).

The major difficulty in identifying groups from the late 2nd- to early 3rd century lies in the apparent lack of evolution of the local pottery industries after the Hadrianic period. Antonine activity is indicated by the samian and perhaps by a white-slipped *mortarium* of probable south-west origin, no 284 from pit (245), but none of the grey ware vessel types can be definitely isolated to this period.

Building V (illustrated vessels nos 258–263)

Very little of the pottery from this phase in the life of the site came from building V itself and it would seem, as in the previous period, that the building was kept clean with little material being allowed to accumulate.

The building was reworked and extended during this period. This involved the rebuilding of wall (255). The foundation of the new wall (155) contained an Oxfordshire *mortarium* (no 259) of type M18, indicating a date of at least c AD 240 for the early stages of activity. A Black-Burnished ware jar (no 263), probably of 3rd-century date, was set in the period 6 floor in room 2a of the building. While it is possible that this vessel was inserted into the floor at a later date it is more likely that it was an original feature. The lack of domestic rubbish within the newly extended building and the gully and basin arrangement (259)/(234) (see stratigraphic discussion above) – which contained a very small group of pottery much of which had been

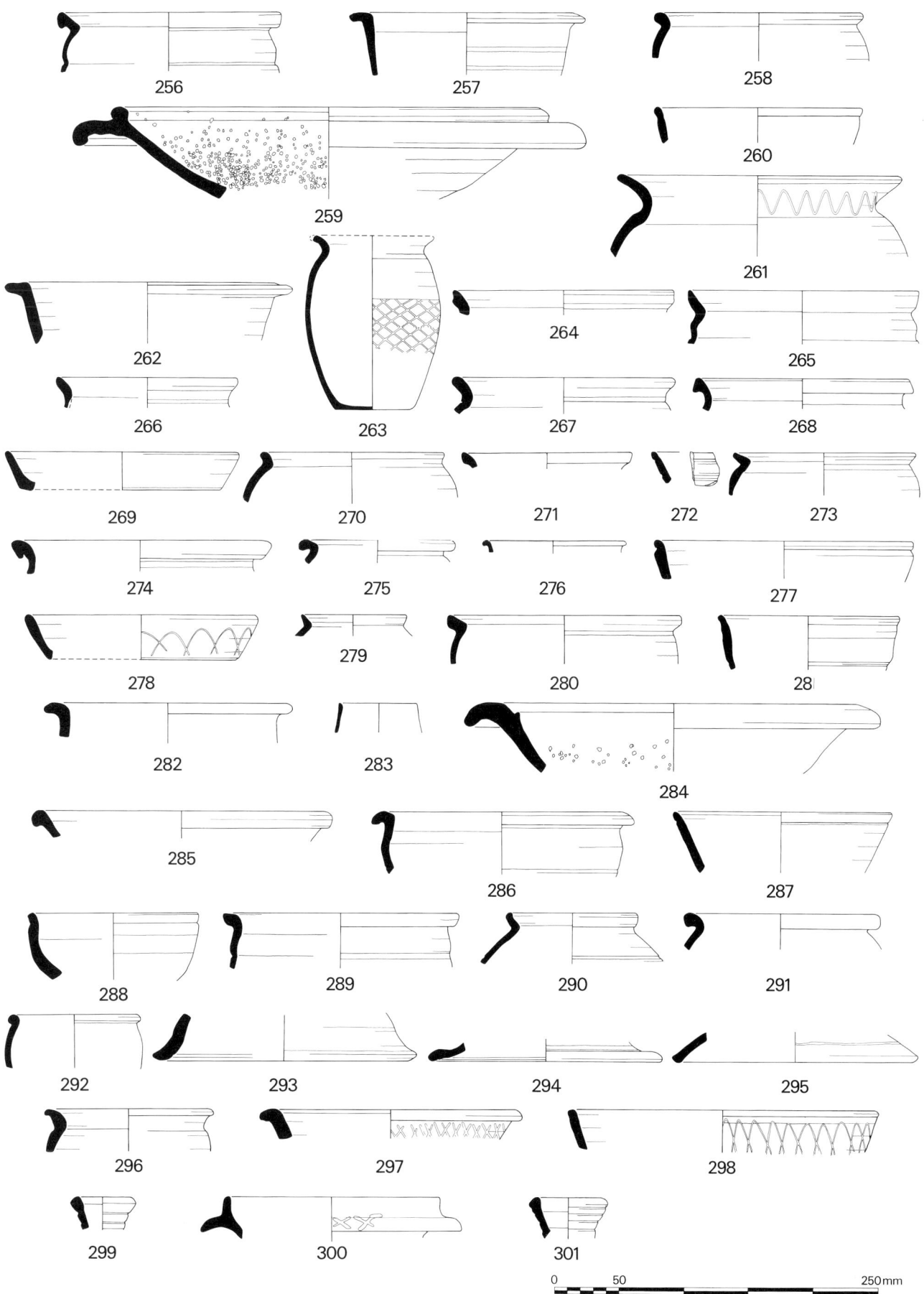

Figure 132 Roman pottery (AES 76–7), nos 256–257, period 5, and nos 258–301, period 6

Explosion site finds (AES 76-7)

coated with a ferrous residue after breakage – suggest that this part of the building may not have had a domestic use.

Building dump (232) (illustrated vessels nos 264–270)

Layer (232) was one of a group of features external to building V at its eastern end from which most of the pottery derived at this time. The dump itself contained a small group of material most of which was undiagnostic but probably contemporary and was dated to the early to mid-3rd century by a sherd from a Nene Valley scale beaker. There was also a flange fragment from a Verulamium region *mortarium*. This last piece was worn and certainly residual.

Pit (245) (illustrated vessels nos 283–298)

This pit, backfilled with building debris, was a re-cut of the earlier feature (245). Consequently the pottery group contained some Hadrianic–Antonine and earlier material. The flagon, no 207, part of which occurred in a period 4 context ((224), see above) and the white-slipped *mortarium* no 284 were of particular interest as good examples of Hadrianic–Antonine types. The pit also contained two Spanish *amphorae* in different fabrics, Verulamium region *mortaria*, and Nene Valley colour-coated ware (eg no 283) as well as Severn Valley wares, local grey wares, and Malvernian material. The Severn Valley wares included nos 286 and 287, both types which may be assignable to the 3rd century.

Layer (227) (illustrated vessels nos 299–383)

This layer covered the south-east corner of the site but its relationship to building V could not be ascertained. The bulk of the pottery in this period derived from (227). Of this 75% was made up of grey wares mainly in the form of rusticated jars (eg nos 316–324 and probably 325–339). Vessels such as no 321 marked the culmination of the development of this type. This group contained a small collection of Oxfordshire colour-coated material and some Oxfordshire *mortaria*, dating the context to around the middle of the 3rd century, contemporary with the rest of the deposits of this period.

Apart from the Oxfordshire products and vessels such as the Severn Valley tankard no 312, and Black-Burnished ware dishes nos 379 and 380, there was little material of conclusively 3rd-century date. A possible explanation for this would be that the spread consisted of redeposited material laid as a new yard surface. The 3rd-century pottery was then acquired during the course of period 6. Its small quantities can be attributed to the way in which the whole area was kept clean. This also explains why (227) was the only really large group from period 6. The idea of (227) being dumped at one time is supported by the fact that very few of the sherds were worn although many were small. It is noticeable that the percentage of weight for this period (10.8% of the site total) was rather less than that based on the sherd total (14.6%). A below average sherd size would probably be consistent with the material having been redeposited.

Period 7 AD 250/260–270 (580 sherds, 2.3%; 7.76 EVEs, 2.3%)

Illustrated vessels 384–414: 384–388, (211); 389–391, (228); 392–394, (161); 395, (162); 396–397, (230); 398, (218); 399, (222); 400–401, (120); 402, (173); 403, (225); 404–409, (198); 410–411, (206); 412, (202); 413–414, (II 19) (Figs 134–135)
 Catalogue: 384, R30; 385, R01; 386, R30; 387, R01; 388, R40; 389, O21; 390, O25; 391, R30; 392, O23; 393, B11; 394, R70; 395, O23; 396, O27; 397, R80; 398, O32, 399, R01; 400, F52; 401, O21; 402, B11; 403, R01; 404, O24; 405, O51; 406, R40; 407, R30; 408, R01; 409, R50; 410, O27; 411, R01; 412, O24; 413, W12; 414, O25

As in the earlier periods on the site very little pottery was associated with structures. The only large groups came from the gravel surface (161) and its make-up layers (211) and (228) which lay between buildings V and VI. None of the groups from period 7 was particularly large, perhaps suggesting that this period of the site's development was relatively short.

The assemblage still contained many elements which must have derived from earlier periods, such as *amphorae* and Malvernian vessels. However, despite this and the prevalence (still) of residual rusticated jars, the group had acquired a more definite 3rd-century character. Grey wares declined markedly in numbers from the previous period, to 34.1% of the total. They were now surpassed by Severn Valley wares (41.6%) and Black-Burnished ware increased to 11.6% of the assemblage. The abruptness of this change in the relative importance of the major fabric groups might suggest that there were some peculiarities about the composition of the period 7 group, perhaps supporting the view that a high proportion of the pottery in (227) consisted of material which was not only redeposited, but also highly residual.

Severn Valley ware flanged bowls first appeared in period 7 and 3rd-century Black-Burnished ware types such as no 402 were also present.

Building V reconstruction (illustrated vessels nos 396–402)

There was evidence for a certain amount of disturbance within the building during this period. Part of a Nene Valley flagon, no 400, was redistributed from the period 6 wall foundation (155) to the dump (120) adjacent to it. The Severn Valley ware strainer, no 401, of which pieces were found in slot (157A) and on the period 6 mortar floor (131), had also been swept into (120). Apart from the fragments of these two ves-

Explosion site finds (AES 76-7)

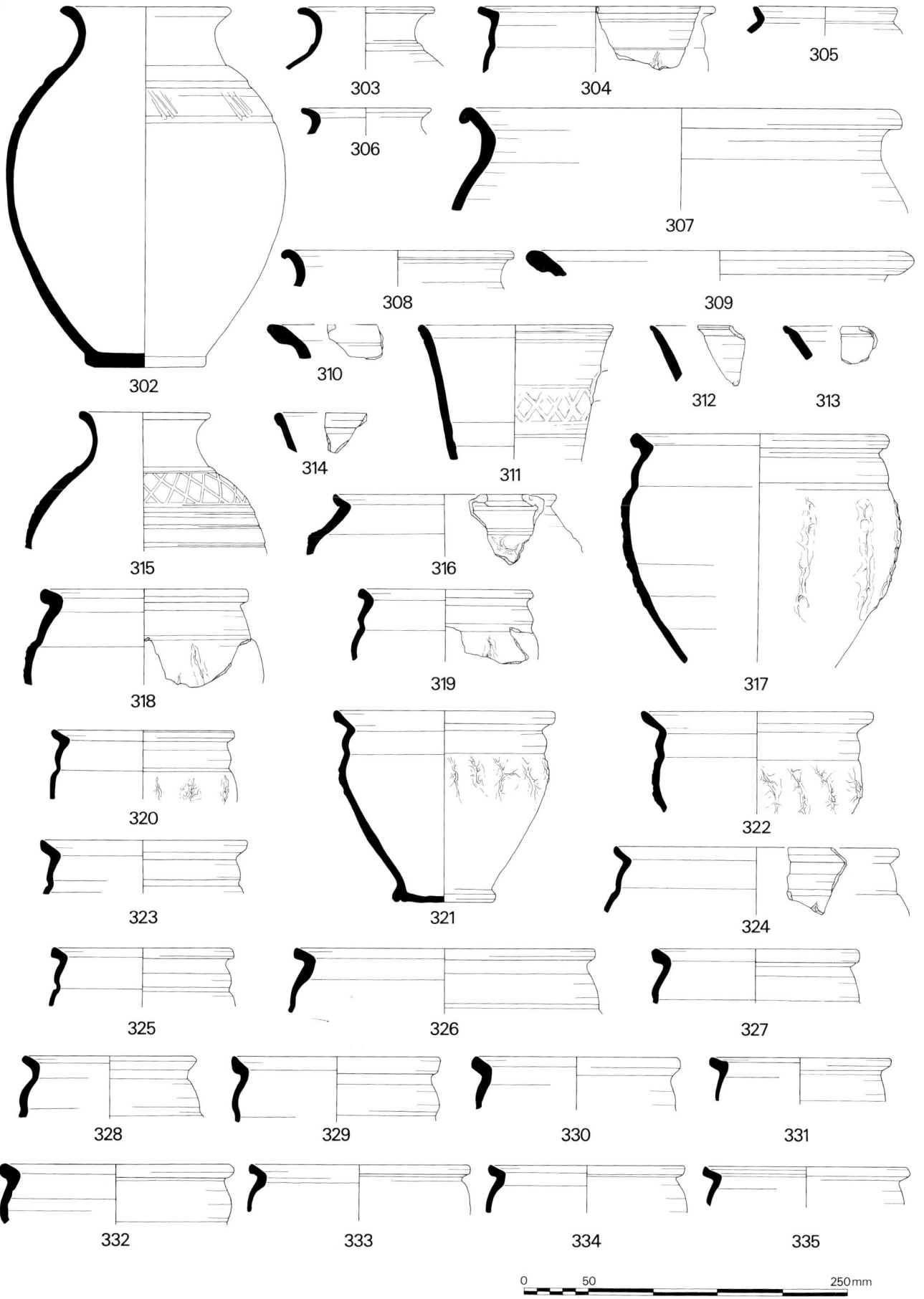

Figure 133 Roman pottery (AES 76–7), nos 302–335, period 6

Explosion site finds (AES 76-7)

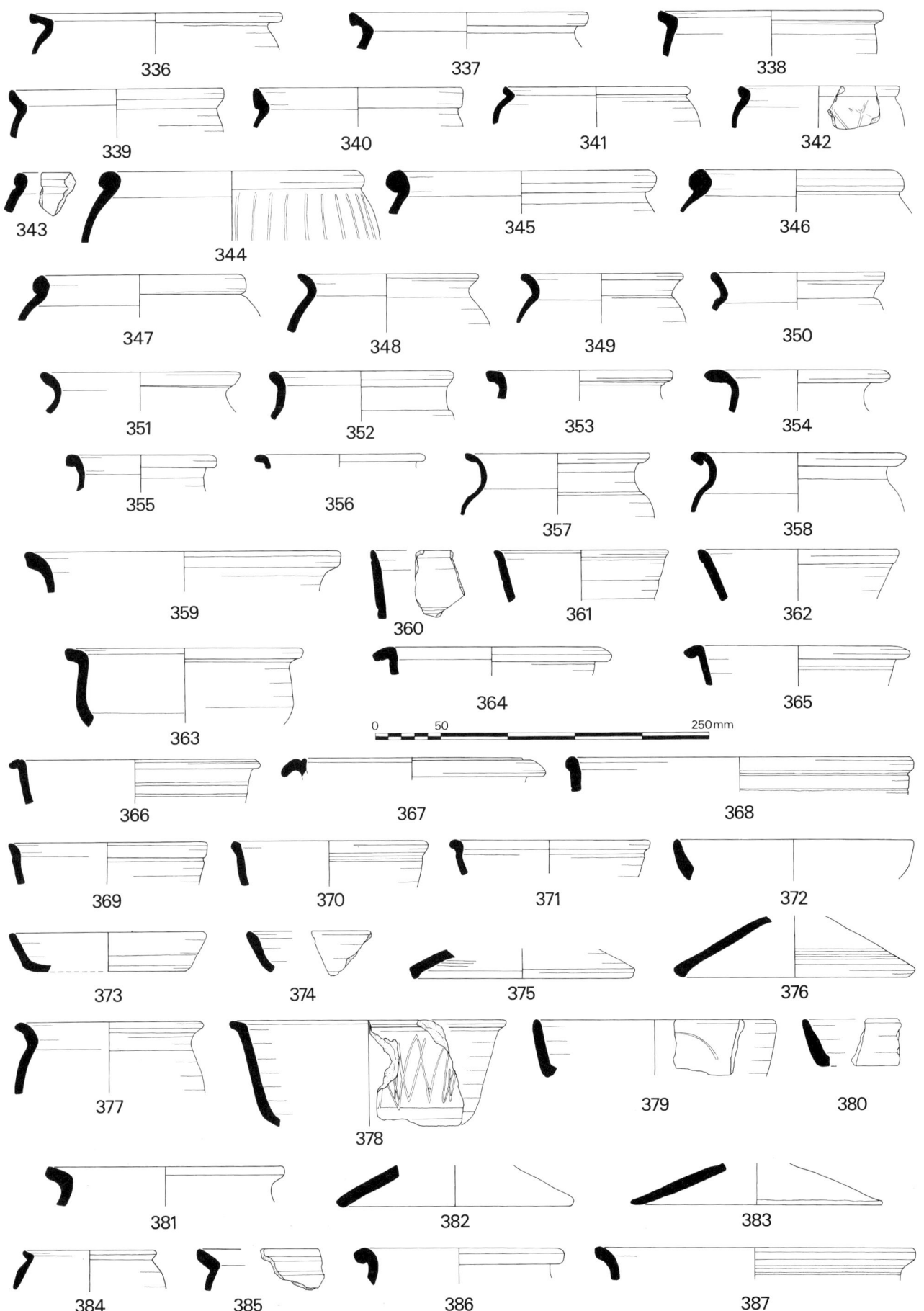

Figure 134   Roman pottery (AES 76–7), nos 336–383, period 6, and nos 384–387, period 7

Table 23 Stratified samian ware (AES 76–7, period 6)

Context	Source	Form	Date	Comments
145	SG	27	Fl–Tr	
155	CG	33	Antonine	
155	CG	38 or 44/81	Antonine	
157	CG	18/31	Had–Ant	
157	CG	37	Had–Ant	
157	CG	31	Mid–Ant	
186	M de V	18/31R	Tr–e Had	
197	CG	?	Had or Ant	
210	CG	37	Hadrianic	
210	?M de V	37	AD 135–160	
216	SG	R dish	Fl–Tr	riveted
216	M de V	27	Tr–e Had	
226	SG	27	1st C	
226	SG	29	1st C	
226	M de V	Curle 11	Tr–e Had	?same vessel as 224
226	M de V	46	1st h 2nd C	
226	CG	37	Had–e Ant	
226	CG	18/31 or 31	Antonine	
226	CG	30 or 37	Antonine	
226	CG	31	Antonine	
226	CG	33	Antonine	
226	CG	36	Antonine	
226	CG	37	Antonine	
226	CG	38 or 44	Antonine	
226	CG	Curle 21	Antonine	
226	CG	Closed form	Antonine	
226	CG	Ink well	Antonine	
227	SG	15/17–18	Neronian	
227	SG	29 or 30	Fl–Tr	
227	SG	37	Fl–Tr	
227	M de V	18/31 (2)	Tr–e Had	
227	M de V	27	Tr–e Had	
227	M de V	36	Tr–e Had	
227	M de V	37 (2)	Tr–e Had	1 by Drusus i
227	M de V	42	Tr–e Had	
227	M de V	Dish	Tr–e Had	
227	CG	18/31R–31R	Antonine	
227	CG	30 or 37	Antonine	
227	CG	36	Antonine	
227	CG	38	Antonine	
227	CG	79 or Lud.Tg	m–l Ant	
227	CG	45	AD 170–200	

Explosion site finds (AES 76-7)

Table 23 (*cont.*) **Stratified samian ware (AES 76–7, period 6)**

Context	Source	Form	Date	Comments
232	SG	Curle 11	Flavian	
232	CG	18/31 or 31	Had–e Ant	
232	CG	31R	m–l Ant	
234	CG	?	?Antonine	
245	SG	18R	Ner–Fl	
245	SG	18/31	Ner–Fl	
245	SG	29	Ner–Fl	
245	M de V	33a	Tr–e Had	
245	CG	37 (2)	Had–e Ant	
245	CG	42	Had–e Ant	
245	CG	31 (2)	m–l Ant	
245	CG	38	m–l Ant	
263	M de V	Dish or bowl	Tr or Had	
II 31D	SG	36	Neronian	
II 31D	SG	37	Fl–Tr	
II 31D	M de V	37	AD 135–160	Fig 122, no 29
II 35	SG	15/17 (2)	Neronian	
II 35	CG	33	Antonine	
II 35	CG	45	AD170–200	

sels (120) only contained two Antonine samian sherds, one of which was burnt. The dump is described as the 'main feature' in room 1 of building V at this time and contained a quantity of building debris. The low incidence of pottery in the building combined with the presence of refuse of other types may be seen as an indicator of non-domestic use. Some rubbish evidently was cleared out of the building, however, as vessel no 406, a greyware narrow-mouthed jar, seems to show. This pot probably originated in the small layer (94) within building V, but fragments were also found in (198), a hollow feature within the gravel surface (161).

Apart from layer (120) in room 1, evidence for the reconstruction of building V consisted of post-pits (231), (230), and (222). The pits were cut through the rubble and mortar floors of the period 6 work on building V and presumably the residual component of these small assemblages derived from this rebuilding. It was difficult to establish the size of this component but the fragments of Spanish *amphora* must have been residual by this stage and no 399, a carinated bowl, had probably already been redeposited before it reached the group. The post pits also contained some contemporary material. Vessel no 398 demonstrated some connection between the filling of post-pit (222) and the slag deposit (218) by being distributed between the two features.

Gravel surface (161) and make-up layers (illustrated vessels nos 384–394)

As with earlier gravel surfaces (161) contained re-deposited material, including a large fragment of a Malvernian storage jar (no 394), some Flavian rusticated jars, a handmade vessel and part of a possible north-east Gaulish *amphora*. Both (161) itself and the make-up layer (228) contained 3rd-century Severn Valley ware bowls, nos 392 and 390 respectively.

Period 8 AD 270–280/290 (1363 sherds, 5.5%; 15.28 EVEs, 4.5%)

Illustrated vessels 415–455: 415–441, (128); 442–452, (164–6); 453, (130); 454, (260); 455, (130A) (Figs 135–136)
Catalogue: 415, M23; 416, M23; 417, W13; 418, O25; 419, O50; 420, O24; 421, O23; 422, O28; 423, O24; 424, O27; 425, O23; 426, O23; 427, O24; 428, R40; 429, R40; 430, R01; 431, R01; 432, R30; 433, R40; 434, R30; 435, R30; 436, R15; 437, R30; 438, R40; 439–441, B11; 442, F51; 443, M23; 444, W13; 445, O23; 446, O23; 447, O27; 448, R01; 449, R40; 450, R40; 451, R01; 452, G44; 453, R30; 454, B11; 455, G44

From this time until the end of the Roman period the pottery assemblage took on the characteristic appearance of all late 3rd- to 4th-century groups from the town in which the local grey wares were

Explosion site finds (AES 76-7)

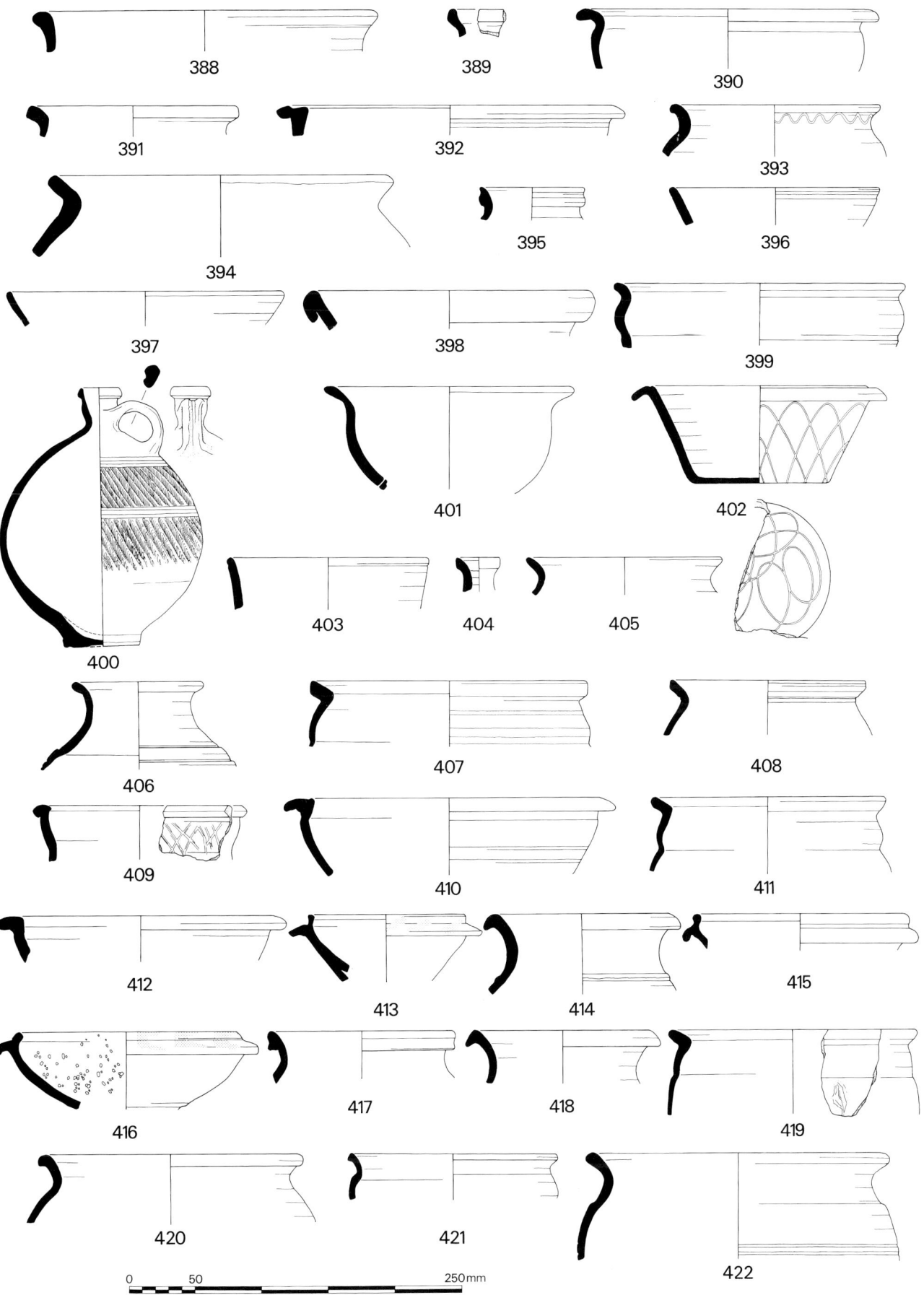

Figure 135   Roman pottery (AES 76–7), nos 388–414, period 7, and nos 415–422, period 8

Explosion site finds (AES 76-7)

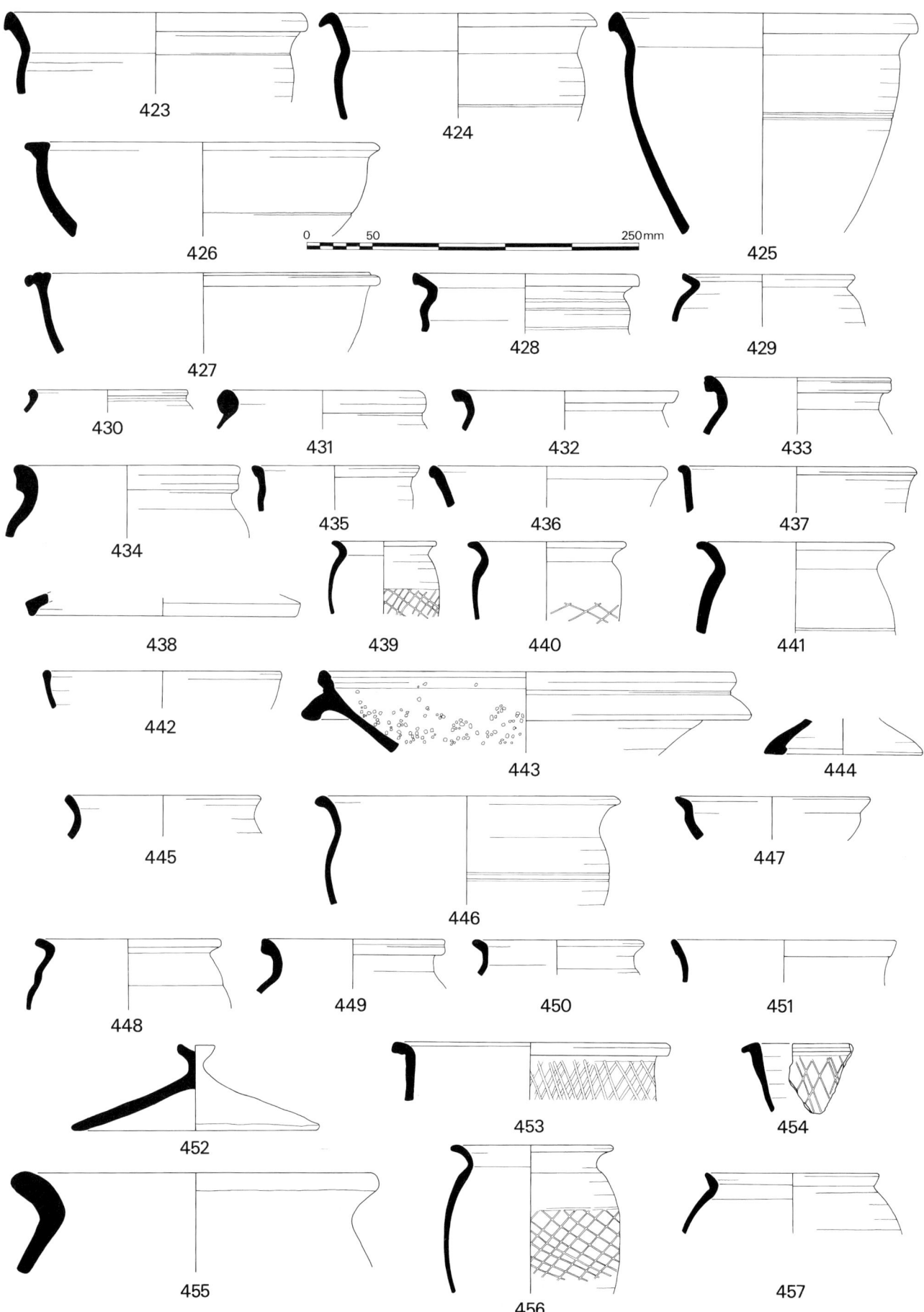

Figure 136 Roman pottery (AES 76–7), nos 423–455, period 8, and nos 456–457, period 9

never more than equal in importance to the Severn Valley wares and Black-Burnished ware was present in ever increasing quantities. Grey wares now amounted to 26.1% of the assemblage and Severn Valley wares to 40.1%. Black-Burnished ware comprised 16.8%. Both samian and white wares were relatively well-represented (6.5% and 4.6% respectively), and while fine wares only constituted 2.1% they were now beginning to increase in importance towards their much higher late Roman level. Jar types, at 57.8%, were very close to the level at which they had occurred in the previous period, rather less important than in the 2nd century. Medium-mouthed jars were marginally the most important jar type, but wide-mouthed jars in Severn Valley ware became prominent for the first time. Cooking pots likewise increased in popularity in this period, in line with the growth of Black-Burnished ware. Bowls and dishes were also more important than earlier, at 15.5% and 8.3% respectively, probably for the same reason. Tankards were now 5.4%, their rise in popularity, first discernible in period 7, being maintained, reflecting the increased significance of Severn Valley wares.

There was still quite a large proportion of residual material: 8% of the grey wares were from rusticated jars, and Spanish and Gaulish *amphorae*, Verulamium region white wares, white-slipped flagons, and sherds from roughcast beakers of Hadrianic–Antonine date were still present. The contemporary fine wares consisted of Oxfordshire and Nene Valley colour-coated fabrics, white ware flagons from Oxfordshire and Mancetter-Hartshill, and Lezoux ware.

Buildings IV, V, and VI (illustrated vessels nos 453–455)

Little pottery came from these structures. Within building V there continued to be disturbance of earlier deposits leading to the redeposition of sherds from the suggested period 7 vessels 400 and 401 in the possible floor layer (130). Vessels 453–455 were all residual in later 3rd-century contexts.

Yard areas (illustrated vessels nos 415–452)

The deposit which yielded most pottery in this period was (128), a layer which contained 44% of all the pottery from period 8. The group from (128) (nos 415–441) was made up of a mixture of residual and contemporary material. This is the earliest appearance of the Severn Valley ware wide-mouthed jar (nos 423–425). Substantial sherds of these vessels were found. Very little of the pottery from (128) was worn and it would seem that much of the assemblage was simply dumped in a single action. This might indicate a period when part of the yard area between the buildings was out of use. A fixed date is given for this group by the presence of sherds of an Oxfordshire col-our-coated beaker dated after c AD 270 (Young 1977, 152, type C23). Other Oxfordshire vessels included two examples of the *mortarium* type M20 (nos 415 and 416). Black-Burnished ware of late type was also present (eg no 440).

The deposit (128) was overlain by gravel surfaces (164–6). These contained an assemblage only half the size of that from (128) but its composition was much the same (nos 442–452). It contained a bowl in Oxfordshire colour-coated fabric (no 442) and an Oxfordshire M18 *mortarium* (no 443) dated c AD 240–300 (Young 1977, 72). The group also included the complete profile of a Malvern ware lid (no 452).

Later 3rd and 4th centuries (periods 9–10)

The pre-eminence of the major industries established from period 7 onwards was even more marked during the later occupation of Alcester. In the 4th century, local producers were responsible for less than 20% of the material found at the Explosion site, a situation which is paralleled in other late groups from the town (Ferguson, in Cracknell 1996).

The significant developments in pottery supply during the late Roman period were mainly regional. They consisted firstly of the increase in importance of the trade with Oxfordshire. This involved not only larger volumes of material but also a greater variety of fabrics (parchment ware, the white-coated fabric, and 'burnt' white ware as well as the colour-coated and white *mortarium* fabrics). The second development was the establishment of trading contacts with Northamptonshire and the east and south-east Midlands: both shell-gritted (fabric C11) and pink grogged ware (G11) were regular, though not numerous, components of later Roman groups from the town.

Further afield, Black-Burnished ware was the fabric traded in the largest amounts but the quantities of Nene Valley colour-coated material continued to increase and some sherds of New Forest ware were also found. Rhenish wares were probably the only material brought in from abroad although it is possible that some *amphorae* from the eastern Mediterranean reached the town at this period.

Period 9 AD 280/290–340/350 (7291 sherds, 29.5%; 103.53 EVEs, 30.4%)

Illustrated vessels 456–746: 456, (124M); 457, (124J); 458–461, (124L); 462–464, (124I); 465–466, (124H); 467–475, (124C); 476–519, (124); 520–537, (124A); 538, (125); 539–540, (115); 541–543, (123); 544, (41); 545–546, (40); 547, (39); 548, (76); 549–552, (170K); 553–554, (170F); 555–567, (170D); 568–571, (170C); 572–615, (170); 616–625, (207); 626–627, (249); 628–675, (86); 676–729, (II 10); 730–746, (II 22) (Figs 136–147)

Catalogue: 456, B11; 457, R30; 458, M23; 459, O21; 460, B11; 461, B11; 462, O24; 463, R01; 464, R30; 465, 024; 466, O23; 467, O80; 468, O24; 469, O25; 470–475, B11; 476, F33; 477, F32; 478, F33; 479–481, F52; 482, A21; 483, M23; 484, M23; 485, M22; 486,

Explosion site finds (AES 76-7)

W13; 487, O25; 488, O23; 489, O23; 490, O24; 491, O23; 492, O24; 493, O25; 494, O23; 495, O25; 496, O23; 497, O24; 498, O27; 499, O24; 500, O25; 501, R50; 502–517, B11; 518, G44; 519, G44; 520, F51; 521–523, F32; 524, M23; 525, O23; 526, O23; 527, O24; 528–530, O23; 531, R30; 532, R40; 533, R30; 534–537, B11; 538, O24; 539, Q25; 540, O23; 541, R40; 542–544, B11; 545, F74; 546, R30; 547, O24; 548, O25; 549, M23; 550, W12; 551, R01; 552, G44; 553, W13; 554, B11; 555, O24; 556, O23; 557, O24; 558, O23; 559, O25; 560, R01; 561, R40; 562, R01; 563, R40; 564–567, B11; 568, W13; 569, O25; 570, R40; 571, B11; 572, F52; 573, F23; 574, F23; 575, W12; 576–578, O23; 579, O27; 580, O27; 581, O25; 582–584, O23; 585, O25; 586, O23; 587, O25; 588, O21; 589, O24; 590, O25; 591, O23; 592, O24; 593, O27; 594, O25; 595, R01; 596, R30; 597, R01; 598, R30; 599, R40; 600, R30; 601–611, B11; 611–614, C11; 615, G44; 616, O24; 617, R15; 618–620, R01; 621, R50; 622, R30; 623, R01; 624, R30; 625, R40; 626, O21; 627, R80; 628, F52; 629, A22; 630–632, M23; 633, M71; 634, W12; 635, O24; 636, O21; 637, O23; 638, O23; 639, O24; 640, O23; 641, O24; 642, O23; 643, O24; 644, O21; 645, O24; 646, O23; 647, O21; 648, O23; 649, O23; 650, R40; 651, R40; 652, R19; 653, R40; 654, R30; 655, R01; 656, R01; 657, R40; 658, R01; 659, R24; 660, R40; 661, R40; 662–670, B11; 671–672, C11; 673–675, G44; 676, O24; 677, O27; 678–681, O24; 682–684, O25; 685, O24; 686, O25; 687, O24; 688, O21; 689, O21; 690, O25; 691, O24; 692, O27; 693, R01; 694, R30; 695, R40; 696, R30; 697, R40; 698, R40; 699, R01; 700, R40; 701, R30; 702, R40; 703, R30; 704, R01; 705, R30; 706, R40; 707, R01; 708, R40; 709, R30; 710–725, B11; 726–729, G44; 730, M43; 731, O23; 732, O24; 733, O27; 734; O21; 735, O24; 736, O24; 737, O21; 738, R40; 739, R21; 740–741, R40; 742–746, B11

The features assigned to this period produced more pottery than those from any other period of activity on the site. The areas between buildings V and VI were partly given over to rubbish disposal. About half of the assemblage (3548 sherds) derived from two pits (124) and (170) which occupied part of this area. The size of the group led also to its containing the widest range of fabrics from any period. There was still a high proportion of residual material (as might be expected in a small area in which large pits had been dug). The pits penetrated right to the lowest excavated levels and pottery from the earliest periods, such as the handmade, coarse-gritted, and mica-dusted fabrics were redeposited. Other fabrics, known to have gone out of production by the late 2nd century, appeared in every period on the site and were still present in period 9. These included Verulamium region products, *amphorae* from Spain and possibly northern Gaul, white-slipped flagons, and the imported Hadrianic–Antonine roughcast beakers. There were also 2nd-century vessel types such as the rusticated jar which was still present as around 3% of the assemblage. (This type was more important in certain features: see discussion of (170) below.)

The contemporary material included Oxfordshire products (colour-coated, white, white-slipped, and parchment ware), Nene Valley, New Forest and some unattributed colour-coated fabrics, and Rhenish ware. Fine wares totalled 3.4% of the assemblage (and samian still amounted to 5.7%). Mancetter-Hartshill white wares also occurred, but in percentage terms they were less common than previously and may have been largely residual, though *mortaria* from the same source continued to be supplied.

The coarse wares were largely Severn Valley (36.5%) and Black-Burnished wares (35.2%) but there was also an element of local grey wares (13.6%), not all of which were residual. There was some trade in coarse wares with the eastern Midlands, resulting in the presence of the pink grogged ware (fabric G11) and some shell-gritted fabrics (C11), though these fabrics only amounted to 0.7% of the pottery in this period.

There were also developments in the breakdown of vessel types. For the first time (in a period group large enough to be statistically reliable) jars fell below half of the vessel population, to 44.7%. Of these, over one third were of cooking pot type, reflecting the considerable increase in the importance of Black-Burnished ware at this time. Many of the other jar types were in Severn Valley ware. These included narrow-, medium- and wide-mouthed types, though the latter constituted a smaller proportion of the group than in the previous period. Bowls were the next most numerous vessel type and totalled 17.5%, of which well over half were straight-sided Black-Burnished ware types. Dishes accounted for 9.1% of all vessels; they were followed closely by tankards, which at 8.4% reached their peak of popularity at this time. Beakers also increased in importance (to 6.9%), a result in part of the gradual growth in fine wares.

There was a small amount of pottery from within building V and some from features in the area where building IV had been. The major groups, however, were those from the large pits (124) and (170) and from a general layer (86)/(II 10).

Pit (124) (2477 sherds, 33.43 EVEs) (illustrated vessels nos 456–537)

This pit contained coins dated *c* AD 270+. These, together with vessel types (particularly Oxfordshire) also assigned to a date after AD 270 and the dating evidence for the previous period, suggested a closely dated group within the last quarter of the 3rd century for this feature. Although several successive fills were distinguished, the pit group seems to indicate rubbish disposal over a fairly short space of time, with the possible exception of the uppermost fill (see below). The large, contemporary group of Black-Burnished ware seems to represent one discrete activity.

Two fabric groups made up nearly 73% of this assemblage: Black-Burnished ware (44%) and Severn Valley wares (28.8%). The Black-Burnished ware material comprised a large group of very similar vessels probably closely dated (see above). Nos 456, 460, 470–72, 503–510, and 534 show the range of cooking pots. Most of the bowls were of 'incipient flange' type, for example nos 461, 473, and 511–13. Dropped flange bowls (eg nos 514–15) were rare in this pit; five out of 58 Black-Burnished ware bowls were of this type. Of these, two were certainly and all were probably in the uppermost fill of the pit (124A), which may have been a little later in date than the other fills. (It was noticeable that (124A) was the only fill to contain shell-tempered sherds, which also suggests that there was a chronological distinction between this and the lower fills of the pit.) In any case the evidence suggests that the incipient flanged Black-Burnished ware bowl was in use throughout the 3rd century and was succeeded only at the very end of that century by the dropped flange type. Dishes were generally of simple straight-sided form, typified by nos 474–75, 516, and 535–37. There was only one flanged dish (no 517).

The Severn Valley wares included narrow-mouthed jars such as nos 467 and 487–88, wide-mouthed jars of the types seen in the previous period (eg nos 465–66 and 490–94), of which one (no 465) was a particularly large example, and tankards (nos 469 and 497–98).

Of the remaining 27% of the pottery just over half consisted of local reduced fabrics (7.7%) and samian (6.5%). Other coarse wares present as less than 1% of the group were shell-gritted, Malvernian, coarse-gritted, and local oxidised fabrics. Of these, only the shell-gritted sherds are likely to have been contemporary with the rest of the material. Apart from the samian, fine wares were only present in relatively small amounts. The Oxfordshire and Nene Valley colour-coated fabrics and the Rhenish/Central Gaulish fabrics represented between 1–2% whilst the other fabrics (Gaulish and Spanish *amphorae*, Oxfordshire, Mancetter-Hartshill and Verulamium region white wares and *mortaria* and white-slipped flagons) appeared as less than 1% of the assemblage. Nevertheless, Rhenish/Central Gaulish sherds were present in unusually large quantities in comparison to other Alcester sites (nos 476–78 and 521–23). The Nene Valley wares nos 479–481 included a large part of a fine hunt cup (no 481). The samian, *amphorae*, white-slipped flagons, and Verulamium region and Gaulish *mortaria* must all have been residual. This means that at least 13% of the assemblage was residual before the earliest products of industries still in operation in the late 3rd century are taken into account.

Mortaria were principally from Oxfordshire. Vessels included the first instance on the site of type M22 (no 458), which became the leading 4th-century Oxfordshire type (Young 1977, 76), among earlier forms (nos 483–84 and 524). Mancetter-Hartshill *mortaria* also continued to be found: no 485 was a characteristic late 3rd- to 4th century type.

Amongst the vessel types, the most important were cooking pots (23.7%), bowls (19%), beakers (10.2%), and dishes (10%). These figures are likely to have reflected the importance of Black-Burnished ware. The proportion of beakers was unusually high but may be accounted for by the relative importance of Rhenish wares and the Oxfordshire and Nene Valley colour-coated fabrics among the fine wares. Vessel types which were definitely no longer current by this period were the rusticated, everted rim jars (1.7%) and carinated bowls (less than 0.1%).

Pit (170) (1071 sherds, 24.95 EVEs) (illustrated vessel nos 549–615)

As with all major groups of this period Black-Burnished ware and Severn Valley wares made up the bulk of the collection. Their relative proportions were, however, quite different from those in pit (124). Figs 140 and 141 present in graphical form the comparison between pits (124) and (170) in terms of fabrics and vessel types. In (170) Severn Valley ware amounted to 39.8% of the pottery and Black-Burnished ware 27.6%. The only other fabric groups which made up more than 10% were local reduced wares (13%) and samian (10.7%). Malvernian and shell-gritted fabrics were present at between 1–2% of the assemblage, as was Mancetter-Hartshill white ware. There was then a wide range of fine wares which were proportionately less than 1%. These included British colour-coated wares (amongst which New Forest ware appeared for the first time) and Rhenish wares, Oxfordshire *mortaria*, and several *amphora* fabrics of which the last are all likely to have been redeposited. The same was true of the mica-dusted vessels nos 573 and 574. These were in a different fabric from the earlier material with the same finish and the curious variant of Dr 38 is an unusual form in this fabric. This type did not, for example, occur in the extensive repertoire of mica-dusted forms produced at London in the early 2nd century (Marsh 1978). These vessels may have dated from the second half of the 2nd century.

From the study of the fabrics at least 14.6% of the collection must have been residual (the samian was the most significant residual element). Of the vessel types about 6% (apart from samian ware forms) were residual (rusticated everted rim jars 4.5%, globular jars 0.6% and carinated bowls 1.1%).

The most significant individual vessel types were tankards (20.9%), bowls (18.5%), cooking pots (13.3%), and dishes (11.1%). None of the other categories was present as more than 10% of the total. The most notable feature of the (170) assemblage was the importance of Severn valley ware tankards (eg nos 558–59 and 585–590). These occurred in a range of sizes and all appeared to be of similar date. Other Severn Valley ware vessels included wide-mouthed jars (eg nos 556, 569, and 580–584) and bowls (eg nos 592–93). The Black-Burnished ware types were similar to those in (124), comprising cooking pots in a range of sizes (nos 554, 564–65, and 601–02), bowls (nos 571 and 604–08) and dishes. The grey wares included a few vessels of distinctively late type, of which the narrow-mouthed jar no 585, perhaps from the Wappenbury kilns, was the most characteristic. It was from this pit that the only substantial remains of shell-gritted jars in this period derived (nos 612–14). The vessels were all large baggy jars, some decorated with incised wavy lines. There is some variation in rim type.

On the whole (170) seemed to contain a higher proportion of redeposited material than (124). The quantities of samian, reduced, and Malvernian fab-

Explosion site finds (AES 76-7)

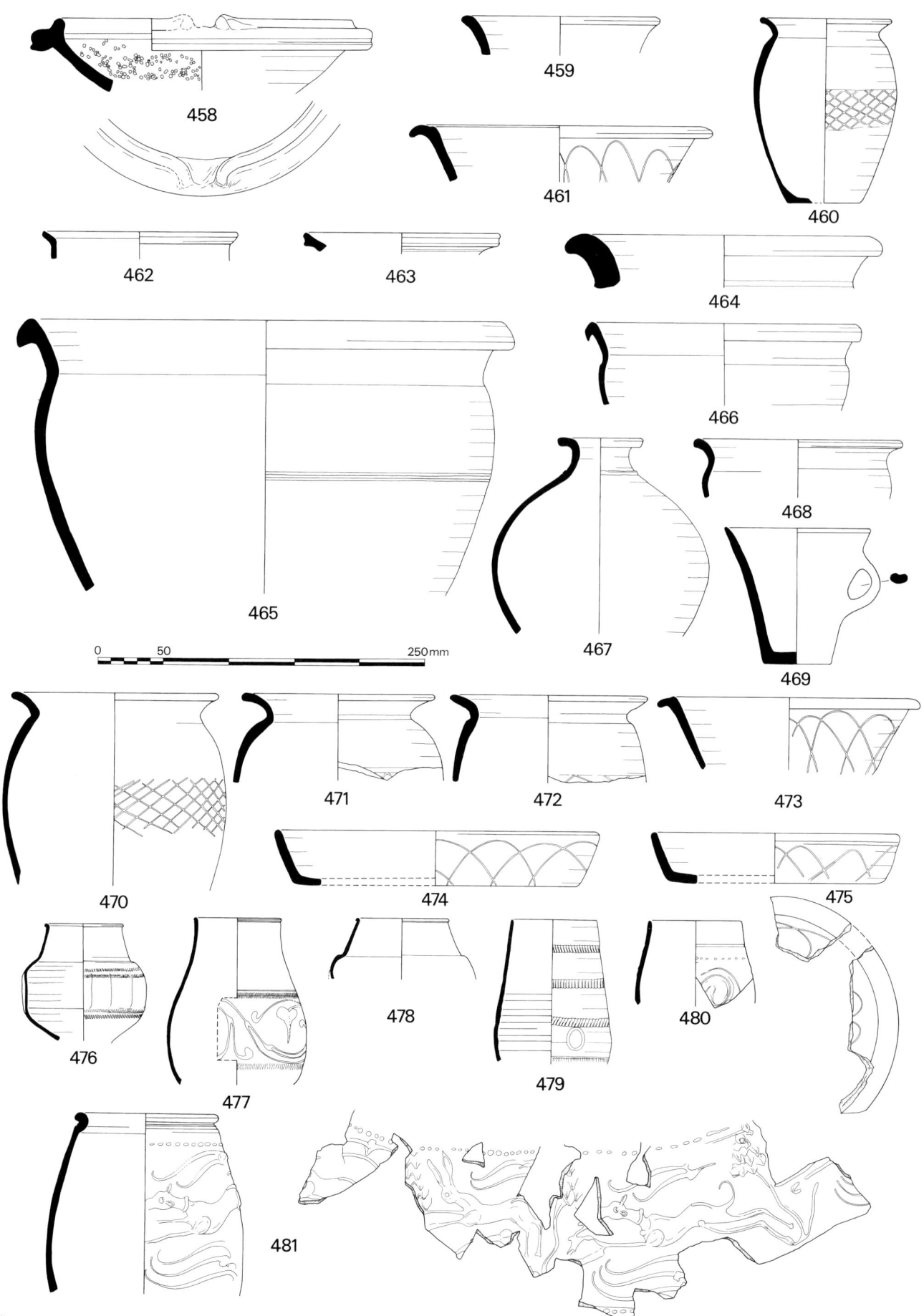

Figure 137   Roman pottery (AES 76–7), nos 458–481, period 9

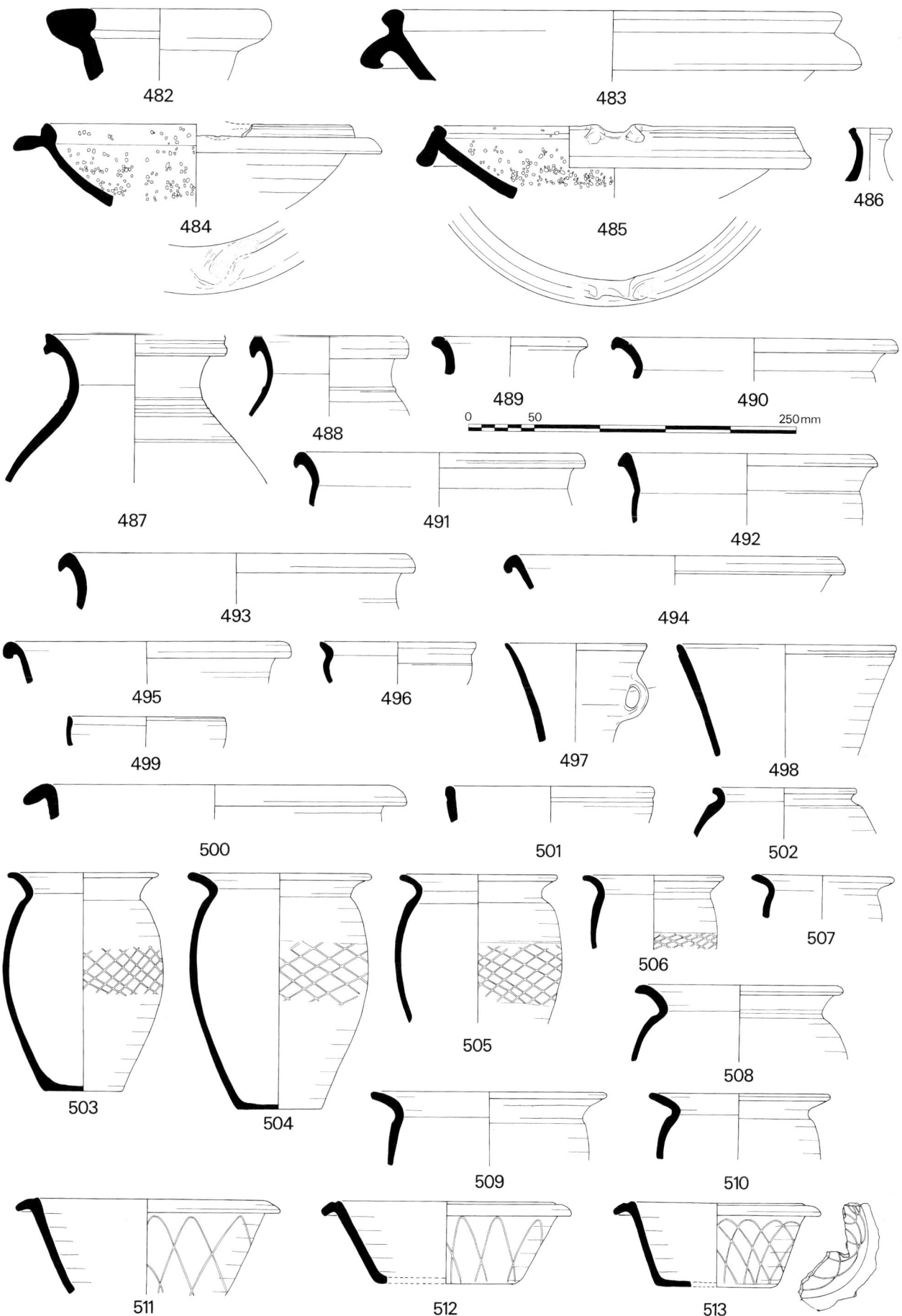

Figure 138   Roman pottery (AES 76–7), nos 482–513, period 9

Explosion site finds (AES 76-7)

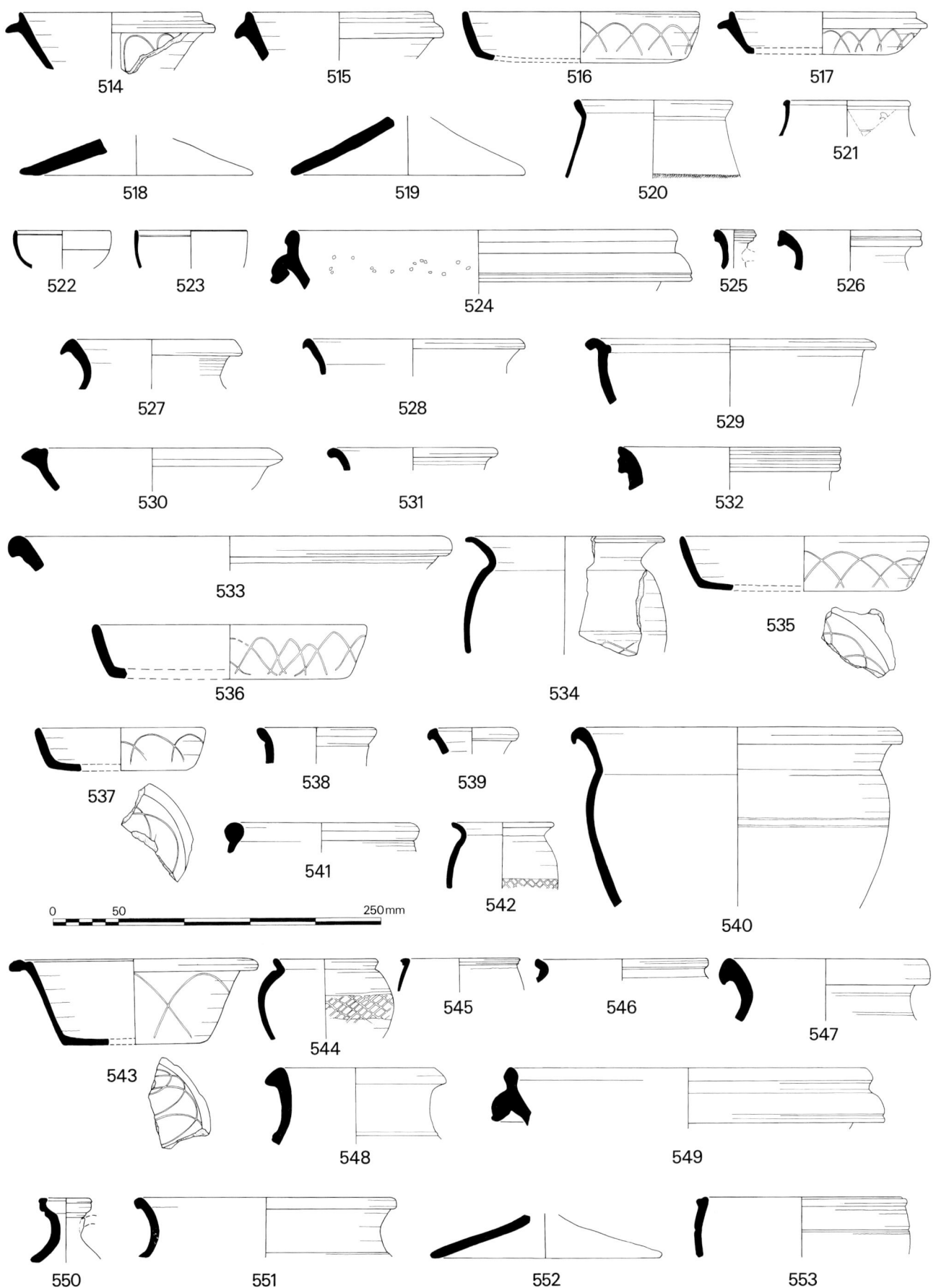

Figure 139   Roman pottery (AES 76–7), nos 514–553, period 9

Explosion site finds (AES 76-7)

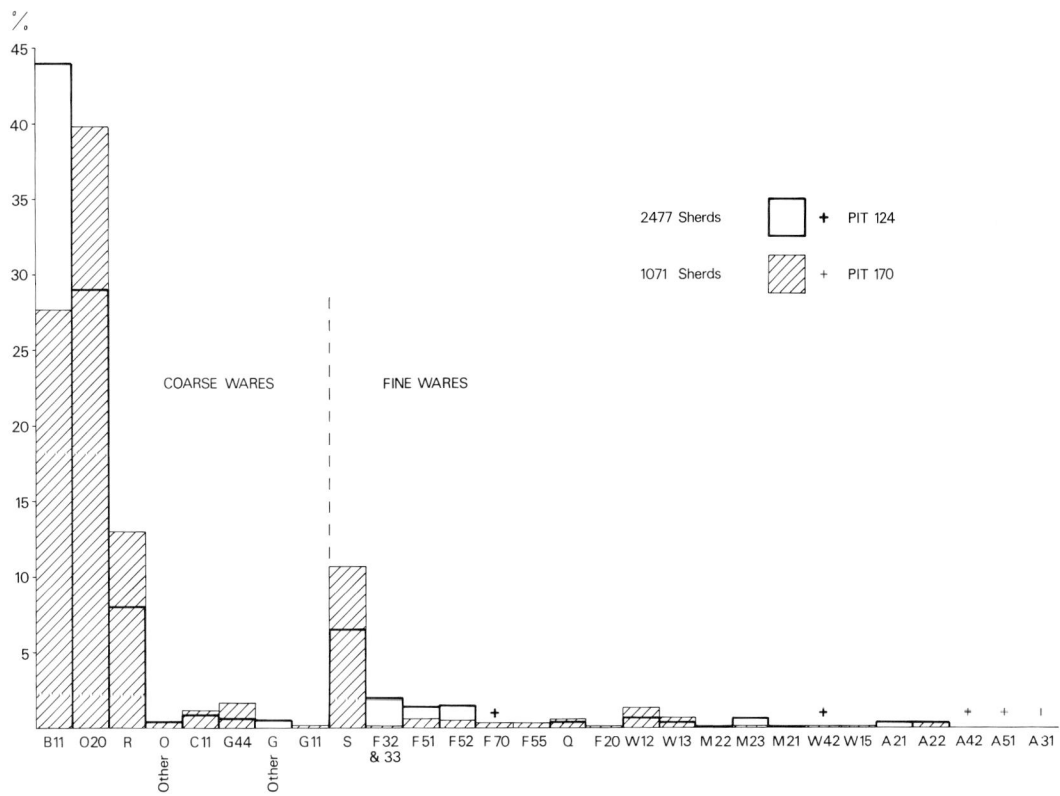

Figure 140 Comparison of Roman pottery assemblages in pits 124 and 170: fabrics (AES 76–7)

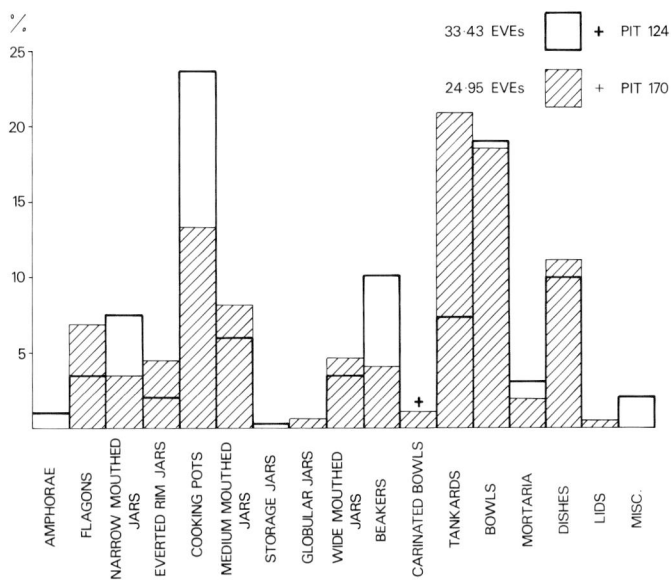

Figure 141 Comparison of Roman pottery assemblages in pits 124 and 170: vessel types (AES 76–7)

rics and the greater importance of earlier vessel types supports this. The difference between the two assemblages might be explained by the gradual backfilling of (170) with rubbish brought from a variety of sources. This would have been possible for a pit positioned in a narrow gap between two buildings as (170) was. A pit such as (124) which intruded more into the yard area would have needed to be filled quickly to avoid inconvenience.

Layer (86) and (II 10) (illustrated vessels nos 628–729)

This layer contained the only other large group of pottery from period 9. The material reflected the pattern of fabric distribution found in the two large pits, but the layer probably accumulated over a longer period of time than that in which the pits were filled and it clearly extended well into the 4th century.

Explosion site finds (AES 76-7)

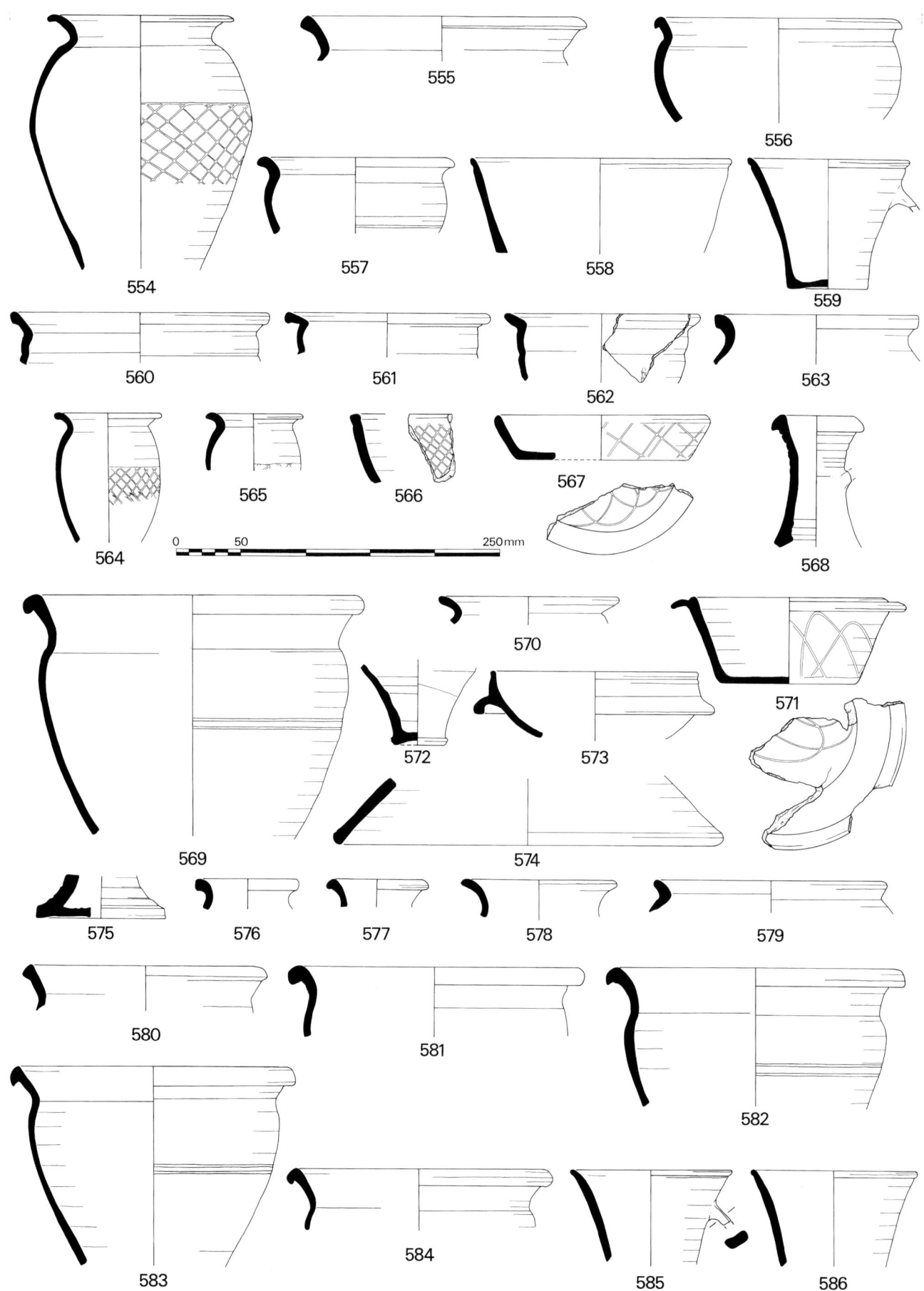

Figure 142   Roman pottery (AES 76–7), nos 554–586, period 9

Explosion site finds (AES 76-7)

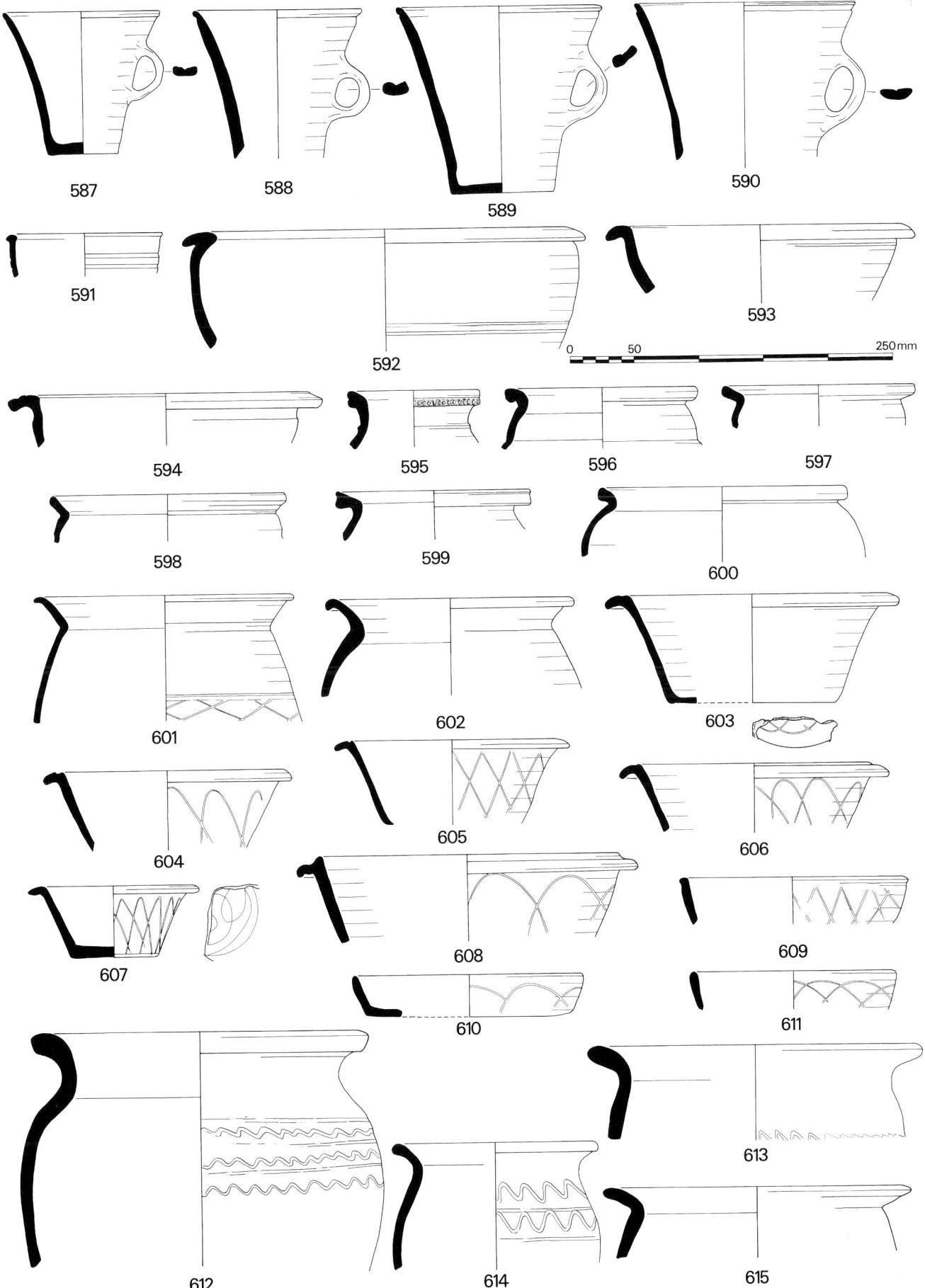

Figure 143 Roman pottery (AES 76–7), nos 587–615, period 9

Explosion site finds (AES 76-7)

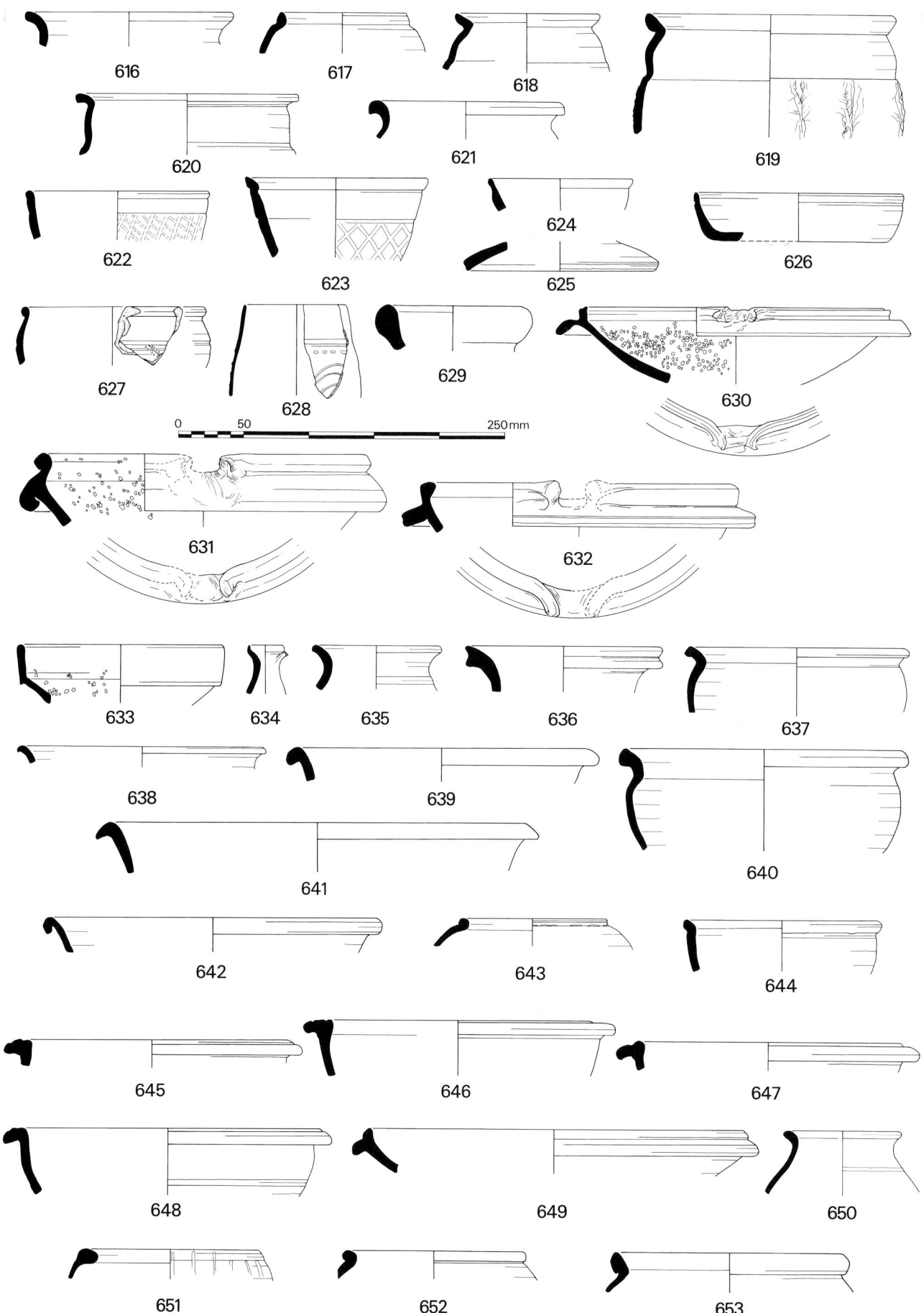

Figure 144   Roman pottery (AES 76–7), nos 616–653, period 9

Explosion site finds (AES 76-7)

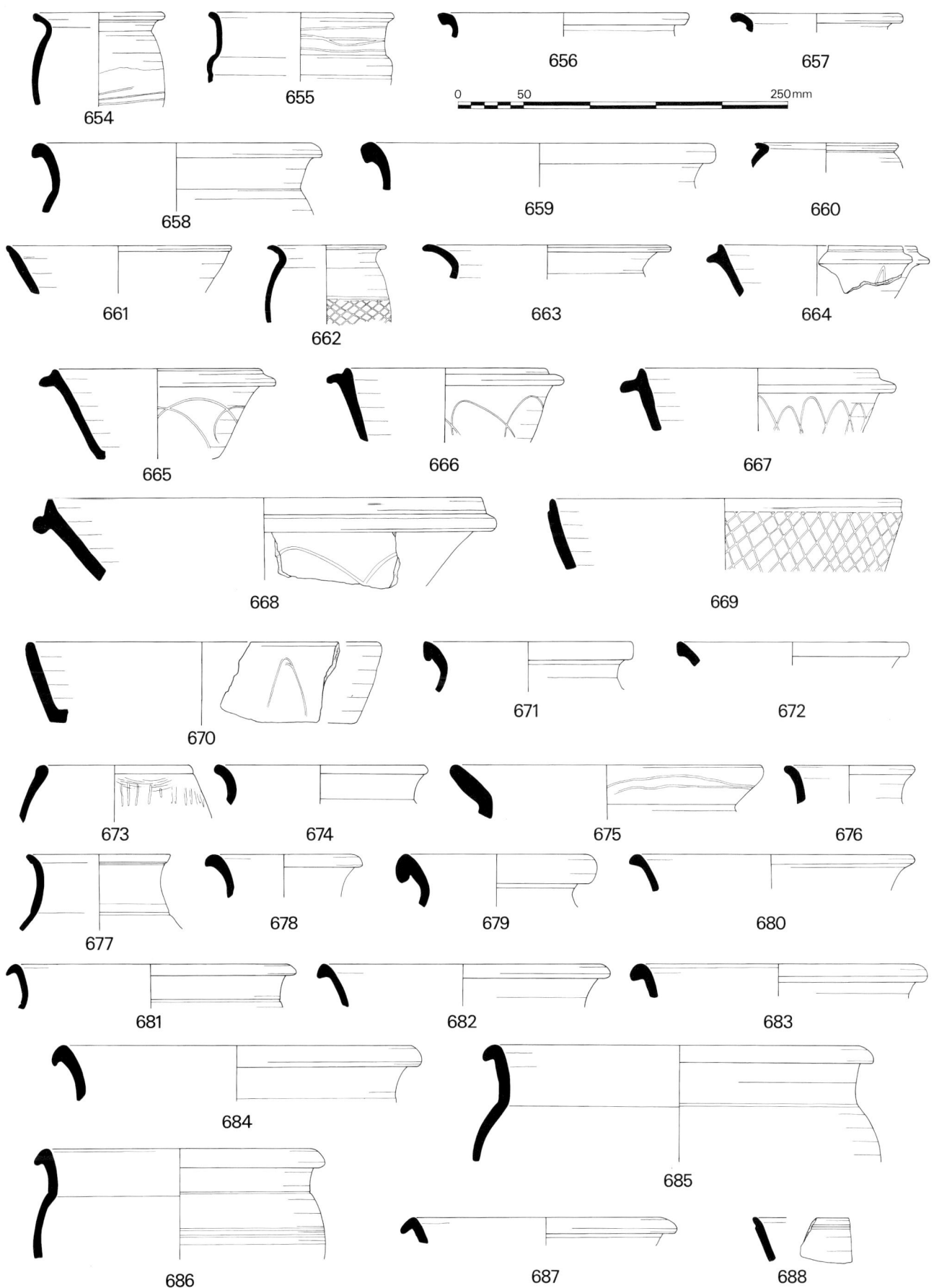

Figure 145   Roman pottery (AES 76–7), nos 654–688, period 9

Explosion site finds (AES 76-7)

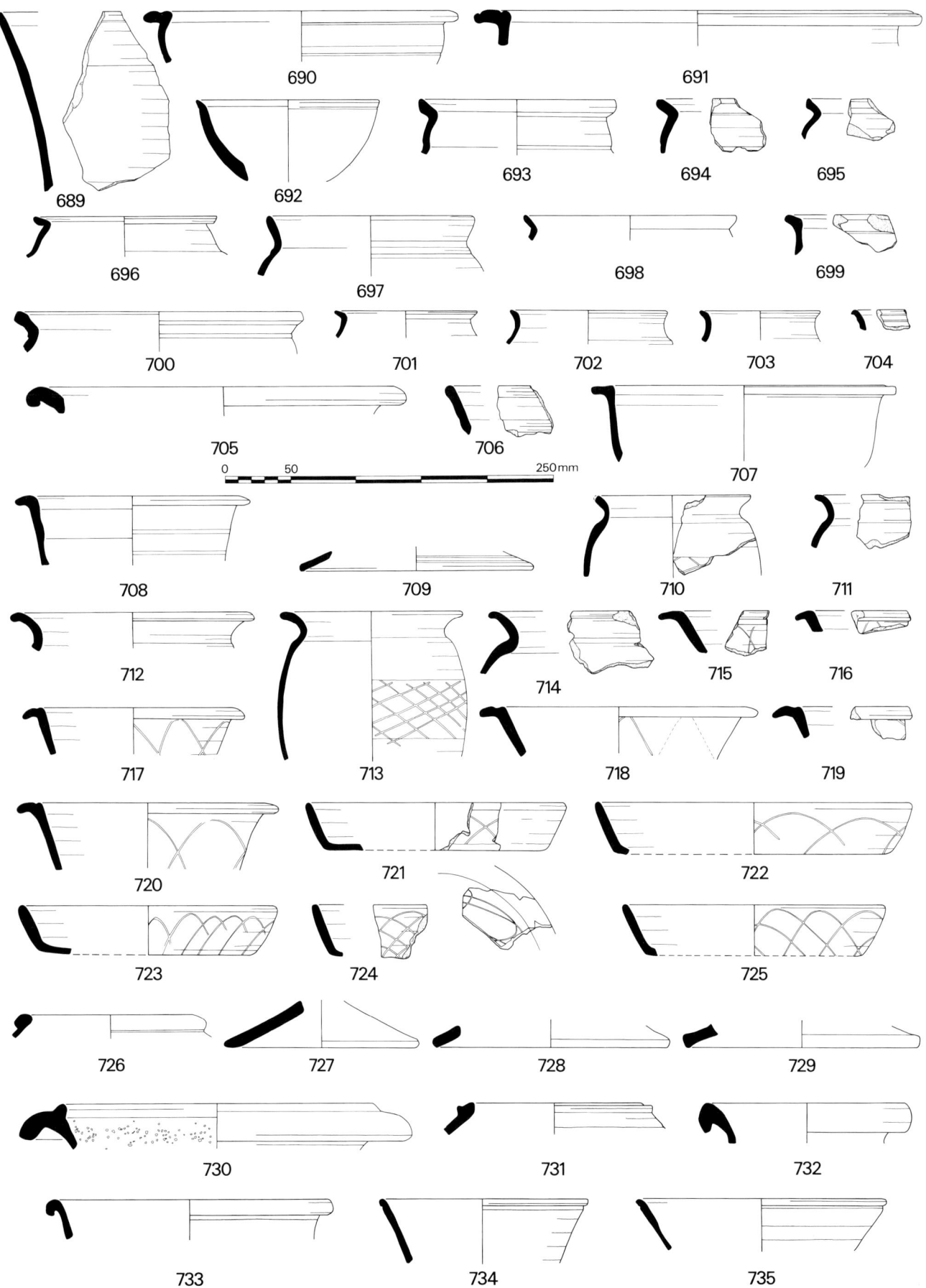

Figure 146   Roman pottery (AES 76–7), nos 689–735, period 9

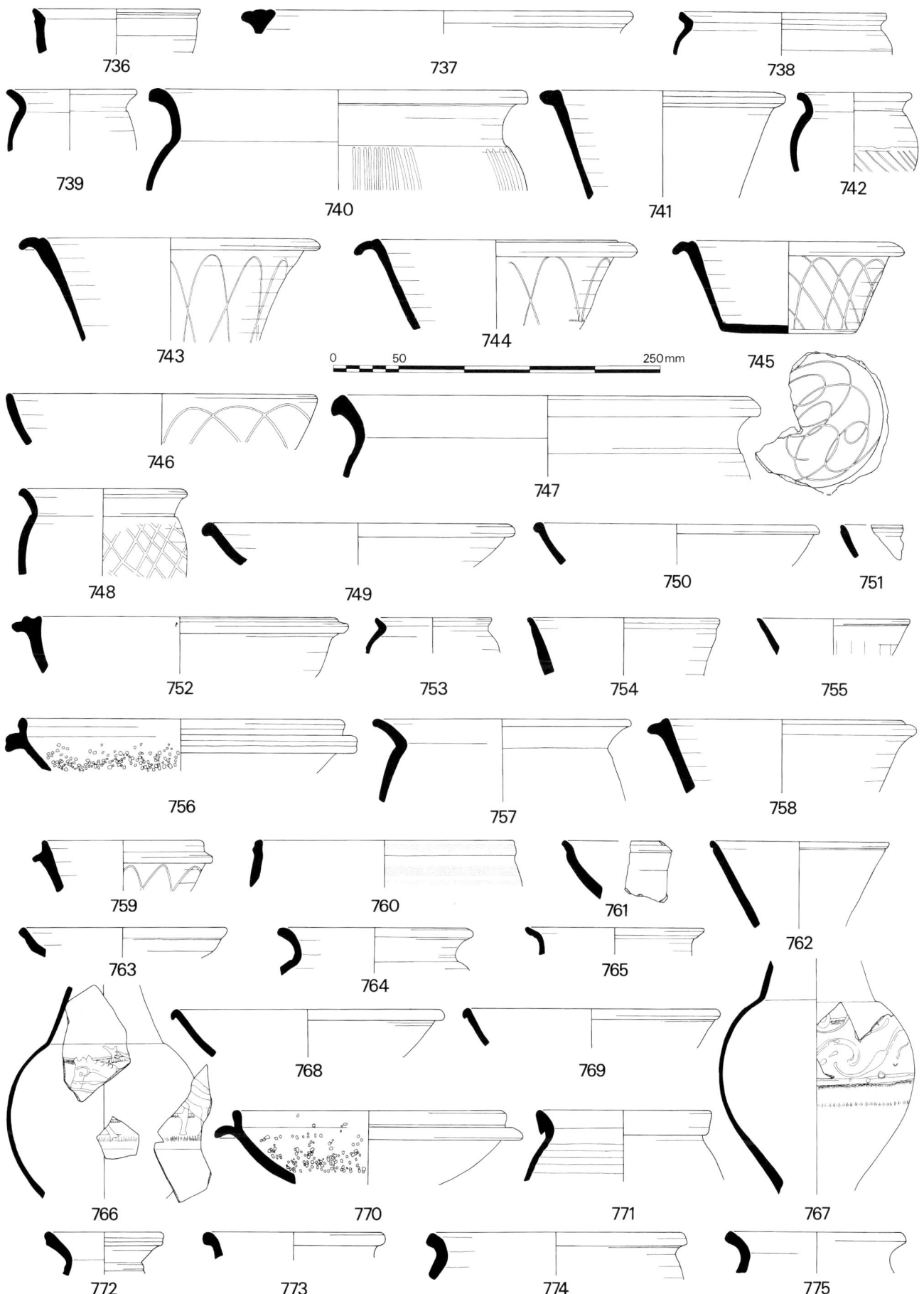

Figure 147 Roman pottery (AES 76–7), nos 736–746, period 9, and nos 747–775, period 10

Explosion site finds (AES 76-7)

Severn Valley and Black-Burnished wares were the most important fabric types. There was some survival of samian, local reduced fabrics (eg nos 651–53 from (86)), and Malvernian material (nos 673 and 675). Some local variation could be observed in this group in that 4th-century Black-Burnished ware types were concentrated in (86) (nos 664–68), whilst (II 10) contained a good group of 3rd-century examples (nos 715–720). It was also noticeable that most of the reduced wares in (II 10) were probably residual in a late 3rd- to 4th-century context.

Period 10 AD 340/350-?400+ (3238 sherds, 13.1%; 51.20 EVEs, 15.1%)

Illustrated vessels 747–915: 747–748, (88); 749, (6); 750, (28); 751–753, (II 8); 754, (II 9); 755, (II 5); 756–759, (II 7); 760, (II 15); 761–765, (15); 766–784, (2); 785–787, (26); 788–790, (91); 791, (111); 792–794, (64); 795–801, (75); 802–813, (87); 814–820, (104); 821–827, (24A); 828–831, (24); 832–838, (122); 839–840, (223); 841–857, (49); 858–866, (78); 867–868, (170A); 869, (118); 870–874, (142); 875–915, (4) (Figs 147–151)

Catalogue: 747, O24; 748, R40; 749, F51; 750, O20; 751, Q16; 752, O24; 753, R30; 754, O25; 755, O27; 756, M23; 757–759, B11; 760, W15; 761, O20; 762, O25; 763, O21; 764, R40; 765, R30; 766–769, F51; 770, M43; 771, W13; 772, O23; 773, O24; 774, O24; 775, R40; 776, R01; 777, R01; 778, R30; 779, R01; 780, R30; 781, R30; 782–783, B11; 784, C11; 785, O27; 786, R40; 787, B11; 788, M22; 789, W11; 790, R40; 791, B11; 792, O24; 793, B11; 794, G44; 795, F51; 796, M23; 797, O24; 798, O21; 799, O24; 800, R01; 801, R01; 802, F52; 803, F51; 804, F52; 805, F52; 806, F51; 807, O24; 808, O25; 809, O25; 810, O24; 811, R01; 812, R40; 813, R40; 814, F51; 815, O24; 816, O24; 817, ?R80; 818, O23; 819, R01; 820, B11; 821–822, O23; 823, O24; 824–826, B11; 827, C11; 828, F52; 829, O24; 830, B11; 831, C11; 832, M13; 833, O21; 834, O25; 835, R30; 836, R30; 837, B11; 838, B11; 839, O27; 840, R30; 841, M71; 842, M23; 843, W13; 844, O23; 845, O24; 846, O21; 847, O21; 848, R40; 849, R30; 850, R40; 851, R01; 852, R30; 853, R15; 854–857, B11; 858, F51; 859, M23; 860, W13; 861–862, O23; 863, O25; 864, O24; 865–866, C11; 867, O25; 868, B11; 869, R40; 870, Q25; 871, O24; 872, O23; 873, R01; 874, R30; 875–880, F51; 881, M71; 882, M23; 883, W17; 884, O23; 885, O22; 886, O23; 887, O21; 888, O27; 889, O24; 890, O27; 891, R40; 892, R01; 893, R30; 894, R30; 895, R40; 896, R30; 897, R01; 898, R30; 899–908, B11; 909–913, C11; 914–915, G44

The figures for this period include those from contexts assigned to a later subphase (period 10A).

The range of fabrics present in this period was as diverse as in period 9 whilst the element of residual material seems to have been slightly reduced. Black-Burnished ware and Severn Valley wares were still the most important fabric types (30.7% and 27.6% respectively). The other major coarse ware group, the local grey wares, represented a higher proportion of the assemblage (19.0%) than previously. This seems to result from a new impetus in the local industries as they produced imitations of 4th-century Black-Burnished ware forms and vessel types such as those manufactured at Wappenbury (Stanley and Stanley 1964) during the late 3rd- to 4th centuries.

Another major component of the later 4th-century assemblage was colour-coated wares, which increased considerably in importance in this period. Oxfordshire and Nene Valley colour-coated fabrics (6.8% and 2.9% respectively) were the most significant of these fabrics. Several other of the Oxfordshire products (white, parchment and white-coated wares) continued to occur as in earlier periods and 'burnt white ware' appeared for the first time. Shell-gritted fabrics now amounted to 2.4% and a further element of the 4th-century assemblage was pink grogged ware. Although never present in large quantities this fabric was a constant element in groups of this period throughout Alcester and at most other Warwickshire sites. Rhenish ware, New Forest ware, and other unattributed colour-coated fabrics continued to be present in very small amounts. Amongst those fabrics which must have been residual or redeposited in this period the most important were the Malvernian material (0.8%) and the *amphorae* fabrics (Rhodian *amphorae*: 0.6%; Gaulish *amphorae*: 0.6%; Spanish *amphorae*: 0.5%). Quantities of *amphorae* were nearly three times greater than in period 9. Other residual fabrics included locally made oxidised wares, some white-slipped flagon fabrics, Verulamium region wares, a possible Italian *mortarium* fabric, and sherds from Hadrianic roughcast beakers.

Building V (illustrated vessels nos 747–750)

The only deposit to yield much pottery from the last phase of building V was the destruction layer (6). Even this was a very small group (55 sherds) consisting mainly of Black-Burnished ware with some Severn Valley and reduced wares, Oxfordshire (no 749) and Nene Valley colour-coated fabrics, and a large sherd from a Rhodian *amphora*. Most of the material from the other contexts, including that from the robber trench (88) (nos 747–48) seems to have been redeposited from the occupation of building V. No 750, from layer (28), appears to have been a Severn Valley ware imitation of the Oxfordshire version of Dr 31.

Building VI/VIA (illustrated vessels nos 751–760)

There was very little pottery from this building, perhaps because relatively little of the building itself was excavated. The group of material was different from other period 10 assemblages in that it was largely made up of Severn Valley wares and local reduced fabrics with some Oxfordshire and Nene Valley colour-coated wares but with very little Black-Burnished ware. Within the building the overall character of the assemblage was 2nd- to early 3rd century rather than late 4th century suggesting, perhaps, that activity in this area of the site at this time was not domestic and that most of the pottery assemblage derived from the earlier use of the area. The group from the robber trench (II 7), however, (nos 756–59) was clearly of later 4th-century character and no 760, one of relatively few parchment ware vessels from the site, from a posthole adjacent to the building, was probably of similar date.

Yard area and building III (illustrated vessels nos 788–820)

Most of the pottery from and adjacent to building III was found in the rubble deposits (64)/(77), (75), (38), (104), and (87). Of these (87) yielded the largest group (396 sherds). The assemblages from (87) (nos 802–813) and (104) (nos 814–820) were the only two in this group which contained material which could be conclusively dated to the last half of the 4th century. The group from (87) consisted mainly of Black-Burnished ware and Severn Valley wares with some reduced fabrics, shell-gritted ware, Mancetter-Hartshill white ware (including *mortaria*), Oxfordshire colour-coated (nos 803–806), white and parchment wares, and Nene Valley colour-coated fabric. Particularly noticeable in the group was the high proportion of 4th-century Black-Burnished ware bowls (none illustrated) which were not found in other building III deposits (apart from the single sherd no 791 in post-hole (111)) and the presence of late 4th-century types amongst the Oxfordshire colour-coated wares (eg no 805) (Young's type C38 dated c AD 340–400). Other Oxfordshire wares, including the beaker no 795, were found in the layers associated with building III. These layers also produced a late Mancetter-Hartshill *mortarium* no 788.

The characteristic of the group from the rubble spread (104) which identified it as a later 4th-century assemblage was the importance of the Oxfordshire colour-coated fabric (eg no 814). Within the area of Alcester's defences (Ferguson, in Cracknell 1996) this fabric was of particular importance at the end of the Roman period. This importance is reflected at the Explosion site in the survival of large quantities of such pottery in immediately post-Roman assemblages (see layer (12) below). The remainder of the pottery in period 10 seems to have been material brought in to the site with the rubble used to build up the platforms for the late timber buildings.

Late pits (illustrated vessels nos 821–915)

Each of the pits which were grouped in the western area of the site in period 10 contained an amount of pottery roughly proportionate to its size. Of these the group from (4) (nos 875–915) was the largest with 648 sherds. Complete vessels nos 900 and 908 were found at the very bottom of pit (4), indicating a mid-4th-century or later date for the earliest stage of the backfilling. The assemblage contained an element of early material such as grey ware rusticated jars and the Malvernian storage jars, nos 914 and 915 which may have derived from the excavation of the pit through earlier deposits. The bulk of the material was contemporary, however, such as Black-Burnished ware bowls nos 903 and 904, shell-gritted ware jars nos 911–913 and the Oxfordshire colour-coated vessel no 880 (type C85 dated after AD 350 (Young 1977, 170) among a good range of Oxfordshire types (nos 875–881). Vessels 891 and 892 are reminiscent of the more elaborate grey ware types manufactured at Wappenbury in the late 3rd and 4th centuries and 897 and 898 were typical of the use of reduced fabrics for flanged bowls as well as jars.

The assemblage from pit (49) (nos 841–857) was very similar in that it contained early material such as the carinated bowl no 853, but examples of very late types, such as Black-Burnished ware cooking pots 854 and 855 and Oxfordshire *mortarium* no 841 dated after AD 350 (Young 1977, 172) were also present. Vessel no 843 was perhaps an Oxfordshire flanged bowl from which the flange had broken off, the pot being 'repaired' by the sanding down of the broken flange to a smooth surface flush with the rest of the pot. Pit (78) (nos 858–866) appeared to be paired with (49) and the group of pottery it contained was very much the same. The only noteworthy vessel, a complete shell-gritted jar no 866, was found at the base of this pit.

The three closely grouped pits (168), (24) (nos 821–831), and (122) (nos 832–838) also contained similar material, as did the two possible latrine pits (170A) (nos 867–868) and (142) (nos 870–874), from which, however, smaller groups were recovered. Amongst them (24) produced characteristic late Black-Burnished ware types (eg nos 824–826). Pit (122) was distinguished by the presence of a large number of sherds from a Gaulish Pélichet 47 *amphora*. The increase in the importance of *amphorae* in this period and the appearance of large sherds from several Rhodian *amphorae* scattered throughout these pits and the rubble platforms on the eastern half of the site might indicate that the fill of the pits and the rubble itself derived from the same source. The Rhodian *amphorae* do not occur in large numbers until period 10 (three sherds are known from period 9) when they must have been redeposited. It may be that the redeposited material in period 10 came from a different source from that in earlier periods.

Period 10A

Building II and surface (2) (illustrated vessels nos 766–787)

The main group of material from building II (26) (nos 785–787) was small but contained the standard range of fabrics found in this period. The group from the possibly related gravel surface (2) (nos 766–784), however, was more distinctive. This may have been one of the latest features on the site, and the pottery had what appear to have been some

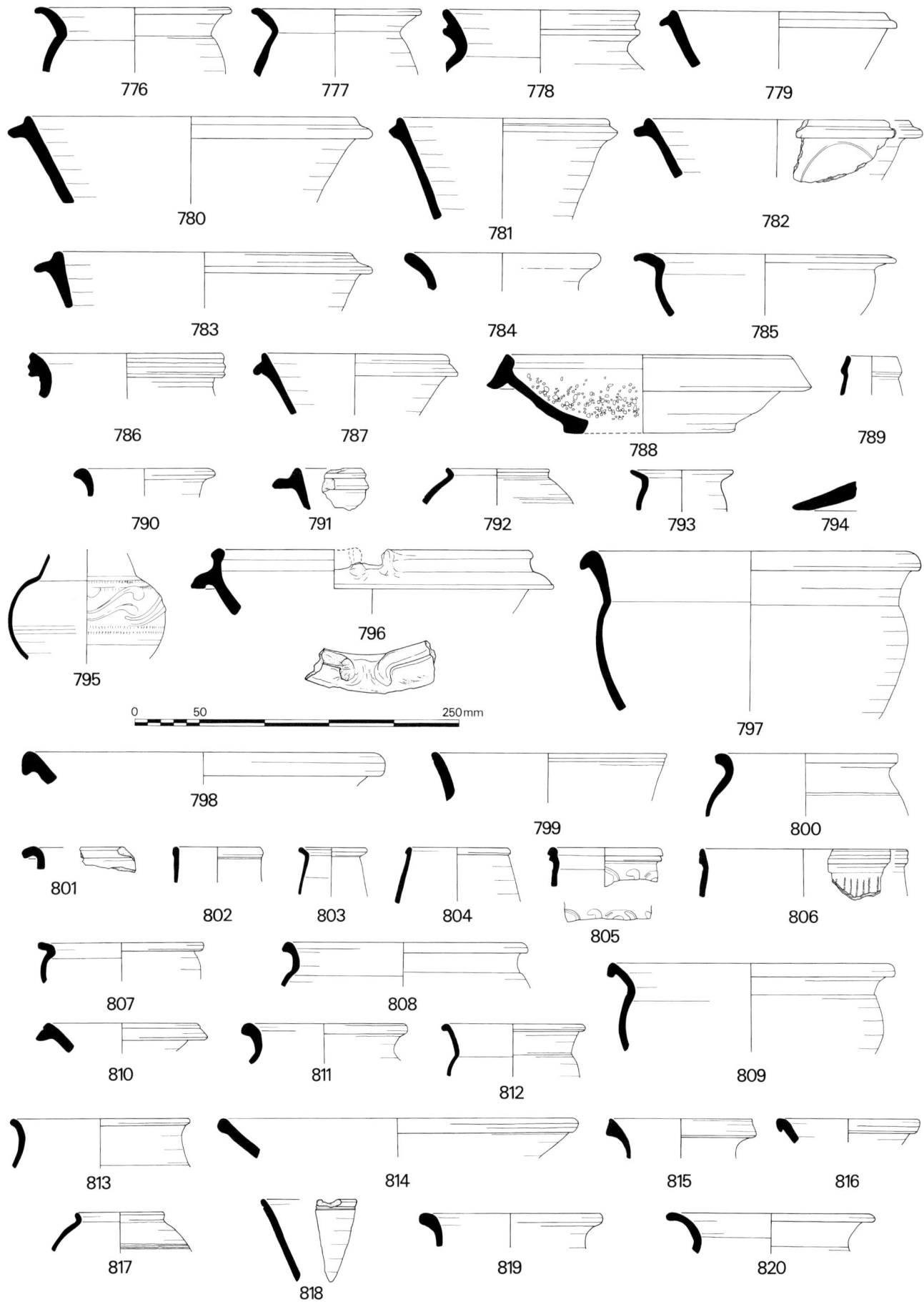

Explosion site finds (AES 76-7)

Figure 148 Roman pottery (AES 76–7), nos 776–820, period 10

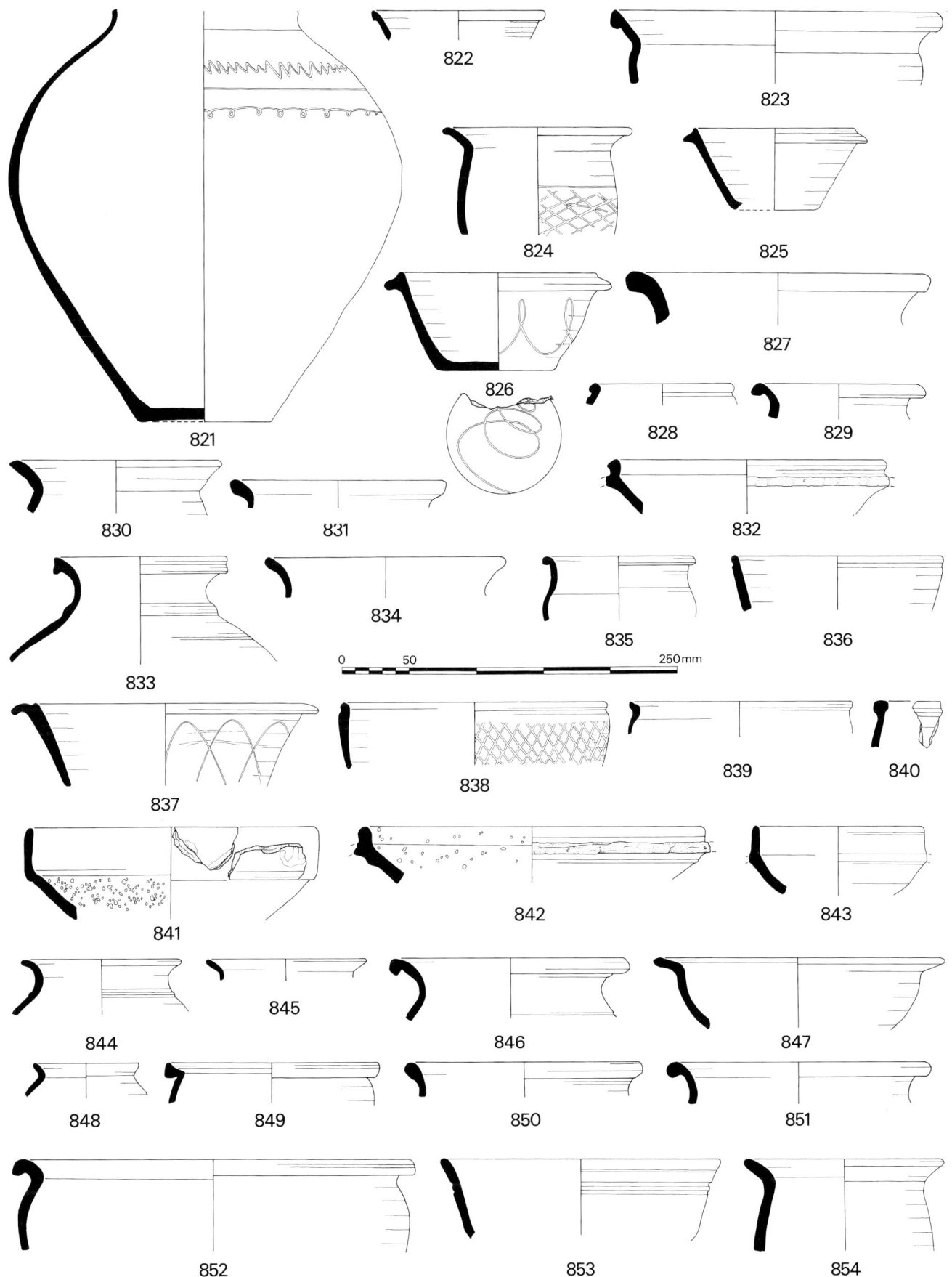

Figure 149   Roman pottery (AES 76–7), nos 821–854, period 10

Explosion site finds (AES 76-7)

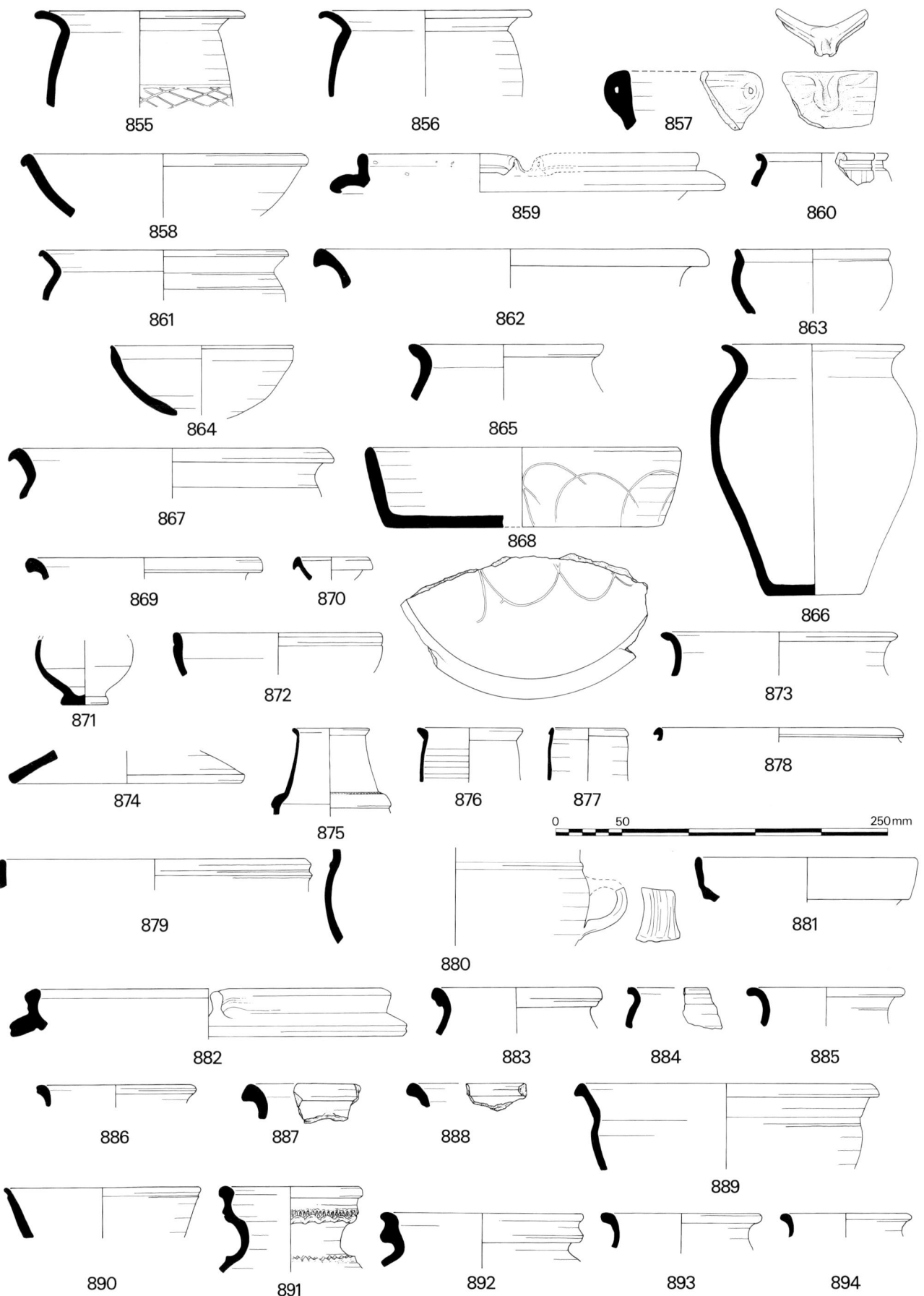

Figure 150   Roman pottery (AES 76–7), nos 855–894, period 10

Explosion site finds (AES 76-7)

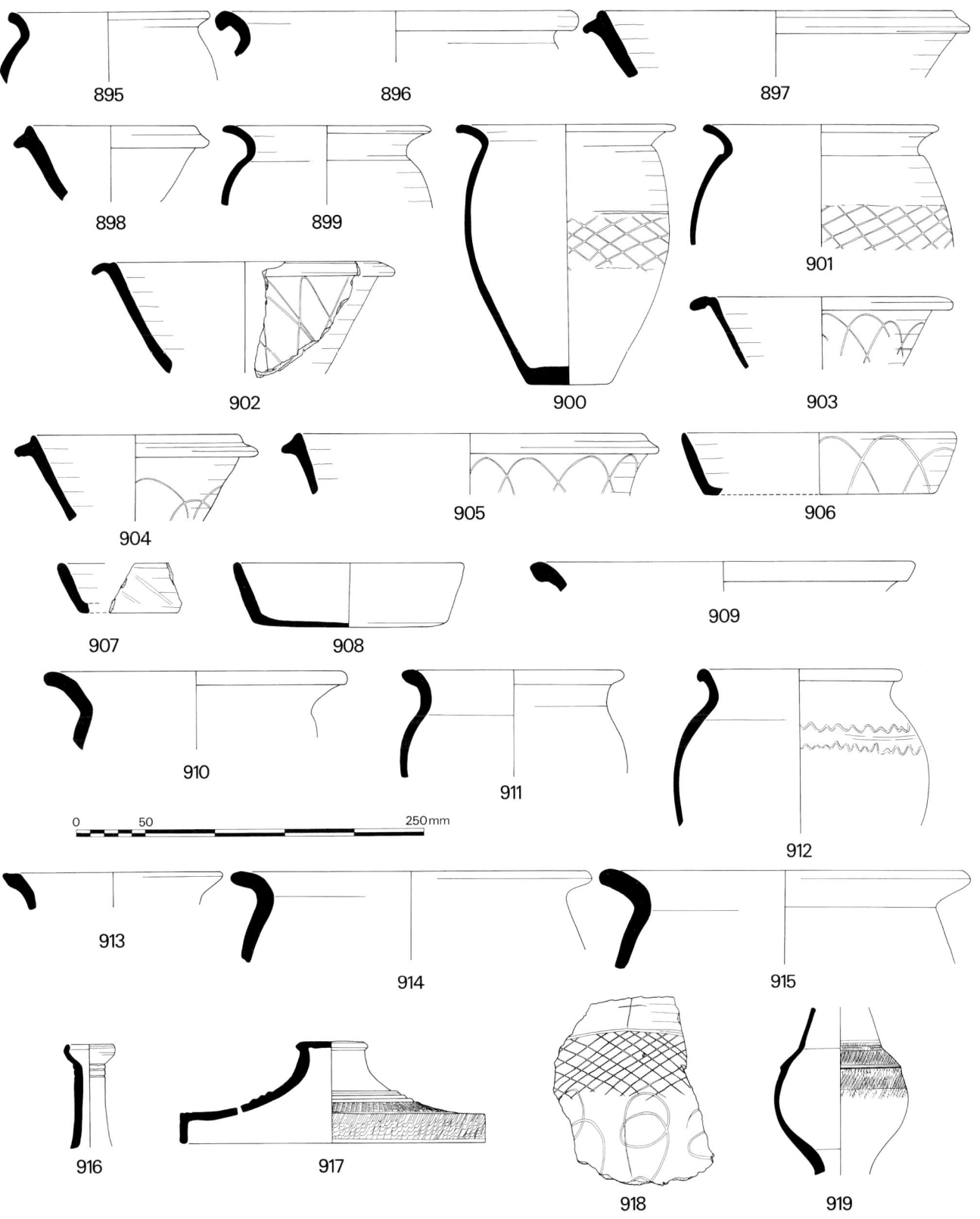

Figure 151   Roman pottery (AES 76–7), nos 895–915, period 10, and nos 916–919, post-Roman

231

Explosion site finds (AES 76-7)

very late characteristics. These included the presence of a relatively high proportion of shell-tempered wares and a high representation of late grey wares, consisting of not only of flanged bowls (eg nos 779–781) and a jar with a double lipped rim (no 778), but also of 'cooking pot types' (nos 776–777) which may have begun to replace Black-Burnished ware examples. Though this type did still occur in Black-Burnished ware most of the examples were small (and perhaps residual) sherds. Flanged bowls were still found in this fabric, however (eg nos 782–783). The most notable feature amongst the fine wares (both Oxfordshire and Nene Valley sherds occurred) was the presence of barbotine decorated beakers (766 and 767). There was some doubt that these vessels were Oxfordshire products, since neither the fabric nor colour-coat was exactly typical, but the sherds had so many similarities with Oxfordshire products that they were grouped with them in the absence of compelling evidence to the contrary. Vessels in a very similar fabric occurred elsewhere in this phase and later (nos 795 and 919). All were consistent in their use of rouletted and/or barbotine decoration. The most distinctive was no 766, which appeared to depict a mounted warrior or huntsman, if, as seems likely, the piece of barbotine above the horse's head is to be interpreted as a spear. Sherds of both 766 and 767 were also found in post-Roman contexts. Other Oxfordshire products included colour-coated and white-slipped *mortaria* (no 770 was a good example of the latter) and Burnt white ware (eg no 771).

Roman pottery from post-Roman contexts (periods 11–14)

Large quantities of Roman pottery are found in medieval and later groups throughout Alcester. At the Explosion site it seems likely that a layer forming in the late Roman period (12) continued in use during the medieval period. This may well also be an explanation for the large groups of Roman material in post-Roman contexts from other sites in the town, such as on the south-west corner of the defences (Ferguson, in Cracknell 1996). These groups all have a very similar character which must reflect pottery assemblages in the last quarter of the 4th century and perhaps the early 5th. Their most striking characteristic is the very high representation of Oxfordshire products, especially the colour-coated fabric (F51), which varies from between about 9%–13% of the assemblage. This continues the trend begun in period 10 at the Explosion site when F51 increased from about 1% to almost 7%.

The other major components of these very late groups were Black-Burnished ware, Severn Valley wares, Nene Valley colour-coated ware, shell-gritted ware, pink grogged ware (fabric G11), and slightly increased quantities of local grey wares.

Post-Roman periods (5376 sherds, 21.8%; 79.07 EVEs, 23.3%)

Illustrated vessels: period 11 – 916–918: 916, (29); 917–918, (12); period 14 – 919, (1) (Fig 151)
   Catalogue: 916, O20; 917, F52; 918, B11; 919, F51

Numbers 916–919 illustrate selected unusual vessels which occurred in post-Roman contexts. These included a further beaker in the late Roman, possibly Oxfordshire group discussed above (no 919). No 918, in Black-Burnished ware, was an unusual example of the use of a decorative technique, usually found on bowls and dishes, on the side of a jar below the standard lattice decoration. This piece also carries a graffito + on the shoulder. No 916 was an uncommon flask/flagon form in Severn Valley ware.

Medieval pottery (AES 76–7)
Stephanie Ratkai

The full description and interpretation of the medieval pottery can be found in microfiche M2:D7–D12. Fig 152 shows the distribution of medieval pottery fabrics in stratified contexts in periods 11 and 12 (for fabric descriptions, see Table MT13 (microfiche M2:D11)

Illustrated medieval pottery vessels (Fig 153)

1 Fabric 32, twisted handle, light green glaze. (1)
2 Fabric 32, cooking pot/jar. (1)
3 Fabric 32, lamp base. (1)
4 Fabric 1, cooking pot/jar. (II 14A)
5 Fabric 1, strap handle, patchy light green glaze. (1)
6 Fabric 1, cooking pot/jar. (1)
7 Fabric 1, cooking pot, distorted rim, interior and exterior sooting. Drilled hole in body. (II 13)
8 Fabric 1, cooking pot/jar. (II 30)
9 Fabric 1, cooking pot/jar. (3)
10 Fabric 1, cooking pot/jar. (II 12)
11 Fabric 34, jug with corrugated neck, exterior dark green patchy glaze. (II 14)
12 Fabric 35, cooking pot, exterior sooting. (II 11)
13 Fabric 112, jug with vertical lines of white slip, exterior olive glaze. (II 12)
14 Fabric 104, Boarstall-Brill jug with vertical bands of iron rich slip and thinner lines of self slip, olive green glaze. (II 14)

Copper alloy (AES 76–7)
Glenys Lloyd-Morgan

Although bracelets are well represented amongst the copper alloy finds, as they are also amongst the bone, jet, and shale finds, it is curious to note that only two brooches have been identified. The late 3rd-century crossbow type links up well with the strong bias towards personal items of the later Roman period. Toilet items, such as the tweezers and the less common form of nail cleaner no 26, can be paralleled from Alcester and other sites in the

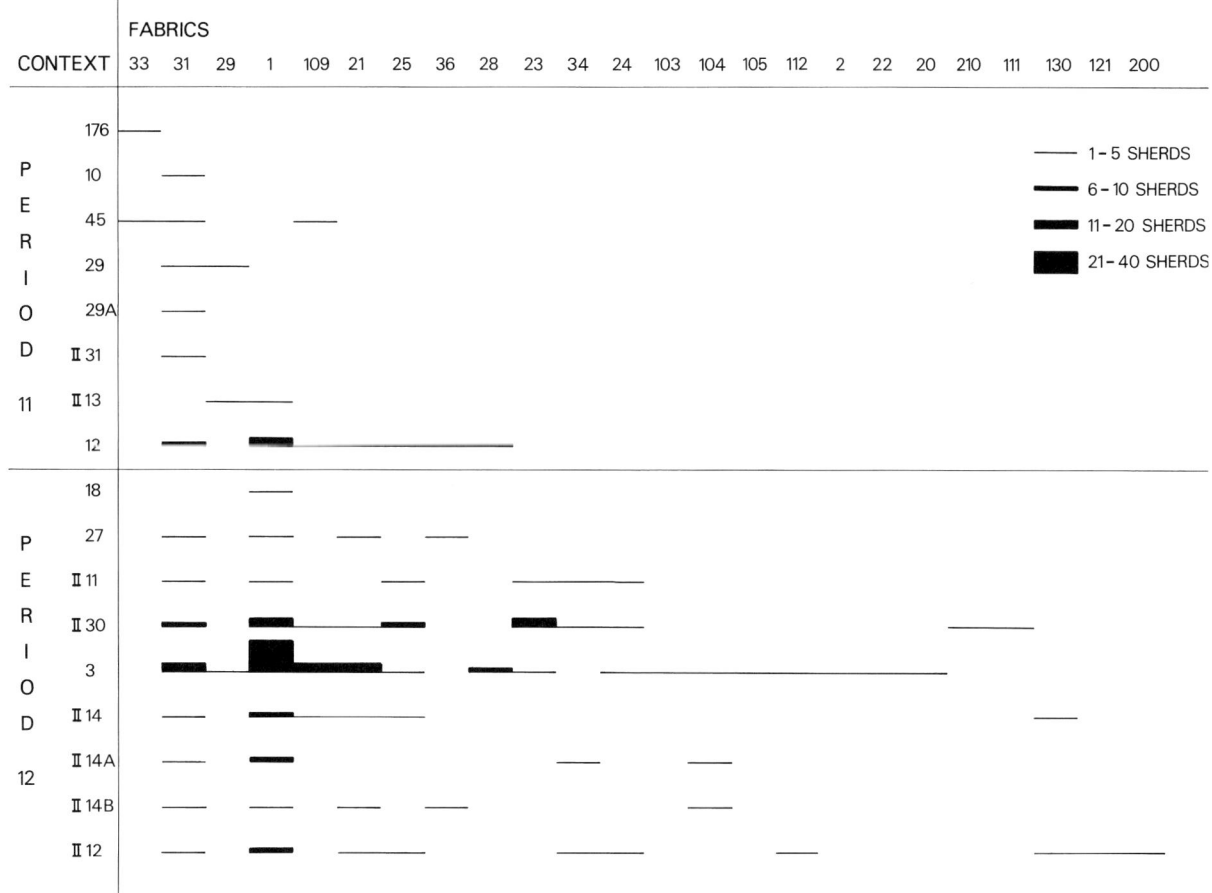

Figure 152 Medieval pottery fabrics in stratified contexts (AES 76–7)

region, but the find of two mirror fragments, nos 20 and 21, is noteworthy. Both are dated to the 1st century AD and can be classed with the other luxury items which, however fragmentary, are beginning to show just how prosperous sections of the local community were. To some extent this can be attributed to the military presence in Alcester during the early years of the Roman period. This is attested by the two pieces, nos 43 and 44, as well as the decayed pendant no 45. The fish hook, no 33, is another find which should help to throw some light on one aspect of the local economy of the Roman period, however small scale.

It is greatly regretted that it was not possible for further conservation to be done on the finds, not only in the interests of preserving the more significant representative objects, but also to confirm the identification and closely date more of the items than has hitherto been possible.

Illustrated copper alloy (Figs 154–156)

A full catalogue of all copper alloy can be found in microfiche M2:D13–E6.

1 Polden Hill type *fibula*, the head and upper section of the bow only have survived with the spring, chord, and much of the pin which are still *in situ*. The upper part of the bow is decorated with a regular, deeply incised herring bone pattern. Present length 24mm. An identical piece, complete but for the spring and pin, was found during excavations at Brown's Basement, Eastgate Street, Chester 1960. The site is unpublished apart from a brief notice in *J Chester Archaeol Soc* 48 (1961), where brooches are referred to in passing. Compare also the related *fibula* from Tiddington (M10) which has a broader spaced and heavier raised herringbone pattern down the bow. (SF 384, 130B, period 8)

2 *Fibula* of the early crossbow type with slight knobs at either end of crossbar, and a more pronounced knob projecting from the head of the steeply arched bow just above the cross bar. The bow is roughly hexagonal in cross-section with slight mouldings just above the elongated foot. The hinged pin is lost. Length c 57mm. Compare the examples from Richborough (Bushe-Fox 1928, 34–4, plate XVII no 15); Verulamium where one example comes from a context dated AD 280–360 (Frere 1984, 29–30, Fig 9, no 54, compare also Fig 9, no 53, unstratified); and Dover, the context being dated probably AD 210–270 (Philp 1981, 153, Fig 33, no 82). Another example in the collection of the Musee Denon at Chalon-sur-Saone is dated by Feugère to the end of the 3rd century (1977, 126, plate 18, no 106). (SF 132, 12, period 11)

3 Fragment of a bracelet with rectangular cross-section, the outer, narrow edge has a notched 'cog wheel' pattern in profile. Corroded. Length 85mm. Compare the similar pieces from Nettleton, Wilts (Wedlake 1982, 212, 214, Fig 90, no 11) and Coventina's Well on Hadrian's Wall (Allason-Jones and McKay 1985, 28, no 64 and Fig on p 27). (SF 95, 1, period 14)

4 Two fragments of bracelet, with narrow rectangular cross-section and notched decoration on each angle of the narrow face to give a neat zigzag type of decoration. Corroded. Length 28mm and 29mm. Two parallel examples have been reported from the Lankhills cemetery, Winchester dated AD 350–370 and AD 310–350/370 respectively (Clarke 1979, 306, no 141, Fig 37 and Fig 75,

Explosion site finds (AES 76-7)

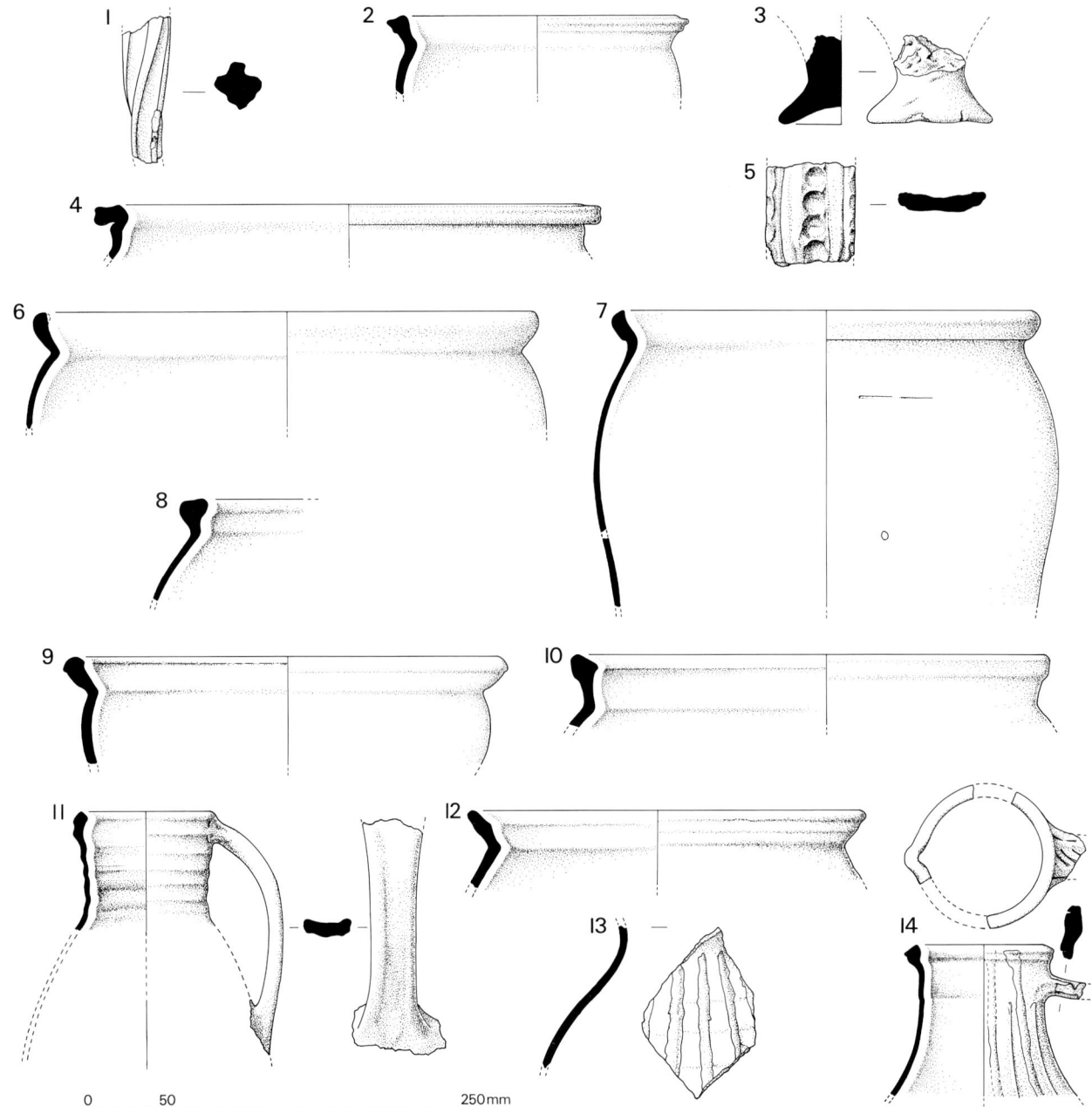

Figure 153 *Medieval pottery (AES 76–7), nos 1–14*

Grave 117; p 306, no 196, Fig 78, Grave 155). Other examples have been reported from Gestingthorpe, Essex (Draper 1985, 29, Fig 10, no 37) and South Shields (Allason-Jones and Miket 1984, 130, nos 3.233, 3.233, 3.234, 3.235 Fig on p 129). (SF 276, 87, period 10)

5 Fragment of bracelet with rectangular cross-section, similar to nos 3 and 4 above, but with no traces of decoration visible on the narrow outer face. Corroded. Length *c* 60mm. (SF 128, 12, period 11)

6 Heavily corroded ring shaped in three adjoining fragments, with originally a rectangular cross-section, possibly from a bracelet similar to the example above. Length *c* 63mm. (SF 141, 4, period 10)

7 Curved strip, which might have been part of a bracelet as above, but too decayed for secure identification. Length 37mm. Max cross-section *c* 1mm × 3mm. (SF 319, 86, period 9)

8 Wire with remains of two fine loops wound round it, possibly part of a bracelet with sliding knot fastening. Length 57mm. Max cross-section 1.5mm. Compare the example from Woodeaton, Oxon. (Kirk 1949, 20, no 17, Fig 5, no 1). (SF 443, II 10, period 9)

9 Bracelet made of three fine wires twisted together, two fragments only. Length 32mm and 19mm. Cross-section *c* 2mm. Compare the pieces from Woodeaton, Oxon. (Kirk 1949, 20, nos 18–22, Fig 4, no 13); and two from a late 4th-century context at Shakenoak (Brodribb *et al* 1968, 88, Fig 30, nos 25 and 26). Other examples from Warwickshire include Coleshill GH78, SF 90; GH 79 SF 558 and Tiddington TD81, SF 498, 719, 971. (SF 107, 1, period 14)

13 Curved wire with rounded cross-section, flattening out into a loop. Length 49mm, maximum cross-section 16mm × 2.5mm. Possibly the loop fastening and part of hoop of a simple wire bracelet (as Allason-Jones and Miket 1984, 128, no 3.224, Fig on p 127); or a fragment of a small toilet implement from a chatelaine? (SF 549, 4, period 10)

14 Crude ring, rather encrusted. Diameter 22mm, depth 3.4mm. (SF 452, 227, period 6)

16 Ring fragment or fitting. Diameter 22.5mm, depth 2.3mm. (SF 16, 1, period 14)

17 Pin with faceted cuboid head, shaft bent but otherwise com-

Explosion site finds (AES 76-7)

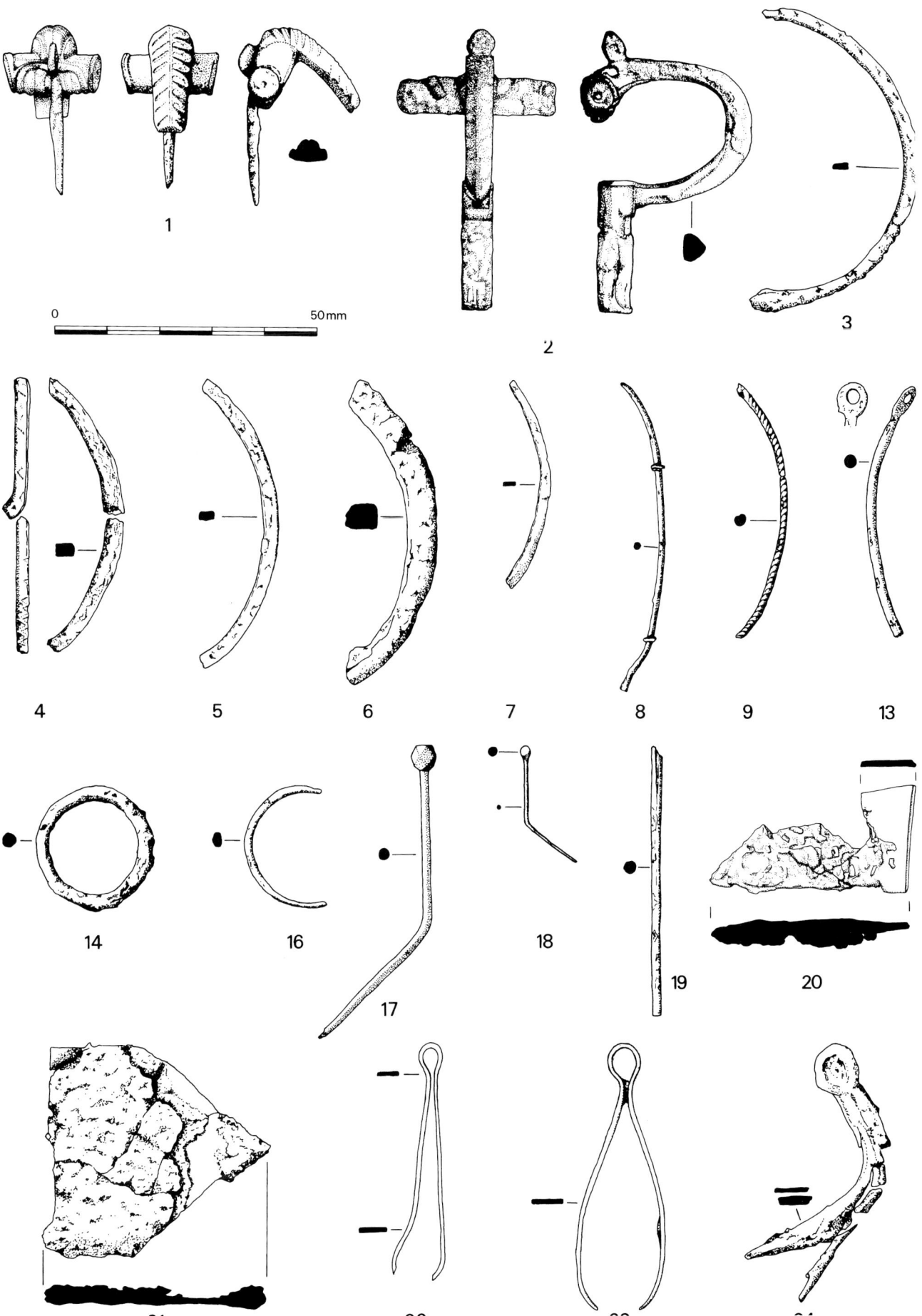

Figure 154   Copper alloy (AES 76–7), nos 1–24

Explosion site finds (AES 76-7)

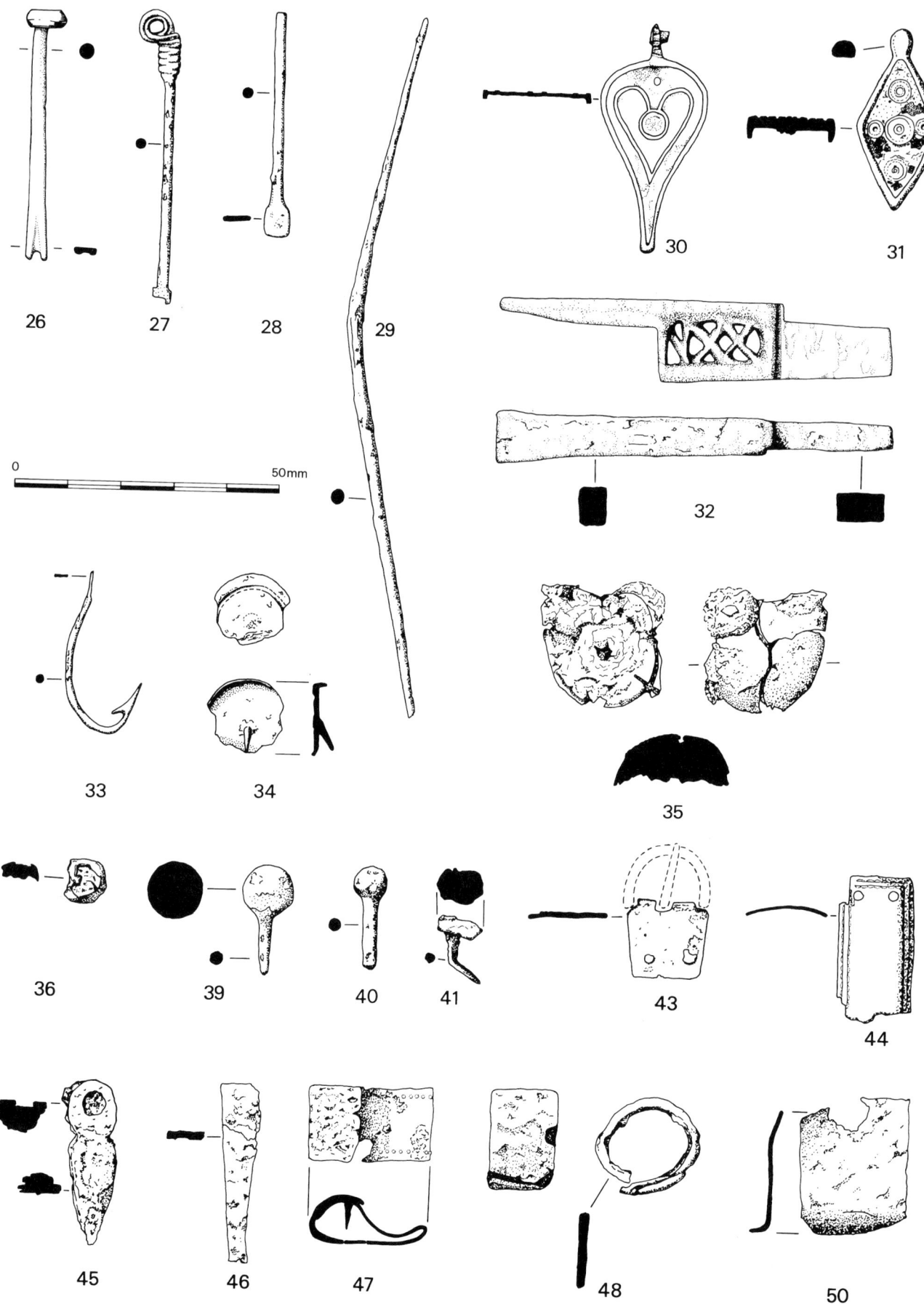

Figure 155   Copper alloy (AES 76–7), nos 26–50

plete. Length 63mm, cross-section of head 3.8mm × 3.8mm. One example from Verulamium comes from a context dated AD 360–370, whilst a second piece was found in a context dated 2nd–3rd century AD (Frere 1984, 43, fig 16, nos 131 and 132 respectively), another from Colchester came from a medieval robber trench (Crummy 1983, 29, no 487, fig 29). Compare also the bone pins AES 76–7 SF 2 and SF 53 of Crummy type 4 dated c 250 to late 4th/early 5th century; and the jet pin no 188 below with the same type of head. (SF 83, 1, period 14)

18 Dress-maker's pin, with head made of fine wire wound round the shaft. Length 27mm. Compare the examples from Southampton found in medieval contexts (Platt and Coleman-Smith 1975, 258, no 170, Fig 241, context dated AD 1375–1425; p 264, nos 1832–1837, Fig 244, context dated AD 1550–1650); and the piece from Tiddington TR82, SF 151. (SF 513, II 17, period 7)

19 Fragment of ?needle broken just below eye, tip lost. Length 53.7mm. (SF 487, 168, period 10)

20 Rectangular mirror fragment with part of edge bevelled to reflecting side. The presence of the straight edge identifies the type. In three adjoining fragments. 22.5mm × 22.5mm, thickness 1.3mm. Further fragment 14mm × 15mm. Compare Lloyd-Morgan Group A, rectangular mirrors (1981a, 3–20) for a brief discussion of this 1st-century type. Note also the near complete rectangular mirror with a large fragment of wooden backing plate from excavation at Towcester, with further parallels (Lloyd-Morgan, in Brown and Woodfield 1983, 106, 108, Fig 38, no 44). (SF 650A, 279, period 2)

21 Internal fragment of a mirror, possibly a rectangular or simple disc type, but with no remains of the edging which would identify the shape. One side retains traces of the finished reflecting surface, the other is pocked and unfinished. 41mm × 39mm, thickness 0.8mm. Lloyd-Morgan 1981a, 107–8, Group Za fragments, 1st century AD. (SF 450, 227, period 6)

22 Small pair of undecorated tweezers, well preserved. Length 44mm. Originally noted by Booth (1980, Fig 8, no 6). The type is not uncommon on Roman sites and has been reported from Fishbourne (Cunliffe 1971, 110, Fig 42, nos 61, 63, 65, 66); Chilgrove Villa (Down 1979, 151, Fig 45, no 17); Shakenoak (Brodribb et al 1968, 86, Fig 29, no 18 dated late 4th century; Brodribb et al 1971, 108, Fig 46, no 64 dated later 3rd century); and from Coleshill, Warwickshire GH79 SF 527, SF 824; and Tiddington SF M46, M514, M690 + M692 (one piece), TD81 SF 379, 480, 496, and 801. (SF 317, 86, period 9)

23 Undecorated tweezers, corroded but complete, as above. Length 49mm. (SF 274, 12, period 11)

24 Tweezers, bent and decayed, probably undecorated as above. Length c 54mm. (SF 275, 64, period 10)

26 Nail cleaner with small, bone disc-shaped head. Length 46mm, diameter of head 7.8–8.4mm. Compare the examples from Woodeaton (Kirk 1949, 25, no 1, Fig 6, no 5); Nettleton, Wiltshire, said to come from 3rd- to 4th-century levels (Wedlake 1982, 219, Fig 94, nos 8 and 11, also no 7 now lacking the bone disc); Cirencester (Wacher and McWhirr 1982, 103, Fig 30, no 71) and Alcester (see above, ALC 72/2, no 17) An example, unpublished, was found by L P Wenham during excavations at Malton, Yorkshire, 1968–9. (SF 677, 122, period 10)

27 Toilet implement, the upper section of wire coiled around twice to make a suspension loop, and then wound neatly around the shaft. The small spoon-shaped end is broken. Present length 53mm. Compare the piece from Woodeaton, Oxon. (Kirk 1949, 24, no, 2, Fig 6, no 4), and from a 2nd-century context at Caerleon (Zienkiewicz 1986, 183, Fig 60, no 139). (SF 535, 266F, period 1)

28 *Ligula*, with small flat spatulate end, and most of shaft lost. Length 40.7mm. Compare the examples from Gadebridge Park (Neal 1974a, 143, nos 200–3, 206–8, Fig 63); Chichester (Down 1981, 169, no 46, Fig 8.32); and from Coleshill, Warwickshire GH78 SF 66; Tiddington SF M28; SF M672; TD80, SF 37; TR82, SF 135; and Alcester (ALC 69, no 18). (SF 504, II 22, period 9)

29 Shaft from ?toilet implement, bent, incomplete. Length 131mm. (SF 534, 207, period 9)

30 Seal box lid, leaf or drop-shaped, the base is now lost, but part of the hinge and swivel is still *in situ*. Set with enamel in a leaf-shaped design. Length 41.4mm, maximum width 20mm. Originally noted by Booth (1980, Fig 13, no 1). This well known design is recorded from Colchester (Crummy 1983, 104, Fig 106, no 2525); *Segontium*, where it is stated that it came from a context 'not later than AD 230' (Wheeler 1923, 141, Fig 61, no 18), Brancaster, Norfolk (Hinchcliffe and Sparey Green 1985, 213, Fig 90, no 60); and South Shields, where further examples are noted by Allason-Jones and Miket (1984, 152, no 3.374 and fig on p 153). (SF 217, 12, period 11)

31 Diamond-shaped seal box lid, the base and hinge now lost, set with blue enamel in the main field. The smaller panels of enamel in the circular and ring-shaped fields, making three dot-and-circle patterns down the length of the box, and the two smaller dots, one on either side, are now too decayed and discoloured for the original colour to be identified. 33mm × 16.3mm, depth 4.5mm. Originally noted by Booth (1980, Fig 13, no 2). Compare the similar patterned seal box lid from Caerleon found in a context dated c AD 100/110–230 (Zienkiewicz 1986, 186, Fig 61, no 154). (SF 414, II 1, period 14)

32 Lock bolt, complete. 73.4mm × 14.7mm, maximum width 8.3mm. Originally noted by Booth (1980, Fig 9, no 3). Similar examples have been found at the Park St Villa, St Albans (O'Neil 1945, 65, no 13, Fig 8); and Dover (Philp 1981, 173, Fig 45, no 275 from a context no later than the first quarter of the 3rd century, and no 276 from demolition layers dated to after AD 150/155). (SF 483, 247, period 3)

33 Fish hook in one piece, the flattened upper section would have been pierced to take the line. Length 27.7mm. Compare the examples from Chichester (Down 1981, 169, Fig 8.31, no 27); a 5th-century context at Verulamium (Frere 1984, 58, Fig 23, no 214); and from the fortress at Longthorpe, which was occupied between c AD 44/8 and c AD 62 (Frere and St Joseph 1974, 62–3, Fig 32, no 84). (SF 336, 124, period 9)

34 Stud with a flat head and edge turned back, with a single incised concentric circle turned as border decoration just inside the edge. Incomplete. Diameter c 16mm, height c 6.5mm. One example from the legionary baths at Caerleon comes from a context dated earlier than AD 100/110 (Zienkiewicz 1986, 173, Fig 56, no 16); another from the amphitheatre at Chester was unstratified (F H Thompson 1976, 195, Fig 28, no 46). (SF 538, 266, period 1)

35 Hollow dome-headed stud with lead alloy filler, now decayed. The iron pin is now completely decayed and lost. Diameter was c 24mm, height c 8mm. (SF 47, 1, period 14)

36 Stud with hollow domed head; the pin and part of the head are now lost. Diameter 8mm, height 3.5mm. (SF 58, 12, period 11)

39 Pin or nail with heavy sub-spherical head. Diameter of head 10.5mm, height 21.2mm. Compare the related pieces from Caerleon from a context dated c AD 160–230 (Zienkiewicz 1986, 178, Fig 59, nos 80, 83, and 84). (SF 64, 12, period 11)

40 Pin or nail with sub-spherical head, tip lost, as number 39 above. Diameter of head 6.5mm, height 18.5mm. (SF 509, II 22, period 9)

41 Stud or tack with solid, domed head, pin bent. Diameter of head 7mm × 8.4mm, height 14.3mm. (SF 87, 1, period 14)

43 Buckle plate, broken across loops or swivel, with remains of two rivets *in situ*. Undecorated and incomplete, probably from a *lorica segmentata*. Max width 15mm. Present length 14.2mm. Compare the more complete, unstratified piece from Caerleon (Zienkiewicz 1986, 188, Fig 63, no 175). (SF 134, 3, period 12)

44 Rectangular belt plaque, one end lost, with rivet-hole inside each of the surviving corners, and decorated with two parallel lines of incised dashes as a border. Present length 26.4mm, width c 15mm. Compare the better preserved piece from Chichester (Down 1974, 82, Fig 7.5, no 4); and another from the mid-1st-century fort at Woodcock Hall, Norfolk (Brown 1986, 49, Fig 30, no 225). (SF 255, 61, period 5)

45 Small military pendant cut out of sheet metal, now rather corroded. Present length c 29mm. Compare the incomplete piece from Balkerne Lane, Colchester from a late 3rd-century context (Crummy 1983, 165, Fig 204, no 4645). (SF 375, 124A, period 9)

Explosion site finds (AES 76-7)

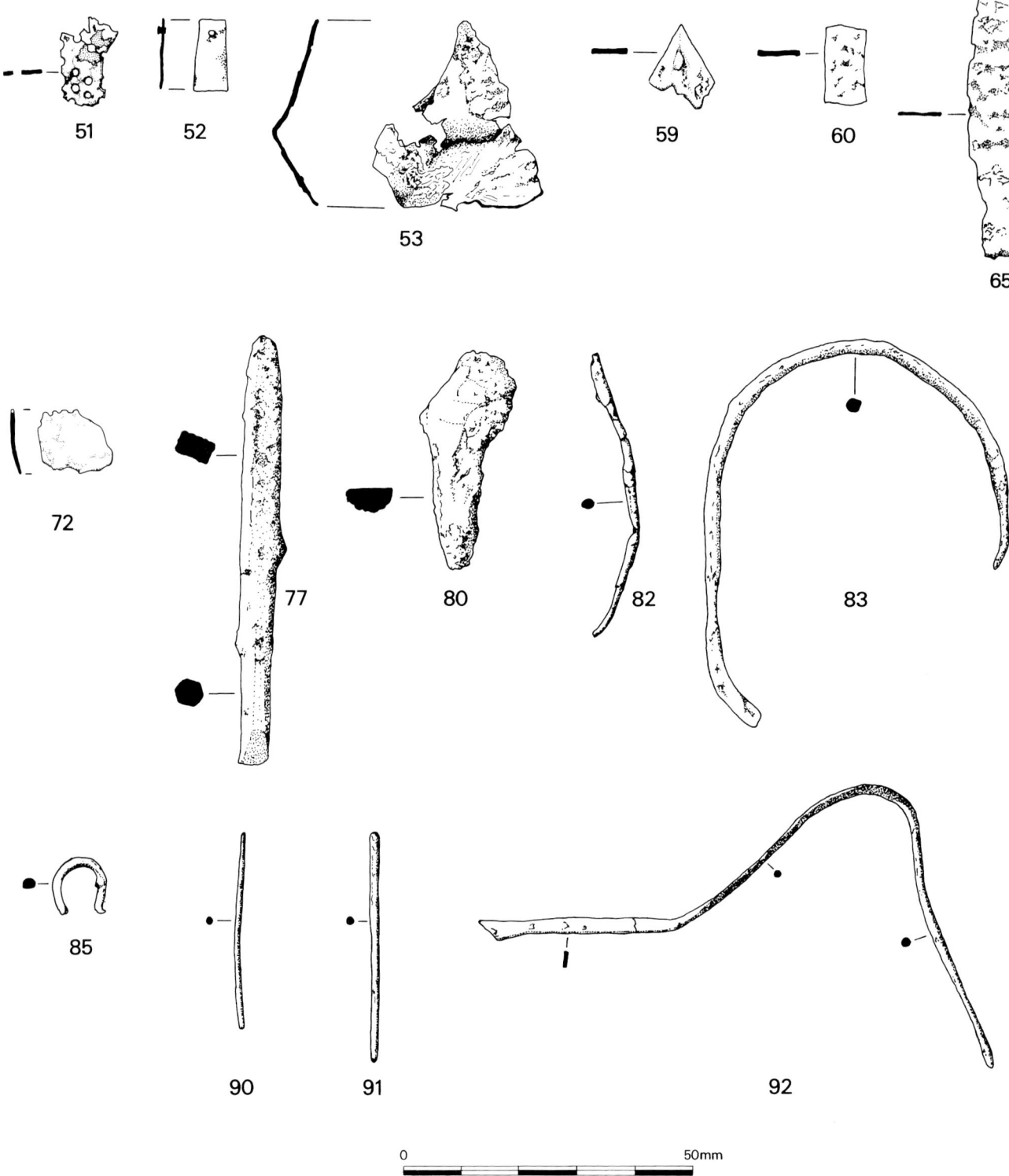

Figure 156 Copper alloy (AES 76–7), nos 51–92

46 Fitting or ?pendant in two adjoining pieces, incomplete and corroded. Length 32.7mm. (SF 442, 227, period 6)
47 Decorative binding strip with fine repousse dots as a border, remains of an iron nail or tack *in situ*. Now rather bent. Width 13mm. Compare the similarly decorated plaques from Nettleton, Wilts (Wedlake 1982, 210, Fig 88, no 37); Nor'nour, Scilly (Dudley 1967, 22, Fig 9, no 29); Coleshill, Warwickshire GH79, SF 215; and Tiddington SF M622. (SF 125, 4, period 10)
48 Crude collar or strip rolled into ring. Height 13mm, diameter 17.5mm × 19mm. (SF 297, 12, period 11)
50 Shield-shaped appliqué or strap end, the hole for attachment at the upper edge now broken. Length *c* 25mm, width 20.3mm. (SF 189, 27, period 12)
51 Two fragments of sheet metal with circular perforations overall. 7.4mm × 12.3mm and 5.2mm × 6.4mm, thickness 0.7mm. (SF 500, II 23, period 7)
52 Strip or plaque, incomplete with one rivet remaining *in situ*. 6mm × 11.8mm. (SF 41, 1, period 14)
53 Sheet metal fragment, encrusted. 31mm × 30mm, thickness *c* 0.5mm. (SF 70, 1, period 14)
59 ?Seven sheet metal fragments. Thickness 0.8mm. Largest piece measures 11.6mm × 14mm. (SF 245, 12, period 11)

Table 24 Copper alloy by period (AES 76–7)

Category	Period – (Roman)								(Post-Roman)						Total
	1	2	3	4	5	6	7	8	9	10	11	12	13	14	
Brooches	–	–	–	–	–	–	–	1	–	–	1	–	–	–	2
Bracelets	–	–	–	–	–	–	–	–	2	3	3	–	–	3	11
Rings	–	–	–	–	–	1	–	–	–	–	–	–	–	2	3
Pins	–	–	–	–	–	–	1	–	–	–	–	–	–	1	2
Needle?	–	–	–	–	–	–	–	–	–	1	–	–	–	–	1
Mirrors	–	1	–	–	–	1	–	–	–	–	–	–	–	–	2
Tweezers	–	–	–	–	–	–	–	–	1	1	1	–	–	1	4
Toilet implements	1	–	–	–	–	–	–	–	2	1	–	–	–	–	4
Seal box lids	–	–	–	–	–	–	–	–	–	–	1	–	–	1	2
Lock bolt	–	–	1	–	–	–	–	–	–	–	–	–	–	–	1
Fish hook	–	–	–	–	–	–	–	–	1	–	–	–	–	–	1
Studs	1	–	–	1	–	–	–	–	1	–	2	–	–	2	7
Pin/nail	–	–	–	–	–	–	–	–	1	–	1	–	–	–	2
Military items	–	–	–	–	1	–	–	–	1	–	–	–	1	–	3
Fitting/pendant	–	–	–	–	–	–	1	–	–	–	–	–	–	–	1
Binding/strip	–	–	–	–	–	–	–	–	–	1	2	–	–	1	4
Appliqué/strap end	–	–	–	–	–	–	–	–	–	–	–	–	1	–	1
Sheet/strip frags	–	–	–	–	–	1	1	–	9	3	6	–	–	1	21
Bar/offcut, etc	–	–	–	–	–	–	–	–	6	1	1	–	–	–	8
Wire	–	1	–	–	–	–	–	–	6	1	2	–	–	2	12
Lumps/waste	2	–	1	–	–	1	–	–	4	2	6	–	–	–	16
Total	4	2	2	1	1	5	2	1	34	14	26	2	–	14	108

60 Offcut, rather corroded. 7.7mm × 13mm. (SF 250, 12, period 11)
65 Sheet metal offcut. 44mm × 8.5mm. (SF 339, 49, period 10)
72 Two adjoining fragments of strip with decorative notched edge, folded and encrusted. 24mm × 12mm. (SF 467, II 10, period 9)
77 Crude bar, corroded. 71.4mm × 4.4mm × 6.5mm. (SF 447, II 10, period 9)
80 Waste or heavy offcut, corroded. 32mm × 22mm × 7mm. (SF 502, II 52, period 9)
82 Wire, corroded. Length 52mm. (SF 102, 12, period 11)
83 Wire, irregular, bent. Length c 135mm. (SF 187, 1, period 14)
85 Wire loop or twist, incomplete. Length 27mm, cross-section 1.6mm × 2mm. (SF 292, 86, period 9)
90 Wire. Length 32.8mm. (SF 454, II 10, period 9)
91 Wire. Length 38.5mm. (SF 485, 168), period 10)
92 Wire or offcut flattening out at one end. Length c 145mm. (SF 525, 12, period 11)

Lead (AES 76–7)
Paul Booth

Only one object can be assigned a specific function, this is the weight or plumbob, no 109. The remaining pieces seem to be strip or offcut fragments or waste, in some cases apparently partly molten. Many pieces occurred in late or post-Roman contexts, but a few were found in earlier phases. Most notable of these was the triangular nailed sheet fragment (no 110) from a period 1 layer (292).

Illustrated leadwork (Fig 157)

A full catalogue of lead can be found in microfiche M2:E6–E7.

109 Weight or plumbob. Roughly spherical but with top drawn out. Corrosion suggests attachment to an iron hook or loop at the top. Height 42mm, diameter 43mm. Weight c 392g. The weight bears little obvious relationship to any known system of Roman weights, the Roman pound (*libra*) equalling approximately 327.45g. (SF 225, 12, period 11)
110 Triangular plate ?cut from corner of sheet. Crude ?nail hole c 5mm across in right-angled corner. Sides at right angles 35mm and 36mm long. (SF 532, 292, period 2)
111 Curved length of ?rod. Total length c 60mm. (SF 66, 1, period 14)
112 Sheet c 1mm thick roughly rolled to form tube or pipe of c 7mm diameter. Length 37mm. (SF 239, 12, period 11)
115 Disc c 1mm thick with slightly roughened surfaces. Function unknown. Diameter 33mm. (SF 492, 245, period 6)
116 Rectangular lump with very irregular surfaces, possibly

Explosion site finds (AES 76-7)

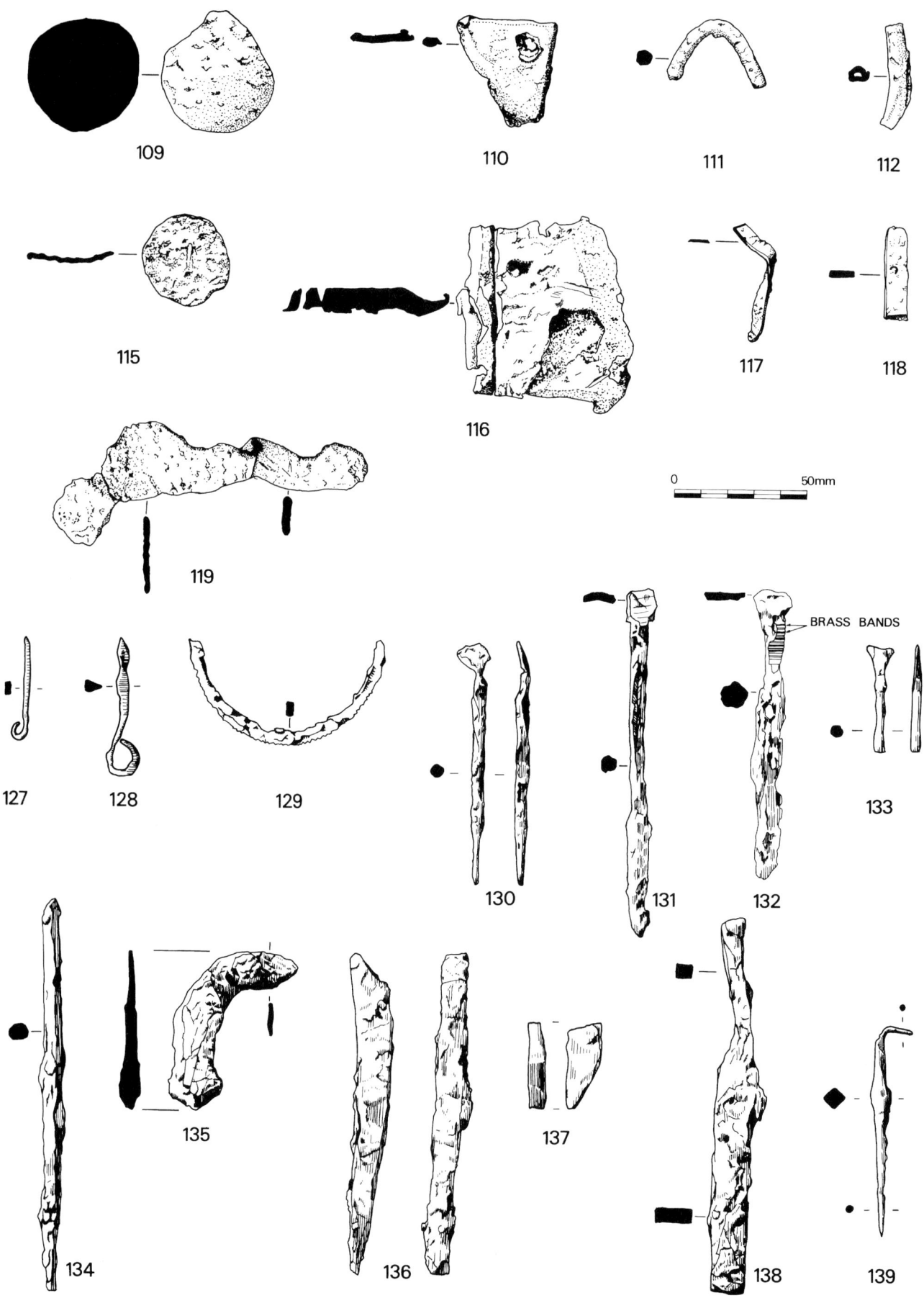

Figure 157   Lead, nos 109–119, and iron, nos 127–139 (AES 76–7)

formed of molten lumps fused together. Two sides have been trimmed, perhaps by cutting off small strips for use. One such strip still survives, almost cut through. *c* 65mm × 60mm. (SF 74, 1, period 14)

117 Strip/offcut. Tapering bent strip, 1mm thick. Long sides and one end crudely cut, suggesting that this is scrap. Length 51mm. (SF 484, 247, period 3)

118 Slightly rounded strip *c* 2.5mm thick. One straight end broken or cut off. Length 34mm. (SF 521, II 52, period 9)

119 Irregular bent ?strip with rounded edges, presumably a result of partial melting. Variable width and thickness. Length 99mm. (SF 439, 227, period 6)

Iron (AES 76–7)
Quita Mould

Introduction (Figs 157–161)

Approximately 175 iron objects were examined from the Explosion site. They had been radiographed and a small number of the more interesting objects had been cleaned some years previously. Much of the iron was found to be flaking badly so that inevitably some sections and details had been lost. The quantity of iron objects found within each period is given in Table 25 and proportionally illustrated in Fig 161.

A relatively large quantity of timber nails, hobnails, and small fragments with no distinguishable features was also recovered from the site, see Table 25; however, it was not considered sufficiently worthwhile for their detailed study to be undertaken in the light of the resources available.

Nearly three-quarters (72%) of the iron finds occurred in contexts dating from the later 3rd to the end of the 4th century. This was chiefly a reflection of the nature of the deposits; later 3rd- and 4th-century contexts comprised principally rubbish pits and large accumulation layers whilst fewer and smaller contexts were excavated from the earlier periods. It is clear that a proportion of the iron found in medieval and post-medieval contexts was also of Roman date occurring residually.

The different functional categories of ironwork found on the site are given in Table 26. In order to avoid the bias created by the relatively large quantities of hobnails, nails, and unidentifiable fragments recovered they have been omitted from the percentage calculations of functional categories represented which are given in the text.

The majority of the ironwork found fell within the miscellaneous category, chiefly due to the amount of broken strap and strip fragments recovered. These, together with the small unidentifiable fragments found, may reflect ironwork scrap. Other ironwork comprised principally domestic items and structural fittings along with a small quantity of tools, writing equipment, and possible items of dress. Evidence of transport such as cart fittings or horse harness was absent. Despite the proximity of the site to a possible early fort, no items of military ironwork were found.

The iron found represents a generally domestic assemblage of household items and fittings. The presence of the *styli* indicates literacy, whilst the occurrence of the lock fittings and a window grille fragment suggests that sufficient property was owned during the later 3rd and 4th centuries to require protection; the decorated stylus no 132 being a higher quality and, therefore, prized item.

What follows is a brief discussion of the various functional categories of ironwork found and some indication of the periods within which this material occurred. Illustrated pieces are simply referred to by the illustration number. Other items mentioned in the text are identified by the excavation small find (SF) number. A more detailed outline of the material found within each period is contained in microfiche M2:E8–E10.

Items of dress

A small number of hobnails from nailed footwear were found in periods 6 and 8 and residually in medieval deposits and topsoil; large quantities were found in periods 9 and 10 occurring principally within large rubbish pits (see Table 25).

A fine stem and looped terminal (no 127) from a pit in period 10 is likely to be a buckle pin. A larger example (no 128) from a pit in period 9 may be broken from a large buckle, possibly from a harness, or a loop spike.

A fragment of a possible bracelet (no 129) with rectangular section and a decorative exterior edge was found in a medieval deposit. Plain, round-sectioned iron bracelets are known, such as the five examples from graves in the Butt Road Cemetery, Colchester (Crummy 1983, 1733–1737 and Fig 48; one example from a grave dated from 2nd century to *c* AD 320; four examples from graves dated *c* AD 320–450) and an example in the Durben Collection likely to be of Iron Age date (Manning 1985, J10, 78 and plate 33). An expanding iron bracelet found associated with coins and samian of 1st-century date has been found from London (*ibid*, J11) but no similarly decorated bracelets are known to the author.

Writing equipment

Four *styli* were found from the excavations. Two *styli* (nos 130 and 131) were of simple form of Manning's type II (1976, 34–5, Fig 10; 1985, 85, Fig 24), the stem of a third (no 132) had decorative mouldings with inlaid brass bands, being of Manning's type IV (*ibid*). An eraser (no 133) broken from a fourth stylus occurred residually in a medieval deposit. Two fine, round-sectioned stems (no 134 and SF 364) found may be simple *styli* stems or possibly needle stems or heckle teeth.

Explosion site finds (AES 76-7)

Table 25 Ironwork by period (AES 76–7)

Period	Date	Object	Hobnail	Nail	Nail frag	Unid	Total
1	?70–80/85	–	–	1	4	1	6
2	80/85–125/40	5	–	24	8	3	40
3	125/40–140/50	4	–	4	16	1	25
4	140/50–150/70	5	–	11	13	5	34
5	150/70–240	–	–	10	6	–	16
6	240–250/60	12	24	71	100	57	264
7	250/60–270	8	–	21	24	24	77
8	270–280/90	30	2	96	98	72	298
9	280/90–340/50	31	866	414	403	237	1951
10	340/50–?400+	37	340	415	235	86	1113
11	Medieval	22	5	240	157	58	482
12	Medieval	4	1	20	14	12	51
13–14	Post med–modern	16	2	152	112	13	295
U/S		1	–	1	1	–	3
Total		175	1240	1480	1191	569	4655

Tools

The few tools recovered represent agricultural, carpentry, and leatherworking implements; the two broken stems possibly from textile working have been mentioned above.

A small hooked blade (no 135), likely to have been used as a reaping tool for crops and animal fodder, found in period 8 and a rake tooth (no 136) from a medieval deposit are from agricultural tools. A bevelled edge (no 137) possibly broken from a mortise chisel or a small crowbar (see Manning 1985, C19, 32, plate 14) occurred in period 8, whilst a more complete mortise chisel (no 138) was found in a medieval context. An awl (no 139) was found in topsoil.

Two collar ferrules (nos 140 and 141) and a spiral ferrule (SF 644) from Roman contexts may have been used to secure the handles on a variety of hafted implements.

Domestic implements

Of the ironwork found, 13% represented domestic implements. Six blades and various blade fragments were recovered. The earliest example found (no 142), from period 3, was a small knife, the straight back and edge now indistinguishable from each other through corrosion. A fragment from a larger blade (no 143) from period 9 had the back dropping to meet the edge at a pointed tip, while a knife from period 9 (no 144) had a straight back edge with a centrally placed tang. An unusual long, narrow blade (no 145) came from a period 10 pit; although having a distinctly thick triangular section no edge was apparent on the object or visible in radiograph suggesting that the object may have been a steel or possibly a partially worked blank rather than finished blade. A number of possible blade fragments (nos 146–149 and SFs 594, 599, and 631) were also recovered.

A fragment of a handle mount (no 150) and a handle strap (no 151) from a bucket were found separately in Roman deposits.

A long shank with a knobbed terminal (no 152) and a swivel loop (no 153) were found in the same layer (86) within period 9. Swivel loops are found frequently on the end of suspension chains for cooking pots. The shank may have acted as a suspension bar on a cauldron chain or a hanging lamp, the knobbed end articulating with a pierced swivel loop or the lamp handle. The arms of a steelyard or balance are similarly knobbed to prevent the counter balancing weight from slipping off and whilst iron examples are not common they do occasionally occur, see for example that from Icklingham, Suffolk (Manning 1985, 107, no 45, plate 52).

The strap with a knobbed terminal (no 154) from a period 10 context is similar to a drop handle from Baldock (Manning and Scott, in Stead and Rigby 1986, Fig 67, no 550), however, this example would seem to be unusually wide in the handle.

A simple tripod candlestick (no 155) occurred in a medieval context (12). Such a simple household object may have been made at any date, however it is comparable to a short legged example from Verulamium (see Manning, in Frere 1972, 178, Fig 65, no 51, where a number of other Roman examples are quoted). A long, twisted handle from a ladle or possibly a fire shovel (no 156) was found in the same context; again a medieval or Roman date for this implement is equally possible.

Explosion site finds (AES 76-7)

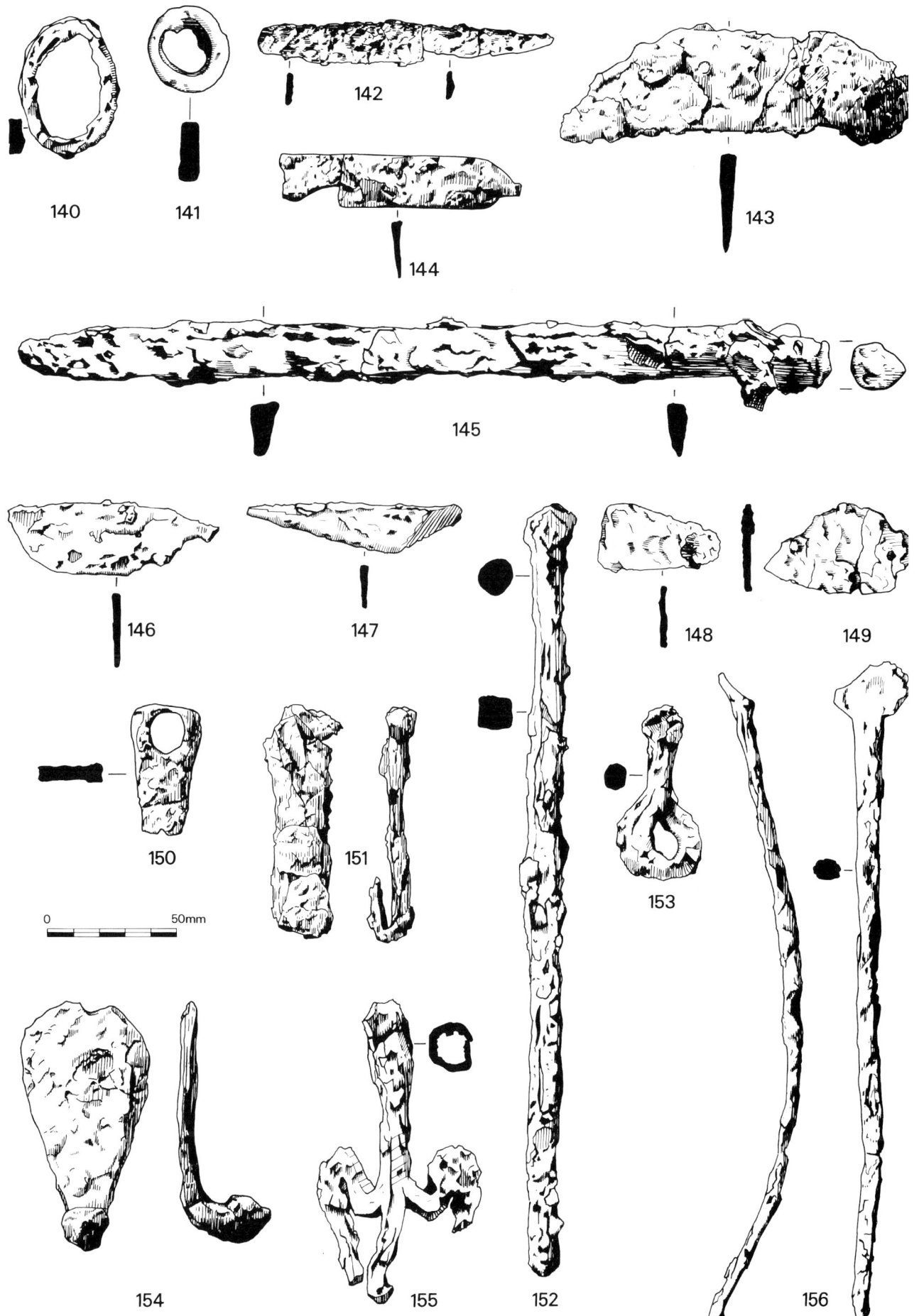

Figure 158   Iron objects (AES 76–7), nos 140–156

Explosion site finds (AES 76-7)

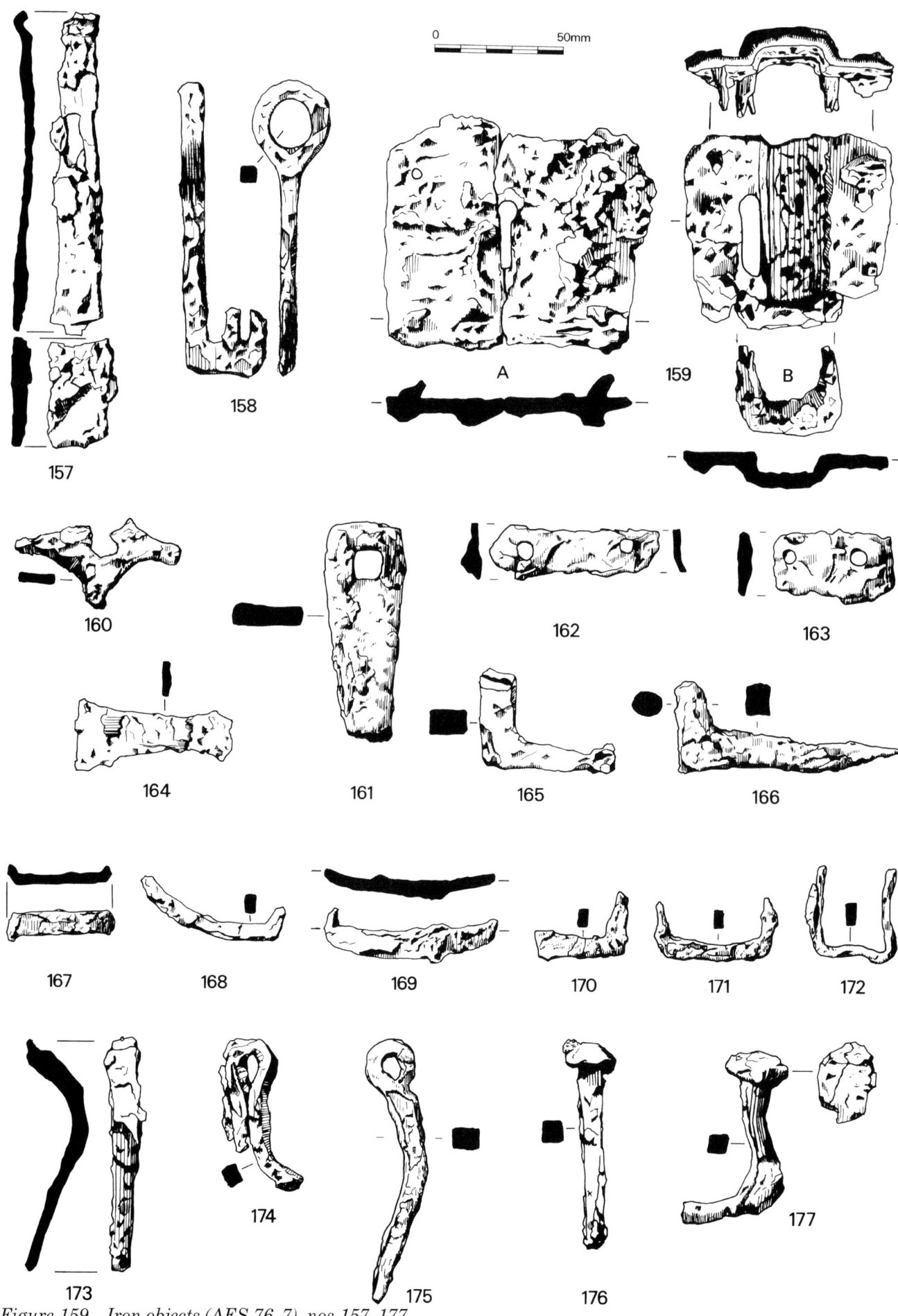

Figure 159   Iron objects (AES 76–7), nos 157–177

Explosion site finds (AES 76-7)

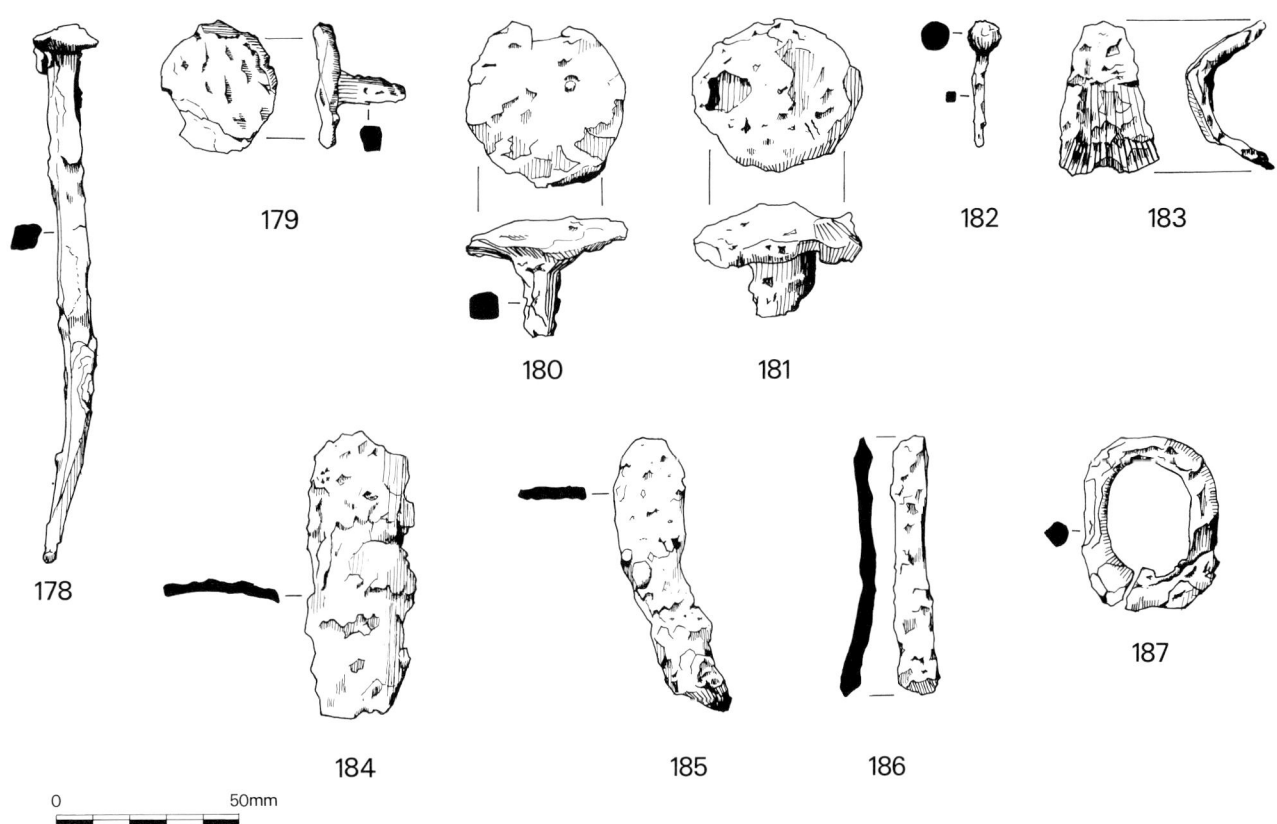

Figure 160   Iron objects (AES 76–7), nos 178–187

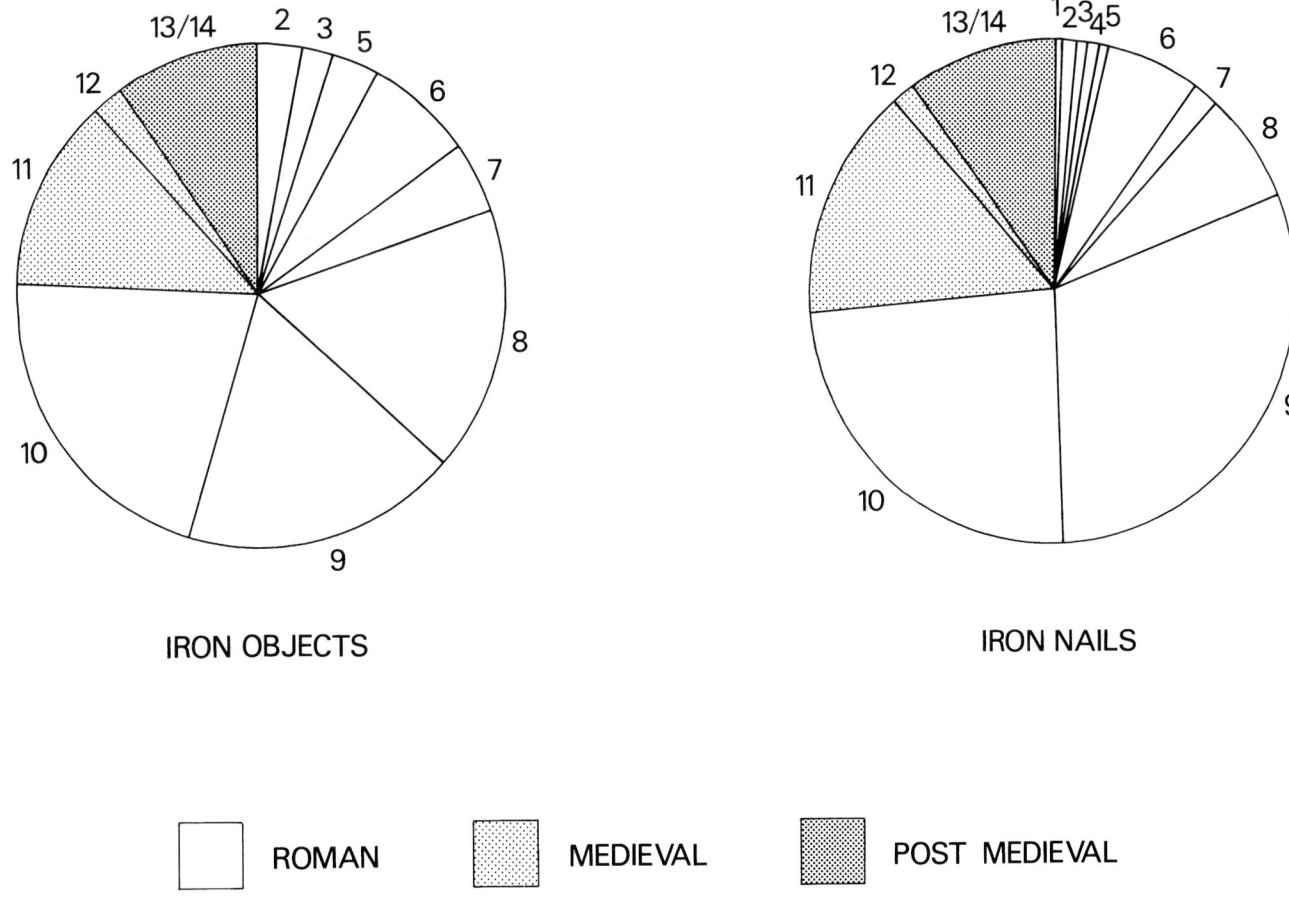

Figure 161   Iron objects and iron nails by period (AES 76–7)

Explosion site finds (AES 76-7)

Table 26   Ironwork by functional category (AES 76–7)

Items of dress		*Structural fittings*	
Bracelet	1	Binding, nailed	17
Buckle Pin	1	Cleat	2
Hobnail	1240	Hinge strap	1
Writing equipment		Joiner's dog	9
Stylus	4	L-shaped hinge staple	2
Tools		Loop headed spike	3
Awl	1	Nail	1480
Chisel, mortise	2	Nail fragment	1191
Ferrule, collar	2	Split spiked loop	3
Ferrule, spiral	1	T-staple	1
Hooked blade	1	U-shaped staple	1
Rake tooth	1	Window grille cross	1
Domestic items		*Miscellaneous items*	
Blade	6	Bar	1
Blade/steel	1	Fragment	569
?blade	2	Link	1
Bucket handle mount	1	Offcut shank	1
Bucket handle strap	1	Ring	1
Candlestick	1	Ring terminal	1
Handle, twisted	1	Sheet	3
?handle, knobbed strap	1	Sheet, nailed	1
Key	3	Sheet, rolled	1
Knobbed shank	1	Stem	3
Lock casing	1	Strap	47
Lock plate	1	Strap/?blade	2
Swivel	1	Strip	36
Tang	2		

Locking mechanisms

Three keys were found: a barb-spring padlock key handle (no 157) in period 8, an L-shaped tumbler-lock lift key (no 157) in a medieval context, and a possible broken key bow and stem (SF 652) which occurred in topsoil. No 157 is a common Roman form occurring residually.

A flat lockplate from a lever lock and its lock casing (no 159a and b) were found together in a period 10 deposit, both having large quantities of minerally preserved wood, identified as probably lime (*Tilia*), present on their internal surfaces from the chest or cupboard to which they have been attached. Lever lockplates are not commonly found in Roman contexts, but an example of similar 3rd- or 4th-century date comes from Baldock (Manning and Scott, in Stead and Rigby 1986, Fig 67, no 553), whilst another dated c AD 235 is known from Vindolanda (Jackson, in Bidwell 1985, Fig 54, no 108).

Structural fittings

Of the ironwork recovered, 23% came from structural fittings other than nails. A broken star or cross from the junction of window grille bars (no 160) occurred in a late 3rd-century pit.

Fragments of nailed binding (eg nos 161–163) were found in periods 2, ?3, 7, 8, 9, and 10, and in medieval deposits. One fragment from a period 9 pit (no 164) appears to be from the arm of an angled binding or possibly a hinge strap. A hinge strap fragment (SF 180) and two L-shaped hinge staples (nos 165 and 166) were also found along with several examples of joiner's dogs (eg nos 167–171), a U-shaped staple (no 172), fragments of cleat (no 173, SF 79, and SF 570), split spiked loops (no 174, SF 571, and SF 616), loop-headed spikes (no 175, SF 588, and SF 665) and a T-staple (SF 241).

Nails

Approximately 1480 nails and a further 1191 possible nail fragments were found from the excavation (see Table 25). The vast majority were flat headed (eg nos 176–178) of Manning's type 1B (1985, 134–5, Fig 32), the most commonly occurring nail type; type 2 (eg SF 233), type 7 (eg nos 179 and 180), type 8 (eg no 181), and an unusual small nail with a globular head of type 9 (no 182) were also noted in the assemblage. Nails and nail fragments occurred in all periods. The majority were found in periods 9 and 10 (31% and 24% respectively) belonging to the late 3rd and the 4th century; a further 15% came from period 11 medieval deposits (see Fig 161).

Miscellaneous

The majority of the iron fell within the miscellaneous category, principally comprising fragments of broken strap (eg nos 183 and 184, drawn), and strip (eg nos 185 and 186) and a quantity of small fragments with no distinguishing features.

Along with a fragment of bar (SF 607) and a shank offcut (SF 200) with a chisel cut end, they appear to be scrap associated with ironworking. Smithing slag has also been found on the site (particularly in period 8 layer (128) which contained 16% of the miscellaneous ironwork).

Individual items such as the ring (SF 402), link (no 187), and ring terminal (SF 230) may have had a variety of functions and, therefore, could not be placed within one of the other categories.

Jet and shale (AES 76–7)
Glenys Lloyd-Morgan

These pieces, which can be classed as luxury items, can now be compared with earlier finds from excavations at Alcester in 1969 and 1973, helping to set them in a wider context. Although jet pins such as no 188 can be paralleled elsewhere, the decoration on beads nos 191 and 192, especially the former, is unusual and of some quality. The better-known types of undecorated shale bracelets are well represented, and with the less common examples 195 and 196 with notched decoration, they suggest a fairly widespread prosperity. The most unusual find is the shale vessel fragment, no 205, which may have been an unsophisticated form of pyxis related to the example from Thetford 1979, but with a certain robust and naive charm which is, as yet, unparalleled. The collection thus represents a mixture of both sophisticated luxury goods for conspicuous display, and the simpler items which reinforce an impression of successful long distance trading and contact in the later Roman period.

Jet (Fig 162)

188 Pin with faceted cuboid head, the tip and most of shaft now lost. Cross-section of head 5.7mm × 7.8mm, length 19.9mm. Originally noted by Booth (1980, Fig 8, no 7). Similar examples have been found on a wide range of sites in Britain, as for example Wroxeter (Bushe-Fox 1914, 22, plate X, Fig 2); Silchester (Lawson 1976, 258, Fig 7, no 65 a–d); Scole, Norfolk (Rogerson 1977, 148, Fig 63, no 5 from a context of period III dated mid-Antonine to late 3rd century AD); and Vindolanda (Bidwell 1985, 128, Fig 45, no 10 unstratified). Compare the bone nos 237 and 238 below, of Crummy (1979) type 4 and dated by her to *c* AD 250 to late 4th/early 5th century AD. (SF 57, 12, period 11)

189 Jet (or shale?) disc-shaped bead with two near-parallel holes running chord-wise through it. The disc is flattened at the edge where the perforations enter and emerge. The upper surface is slightly convex, turned with a circle as border and has a centring hole for the lathe. The underside is flat. The bead is virtually complete apart from the loss of a small chip on the upper edge. Diameter 19.7mm, depth 4.8mm. Compare the examples from Silchester (Lawson 1976, 244, Fig 1, no 7); South Shields (Allason-Jones and Miket 1984, 308, nos 7.64, 7.65 with figs on p 307); and from Richborough (Bushe-Fox 1949, 148, pl LV no 230 (shale) and no 232 (jet)) where both were unstratified. Bushe-Fox makes reference to finds of similar beads from Lydney which were said to have come mainly from contexts dated late 3rd to 4th century. (SF 147, 3, period 12)

190 Disc-shaped bead perforated by two near-parallel holes running chord-wise through it, in similar fashion to 189 above. The disc is flattened at the edge where the perforations enter and emerge, as well as at right angles to the line of the holes, giving a sub-octagonal appearance. The upper surface has been turned to give a sunken ring around the central area, where the centre point for the lathe can be clearly observed. The underside is flat, but a little chipped and damaged at the lower edge. Diameter 17.3mm, depth 5.1mm. Compare the example from Silchester which, with five related examples, is now in the Reading Museum (Lawson 1976, 244, 246, Fig 1, no 8d); and another, slightly smaller than ours, from South Shields (Allason-Jones and Miket 1984, 306, no 7.62, fig on p 307, with further parallels noted). (SF 213, 12, period 11)

191 Flat, semi-circular bead from a bracelet. The outer curved edge is decorated at the centre with a stylised scroll pattern, now broken across one of the perforations. Present size 21.4mm × 25.7mm, thickness 4mm. Beads of this type are more commonly wedge-shaped, and when threaded would have made an eye-catching chunky bracelet, as the example from Grave Group LXII at Ospringe, Kent which had 24 beads strung on 'twisted bronze wire' (Whiting *et al* 1931, 99–100, plate LVII, Fig 2, found in urn no 212); or the two 'almost complete articulated bracelets' from Blossom St, York 1852 and The Mount, noted in *Eburacum* (RCHM 1962, 143a, plate 70). Another similar bead, from a grave group dated AD 320 from Bootham 1845 is also listed. This is now in Sheffield Museum, no J93-736 (Howarth 1899, 228 with fig). Compare also the similar wedge form of bead from Alcester 1970, SF 19. None of these examples has the same scroll type edge decoration as ours. (SF 277, 87, period 10)

192 Rectangular bead, pierced laterally by two near-parallel holes. The upper side is convex and incised to suggest a twisted pattern. The underside is flat. 8.1mm × 17.2mm, thickness 5.4mm. Originally noted by Booth (1980, Fig 8, no 8). Compare the related examples from Silchester (Lawson 1976, 246, Fig 2, no 14); and South Shields, where the incisions are parallel to each other and the line of thread holes. It is also decorated on the narrow ends, unlike ours (Allason-Jones and Miket 1984, 310, no 7.84, fig on p 309). (SF 92, 1, period 14)

Explosion site finds (AES 76-7)

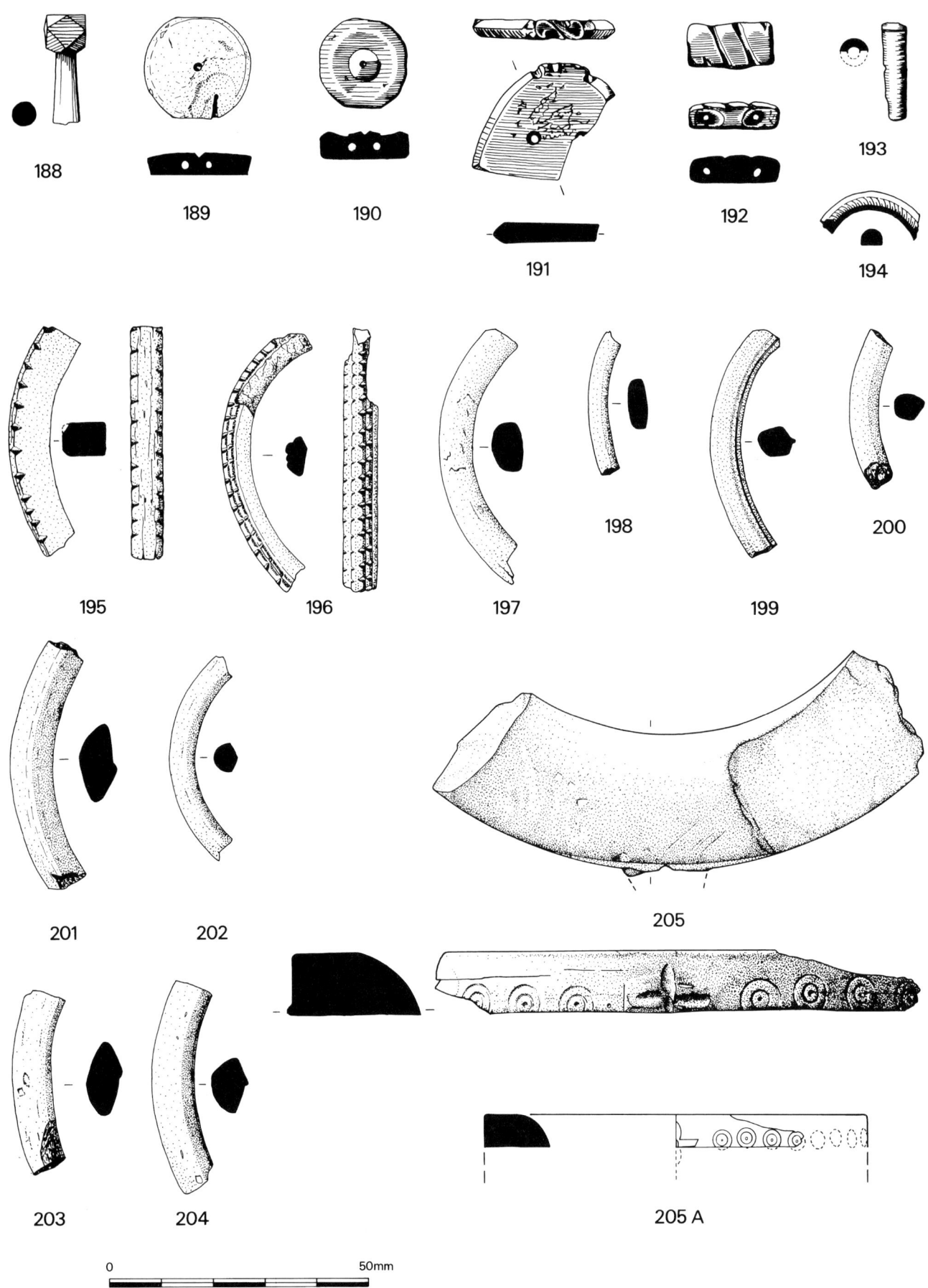

Figure 162   Jet, nos 188–194, and shale objects, nos 195–205 (AES 76–7)

Explosion site finds (AES 76-7)

Table 27 Jet and shale objects by period (AES 76–7)

Period	1	2	3	4	5	6	7	8	9	10	11	12	13	14	Total
Jet															
Pin	–	–	–	–	–	–	–	–	–	–	1	–	–	–	1
Beads	–	–	–	–	–	–	–	–	–	1	2	1	–	1	5
Ring	–	–	–	–	–	–	–	–	1	–	–	–	–	–	1
Total	–	–	–	–	–	–	–	–	1	1	3	1	–	1	7
Shale															
Bracelets	–	–	–	–	–	–	–	1	2	1	–	–	–	6	10
Vessel	–	–	–	–	–	–	–	–	–	–	–	–	–	1	1
Total	–	–	–	–	–	–	–	1	2	1	–	–	–	7	11

193 Fragment of a cylindrical bead which may taper towards the broken end, suggesting that it may have been the terminal bead to an elaborate necklace or collar. The one surviving end is marked by a lightly incised collar. Present length 17.8mm, diameter *c* 4.9mm. Compare the cylindrical beads from South Shields (Allason-Jones and Miket 1984, 303 especially no 7.17, length 38mm, fig on p 305). (SF 210 (12) period 11)

194 Fragment of an undecorated ring with D-shaped cross-section. Length *c* 24mm, original diameter *c* 22mm, depth 4mm, thickness 3mm. Compare the piece of similar size from South Shields (Allason-Jones and Miket 1984, 312, no 7.103, fig on p 311); another from a 4th-century context at Winterton, Lincs. (Stead 1976, 204, no 62, Fig 105); and a slightly larger unpublished piece from Abbey Green, Chester 1975–8 SF 394. A fine example in shale from a grave dated AD 360–370/380 was reported from Winchester (Clarke 1979, 318–319, Fig 98, Grave 438, no 563, and note also no 564 from the same grave). (SF 314 (86) period 9)

Shale (Fig 162)

195 Bracelet fragment with rectangular cross-section, the outer two angles decorated with a series of neat V-shaped notches. Length 45mm, diameter 76mm, height 5.5mm, thickness 7.5mm. Originally noted by Booth (1980, Fig 8, no 11). The type is not uncommon and examples have been noted at Silchester (Lawson 1976, 254, Fig 6, nos 47, 51); London (Wheeler 1930, 102, plate XL no 1, Mus no 11037, from Southwark St); and from a context dated AD 350–410+ at Verulamium (Frere 1972, 152, Fig 57, no 220). (SF 1 (1) period 14)

196 Bracelet fragment with a stepped profile to the outer face, each angle of which is decorated with small V-shaped notches. The inner face has been rather carelessly cut, removing part of the profile which does not, therefore, quite match those of the other better turned examples noted below. Length *c* 52mm, diameter 58mm, height 5.6mm, thickness *c* 5.5mm. Compare the example from Silchester (Lawson 1976, 256, Fig 6, nos 55a, c, d); and Cirencester (McWhirr 1986, 116, no 244, Fig 85). (SF 8 (1) period 14)

197 Undecorated bracelet fragment with heavy ovoid or sub-rectangular cross-section. Length *c* 52mm, diameter 61mm, height 9mm, thickness 6.3mm. Exact parallels have not been listed for this or the seven other undecorated shale bracelets which follow, but similar pieces can be seen, for example, amongst the old collections from Silchester (Lawson 1976, 250, 252, nos 19–31, Fig 4); South Shields (Allason-Jones and Miket 1984, 313–314, nos 7.121–7.139, figs and cross-section on p 315); and Chester (Lloyd-Morgan 1981b, 42, 44, nos 8, 10, and 13, Fig 1 B, D). (SF 14 (1) period 14)

198 Bracelet fragment, undecorated, with neat elongated ovoid cross-section. Length 27mm, diameter *c* 76.8mm, height 9mm, thickness 3.8mm. (SF 37 (1) period 14)

199 Bracelet fragment, undecorated, with trapezoidal cross-section and untrimmed internal flange. Length 38mm, diameter *c* 66.5mm, height 4.8mm, thickness 5.8mm. (SF 94 (1) period 14)

200 Bracelet fragment, undecorated, with irregular D-shaped cross-section, a little worn. Length 29mm, diameter *c* 58mm. height 5.3mm, thickness 5.5mm. (SF 122 (1) period 14)

201 Bracelet fragment, undecorated, with angular ovoid cross-section similar to no 203 below. Length 50mm, diameter 92mm, height 12.8mm, thickness 7mm. (SF 220 (43) period 9)

202 Bracelet fragment, undecorated, with angular D-shaped cross-section. Length 43mm, diameter 44mm, height 5mm, thickness 4.7mm. (SF 346 (108) period 8)

203 Bracelet fragment, undecorated, with angular ovoid cross-section similar to no 201 above but not belonging to it. Length 34mm, diameter 101.7mm, height 12.5mm, thickness 7mm. (SF 438 (18) period 9)

204 Bracelet fragment, undecorated, with angular ovoid cross-section. Length 41mm, diameter *c* 82mm, height 9.8mm, thickness 7.5mm. (SF 519 (168) period 10)

205 Fragment, probably the rim of a shale vessel, with remains of a vertically pierced lug. The remaining upper section of the outer ?vertical rim wall is decorated with dot-and-double circle motifs. Diameter *c* 143mm, width *c* 25mm, present height 12.7mm. The piece is too heavy to be interpreted as a cup and too small in diameter to be totally satisfactory as a bowl. It may perhaps have been part of a more elaborate form of vessel, such as a small pyxis of the type found in 1979 with the late Roman treasure at Thetford (Johns and Potter 1983, 131, no 83, Fig 45, plate 13), though differing in size and style. It is also worth noting here the fragment of a shale *patera* from excavations at Alcester 1973, SF 28. (SF 99, 1, period 14)

Worked bone (AES 76–7)
Glenys Lloyd-Morgan

The high proportion of worked bone items used for personal adornment is perhaps not entirely surprising and, as with the finds of jet and shale, they are predominantly late in date. The 4th-century bone bracelets, especially the less common decorated examples, again underline the prosperity and general well being of the community at this time.

The following catalogue describes only the items illustrated (Figs 163–165). A full version can be found in microfiche M2:E11–F3.

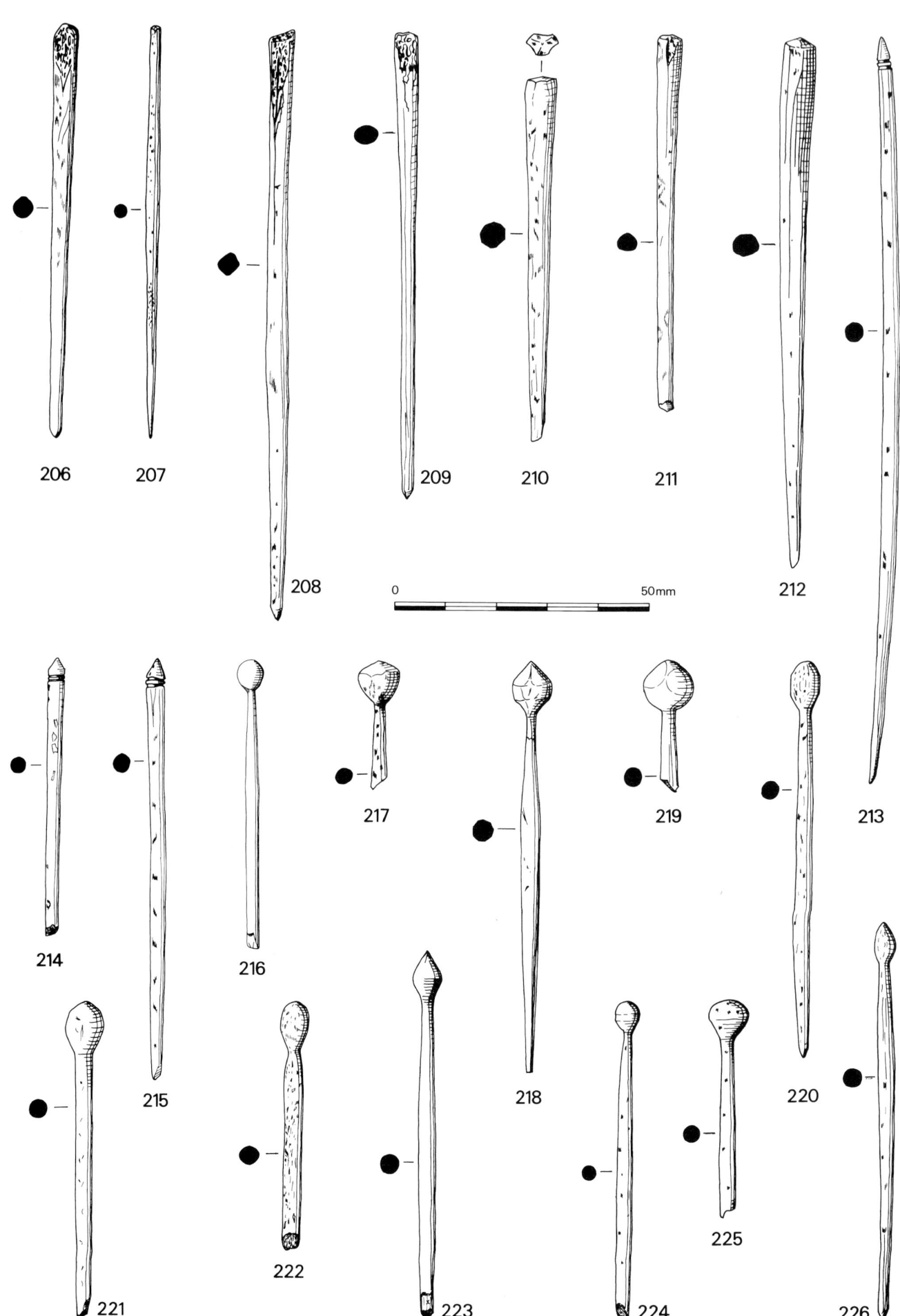

Figure 163   Bone objects (AES 76–7), nos 206–226

206 Complete pin terminating as a low cone and without any further elaboration to the head. The other end tapering to a crude point. Length 78.6mm. Crummy type 1 dated AD 70–200/250 (1979, Fig 1, no 1, pp 159–160). Other examples have been reported from Dover (Philp 1981, 157, Fig 36, nos 148–151; nos 148 and 150–1 come from period III contexts dated AD 190/200–208); two examples from alignment 1a in the sewer at York have been dated to no later than late 2nd or early 3rd century AD (MacGregor 1976, 12, 23, nos 128, 129, Fig 9). Compare the finds from Tiddington, Warwickshire, TD81, SF 784; and Alcester 1972 (see above, ALC 72/2 no 2). (SF 362, 142, period 10)

207 Pin of Crummy type 1, as above with flat head, virtually complete. Length 78.3mm. (SF 46, 1, period 14)

208 Pin of Crummy type 1, as above, but with head section almost flat, complete. Length 112.3mm. (SF 361, 142, period 10)

209 Pin of Crummy type 1, as above, with flat top and damaged patch of cancellous bone along part of upper section, otherwise complete. Length 88.7mm. (SF 387, 124M, period 9)

210 Pin of Crummy type 1, as above, tip and lower part of shaft lost. Length 69mm. (SF 432, 10, period 9)

211 Pin of Crummy type 1, as above, tip and lower part of shaft lost. Length 71.4mm. (SF 463, 10, period 9)

212 Pin of Crummy type 1, as above, with low conical head, complete. Length 101mm. (SF 475, 22, period 9)

213 Pin with conical head and slight collar beneath indicated by two grooves. In two adjoining pieces, complete. Diameter of head c 3mm, length 143.6mm. Crummy type 2 pin dated c AD 50–200/250 (1979, 160–1, Fig 1, no 2). One example from Leicester comes from a context with 2nd-century samian and stamped mortarium dated c AD 135–145 (Hebditch and Mellor 1975, 49, Fig 21, no 36, cf p 25 for context dating); another from South Shields is from a 4th-century context (Miket 1983, 136, Fig 81, no 15). Note also the examples from Tiddington, Warwickshire, SF M715, SF M716, and SF M721 and TD81 SF 805; and Alcester (see above, ALC 69 no 4). (SF 397, 156, period 6)

214 Pin of Crummy type 2, as above, tip and lower part of shaft now lost. Diameter of head 3.3mm, length 52.3mm. (SF 522, 54, period 5)

215 Pin of Crummy type 2, as above, tip rather crudely finished but otherwise complete. Diameter of head 4.1mm, length 80mm. (SF 524, 66, period 4)

216 Pin with sub-spherical head, tip and lower part of shaft lost. Diam of head 5.8–6.1mm, length 54.9mm. Pin of Crummy type 3 dated c AD 200 to late 4th/early 5th century. Three examples from Shakenoak, Oxon. are said to have come from late 4th-century deposits (Brodribb et al 1973, 142, Fig 73, nos 122, 123, and 124); another from Wadham House, Dorchester, Dorset, came from an early 4th-century context (Draper and Chaplin 1982, 24, Fig 12, no 5). Compare the examples from Tiddington, Warwickshire, SF M602, SF M722, SF M723, SF M937, SF M938, SF M939; TD80, SF 5; TD81, SF 880; and Alcester ALC 69 and 1972 (see above, ALC 69 no 8, and ALC 72/2 no 4). (SF 3, 1, period 14)

217 Pin of Crummy type 3, as above, head and upper part of shaft only. Diameter of head 8.2–8.7mm, length 24.3mm. (SF 36, 1, period 14)

218 Pin of Crummy type 3, as above, with pointed sub-spherical head, in two adjoining pieces, tip lost. Diameter of head 8–8.7mm, length 81mm. (SF 136, 4, period 10)

219 Pin of Crummy type 3, as above, with irregular sub-spherical head and only upper part of shaft surviving. Diameter of head 8.7–9.3mm, length 25mm. (SF 161, 2, period 10)

220 Pin of Crummy type 3, as above, with crude sub-spherical head, complete. Diameter of head 5.2–6.2mm, length 80.7mm. (SF 209, 12, period 11)

221 Pin of Crummy type 3, as above, with sub-spherical head, lower part of shaft and tip lost. Diameter of head 7.6–8.2mm, length 60mm. (SF 259, 12, period 11)

222 Crude pin of Crummy type 3, as above, with sub-spherical head, lower part of shaft and tip lost. Diameter of head 5.6–6.2mm, length 46mm. (SF 283, 87, period 10)

223 Pin of Crummy type 3, as above, with pointed spherical head, tip and lower part of shaft lost. Diameter of head 5.1–5.6mm, length 69.1mm. (SF 284, 87, period 10)

224 Pin of Crummy type 3, as above, with sub-spherical head, lower part of shaft and tip lost. Diameter of head 5mm, length 59.8mm. (SF 313, 86, period 9)

225 Pin of Crummy type 3, as above, with sub-spherical head, lower part of shaft and pin lost. Diameter of head 7.3–7.7mm, length 40.5mm. (SF 331, 124, period 9)

226 Pin of Crummy type 3, as above with ovoid head, complete. Diameter of head 4.4–4.7mm, length 69.9mm. (SF 406, 170, period 9)

227 Pin of Crummy type 3, as above, with spherical head, complete. Diameter of head 5.5–5.9mm, length 62.7mm. (SF 413, 1, period 14)

228 Pin of Crummy type 3, as above, with sub-spherical head, complete. Diameter of head 6–6.8mm, length 82.1mm. (SF 431, 10, period 9)

229 Pin of Crummy type 3, as above, with sub-spherical head, tip and lower part of shaft lost. Diameter of head 5.2–6mm, length 52.7mm. (SF 441, 10, period 9)

230 Pin of Crummy type 3, as above, with ovoid head, complete. Diameter of head 5.9mm, length 115.4mm. (SF 477, 22, period 9)

231 Pin of Crummy type 3, as above, with ovoid head, tip and lower part of shaft lost. Diameter of head 4.6–5.2mm, length 41.2mm. (SF 478, 22, period 9)

232 Pin of Crummy type 3, as above, with sub-spherical head, a little eroded otherwise complete. Diameter of head 6.3–7.4mm, length 69.2mm. (SF 505, 22, period 9)

233 Pin of Crummy type 3, as above, with sub-spherical head, tip and lower part of shaft lost. Diameter of head 4.9–5.2mm, length 80.6mm. (SF 517A, 170D, period 9)

234 Pin of Crummy type 3, as above, with sub-spherical head, tip and lower part of shaft lost. Diameter of head 4.2–4.7mm, length 51mm. (SF 517B, 170D, period 9)

235 Pin of Crummy type 3 with crude disc-shaped head, tip and lower part of shaft lost. Diameter of head 6.2–6.6mm, length 44.7mm. Compare the examples from Lydney dated late 3rd to 4th century (Wheeler and Wheeler 1932, 84, Fig 18, no 69); Gadebridge Park (Neal 1974a, 155, Fig 67, no 317) and Gestingthorpe (Draper 1985, 71, Fig 33, no 382). (SF 231, 12, period 11)

236 Pin with cylindrical head. Diameter of head 5.2–6.5mm, length 101.7mm. Probably a crude version of a Crummy type 3 pin as above. (SF 368, 124A, period 9)

237 Pin with irregular faceted cuboid head, tip and lower part of shaft lost. Cross-section of head 5.5mm × 5.3mm, length 39.5mm. Pin of Crummy type 4 dated c AD 250 to late 4th/early 5th century (1979, 161–2, Fig 1, no 5). An example from Lydney is said to have been found 'with late 3rd- and 4th-century coins' (Wheeler and Wheeler 1932, 84, no 70, Fig 18); another from Dover was unstratified (Philp 1981, 157, no 121, Fig 36); two pieces are reported from Verulamium, one, unillustrated, is said to have come from a context dated AD 290–310 (Frere 1984, 71, no 265, Fig 30). Note also two unpublished examples from Droitwich Bays Meadow, Worcestershire 1974 VIII, SF 783 and VIII, SF 899. (SF 2, 1, period 14)

238 Pin of Crummy type 4, as above, with irregular faceted cuboid head, the tip and lower part of the shaft lost. Cross-section of head 6.4 × 6.7mm, length 56.5mm. (SF 53, 1, period 14)

239 Pin with pointed conical head and a neat, well defined collar beneath, part of the head damaged and most of shaft lost. Diameter of head c 5.3mm, length 12.4mm. Pin of Crummy type 5 dated c AD 250 to late 4th/early 5th century (1979, 162, Fig 1, no 7). Compare the example from Verulamium from a context dated AD 300–370 (Frere 1984, 71, Fig 30, no 270); examples from Gestingthorpe (Draper 1985, 68, nos 366–369, Fig 32;) the heavier piece from South Shields (Allason-Jones and Miket 1984, 87, no 2.543, Fig on p 85); and the unpublished piece from Droitwich Bays Meadow, Worcestershire, 1967 II, SF 41. (SF 17, 1, period 14)

240 Pin of Crummy type 5, as above, with pointed ovoid head and well defined collar beneath, tip and most of shaft lost. Diameter of head 5mm, length 28.3mm. (SF 52, 1, period 14)

241 Pin of Crummy type 5, as above, with elongated pointed ovoid

Explosion site finds (AES 76-7)

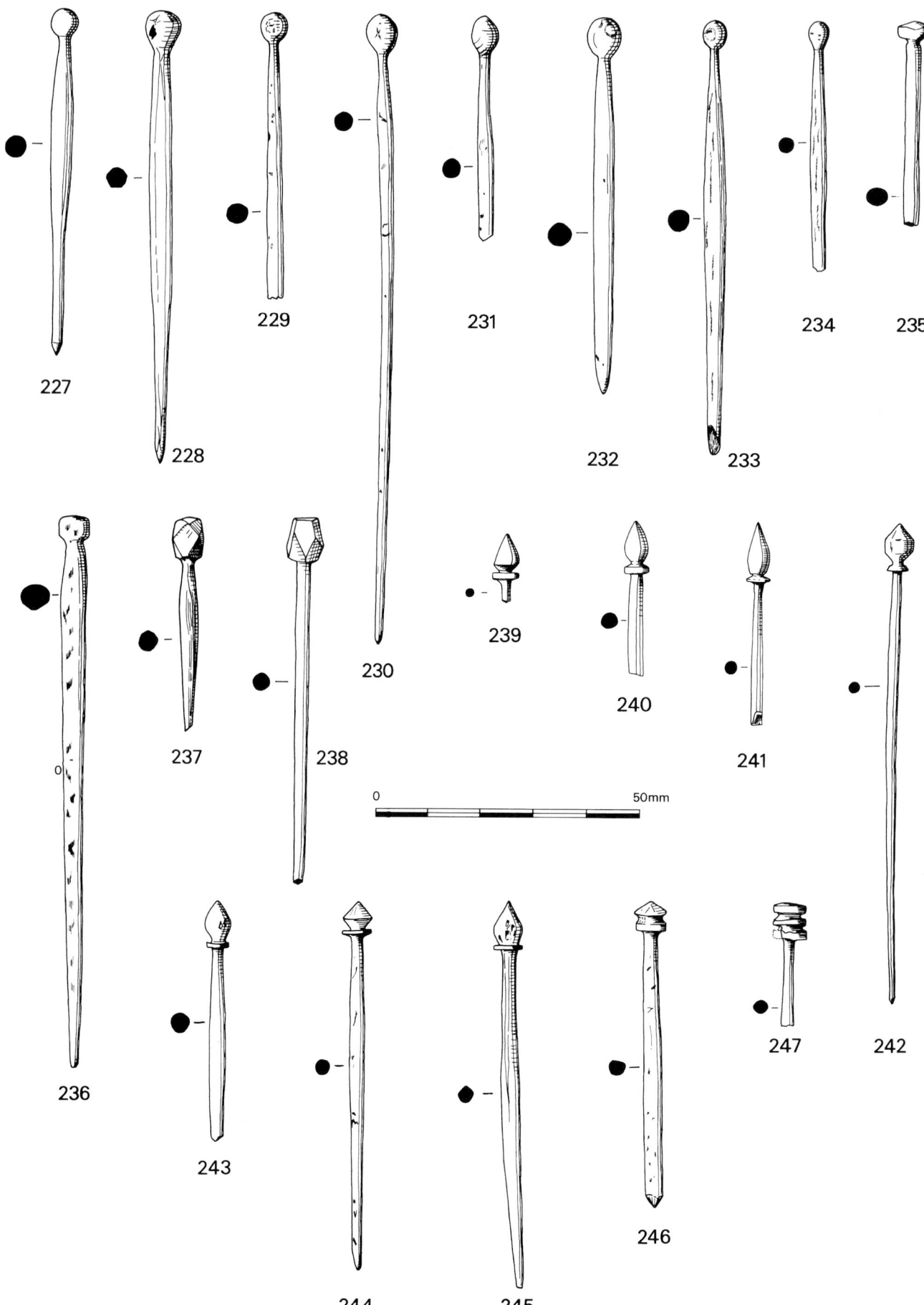

Figure 164   Bone objects (AES 76–7), nos 227–247

Table 28 Bone objects by period (AES 76–7)

Period	1	2	3	4	5	6	7	8	9	10	11	12	13	14	Total
Pins: type 1	–	–	–	–	–	–	–	–	4	2	–	–	–	1	7
type 2	–	–	–	1	1	1	–	–	–	–	–	–	–	–	3
type 3	–	–	–	–	–	–	–	–	11	4	3	–	–	3	21
type 4	–	–	–	–	–	–	–	–	–	–	–	–	–	2	2
type 5	–	–	–	–	–	–	–	–	–	2	2	–	–	4	8
type 6	–	–	–	–	–	–	–	–	–	–	1	–	–	–	1
Pin/needle Frags	–	–	–	–	–	–	–	1	7	5	6	–	–	11	30
Bracelets	–	–	–	–	–	–	–	–	–	1	1	–	–	1	3
Knife handle	–	–	–	–	–	1	–	–	–	–	–	–	–	–	1
Gaming counters	–	–	–	–	–	–	–	–	1	1	–	–	–	1	3
Total	–	–	–	1	1	2	–	1	23	15	13	–	–	23	79

head and well defined collar beneath, tip and lower part of shaft lost. Diameter of head 4.7mm, length 37.4mm. (SF 73, 1, period 14)

242 Pin of Crummy type 5, as above, with pointed ovoid head and angular collar beneath, complete. Diameter of head 5.1mm, length 88.1mm. (SF 139, 1, period 14)

243 Pin of Crummy type 5, as above, with pointed ovoid head and neat collar beneath, tip and lower part of shaft lost. Diameter of head 5.4mm, length 43.5mm. (SF 177, 12, period 11)

244 Pin of Crummy type 5, as above, with biconical head and chipped angular collar beneath, complete. Diameter of head 4.6–5.2mm, length 68.2mm. Originally noted by Booth (1980, Fig 8, no 12). (SF 185, 4, period 10)

245 Pin of Crummy type 5, as above, with biconical head and well-defined collar beneath, tip lost. Diameter of head 4.7–5.6mm, length 75.4mm. (SF 372, 122, period 10)

246 Pin with low conical head and crude collar beneath, complete. Diameter of head 5.7–6.4mm, length 56mm. A coarser version of the Crummy type 5 pin, as above. (SF 211, 12, period 11)

247 Pin, the head consisting of three narrow discs, now a little damaged, tip and lower part of shaft lost. Diameter of head 5.1–6.4mm, length 22mm. Pin of Crummy type 6 dated c AD 200 to late 4th/early 5th century AD (1979, 162, Fig 1, no 8). Compare the example from Winterton from a context dated 3rd or 4th century (Stead 1976, 207, Fig 107, no 86); Chichester (Down 1978, 312, no 192, Fig 10.44) and the temple site at Nettleton, Wiltshire (Wedlake 1982, 201, no 26, Fig 82). (SF 184, 12, period 11)

278 Bracelet in two adjoining pieces and virtually complete with remains of the copper alloy collar used to hold the ends together. One end is broken across the rivet-hole used to secure it in place. Undecorated and with an angular D-shaped cross-section. Length c 192mm, height 3.7–4.1mm, thickness 2.2–2.3mm. An example from the Baths at Caerleon comes from a 4th-century context (Zienkiewicz 1986, 211, no 32, Fig 76). The most extensive collection of undecorated bone bracelets from any one site is probably that from the Lankhills Cemetery, Winchester, where bracelets of bone and ivory have been found with connecting collars of silver, iron, and copper alloy. Only these last will be noted here with the dating of their respective graves which confirms the popularity of the type in the 4th century (Clarke 1979, 313–4 for discussion of the type and variants in the mechanics of holding the ends together. Grave 63, Fig 70, no 49, AD 370–380; Grave 134, Fig 74, no 123, AD 310–370; Grave 143, Fig 77, nos 157, 160, 161, and 293, with three other bone bracelets, AD 350–370; Grave 265, Fig 82, no 286, AD 390–395; Grave 336, Fig 89, nos 344, 348, and 349 with one other example, AD 350–370; Grave 337, Fig 91, nos 417 and 418 with three other examples, AD 330–350). (SF 168, 2, period 10)

279 Fragment of bone bracelet with remains of copper alloy collar at one end. D-shaped cross-section and decorated at each edge with a notched border marked off by a lightly engraved line. Length 35mm, height 4mm, thickness 2.5mm. A virtually complete example comes from Richborough with identical decoration along the main portion of the band, but with the addition of small panels of patterning at the ends next to the remains of the iron fastenings (Bushe-Fox 1926, 46, plate XIV, no 20); Another example from Portchester Castle comes from a period 4 context dated AD 325–345 (Cunliffe 1975, 218, no 99, Fig 117, cf p 61 for dating). (SF 11, 1, period 14)

280 Fragment of bone bracelet with incised diagonal pattern on outer face suggesting twisted cord decoration. Length 61mm, height 5.1mm, thickness 3mm. Compare the example from Portchester Castle (Cunliffe 1975, 220, no 100, Fig 117), and Lankhills cemetery, Winchester from a grave dated AD 350–370 (Clarke 1979, 314, Grave 122, Fig 71, no 101). (SF 293, 12, period 11)

281 Bone knife handle with figure-of-eight-shaped cross-section and bevelled on either side of the upper section to meet the plane of the knife blade. Remains of the iron tang and a portion of the blade are still *in situ*. Present length 59.4mm, cross-section 9.4mm × 14.3mm. A similar form of knife handle in copper alloy was found with late 1st/2nd century material at Traprain Law in 1914 (MacGregor 1976, vol I, 144, vol II, no 278 with fig). Compare also the related examples of bone knife handles with figure-of-eight cross-sections discussed by Greep, where a 1st-century date, probably no later than Flavian, is suggested (1982, 93, 95, Fig 3, nos 8–11, catalogue p 99). (SF 516, 49, period 6)

282 Gaming counter, concave side has a central depression for the lathe, the flat side is marked with a cross and subsidiary small cuts. Diameter 17.5–18mm, depth 3.2mm. Kenyon type A counter (1948, 266, nos 9–11, Fig 91). Compare the example from the Deanery Fields, Chester 1928 where a cross made of double lines is incised (Droop and Newstead 1931, 135, no 76, plate XLVII); and from Dover (Philp 1981, 169, Fig 42, no 228; 169, Fig 42, no 230 with graffito from a period III context ie AD 190–200 to AD 208). (SF 181, 36, period 14)

283 Gaming counter, the concave side has a roughly central depression for the lathe, the other side is flat and undecorated. Diameter 22.2–22.7mm, depth 4mm. Kenyon type A counter as above. (SF 353, 24, period 10)

284 Gaming counter, the concave side has a central depression for the lathe, the other flat side has on it some five intersecting lines and four small pecked or punched holes. The edge is marked with four sets of slashes. Diameter 17.7mm, depth 3.8mm. Kenyon type A counter as above. (SF 392, 124F, period 9)

Explosion site finds (AES 76-7)

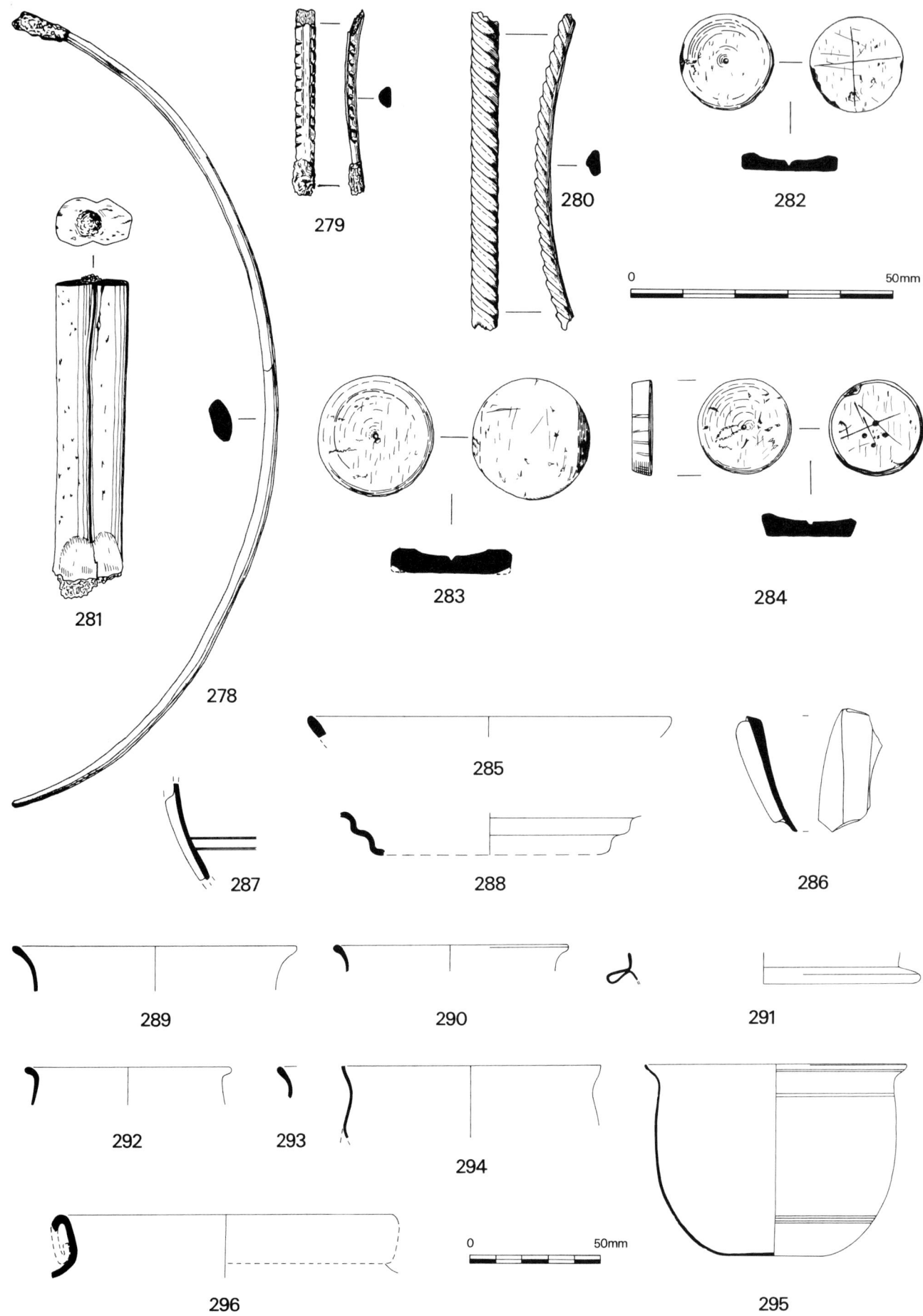

Figure 165 Bone objects, nos 278–284, and glass vessels, nos 285–296 (AES 76–7)

Glass (AES 76–7)
Denise Allen

The excavations produced 133 fragments of vessel glass, 11 fragments of window glass, eight beads, and one gaming piece.

The vessel glass is predominantly of the natural blue-green colour used both for containers and tableware throughout most of the Roman period. This totals 88 fragments, of which 19 could be recognised as bottles of common 1st- and 2nd-century forms. In addition there were 36 fragments of the colourless glass popular for tableware from the Flavian period on. The remaining vessel fragments comprise five pale green, two yellow-green, one olive green, and one dark blue. The last was the only example of the brightly coloured glass most popular for tableware during the 1st century, and this date is supported by the evidence of the rim fragment itself (no 285).

All the glass is extremely fragmentary, and even the catalogued pieces cannot always be assigned with certainty to a specific vessel type or date. What it does offer, though, is a hint of the range of glassware in use on the site: cast and ground bowls (nos 285–287), a mould-blown vessel of uncertain form (no 288), and a good range of blown bowls, beakers, and cups, some of them decorated with folded ridge (no 291), indents (no 294), and wheel-cut lines (no 295). In addition there is a jar rim (no 296), a spouted jug (no 297), the bottles already cited, and vessel fragments with linear wheel-cutting (no 300) and trailing (nos 301–309). The date range for these fragments spans the early Flavian period to possibly the 4th century (no 300). The great majority of these vessels would have been imported, probably from the Seine-Rhine region.

The beads are all small and undecorated, and those that can be closely dated belong to the later Roman period. The gaming piece, too, is dated by its decoration to the 4th century. It should be noted that the vessel base no 311 has been worked for re-use, presumably as a gaming piece or counter.

All the window glass is of the cast matt-glossy variety, in use until about AD 300; late Roman cylinder blown window panes are not represented.

Cast and ground (Figs 165–166)

285 Rim fragment of a bowl of dark blue glass. Cast and rotary-polished; sides steeply sloping. Diameter of rim *c* 140mm. (SF 514, II, U/S)
286 Fragment from the side of a pillar-moulded bowl of blue-green glass. Moulded, inner surface rotary-polished, outer surface fire-polished. Part of one rib extant, diameter of vessel indeterminable. (168F, period 2)
287 Fragment from the side of a pillar-moulded bowl of blue-green glass. Manufacturing details as above, with the addition of two horizontal wheel-cut lines on interior. (231, period 7)

Pillar-moulded bowl fragments represent one of the commonest glass finds on sites occupied during the 1st century AD, partly because of their widespread popularity and partly because even very small pieces are easy to recognise! The ribs may have been formed in a mould, or alternatively by pressing a hot flat disc of glass with a disc-shaped tool which had gaps radiating from the centre so that the glass squeezed through the gaps to form raised ribs. The ribbed disc would then be sagged over a mould to produce the bowl shape (Price 1985, 304). The characteristic finish was produced by rotary-polishing the inside and the rim outside, while the ribbed area was fire-polished. Polychrome and bright monochrome bowls belong to the pre-Flavian period, whilst blue-green vessels, like nos 286 and 287, were the most numerous, and continued to be made into the Flavian period, with some surviving into the early 2nd century. The blue rim fragment, no 285, may be from another pillar-moulded bowl, or alternatively from a plain cast and ground bowl, as at Camulodunum (Harden 1947, 301, nos 38, 38a, 56, 56a). Either way it dates to the pre- or early Flavian period.

Mould-blown glass

288 Lower body fragment of a vessel of pale green glass; some pinhead bubbles within the metal, surfaces iridescent. Sloping profile, with two horizontal mould-blown corrugations extant, the lower one possibly representing the edge of a base, diameter *c* 90mm. (25, period 11)

Mould-blown vessels were made throughout the Roman period, but in greatest number and widest variety during the 1st century AD. This fragment is too small to assign it with any certainty to any one group.

Blown glass

Bowls, beakers, and cups

289 Two joining rim fragments of a beaker of blue-green glass. Rim outflared, fire-rounded, and thickened, diameter *c* 110mm. (SF 35, 1, period 14 and SF 334, 124, period 9).
290 Rim fragment of blue-green glass; surfaces iridescent. Similar to no 4 above, but rim diameter *c* 90mm. (SF 305, 86, period 9)

Neither of these fragments is diagnostic enough to allow close identification.

291 Side fragment from a bowl of blue-green glass. Thin-walled, with part of a decorative horizontal folded loop or flange extant. Maximum diameter *c* 120mm. (SF 190, 29, period 11)

The folded side ridge on this fragment identifies it as belonging to a group of bowls with what is described by Isings as a 'cut out ridge' (1957, 89–90, form 69). The type appears to have been extremely long-lived: early examples have come from the Magdalensberg, dated before AD 45 (Czurda-Ruth 1979, 62–65, plate 3, nos 510–527), from Velsen II, dated AD 40–55 (van Lith 1977, 55, plate 5, no 338). Isings lists Flavian and later finds, and there is also one from an early 4th-century grave at Trier (Goethert-Polaschek 1977, 37–38, form 26, no 102, plate 16, no 176e). British par-

Explosion site finds (AES 76-7)

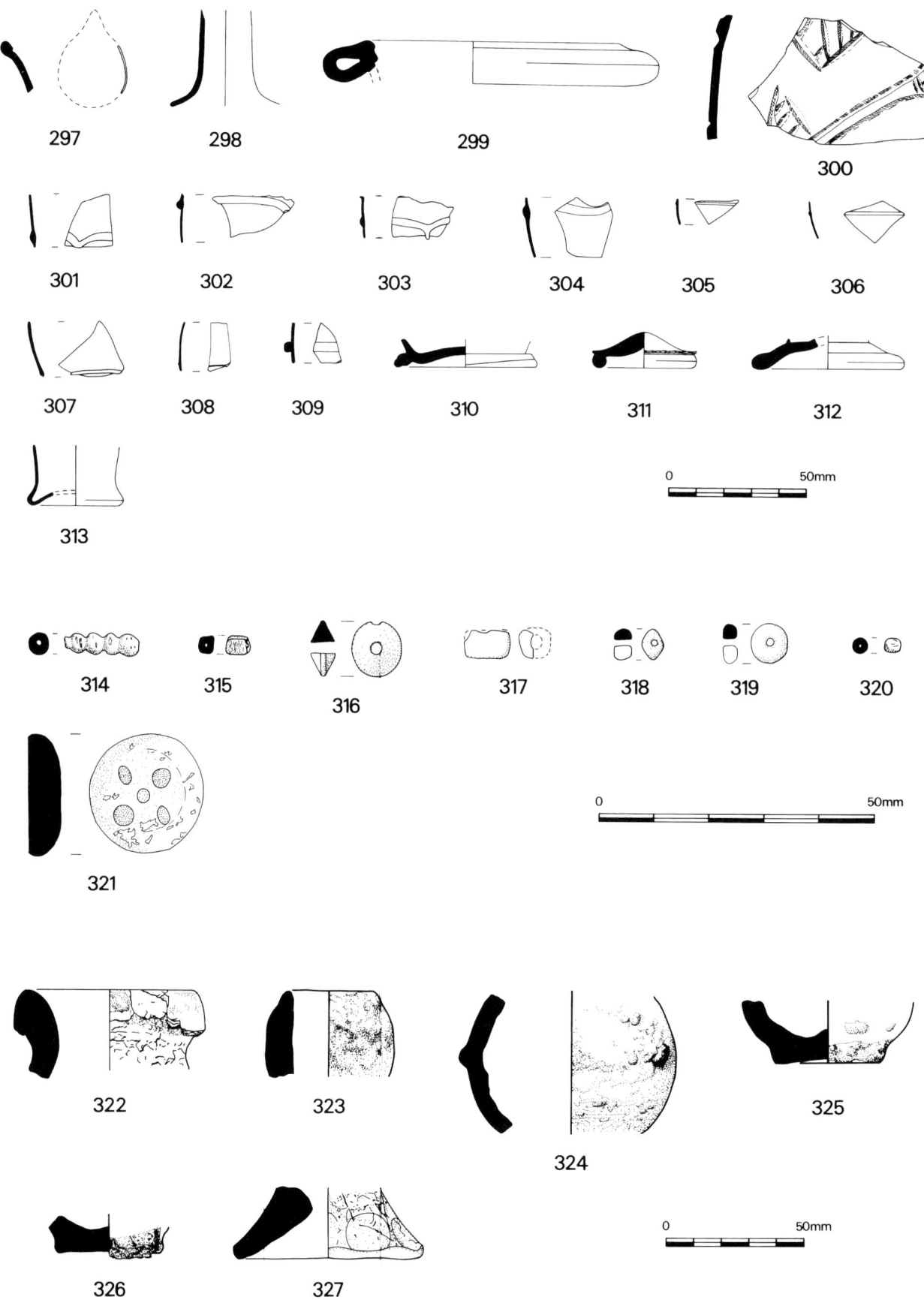

Figure 166 Glass vessels and objects, nos 297–321, and crucibles, nos 322–327 (AES 76–7)

allels include a complete bowl from Felixstowe, Suffolk (British Museum), a fragmentary one from Silchester (Boon 1974, 230–231, Fig 36, no 7), and four fragments from Verulamium (Verulamium Museum).

292 Rim fragment, probably of a beaker, of yellow-green glass; some flaking iridescence. Rim outflared, fire-rounded, and thickened; large accidental air-bubble trapped beneath. Diameter of rim c 80mm. (SF 240, 12, period 11)

293 Small rim fragment of yellow-green glass, similar to no 7 above, diameter indeterminable. (SF 42, 1, period 9)

These fragments are again not closely identifiable.

294 Rim fragment of a cup of greenish-colourless glass; some streaky iridescence. Rim outflared and ground smooth, sides expand slightly downward, the lower part of the surviving profile showing that the vessel was originally decorated with indents, pushed in whilst the glass was still warm and pliable. Diameter of rim c 100mm. (SF 236, 29, period 11)

Glass cups decorated with oval indents were made in a range of shapes and sizes from the Flavian period on. There was variety in the number of indents (from four to 12 or more), the colour, the presence or absence of a base-ring, and the shape of the rim. Numerous British finds include two from 1st-century contexts at Richborough (Bushe-Fox 1926, 49, plate XIX, no 8; Radford 1932, 85, no 61, pl XV), one from a 2nd-century burial at Lower Runhams, Lenham, Kent (Monckton 1979, 120, Fig 2, f), and one from a 3rd-century burial at York (Harden 1962, 140, plate 66, no HG 180).

295 Rim, body, and base fragments revealing a complete profile of a cup of colourless glass; surfaces iridescent. Rim outflared and ground smooth; body hemispherical, decorated with a horizontal wheel-cut line immediately beneath rim, another around top of body, a pair around lower body, and one circle around the edge of the base. The base is flat with usage scratches visible on underside. Height 70mm; diameter of rim c 100mm; diameter of base c 40mm. (SF 544, II 52, period 9)

Hemispherical bowls decorated with linear cutting, as here, and also facet cutting, were popular during the later 2nd and 3rd centuries. A fragmentary example very similar in shape to no 295 was found in a pit dated AD 155–165 at Park Street, Towcester (Price 1980, 63–64, Fig 14, no 2), and there is another, differing slightly in the presence of a small base-ring, from mixed contexts at Verulamium with a *terminus post quem* of AD 150–155/60 (Charlesworth 1972, 206, Fig 77, no 46). A shallower variety of the same type is also known. Three fragmentary examples came from a 2nd-century grave at Skeleton Green, Herts (Charlesworth 1981, 268–270, Fig 105, nos 20a–c).

Jar

296 Broken rim fragment of a jar of blue-green glass. Rim would originally have been folded outward and downward, possibly twice, forming a sloping tubular collar. Diameter of rim c 130mm. (285, period 2)

The surviving part of this rim makes its most likely identification as that of a globular jar, probably with vertically ribbed body and tubular collar (Isings 1957, 88, form 67c). Such vessels were produced in large numbers, in blue-green and other colours such as dark blue and amber, during the period c AD 60–130.

Jugs/flasks

297 Rim fragment of a jug of greenish-colourless glass; surface iridescent. Flaring rim, folded inward and downward, and curvature of extant fragment shows that it has been pulled to form a spout, probably quite pointed in shape. (SF 420, 170, period 9)

Jugs with spouted rims were made in a variety of shapes and sizes from the later 1st to 4th centuries. Some have the spout opposite the handle, whilst others have it to one side, at right-angles to the handle. The spout itself is sometimes quite rounded, often described as a 'trefoil' mouth, in other cases it is more pointed, as is probably the case here. This fragment cannot therefore be closely identified or dated, but since none of the variations was particularly common, it is worth noting its presence on the site.

298 Lower neck fragment of a jug, flask or bottle of colourless glass, now whitish with swirling iridescent surfaces. Diameter of neck c 20mm. (88, period 10)

This piece cannot be closely identified.

Bottles

299 Rim fragment of a large bottle of blue-green glass. Rim folded outward, upward, and inward, and flattened to 'mushroom' shape, diameter c 110mm. (SF 533, 207, period 9)

Mould-blown blue-green bottle fragments almost invariably make up the bulk of the glass found on sites occupied during the first two centuries AD. Here the total is nineteen fragments, of which twelve are from prismatic bottles, five of them certainly square, two are from cylindrical bottles, and five are indeterminate. The square was the longest-lived variety, spanning the second half of the 1st and the 2nd centuries. Production of cylindrical bottles seems to have ceased by the end of the Trajanic period.
Bottle fragments from the following contexts are not described in detail:

1 shoulder fr, prismatic bottle. (266I, period 1)
1 body fr, cylindrical bottle. (244, period 4)
1 body fr, prismatic bottle. (208A, period 5)
1 rim fr. (SF 440, 232, period 6)
1 body fr, cylindrical bottle. (62, period 8)
1 indeterminate base fr. (41, period 9)
1 base fr, prismatic bottle, with 2 circles extant; 2 body frs, square bottles. (124, period 9)
1 rim fr. (SF 586, 124A, period 9)
1 body fr, square bottle. (86, period 9)
1 neck fr. (SF 341, 86A, period 9)
1 body fr, square bottle. (II 10, period 9)
1 body fr, square bottle. (49, period 10)
1 body fr, prismatic bottle. (75, period 10)
1 shoulder fr, prismatic bottle. (SF 223, 12, period 11)

Explosion site finds (AES 76-7)

1 body fr, square bottle. (8, period 12)
1 body fr, prismatic bottle. (1, period 14)

Body and base fragments, vessel types uncertain

300 Body fragment, probably of a bowl or plate, of colourless glass, now whitish and opaque. Outer surface decorated with a series of long and short rotary-cut lines, with polished finish. (1, period 14)

Colourless glass with cut decoration was popular for tableware from the Flavian period to the 4th century. It usually occurs in the form of cups and bowls, but occasionally flasks and bottle-jugs were thus decorated. This piece has been blown rather than cast, and the curvature of the fragment make it most likely to have come from a shallow or deep curved or 'bag-shaped' bowl. The style of cutting, comprising a series of long and short wheel-cut lines, could place it with a 3rd-century group of vessels with geometric designs combining cut lines and circular or oval facets, best exemplified by finds from a cellar deposit at Verulamium (Charlesworth 1972, 208, Fig 78, nos 48–53). Alternatively no 300 could form part of a figured scene, also formed by a series of wheel-cut lines. Vessels bearing such decoration, of which a large number of different styles have been identified, were produced largely in the 4th century. They have been discussed recently with reference to fragments from Lullingstone Villa (Cool and Price 1987, 113–118, Fig 54, nos 338–9).

301 Body fragment of a blue-green glass; some pinhead bubbles within the metal. Part of a looped self-coloured trail extant. (87, period 10)
302 Body fragment of blue-green glass; surfaces iridescent. Part of a curved self-coloured trail extant. (1, period 14)
303 Body fragment of greenish-colourless glass; some pinhead bubbles within the metal, iridescent surfaces. Part of a looped self-coloured trail extant. Diameter of body c 50mm. (80, period 10)
304 Body fragment of greenish-colourless glass; surfaces streaky, some pinhead bubbles. Part of a curved self-coloured trail extant. (24, period 10)
305 Small body fragment, blue-green glass with fine applied self-coloured trail. Diameter of body c 100mm. (SF 235, 64, period 10)
306 Body fragment similar to no 305 above; iridescent surfaces, diameter of body c 120mm. (124, period 9)
307 Body fragment of very bubbly pale green glass, with fine applied self-coloured trail. Diameter of body c 90mm. (86, period 9)
308 Body fragment similar to no 307 above, bubbly pale green glass with black impurity within the metal. (SF 267, 12, period 11)
309 Small body fragment of colourless glass, with relatively thick applied self-coloured trail. (87, period 10)

Self-coloured trails were applied to many vessel forms throughout the Roman period, and small fragments such as nos 301–309 are therefore impossible to identify with certainty.

310 Part of a vessel base of blue-green glass; some pinhead bubbles within the metal. Pushed-in tubular base-ring, with a folded irregularity around part of it. Central base rises to low dome. Diameter of base-ring c 50mm. (1, period 14)
311 Base of a vessel of colourless glass, now very cracked. Pushed-in tubular base-ring, central base rises to low point. Broken vessel walls have been systematically removed by grozing, presumably to allow re-use of the base as a gaming piece or counter. Diameter of base-ring 38mm. (170, period 9)
312 Part of a vessel base of pale green glass; surfaces dulled, iridescent, and very streaky. Tubular-edged foot, formed by blowing another bulb below the vessel body, and pushing it back up inside itself. Diameter of footring 55mm. (SF 80, 1, period 14)
313 Part of a vessel base of pale green glass; surfaces dulled. Pushed-in open base-ring, diameter c 35mm. (12, period 11)

These four base fragments could have originated from many possible vessel forms. Most interesting is no 311, which has been worked for re-use, presumably as a counter or gaming piece. Such re-use of glass was not uncommon in Roman times, and indeed this treatment of vessel base-rings was probably its commonest manifestation. One example came from Fishbourne (Harden and Price 1971, 353, Fig 141, no 77), there are two more unpublished finds from York (Yorkshire Museum), and a deeper base-ring re-shaped to form a shallow dish from a burial group at Colchester (Colchester and Essex Museum).

Beads

314 Segmented bead of ?green glass; surfaces now weathered to yellowish colour. Four segments extant, length 13mm, diameter 4mm. (SF 113, 2, period 10)

Small segmented beads were common in Roman times, occurring in Britain from the 2nd century to the post-Roman period (Guido 1978, 91–93, Fig 37, no 2).

315 Small square-sectioned bead of blue glass. Length 5mm, max width c 3mm. (SF 412, 161, period 7)

Most small square-sectioned beads seem to come from 3rd- and 4th-century contexts (Guido 1978, 96, Fig 37, no 7).

316 Small biconical bead of green glass, surfaces now heavily weathered to pale gold. Diameter 10mm, thickness at perforation 5mm. (SF 493, 263, period 5)

Beads of this type, too, are predominantly late Roman in date (Guido 1978, 97, Fig 37, no 12).

317 Fragments of a bead of ?turquoise glass; surfaces now heavily weathered to yellow/gold. Original shape apparently cylindrical, height c 5mm; diameter c 6mm. (SF 399, 156, period 6)

Cylindrical beads occurred throughout the Roman period (Guido 1978, 95, Fig 37, no 5). Most were green in colour, and if this bead was indeed turquoise it is more unusual. However, it is so heavily weathered its original colour is uncertain.

318 Small diamond-sectioned bead of blue glass. Length c 4mm, max width (point to point) 6mm. (SF 272, 12, period 11)
  This may in fact be a badly shaped example of a square-sectioned bead like no 315 above.
319 Small discoid bead of green glass, surfaces weathered to yellow/gold. Diameter 7mm, thickness 3mm. (SF 531, 282, period 7.
  This is probably a variant of a cylindrical bead, as discussed with relation to no 317 above.

320 Tiny rounded-cylindrical bead of turquoise glass. Diameter 3mm, length 3mm. (SF 333, 86, period 9)
Also, tiny fragment (unillustrated) of a bead of green glass, shape indeterminable. (SF 437, 18, period 9)

Counter or gaming piece

321 Plano-convex counter or gaming piece of opaque black glass. Surfaces now marred with patchy yellowish weathering, but clearly visible on upper surface is a decoration comprising a central opaque red marvered spot, surrounded by a square arrangement of four blue spots. Height 5mm; diameter 21mm SF 303 (49) period 10.

Decorated gaming pieces have been discussed recently with reference to a complete set of 30 found on the lid of a lead coffin at Lullingstone Villa (Cool and Price 1987, 123–125, Fig 57, no 391). The Lullingstone counters comprise 15 opaque white with red, blue, and turquoise spots, and 15 opaque red/brown with blue, yellow-tinged turquoise, and red-tinged turquoise spots. However, Cool and Price cite two further complete sets found, at Lankhills, Winchester (Clarke 1979, plate 1b) and Krefeld Gellep (Pirling 1966, farb taf B), in which the counters are white or black with red or blue spots arranged, as here, with four spots of one colour surrounding one of the other colour. Single finds listed also occur most often in the colours and spot arrangement of no 321 here. These include examples from Richborough, South Shields, Colchester, London, Mancetter, Woodcuts, and Brunehaut Liberchies, Belgium. Where dates are available, the decorated gaming pieces have come from 4th-century contexts, although plain ones seem to have occurred throughout the Roman period.

Window glass

A total of 11 fragments of window glass was found, all of the cast matt-glossy variety in use to about AD 300 (Boon 1966). This was usually blue-green in colour, but colourless fragments are by no means unusual.

1 fr, blue-green, matt-glossy; 1 fr, colourless, matt-glossy. (69, period 6)
1 fr, blue-green, matt-glossy. (226, period 6)
1 fr, blue-green, matt-glossy. (227, period 6)
1 fr, blue-green, matt-glossy. (232, period 6)
2 fr, blue-green, matt-glossy; 1 fr, colourless, matt-glossy. (124, period 9)
1 fr, blue-green, matt-glossy. (78, period 10)
1 fr, blue-green, matt-glossy. (12, period 11)
1 fr, blue-green, matt-glossy. (II U/S)

Metalworking slags and furnace residues (AES 76–7)
Gerry McDonnell

(For a description of individual samples see microfiche M2:F3–F5)
Samples of various types of residues were analysed. They fall into three categories; smithing slag, fuel ash slag, and fragments of furnace lining, all of which are typical residues of ironworking.

Fuel ash slag is characterised by its low density (resulting from its high silica content), highly gassed nature, and light colour (principally grey). It is derived from reactions between the incombustible material (ash) in the charcoal or wood fuel, and siliceous material such as sand, furnace lining, and so on.

Furnace lining survives where the heat of the furnace or hearth has baked and stabilised the clay, the hot face of which sometimes shows reactions with slag or fuel ash slag. The surface is therefore often vitrified and the body clay is burnt red. The surviving heat-affected lining sherds are rarely more than 20mm thick.

The slag occurs as complete or fragmented hearth bottoms. There was no tap or run slag recorded. This indicates that the residues are the result of smithing. The hearth bottoms are hemispherical conglomerations of slag (of a typical fayalite composition, extruded from the wrought iron while it was heated in the smithing hearth), hammer scale, metallic iron, charcoal, and fuel ash slag. They develop at the bottom of the smithing hearth, and hence often have hearth lining adhering to the sides.

In addition to analysis of the slag and related materials two sherds of crucible, a rim sherd and a body sherd with an external lug were examined by X-ray fluorescence analysis. Only the larger body sherd proved satisfactory, results showing that Ca, Fe, Cu, Zn, and Pb were present. Both Ca and Fe derived from the crucible fabric. The remaining elements suggest the working of leaded brasses.

Conclusion

The ironworking residues are typical of those associated with the smithing process. The fuel ash slag and furnace lining can be found in association with any industrial process involving hearths or kilns. The nature of the furnace lining fragments is the result of their being attacked by the slag and also exposed to high temperatures. The slag itself occurs in typical hearth bottom forms, which are atypical in that the magnetite content is either extremely low or absent. The magnetite can be derived from hammer scale (which is often found as a separate deposit on sites), or from oxidation of the slag *in situ* in the hearth.

Besides ironworking it is apparent from the crucibles that copper alloys (probably brasses) were also worked on this site.

Crucibles (AES 76–7)
Paul Booth

Thirteen crucible fragments were found on the site (Fig 166), all but one in the period 9 pit (124). They included five rim sherds and three bases. The number of crucibles represented is uncertain; four of the rims,

Explosion site finds (AES 76-7)

all very small fragments, could have come from a single vessel perhaps no more than c 40mm in diameter, but equally there may have been more than one vessel. The fifth piece is from a rather larger crucible (no 322), c 65mm in diameter, with a thickened rather than a tapered rim. All the remaining fragments are probably from crucibles of the smaller type (eg no 323). A base of one of these occurred in the period 10 pit (168). One body sherd in (124), apparently of this type, had a small rounded boss or lug (no 324).

The fabric of the crucibles, where it was not grossly modified by continual heating, was quite consistent; light grey in colour and hard fired, with moderate quantities of fairly fine-grained quartz sand. The larger rim contained more sand. The base in (168) (no 325) was clearly wheelthrown, as was the large rim. Many of the other fragments were irregular, but this was probably a result of firing and refiring during use, rather than of different manufacture.

Also in (124) were three fragments of a possible crucible lid (no 327), one of which had a spot of green 'glaze', presumably derived from a molten copper alloy, adhering to the rim. These pieces were clearly handmade in a clay distinct from that of the crucibles themselves, less sandy and with a high mica content. A further, similar fragment (though possibly from the rim of another small crucible) was found in (224), along with a grey ware pottery sherd which had been very heavily heated and partly vitrified, though this may have been accidental.

The use of the crucibles for melting copper alloys is discussed by Gerry MacDonnell above.

322 Rim fragment of large crucible. (124, period 9)
323 Rim fragment of small crucible. (124A, period 9)
324 Body fragment of small crucible with lug. (124, period 9)
325 Crucible base. (168, period 10)
326 Crucible base. (124, period 9)
327 Possible crucible lid. (124, period 9)

Stone objects (AES 76–7)
Paul Booth including identifications by John Crossling

Querns (Fig 167)

Four principal stone types were identified. Three fragments of imported querns of Niedermandig lava, from the Eifel region, occurred, two in the late 2nd- to mid-3rd-century layer (227) and the third (no 328) in the period 10 pit (168). This piece may have derived from the late 1st- to early 2nd century well (168A), cut by the pit. The most important material for querns at this site was a probable Millstone Grit. Four pieces of this were found (from three stones), one (no 329) in the later 2nd- to mid-3rd-century context (227). The other pieces, including the finer-grained no 330, occurred in late Roman features (170) and possibly (12) or (170). These pieces are likely to have come from the Carboniferous regions of Derbyshire or Staffordshire. A conglomerate was also used, for which the Forest of Dean seems to be the most likely source. Two pieces of this stone occurred at the Explosion site, a coarse conglomerate in the period 1 context (267) and a relatively fine conglomerate in (90). Querns thought to be from this source were an important component of the stone assemblage at the nearby settlement of Tiddington. The only remaining stone was a small fragment of perhaps local Triassic sandstone, deeply scored, occurring in a post-Roman context (12), but likely, along with most of the other finds from this layer, to have been of Roman date.

328 Quern fragment of Niedermandig lava. (168B, period 10)
329 Quern fragment. Upper stone of Millstone Grit. (227, period 6)
330 Quern fragment. Upper stone of fine Millstone Grit. (170, period 9)

Other objects (Fig 167)

331 A rough disc of white Oolitic limestone, perhaps from a relatively local source, of uncertain function. (SF 646, 227, period 6)
332 A whetstone fragment, probably Blue Lias and therefore from a local source. (SF 411, 199, period 9)

Building stone (AES 76–7)
Paul Booth including identifications by John Crossling

Arden Sandstone was used for the foundations and walls of the main buildings on the site, ie from period 5 onwards. This was obtained locally, probably from Primrose Hill, only c 0.5km south-east of Alcester. Quarry pits, albeit of uncertain date, are known here.

A variety of stones was used for roofing of Roman buildings (Fig 167). The quantity of this material precluded its recovery on a systematic basis. It occurred almost exclusively in site I, though it was fairly certainly used on both buildings V and VI, the latter extending into site II. The most common material was Jurassic Blue Lias 'slates' which were widely used, particularly in the later periods. Its earliest occurrence was a single fragment in a period 4 layer (224), otherwise it did not appear before period 6. In any case there can be no doubt that building V (period 5) was roofed with tile for at least part of its life. It is possible that in the 4th-century tile was used alongside stone on some of the roofs, perhaps particularly for ridges, etc. Blue Lias was quarried at Wilmcote, 7km east of Alcester, and at Binton, 6km south-east, from medieval times and both of these sources could have been exploited in the Roman period. Blue Lias was used not only for roofing but also (probably) for a whetstone (no 332 above). A single well-shaped *tessera* of this stone was found in the period 9 pit (II 22). Occurring in isolation, this is unlikely to have derived from the Explosion site itself.

A white Oolitic Jurassic limestone also occurred, used alongside the lias for roofing. This stone does not occur locally, but is found particularly to the

Explosion site finds (AES 76-7)

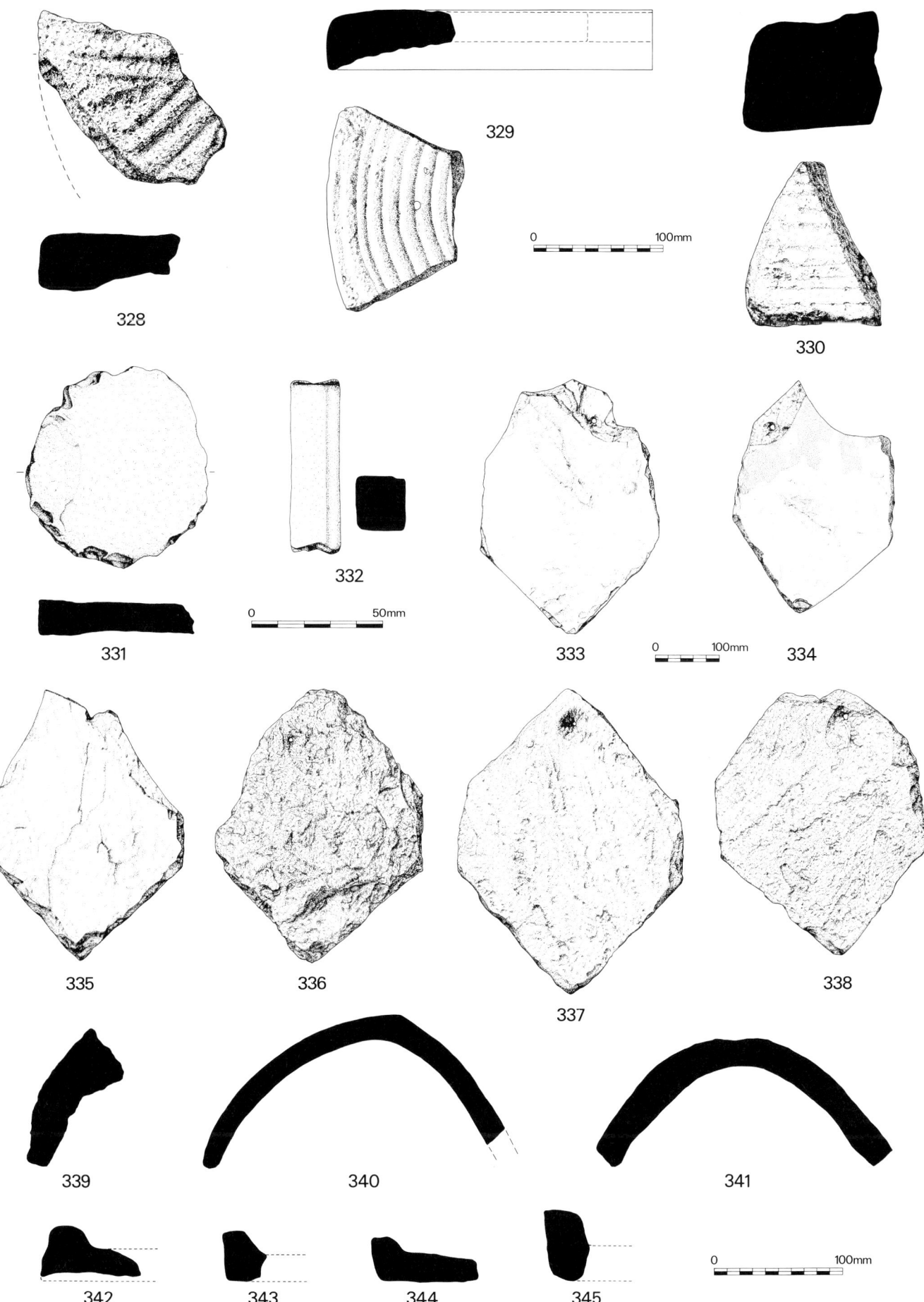

Figure 167 Stone objects, nos 328–332, stone building material, nos 333–339, and tile, nos 340–345 (AES 76–7)

Table 29 Roman tile fabric quantification (AES 76–7) (number of fragments/weight in grams)

	Tile type	Tegula	Imbrex	Box flue	Floor	Unidentified	Total
Fabric	1	9/1320	5/330	3/270	–/–	120/4150	137/6070
	2	53/18360	73/8350	6/610	21/4520	1145/53330	1298/85170
	3	–/–	11/1090	–/–	4/640	50/1980	65/3710
	4	55/16480	139/21560	9/880	15/5110	656/31830	874/76220
	5	1/90	1/60	–/–	1/420	21/890	24/1460
	6	–/–	1/2030	–/–	–/–	–/–	1/2030
Total		118/36610	230/33420	18/1760	41/10690	1992/92180	2399/174660

It should be noted that *tegulae* will tend to be under-represented in the above figures as the centre parts of *tegulae* with no distinguishing features were recorded as type unidentified.

south-east of Alcester, for example in Oxfordshire, where rock of this description is found in the Great Oolite series. This stone was quite common in the later Roman period. Occurring in much smaller quantities was a honey-coloured limestone typical of the Jurassic Inferior Oolite series. Fragments of this stone were found in period 2 contexts, but otherwise the only noteworthy piece was part of a possible *imbrex*-like ridge piece (no 339) from the period 10 pit (4). The nearest outcrop of this type of stone is at the top of Ebrington Hill, near Stratford-upon-Avon, though there is no certainty that the Alcester pieces originated there and they could have come from any one of a large number of sources in the Cotswolds. A further stone type, superficially similar to the Blue Lias, is a limestone containing fine silt grains which mark it as distinct from other material. 'Slates' of this stone occurred in a late 3rd- to 4th-century pit (II 52); its source is unknown.

A further stone used for roofing was a good quality dark, possibly Carboniferous, sandstone. This is a distinctive medium-grained stone with a very high iron content. Its source is unknown but the nearest possibility is in the Enville Beds, of appropriate date, located to the north-east of Coventry, though there is at present no evidence that the Romans exploited this source for building material. Two complete hexagonal 'slates' of this stone (nos 337 and 338) were found in the period 10 pit (4), together with much other roofing material (all the illustrated 'slates' were from this context).

Small quantities of tufa were found on the site, fourteen probable fragments being identified. These were concentrated in period 4 features in site II, (II 67) and (II 67A) and the overlying period 5 layer (II 54), with a further fragment in the period 3 feature (II 53). Isolated fragments occurred in later contexts in site I. Tufa was sometimes used in bath buildings, and its presence here may indicate the existence of such a building in the vicinity of the site, or may suggest that materials from such a building were reused more widely in the town after its demise. The probable mid-2nd-century date of the majority of instances is interesting, suggesting the possible existence of a bath building at this or an earlier date, perhaps in the central part of the town.

333 Roof slate of Blue Lias. (4, period 10)
334 Roof slate of Blue Lias. (4, period 10)
335 Roof slate of Blue Lias. (4, period 10)
336 Roof slate of white Oolitic limestone. (4, period 10)
337 Roof slate of possibly Carboniferous sandstone. (4, period 10)
338 Roof slate of possibly Carboniferous sandstone. (4, period 10)
339 Fragment of possible ridge piece of Inferior Oolitic limestone. (4, period 10)

Roman tile (AES 76–7)
Peter Cheer and Paul Booth

A moderate quantity (174.66kg) of tile was recovered from Roman and later contexts. The initial examination of this material was carried out by Peter Cheer. This involved recording the fragment count, weight, tile type, and flange type (where applicable) of six tile fabrics. The fabrics were distinguished solely on macroscopic criteria of colour, sandiness, and clearly visible inclusion types. Only two fabrics (2 and 4) occurred in large quantities, the principal difference between them being the presence of black iron inclusions in fabric 4.

Fabrics

1. Cream to light pink surfaces and margins; orange core. Fine, even matrix of small quartz; streaky veins and inclusions of white clay; moderate medium red ironstone
2. Orange to dark red surfaces and margins; orange, dark red, or grey core. Frequent fine and sparse medium quartz grains
3. Dark red to grey throughout. Frequent medium and sparse large quartz grains, sparse medium black ironstone
4. Dark red to orange or grey throughout. Frequent small and moderate medium to large quartz grains. Sparse to moderate medium black iron ore. This fabric appears to lie between fabrics 2 and 3
5. Bright red throughout. Similar to fabric 4 but distinctive because of its colour and laminar fracture
6. Orange surfaces and margins; grey core. Frequent fine and sparse moderate quartz grains. Sparse

Explosion site finds (AES 76-7)

Table 30 **Roman tile types by period (AES 76–7)** (weight in grams)

Period	1	2	3	4	5	6	7	8	9	10	11	12	13	14	Total
Tegula	5140	160	3030	190	1990	9510	870	1690	4970	4100	1750	1300	–	1910	36610
Imbrex	700	690	120	–	480	11190	200	1960	5260	7140	3600	190	–	1890	33420
Box flue	–	–	–	–	–	110	–	–	970	420	160	40	–	60	1760
Flat	–	–	–	180	390	4050	60	630	2280	1480	–	1580	–	–	10690
Unidentified	1320	2400	1410	640	2820	24450	3780	4720	23300	15020	8130	1480	100	2610	92180
Total	7160	3250	4560	1010	5680	49310	4910	9000	36820	28160	13640	4590	100	6470	174660

Table 31 **Roman tile fabrics/types by period** (weight in grams)

Period	1	2	3	4	5	6	7	8	9	10	11	12	13	14	Total
Fabric 1															
Tegula									140	430	40	440		270	1320
Imbrex										210				120	330
Box flue										250				20	270
Flat															
Unident.						130		220	940	1550	430	250		630	4150
Subtotal						130		220	1080	2440	470	690		1040	6070
Fabric 2															
Tegula	1890	160	3030	190	990	5010	320	560	2000	2730	790			690	18360
Imbrex		90			20	900	160	960	2510	2060	880			770	8350
Box flue									540	70					610
Flat				180	390	2300			1450	200					4520
Unident.	1020	1480	770	470	1670	16380	2440	1610	12880	7890	4540	790	60	1330	53330
Subtotal	2910	1730	3800	840	3070	24590	2920	3130	19380	12950	6210	790	60	2790	85170
Fabric 3															
Tegula															
Imbrex						380	40	160	370	30				110	1090
Box flue									40	600					640
Flat															
Unident.			290			270	20	80	360	740	150	10		60	1980
Subtotal			290			650	60	240	770	1370	150	10		170	3710
Fabric 4															
Tegula	3250				1000	4500	550	1130	2830	940	920	860		860	16840
Imbrex	700	600	120		460	9910		840	2320	2810	2720	190		890	21560
Box flue						110			430	100	160	40		40	880
Flat						1750	60	630	830	680		1160			5110
Unident.	300	920	350	170	1150	7580	1320	2800	8860	4570	2990	200	40	580	31830
Subtotal	4250	1520	470	170	2610	23850	1930	5400	15270	9100	6790	2450	40	2370	76220
Fabric 5														90	90
Tegula															
Imbrex										60					60
Box flue															
Flat												420			420
Unident.						90		10	260	270	20	230		10	890
Subtotal						90		10	320	270	20	650		100	1460
Fabric 6															
Imbrex										2030					2030
Subtotal										2030					2030
Total	7160	3250	4560	1010	5680	49310	4910	9000	36820	28160	13640	4590	100	6470	174660

Explosion site finds (AES 76-7)

large grey angular grog lumps. This fabric is distinguished by the use of red paint on its surfaces

The source of fabrics 1–5 is unknown, though it is likely to have been quite local. The nearest known tileries are at Lapworth and Chase Wood, Kenilworth, respectively 16 and 23km distant. While these sources could have supplied Alcester, more local production is also likely, and is suggested by the appearance elsewhere in the town of tiles stamped TCD (three examples) and]ERNI (two examples), both of which stamps are unique to Alcester. Tile fabric 6 is of considerable interest as it is the same as pottery fabric G11 and originates most probably in the vicinity of Milton Keynes, where it is extremely common (Zeepvat 1987, 120; Booth and Green 1989, 82, see also below). The distinctive nature of this fabric and the use of red paint, which is also found in Buckinghamshire and Northamptonshire, leave no doubt about its identification.

Tile types (Table 30)

Despite the under representation of *tegulae* they were still the most common identified tile type in terms of weight, though outnumbered 2:1 by *imbrex* fragments. Both *tegulae* and *imbrices* occur on the site from period 1. Tiles with a thickness greater than 33mm have been assumed to be 'flat' when no other identifying feature was present. Such tiles were found in small quantities from period 4 onwards. Box flue tiles were even less common and apart from a single occurrence in period 6 were found only in late Roman contexts. It seems certain that none of the excavated rooms of buildings V and VI was heated. Flue tiles may therefore have come from parts of these structures lying outside the excavated area or have been derived from adjacent buildings.

Dimensions

For most fragments, thickness was the only meaningful dimension surviving. Thicknesses were recorded but showed nothing outside the range encountered on other sites (Table 32).

A late 4th-century pit (4) produced fragments of an exceptionally large *imbrex* with a width of *c* 220mm. This unique tile was in fabric 6 (see above), and was the only example of this fabric from the site. It has been suggested that it may have been intended as a ridge tile for use in conjunction with limestone 'slates' (G Brodribb pers comm). From the same context was a complete *imbrex* of fabric 4. Its dimensions were: length 395mm, width 130–170mm, thickness 15mm; it weighed 1500g.

Four different flange types were noted on *tegulae*. The total length of each type was recorded as follows: type 1, 880mm; type 2, 3395mm; type 3, 1748mm; type 4, 1580mm. This form of quantification is little used but provides the best means of comparing the propor-

Table 32 Roman tile thicknesses (AES 76–7) (mm)

	Imbrices	Tegulae	Box flue	Flat
Range	10–30	13–30	10–28	31–70
Mean	16.9	22.9	16	41.8
Mode	15	25	15	35

tions of different flange types. The significance of the variations in type is, however, uncertain. All types are found in fabrics 2 and 4 and types 1–3 also occur in fabric 1. Type 2 was most common in fabric 2, but for all other flange types fabric 4 was the principal fabric.

340 Incomplete section of large *imbrex* (fabric 6). (4, period 10)
341 Section of complete *imbrex* (fabric 4). (4, period 10)
342 *Tegula* flange type 1 (fabric 1). (1, period 14)
343 *Tegula* flange type 2 (fabric 5). (1, period 14)
344 *Tegula* flange type 3 (fabric 2). (1, period 14)
345 *Tegula* flange type 4 (fabric 1). (4, period 10)

Animal prints

Three prints were identified; two were probably dog and the third was of a cat. In addition there was one unidentified probable print.

Discussion

The earliest buildings on the site had tiled roofs, as is evidenced by the occurrence of *tegulae* and *imbrices* from period 1 onwards. Fabrics 2 and 4 were the principal fabrics in use throughout the Roman period. There was an isolated instance of fabric 3 in period 3 (late 1st to early 2nd century), but otherwise the full range of fabrics (apart from 6, which was only found in a single later 4th-century context) only occurred from period 6 onwards. This was a period which saw major reconstruction work to building V, and more tile survived from contexts of this than of any other period. The main occurrences of tile after period 6 were in periods 9 and 10, which saw further reworking and demolition of tile-roofed structures. The use of tiles for purposes other than roofing was rare and such tiles may have derived from adjacent sites. The source(s) of the tiles are, with one unusual exception, unknown. They may have been locally produced, but the absence of underfired and overfired tiles shows that such production must have taken place at some little distance from the site where they were used.

Other building materials (AES 76–7)
Paul Booth

Daub

Of the 210 fragments of daub recovered from the site, 63 occurred in the very limited areas of period 2 deposits examined. There can be little doubt that a timber-framed building or buildings with wattle and daub infilled walls stood on or close to the site at this time. Subsequent occurrences of daub were probably largely residual, either in large build-up layers or in the period 9 and 10 pits which cut earlier deposits. Most of the daub from site II was found in period 4 contexts, possibly indicating the demolition of nearby structures at this time.

The daub fragments from period 2 preserved some structural details. Several rounded wattle impressions of c 20mm diameter survived. Some pieces of daub were faced on both sides; where this was so one side was rougher than the other, perhaps indicating that the daub had been plastered up against upright structural timbers in the wall while the smoother face represented the exposed, hand-finished surface. The 'double-faced' pieces ranged in thickness from c 24–27mm. A few of the daub fragments were less regular; one piece with both faces of similar (smooth) appearance ranged from 18–23mm in thickness.

Plaster

There were 328 fragments of plaster from the site, of which only four, from late 3rd- to 4th-century contexts, were painted. Five fragments in total came from period 3–6 contexts and possibly derived from the early timber buildings on the site. The majority of all the plaster fragments (53%) were from period 7 contexts in site I, particularly layer (120), within the southerly room of building V. This seems to have been a dump of material, presumably indicating re-plastering of this room at this time, or possibly relating to the reconstruction of building V in the previous period. The relatively large amounts of plaster in contexts of periods 9–11 will have been derived from the final decay and demolition of the building, and perhaps also from building VI. The extreme rarity of painted fragments suggests that the rooms of buildings V and VI, certainly those which occurred within the excavated area, were plastered but not painted. Samples of the plaster and mortar were analysed by Graham Morgan (see microfiche M2:F5–F8). The analysis showed that the plasters were very similar and closely comparable to those from some other sites in Alcester. Most had two lower layers and two *intonaco* layers.

Opus signinum

Five fragments of opus signinum were recorded. Four were from late 3rd- to 4th-century contexts in site II; perhaps the most significant occurrence was of a relatively large piece (130gm) from (291), one of the earliest period 2 layers and likely to be of 1st-century date. This cannot have come from a structure within the excavated area but was presumably from one situated nearby.

Faunal remains (AES 76–7)
Mark Maltby

Introduction

Animal bones from the excavations were examined using the modern comparative collection in the Department of Prehistory and Archaeology, University of Sheffield during the summer of 1977 (the report text was revised in 1989). Detailed records were made of the types of fragment and the minimum numbers represented by each skeletal element in each context. Tooth eruption and epiphyseal fusion data were recorded where applicable to enable the analysis of the ages of the animals represented to be undertaken. Metrical data were recorded using a pair of vernier callipers to an accuracy of 0.1mm. An osteometric board was employed for the larger measurements. Notes were made of preservation, butchery, and pathology.

The faunal sample was analysed in three groups dated to the earlier Romano-British period, the later Romano-British period, and the medieval period respectively. The division of the Romano-British material was based on the pottery and stratigraphic evidence and broadly separates deposits dated to the 1st–2nd centuries AD from those dated to the 3rd–4th centuries AD. Contexts that contained a large amount of residual pottery (eg 12) are not considered in this report. The subdivision of the Romano-British material is an arbitrary one and it will be shown that there was comparatively little variation between the assemblages of the two periods. The majority of the bones were dated to the later Romano-British period and these will be discussed in the greatest detail. In contrast, very few bones belonged to the medieval period and these merit only brief comment.

Following a brief discussion of the number of fragments identified to species in each period, the report deals with the quantitative data derived from the identification of the different skeletal remains of the major domestic species, concentrating on the later Romano-British deposits. This examines the nature and variability of the animal bone accumulations in the deposits. The following sections on the cattle, sheep/goat, and pig remains concentrate on the information these remains have provided about the exploitation of these species. Some of the tables associated with these sections (Tables MT15–MT25) are located in microfiche (M2:F9–G4). Briefer summaries are provided for the other species of mammal, birds, and fish, whose bones were found in much smaller quantities. The report concludes with an assessment of the importance of the material, the implications of the analysis, and suggestions of the types of future research that may prove profitable.

Analysis of species and fragment representation

Over 23,000 fragments of animal bone form the basis

Explosion site finds (AES 76-7)

Table 33 Number of animal bone fragments identified to species (AES 76–7)

	Early Roman		Late Roman		Medieval	
	n	**%**	**n**	**%**	**n**	**%**
Mammal						
Cattle	843	59.4	6834	61.7	129	58.9
Sheep/goat	445	31.4	2335	21.1	51	23.3
Pig	70	5.4	1186	10.7	25	11.4
Dog	8	0.6	311*	2.8	4	1.8
Cat	–		25*	0.2	1	0.5
Horse	8	0.6	23	0.2	–	
Red deer	–		15	0.1	–	
Roe deer	–		2	0.02	–	
Fallow deer	–		–		1	0.5
Hare	1	0.1	18	0.2	1	0.5
Badger	1	0.1	3*	0.03	–	
Total mammal	1376		10752		212	
Bird						
Domestic fowl	27	1.9	247	2.2	4	1.8
Greylag/Domestic goose	–		12	0.1	–	
Mallard/domestic duck	1	0.1	8	0.1	1	0.5
Woodcock	1	0.1	22	0.2	1	0.5
Golden plover	–		1	0.01	–	
Small duck species (cf teal)	–		1	0.01	–	
Woodpigeon	–		2	0.02	–	
Stock dove/pigeon	–		2	0.02	–	
Small goose species	–		3	0.03	–	
Jackdaw	–		4	0.04	–	
Raven	6	0.4	26*	0.2	–	
Total bird	35		328		6	
Fish and amphibians						
Cod	–		–		1	0.5
Pike	–		1	0.01	–	
Trout/salmon	–		1	0.01	–	
Amphibian	–		1	0.01	–	
Total fish and amphibians	0		3		1	
Total Identified	1411		11083		219	

n = number of fragments,   % = percentage of identified fragments,   * = includes bones of articulated skeletons

of this report, the large majority being of late Roman date (Table 33). In both the Roman samples cattle fragments dominated the assemblage, followed by sheep/goat and pig. The totals include all identifiable fragments including loose teeth, skull fragments, and shaft fragments of longbones. However, the atlas, axis, and sacrum were the only vertebrae included in the counts. The other vertebrae and ribs were assigned to the large mammal and sheep-sized mammal categories, along with other unidentifiable fragments as shown in Table 34. Other domestic mammals (dog, cat, and horse) were present but in much smaller numbers. The number of dog bones was swollen by the presence of several complete or partial

Table 34 Number of unidentified animal bone fragments (AES 76–7)

	Early Roman	Late Roman	Medieval
Large mammal ribs	293	2324	50
Sheep-sized mammal ribs	203	1317	22
Dog ribs	–	65	–
Bird ribs	–	5	–
Large mammal vertebrae	136	1014	22
Sheep-sized mammal vertebrae	48	293	5
Dog vertebrae	–	35	–
Bird vertebrae	–	1	–
Unidentified fragments	622	4079	102
Total	1302	9133	201

* = includes bones from articulated skeletons.
Totals of vertebrae exclude fragments of atlas, axis and sacrum identified to species.

skeletons in the deposits. Domestic fowl dominated the bird bones assemblage. Fragments of wild mammals, birds, and fish were present only in small numbers.

Table 35 shows the number and percentages of cattle, sheep/goat and pig fragments in the major Roman deposits together with the cumulative totals from the smaller assemblages. Cattle fragments were the most common in nearly all the deposits. In only three of the early Roman and three of the late Roman assemblages did the percentage of cattle fragments fall below 60% of the total cattle, sheep/goat, and pig assemblages. Indeed, ten of the deposits contained over 70% cattle fragments, and overall, 62% of the early Roman and 66% of the late Roman fragments belonged to cattle. Sheep/goat fragments outnumbered those of cattle in only one deposit (II 22). This deposit produced the highest percentage of sheep/goat fragments (43%) in any late Roman feature. In most assemblages of that date the percentage of sheep/goat fragments lay between 14–26%, with an overall percentage of 25%. This was lower than the figure obtained in the early Roman deposits (33%), in which only one of the large assemblages (II 67) produced a figure of less than 26%. This decrease was matched by rises in the percentages of both cattle and pig fragments which rose from 5% to 12%.

Such changes in the relative frequencies of fragments of the major domestic species could reflect changes in the meat diet with pork and beef becoming relatively more important in the late Roman period. However, changes in fragment representation could be due to other factors, such as differential recovery rates, preservation conditions, or disposal strategies in the two periods. It is necessary to study the types of fragment represented to understand the nature of the faunal assemblage. Tables 36, 38, and 40 list the number of fragments represented in each of the major assemblages of Roman date for cattle, sheep/goat, and pig respectively. They also list the number of articular surfaces of the major limb bones recovered.

Cattle assemblage

It is clear from Table 36 that the cattle assemblage was dominated by skull fragments. Table 37 expresses the figures given in Table 36 as percentages of the total cattle assemblage in each deposit. In the early Roman deposits they provided 18% of the cattle assemblage and this figure rose to 22% overall in the late Roman deposits. If the maxilla fragments are added to the other skull fragments, the figures rise to 24% and 28% in the early and late Roman periods respectively. Mandible fragments were also well represented in most deposits, providing 15% of the fragments in the early Roman deposits and 8% in late Roman contexts. The predominance of fragments from the area of the skull and jaws was completed by the number of loose teeth recovered (providing 9% and 8% of the early and late Roman assemblages respectively). Together, mandible, maxilla, other skull fragments, and loose teeth formed 48% and 47% of the early and late Roman samples respectively. Such a high proportion of such bones is in fact not unusual in archaeological samples. The skull tends to break up into more identifiable fragments than other bones. In addition, fragmented cattle jaws may release up to 10 loose teeth, which may be counted separately. Both loose teeth and mandibles are dense elements and survive better than many other parts of the skeleton. It is also the case that disposal strategies in Romano-British towns on occasions left concentrations of these bones dumped together after primary butchery of cattle carcasses. Several examples of such accumulations have now been recorded on Romano-British urban settlements (Maltby 1984, 128–32). These assemblages are also sometimes distinguished by low numbers of the major meat-bearing upper

Explosion site finds (AES 76-7)

Table 35 Number of fragments of the major species in Roman contexts (AES 76–7)

Context	Cattle		Sheep/goat		Pig	
	n	%	n	%	n	%
Early Roman						
227	426	70	167	27	17	3
168A–M	63	47	61	45	11	8
245	83	49	68	40	19	11
224	70	61	42	37	3	3
II 54	48	64	22	29	5	7
II 67	61	84	12	16	0	–
Other contexts	92	51	73	41	15	8
Total	843	62	445	33	70	5
Late Roman						
2	40	41	32	33	24	25
4	755	67	247	22	120	11
24/24A	88	66	25	19	21	16
26	135	83	17	10	11	7
42	60	65	22	24	10	11
49	429	71	114	19	64	11
64	127	77	24	15	15	9
78	497	75	108	16	60	9
86/86A	617	63	241	25	122	12
87	208	64	58	18	59	18
122	177	78	32	14	19	8
124	1313	66	439	22	232	12
161	70	78	17	19	3	3
164–166	120	62	50	26	23	12
168	77	68	24	21	13	11
170	1022	65	373	24	172	11
226	133	78	29	17	9	5
II 10	451	55	264	32	103	13
II 22	96	40	104	43	41	17
Other contexts	419	70	115	19	65	11
Total	6834	66	2335	23	1186	12

limb bones, but relatively high numbers of metapodia, broken open for marrow but subsequently discarded because of their low meat value. The skulls too had often been broken open to remove the brain, and the tongues were no doubt also removed from the mandibles before disposal. Although there were high percentages of skull and mandible fragments at the Explosion site, the percentages of metacarpi and metatarsi (3% and 4% respectively in the late Roman sample) were not particularly high, and indeed were generally no more common than fragments of the major meat-bearing limb bones (humerus – 4%, femur – 4%, tibia – 6%). Counts of the articular surfaces of the major limb bones (Table 36) on the other hand, showed a greater proportion of metapodia. However, this method of analysis favours the epiphyses of early fusion age (such as the distal scapula) and those already fused at birth (the proximal metacarpus and metatarsus). Elements with late fusion ages (proximal humerus and tibia, both ends of the femur) were poorly represented. There is therefore no clear evidence that there was a bias towards the disposal of metapodia on the site. The phalanges were moderately represented and there is

Table 36 Cattle fragment numbers identified (AES 76-7)

	Early Roman									Late Roman													
Bone\Context	227	168A	245	224	II54	II67	Other	Total	2	4	24	26	42	49	64	78	86	87	122	124	161	164	168	170	226	II10	II22	Other	Total
Mandible	72	9	13	11	3	3	17	128	4	107	11	11	5	43	9	27	74	16	21	152	11	14	3	143	8	44	3	46	752
Maxilla	24	–	5	3	–	12	3	47	1	40	6	24	–	17	1	35	26	3	15	108	2	10	–	88	12	8	3	12	411
Skull frags	75	8	9	8	14	22	15	151	9	139	8	37	8	92	41	223	124	26	30	273	6	22	30	182	66	48	7	104	1475
Loose teeth	39	2	7	12	–	6	6	72	3	79	5	16	1	19	8	25	52	20	15	113	7	12	1	61	4	54	13	32	540
Scapula	20	3	1	1	1	3	5	34	1	54	11	3	16	27	4	13	30	11	18	96	–	4	5	90	4	26	5	21	439
Humerus	21	4	7	4	5	2	2	45	2	36	1	5	1	25	5	15	28	15	7	37	7	3	3	39	3	19	5	15	271
Radius	14	3	2	3	3	1	2	28	3	27	–	3	3	18	3	11	24	11	4	23	5	7	3	32	4	15	2	14	212
Ulna	5	1	2	2	2	2	1	15	–	12	1	–	1	9	1	6	11	5	6	19	2	2	2	10	1	5	2	9	104
Pelvis	16	4	3	3	–	1	3	30	4	39	9	4	5	27	4	19	35	10	12	64	6	11	6	49	2	19	8	17	350
Femur	20	4	6	2	6	–	3	41	1	35	4	5	2	22	4	20	32	6	4	57	2	7	3	34	6	15	3	13	276
Tibia	49	9	8	6	6	6	9	93	5	58	9	10	2	31	8	33	38	11	7	70	5	7	5	51	6	39	5	29	429
Astragalus	3	–	1	1	1	–	1	7	–	14	2	–	–	2	–	3	4	2	3	6	1	1	–	14	2	5	1	4	64
Calcaneus	3	1	1	–	1	–	1	7	–	8	–	2	–	6	–	4	3	4	4	15	–	1	–	20	2	8	2	7	86
Other tarsals	–	–	3	–	–	–	1	4	–	7	2	–	–	–	1	1	2	2	2	5	–	1	–	4	1	2	–	1	30
Carpals	1	–	–	–	–	–	1	2	–	5	3	1	–	1	2	5	5	2	–	7	–	–	1	1	–	5	2	–	39
Metacarpus	10	4	3	2	1	1	3	24	1	25	2	–	3	12	4	7	12	8	10	45	4	1	2	46	1	30	6	20	239
Metatarsus	18	5	6	1	4	–	4	38	–	24	3	1	3	24	1	4	26	9	3	45	3	9	6	46	4	21	10	15	257
Metapodial	3	–	1	–	–	–	–	4	1	3	–	–	–	2	2	–	–	1	–	3	–	–	–	–	–	1	1	2	16
1st phalanx	16	4	2	8	1	1	7	39	4	13	7	6	6	26	12	22	31	18	10	65	4	3	2	64	2	32	8	23	358
2nd phalanx	7	–	2	1	–	–	3	13	1	11	2	2	–	9	9	9	25	11	3	56	4	3	–	12	1	31	4	19	212
3rd phalanx	8	1	1	2	–	–	3	15	–	11	1	2	4	9	7	9	28	11	–	43	1	1	2	26	4	17	5	12	193
Others	2	1	–	–	–	1	2	6	–	8	1	3	–	8	2	6	7	7	3	11	–	–	3	10	–	7	1	4	82
Total	426	63	83	70	48	61	92	843	40	755	88	135	60	429	127	497	617	208	177	1313	70	120	77	1022	133	451	96	419	6834
Scapula d.	6	–	–	1	–	2	2	11	–	22	4	1	6	7	1	1	9	3	10	32	–	3	3	28	3	8	–	7	148
Humerus p.	–	–	–	–	–	–	–	–	–	–	–	–	–	–	–	2	4	2	–	4	1	–	–	3	–	1	–	–	29
Humerus d.	4	–	4	1	1	1	1	12	–	10	–	1	–	6	1	6	8	6	1	5	4	–	1	13	–	5	1	1	69
Radius p.	5	2	–	1	1	1	–	10	–	13	–	–	2	8	–	6	8	4	1	11	2	4	–	7	2	3	–	6	79
Radius d.	3	–	–	1	1	–	–	5	1	5	–	1	–	3	1	1	3	4	1	5	1	–	1	10	–	3	–	1	41
Femur p.	2	–	2	–	–	–	–	2	–	2	2	–	–	2	2	1	6	2	1	6	1	–	–	4	2	1	–	1	32
Femur d.	–	–	–	1	–	–	–	–	–	5	2	–	–	3	–	–	3	–	1	6	–	–	–	3	1	4	–	–	32
Tibia p.	4	–	–	1	–	–	–	4	–	6	3	2	–	5	1	4	2	4	1	3	–	1	–	–	2	2	1	1	35
Tibia d.	8	1	1	1	–	1	2	13	–	10	3	3	–	4	3	3	3	2	1	5	1	1	–	11	–	–	–	2	50
Metacarpus p.	4	2	1	1	1	–	1	9	–	15	1	–	2	7	2	5	9	4	5	29	1	–	1	23	–	15	2	8	129
Metacarpus d.	4	1	–	1	1	1	–	8	1	7	1	–	1	3	–	2	2	2	3	11	3	–	2	23	–	8	–	7	76
Metatarsus p.	5	1	1	–	1	–	2	12	–	15	1	–	1	11	1	1	9	5	3	22	1	4	4	19	2	8	7	7	121
Metatarsus d.	2	1	1	–	–	–	3	7	–	8	–	–	–	4	–	2	9	3	–	12	1	2	1	15	1	4	–	4	66

p. = proximal articulation; d. = distal articulation

269

Table 37 Percentage of cattle fragments in Roman deposits (AES 76–7)

Bone\Context	Early Roman								Late Roman																				
	227	168A	245	224	II54	II67	Other	Total	2	4	24	26	42	49	64	78	86	87	122	124	161	164	168	170	226	II10	II22	Other	Total
Mandible	17	14	16	6	5	16	18	15	10	14	13	8	8	10	7	5	12	8	12	12	16	12	4	14	6	10	3	3	11
Maxilla	6	–	4	–	20	6	3	6	3	5	7	18	–	4	1	7	4	1	8	8	3	8	–	9	9	2	3	3	6
Skull fragments	18	13	11	29	36	11	16	18	23	18	9	27	13	21	32	45	20	13	17	21	9	18	39	18	50	11	7	25	22
Loose teeth	9	3	17	–	10	8	7	9	8	10	6	12	2	4	6	5	8	10	8	9	10	10	1	6	3	12	14	8	8
Scapula	5	5	1	2	5	1	5	4	3	7	13	2	27	6	3	3	5	5	10	7	–	3	6	9	3	6	5	5	6
Humerus	5	6	6	10	3	8	2	5	5	5	1	4	2	6	4	3	5	7	4	3	10	3	4	4	2	4	5	4	4
Radius	3	5	4	6	2	2	2	3	8	4	–	2	5	4	2	2	4	5	2	2	7	6	4	3	3	3	2	3	3
Ulna	1	2	3	4	3	2	1	2	–	2	1	–	2	2	1	1	2	2	3	1	3	2	3	1	1	1	2	2	2
Pelvis	4	6	4	–	2	4	3	4	10	5	10	3	8	6	3	4	6	5	7	5	9	9	8	5	2	4	8	4	5
Femur	5	6	3	13	–	7	3	5	3	5	5	4	3	5	3	4	5	3	2	4	3	6	4	3	5	3	3	3	4
Tibia	12	14	9	13	10	10	10	11	13	8	10	7	3	7	6	7	6	5	4	5	7	6	6	5	5	9	5	7	6
Astragalus	1	–	1	2	–	1	1	1	–	2	2	–	–	–	–	1	1	1	2	–	1	1	–	1	2	1	1	1	1
Calcaneus	1	2	–	2	–	1	1	1	–	1	–	1	–	1	–	1	–	2	2	1	–	–	–	–	2	2	2	2	1
Other tarsals	–	–	–	–	–	4	1	0.5	–	1	2	–	–	–	–	–	–	1	1	–	–	1	–	–	1	–	–	–	0.4
Carpals	–	–	–	–	–	–	1	0.2	–	1	3	1	–	–	2	1	1	–	–	1	–	–	1	–	–	2	–	–	0.6
Metacarpus	2	6	3	2	2	4	3	3	3	3	2	–	5	3	3	1	2	4	6	3	6	1	3	5	1	7	6	5	3
Metatarsus	4	8	1	8	–	7	4	5	–	3	3	1	5	6	1	1	4	4	2	3	4	8	8	5	3	5	10	4	4
Metapodial	1	–	–	–	–	1	–	0.5	3	–	–	–	–	–	2	–	–	–	–	–	–	–	–	–	–	–	1	–	0.2
1st phalanx	4	6	11	2	2	2	8	5	10	2	8	4	10	6	9	4	5	9	6	5	6	3	3	6	2	7	8	5	5
2nd phalanx	2	–	1	–	–	2	3	2	3	1	2	1	–	2	7	2	4	5	2	4	6	3	–	1	1	4	7	5	3
3rd phalanx	2	2	3	–	–	1	3	2	–	1	1	1	7	2	5	2	5	5	–	3	1	1	3	3	3	4	5	3	3
Others	–	2	–	–	2	–	2	0.7	–	1	1	2	–	2	2	1	1	3	2	1	–	–	1	4	1	–	2	1	1

some evidence to suggest that their small size, particularly of the smaller second and third phalanges, led to their under-representation due to recovery bias. This would also account for the rare recovery of other small bones, particularly the carpals and the smaller tarsals.

Statistical analysis was undertaken to investigate the variability of the cattle assemblage in the late Roman deposits. Table MT15 (microfiche M2:F9) shows the Pearson's *r* correlation coefficients for the skeletal elements in these deposits. The results were obtained employing the SPSS statistical package (Nie *et al* 1975, 280–88). The analysis compared the percentage figures given in Table 37. As would be expected, the major variability is accounted for in the fluctuations of the percentage of skull fragments. As a result, skull fragments were negatively correlated with most of the other skeletal elements, whereas the majority of other correlations were positive.

Several interesting correlations emerged from this analysis, for example, the high correlations between the humerus and the radius and ulna, and between the femur and tibia, suggesting that the major meat-bearing limb bones were often closely associated; several Roman urban and military sites have now produced concentrations of upper limb bones dumped together (Maltby 1989). In addition, the metatarsus and pelvis had quite strong correlations with the other major bones of the hindlimb, perhaps suggesting that all the hindlimbs were often dumped together. The phalanges had high correlations with each other, indicative not only of their close association during disposal but also of variable recovery rates between features.

Table MT16 (M2:F11) shows the correlation coefficients of the cattle assemblages in each of the late Roman deposits. The analysis was designed to test how similar the different assemblages were and employed the Clustan statistical package (Wishart 1978). It can be seen that the coefficients of similarity (max 1.0) were quite high, showing that the assemblages were indeed quite similar. This is to be expected since most of them were dominated by skull fragments. A few deposits, however, did have consistently lower coefficients, notably (42) and (II 22). In the former instance this reflects the unusually low percentage of skull fragments and the very high percentage of scapula fragments (27%) in a small sample (Table 37). This also accounts for the fact that the scapula did not have any close correlations with any of the other bones (Table MT15, M2:F9). (II 22) had unusually low percentages for both the mandible and skull fragments (Table 37). It is interesting that this feature produced the lowest percentage of cattle fragments in the late Roman deposits.

It is possible, therefore, that the high incidence of skull fragments in some deposits suggests that the area was used for the disposal of cattle primary butchery waste. However, it was by no means used solely for that purpose since good meat bones were also represented in some numbers.

Sheep/goat assemblage

The Roman sheep/goat assemblages were noticeably biased both by differential preservation of the skeletal elements and by variable recovery rates. The elements represented in the early and late Roman deposits are shown in Table 38 and the percentages of the different elements with assemblages of over 100 sheep/goat fragments are given in Table 39. The most common fragments were those of the tibia, mandible, and metapodia. These are dense elements that withstand better attrition from canid scavenging, weathering, and trampling than more fragile elements of the sheep/goat skeleton. Even these bones had suffered some destruction by these agencies. As in the case of cattle, the later-fusing articular surfaces were under-represented in comparison with earlier-fusing ones, but the bias was much more marked (Table 38). For example, only six proximal and seven distal ends were recorded amongst the 160 femora fragments of late Roman date. In the same sample, only ten proximal ends of tibiae were recorded compared to 73 distal ends; 314 shaft fragments possessed neither articular surface, suggesting that many distal ends were also destroyed. Such a high degree of fragmentation indicates that canid scavenging had destroyed much of the assemblage, a fact supported by observations of tooth and claw marks on many of the bones of all species. Comparisons with the fragmentation and articulation survival of sheep/goat tibias from other British sites has shown that the Explosion site sample was quite poorly preserved (Maltby 1985). Given this fact, it is surprising that the percentage of loose teeth was comparatively low. Loose teeth usually survive in greater quantities than any other element in poorly preserved assemblages. However, the explanation could lie in the fact that many of the loose teeth at the Explosion site were overlooked during excavation. Support for this explanation comes from the observation that other small bones of sheep/goat are grossly under-represented. No carpals were recorded in the Roman assemblage and only two second phalanges and a single third phalanx were recovered in comparison with 49 of the slightly larger first phalanges. The most likely reason for such discrepancies is recovery bias in favour of larger bones and fragments (cf Maltby 1985, 1). It is also likely that many sheep/goat loose teeth were overlooked.

In general, it seems that sheep/goat were not the subject of the same large-scale primary butchery processes evidenced for cattle in several Romano-British towns. The assemblage on this site could in fact have originally derived from the disposal of butchered complete skeletons which then suffered severe modification by various attritional agents before the surviving portion was buried. The sample was too small for detailed statistical analysis of the variations of element representation in the different deposits. However, most of such variability could be accounted for by differential recovery rates and variable preservation.

Table 38 Sheep/goat fragment numbers identified (AES 76–7)

Bone\Context	Early Roman							Late Roman													
	227	168A	245	224	II54	II67	Other	Total	2	4	24	26	42	49	64	78	86	87	122	124	161	164	168	170	226	II10	II22	Other	Total
Mandible	22	6	5	6	–	1	6	46	3	44	2	3	6	11	2	12	27	3	3	60	5	8	5	64	2	35	13	17	325
Maxilla	7	–	1	–	1	3	2	14	–	8	2	–	2	2	2	2	6	1	2	12	–	–	–	8	–	9	3	1	60
Skull fragments	10	1	7	1	2	2	2	25	1	18	3	1	–	12	–	6	13	3	3	36	–	2	3	22	1	15	8	5	152
Loose teeth	12	2	6	6	1	–	2	29	1	28	3	2	2	8	3	16	25	3	1	18	–	5	2	14	4	32	10	5	182
Scapula	7	4	4	–	1	1	2	19	2	14	–	1	–	6	1	8	5	5	–	21	–	1	–	26	–	8	8	3	109
Humerus	24	3	4	1	2	–	4	38	3	14	1	–	–	7	2	3	13	2	6	28	–	3	1	15	2	20	6	11	137
Radius	10	10	3	6	2	1	4	36	3	19	2	–	2	5	4	1	20	4	2	34	4	4	1	20	1	12	6	12	156
Ulna	–	2	1	2	1	1	–	7	–	1	–	–	–	1	–	1	–	1	–	5	–	1	–	7	1	4	2	1	25
Pelvis	10	4	3	2	2	–	4	25	3	7	1	–	3	6	–	4	11	4	1	24	3	1	–	16	1	9	3	5	102
Femur	15	5	9	6	2	1	7	45	3	19	4	–	1	5	1	10	10	5	–	22	1	6	–	20	3	25	14	11	160
Tibia	32	10	10	6	3	2	14	77	7	37	3	2	3	26	4	21	41	13	4	73	2	10	6	66	5	39	13	20	395
Astragalus	–	–	–	–	–	–	1	1	–	2	–	1	–	–	–	–	–	–	–	7	–	–	–	–	–	2	–	1	13
Calcaneus	3	1	2	–	–	–	6	–	4	–	–	–	1	1	–	6	5	1	1	8	–	–	–	2	–	7	2	2	39
Metacarpus	8	4	5	–	3	–	6	26	3	10	3	1	–	8	1	10	33	2	3	34	1	2	4	41	2	17	11	9	195
Metatarsus	6	9	7	6	2	–	13	43	1	14	1	3	2	12	2	7	24	6	5	46	1	3	2	48	6	22	4	7	216
Metapodial	–	–	–	–	–	–	–	–	–	1	–	–	–	–	–	–	1	–	–	–	–	–	–	–	–	–	–	–	2
1st phalanx	1	–	1	–	–	–	4	6	2	7	–	2	1	2	–	1	4	3	–	8	–	2	–	1	1	5	–	4	43
2nd phalanx	–	–	–	–	–	–	–	–	–	–	–	–	–	–	–	–	–	1	–	–	–	–	–	–	–	–	1	–	2
3rd phalanx	–	–	–	–	–	–	–	–	–	–	–	–	–	–	–	–	–	–	–	1	–	–	–	–	–	–	–	–	1
Others	–	–	–	–	–	–	2	2	–	–	–	1	–	2	2	–	3	1	1	2	–	2	–	3	–	3	–	1	21
Total	167	61	68	42	22	12	73	445	32	247	25	17	22	114	24	108	241	58	32	439	17	50	24	373	29	264	104	115	2235
Scapula d.	2	–	–	–	1	–	–	3	–	1	–	–	–	1	–	2	–	–	–	1	–	–	–	3	–	2	2	–	12
Humerus p.	1	–	–	–	–	–	–	1	–	–	–	–	–	–	–	–	–	–	–	–	–	–	–	1	–	–	–	1	3
Humerus d.	9	3	1	–	–	–	2	15	–	7	–	–	–	3	1	2	4	1	–	8	–	1	–	5	1	7	2	4	46
Radius p.	1	–	1	–	1	–	1	4	–	2	–	–	–	2	–	1	2	–	–	1	3	1	–	4	–	4	1	4	25

272

Table 38 (*continued*) Sheep/goat fragment numbers identified (AES 76–7)

	Early Roman								Late Roman																				
Bone\Context	227	168A	245	224	II54	II67	Other	Total	2	4	24	26	42	49	64	78	86	87	122	124	161	164	168	170	226	II10	II22	Other	Total
Radius d.	1	1	–	1	1	–	1	5	–	4	–	–	–	–	–	–	2	1	–	2	–	–	1	5	–	2	–	1	18
Femur p.	–	1	2	–	–	–	–	3	–	–	–	–	–	–	–	1	1	–	–	1	–	–	–	1	–	1	–	1	6
Femur d.	–	–	–	–	1	–	–	1	1	1	–	–	–	–	–	1	1	–	1	1	–	–	–	–	–	–	1	–	7
Tibia p.	1	–	–	–	–	–	–	1	–	2	–	–	1	–	–	–	4	1	1	–	–	–	1	–	–	–	–	–	10
Tibia d.	4	3	1	–	1	1	3	13	–	8	–	1	1	5	–	1	6	4	–	8	–	1	2	24	–	5	1	6	73
Metacarpus p.	3	–	2	–	1	–	2	8	2	2	1	1	–	–	–	6	12	2	–	8	–	–	2	18	2	4	1	4	65
Metacarpus d.	1	1	1	–	–	–	1	4	–	1	2	–	–	2	–	1	4	–	–	4	–	1	1	8	–	4	2	–	30
Metatarsus p.	–	3	–	1	–	–	4	8	–	4	–	–	2	4	1	3	10	4	–	17	1	–	1	21	1	7	2	1	79
Metatarsus d.	–	2	1	–	–	–	2	5	–	1	–	–	1	–	–	1	3	1	–	4	1	–	1	11	–	2	1	–	27

p. = proximal articulation; d. = distal articulation

Explosion site finds (AES 76-7)

Table 39 Percentage of sheep/goat fragments identified (AES 76–7)

Bone\Context	Early Roman Total	Late Roman								Total
		4	49	78	86	124	170	II10	II22	
Mandible	10	18	10	11	11	14	17	13	13	15
Maxilla	3	3	2	2	2	3	2	3	3	3
Skull fragments	6	7	11	6	5	8	6	6	8	7
Loose teeth	7	11	7	15	10	4	4	12	10	8
Scapula	4	6	5	7	2	5	7	3	8	5
Humerus	9	6	6	3	5	6	4	8	6	6
Radius	8	8	4	1	8	8	5	5	6	7
Ulna	2	–	1	1	–	1	2	2	2	1
Pelvis	6	3	5	4	5	5	4	3	3	5
Femur	10	8	4	9	4	5	5	9	13	7
Tibia	17	15	23	19	17	17	18	15	13	18
Astragalus	0.2	1	–	–	–	2	–	1	–	0.6
Calcaneus	–	2	1	6	2	2	1	3	2	2
Metacarpus	6	4	7	9	14	8	11	6	11	9
Metatarsus	10	6	11	6	10	10	13	8	4	10
Metapodial	–	–	–	–	–	–	–	–	–	0.1
1st phalanx	1	3	2	1	2	2	–	2	–	2
2nd phalanx	–	–	–	–	–	–	–	–	–	0.1
3rd phalanx	–	–	–	–	–	–	–	–	–	0.1
Others	0.4	–	2	–	1	–	1	1	–	1

Total includes all deposits but no calculations were made for individual features with <100 sheep/goat fragments.

Pig assemblage

The pig fragments identified are listed in Table 40 and for the largest samples these figures are expressed as percentages in Table 41. As in the case of cattle, mandible, loose teeth, and skull fragments were the most common elements. This again can be attributed mainly to differential preservation and fragmentation of the pig skeleton. Most of the pig bones belonged to immature animals and therefore the fragile later-fusing articulations were especially susceptible to destruction (Table 40). The under-representation of the pig postcranial skeleton is a common feature of most archaeological assemblages, including those of Romano-British date (King 1978). Nevertheless, at the Explosion site the major meat-bearing limb bones were reasonably well represented. Certain deposits also produced quite high percentages of metapodials (eg (86) and (124), Table 41). Although pigs possess four metapodia on each limb which would favour them in this analysis, their small size, particularly of the lateral metapodials, would tend to counteract this bias because they would have had a greater chance of being overlooked during excavation than many of the other bones. If all the metapodial categories in Table 41 are added together, it can be seen that they constituted 16% of the pig assemblage in the late Roman deposits. This high figure compares well with those obtained from various Roman assemblages in Exeter (Maltby 1979a: 103). In some deposits at Exeter it was clear that pig metapodia (and phalanges) had been dumped in large quantities as trotters were discarded presumably during butchery (Maltby 1979a, 13). Large numbers of pig metapodials were dumped in a well of Roman date at Nazeingbury, Essex (Huggins 1978). On this site it seems likely that pigs' trotters were also thrown away in some numbers in certain layers, but as in the case of cattle such butchery waste was admixed with kitchen and table waste.

Conclusions

Considering the relatively small area of excavation, the Roman samples were quite substantial. Such a dense accumulation implies that deliberate disposal of bones took place in that area over a considerable period of time. It is likely, however, that many of the bones were not buried immediately but were accessible to dogs and other destructive agents, which radically modified the assemblages. On the other hand, it seems likely that some features were filled, at least in part, with bones that had not lain exposed for any length of time. If this was the case, it is possible that the bones from the larger-scale primary butchery activities may have been deliberately buried more commonly than those bones derived from household waste. This would account for the concentrations of cattle skull fragments and, to a lesser degree, the accumulation of pig metapodials.

What implications does the analysis of element representation have for the interpretation of species abundance in the deposits? At first sight, the high incidence of cattle fragments would fit nicely into the pattern put forward by King (1984) that in the Romano-British period, Romanised urban settlements consumed a large proportion of beef in their diet. Urban and military assemblages of this date have often produced over 60% cattle fragments. The increases in the percentages of cattle and pig in the late Roman deposits would also fit King's hypothesis of dietary change being largely the effect of 'Romanising' influences. However, we must be careful about comparing samples simply by fragment counts. We have seen that the Explosion site sample was biased by differential recovery rates and preservation and probably by deliberate dumping of particular types of bone. All these factors would have favoured cattle at the expense principally of sheep/goat. Fewer cattle fragments are likely to have been overlooked during excavation; the analysis of articular surface survival indicated that sheep/goat and pig were more severely affected by canid scavenging; finally there is a strong possibility that some moderately large-scale disposal of cattle skulls took place at times on the site. It is likely therefore that the dominance of cattle may be more apparent than real, although it is very difficult to judge the degree of bias. Clearly, other faunal samples in the Explosion site need to be compared to establish how typical these assemblages were of the town as a whole. This does not imply that cattle were not the dominant species in the meat diet (they would certainly have provided the most meat weight), but more rigorous analysis of contemporary samples are required before we can place a great deal of confidence in these results.

Cattle sample

The predominance of cattle in the sample enabled detailed analysis of their exploitation to be undertaken. The ageing data were derived from the examination of the eruption and wear stages of the mandibular cheek teeth and from the epiphyseal fusion of the long bones. The late Roman deposits provided abundant evidence of butchery practices and the metrical characteristics of the bones. All these aspects will be discussed in this section.

Tooth eruption data

The great majority of cattle mandibles represented belonged to adult animals (Table MT17, M2:F13). Of the 155 of late Roman date that provided ageing data, a maximum of ten (6.5%) did not have all their molars in wear and only a maximum of 44 (28.4%) had not completed their tooth eruption sequence, which is marked by the eruption of the fourth permanent premolar. In modern breeds this occurs between four and five years of age. However, present methodology precludes the absolute ageing of these animals. The rapidity of tooth eruption is dependent on breed and the plane of nutrition of the stock and it is possible that the dental development of Roman cattle was slower than that of improved modern breeds. The seventeen ageable specimens of early Roman date included a higher proportion belonging to young cattle. Nine mandibles belonged to animals that died before their tooth eruption sequence was completed. However, the sample was too small to show conclusively that there was a significant change in the ages of cattle represented in the two periods.

Although absolute ageing is hazardous, standardisation of recording methods enables relative comparisons between ageing data from different sites to be made. The method used here followed that employed at Portchester Castle (Grant 1975). This involves the study of the eruption and surface wear on the three molars (M1–M3) and the deciduous and permanent fourth premolars (p4, P4). A numerical value is assigned or estimated for each mandible based on the stages of eruption or wear of the three molars. Each successive stage carries a higher numerical value and hence the oldest mandibles have the highest values. Fig 168 compares the ageing evidence of the mandible from the late Roman deposits at the Explosion site with that of the Roman mandibles from Portchester Castle. The samples showed similar patterns: 8.4% of the Explosion site and 10.0% of the Portchester Castle mandibles had numerical values of 30 or less (M3 not in wear). Most of the Explosion site specimens had numerical values of 38–46, whereas the main concentration of Portchester Castle mandibles had values of 39–48. However, there were differences within these concentrations. At the Explosion site 86 (55.5%) of the mandibles had values of 40 or less compared to only 34 (28.3%) of the Portchester specimens; 143 (92.3%) of the Explosion site mandibles but only 88 (73.3%) from Portchester had numerical values of 45 or less. In other words, more of the Explosion site mandibles possessed fourth premolars in an early stage of wear. There are three possible explanations for this:

i) the cattle represented at Portchester Castle had on average a rather longer life expectancy than those at the Explosion site, although most were fully mature animals;
ii) the rate of wear on the molars was greater on the Portchester mandibles;

Table 40 Pig fragment numbers identified (AES 76–7)

Bone\Context	Early Roman								Late Roman																				
	227	168A	245	224	II54	II67	Other	Total	2	4	24	26	42	49	64	78	86	87	122	124	161	164	168	170	226	II10	II22	Other	Total
Mandible	1	1	3	–	2	–	4	11	4	13	5	1	–	17	1	8	22	5	–	23	–	2	1	24	1	10	3	7	147
Maxilla	1	2	–	–	–	–	–	3	1	10	–	1	–	5	–	7	5	5	1	13	–	1	–	8	–	6	–	3	66
Skull fragments	3	3	–	–	–	–	1	7	1	13	–	–	–	4	3	6	8	6	1	19	–	2	1	24	–	6	4	5	102
Loose teeth	–	–	–	–	–	–	1	1	2	7	5	–	–	5	2	7	14	7	1	25	1	3	–	19	1	8	9	11	127
Scapula	3	–	3	–	1	–	1	8	–	11	3	–	2	5	1	1	9	9	4	8	–	1	2	15	–	4	1	3	81
Humerus	2	–	1	–	–	–	1	4	4	13	–	1	1	3	3	6	9	2	1	14	–	1	3	16	4	6	6	5	98
Radius	1	1	–	–	–	–	2	4	–	8	1	–	1	1	–	4	2	4	–	10	–	2	–	5	–	2	–	2	42
Ulna	1	1	–	–	–	–	1	3	1	2	–	–	1	3	–	2	4	–	–	9	–	1	2	8	–	6	3	4	46
Pelvis	–	–	–	–	–	–	–	–	2	9	3	–	–	2	–	1	7	1	–	3	–	1	–	8	–	1	–	–	41
Femur	–	2	4	–	–	–	–	6	–	4	–	–	–	3	–	2	6	3	–	7	1	1	1	7	–	14	3	7	60
Tibia	1	–	4	–	1	–	1	7	3	13	2	–	1	5	2	1	3	4	4	26	–	2	1	10	–	11	3	2	93
Astragalus	–	–	–	–	–	–	–	–	–	–	–	–	–	–	–	2	–	–	2	2	–	–	–	1	–	1	–	–	8
Calcaneus	1	–	–	1	–	–	1	3	–	–	–	1	–	1	–	3	1	1	–	–	–	2	–	2	–	2	1	1	17
Other tarsals	–	–	–	–	–	–	–	–	1	–	–	–	–	–	–	–	–	–	–	–	–	–	–	–	1	–	–	–	2
Carpals	–	–	–	–	–	–	–	–	–	–	–	–	–	–	–	–	–	–	–	1	–	–	–	–	–	–	–	–	1
Metacarpals	–	–	2	–	1	–	–	3	2	4	–	–	–	1	1	1	8	4	3	17	–	1	1	7	1	2	–	4	57
Metatarsals	–	–	–	1	–	–	–	1	–	2	–	–	–	3	–	3	11	3	–	13	–	–	–	7	–	4	1	–	50
Metapodial	1	1	1	–	–	–	2	5	–	5	1	1	1	2	1	1	9	3	1	28	–	1	–	4	1	8	2	10	79
1st phalanx	–	–	–	–	–	–	–	–	–	3	–	–	–	1	–	2	–	1	–	3	–	2	–	2	–	1	–	–	16
2nd phalanx	–	–	–	1	–	–	–	1	–	1	–	–	–	–	–	1	–	–	–	1	–	–	–	–	–	–	–	–	3
3rd phalanx	–	–	–	–	–	–	–	–	–	1	–	–	–	–	–	–	1	–	1	1	–	–	–	–	–	1	–	–	4
Others	2	–	–	–	–	–	–	3	1	2	1	1	1	3	1	2	3	1	1	9	–	–	–	5	–	9	5	1	46
Total	17	11	19	3	5	0	15	70	24	120	21	11	10	64	15	60	122	59	19	232	3	23	13	172	9	103	41	65	1186

Table 40 (cont.) Pig fragment numbers identified (AES 76–7)

Bone\Context	Early Roman								Late Roman																					
	227	168A	245	224	II54	II67	Other	Total	2	4	24	26	42	49	64	78	86	87	122	124	161	164	168	170	226	II10	II22	Other	Total
Scapula d.	–	–	–	–	1	–	1	2	–	–	–	–	–	1	–	–	2	3	3	–	–	–	1	2	–	–	1	–	13
Humerus p.	–	–	–	–	–	–	–	–	1	1	–	–	–	–	–	2	–	–	–	–	–	–	–	–	–	2	–	–	6
Humerus d.	1	–	–	–	–	–	1	2	1	4	–	–	–	1	1	2	–	–	–	4	–	–	–	4	4	2	2	–	25
Radius p.	–	–	–	–	–	–	2	2	–	5	–	–	1	1	–	2	–	1	–	4	–	–	–	2	–	–	–	1	17
Radius d.	–	–	–	–	–	–	–	–	–	–	–	–	–	–	–	1	1	–	–	2	–	–	–	–	–	–	–	1	5
Femur p.	–	–	–	–	–	–	–	–	–	1	–	–	–	–	–	–	–	–	–	–	–	–	–	1	–	–	–	1	3
Femur d.	–	1	–	–	–	–	–	1	–	–	–	–	–	–	–	–	2	–	–	–	–	–	–	1	–	2	–	–	5
Tibia p.	–	–	–	–	–	–	–	–	–	–	–	–	–	–	–	1	–	–	–	–	–	–	–	1	–	–	–	–	2
Tibia d.	–	–	–	–	–	–	–	–	1	3	1	–	–	–	–	1	–	1	–	4	–	–	–	4	–	4	–	–	19
Metacarpals p.	–	–	2	–	1	–	1	4	2	4	–	–	–	1	1	1	7	1	2	15	–	1	1	7	1	–	–	4	48
Metacarpals d.	–	–	–	–	1	–	1	2	–	3	–	–	–	1	1	–	4	1	2	4	–	–	1	4	1	–	–	1	23
Metatarsals p.	–	–	–	1	–	–	–	1	2	2	–	–	1	3	–	3	11	3	–	11	–	–	–	7	–	4	1	–	48
Metatarsals d.	–	–	–	–	–	–	–	–	–	1	–	–	–	2	–	1	7	1	–	1	–	–	–	4	–	3	–	–	20

p. = proximal articulation; d. = distal articulation

Explosion site finds (AES 76-7)

Table 41 Percentage of pig fragments identified (AES 76–7)

Bone\Context	Late Roman					
	4	86	124	170	II10	Total
Mandible	11	18	10	14	10	12
Maxilla	8	4	6	5	6	6
Skull fragments	10	6	8	14	6	9
Loose teeth	6	11	11	11	8	11
Scapula	9	7	3	9	4	7
Humerus	11	7	6	9	6	8
Radius	7	2	4	3	2	4
Ulna	2	3	4	5	6	4
Pelvis	8	6	1	5	1	3
Femur	3	5	3	4	14	5
Tibia	11	2	11	6	11	8
Astragalus	–	–	1	1	1	1
Calcaneus	–	1	–	1	1	1
Other tarsals	–	–	–	–	1	0.2
Carpals	–	–	1	–	–	0.1
Metacarpals	3	7	7	4	2	5
Metatarsals	2	9	6	4	4	4
Metapodials	4	7	12	2	8	7
1st phalanx	3	–	1	1	1	1
2nd phalanx	1	–	1	–	–	0.3
3rd phalanx	1	1	1	–	1	0.3
Others	2	2	4	3	9	4

Total includes all deposits but no calculations were made for individual features with <100 pig fragments.

iii) the rate of tooth eruption was faster at Portchester.

The second of these explanations can probably be ruled out since the two samples showed a consistent pattern of wear on the molars in relation to the eruption of the other teeth, particularly the P4. Conversely, if there were major discrepancies in the rates of tooth eruption, one would expect contrasts in the wear patterns of the earlier teeth (M1, M2) in relation to the eruption of the M3 and P4. The fact that there was no evidence of this argues against the third explanation. This leaves the first explanation as the most likely, although the other two cannot be entirely ignored. Little is known in detail of the processes of surface wear on teeth and it is likely that there was a degree of variability within both samples. Nor can the present methodology give the absolute ages of these animals. The time span for each wear stage is variable and the rate of change of the later wear patterns is generally slower than those of the earlier stages. The concentration of mandibles with numerical values of 38–48 probably covers animals of quite a large range in age. Employing the ages of tooth eruption given by Silver (1969), Grant (1975, 396) suggests that these animals would have been 3.5 to 5 years old.

The cattle tooth eruption data from Roman Exeter also showed similar patterns to the Explosion site. Jaws of young animals were almost absent and probably no more than 25% had completed their tooth eruption sequence in a sample of 132 jaws dated to the first three centuries AD. It is interesting, however, that the late Roman deposits at the Explosion site did not produce similar evidence to that of the 4th-century levels at Exeter, where the number of immature cattle jaws increased significantly (Maltby 1979a, 30–1). The significance of these mortality rates will be discussed at the end of the section.

Epiphyseal fusion data

The epiphyseal fusion data for cattle from the site can be found in Table MT18 (M2:F13). Epiphyses

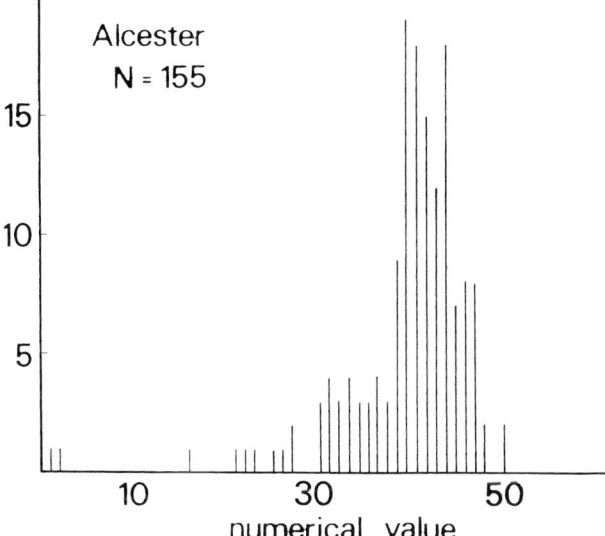

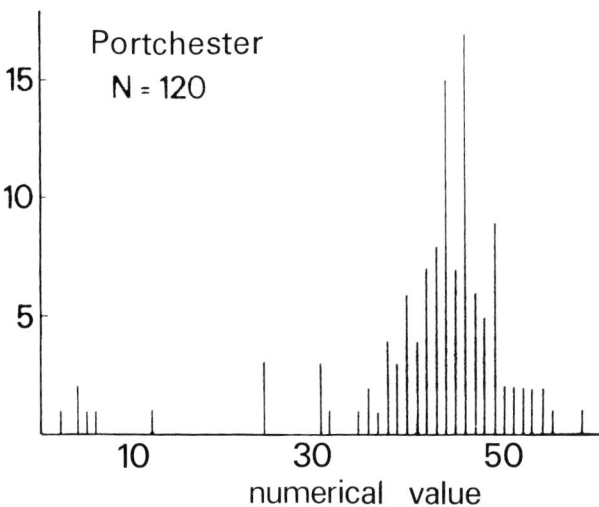

Figure 168 Ageing values of cattle mandibles from Alcester (AES 76–7, late Roman) and Portchester Castle (Roman) (data adapted from Grant (1975, 443–444); method based on Grant (1975), estimated numerical values are added)

fuse at different ages and as a guide the fusion ages cited by Silver (1969, 285–6) are given in the table. These may underestimate the actual age of fusion because of the slower development of Roman cattle. The fusion evidence supports that of the tooth eruption data. Few young unfused bones were recovered in the large late Roman sample. The number of unfused distal tibiae and metapodia ranged from 3.8% to 11.3% implying that most of the animals represented survived at least three years employing modern analogies. Analysis of the late-fusing group of epiphyses (proximal humerus, etc) showed that the number of unfused specimens ranged from 18.2% to 36.7%. The majority of these epiphyses therefore belonged to animals over four years of age. The fusion evidence from the earlier Roman deposits was more limited, but there are indications that the number of immature cattle represented was larger, supporting the tooth eruption evidence.

One may expect that an identical analysis of the Roman cattle fusion evidence from Portchester Castle would have indicated a slightly lower proportion of unfused late-fusing epiphyses, thus supporting the tooth eruption evidence, which suggested a somewhat later peak of slaughter. However, in a sample of 631 late-fusing epiphyses (combining Groups 1–5 at Portchester) 37.4% were unfused (Grant 1975, 393) compared with 26.7% at the Explosion site. It is possible that these epiphyses fused before the main peak of slaughter began and therefore the differences can be explained as variability in relatively small samples of immature animals. More likely, however, is the possibility that differential preservation at the two sites biased the results. The major disadvantages in the detailed analysis of epiphyseal fusion data is the fact that the late-fusing epiphyses are very vulnerable to destruction by attritional forces (Binford and Bertram 1977). The data (Table MT18, M2:F13) show that 71 fragments of the denser and early-fusing distal humerus survived from the late Roman deposits at the Explosion site, whereas only 30 of the proximal ends were recovered. Similar variability was observed in the survival of the early- and late-fusing epiphyses of the radius and tibia. Comparable patterns can be shown for the Portchester Castle and Exeter samples (Grant 1975, 388; Maltby 1979a, 158) and indeed in any large assemblage of animal bone studied in this manner. There are differences in detail, however. For example, a relatively large number of proximal humeri were recovered at the Explosion site in comparison with both Exeter and Portchester, whereas a relatively large number of distal radii were found at Portchester. The question of epiphyseal survival is a complex one. All too little is known of the disposal mechanisms resulting in the animal bone assemblages recovered from archaeological sites. Until such processes are better understood, epiphyseal fusion data should only be employed as a general guide to ageing. It has to be accepted that the results of such studies are probably biased in favour of older animals, whose epiphyses are fused and less vulnerable to destruction. It is therefore important to stress that the percentage figures given in Table MT18 (M2:F13) do not necessarily equate with the actual percentage of stock represented by the various age groups. It can be said that the fusion data support the tooth eruption data in that the majority of cattle represented were adult but direct comparisons with fusion data from other sites cannot be made without a detailed knowledge of the preservation conditions, butchery, and disposal practice of each site.

Sexual dimorphism

The high proportion of adult cattle represented at the Explosion site leads to the question of why so

Explosion site finds (AES 76-7)

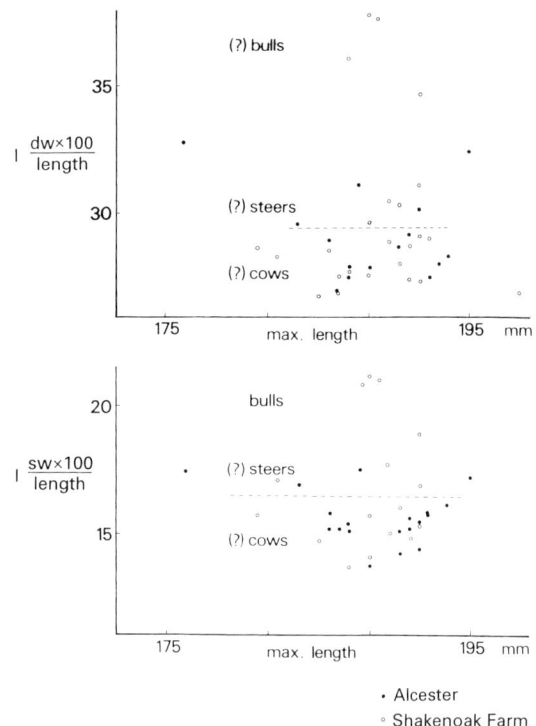

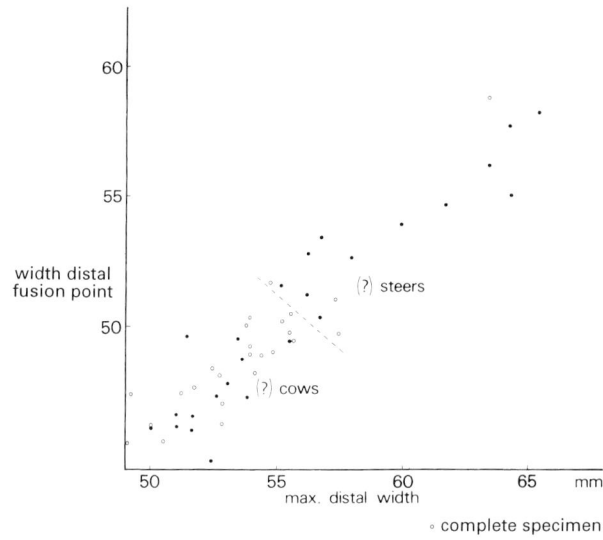

Figure 170 Scatter diagram of late Roman cattle metacarpi distal epiphyses (AES 76–7)

Figure 169 Distal and shaft width indices of cattle metacarpi from Alcester (AES 76–7, late Roman) and Shakenoak Farm, Oxon (data adapted from Cram (1973, 160; 1978, 149)

many animals were allowed to reach maturity. Adult cows can be kept for dairy or breeding purposes (and indeed as draught animals). Steers can be kept as working animals and some bulls would be required for breeding. Any deliberate culling of young stock is usually at the expense of young males, which are surplus to the breeding stock. Given such a high proportion of adult cattle, one would expect a relatively large number of adult steers and bulls to be represented, if the sample provides a true reflection of cattle exploitation in the area.

Metrical analysis of cattle metapodia has been undertaken on several sites in the belief that these bones display sexual dimorphism. Fock (1966) has shown that although the sexes can be differentiated by the use of specific measurements and indices, the variability between modern breeds is great and the pattern is not always predictable. Generally, however, the metapodia of bulls are shorter and broader than those of cows in the population, and those of castrates have breadth and depth measurements larger than cows but their bones are more slender than bulls. Despite various attempts at using such data on archaeological material (Higham 1967; Grant 1975; Maltby 1979a), the analysis of cattle metapodia on British sites has not demonstrated conclusively that sexual dimorphism can be monitored on these bones. The Explosion site material therefore offers another opportunity to test the methodology. The following measurements were used in the analysis of both metacarpi and metatarsi: length, maximum proximal width, maximum proximal depth, minimum width of the shaft (diaphysis), maximum distal width, width at distal fusion point, and depth at distal fusion point. Space prevents the publication of all the data but the scatter diagrams presented here are representative of the results obtained. Fig 169 shows the metrical analysis of complete, fused metacarpi from the late Roman levels. As the distal epiphyses of these bones do not fuse until c 2–2.5 years even in modern cattle (Silver 1969, 285), these belong to animals at least that age and probably substantially older in many cases. It can be seen that the Explosion site metacarpi fell into two groups. The majority had distal width indices of less than 29.5 and minimum shaft indices of below 16. A small group, however, stood apart from these and were distinguished both by their greater distal width indices (29.5–33) and minimum shaft indices of over 16.9. Similarly most metatarsi had distal width indices of less than 25 and minimum shaft indices of under 12.5. These were separated from a small group of larger specimens with distal width indices of 26 and over and minimum shaft indices of over 13. Indices of the proximal width also separated out the same specimens in both the metacarpi and metatarsi samples. Provisionally, the more slender specimens were designated as belonging to cows and the larger ones to steers or bulls. To increase the size of the samples, the maximum distal width of the bones was plotted against the maximum width of the fusion point (Figs 170–171). These therefore included broken specimens with just the distal portion of the bone present. The provisionally sexed complete specimens are indicated in the scatter diagrams and apart from one anomalous 'male' metacarpus which fell within the 'cow' grouping, there was no overlap. The provisionally sexed metatarsi specimens fell within two distinct groups. If the sex classifications are correct, only about one-third of the fused distal metacarpi and c 20% of the metatarsi belonged to steers or bulls.

Comparisons can be made with the results of

similar metrical analyses from other Romano-British assemblages. At Portchester Castle 65% of 119 metacarpi were classified as cows, 17% as castrates (steers), 7% as either cows or castrates, 6% as bulls and 5% as either bulls or castrates (Grant 1975, 399–402). A similar high proportion of 'cows' was monitored in the deposits dated to the first three centuries AD at Exeter. The smaller 4th-century sample from the Trickhay Street site, however, showed a decline in the proportion of probable steer and bull specimens corresponding with an increase in the number of unfused distal metacarpi, suggesting that more of the steers and bulls tended to be killed immature (Maltby 1979a, 34). No such kill-off pattern was found in the Explosion site sample, yet the majority of cattle in this as well as the other samples cited above were classified as female. Given the evidence of very low immature mortality rates, the small representation of specimens classified as steers or bulls has to be explained. The following explanations can be put forward:

i) none of the methods of assessing sexual dimorphism is applicable to these Roman populations;
ii) other variables such as differences in breed and the planes of nutrition may have masked the effects of sexual dimorphism;
iii) preservation and recovery have biased the samples towards mature animals and the metapodia of young steers and bulls are under-represented;
iv) the bones do show sexual dimorphism but the site was not typical of the rest of Alcester;
v) the sample from the site is not representative of the cattle kept in the surrounding countryside.

If either of the first two explanations are correct, the results of such analyses would be limited and would call into question the application of these techniques on archaeological material. The analysis at the Explosion site did successfully separate the bones into two groups and the small group of larger specimens probably did belong to steers or bulls. It is conceivable, however, that the group provisionally classified as cows does contain specimens from castrated males, which cannot be distinguished from cows using these particular sets of measurements and indices. Differential preservation may have had some effect on the results but it is unlikely to account for all the anomalies and much more fragile bones than unfused distal metapodia did survive in greater numbers. Whether the sample is typical of Alcester can only be established by comparison with other parts of the Roman town. The final explanation would be the most interesting, if correct. The low representation of steers and bulls in centres such as Alcester and Exeter may suggest that market pressures played some part in the types of cattle brought to the town. One hypothesis is that old plough animals and bulls were not in great demand

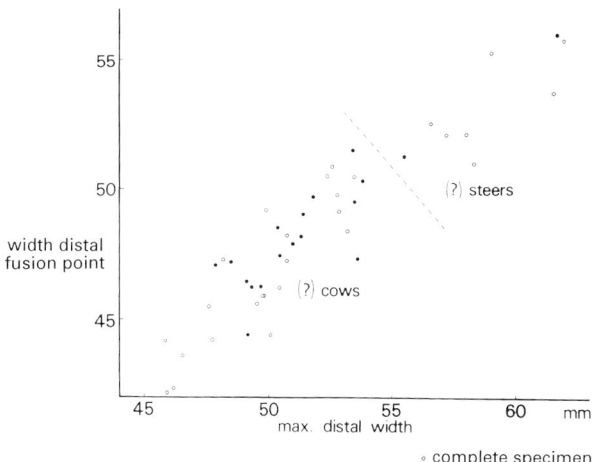

Figure 171 Scatter diagram of late Roman cattle metatarsi distal epiphyses (AES 76–7)

in urban markets and perhaps are to be found more commonly on rural sites. Urban centres may have favoured the marketing of cows no longer required for breeding but still young enough to produce tender meat. This may also explain the low number of very old jaws in the samples, although most belonged to adult animals. To test this hypothesis, comparable material is required from rural settlements near to the town in question and unfortunately this material is not as yet available. It is interesting to note, however, that in a small sample of 15 complete metacarpi from the Roman villa at Shakenoak Farm, Oxfordshire, (Cram 1973, 160; 1978, 149) four could be sexed as bulls and stood apart from the Explosion site specimens, although others fell in the other two provisionally sexed groupings (Fig 169). This and other samples from Roman villa and other rural settlements in southern Britain are as yet too small for any confident conclusions to be made but it should be possible to monitor this possible classification between the relative proportions of cows, steers, and bulls represented on different types of Roman sites.

Other metrical analysis

Metrical and morphological analysis of cattle horn cores was undertaken. Analysis of the overall size of the cores revealed that although 'small-horned' and 'medium-horned' cattle were present, the majority were 'short-horned', as defined by Armitage and Clutton-Brook (1976, 331).

Converting the lengths of complete metapodia into an estimation of withers height using the intermediate conversion factors of Fock (1966, 73), it was found that these ranged from 1.02m–1.225m, with a mean of *c* 1.14m–1.15m (for the range, mean, standard deviation, and the coefficient of variation of all cattle measurements see Table MT19, M2:F14). These fell within the range of measurements made for the metatarsi at Portchester (Grant 1975, 401)

Explosion site finds (AES 76-7)

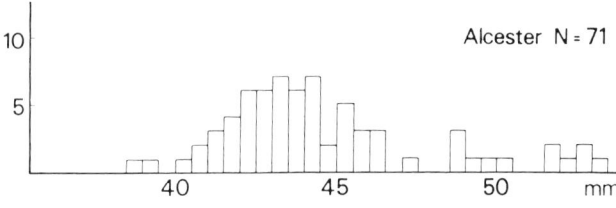

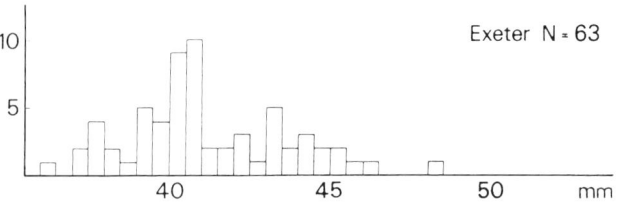

Figure 172 Maximum proximal width measurements of cattle metatarsi from Alcester (AES 76–7, late Roman) and Roman Exeter

but were much larger on average than those at Exeter (Maltby 1979a, 167). Indeed regional variation in the size of cattle in the Roman period can be demonstrated in Fig 172, which compares the maximum proximal width of the metatarsi from the Explosion site and Exeter. The cattle found in the late Roman deposits at the Explosion site were consistently larger. This was typical of most of the other measurements taken on both cattle assemblages. The larger and more reliable samples usually showed the Explosion site mean to be over 5% greater than that at Exeter. The size differences may be due either to regional variation in the types of cattle kept or the result of differential planes of nutrition. Detailed comparisons with other Romano-British cattle assemblages are required, however, before the pattern of regional variation can be better understood.

Butchery evidence

Abundant evidence of knife cuts and chop marks on cattle bones was found. The following basic pattern of butchery in the later Roman period was observed.

Skull and mandible

Despite their quantity, relatively few butchery marks were observed on skull fragments. One skull showed clear evidence of pollaxing and several revealed signs of skinning marks. The fragmentation of the skull material may have been due partly to post-depositional processes but it does seem likely that the cranial cavity was split open to remove the brain. The mandible was commonly cut with a knife on the posterior condyle. These cuts were probably made during the detachment of the mandible from the skull. Knife cuts along the diastema and below the cheek teeth appeared more rarely and are perhaps associated with skinning or the removal of meat from the cheek.

Girdle bones

The cattle assemblage was notable for the large number of complete, or nearly complete, scapulae recovered. Few cuts were found on the proximal or the blade of these bones but many of the distal portions showed knife cuts or chop marks. Many had been chopped through the glenoid notch and knife cuts were commonly located both on the glenoid cavity (distal epiphysis) and nearby on the lateral aspect of the neck of the bone. These would all indicate that the shoulder blade was severed from the fore limb at this point. The pelvis also showed abundant evidence of butchery. The number of knife cuts on the acetabulum and nearby on the ilium, pubis, and ischium show that the hind limbs were removed at the hip joint.

Long bones

The major meat-bearing long bones (humerus, radius, femur, and tibia) were nearly always broken. In a sample of nearly 1200 fragments, only seven complete bones were recovered. Although erosion, gnawing, and breakage during and after disposal caused some of the fragmentation, it is clear that these bones were intensively butchered. Their high level of fragmentation was the result not only of butchery for meat but also of the extraction of marrow. The evidence for butchery is supported by the common occurrence of knife cuts and chop marks on these bones. The chop marks appeared most commonly around the elbow joint and it is clear that the fore limb was often severed at this point. On several specimens the distal articulation of the humerus was found to have been chopped through completely and thus divided into its medial and lateral halves. Corresponding butchery sometimes severed the proximal radius into two halves and some of the ulnae had been chopped across the olecranon just above the articulation with the humerus. Axial splitting of upper limb bones was a common feature of Romano-British specialist butchery (Maltby 1989). On other specimens a knife was used to remove the meat from the elbow joint, as indicated by cut marks on the distal humerus, the olecranon of the ulna, and the medial aspect of the proximal radius. The rare occurrence of the proximal part of the humerus prevented the survival of butchery evidence corresponding with the cut marks on the distal scapulae made during the disarticulation of the forelimb at the shoulder. Butchery marks on the proximal femur were found more regularly and many were the result of the same process that produced cuts on the pelvis. Sometimes just the proximal articulation was found and this had been chopped off when the hindlimb was severed at the hip joint. A concentration of such fragments has been recorded from late Roman levels in Gloucester (Maltby 1979b). Rather more common, however, were knife cuts on the third trochanter and the knife seems to have been the tool more commonly used in the disarticulation of this joint. Knife cuts were also found occasionally on the shafts of all the long bones and presumably were made during the removal of meat from the bones.

Tarsals

Chop marks and knife cuts were found on the astragalus and calcanus in sufficient numbers to infer that this area was another common point for the severing of the hindlimb. A few of the astragali were chopped across separating the bone into proximal and distal portions, and chop marks were also found occasionally on the bone's lateral aspect. The calcaneus was most commonly cut chopped between the articular surface and the tuber calcis.

Metapodia and phalanges

Only c 11% of the metacarpi and metatarsi recovered were complete, a figure comparable to the Roman assemblages at Exeter (Maltby 1979a, 170). Less meat can be obtained from these bones but they are a good source of marrow and useful raw material for bone tools and these factors could account for much of their fragmentation. The metatarsi in particular commonly had butchery marks just below their proximal epiphysis on the posterior aspect. These were made during the removal of the tarsals from the feet. Several of the metapodia had knife cuts near the distal epiphysis as well. Despite the relatively large number of phalanges recovered from the site, very few had butchery marks on them. These bones provide little meat or marrow. It is no surprise, therefore, that they were thrown away whole, especially if they were not required in the production of glue or other products.

Vertebrae and ribs

The vertebrae were not commonly chopped down their central axis as in modern practice and there is no evidence for the division of the carcass into sides of meat. Knife cuts appeared on several examples but no clear pattern was discerned. Cut marks on several of the atlases (first cervical vertabra) were made during the removal of the skull from the backbones. Butchery marks on ribs consisted mostly of knife cuts and these were liable to occur both on the medial and lateral aspects of the shaft.

Discussion

Butchery evidence is a subject which requires greater consideration than it usually receives in faunal studies. Not only does butchery have a direct bearing on any quantitative analysis by to a large extent creating the number and types of fragments recovered, but the analysis of such evidence taken in conjunction with the distribution of different bone elements can provide information about the organisation of the meat supply. Work on present hunter communities has shown that detailed examination of butchery techniques can provide an important aid to the understanding of subsistence strategies (Binford 1978). Similar work on archaeological material in Britain could improve our understanding of meat processing, marketing, and other related topics. Comparisons with other bone samples within Alcester should establish how typical this pattern of butchery was in the Roman period and this study can provide a basis for more detailed surveys of butchery and meat distribution within different parts of the town. The evidence from the more limited early Roman sample suggests that the pattern of butchery may have remained consistent throughout a good deal of the Roman period. Chop marks and knife cuts on some scapulae, calcanei, astragali, radii, and mandibles were similar to those described for the late Roman cattle bones.

Pathology

Pathological conditions on the cattle bones were rarely observed. A metatarsus in pit (170) had the second and third tarsal fused to its proximal surface. This arthropic condition may be an indication that the animal in question was relatively old, as such conditions are more likely to occur in mature animals. Exostosis on the articulations and shafts of several of the phalanges may also be a condition developed in old age. Twelve out of 116 mandibles with the M3 present had only, at most, vestigial remains of the most posterior column developed. This is probably a congenital absence and similar mandibles have been discovered elsewhere (eg Andrews and Noddle 1975, 140; Maltby 1979a, 40). Eight fully developed mandibles possessed no permanent second premolars, a condition found relatively commonly in many ruminant species (Andrews and Noddle 1975).

Summary – exploitation of cattle

As discussed in the previous section, cattle were by far the most important source of meat in Roman Alcester. Nevertheless, the exploitation for meat was not a particularly intensive one. Fattening up of cattle for slaughter whilst immature would appear to have been little practised. The ageing evidence suggests that most of the cattle represented were not slaughtered until at least four years of age. Limitations in the methods of ageing cattle teeth are a severe handicap in the interpretation of peak periods of culling. There does, however, appear to have been a deliberate selection of animals for slaughter. The concentration of mandibles possessing fourth premolars in an early stage of wear and the lack of many very old cattle would support this view. Absolute ageing is at the moment little more than educated guesswork but it is possible that animals between c 4–8 years of age made up the majority of cattle represented. Preferred selection for cows rather than steers or bulls may also be indicated by the metrical analysis of the metapodia, although some doubts must still remain about the reliability of the methods used for determining sexual dimorphism. Because of the predominance of adult 'cows' it is tempting to suggest that dairying may have been an important aspect in cattle exploitation. However, if dairying was of major importance, one would have expected a much larger proportion of calves to be represented in the sample, since these would have been slaughtered to ensure the milk supply for human consumption. Although dairying on some scale no doubt did take place, it was not as intensive as, for example, milk production in the post-medieval period in Exeter (Maltby 1979a, 32). It is more likely that many of the cows represented were important as breeding stock and were not slaughtered until they had reared several calves. The comparative scarcity of very old cattle (if typical of the rest of Alcester) is indicative that there was a balance struck between the production of calves and the need for plough animals and the provisioning of the town. It is likely that the system of marketing cattle in the late Roman period was a sophisticated one. However, until the bones from urban, villa, and small farming settlements within a specific region are compared, interpretation of cattle exploitation and marketing must remain tentative.

The cattle brought to Alcester were of a good size for the Roman period and larger than those reared in parts of south-west England at the same date. The butchery evidence suggests than many cattle were slaughtered in the town and that the carcasses were butchered systematically for their meat and marrow. Other cattle products, particularly their skins, would also have been important in their exploitation.

Sheep/goat sample

Proportion of sheep to goat

Fragmentary archaeological material makes it impossible to differentiate totally between sheep and goat bones. It is essential, however, to have some indication of the proportion of each species present, since they could have been exploited in different ways. Certain bone elements are more diagnostic than others and all these suggested that sheep predominated.

Sheep and goat horn cores are relatively easy to distinguish. Of the seven recovered from the early Roman levels, five belonged to sheep and two to goat. There were also two skulls of polled sheep. In the larger late Roman sample, only one goat horn core was identified, whereas sheep were represented by 28 horn cores and 13 hornless skulls. The evidence from horn cores alone should be treated with caution, however, since horn could have been in use industrially and the cores may not accurately reflect the proportion of sheep and goat exploited at a site for meat.

The distal metapodia are also diagnostic to species when fused and metrical tests can be used to confirm the morphological observations (Boessneck et al 1964, 115–116). No fused distal epiphyses of goat metacarpi were found, whereas those of fourteen sheep were identified in the late Roman deposits. Thirteen sheep distal metatarsi were identified but none of goat was recovered. The same pattern was apparent for the rest of the ovicaprine assemblage. In specimens where morphological distinction was possible, very few could be assigned to goat, whereas many had characteristics diagnostic of sheep.

Tooth eruption evidence

Once again the late Roman sample was the only one large enough for detailed study. Table MT20 (M2:G1) summarises the tooth eruption evidence from 157 mandibles from this period. Sheep and goat mandibles cannot easily be distinguished morphologically but it is assumed that the large majority of these jaws belonged to sheep. It can be seen that many more immature individuals were present than in the case of cattle. A minimum of 10.2% of the mandibles examined did not have the first molar in wear; a minimum of 20.4% did not have their second molar fully erupted; and 59.2% belonged to animals that died before their third molar came into wear. Modern estimates would place these three stages at c 3–6 months, 12 months, and 24–30 months, although these probably underestimate the actual age of the unimproved Roman sheep under consideration. It seems, however, that the majority of jaws belonged to sheep killed at under three years.

Such a mortality pattern was also observed at Exeter where over 60% of the sheep/goat jaws represented in Roman levels did not have their third molars in wear (Maltby 1979a, 171). Detailed comparisons with the Roman Portchester Castle sheep/goat mandibles using Grant's method of tooth wear analysis (1975, 437–450) show close similarities between the two samples (Fig 173). Both have peaks in the number of mandibles with numerical values of 21–27 (M2 in early wear but M3 and premolars not in wear) and 31–35 (M3 in early stages of wear). The apparent bimodality may be misleading, however, since mandibles with numerical values of 28–30 are dependent on the short-lasting stages between the eruption and the early wear of the M3.

Explosion site finds (AES 76-7)

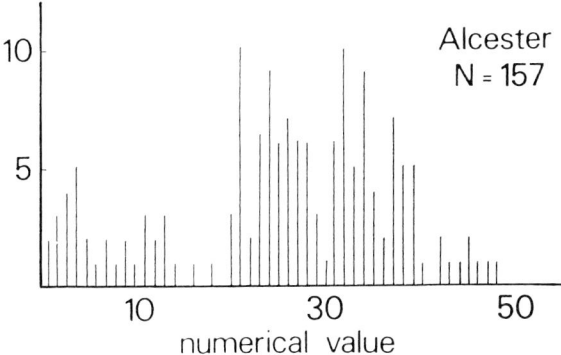

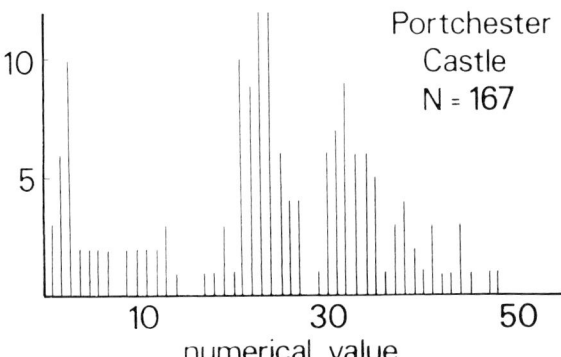

Figure 173 Ageing values of sheep/goat mandibles from Alcester (AES 76–7, late Roman) and Portchester Castle (Roman) (data adapted from Grant 1975, 447–448; method based on Grant (1975), estimated numerical values are included)

The size of the samples, the variability in the ages of tooth eruption and wear, and the limitations of the methodology do not allow detailed peaks in the slaughter pattern to be determined and precludes discussion of seasonal variations in the mortality data. It can be said, however, that the main period of slaughter among the sheep/goat represented on both sites probably lay between 18 months and three or possibly four years. Both these sites and Exeter produced mandibles belonging to lambs that died or were killed in the first year but the number of neonatal deaths was greater at Portchester Castle. There, the proportion of such animals was enhanced by the disposal of several of the carcasses in wells (Grant 1975, 398). No such concentrations were discovered at the Explosion site but the example demonstrates that intra-site variability can also affect the ageing data and samples derived from a limited area of a settlement may not be representative of the mortality rates of the flocks exploited by the inhabitants as a whole (Maltby 1982). About 20% of the late Roman Explosion site mandibles had reached the stage of heavy wear on one or more of their molars. These belonged to adult animals kept either for breeding, dairy, or wool production before being butchered for meat.

Only 21 mandibles of early Roman date provided tooth eruption evidence (Table MT20, M2:G1). The sample was too small for detailed analysis but it is noticeable that this sample was also dominated by mandibles of immature animals, perhaps indicating similar exploitation policies and disposal practices throughout the Roman period.

Epiphyseal fusion evidence

The sheep/goat epiphyseal fusion data from Roman levels at the Explosion site again demonstrate the problems of using such data on archaeological material (Table MT21, M2:G1). It can be seen that the epiphyses with late fusion ages are poorly represented in comparison with those of younger fusion age and the proximal humerus and tibia are particularly scarce. This is a direct result of differential preservation of the bone elements. Bones with unfused epiphyses in all groups are probably underrepresented and it should also be noted that the ages of fusion given in the table probably underestimate the actual age of fusion of the animals involved. There are discrepancies in the percentages of unfused specimens of similar fusion ages, notably those of the distal metacarpus (44.8%) and the distal metatarsus (42.9%) compared with those of the distal tibia (9.2%). All of these fuse at between 18 and 30 months on modern estimates. A similar discrepancy between these epiphyses was discovered in the Roman sheep/goat sample from Exeter (Maltby 1979a, 43). This may be due in part to differential preservation but the use of fused distal metapodia as raw material for boneworking may have biased the samples in favour of the unfused specimens, which are less suitable for industrial purposes and therefore more likely to have been thrown away with other butchery or kitchen refuse.

A comparison with the Exeter data is also interesting in that it suggests that the preservation of the sheep/goat samples was better in Exeter than at the Explosion site. The tooth eruption evidence from both sites suggested that a similar high number of immature animals was represented, yet there are substantial differences in the epiphyseal fusion evidence. Assuming that the long bones and the mandibles on both sites came from roughly the same populations of sheep/goat, the percentage of unfused bones of the latest group of epiphyses to fuse (the proximal humerus, etc) should be substantially over 50%. This is the case in the Exeter sample but it is clear that the poor survival of these at the Explosion site has made the data there more unreliable. Indeed, to take the fusion data as a whole, with the exception of the calcaneus and the very small samples of the proximal ulna and tibia, the percentage of unfused specimens represented at the Explosion site is less than the corresponding fusion point in the Exeter samples. This, however, does not necessarily imply that the immature mortality rate was any greater in Exeter. Similarly the Portchester Castle epiphyseal fusion evidence showed consistently higher percentage of unfused bones of all fusion ages (Grant 1975, 394) despite many similarities in the tooth eruption data (Fig 173). The evidence from these sites would indicate that the use of epiphyseal fusion evidence as a guide to ageing without reference to toothwear evidence and preservation conditions is extremely suspect. Much more research is needed before such methods can be considered reliable for use on archaeological material.

Metrical analysis

Measurements were taken where possible but only the late Roman sample provided enough material for detailed study (Table MT22, M2:G2). The sheep represented were much smaller and their bones more slender than their modern counterparts but possibly of a good size for the period. It is interesting to compare them with those from the Roman levels from Exeter (Maltby 1979a, 181–5), for it is clear that the sheep represented at the Explosion site were on average somewhat larger animals. Fig 174 compares the size of the distal width of the tibia from the sites. In both cases the majority of these belonged to sheep, although one or two goats may be represented. Although some of the Explosion site specimens were as small as those from Exeter, the mean for the measurement was 25.5mm compared to Exeter's mean of 23.4mm. This size difference is typical of all the sheep measurements taken on both sites. The sheep brought to Alcester were therefore larger and able to provide more meat per animal and possibly a heavier fleece. The reasons for the size difference require further study. It is possible that there were regional variations in the types of sheep kept in Roman Britain. In support of this may be the fact that the number of polled sheep in the Explosion site sample was quite high in comparison with Exeter, although the skull sample studied there was small (Maltby 1979a, 41). Horned and polled specimens do not necessarily imply that different breeds or types of sheep were present (Armitage and Goodall 1977). Alternatively, the planes of nutrition of the two sheep populations may have been different. It is conceivable that the land around Alcester provided better quality grazing than was the case of the sheep brought to Exeter. Unfortunately, published detailed metrical analysis of other Roman sheep assemblages in central and southern England is virtually lacking. The sheep from Shakenoak Farm, Oxfordshire, also seem to have been generally larger than those from Exeter and similar in size to those at Alcester (Fig 174; Cram 1973, 161 and 1978, 152–153). Future work should establish a much clearer picture of the variety of the types of sheep kept in Roman Britain and conclusions about the Alcester material should perhaps wait until more evidence is forthcoming.

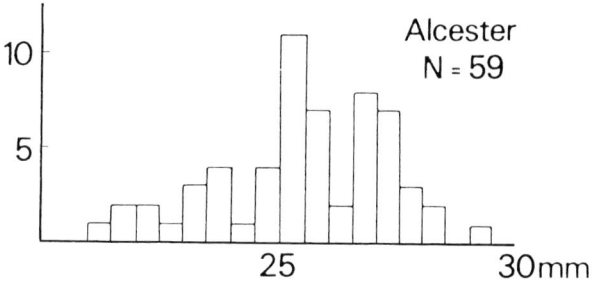

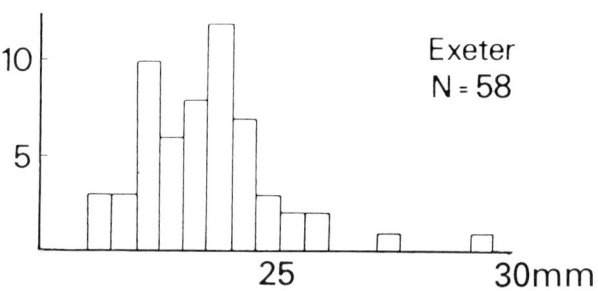

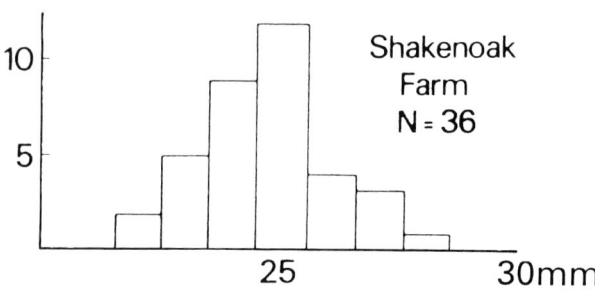

Figure 174   Maximum distal width measurements of sheep/goat tibiae from Alcester (AES 76–7, late Roman), Roman Exeter, and Shakenoak Farm, Oxon (data from Maltby 1979 and Cram 1973, 161; 1978, 152–153)

Butchery practices

Much less butchery was observed on the sheep/goat bones than on those of cattle. This is not surprising because their smaller carcasses require less butchery. Nevertheless, of all the major meat longbone fragments, only two bones (a humerus and a femur) were complete. Of course much of the fragmentation was caused by breakage after disposal, by erosion or gnawing of the bone, and during the excavation itself but the evidence for intensive butchery of the bone is overwhelming. Knife cuts and chop marks were found quite commonly on these bones, although many seem simply to have been smashed crudely for the extraction of marrow, leaving no trace of butchery marks. It is very difficult to decide whether such fragments were broken before or after disposal. As in the case of cattle, knife cuts and chop marks were found frequently on the pelvis, in particular on the ilium and around the acetabulum, where the hindlimb was severed from the rest of the carcass. The metapodia showed less evidence of butchery marks and c 8% of their fragments were complete. Similar fragmentation of sheep/goat long bones occurred in the Exeter deposits (Maltby 1979a, 53–4). A feature of the Explosion site late Roman sheep/goat assemblage was the practice of splitting the cranium down the centre, presumably for the extraction of the brain as a food resource. There was no evidence, however, for the systematic chopping of the vertebrae down the central axis of the spine to obtain sides of meat, although knife cuts were occasionally noted on these bones.

Pathology

Several old jaws of sheep/goat showed evidence of malocclusion of the cheek teeth and several showed signs of periodontal disease, in which the teeth have become loose in their sockets due to reduction of the bone supporting their roots. This is often thought to be caused by nutritional deprivation and results in the infected animal having difficulty in feeding. Few signs of pathology were found on the postcranial skeleton. Two metatarsi did, however, have slightly distorted shafts, although the cause of this condition is unclear.

Summary – exploitation of sheep/goat

The large majority of the ovicaprine assemblage belonged to sheep and most of those represented died or were slaughtered immature for their meat. Provided that the estimated ages of tooth eruption and wear are not wildly inaccurate, it would appear that the majority of sheep were killed between two and four years of age. It is sensible husbandry practice to kill off sheep not required for breeding or wool-producing purposes in their second or third years, since by then they will have grown almost to full size. Older sheep kept principally for breeding and wool would appear to be much more poorly represented. Indeed specialisation in wool production does not seem to have prevalent according to this and other Roman samples as yet examined in detail, although it must be stressed that by no means an adequate sample of Roman sites has been taken. On the other hand, the quick fattening of lambs for slaughter seems to have played a relatively small part in sheep exploitation in Alcester. Present methodologies do not allow estimates of seasonal variability in the slaughter pattern to be made and it has been shown that epiphyseal fusion data can be misleading in the interpretation of sheep/goat mortality rates.

The late Roman mandible sample was quite large but it remains to be seen if it is typical of the rest of the town. Little intra-site variation was noted in the age structure of the mandibles and no concentrations of neonatal mortalities were discovered. This may be due to chance but the absence of such animals from an urban centre is perhaps to be expected. Only those sheep destined for the meat market would have been brought to Alcester and, unless large numbers of sheep were kept within the environs of the town itself, neonatal mortalities would be under-represented. Certainly, if the sheep represented in Alcester were a cross-section of the herd structure, one would have expected a much larger number of such mortalities. Medieval sheep flocks suffered greatly from disease and there is no reason to assume that the situation was different in Roman times. Perhaps there is a contrast to be made between urban centres such as Alcester and Exeter, where neonatal deaths are under-represented, and sites such as Portchester Castle, where the inhabitants in the late Roman period may have been more self-supporting in their agricultural stock (Grant 1975, 406). It also remains to be seen how typical the Explosion site sheep/goat assemblage is of sites in its region and whether its status as a market centre encouraged farmers to send there sheep specifically raised for meat or whether the stock represented in the deposits was an accurate cross-section of the animals exploited in the region.

Metrical analysis has demonstrated clearly that there were regional variations in the size of sheep in Roman Britain. The sheep in Alcester were larger than those in Exeter, although small by modern standards. How they compared with other regions of Roman Britain and the origins of the stock remains for future research to clarify.

Pig sample

Tooth eruption evidence

Most of the pigs represented in all phases were immature, although only detailed analysis was carried out on mandibles from the late Roman deposits. Of the mandibles of this date, 73 produced evidence of tooth eruption. A maximum of fifteen (20.6%) did not have their M1 in wear; a maximum of 27 (37.0%) did not have their M2 in wear; and a maximum of 63 (86.3%) did not have their M3 in wear (Table MT23, M2:G3). Concentrations of immature pig mandibles are to be expected, since the high reproductive rate of pigs enables most of the stock to be fattened for slaughter at a young age. As pigs are valued mainly for their meat and lard, it is to be expected that most of the stock would be killed immature. Detailed examination of wear patterns on the mandibular cheek teeth, using Grant's (1975) method of analysis, showed that the majority of the mandibles had numerical values of less than 30, with the main concentration lying between 17 and 24. This coincides with the early wear of the M2 and the eruption of the P4. This evidence would suggest that there was a peak of slaughter of second-year animals, if modern ageing estimates are applicable to Romano-British tooth eruption rates. The peak of numerical values at the Explosion site is slightly earlier than at Portchester Castle (Grant 1975), where the main concentration of Romano-British mandibles had numerical values of 20–30.

Explosion site finds (AES 76-7)

This need not necessarily imply that the peak of pig slaughter was earlier at the Explosion site. It is possible that difference in rates of tooth wear, nutrition, and breeding may account for minor variations in the ages of tooth eruption and wear in different herds. Perhaps more significant is the larger proportion of mandibles with numerical values of over 30 at Portchester Castle. Of the ageable mandibles, 33 (25.8%) possessed the M3 in wear (n.v. = 30+), whereas only 10 mandibles (13.7%) from the Explosion site had reached this stage. Most of these specimens from both sites had relatively little wear on the M3 and probably belonged to animals aged between 2–3 years. The causes of the variation are unclear. It is possible that the intensity of exploitation of pigs was greater at the Explosion site, resulting in a policy of fattening more animals in their first and second years, possibly by the introduction of sty husbandry. Alternatively, we may be observing a function of marketing practice, which saw a greater concentration of younger animals being brought for consumption in the town of Alcester. Obviously the questions cannot be answered without recourse to comparative data from other settlements in both areas.

Epiphyseal fusion data

The value of the pig epiphyseal fusion data was limited by the constraints of differential preservation. The results, however, did confirm that most of the pigs represented were immature. None of the latest-fusing articulations had in fact fused and even the youngest-fusing group included a large number of unfused specimens (Table MT24, M2:G3). Using modern fusion data (Silver 1969, 285–6), the latter would have belonged to animals under a year old. Comparable results were obtained from Portchester Castle (Grant 1975, 394) and Exeter, where the fusion data implied that the proportion of first-year killings was greater in the Romano-British phases than in the medieval period (Maltby 1979a, 189–90). The percentage of unfused distal tibiae at the Explosion site in the late Roman deposits (33.3%) and of unfused distal metacarpals (75.0%) was also high. The discrepancy between the proportion of unfused specimens of these two fusion points, which both fuse at about two years of age on modern estimates, again demonstrates the limitations of placing too much emphasis on this type of data in reconstructing kill-off patterns. Nevertheless, both ageing methods indicate that pigs were quite intensively exploited in Alcester and comparatively few appear to have survived into their third year.

Metrical analysis

The presence of so many immature bones meant that very few pig bones were measurable. Eight late Roman radii had a mean proximal width of 29.5mm, ranging from 26.7mm to 32.4mm. Eight tibiae of the same date had a mean maximum distal width of 28.8mm, with a range of 25.5–30.7mm. Both means were greater than their equivalents from Roman Exeter (Maltby 1979a, 193–194) but the evidence is too limited to place much weight upon these results. None of the few measurements of the length of the lower third molar fell into the range of wild boar (*Sus scrofa*) and none of the limb bones could be ascribed to the wild form of the species.

Butchery evidence

Most of the pig bones were in a fragmentary condition. Only 2.8% of the late Roman humeri, radii, femora, and tibiae were complete. The rest had been fragmented before or after disposal. Many of these bones must have been broken open to release the marrow. Chop marks and knife cuts were discovered on all the major limb bone types and on the mandible and skull. Not enough were discovered, however, to ascertain whether there was a standard practice of butchery.

Other species

Horse

Horse was extremely poorly represented on the site. Only 31 fragments were recovered from all phases. The 23 from the late Roman deposits represent only 0.2% of the identifiable mammalian fragments. It seems that horsemeat was a very rare food resource in Alcester, if these deposits are typical of the rest of the settlement. No butchery marks were found on any of the bones, although that does not prelude the horse's use as an occasional meat resource. The low representation of horse bones is typical of other large Roman samples (eg Portchester Castle – Grant 1975, 382; Exeter – Maltby 1979a, 61, 95–101). However, some rural and villa sites have produced a higher proportion of horse bones (eg Shakenoak Farm – Cram 1978) and it is possible that we are beginning to see a dichotomy in the distribution of horse bones on Romano-British sites. Horses would have been kept for their working qualities on a farm or villa estate or as a transport animal, particularly by the occupying army. They were not, however, systematically slaughtered for meat markets and hence their virtual absence from deposits derived principally from food refuse in towns.

Dog

The excavations recovered 323 fragments of dog but this number was inflated by the presence of several partial skeletons in the late Roman deposits. Out of 311 fragments (excluding vertebrae and ribs) dated to this period, 198 belonged to thirteen partial skeletons. Many of the remaining bones also probably belonged to relatively few individuals, for there were comparatively few fragmentary bones and no evidence of butchery was found on any of the specimens. The reason for the incomplete nature of most of these skeletons may be the disturbance of the carcasses before or after deposition or to the failure to recover some of the bones, particularly the small carpals, tarsals, and phalanges, during excavation. Whatever the explanation, there is no evidence for the exploitation of dogs for meat. It seems likely that the dog skeletons were dumped amongst other rubbish. Most of the animals represented were adults, although one of the partial skeletons (in (86)) belonged to a dog that died under a year old. Metrical analysis of the lengths of the longbones of ten of the skeletons produced estimated shoulder heights of 250–570mm, using the conversion factors of Harcourt (1974, 154). The three smallest specimens fall into the size range of small household or lap dogs, which have been found commonly in the Romano-British period (Harcourt 1974, 164). The larger dogs could have had a variety of uses or may simply have been scavengers.

Cat

All but one of the 26 domestic cat bones were of late Roman date. They included three limb bones of an immature animal in (24A), nine fragments of another immature specimen in (170), and three metacarpals and a first phalanx of one animal in (II 5).

Deer

Only 15 fragments of red deer (*Cervus elaphus*) were recovered, all of late Roman date. The only measurable specimens were a radius with a maximum proximal width of 59.9mm and a metatarsus with a maximum distal width of 39.7mm. Two antler fragments were found, one of which had been sawn. Roe deer (*Capreolus capreolus*) was represented by just two fragments of late Roman date. The only occurrence of fallow deer (*Dama dama*) was in a medieval deposit (II 14), in which a complete metacarpus (maximum length 197mm) was recovered. It appears that venison was a very rare addition to the diet of the people who deposited these bones.

Hare

Twenty fragments of hare (*Lepus sp.*) were identified, eighteen of late Roman date. Too few specimens were available to determine whether the bones belonged to the brown hare (*Lepus capensis*) or the mountain hare (*Lepus timidus*). Hare would have provided an occasional source of meat.

Badger

Three bones of badger (*Meles meles*), all belonging to the same individual, were found in (170). These consisted of a pair of radii and an ulna.

No bones of small mammals were discovered, as a result of the lack of sieving on the site, although a bone of an unidentified amphibian was recovered from the late Roman levels.

Bird remains

The site produced 370 bird bones fragments, of which 328 were of late Roman date. Domestic fowl predominated, contributing 27 of the 36 early Roman bird bones and 247 of the late Roman fragments. The metrical analysis of the complete bones of late Roman date produced samples that are too small to make a detailed assessment of their size (Table MT25, M2:G4). They are in general comparable to the size of domestic fowl bones recovered from Roman Exeter (Maltby 1979a, 210) and the range in the lengths is similar to the bones from Fishbourne (Eastham 1971, 392). Occasional butchery marks were found on fowl bones. It seems likely that domestic fowl were the only poultry kept in any numbers. Bones of the domestic duck/mallard (*Anas platyrhychos*) and the domestic goose/grey lag goose (*Anser anser*) were represented by only ten and twelve fragments respectively, mostly of late Roman date (Table 33). It was not possible to tell from these few bones whether the domesticated variety of these species was represented. The poor representation of grey lag/domestic goose is a common feature of Romano-British samples.

The presence of woodcock (*Scolopax rusticola*), golden plover (*Pluvialis apricaria*), woodpigeon (*Columba palumbus*), stockdove/pigeon (*Columba oenas-livia*), and bones of an unidentified small duck and small goose species indicate that wildfowl provided an occasional supplement to the diet. Of these species, woodcock (24 fragments in all deposits) was the most commonly found. The same species was also relatively common in Roman deposits at Exeter (Maltby 1979a, 72). Two corvid species were identified: jackdaw (*Corvus monedula*) and raven (*Corvus corax*). Ten of the raven bones belonged to one bird found in (170). Raven skeletons are not uncommon on Romano-British sites (Maltby 1979a, 73) and it has been suggested that some may have been kept as pets. These and other corvids, however, would also have been attracted as scavengers.

Fish bones

Only three fish bones were recovered and these have been identified by Mike Wilkinson. A dentary of a large pike (*Esox lucius*) of about 700mm in length and a centrum of a large trout or small salmon (*Salmo sp.*) were found in late Roman deposits. The

Explosion site finds (AES 76-7)

Table 42 Incidence of (oyster) shell fragments by period (AES 76–7)

Period	1	2	3	4	5	6	7	8	9	10	11	12	13	14	Total
Number of frags	–	3	–	1	6	49	9	39	592	118	84	–	–	10	911

medieval deposits produced a precaudal centrum of a large cod (*Gadus morhua*). Preservation and excavation conditions may have precluded the recovery of other fish bones.

Conclusions

The Romano-British sample from the Explosion site is one of the largest so far investigated for this period. The analysis has again demonstrated the complex nature of bone accumulations in urban deposits. It was possible to monitor some of the disposal practices in this area of the town but it remains to be seen how typical they were of the rest of the town. Similarly, the exploitation patterns of the major domestic species have been discussed in detail. They cannot fully be understood in isolation, however, and it will only be possible to assess them properly when contemporary samples from rural settlements in the surrounding area are compared. There is now evidence for substantial variation in species representation, size, mortality rates, and butchery techniques in the Iron Age and Roman periods in Britain. The Explosion site sample adds an important set of data to the overall picture of Romano-British animal husbandry. Its full value will only be realised when more samples from within the town and from the surrounding region are compared.

Oyster shells

A total of 911 fragments (*c* 8kg) of shell, mainly, if not entirely, of oyster, was recovered from the site (Table 42). These were not examined in detail. One fragment apparently came from the primary fill of the possibly late 1st- to early 2nd-century (period 2) well, with two others from the upper fills of the same feature. Thereafter there were very small numbers in periods 4 and 5, and only in period 6 did the use of oysters, or rather, their disposal on the site, become established. Nearly two-thirds (65%) of all the fragments occurred in period 9, and exactly one-third of all the oyster shells from the site were contained in a single pit (124). Quantities of oysters in period 10 were much lower than in period 9. Their post-Roman incidence, apart from in the period 11 layer (12), was very low.

Although relatively scarce in absolute terms the quantity of shells in period 9 deposits indicates that oysters could at times have been an important supplement to the diet of the inhabitants of Roman Alcester.

Plant remains from the period 2 well 168A (AES 76–7)
Susan Colledge

The well was cut to a depth of about 3m in the natural gravels. Its upper part had been disturbed by being re-cut as a pit in perhaps the later 4th century (period 10) but the well itself was probably of late 1st- to early 2nd-century date (see above). The well fill produced evidence of several distinct strata. A bulk sample was taken from one of the uppermost layers in the well, then at the bottom of the shaft a thin layer of organic material was discovered, and sampled by the excavation director. Sampling was considered important because wells can provide information about the environment from both floral and faunal aspects; they act as traps for insects living on the surface. Also, once the well is abandoned it can be a useful tip for domestic waste. The bulk samples were investigated for their macroscopic remains: they were washed down and sieved then paraffined (Buckland 1976). Preservation in the organic layer (168L) was good, from a sample of about 7 or 8kg. There were over a thousand seeds and some coleopteran remains but not as many as were expected. The Alcester well was disappointing in this respect. It is conceivable that the well was covered in some way while it was in use or perhaps had a surrounding parapet which would have helped prevent faunal contamination.

The seeds were grouped according to habitat preference (Table 44). By far the largest group was that of plants which live on cultivated and waste ground, including cornfield weeds such as *Papaver argemone*, the long prickly headed poppy, and *Valerianella dentata*, a member of the Valerian family. No cereal grains were discovered in layer 168L, but there were some charred grain spikelet fragments, and a pollen sample which was prepared from the deposit showed the presence of cereal pollen (Table 43). There were weed species represented which are common on ploughed land, for example *Aethusa cynapium*, fool's parsley and *Thlapsi arvense*, field pennycross. Somewhere nearby there were cultivated fields and these weeds were probably gathered in with the crops and then sorted out from the grain at some stage; they could have become incorporated with waste from a threshing floor. The bringing of hay to the site for bedding material may well be responsible for the presence of seeds of plants from meadow and pasture land, such as *Ranunculus acris*, the meadow buttercup, and *Potentilla anserina*, silverweed. Grass pollen made up 60% of the total pollen sum from layer 168L. Other plant groups represented by the seeds in the layer were those of hedgebanks and paths, waste places, and

Explosion site finds (AES 76-7)

Table 43 Well 168A pollen spectra (AES 76–7)

	168L		168M	
	No of grains	% of total pollen	No of grains	% of total pollen
Tree pollen				
Alnus	3	+	12	9
Betula	1	+	3	2
Corylus	6	1	10	7
Quercus	7	1	1	1
Sambucus nigra	5	1		
Tilia			1	1
Non-tree pollen				
Cerealia	16	2	1	1
Campanulaceae	1	+		
Caryophyllaceae	6	1	3	2
Chenopodiaceae	17	2	2	1
Compositeae:				
Centaurea nigra	20	3	1	1
Liguliflorae	20	3	15	11
Tubuliflorae	32	4	3	2
Cruciferae	2	+		
Dipsacaceae	4	1		
Ericales	1	+		
Gramineae	439	60	78	57
Labiateae	3	+		
Leguminosae	15	2	2	1
Plantago lanceolata	24	3	1	1
Polygonum aviculare	29	4		
Ranunculaceae	9	1	1	1
Rosaceae:				
Filipendula ulmaria	8	1		
Potentilla	37	5		
Rubiaceae	1	+	1	1
Rumex	1	+		
Umbelliferae	5	1		
Urticaceae	12	2	1	1
Aquatic Pollen				
Cyperaceae	12	2	1	1
Sparganium	1	+	1	1
Totals	737		138	

Explosion site finds (AES 76-7)

Table 44 Well 168A seed list (AES 76–7)

		Layer				
		Seed nos		Pollen %		
		168L	168M	168L	168M	
Species of cultivated and waste land						
Aethusa cynapium L.	Fool's parsley	2	–	1	–	
Atriplex patula L.	Common orache	6	1	2	1	
Chenopdium album L.	Fat hen	74	12	2	1	
Hyoscyamus niger L.	Henbane	14	3	–	–	Farmyards
Papaver argemone L.	Long prickly headed poppy	75	23	–	–	Light soils
Polygonum aviculare agg.	Knotgrass	7	9	4	–	
Polygonum convolvulus L.	Black bindweed	2	–	–	–	
Polygonum persicaria L.	Red shank	1	1	–	–	Near ponds
Senecio vulgaris L.	Groundsel	–	1	4	2	
Stellaria media (L.) Vill.	Chickweed	285	4	1	2	
Thlapsi arvense L.	Field pennycress	4	–	+	–	
Urtica dioica L.	Stinging nettle	40	8	2	1	
Urtica urens L.	Small nettle	c500	34	2	1	
Valerianella dentata (L.) Pool		3	–	–	–	Cornfield weeds
Species of pasture and meadow						
Daucus carota L.	Wild carrot	5	3	1	–	Chalk soils
Isolepis setacea (L.) R. Br.	Bristle scirpus	1	1	1	1	
Potentilla anserina L.	Silverweed	75	1	5	–	
Ranunculus acris L.	Meadow buttercup	33	–	1	1	
Ranunculus repens/bulbosus		52	9	1	1	
Species of hedgebanks and trodden places						
Balleta nigra L.	Black horehound	2	1	1	–	
Ranunculus parviflorus L.	Small flowered buttercup	1	1	1	1	Dry banks
Rubus idaeus L.	Raspberry	2	–	–	–	
Sambucus nigra L.	Elder	1	–	1		
Torilis japonica (Houtt) D.C.	Upright hedge parsley	1	1	1	–	
Species of wet places, streamsides and marshes						
Apium graveolens L.	Wild celery	2	–	1	–	
Carex cf disticha Huds	Brown sedge	7	–	1	1	
Carex cf flava	Yellow sedges	c 175	4	1	1	
Carex cf otrubae Podp.	False fox sedge	1	1	1	1	
Carex cf panicea L.	Carnation sedge	5	–	1	1	Base soils
Carex cf reparia Curt.	Greater pond sedge	1	–	1	1	
Carex cf sylvatica Huds.	Wood sedge	c 50	2	1	1	In woods
Conium maculatum L.	Hemlock	2	1	1	–	
Eleocharis cf. uniglumis/palustris		22	3	1	1	
Senecio aquanticus Hill.	Marsh ragwort	1	–	4	2	
Stachys palustris L.	Marsh woundwort	1	–	+	–	
Species of heathland						
Potentilla argentea L.	Hoary cinquefoil	2	4	5	–	Dry sandy grassland
Stellaria graminea L.	Lesser stitchwort	33	3	1	2	

Explosion site finds (AES 76-7)

Table 45 Incidence of coal by period (AES 76–7)

Period	6	7	8	9	10	11	12	13	14	Total
Weight of coal (g)	6	55	40	452	49	145	26	–	11	784

heathland. One rather rare plant was found, *Ranunculus Parviflorus* the small flowered buttercup, which grows on waysides. Godwin (1975) records it from only four Flandrian sites – all Roman. There were over 200 sedge seeds in the deposit; it seems improbable that sedges were growing on the site, but were more likely to have been transported in with other water plants, for example reeds, for purposes such as flooring.

The layer below 168L which was labelled 168M was also investigated for remains, it was not as rich as the organic deposit above; all the results are recorded in Tables 43 and 44.

Charcoal and coal (AES 76–7)
Paul Booth incorporating identifications by Pam Copson

Small quantities of charcoal and coal were recovered. Charcoal was not collected systematically and was not examined in detail, as it was not thought likely to amplify the environmental information available from the study of the well (168A). Some of the material, particularly that from period 2 deposits (275) and (285) (which produced the bulk of the charcoal from the site), probably derived from structural timbers, principally of oak, though some fragments of what may have been lime were found in (275) and also in (278), a layer associated with (275) and (285).

Much of the remaining charcoal was also of oak, though lime and ash (the latter species not represented at all in the pollen record from well (168A)) occurred in small quantities in period 9 contexts (86) and (124A), with the possibility that pear was also represented in (86). One non-carbonised fragment from well (168A) was perhaps from a climbing plant, possibly honeysuckle.

After its early concentration in period 2 deposits charcoal occurred sporadically in contexts dating up to the end of the Roman occupation, particularly in periods 9 and 10.

A total of 784g of coal was recovered. It occurred in Roman contexts from period 6 onwards, but 452g (57.5%) was found in period 9, much of it in pits (124) and (170). Coal may have been used for domestic heating, but it commonly occurred in contexts with a high incidence of slag, suggesting an association with iron smithing (see report on iron slag). One piece of coal in (218), a period 7 layer with a very high concentration of slag, actually had slag adhering to its surface. The source of the coal has not been established, though the North Warwickshire coalfield is the most likely place of origin (Brodribb *et al* 1968, 42).

Explosion site discussion (AES 76–7) *Paul Booth*

Chronological development of the site

Roman period

It is unfortunate that so little of the earliest deposits on the site could be excavated since the question of the site's origin remains unresolved as a result. The excavations at the Explosion site add three further pieces to the inventory of military metalwork from the town (nos 43–5 above), but all were residual in 2nd-century or later contexts. The excavated period 1 features at the site cannot be dated before c AD 75 at the very earliest as they contain Flavian samian ware. It has to be admitted that there could have been earlier features on this site which were not encountered in the very limited 'key-hole' cut into the earliest deposits. Period 1 and 2 contexts produced an appreciable quantity of Neronian samian ware which could have been derived from such features.

There is insufficient evidence to characterise this earliest activity. Neronian and Flavian features at the Baromix sites to the south are interpreted as military and it is possible that military occupation extended as far north as the Explosion site. The limited evidence of the possible gully (270) suggests, however, that the prevailing north-west/south-east alignment on the present site was already established in period 1, contrasting markedly with the north–south/east–west alignment of the probable military features. On this evidence it may be that period 1 represents civilian activity, presumably contemporary, in the first instance, with military activity close by to the south. Material such as Neronian samian could have derived from the military site or perhaps from early civilian settlement associated with it.

The presence of buildings on or near the site in period 1 is indicated by the occurrence of tile in pit (267). These buildings, however, may not have been the same as the structure or structures evidenced in period 2. The absence of structural features such as timber slots or postholes makes it uncertain whether the period 2 building stood exactly where the debris derived from it was located, but the size of the excavated area is such that no conclusions can be drawn.

The nature of the period 2 building is uncertain. It had a clay floor, wattle and daub walls, and probably a tiled roof, though the quantities of tile recovered from period 2 deposits were not great. The use of tile probably means that the building was of rectilinear plan. By contrast it is known that site E in Birch Abbey, excavated by C M Mahany in 1965, was occupied at about this time in part by successive phases of circular timber structures in an Iron Age building tradition. These buildings probably had a domestic function (Mahany 1994). At Baromix, however, there was a succession of rectangular timber buildings dating, like the Explosion site, from the early Flavian period onwards. One of these, structure 3 ALC 69, was destroyed, perhaps accidentally, by fire in the early 2nd century. The period 2 buildings at the Explosion site may also have been damaged by fire since quantities of burnt material occurred on the site. Such burning could, alternatively, have been part of a process of deliberate demolition on the site prior to alterations in its layout.

Whether or not the destruction of the period 2 building was deliberate, period 3 certainly saw a major alteration in the use of the site, with the laying of gravel surfaces over the probable site of the former building. Associated with the gravel surfaces was the enigmatic building VII, of roughly circular plan, apparently defined by a gully perhaps some 8m in diameter. It is unclear whether or not this was a roofed structure. If so, the re-emergence of a 'native' building tradition in place of a 'Romanised' one is notable, and may underline the association of the earliest structures on the site with the military establishments to the south. Comparable circular structures are known in Alcester at this date. While it may be that structures of this type had a very specific function which leaves no readily identifiable trace in the archaeological record, there is no particular reason to believe that they were not 'normal' domestic buildings.

Period 3 activity was probably quite short-lived, as was the succeeding period 4, very similar in character, in which more gravel surfaces were laid in site I. Building VII, at least in its original form, was out of use, though it may have been at this time that it served as a depository for domestic rubbish. In period 4 there was little evidence for structures or features associated with the major gravel surface (235). In site II, ditches were dug on a north-east/south-west alignment substantially similar to that of most of the features in site I. Their nature is uncertain, though it is possible that they could have defined a track or roadway along the eastern side of the site. A road in this position would have been on approximately the same alignment as the road located by S J Taylor at ALC 69 (see above). However, although the road at ALC 69 was re-sited a few metres to the west after destruction of the buildings fronting it, there is no such evidence from the Explosion site, and no suggestion that the trackway here was ever surfaced or was in use for anything other than a short while.

The construction of building V in about the middle

of the 2nd century (period 5) marked a major new development of the site. The alignment of this structure, however, followed that laid down perhaps as early as period 1 and apparently retained throughout the Roman period. Building V used a variety of construction techniques, with adjacent rooms having their walls based on stone and timber. Only the northern part of the building lay within the excavated area; its extent to the south is unknown. In its basic form (Fig 175) it seems to have consisted of two rectangular rooms (1 and 2), with a smaller room or rooms on the east side and perhaps a veranda or lean-to structure up to c 4m wide on the north side. In period 6 the building was enlarged on the west, a substantial, possible external wall being constructed c 1.10m from the original west wall. This presumably added no more than a corridor or passage to this side of the building. This construction phase also included the reworking of the small room(s) on the east side of the building and the partition of the original north room into two. Room 1 contained a hearth, perhaps from as early as period 5, and it is possible that this feature was retained throughout the life of the building since a period 9 feature (42) may have been a late version of the hearth. Only a small part of this and its predecessors occurred within the excavated area; they may have been almost centrally placed within room 1. In its expanded form the building was c 11.2m wide and had a minimum length of 11.5m (not including the possible veranda on the north side), though it was probably considerably longer.

Although at one time it was thought that the period 6 reconstruction followed fairly closely on the period 5 building it is now clear that this could not have been the case. Building V in its original form must have been in use for almost a century before being expanded, since the evidence for period 6 was quite consistent in suggesting that this period could not have commenced significantly before c AD 240 at the earliest. As a result of the redating of period 6 both it and the following period are seen as relatively short-lived phases of quite intense construction activity.

Outside building V the yard surface (235), which seems to have been kept clean since it was laid in period 4, was eventually covered in period 6 with a layer containing quantities of pottery and other rubbish (227). The nature of this layer is uncertain. It seems unlikely that such a deposit would have been allowed to accumulate over a long period of time and it is possible that it represents a deliberate deposit of refuse, some of it much earlier than the date of the deposition of the layer. This was perhaps intended to raise the ground level, shortly before the construction of the substantial period 7 gravel surface (161) which sealed (227).

Period 7, dated just after the middle of the 3rd century, was a time of major development on the site. Approximately contemporary with the laying of the new gravel yard was the demolition of rooms 3 and 4 on the east side of building V. The northern veranda or lean-to was demolished either at this time or more likely a little later. Shortly after the gravel was laid a new building, building VI, was constructed at an angle 10 degrees from the perpendicular with building V and to its north and east (Fig 175). The significance, if any, of the alignment is uncertain but may have related to that of a road to the east of the site (see below).

Building VI presents some problems of interpretation as a result of the fragmentary nature of the excavated plan. The principal feature of this building to the east was a pair of parallel walls (site II) c 4m long and 1.80m apart which are presumed to have terminated at the eastern end of the building. These may have formed some sort of entrance passage into the building, flanked by a room on the south side and with a threshold at the inner end of the passage. It is possible that the passage was centrally placed in the short axis of the building, with a room on either side, in which case the whole structure would have been some 14.4m wide. This would have been a very large span for such a building and it is perhaps more likely that the north wall of the passage served as the north wall of the whole structure; the building would thus have been c 9m wide. Its surviving length was 16.5m. There are two reasons to suggest that it is unlikely to have been much longer than this. Firstly, the south-west corner of the timber lean-to against the south wall of the building (site I), may have been in line with the west end of the building. Secondly, the period 9 pit (170) seems to have been placed so as to leave a gap between itself and the west end of building VI. Neither of these pieces of evidence is conclusive, however, and the building could have been longer than is shown on the hypothetical plan (Fig 175).

The passageway and the central room (the part of the building mostly occurring within the excavated area) were floored with the gravel surface (161)/(II 20) which had preceded the construction of the building, and there were no subsequent floor surfaces of any kind. There was some evidence for a mortar floor in the west room, of which only the corner projected into the excavated area, but little indication of other surfaces. The absence of floor layers within the central room was considered to be a possible indicator that this room was not roofed, but the balance of probability is against this suggestion. It is more likely that the absence of floors is indicative of the function of the building. The somewhat irregular timber slot (II 23) probably represented an internal partition dividing the central room into two parts, respectively c 3m and c 5.5m wide and both (presumably) some 7.5m north–south.

South of these rooms a lean-to timber structure against the south wall of the building was probably an original feature. The structure could have been open-fronted or have had timber walls, the position of which was respected by a later gravel surface (164). In its initial form it probably had a drain (201) along its front.

After period 7 there is no evidence for significant alterations to either building V or VI until the late

Explosion site discussion

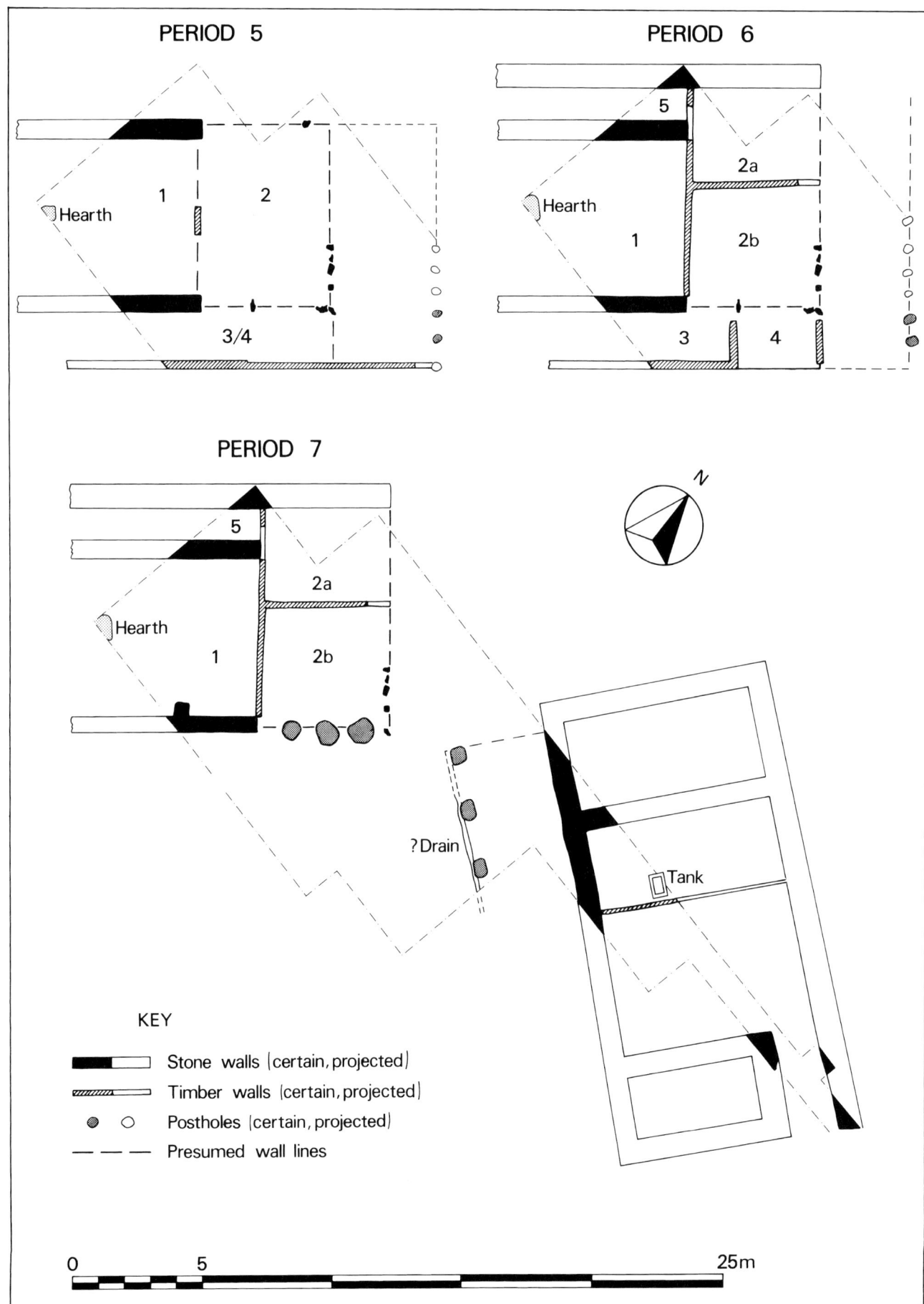

Figure 175 *Reconstruction plans of buildings V, periods 5–7, and VI, period 7 (AES 76–7)*

3rd century at the earliest. Most of the identifiable activity in period 8 took place in the yard area between the two buildings, where several layers were attributed to this period. The gravel surfaces (164–166) fronted and were probably associated with a structure, building IV, at the south edge of the site, situated to the east of building V. The building was apparently of timber on a crushed sandstone base, but so little of it was found within the excavated area that nothing can be said about its nature or function. In any case it was not in use for long since it was cut by a period 9 pit (115).

In period 9 the timber partition wall between rooms 1 and 2 of building V was renewed; it seems to have rested on vertical posts set on clusters of stone (114), (183), and the position of the horizontal timber which had supported the earlier partition was sealed with clay. A very large pit (170), dug right against the north wall of the building, was perhaps intended to be structurally related to it, but its plan was sufficiently irregular to make it unlikely that it could have represented an attempt to construct a cellar. The feature may have been only short-lived, and was perhaps abandoned before completion.

In building VI the only activity attributable to this period was pit-digging, both within the central room and (probably) in the lean-to structure to the south. It is not clear whether these parts of the building were out of use at this time. The pits were, however, of a fairly distinctive sub-rectangular plan and may have had a specific function not incompatible with their location within standing structures. There is little indication from their contents as to what such a function might have been, but pit (II 22), within the central room of the building, was noteworthy for containing an abnormally high proportion (c 43%) of bones of sheep/goat, the only group from the site in which cattle were less important than sheep/goat. The significance of this is not clear. In period 9 the yard area between the two buildings was also affected by pit-digging. Pit (124), cut in the centre of the yard area, may have been excavated as a gravel pit and was backfilled with rubbish.

In period 10, which may have commenced in about the mid-4th century, the appearance of the site was transformed. While a considerable degree of organisation seems to be implied by the layout, its character was clearly different in some ways from that of preceding periods. Some major activities such as animal butchery may have been continued, however, and there was no significant difference between the nature of the pottery assemblage in this period and that of period 9.

The western end of building VI was still standing, but at least part of the central room may have been demolished at this time, and building V was completely removed. Timber structures replaced building V and may have occupied the central part of building VI. Only on the south side of the site, however, could the nature and construction of these buildings be determined with confidence, and none lay entirely within the excavated area. Buildings III and II were both at right angles to building V and overlaid its east wall. Building III, of which there may have been two phases, was of standard post-in-pit construction. The principal posts probably supported the outer walls as well as the roof structure, but it is possible that the building was aisled, though if this was the case there is no evidence of any kind for the external walls. Only the posts of the north side of the building were discovered; neither its length or width are known, but the former was in excess of 6.3m. An internal wall or partition is indicated by three lesser postholes roughly parallel to the north wall.

Building II, which exactly replaced building III, was of completely different construction, resting entirely on a platform of carefully selected rubble, apart from the truss at the west end which was set on the ground. Other possible structures, including one on the east side of the yard area and one (building VIA) within the central room of building VI, were also set on rubble bases. The nature of building VIA remains uncertain, but lines of crushed sandstone c 0.70m wide may have been used to support timber walls, presumably of sleeper beam construction. Associated floor surfaces were of poor quality, incorporating gravel and clay. The function of this possible building is uncertain, but buildings II and III may be assumed to have been domestic. It is not known how many of these late structures were in contemporary use. Associated with them were groups of pits which seem to have been carefully zoned according to shape and therefore, presumably, function as well. The primary functions of the pits are unknown, but most of them contained large quantities of animal bone.

A well (240) was located between buildings II/III and VI. It may have cut the rubble spread (104) which possibly represented another timber building facing the yard area of the site. This building must have belonged to the earlier part of period 10 since it was sealed by a late Roman gravel surface (2) which is likely to have been related to building II. The surface was laid round the well-head.

Medieval period

The late Roman surface (2) was one of several layers which provided a link with the medieval occupation of the site. These layers produced medieval pottery from their surfaces, and it is possible that features such as well (240) continued in use into the medieval period, but there is no indication of early medieval settlement. The earliest medieval activity may have been of the 11th century, but most features were probably of late 12th- to 14th-century date. This date may correlate with the documentary evidence for the development of the medieval town, which was probably a borough from at least the 12th century. The earliest reference to burgage tenure is in 1207, and in 1251 the town was described as having been a free borough from the time of Henry I

Explosion site discussion

(*VCH* 1945, 13), though there is no evidence for the reliability of this statement. The evidence of burgage plots still survives, and the north end of Bleachfield Street seems to have been included within the part of the town in burgage tenure. Whether the Bleachfield Street plots were laid out as early as the 12th century is uncertain. They differ considerably in character from the irregular, deep plots fronting High Street, Church Street, and Henley Street which indicate unplanned growth (Slater 1982, 192), being more regular and of much reduced depth. It is perhaps likely that they represent a later addition to the burgage series, though if the High Street plots were of early 12th-century date the addition could have still have taken place in the 12th century. The dimensions of the plot at 1–5 Bleachfield Street (on the basis of the modern boundaries) are c 60m × 17.5m at the street frontage, which makes this plot almost exactly the same size as those of the planned town at Stratford-upon-Avon (12 perches × 3.5 perches, or 60m × 18m), established in 1196 (*VCH* 1945, 247). Bleachfield Street itself was almost certainly in existence by 1232 (Gover *et al* 1936, 194). All the identifiable medieval features at the Explosion site follow the east–west alignment of the burgage plots, in marked contrast to that of the underlying Roman features, some of which, such as ruinous stone walls, must still have been visible when the burgage plots were laid out.

The principal period 11 structure, based on walls (10) and (45), is difficult to interpret, but may have been related to the hearth (60). This does not seem to have been a domestic feature, but its precise function is unknown. Further east were the two short walls (II 13). Since most of the feature to which they belonged lay beyond the excavated area interpretation is difficult, but it is possible that the walls represented the flue of some kind of oven or kiln, perhaps a malting kiln of the type excavated by S J Taylor (further south at ALC 69, see above), C M Mahany (1965, 4), and S Cracknell (at Meeting Lane in 1984 (Cracknell 1989b)).

Period 12 saw the replacement of the hearth and stone walls by a rectangular building (building I) of 14th-century date. This building was small, c 6.45m × 2.50m, and of relatively insubstantial structure. It appeared to have had a porch on the south side. The absence of a hearth presumably precludes a domestic function, and it is assumed that domestic structures were sited at or towards the street frontage. The function of the building remains uncertain. Pits of this period were located in the northern part of the plot westwards from a point c 26m from the (present-day) street frontage. While medieval layers in the site II trench could have been truncated by post-medieval activity it is unlikely that pits would have been completely removed; negative evidence therefore suggests that pit digging was confined to the central part of the plot and did not extend either towards the street frontage or beyond the western end of the site II trench.

Post-medieval period

Most of the excavated features assigned to these phases could be related to the buildings of 1–5 Bleachfield Street at the front of the site. These buildings still stood at the time of the excavation but were demolished in 1978. The main house, originally of 17th-century date, had been reduced in size in the 18th century, and a cobbled surface found in the site II trench probably related to the building in this form. Also found in the trench were the foundations of brick outbuildings against the northern side of the site, possibly of 19th-century date. To the south, substantial outbuildings attached to the main house were still extant. It was probably one of these buildings which housed the smithy known to have been located at the site in the 19th and early 20th centuries (Johnson 1986, 82–3).

Function and economy of the site

Little can be said about questions of function and economy before period 5 because of the limited excavated evidence. The nature of the early buildings is uncertain, though it is presumed to have been domestic. The principal economic evidence is from the period 2 well. Plant remains from the well suggest that weeds of cultivated fields may have been separated from grain on the site. Grain itself was represented by charred spikelet fragments, but in small quantities which do not necessarily indicate crop processing on the site. The presence of hay, inferred from the seeds of pasture and meadowland plants, may indicate that animals were stalled from time to time on the site. The well, however, being of period 2, need not reflect activity which was sustained through the Roman period.

From period 5 onwards the site seems to have developed as a single unit. Both buildings V and VI may have consisted of domestic accommodation combined with non-domestic activities. Room 1 of building V, with a central hearth and many successive floor surfaces, presumably had a domestic function, although there were some features (eg (234) and (259)) whose interpretation in a domestic context is uncertain, but room 2 was of different character. Building VI was perhaps entirely non-domestic in function, with the possible exception of the room at the west end, which may have had a mortar floor.

Buildings V and VI were substantial, and employed a variety of construction techniques. Timber and local stone were used for walling, and a range of materials was used for roofing, particularly in the later Roman period. Earlier, tile was the principal material, and was presumably locally produced, but one tile in a late Roman context was almost certainly from a source in Buckinghamshire. Among the stone roofing material the presence of sandstone slates is noteworthy. These were not common on the site, and are not known elsewhere in the county. They were presumably used on building V, and while it is possible that they covered one particular part of the roof it is tempting to speculate that they were used for decorative effect in single rows contrasting with the light-coloured slates of Blue Lias and Oolitic limestone. Slates of all these materials were found together in pit (4). Some windows were glazed from at least as early as period 6, though the absence of late Roman window glass may indicate that the 4th-century buildings did not have glazed windows. Part of an iron window grille was also found. Keys indicate that security was a consideration. Furniture within the buildings included a chest or cupboard of limewood with an iron lock.

The activities carried out in these buildings are uncertain, but are likely to have been in part agricultural. Agricultural tools from the site included a reaping hook and a rake tooth. Early Roman arable agriculture evidenced by material from the well may have continued. However, the pattern of activity indicated by the animal bones is consistent throughout the Roman period, with the only difference between the early and late periods being one of scale. The evidence seems to show that primary butchery and presumably slaughtering, particularly of cattle, was carried out on the site. This was primarily the case in the later Roman period, but the majority of artefacts and other objects of all kinds were recovered from these deposits, perhaps because of changes in the pattern of disposal of rubbish in the later Roman period, so it is possible that the impression of more intense activity in the later period is more apparent than real. The quantity of bone fragments, however, certainly suggests that in the later 3rd and 4th centuries butchery was a regular and perhaps major activity on the site.

The evidence for slaughtering does not necessarily indicate that the Explosion site was the centre of a farm concentrating on cattle rearing, though it is likely that this was an important component of the agricultural regime based on the site. It is possible, though perhaps less likely, that butchery of cattle was a specialist activity carried out here on a contract basis because of the proximity of the site to a possible main market area. While sheep were also important at this site they may not have been the subject of the same large-scale primary butchery indicated for cattle. Some sheep bones, and those of the less common species found, presumably reflect the diet of the site's inhabitants, which included pork, game, domestic fowl, and occasionally fish, supplemented by shellfish.

There is no direct evidence for the quartering of animals on the site. It is possible that building VI could have been used for such a purpose, but feature (II 23) does not seem sufficiently substantial to have been a drain, and there is little evidence for heavy wear on the internal gravel surface (II 20), which would be expected had the building served as a byre. This building is perhaps more likely to have been used as a general barn/store, with a doorway wide enough to have admitted small vehicles or implements if necessary, though the lean-to structure on the south side is more likely to have been used for such items.

Other activities on the site included iron smithing and copper alloy working, but neither on a large scale. They occurred at a level which would have been consistent with the periodic requirements of an agricultural establishment, though copper alloy working would not necessarily have been essential and its presence might imply that the site had a more diverse economic base than being purely agricultural. The presence of a piece of sawn antler suggests boneworking, a suggestion which might be supported by the large numbers of bone pins and pin fragments found, but the actual evidence for manufacture is limited.

The finds indicate a good level of prosperity. The majority of objects of all types occurred in deposits of periods 9 and 10. Some of these objects may have been residual, but the evidence suggests that there was a genuine preponderance of later Roman items. Finds of some classes of material occurred most commonly in post-Roman deposits. In the case of shale bracelets this probably indicated a generally late date for their currency on the site (the earliest occurrence was in period 8 – later 3rd century) and the same may be true of jet objects (four out of five jet beads occurred in post-Roman contexts). A fragment of a shale vessel, found in topsoil, was particularly noteworthy. Bone pins were certainly more common in the later period; ten examples were of types dated 1st to early/mid-3rd century, but there were 32 examples of 3rd–4th-century types.

Noteworthy among the copper alloy objects were two mirror fragments (Fig 154, nos 20 and 21), both of 1st-century types. These are relatively unusual finds which indicate a considerable degree of prosperity in the town within a very short time of its foundation. It is of course likely that this earliest settlement received a considerable stimulus from the presence of the military garrison, and objects such as the mirrors may have originated in a context contemporary with the later years of the military presence. Personal items were common in a variety of materials, with, for example, bracelets in copper alloy, iron, bone, and shale. Literacy is evidenced by the presence of several *styli*, including one decorated example, and also by two seal-box lids.

The pottery also demonstrated that the inhabitants of the site were quite prosperous. The contrast between the Explosion site assemblage and that from nearby rural sites such as Tiddington and Wasperton was marked (see above) and the pottery emphasises the grouping of Alcester with other major settlements in the county such as Tripontium and Chesterton. The range of pottery at the Explosion site indicated that the Alcester markets drew on a widespread trade network. This included sources for *amphorae* as far afield as Italy and the eastern Mediterranean as well as the more common vessels originating from Spain and France and used to transport olive oil and wine. Early imported fine wares may have included mica-dusted ware. Later

Explosion site discussion

on, fine wares from Central Gaul and Trier were unusually common in comparison to other Warwickshire sites.

Within Britain the sources of supply, while various, were mainly standard ones, with coarse wares drawn from local producers (most of the grey wares), Malvern, the Severn Valley region, Dorset, and (in the 4th century) possibly Northamptonshire and Buckinghamshire (for shell-tempered and pink grogged wares respectively). Mancetter-Hartshill, in north Warwickshire, was important for *mortaria* and white wares and such vessels were also obtained from the Verulamium region. In the later Roman period, however, the products of these sources were outnumbered by those of the Oxfordshire industry, which dominated both *mortarium* and fine ware supply. The Nene Valley was the other main late Roman fine ware supplier and a sherd of the much less common Nene Valley white ware was also found, though mortaria from the same source were apparently absent. Other fine wares were from unknown sources. The most unusual British fine ware, apart from two mica-dusted vessels of unknown origin, was New Forest ware, which was found in small quantities well beyond its normal distribution range. Such occurrences indicate the importance of trading centres such as Alcester in attracting goods from diverse and far-flung sources.

Other classes of imported material included lava querns from the Eifel region of Germany, and glass. The glass came mainly from the north-western provinces of the empire. There were no particularly unusual pieces, but the material was noteworthy as much for its quantity as for other characteristics. The comparison with Tiddington has already been made with relation to differences in the pottery assemblages from the two sites. In terms of glass the comparison is extremely marked. There are 122 recorded pieces from Tiddington, including counters and beads. These come from two very extensive area excavations carried out in 1980 and 1982 and a large collection derived from pre-war excavations (Fieldhouse *et al* 1931; Palmer 1982). The corresponding number of fragments from the Explosion site, a much smaller excavated area, is 153. Superficially at least, this kind of contrast suggests a considerably higher level of prosperity at Alcester than at Tiddington. It may be the case that the contrasts were more marked in some classes of item than others, and imported glass may have been one of the classes which was found in relatively large quantities only at the major market centres. Nevertheless much of the evidence from the Explosion site indicates that this site was integrated into a market system which had not only wider ranging contacts than the lesser market centres such as Tiddington but also access to larger quantities of traded goods.

The northern suburbs and the development of Roman Alcester *Paul Booth and Jeremy Evans*

All the sites discussed in this volume lie in what became the northern extramural area of the town, south of the peninsula surrounded by the river and marshland which was enclosed with earthwork defences around the beginning of the 3rd century, and north of the Salt Way (street A, Fig 3). In the southern suburbs occupation seems to have commenced in the early to mid-AD 60s (Hartley et al 1994; Brickstock and Casey 1994) and the earliest activity in the northern suburbs seems to have commenced around the same time.

The origins and development of the Roman town has been summarised previously by Booth (1994). That summary was prepared before detailed work on the artefactual material from the Mahany excavations and the Baromix sites had been completed. The effect of this subsequent work has been to alter the interpretation of the early development of the town in several significant details. The most important change is the suggestion from the Baromix excavations that military occupation may have continued into the 2nd century AD.

Origins of the town

There is remarkably little evidence of Iron Age activity in the area of the Roman town, there being a few sherds of middle Iron Age pottery from pits at Tibbet's Close (Ferguson 1989), and several more from pits at Mahany's site M (Evans 1994b) and a pit at Gas House Lane (Evans 1996, 59). In the southern suburbs none of the features is assigned to a pre-conquest date (Mahany 1994), but Mahany's excavations produced seven pre-conquest brooches (Mackreth 1994), one from the site M III trench in the defended area and six from the southern suburbs, most (five out of six) being concentrated in areas D and G, possibly suggesting some pre-conquest activity in the town.

This Iron Age activity perhaps attracted the Roman military to the area. The earliest fort seems likely to have been the one located 400m south of the River Arrow at Lower Oversley Lodge, revealed by aerial photographic evidence (Webster 1981, plate 11). This fort, with an area of c 1.6ha, had early morphological characteristics and might belong to the conquest period. It presumably had a fairly brief occupation, not least as it lacks evidence of associated civil settlement. In the town there is no real evidence of activity before the AD 60s. Some brooches could be earlier (Mackreth 1994) with a suggested start date range of AD 50/55–60/65 being given, but the samian suggests the AD 60s (Hartley et al 1994), and the preponderance of worn, light Claudian copies amongst the early coinage (Brickstock and Casey 1994) suggests a date early in the AD 60s. Apparently contemporary with these finds, and probably the reason for their occurrence, there would seem to be a fort in the northern suburbs, of which the principal excavated areas are the Baromix sites. Unfortunately the existence of the fort cannot be proven beyond doubt as the defences have yet to be located and no recent excavations of any substantial area have been undertaken within it. However, the very high proportion of military metalwork from the Baromix sites relative to other small finds and the fact that these sites have the highest proportion in the town of pre-Hadrianic compared with later 2nd- to mid-3rd-century coinage are both very suggestive. This is particularly so when combined with the evidence for three phases of pre-Hadrianic rectilinear timber buildings aligned north to south found across all three sites. Although military finds have been made on purely civilian sites (Millett 1990, 60) the concentration at Alcester seems far too great for this to have been the case here, with five from the Taylor Baromix sites (ALC 69 and ALC 72/2), one from the 1988–89 Baromix excavation (AL 28), three from the adjacent Explosion site (AES 76–7), ten from the southern suburbs (Cracknell and Mahany 1994), and one from the Magistrates Court site between Priory Road and Seggs Lane (Seaby 1945, 45, no 53). Fig 176 indicates the area in which the fort might be located. The north-east to south-west orientation of features on the Explosion site and at Lloyds Bank, in contrast to the north-north-east to south-south-west orientation of features on the Baromix sites, and the nature of the features on the Lloyds Bank site, suggests that both of these lay beyond the northern limit of the putative fort. It is unfortunate that only a very small area of deposits of this period was examined on the Explosion site, which results in the nature of activity on this site at this time being poorly understood. It does, however, seem likely that the Explosion site lay very close to the northern limit of the defences, and the burnt clay deposit, layer 290, from period 2 on site I of the site may have been the equivalent of the burnt clay found as a demolition horizon on ALC 69 and 72/2. The Baromix sites, ALC 69 and 72/2, are clearly within the putative fort, as are the trenches of Baromix AL 28 to judge by the alignment of the timber slots, the oven, the three pre-Hadrianic phases, and the military metalwork. To the west the site at

6 Birch Abbey (AL 10; Cracknell 1989b, 25–38) would seem to be beyond the fort defences, although it has two enigmatic parallel early east to west slots which would appear to match the fort alignments.

To the east Mahany's site L (Mahany 1994) shows no indication of military type features, trenches L V–VII, the nearest, being disturbed by post-medieval quarrying, whilst L I, L XIII, and L XI show features on a north-east to south-west alignment similar to that found on the Explosion site and Lloyds Bank. The limits of the putative fort to the south are a little harder to establish. Certainly no features in Mahany's site G south of the line of street A seem to be of this nature.

At 64B–D Bleachfield Street (Cracknell and Ferguson 1989) street A was located and sectioned and to its north a Flavian–Trajanic pit was recorded, but no trace of fort defences or beam slot buildings on the 'fort's' alignment, suggesting these were located north of this site. Other pits were also found cutting the natural gravel but were not excavated or planned in detail. Immediately to the north of this at 64 Bleachfield Street (Booth 1989) both Neronian–Flavian pits and some beam slots and gullies aligned approximately north–south and east–west, like those on the Baromix sites, were recorded. These features are similar to those with a suggested military association at Baromix but lack evidence of the three phases of activity noted there. It seems unlikely that they were actually situated within the 'fort' as there is no evidence of early defences on 64B–D Bleachfield Street immediately to the south, but they may have been *vicus* structures immediately south of it. Alternatively the first military phase, of Neronian to early Flavian date, may just possibly have been of a different layout to the subsequent ones. The little dating evidence from 64 Bleachfield Street would be consistent with the assignment of features here to this phase, although the failure to locate evidence of defences to the south of the site counts against this.

On the basis of the above evidence, an area of roughly 120m north–south by 120m east–west could have been occupied by military features, assuming that the 64 Bleachfield Street sites lay outside the fort to the south. This space would have been adequate for an auxiliary fort which at about 1.5ha would have been closely comparable in size to that at Lower Oversley Lodge. This is not to suggest, however, that the two sites were necessarily garrisoned by the same unit, or that the whole of the potentially available area around Bleachfield Street was occupied by military features.

The orientation of the fort is uncertain, though the survival of the north–south street into the post-military period as street D might suggest that this was already a through road and thus most likely to have been the *via principalis* of the fort. If the earliest Baromix buildings were barrack blocks aligned north–south, as is possible, it is conceivable that the suggested space/street at their northern end was on the central east–west axis of the fort. These suggestions must remain speculative, however, in the absence of further evidence. Equally the nature of the occupying unit remains unclear, although the items of copper alloy horse trappings (ALC 69 nos 1 and 2, and ALC 72/2 no 1) may suggest the presence of cavalry.

There remains the question of the 'historical' context of the fort. The Roman army probably reached Warwickshire by about AD 47, as it is thought that most of lowland Britain up to the rivers Severn, Avon, and Trent had been occupied by this time. It has been suggested that the Romans intended to establish a frontier along this line and not to advance beyond it. The Fosse Way, which runs across the area, has been seen as an integral part of such a scheme, which has been termed the Fosse Way frontier (eg Dudley and Webster 1973, 98; Webster 1980, 123). The concept of a fixed frontier in Britain at this time is probably an anachronism, however, (eg see Jones and Mattingly 1990, 88–94) and in any case the westward advance under Ostorius Scapula in AD 48 makes the issue incapable of proof either way.

The principal military sites in the region include Baginton to the north-east, Mancetter and Wall further north on Watling Street, and Metchley, like Alcester situated on Ryknild Street, also to the north. To the north-west and west are further sites such as Greensforge and Droitwich. To the south-west the nearest certain military establishments are those at Gloucester and Cirencester.

Mancetter and Wall both have large early (Claudian) establishments, generally accepted as vexillation fortresses, probably connected with the advance of the 14th Legion into the West Midlands. At Wall occupation seems to continue from this period through to the early 3rd century (Jones 1998). At Mancetter traces of a number of different defensive circuits attest a complicated sequence of smaller-scale activity after the abandonment of the vexillation fortress, but there is at present no suggestion that this activity outlasts the early Flavian period. At Baginton early and probably extensive military occupation is attested at Home Farm. This most likely predates the well known fort at the Lunt, thought to have been founded about AD 60 and not to have been occupied after *c* AD 75 (Reece 1975, 24–5). At Greensforge (Webster 1965) there are at least two distinct phases of military activity, but the dating is not very clear. At Metchley recent excavations (A Hancocks pers comm) have demonstrated a more complex sequence of forts than previously thought (Webster 1965), with occupation extending from the mid-1st century to the early 3rd century. The fort at Dodderhill, Droitwich also has two military phases, though with a clear break between them. The first (Claudio-Neronian) fort seems to have been given up *c* AD 70, but the site was reoccupied from *c* AD 120–150, an action perhaps connected with imperial interest in the exploitation of the supply of salt (Burnham and Wacher 1990, 214).

At Cirencester the first fort has been thought to date as early as AD 45 (Wacher and McWhirr 1982,

22), though a rather later date has also been suggested (eg Trow 1990, 112). Military occupation is considered to have ended by *c* AD 75 (Wacher and McWhirr 1982, 22).

Most of these sites follow a broad pattern of early activity (ie Claudian to early Neronian), apparently followed in some cases by a secondary phase or phases lasting into the early Flavian period. The commencement of this secondary phase has in the case of the Lunt, at least, been directly associated with the aftermath of the rebellion of Boudicca (Hobley 1973, 14–15). The dating evidence, which suggests a foundation date in the region of AD 60, may allow Alcester to be fitted into this pattern, but the complexity of military operations in the West Midlands up to the early Flavian period must have provided many opportunities for realignment of the disposition of army units. It is possible, for example, that the foundation of the Bleachfield Street fort at Alcester followed immediately on the abandonment (for whatever reason) of the Lower Oversley Lodge fort, an action which need have had no connection whatsoever with the Boudiccan rebellion.

Alcester is unusual in a West Midlands context in apparently remaining in military occupation into the early 2nd century, whereas the standard model for the development of civilian administration in the province (eg Frere 1987, 192–3) implies the removal of most, if not all military personnel as a prerequisite of attaining self-governing status. There can be little doubt that for the *Dobunni*, the tribe in whose territory Alcester certainly lay, this development occurred in the Flavian period (Frere 1987, 192–3; Wacher 1975, 294). The status of Alcester thus appears anomalous. The military character of the early 2nd-century buildings at Baromix seems established, though the extent of such features is unknown. It is perhaps possible that early civilian structures were built on the same plan as preceding military ones in this part of the town, but while this pattern of development has been noted in some examples of the transformation of legionary fortress into *colonia* (eg at Colchester and Gloucester) there are no known parallels for such a sequence in a small town context. In the absence of more concrete evidence the reason for the unusual prolongation of military occupation must remain unknown. The existence of even a small garrison (primarily in the winter season) is, however, likely to have had its effect on the development of the civilian settlement around. The more recent evidence from Metchley and Wall suggests Alcester was one of a number of forts in the northern West Midlands occupied in the Flavian–Trajanic period. It was probably the earliest abandoned, followed, perhaps by Dodderhill.

Overall the evidence from Alcester would seem to suggest that the town developed from a military *vicus*, conforming more to Millett's model 1 (1990, Fig 20, after Webster 1966) than to his model 2, although the population may have come from a pre-existing concentration in the Iron Age.

Urban topography and the 'fort'

The presence of an early fort in the northern suburbs may do much to explain the topography of the town and parts of the road network. In the southern suburbs, development seems to commence on the north of the site, north of the line of street A in areas E, F, and J (Mahany 1994, Fig 5) and then develops south of street A as a series of enclosures, which suggest more marginal activity. Similarly the activity at Lloyds Bank and the Explosion site starts at the latest in the Flavian period, and probably slightly earlier, on the northern margins of the putative fort. To the west, 1st-century structural activity is noted at 6 Birch Abbey (Cracknell 1989b, 25–38) close to the western margins of street C. This street extended north from Mahany's site E to the west of 6 Birch Abbey and was laid out in the mid- to late 1st century (Mahany 1994, Fig 5, this volume, Fig 3). To the east of the 'fort' area the Hockley Chemical site (Cracknell 1989a) shows occupation from the Flavian period. Interestingly, as the focus of the town develops to the south of the line of street A in the later 2nd century, occupation on this site recedes to the south, towards the northern side of the line of street A. In summary the earliest activity in much of the town seems to have been concentrated in a zone closely surrounding the putative fort and only later do the southern suburbs seem to have developed as one of the principal *foci*.

The main axis of the 'fort' would seem to have been street D, running approximately north to south from ALC 69. This has previously been indicated as running north-east from street A to a hypothetical gateway in the defended area situated under the present High Street (cf Cracknell 1989b, Fig 2), however, this must be mistaken. This street on the ALC 69 site ran north to south, as the other features, and its junction with the line of street A, leaving aside the date of the latter for the moment, must have been to the east of Mahany's site G upon which there was no sign of its continuation; the probable candidate for the continuation of street D to the south in fact being street B. North of ALC 69 the difficulty with the alignment of street D appears to be the lack of evidence of its crossing trench II at the Explosion site. However the north-east to south-west alignments on both the Explosion site and Lloyds Bank (and even on a number of the Hockley Chemical site trenches), consistently held throughout the Roman period, suggests that these property boundaries ought to be parallel to the street, as are those on the Baromix sites, and the obvious suggestion must be that the street turns north-east out of the fort's north gate to cross onto the island of relatively high ground to the north, crossing at its highest point, dictated by topography to be the course of the present High Street.

Approximately parallel to street D, and also of mid- to late 1st-century date, was street C (Mahany 1994, Fig 5, this volume, Fig 3) which seems to have run parallel to the western side of the fort, some distance from it. A further street (street E) may have

The northern suburbs and the development of Roman Alcester

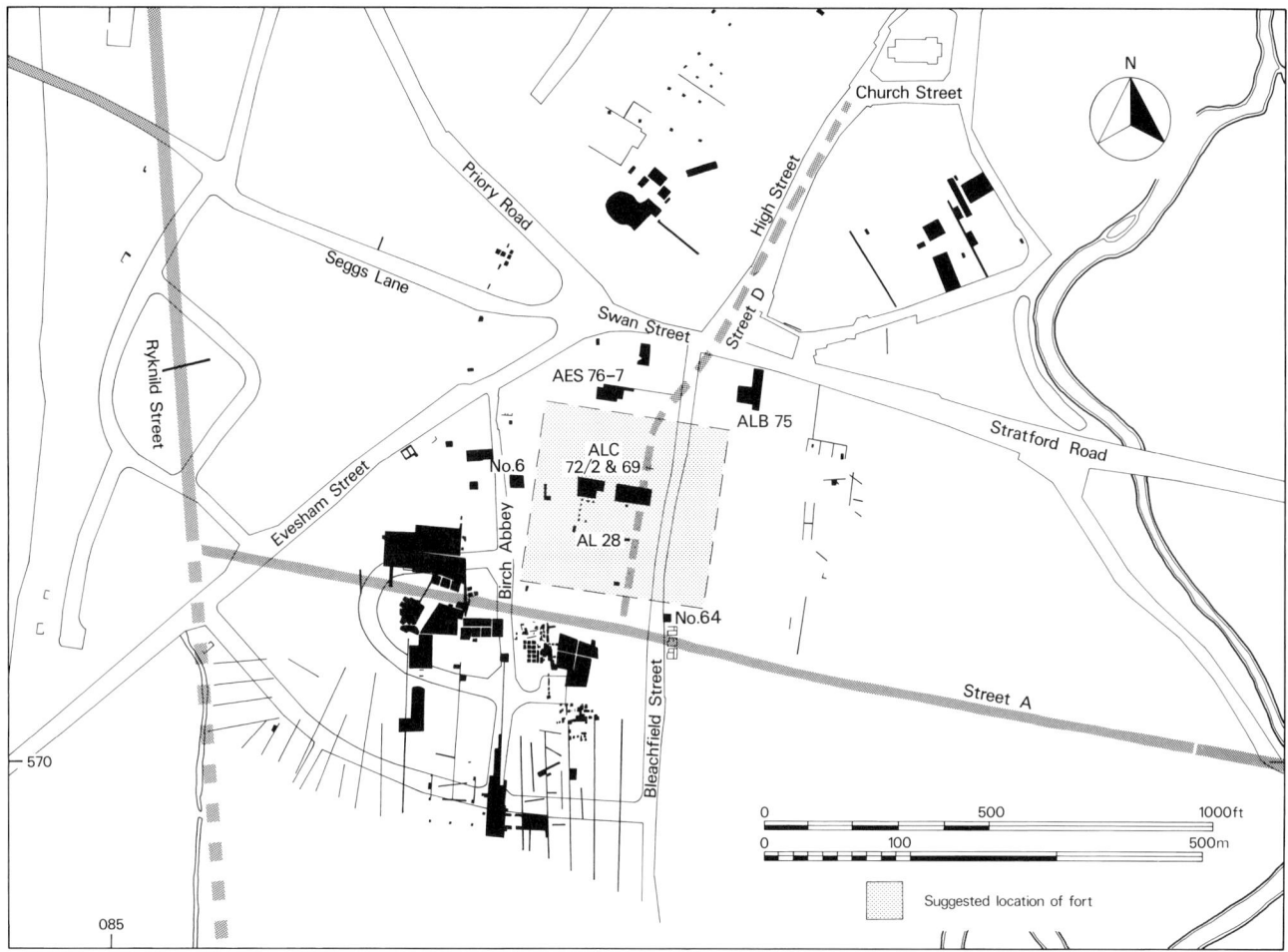

Figure 176 The northern suburbs and the approximate location of the proposed fort

run east-south-east to west-north-west to the north of the fort. Hughes (1960, 15) identified this at Swan Street where 'a section was cut across a road running approximately east–west; the 25ft [7.6m] exposed was incomplete . . . The road lay on a prepared clay surface and the original southern ditch was sufficiently well-defined to give an alignment which was in very close agreement with the line of the present Seggs Lane . . . The remains of the road were about 4ft [1.2m] thick consisting of successive layers of heavy pebble, gravel and clay with sandy partings.' However, this evidence is generally dismissed, mainly because if it extended east-south-east along the course of the present Stratford Road it would descend into ground subject to flooding.

Within the area of the 'fort' two possible road/track lines have been observed. One is along the northern side of the ALC 69 and 72/2 sites, running east to west where buildings generally fail to encroach in the early phases. The other is at right angles to this in the canopy foundation pits observed in a watching brief on the Baromix site by P Booth (nos 1–8 located between ALC 72/2 and AL 28 trench 3, Fig 2). Here pits 1 and 7, some 4.50m apart, both contained gravel and cobble surfaces flanked, respectively on the west and east, by north–south linear cut features. A westward extension of street F might also be potentially

related to the east–west axis of the fort, although nothing of this was observed in Mahany's trenches L V–VII, but these had been extensively disturbed by later quarrying.

South of the fort was street A, which seems to have been part of the road from Stratford to Alcester. As Booth (in Mahany 1994) points out the staggered junction with Ryknild Street (Fig 3), which presumably precedes the town, suggests that the Droitwich road and the Stratford Road were laid out at different times. The location of street A probably owes little to the fort as there is no evidence that it was laid out so early. Despite its illustration on earlier phase plans (eg Mahany 1994, Figs 65–74 and 76) there is no clear evidence of its existence on her site F in the form of metalling or roadside ditches before phase F XII in the 4th century and on Mahany's site D IV a gully runs beneath its first surface. Similar evidence was recorded from Hughes' examination of the street close to the point where its alignment shifts to one closer to due east (1960). Hughes noted that the gravelled surface 'had been laid on turf containing sherds of rustic ware' (of later 1st- to mid-2nd-century date) and that 'subsequently a large (stone) building had been built over the road' (1960, 15–16). Booth (1994) suggests street A 'must have been a very early, if not primary, feature' but the evidence he suggests for alignments based on it is not very strong.

At 64B–D Bleachfield Street (Cracknell and Ferguson 1989) street A was located and sectioned, although unfortunately no clear dating evidence was recovered from the sequence. Here the first gravelled road sat on a soil layer (55) tentatively identified as a buried soil horizon which may have been cut by a pit containing Flavian–Trajanic material. This first surface was overlain by a silty clay loam (48) which sealed it and the Flavian–Trajanic pit, and this was followed by further resurfacings. This loam layer (48) seems very similar to the sandy loam layer (61, 62) from 64 Bleachfield Street (Booth 1989, 12), which sealed Neronian–Flavian features across that site and which contained Hadrianic–Antonine samian. This evidence may suggest that the first road had fallen into disuse by the mid- to late 2nd century. Cracknell and Ferguson (1989, 130) suggested that the 64B–D Bleachfield Street sequence might be equated with Hughes' turf layer beneath the road (1960, 15), with late 1st- to mid-2nd-century dating evidence, although this could just as well have been related to their buried soil horizon (56).

Overall there seems no evidence that street A was laid out before the 2nd century AD and it might well, therefore, be subsequent to the demolition of the 'fort' in the early Hadrianic era.

Civil development of the northern suburbs

Evidence for the development of sites in the northern suburbs varies. To the north of the putative fort, evidence of activity on both the Lloyds Bank and Explosion sites is continuous from the 1st to the 4th centuries although much more intense on the Explosion site, and the Lloyds Bank site seems to have become a marginal area within the 4th century. To the south of these, activity on the street D frontage on ALC 69 seems to suggest an initial burst of timber buildings in the mid-2nd century, tailing off by the end of the century, with the frontage being abandoned by the 3rd century. South of this, the AL 28 site produced some suggestion of 2nd-century timber structures and the evidence from trench 2 suggested a 3rd-century stone structure close to the road line. At 64 Bleachfield Street (Booth 1989; Cracknell and Ferguson 1989), to the south of the fort, as at Lloyds Bank, there is evidence of Flavian activity in the form of pits and some slots, probably of a civil nature, but this seems to have been followed by a hiatus, indicated by soil accumulations. Later, on the 64B–D Bleachfield Street site (Cracknell and Ferguson 1989) a stone building was constructed facing onto street A. This is not closely dated, but by analogy seems unlikely to precede the 3rd century. Just to the north of this at the 64 Bleachfield Street site (Booth 1989) an east–west road with a Hadrianic–Antonine *terminus post quem* was laid down, parallel to street A. This could have been to give access to the rear of the building to the south and is thus more related to the late Roman development along street A than the northern suburbs as such. By the end of the 3rd century much of the area south of the Explosion site and north of street A would appear to have been without major structures.

No doubt the creation of the defended area, which seems to have been quite intensively occupied to judge by the sequence of 3rd-century structures on the Gas House Lane site at its margins (Cracknell 1996), attracted a shift in settlement from elsewhere in the town and the present evidence seems to suggest that this was disproportionately from the northern suburbs. Buildings became scarcer in the northern suburbs but not in the southern suburbs and *de novo* occupation in the defended area would appear to have been intense. This somewhat atypical pattern of development, in which the density of extramural settlement quite clearly declined after the construction of the defences, is in contrast to the more normal picture, in which, for 'small towns' at least, the construction of defences generally had little impact on the remainder of the settlement (Esmonde Cleary 1987). This can be explained by the fact that the newly defended area was, most unusually, almost entirely unoccupied prior to its enclosure. The evidence of less intensive occupation in the northern suburbs combined with the continued development of the stone structure on the Explosion site could be seen in terms of Reece's (1980b) model for the development of towns in the 3rd century. However, the morphology of the town had not changed markedly from the 1st and 2nd centuries, there being at no period intensely packed strip buildings along frontages of the type characteristic of many 'small towns' (cf Burnham 1988, 41–44). There are very few 'strip buildings' from Alcester, despite the large numbers of structures known and their structural diversity (Booth 1994, Figs 109–111).

In the 4th century there is a marked lack of evidence on the ALC 69, ALC 72/2, AL 28, and 64 Bleachfield Street sites for any activity, and whilst some truncation may have taken place there are no pits or foundation trenches clearly of this date and little later Roman pottery in their collections. At Lloyds Bank the area which previously appears to have been a yard seems to have been converted to use as a small cemetery, suggesting its further marginalisation, and only the Explosion site seems to have seen further development. There, the stone founded structures V and VI seem to have survived in use until the mid-4th century, after which they were replaced by timber ones. The continuing activity on this site, and its association with cattle butchery, may have related to its position close to the gates of the defended area and adjacent to the apparently large areas of cobbled surfaces east of street C, which have been tentatively proposed as a market place (Booth 1994).

There is little evidence of early medieval activity from the town, as is usual. In Warwickshire there is no evidence of any pagan Saxon activity from the large medieval town at Warwick (Ratkai pers comm), although there is some from Stratford, and from Worcester (Buteux pers comm) and Droitwich in Worcestershire. At Alcester there are sherds of this date from the Gas House Lane excavations (Ratkai, in Cracknell 1996, 97–99) within the defended area, but no surviving structural evidence. The classic *wic* location is just outside the gates of the late Roman defended area. It is here that Saxon development is found in large towns such as York or London. At Alcester this area includes the Lloyds Bank site. Here the first indications of Saxon structural activity seem to have been found in the form of the beam slot containing a Saxon rimsherd. This is significant given the absence of evidence from many of the larger towns in the county of any activity in this period. However, the Saxon occupation does not seem to have been very extensive given the absence of evidence from the Explosion site, or any of the others in the northern suburbs.

Social and economic evidence

The quality of social and economic evidence from sites in the northern suburbs is very variable, with the Explosion site being the only one to have ecofact evidence and a non-ceramic artefact assemblage of any reasonable size and these are discussed in detail above under the individual site.

The varied finds from all these sites do, however, present a relatively consistent picture of access to a widespread trade network, providing Alcester not only with basic requirements, but also with a number of unusual and potentially high-status items. This would in any case be expected in the early Roman period at the Baromix sites where the presence of a military unit left its mark on the ceramic and artefactual record, as well as in the structures. Evidence for the late Roman period is lacking here, but the Explosion site assemblage makes it clear that a reasonable level of prosperity and trade contacts was enjoyed by the inhabitants of Alcester in the 3rd and 4th centuries.

The most usefully explicit artefact type for suggesting trade links is, however, the pottery. The ceramic assemblages from the Lloyds Bank and AL 28 sites in particular produced evidence of some of the earliest coarse wares found at Alcester. Amongst these assemblages are small quantities of Savernake ware (probably also present at the Explosion site), perhaps because of military associations, and Malvernian Paleozoic Limestone-tempered ware. The latter fabric is much more frequent in the 1st century at the rural site at Bidford Grange to the south west, down the Arrow valley, as is Malvernian metamorphic-tempered ware, suggesting it came to Alcester along this route, whereas Savernake ware is absent there. Distinctive 1st-century types such as butt beakers are found on the Lloyds Bank, Baromix, and Explosion sites as are ring and dot beakers at Baromix, and one of the later grey ware ones from AL 28 (cf Evans 1990). Rustic wares are common in 1st- and early 2nd-century groups, most with the waisted shoulder of the type restricted basically to Warwickshire (Evans 1994a) and some, at least, probably come from the Tiddington kilns as do small quantities of Tiddington oxidised fabrics. The quantities of rustic ware at Alcester are much greater than at the rural site at Bidford Grange, presumably reflecting either supply factors, especially the Tiddington connection, or military demand for the type, or a combination of both of these. The presence of Lyons ware at AL 28 also strongly suggests a military connection, although this is the first example of this fabric at Alcester, perhaps surprisingly given that it was still current in the early Flavian period to judge by the comparatively large quantities from some forts in north-eastern England. Pre-Roman and Claudio-Neronian Belgic style grog-tempered wares (fabric class E) are very scarce at Alcester compared with the major settlement at Tiddington (Booth forthcoming) which probably reflects both chronological factors, with Alcester not being founded before the late Neronian period, and supply ones, with the rural site of Bidford Grange also having a low representation of this fabric class. The bulk of the other reduced wares from 1st- to early 2nd-century deposits are organically tempered grey wares, in both handmade storage jars and wheelmade smaller vessels (fabric class R30). These are probably of fairly local origins with the storage jars being found only occasionally to the west at Worcester (Jane Evans pers comm). A similar, probably local, tradition of organic tempering is seen in the early Severn Valley wares which are predominantly in an organically tempered fabric and comprise the vast bulk of the oxidised wares. The bulk of the early *amphorae* unsurprisingly are South Spanish Dressel 20s with few of the Gaulish Pélichet 47s. The vast bulk of the imported ware is provided by South Gaulish samian, around 10–15% by sherd count on the Baromix sites, but only around 5% at the Explosion site and the small AL 28 group, the concentration on the Baromix site perhaps reflecting its military nature. The *mortaria* from the early groups reflect the usual southern English pattern being basically divided between Pas-de-Calais imports and Verulamium region products, which were also accompanied by some flagons, with only occasional Mancetter pieces.

The sources of pottery in use in the Hadrianic–Antonine era change slightly but slowly. Dorset BB1 appears in small quantities in the Hadrianic period, but at a level of less than 10% and it does not generally reach above *c* 15% by the end of the century. The major reduced wares remain the same and seem to circulate in a similar quantity, although BB copies start to replace rustic ware forms and more dishes and bowls appear. Severn Valley wares also contribute a similar proportion of the assemblage to that in the early 2nd century, although a rather higher proportion on most of the sites than in the Neronian–Flavian period. The types of Severn Valley ware

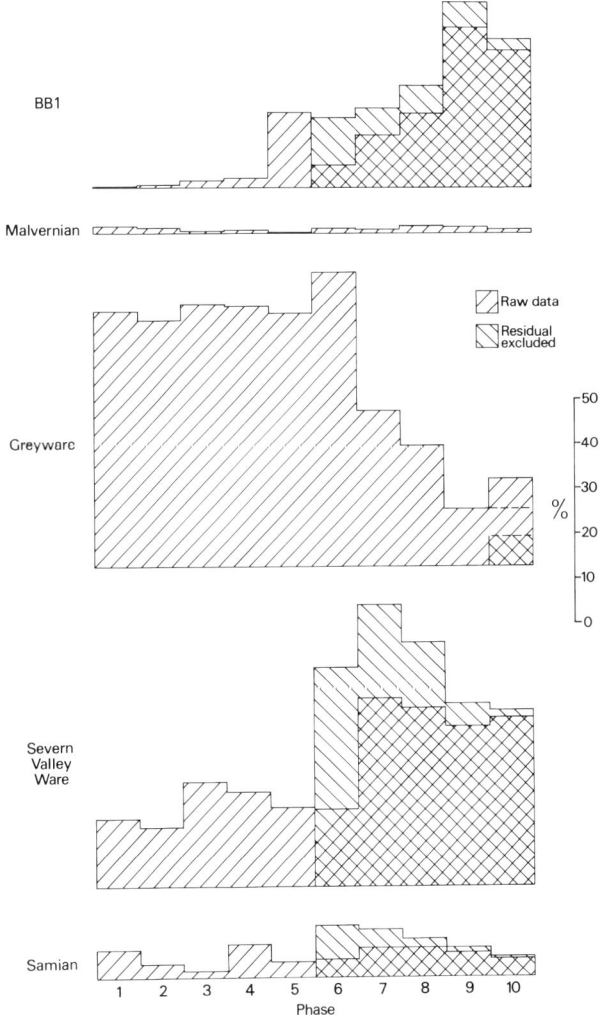

Figure 177 Explosion site (AES 76–7) major pottery fabric classes by phase (with obviously residual material excluded)

fabric vary more with a higher proportion of the non-organically tempered fabrics, some of which at least may come from the Malvern kilns (cf Baromix no 159 with the Great Buckmans Farm kiln products: Waters 1976, no 18). Amongst the *mortaria* there is also some change with Mancetter products becoming predominant, especially when residual earlier material is discounted, and Oxfordshire material making its first appearance.

The 3rd-century figures make an interesting contrast to the preceding ones with evidence of a marked change in supply patterns, one shown even more clearly when the data are contrasted with those from Gas House Lane in the defended area, a site occupied *de novo* around the turn of the century or a little after (Evans, in Cracknell 1996, 58–97). ALC 69 and ALC 72/2 both reflect the major decline in grey ware supply with a marked fall and the Gas House Lane evidence suggests that most of the grey ware industries had probably ceased production at this time, a possible exception being some of those in the R50 fabric class. This evidence offers an important gloss on the Explosion site figures where the period 5 data with a rising BB1 level look a good reflection of contemporary supply, but in period 6 some 65% of the group is composed of residual grey wares. Fig 177 shows the proportions of the major fabric classes from the Explosion site on the same basis as Figs 21 and 22 for the Baromix sites, the different cross-hatched bars showing both the data as recorded, and the proportions as they would be if the grey wares after phase 5 are regarded as residual and the other data recalculated without them. These latter, filtered data, produce a picture much more consistent with the evidence from Gas House Lane, with a peak in Severn Valley ware supply in the mid-3rd century, when it is by far the dominant fabric class, and a steady rise in the proportion of BB1 throughout the century, although the levels are still generally below those at Gas House Lane where BB1 fluctuates around the 30% level. As at Gas House Lane, the organically tempered wares had receded in importance amongst the Severn Valley wares, to be replaced by sand- and possibly limestone-tempered fabrics, the latter quite probably being principally from the Malvern kilns (Adby *et al* in prep). The Explosion site data also show the decline in samian ware through the 3rd century (it was probably being residual by the early 4th), and the consistent minor contribution of Malvernian metamorphic-tempered wares, also seen at Baromix and Gas House Lane. If anything the 3rd-century pattern suggests a reliance on fewer, more distant sources for the bulk of coarse ceramic supply, but also the decline of inter-provincial trade witnessed by the samian ware and *amphorae*.

The early to mid-4th-century data from the Explosion site, providing almost the only reasonable quantified group for this period from the town, suggest a continuation of the 3rd-century pattern of sources of bulk fabric supply, although with continuing changes in the balance between them so that BB1 reached a peak of just over 40% of the group, and Severn Valley wares declined to this level (when the grey wares are excluded). The assemblage from pit 170 (Fig 140) offers a good group confirming this with low levels of residual samian and grey wares and around 45% of BB1 and *c* 30% of Severn Valley wares, with shell-tempered wares appearing at *c* 1%.

The mid- to later 4th-century data from the Explosion site are the only ones from this area of the town, but may be supplemented by an important group from the Gas House Lane site (Evans, in Cracknell 1996, 58–97) and a small group from the Gateway Supermarket site (Ferguson, in Cracknell 1996, 20–31), both in the defended area. The Explosion site groups clearly span the second half of the century, but probably with more emphasis on the earlier part of the range as they contain much higher proportions of fabrics which are clearly residual in the Gas House Lane group dated to the AD 390s. At the Explosion site the decline of Severn Valley wares which started in the late 3rd century continued and BB1 supply started to decline, with new sources such as the shell-tempered wares appearing in minor quantities (*c* 2%) and fine wares starting to appear as bulk ceramics, with around 3% of Nene Valley products, and 6% of Oxfordshire colour-coated wares (excluding *mortaria*).

The shell-tempered ware forms are not those common standard late (after *c* AD 340; Plouviez 1976, 91) types found on the Gas House Lane site, but typologically earlier material which may not be from the Harrold source, from which the late undercut bead rimmed jars and flanged bowls almost certainly originate. The Severn Valley wares were in a similar collection of fabrics to those from the early 4th century, dominated by fabrics O23 and O24, the sources for which are not known, but which are probably not Malvernian. The Gas House Lane evidence shows that the industries producing these had ceased supplying Alcester and had presumably ceased producing before the end of the century. Similarly the decline in Black-Burnished wares, noted above, presages the cessation of supply of this fabric to the town, probably around the same time as Severn Valley ware supply failed. However, little if any of the material in this group from the Explosion site seems to represent the last two decades of Roman rule. Grey wares, regarded here as almost entirely residual in the 3rd and earlier 4th centuries, reappear in the mid- to later 4th century, mainly in sand-tempered fabrics (classes R01 and R40), unlike the 1st–2nd-century emphasis on classes R30 and R50. The sources for these grey wares are not known but are not necessarily local, and it may be significant that no 891, with its notched decoration, has both Oxfordshire (Young 1977, type R9.5) and Lincolnshire parallels (cf Horncastle, Samuels 1983, no 158; Swanpool *et al* 1947, types C40–C48).

In summary, therefore, the ceramic evidence seems to suggest only three major and rapid realignments of suppliers, and possibly dislocation of trading patterns: firstly at the end of the 2nd century; secondly just before the end of the 4th century; and thirdly with the collapse of the pottery supply or usage at the 'end' of Roman Britain. If these are to be related to the structural history of the town then it is an interesting coincidence that the first two of these points seems to coincide with the construction of the town's earthwork and stone defences respectively.

Bibliography

Adby, J, Aspinall, A, Crummett, J, & Evans, J, in prep Neutron activation analysis of some northern Severn Valley wares, *J Roman Pottery Stud*

Adkins, L, & Adkins, R, 1983 An unusual lamp from Beddington, *Britannia*, **14**, 274–8

Allan, J P, 1984 *Medieval and post-medieval finds from Exeter 1971–1980*, Exeter Archaeol Rep **3**. Exeter

Allason-Jones, L, & McKay, B, 1985 *Coventina's Well, a shrine on Hadrian's Wall*. Chesters Museum

Allason-Jones, L, & Miket, R, 1984 *The catalogue of small finds from South Shields Roman fort*, Soc Antiq Newcastle upon Tyne Monogr Ser **2**

Allen, D, 1961 A study of the Dobunnic coinage, in Clifford 1961, 75–149

Anderson, A C, 1980 *A guide to Roman fine wares*, Vorda Research Ser **1**. Heyworth, Wilts

Anderson, A S, & Wacher, J S, 1980 Excavations at Wanborough, Wiltshire: An interim report, *Britannia*, **11**, 115–26

Andrews, A H, & Noddle, B A, 1975 Absence of premolar teeth from ruminant mandibles found at archaeological sites, *J Archaeol Sci*, **2**, 137–44

Armitage, P L, & Clutton-Brock, J, 1976 A system for classification and description of horn cores of cattle from archaeological sites, *J Archaeol Sci*, **3**, 329–48

Armitage, P L, & Goodall, J A, 1977 Medieval horned and polled sheep: the archaeological and iconographic evidence, *Antiq J*, **57**, 73–89

Arthur, P, & Marsh, G, (eds) 1978 *Early fine wares in Roman Britain*, BAR Brit Ser **57**. Oxford

Atkinson, D, 1914 A hoard of samian ware from Pompeii, *J Roman Stud* **4**, 26–64

Avent, R, & Howlett, T, 1980 Excavations in Roman Long Melford 1970–1972, *Proc Suffolk Inst Archaeol and Hist*, **34**(4), 229–49

Bateson, J D, 1981 *Enamel working in Iron Age, Roman and sub-Roman Britain*, BAR Brit Ser **93**. Oxford

Bennett, P, Frere, S S, & Stow, S, 1982 *The archaeology of Canterbury. Vol I: excavations at Canterbury Castle*. Maidstone

Bidwell, P T, 1979 *The legionary bath house and basilica and forum at Exeter*, Exeter Archaeol Rep **1**. Exeter

Bidwell, P T, 1985 *The Roman fort of Vindolanda at Chesterholm, Northumberland*, Engl Heritage Archaeol Rep **1**. London

Binford, L R, (ed) 1977 *For theory building in archaeology*. New York: Academic Press

Binford, L R, 1978 *Nunamiut ethnoarchaeology*. New York: Academic Press

Binford, L R, & Bertram, J B, 1977 Bone frequencies and attritional processes, in Binford 1977, 77–153

Bishop, M C, 1987 The evolution of certain features, in Dawson 1987, 109–31

Blagg, T F C, & King, A C, (eds) 1984 *Military and civilian in Roman Britain: cultural relationships in a frontier province*, BAR Brit Ser **136**. Oxford

Boessneck, J A, Muller, H H, & Teichert, M, 1964 Osteologische Unterscheidungsmerkmale zwischen Schaf (*Ovis aries* Linne) und Ziege (*Capra hircus* Linne), *Kunn-Archiv*, **78**, 1–129

Boon, G C, 1966 Roman window glass from Wales, *J Glass Stud*, **8**, 41–5

Boon, G C, 1973 Finds from Castell Collen Roman fort 1911–1913, *Trans Radnorshire Soc*, **43**, 8–22

Boon, G C, 1974 *Silchester: the Roman town of Calleva*. Newton Abbot

Booth, N B, Webster, G, 1947 A Romano-British pottery kiln at Swanpool, near Lincoln, *Antiq J*, **27**, 61–79

Booth, P M, 1980 *Roman Alcester*. Warwick: Warwickshire Museum

Booth, P M, 1986 Roman pottery in Warwickshire – production and demand, *J Roman Pottery Stud*, **1**, 22–41

Booth, P M, 1989 Excavations at 64 Bleachfield Street, Alcester, Warwickshire, 1981, *Trans Birmingham Warwickshire Archaeol Soc*, **93**, 1983–4, 9–32

Booth, P M, 1994 The excavations in the context of the Roman town, in Mahany 1994, 164–75

Booth, P M, forthcoming Tiddington: the Iron Age, Roman and Anglo-Saxon pottery, in Palmer forthcoming

Booth, P M, & Cracknell, S, 1986 Alcester, from prehistory to the Norman Conquest, in Saville 1986, 5–25

Booth, P M, & Green, S, 1989 The nature and distribution of certain pink, grog tempered vessels, *J Roman Pottery Stud*, **2**, 77–84

Brailsford, J W, 1962 *Hod Hill. Vol 1: antiquities from Hod Hill in the Durden Collection*. London: British Museum

Brandt, E L, 1972 *Antike Gemmen in Deutschen Sammlungen I, Staatliche Münzsammlung München* Part **3**. Munich

Brickstock, R J, & Casey, P J, 1994 The Alcester coins, in Cracknell & Mahany 1994, 157–62

Bibliography

Brodribb, A C, Hands, A R, & Walker, D R, 1968 *Excavations at Shakenoak I*. Oxford, privately printed

Brodribb, A C, Hands, A R, & Walker, D R, 1971 *Excavations at Shakenoak II*. Oxford, privately printed

Brodribb, A C, Hands, A R, & Walker, D R, 1973 *Excavation at Shakenoak IV*. Oxford, privately printed

Brodribb, A C, Hands, A R, & Walker, D R, 1978 *Excavations at Shakenoak V*. Oxford, privately printed

Brown, A E, & Woodfield, C, 1983 Excavations at Towcester, Northamptonshire: the Alcester Road suburb, *Northamptonshire Archaeol*, **18**, 43–140

Brown, R A, 1986 The Iron Age and Romano-British settlement at Woodcock Hill, Saham Toney, Norfolk, *Britannia*, **17**, 1–58

Buckland, P C, 1976 *The environmental evidence from the Church Street Roman sewer system*, The archaeology of York **14**(2). Council for British Archaeology for York Archaeological Trust

Bulmer, M, 1979 An introduction to Roman samian ware, with special reference to collections in Chester and the North-West, *J Chester Archaeol Soc*, New Ser, **62**, 5–72

Burnham, B C, 1988 A survey of building types in Romano-British 'small towns', *J Brit Archaeol Assoc*, **141**, 35–59

Burnham, B C, & Wacher, J, 1990 *The 'small towns' of Roman Britain*. London

Bushe-Fox, J P, 1913 *Report on the excavations on the site of the Roman town at Wroxeter*, Rep Res Comm Soc Antiq London **1**. Oxford

Bushe-Fox, J P, 1914 *Second report on the excavations on the site of the Roman town at Wroxeter, Shropshire 1913*, Rep Res Comm Soc Antiq London **2**. Oxford

Bushe-Fox, J P, 1926 *First report on the excavation of the Roman fort at Richborough, Kent*, Rep Res Comm Soc Antiq London **6**. Oxford

Bushe-Fox, J P, 1928 *Second report on the excavation of the Roman fort at Richborough, Kent*, Rep Res Comm Soc Antiq London **7**. Oxford

Bushe-Fox, J P, 1932 *Third report on the excavations of the Roman fort at Richborough, Kent*, Rep Res Comm Soc Antiq London **10**. Oxford

Bushe-Fox, J P, 1949 *Fourth report on the excavations of the Roman fort at Richborough, Kent*, Rep Res Com Soc Antiq London **16**. Oxford

Casey, P J, Davies, J L, & Evans, J, 1993 *Excavations at Segontium (Caernarfon) Roman fort 1975–79*, CBA Res Rep **90** York: Council for British Archaeology.

Charlesworth, D, 1966 Roman square bottles, *J Glass Stud*, **8**, 26–40

Charlesworth, D, 1972 The glass, in Frere 1972, 196–215

Charlesworth, D, 1979 Glass, in Bidwell 1979, 222–31

Charlesworth, D, 1981 Glass from the burials, in Partridge 1981, 268–71

Clarke, G, 1979 *Pre-Roman and Roman Winchester. Part 2. The Roman cemetery at Lankhills*, Winchester Studies **3**. Oxford

Clifford, E M, 1954 The Roman villa, Witcombe, Gloucestershire, *Trans Bristol Gloucestershire Archaeol Soc*, **73**, 5–69

Clifford, E M, 1961 *Bagendon; a Belgic oppidum, a record of excavations 1954–6*. Cambridge

Cool, H E M, & Price, J, 1987 The glass, in Meates 1987, 110–41

Collis, J R, 1971 Markets and money, in Hill & Jesson 1971, 97–104

Corder, P, 1930 *The defences of the Roman fort at Malton*, Malton and District Rep **2**. Leeds

Cox, J S, 1982 *Romano-British bone hair pins and needles found at Ilchester between 1948 and 1955*, Ilchester and District Occas Pap **36**, 121–32

Cracknell, S, 1989a *The Dennison and Baromix sites; an archaeological brief*. Warwickshire Museum

Cracknell, S, 1989b Roman Alcester: recent archaeological excavations, *Trans Birmingham Warwickshire Archaeol Soc*, **94**, 1985–6, 1–62

Cracknell, S, 1990 Bridge End, Warwick: archaeological excavations of a medieval street frontage, *Trans Birmingham Warwickshire Archaeol Soc*, **95**, 1987–8, 17–72

Cracknell, S, 1994 Archaeological excavation at the Minories, Stratford-upon-Avon, *Trans Birmingham Warwickshire Archaeol Soc*, **98**, 1993–94, 61–71

Cracknell, S, (ed) 1996 *Roman Alcester: defences and defended area*, Roman Alcester Ser **2**, CBA Res Rep **106**. York: Council for British Archaeology.

Cracknell, S, & Bishop, M W, 1992 Excavations at Brook Street, Warwick 1973, *Trans Birmingham Warwickshire Archaeol Soc*, **97**, 1991–92, 1–40

Cracknell, S, Evans, J, & Maclagan, H, 1992 *Roman Alcester Vol 3; the defended area and synthesis: MAP2 proposal*. Warwickshire Museum

Cracknell, S, & Ferguson, R, 1989 The Builder's Yard site, Alcester, 1987: salvage recording, *Trans Birmingham Warwickshire Archaeol Soc*, **94**, 1985–6, 126–32

Cracknell, S, & Jones, M, 1989 Medieval kiln debris from School Road, Alcester, *Trans Birmingham Warwickshire Archaeol Soc*, **94**, 1985–6, 107–22

Cracknell, S, & Mahany, C 1994 *Roman Alcester: southern extramural area. Part 2: finds and discussion*, Roman Alcester Ser **1**, CBA Res Rep **97** York: Council for British Archaeology.

Cram, C L, 1973 The animal bones, in Brodribb *et al* 1973, 145–64

Cram, C L, 1978 Animal bones, in Brodribb *et al* 1978, 117–78

Crummy, N, 1979 A chronology of Romano British bone pins, *Britannia*, **10**, 157–63

Crummy, N, 1983 *The Roman small finds from excavation at Colchester 1971–9*, Colchester Archaeol Rep **2**. Colchester

Cunliffe, B, (ed) 1968 *Fifth report on the excavation of the Roman fort at Richborough, Kent*, Rep Res Comm Soc Antiq London **23**. Oxford

Cunliffe, B, 1971 *Excavations at Fishbourne 1961–69. Vol II: the finds*, Rep Res Comm Soc Antiq London **27**. Leeds

Cunliffe, B, 1975 *Excavations at Portchester Castle. Vol 1 Roman*, Rep Res Comm Soc Antiq London **32**. London

Curle, J, 1911 *A Roman frontier post and its people. The fort of Newstead in the parish of Melrose*. Glasgow

Curwen, E C, 1937 Querns, *Antiquity*, **11**, 133–51

Czurda-Ruth, B, 1979 Die römischen Gläser von Magdalensberg, *Archäologische Forschungen zu die Grabungen auf dem Magdalensburg*, **6**. Klagenfurt

Dannell, G B, 1971 The samian pottery, in Cunliffe, 1971, 260–318

Darling, M J, 1977 Pottery from early military sites in western Britain, in Dore & Greene (eds) 1977, 57–100

Dawson, M, 1987 *Roman military equipment. The accoutrements of war. Proceedings of the third Roman military research seminar*, BAR Int Ser **336**. Oxford

Déchelette, J, 1904 *Les vases céramiques ornés de la Gaule romaine* **ii**. Paris

den Boesterd, M H P, 1956 *Description of the collections in the Rijksmuseum G M Kam at Nijmegen V: The bronze vessels*. Nijmegen

Detsicas, A P, (ed) 1973 *Current research in Romano-British coarse pottery*, CBA Res Rep **10**. London: Council for British Archaeology.

Dickinson, B M, 1984 The samian ware, in Frere 1984, 174–97

Dobson, B, & Jarrett, M G, 1958 Excavations at Binchester in 1955, *Trans Architect Archaeol Soc Durham Northumberland*, **11**(1&2), 115–24

Dore, J, & Gillam, J P, 1979 *The Roman fort at South Shields, excavations 1875–1975*, Soc Antiq Newcastle upon Tyne Monogr Ser **1**. Newcastle upon Tyne

Dore, J, & Greene, K, (eds) 1977 *Roman pottery studies in Britain and beyond*, BAR Int Ser **30**. Oxford

Dore, J, Hartley, B R, Dickinson, B M, Greene, K, & Johns, C, 1979 The samian, in Dore & Gillam 1979, 98–127

Down, A, 1974 *Chichester Excavations* **2**. Chichester

Down, A, 1978 *Chichester Excavations* **3**. Chichester

Down, A, 1979 *Chichester Excavations* **4**. Chichester

Down, A, 1981 *Chichester Excavations* **5**. Chichester

Down, A, & Rule, M, 1971 *Chichester Excavations* **1**. Chichester

Draper, J, & Chaplin, C, 1982 *Dorchester excavations. Vol I*, Dorset Natural History and Archaeol Soc Monogr Ser **2**. Dorchester

Draper, J, 1985 *Excavations by Mr H P Cooper on the Roman site at Hill Farm, Gestingthorpe, Essex*, East Anglian Archaeol Rep **25**. Chelmsford

Droop, J P, & Newstead, R, 1931 Excavations in the Deanery Fields, Chester 1928. II: the finds, *Liverpool Annals of Archaeol and Anthropol*, **18**, 113–47

Dudley, D, 1967 Excavations at Nor'nour in the Isles of Scilly 1962–6, *Archaeol J*, **124**, 1–64

Dudley, D, & Webster, G, 1973 *The Roman conquest of Britain, AD 43–57*. London

Eastham, A, 1971 The bird bones, in Cunliffe 1971, 388–93

Eddy, M R, 1982 *Kelvedon. The origins and development of a Roman small town*, Essex County Council Occas Pap **3**. Chelmsford

Esmonde Cleary, A S, 1987 *Extra-mural areas of Romano-British towns*, BAR Brit Ser **169**. Oxford

Evans, J, 1990 The Cherry Hinton finewares, *J Roman Pottery Stud*, **3**, 18–29

Evans, J, 1993 The finds synthesis, in Casey *et al* 1993

Evans, J, 1994a Discussion of the pottery in the context of Roman Alcester, in Cracknell & Mahany 1994, 144–9

Evans, J, 1994b Iron Age sherds from site M, in Cracknell & Mahany 1994, 153

Evans, J, 1996 The Gas House Lane site: Roman pottery, in Cracknell (ed) 1996, 58–97

Evans, J, 1993 Function and finewares in the Roman north, *J Roman Pottery Stud*, **6**, 95–118

Evans, J, 2001 Material approaches to the identification of different Romano-British site types, in S James & M Millett (eds) *Britons and Romans: advancing an archaeological agenda*, CBA Res Rep **125** 26–35. York: Council for British Archaeology.

Evans, J, Lee, F, & Lindquist, G, 1994 Vessels with incised graffiti, in Cracknell & Mahany 1994, 124–30

Farley, M, 1982 A medieval pottery industry at Boarstall, Buckinghamshire, *Rec Buckinghamshire*, **24**, 107–17

Farrar, R A H, 1973 The techniques and sources of Romano-British black-burnished ware, in Detsicas (ed) 1973, 67–103

Feugère, M, 1977 Les fibules gallo-romaines du Musée Denon à Chalon-sur-Saône, *Memoires de la Societé d'Histoire et d'Archaeologie du Chalon-sur-Saône*, **47**, 77–158

Ferguson, R, 1989 Roman pottery, in Cracknell 1989b, 16–22

Bibliography

Ferguson, R, 1996 Gateway Supermarket site: Roman pottery, in Cracknell (ed) 1996, 20–31

Fieldhouse, W J, May, T, & Wellstood, F C, 1931 *A Romano-British industrial settlement at Tiddington, near Stratford-upon-Avon*. Birmingham

Fock, J, 1966 *Metrische Untersuchungen an Metapodien einiger Europäischer Rinderassen*. Munich: University of Munich

Fowler, E, 1960 The origins and development of the penannular brooch in Europe, *Proc Prehist Soc*, **26**, 149–77

Frere, S S, 1972 *Verulamium excavations. Vol I*, Rep Res Comm Soc Antiq London **28**. Oxford

Frere, S S, 1984 *Verulamium excavations. Vol III*, Oxford Univ Comm Archaeol Monogr **1**. Oxford

Frere, S S, Bennett, P, Rady, J, & Stow, S, 1987 *The archaeology of Canterbury. Vol VIII: Canterbury excavations intra and extra mural sites 1949–55 and 1980–84*. Maidstone

Frere, S S, & St Joseph, J K, 1974 The Roman fortress at Longthorpe, *Britannia*, **5**, 1–129

Friendship-Taylor, R M, 1979 The excavation of the Belgic and Romano-British settlement at Quinton, Northamptonshire: site B 1973–7, *J Northampton Mus*, **13**, 2–198

Fulford, M, 1978 Coin circulation and mint activity in the late Roman empire: some economic implications, *Archaeol J*, **135**, 67–114

Fulford, M, 1984 *Silchester defences 1974–80*, Britannia Monogr **5**. London

Fulford, M, & Huddlestone, K, 1991 *The current state of Romano-British pottery studies: a review for English Heritage*, Engl Heritage Occas Pap **1**

Furtwängler, A, 1896 *Königliche Museen zu Berlin; Beschreibung der Geschnittenen Steine*. Berlin

Gaitzsch, W, 1980 *Eiserne Römische Werkzeuge*, BAR Int Ser **78**. Oxford

Gelling, P S, 1959 Report on excavations at Bays Meadow, Droitwich, Worcestershire, 1954–5, *Trans Birmingham Warwickshire Archaeol Soc*, **75**, 1957, 1–23

Gillam, J P, 1976 Coarse fumed ware in North Britain and beyond, *Glasgow Archaeol J*, **4**, 57–80

Godwin, H, 1975 *History of the British flora*. Cambridge

Goethert-Polaschek, K, 1977 *Katalog der römischen Gläser des Rheinischen Landesmuseums Trier*. Trier

Goodyear, F H, 1968 The Roman villa site at Hales, Staffordshire: an interim report, *N Staffordshire J Fld Stud*, **9**, 104–17

Gould, J, 1966 Excavations at Wall, Staffs 1964–6, on the site of the Roman forts, *Trans S Staffordshire Archaeol Hist Soc*, **8**, 1966–7 (1968), 1–40

Gover, J E B, Mawer, A, & Stenton, F M, 1936 *The place-names of Warwickshire*, English Place-Name Society **13**. Cambridge

Grant, A, 1975 The animal bones/The use of tooth wear as a guide to the age of domestic animals, in Cunliffe 1975, 378–408/437–50

Greene, K, 1978a Imported fine wares in Britain to AD 250: a guide to identification, in Arthur & Marsh (eds) 1978, 15–30

Greene, K, 1978b Mould-decorated Central Gaulish glazed ware in Britain, in Arthur & Marsh (eds) 1978, 31–60

Greene, K, 1979 *The pre-Flavian fine wares*, Report on the Excavations at Usk 1965–1976 **1**. Cardiff: Univ of Wales Press

Greep, S J, 1982 Two early Roman handles from Walbrook, London, *Archaeol J*, **139**, 91–100

Guido, M, 1978 *The glass beads of the Prehistoric and Roman periods in Britain and Ireland*, Rep Res Comm Soc Antiq London **35**. London

Guiraud, H, 1988 *Intailles et camées de l'époque romaine en Gaule*, Gallia suppl **48**. Paris

Harcourt, R A, 1974 The dog in prehistoric and early historic Britain, *J Archaeol Sci*, **1**, 151–76

Harden, D B, 1947 The glass, in Hawkes & Hull 1947, 287–307

Harden, D B, 1962 Glass in Roman York, in RCHM 1962, 136–40

Harden, D B, & Price, J, 1971 The glass, in Cunliffe 1971, 317–68

Hartley, B R, 1972 The Roman occupations of Scotland: the evidence of the samian ware, *Britannia*, **3**, 1–55

Hartley, B R, Pengelly, H, & Dickinson, B, 1994 Samian ware, in Cracknell & Mahany 1994, 93–119

Hartley, K F, 1971 The stamped *mortaria*, in G D B Jones, Excavations at Northwich, *Archaeol J*, **128**, 31–77

Hartley, K F, 1977 Two major potteries producing *mortaria* in the first century AD, in Dore & Greene (eds) 1977, 5–17

Hattatt, R, 1982 *Ancient and Romano-British brooches*. Sherbourne, Dorset

Hawkes, C F C, & Hull, M R, 1947 *Camulodunum*, Rep Res Comm Soc Antiq London **14**. Oxford

Hebditch, M, & Mellor, J, 1973 The forum and basilica of Roman Leicester, *Britannia*, **4**, 1–83

Henderson, A M, 1949 Glass in Bushe-Fox 1949, 158–9

Henig, M, 1978 *A corpus of Roman engraved gemstones from the British Isles*, BAR Brit Ser **8**, 2nd edn. Oxford

Henry, F, 1983 Emailleurs d'Occident, *Studies in early Christian and medieval Irish art. Vol 1: enamels and metalwork*, 9–92; originally published in *Préhistoire* **2** (1933), 65–146

Hermet, F, 1934 *La Graufesenque (Condatomago)*. Paris

Higham, C F W, 1967 Stock rearing as a cultural factor in prehistoric Europe, *Proc Prehist Soc*, **33**, 84–103

Hill, D, & Jesson, M, (eds) 1971 *The Iron Age and its hillforts*. Southampton

Hinchliffe, J, & Sparey Green, C, 1985 *Excavations at Brancaster 1974 and 1977*, East Anglian Archaeol **23**

Hobley, B, 1969 A Neronian-Vespasianic military site at 'The Lunt', Baginton, Warwickshire, *Trans Birmingham Warwickshire Archaeol Soc*, **83**, 1966–7, 65–129

Hobley, B, 1973 Excavations at 'The Lunt' Roman military site, Baginton, Warwickshire, 1968–71, second interim report, *Trans Birmingham Warwickshire Archaeol Soc*, **85**, 1971–3, 7–92

Hobley, B, 1975 'The Lunt' Roman fort and training school for Roman cavalry, Baginton, Warwickshire, *Trans Birmingham Warwickshire Archaeol Soc*, **87**, 1975, 1–56

Howarth, E, 1899 *Catalogue of the Bateman Collection of Antiquities in the Sheffield Public Museum*. London

Howe, M D, Perrin, R J, & Mackreth, D F, 1980 *Roman pottery from the Nene Valley: A guide*, Peterborough City Museum Occas Pap **2**. Peterborough

Huggins, P J, 1978 Excavations of a Belgic and Romano-British farm with Middle Saxon cemetery and churches at Nazeingbury, Essex, 1975–6, *Trans Essex Archaeol Soc*, **10**, 29–117

Hughes, H V, 1960 Recent work at Roman Alcester, *Trans Birmingham Warwickshire Archaeol Soc*, **76**, 1958, 10–18

Hughes, H V, 1961 Recent work at Roman Alcester II, *Trans Birmingham Warwickshire Archaeol Soc*, **77**, 1959, 27–32

Hunter, A G, & Kirk, J R, 1954 Excavations at Campsfield, Kidlington, Oxon 1949, *Oxoniensia*, **17–18**, 1952–3, 36–62

Isings, C, 1957 *Roman glass from dated finds*. Groeningen

Isings, C, 1980 Glass from the *Canabae Legionis* at Nijmegen, *Bericht van de Rijksdienst voor het Oudheidkundig Bodemonderzoek* **3**, 281–346

Ivens, R J, 1982 Medieval pottery from the 1978 excavations at Temple Farm, Brill, *Rec Buckinghamshire*, **24**, 144–70

Jacobs, J, 1913 Sigillatafunde aus einem römischen Keller zu Bregenz, *Jahrb für Altertumskunde*, **6**, 172–84. Vienna

Johns, C, & Potter, T, 1983 *The Thetford treasure. Roman jewellery and silver*. London: British Museum

Johnson, C J, 1986 Trades and industries, in Saville (ed) 1986, 71–92

Johnston, D E, 1972 A Roman building at Chalk, near Gravesend, *Britannia*, **3**, 112–48

Jones, A, 1998 Excavations at Wall (Staffordshire) by E Greenfield in 1962 and 1964, (Wall excavation report 15), *Trans Staffs Archaeol Hist Soc*, **37**, 1–57

Jones, D M, 1980 *Excavations at Billingsgate buildings 'Triangle' Lower Thames Street 1974*, London and Middlesex Archaeol Soc Special Pap **4**. London

Jones G D B, & Mattingly, D, 1990 *An atlas of Roman Britain*. Oxford

Karnitsch, P, 1959 *Die Reliefsigillata von Ovilava*. Linz

Kenyon, K M, 1948 *Excavations at the Jewry Wall Site, Leicester*, Rep Res Comm Soc Antiq London **15**

King, A C, 1978 A comparative survey of bone assemblages from Roman sites in Britain, *Bull Inst Archaeol Univ London*, **15**, 207–32

King, A C, 1984 Animal bones and the dietary identity of military and civilian groups in Roman Britain, Germany and Gaul, in Blagg & King (eds) 1984, 187–217

King, A C & Millett, M J, 1993 The Segontium samian ware, in Casey *et al* 1993

Kirk, J R, 1949 Bronzes from Woodeaton, Oxon, *Oxoniensia*, **14**, 1–45

Knorr, R, 1912 *Südgallische Terra-Sigillata-Gefässe von Rottweil*. Stuttgart

Knorr, R, 1919 *Töpfer und Fabriken verzierter Terra-sigillata des ersten Jahrhunderts*. Stuttgart

Knorr, R, 1952 *Terra-Sigillata-Gefässe des ersten Jahrhunderts mit Töpfernamen*. Stuttgart

Kraskovská, L, 1978 *Roman bronze vessels from Slovakia*, BAR Int Ser **44**. Oxford

Künzl, E, 1983 *Medizinische Instrumente aus Sepulkralfunden der römischen Kaiserzeit*, Kunst und Altertum am Rhein **115**. Cologne

La Baume, P, 1964 *Römisches Kunstgewerbe*. Brunswick

Lawson, A J, 1975 Shale and jet objects from Silchester, *Archaeologia*, **105**, 241–75

Leech, R, 1982 *Excavations at Catsgore 1970–1973. A Romano-British village*, Western Archaeol Trust Excavation Monogr **2**. Bristol

Lloyd-Morgan, G, 1981a *Description of the collections in the Rijksmuseum G M Kam at Nijmegen IX: The mirrors*. Nijmegen

Lloyd-Morgan, G, 1981b Jet and shale in the archaeological collections of the Grosvenor Museum, Chester, *J Chester Archaeol Soc*, **64**, 41–6

LRBC Hill, P, Carson, R, & Kent, J, *Later Roman bronze coinage AD 324–498*, Parts I & II. London

MacGregor, A, 1976 *Finds from a Roman sewer system and an adjacent building in Church Street*, The Archaeology of York **17**(1), Council for British Archaeology for York Archaeological Trust. London

MacGregor, M, 1976 *Early Celtic art in north Britain. A study of decorative metalwork from the third century BC to the third century AD*. Leicester

Mack, R P, 1975 *The coinage of Ancient Britain*. London

Mackreth, D, 1994 Copper alloy and iron brooches, in Cracknell & Mahany 1994, 162–77

McWhirr, A, 1986 *Cirencester excavations III: houses in Roman Cirencester*. Cirencester: Cirencester Excavation Committee

Maddoli, G, 1963 Le Cretule del Nomophylakion di Cirene, *Ann della Scuole Archeologica di Atene*, **41/42**, 1963–4, 39–145

Mahany, C M, 1965 Birch Abbey, *W Midlands Archaeol News Sheet*, **8**, 3–4

Mahany, C M, (ed) 1994 *Roman Alcester: southern extramural area. Part 1: stratigraphy and structures*, Roman Alcester Ser **1**, CBA Res Rep **96**. York: Council for British Archaeology.

Maltby, J M, 1979a *Faunal studies on urban sites: the animal bones from Exeter 1971–1975*. Sheffield: University of Sheffield, Department of Prehistory and Archaeology

Maltby, J M, 1979b The animal bones, in C M Heighway, A P Garrod & A G Vince, Excavations at 1 Westgate Street, Gloucester, 1975, *Medieval Archaeol*, **23**, 159–213

Maltby, J M, 1982 The variability of faunal samples and their effects upon ageing data, in Wilson *et al* (eds) 1982, 81–90

Maltby, J M, 1984 Animal bones and the Romano-British economy, in C Grigson & J Clutton-Brock (eds) *Animals in archaeology 4. Husbandry in Europe*, BAR Int Ser **227**, 125–38

Maltby, J M, 1985 Interpreting patterns in faunal assemblage variability, in G Barker & C Gamble (eds) *Beyond Domestication*. New York: Academic Press

Maltby, J M, 1989 Urban–rural variations in the butchering of cattle in Romano-British Hampshire, in D Sargeantson & T Waldron (eds), *Diets and Crafts in Towns*, BAR Brit Ser **199**, Oxford, 75–106

Mann, J E, & Reece, R, 1983 *Roman coins from Lincoln 1970–1979*, The Archaeology of Lincoln **6**(2), Council for British Archaeology for Lincoln Archaeological Trust

Manning, W H, 1976 *Catalogue of Roman-British ironwork in the Museum of Antiquities, Newcastle-upon-Tyne*

Manning, W H, 1985 *Catalogue of the Roman-British iron tools, fittings and weapons in the British Museum*. London: British Museum

Marsh, G, 1978 Early second century fine wares in the London area, in Arthur & Marsh (eds) 1978, 119–223

Mayes, P, & Scott, K, 1984 *Pottery kilns at Chilvers Coton, Nuneaton*, Soc Medieval Archaeol Monogr Ser **10**. London

Menzel, H, 1966 *Die römischen Bronzen aus Deutschland. Vol II Trier*. Mainz am Rhein

Meates, Lt-Col G W, 1987 *The Roman villa at Lullingstone, Kent II. The wall paintings and finds*. Maidstone: Kent Archaeol Soc

Miket, R, 1983 *The Roman fort at South Shields. Excavation of the defences 1977–1981*. Newcastle-upon-Tyne: Tyne and Wear County Council Museums

Millett, M, 1979 An approach to the functional interpretation of pottery, in M Millett (ed) *Pottery and the archaeologist*, London Inst of Arch Occas Pub **4**. London, 35–48

Millett, M, 1990 *The Romanisation of Britain; an essay in archaeological interpretation*. Cambridge

Millett, M, & Graham, D, 1986 *Excavation on the Romano-British small town at Neatham, Hants*, Hampshire Field Club Monogr **3**. Gloucester

Monckton, A, 1979 Romano-British site at Lower Runhams, Lenham, *Kent Archaeol Rev*, **55**, 118–21

Morin-Jean, 1913 *La verrerie en Gaule sous l'empire romain*. Paris

Mutz, A, 1972 *Die Kunst des Metalldrehens bei den Römern*. Basel and Stuttgart

Mynard, D C, (ed) 1987 *Roman Milton Keynes: excavations and fieldwork 1971–1982*, Buckinghamshire Archaeol Soc Monograph Ser **1**. Aylesbury.

Neal, D S, 1974a *The excavation of the Roman villa in Gadebridge Park, Hemel Hempstead 1963–8*, Rep Res Comm Soc Antiq London **31**. Leeds

Neal, D S, 1974b Northchurch, Boxmoor, Hemel Hempstead Station; the excavation of three Roman buildings in the Bulbourne Valley, *Hertfordshire Archaeol*, **4**, 1974–6, 1–135

Nie, N H, Hull, C H, Jenkins, J G, Steinbrenner, K, & Bent, D H, 1975 *Statistical package for the social sciences: 2nd edition*. New York: McGraw-Hill

Neverov, O, 1971 *Antique cameos in the Hermitage Collection*. Leningrad

Oldenstein, J, 1976 Zur Ausrüstung römischer Auxiliarenheiten, *Bericht der Römisch-Germanischen Kommission*, **57**, 49–284

O'Neil, H, 1945 The Roman villa at Park Street near St Albans, Herts, *Archaeol J*, **102**, 21–110

Oswald, A, 1962 Interim report on the excavations at Weoley Castle 1955–60, *Trans Birmingham Warwickshire Archaeol Soc*, **78**, 1960, 61–85

Oswald, F, 1936–7 *Index of figure-types on* terra sigillata, Liverpool

Oswald, F, & Davies Pryce, T, 1920 *An introduction to the study of* terra sigillata. London

Palmer, N, 1982 *Roman Stratford: Excavations at Tiddington 1980–81*. Warwick: Warwickshire Museum

Palmer, N, forthcoming *Tiddington Roman settlement*

Partridge, C, 1981 *Skeleton Green*, Britannia Monogr Ser **2**. London

Peacock, D P S, 1967 Romano-British pottery production in the Malvern district of Worcestershire, *Trans Worcestershire Archaeol Soc*, 3 Ser, **1**, 15–28

Peacock, D P S, (ed) 1977 *Pottery and early commerce: characterisation and trade in Roman and later ceramics*. New York: Academic Press

Peacock, D P S, & Williams, D F, 1986 *Amphorae and the Roman economy*. London

Philp, B J, 1981 *The excavation of the Roman Forts of the Classis Britannica at Dover 1970–1977*, Rep Kent Monogr Ser **3**. Dover

Pirling, R, 1966 *Das Römisch-Frankische Gräberfeld von Krefeld-Gellep* (2 vols). Berlin

Pitts, L F, & St Joseph, J K, 1985 *Inchtuthil, the Roman legionary fortress excavations 1952–1965*, Britannia Monogr Ser **6**. London

Platt, C, & Coleman-Smith, R, 1975 *Excavations in medieval Southampton 1953–1969. Vol II, the small finds*. Leicester

Plouviez, J, 1976 The pottery, in S E West & J Plouviez, *The Romano-British site at Icklingham*, East Anglian Archaeol Rep **3**. Ipswich, 85–102

Price, J, 1975 The glass vessels from the cremation groups, in A E Johnson, Excavations at Bourton Grounds, Thornborough 1972–3, *Rec Buckinghamshire*, **20**(1), 18–22

Price, J, 1977 The Roman glass in A Gentry, J Ivens, & H McClean, Excavations at Lincoln Road, London borough of Enfield, Nov 1974–March 1976, *Trans London Middlesex Archaeol Soc*, **28**, 154–61

Price, J, 1980 The Roman glass, in G Lambrick, Excavations in Park Street, Towcester, 1963–8, *Northamptonshire Archaeol*, **15**, 63–8

Price, J, 1985 The Roman glass, in Pitts & St Joseph 1985, 303–12

Radford, C A R, 1932 Small objects in metal, bone, glass etc, in Bushe-Fox 1932, 76–93

Rahtz, P, 1966 Kenilworth Castle 1960, *Trans Birmingham Warwickshire Archaeol Soc*, **81**, 1963–4, 55–73

Ratkai, S, 1990 The medieval pottery, in Cracknell 1990, 33–57

Ratkai, S, 1992 Medieval pottery, in Cracknell & Bishop 1992, 8–22

Ratkai, S, 1994 Pottery, in Cracknell 1994, 67–9

Ratkai, S, 1996 Gateway Supermarket site: medieval pottery, in Cracknell (ed) 1996, 31–3

Ratkai, S, 1996 Gas House Lane: post-Roman pottery, in Cracknell (ed) 1996, 97–9

Rawes, B, 1982 Gloucester Severn Valley ware, *Trans Bristol Gloucestershire Archaeol Soc*, **100**, 33–46.

RCHM, 1962 *An Inventory of the Historical Monuments in the City of York. Vol I Eburacum, Roman York*. London: HMSO

Redknap, M, 1985 Twelfth- and thirteenth-century Coventry wares, with special reference to a waster group from the Cannon Park Estate (Lychgate Road), Coventry, *Medieval Ceram*, **9**, 65–78

Reece, R, 1972 A short survey of the Roman coins found on fourteen sites in Britain, *Britannia*, **3**, 269–76

Reece, R, 1975 Coins, in B Hobley 'The Lunt' Roman fort and training school for Roman cavalry, Baginton, Warwickshire. Final report: excavations (1972–73) with conclusions, *Trans Birmingham and Warwickshire Archaeol Soc*, **87**, 23–25

Reece, R, 1980a Religion, coins and temples, in Rodwell 1980, 115–28

Reece, R, 1980b Town and country: the end of Roman Britain, *World Archaeol*, **12**(1), 77–92

Rees, S E, 1979 *Agricultural implements in prehistoric and Roman Britain*, BAR Brit Ser **69**. Oxford

Richardson, K M, 1944 Report on excavations at Verulamium: Insula XVII, *Archaeologia*, **90**, 81–126

RIB II, 8 Collingwood, R, & Wright R, *The Roman inscriptions of Britain,* **II**, instrumentum domesticum, *fasc 8, graffiti on coarse pottery,* S Frere & R Tomlin (eds). Stroud

RIC Mattingly, H, & Sydenham, E, *Roman imperial coinage*. Vols I–X (1923–). London

Rigby, V, 1982 The coarse pottery, in Wacher & McWhirr 1982, 152–200

Robertson, A S (ed) 1975 *Birrens (Blatobulgium)*. Edinburgh

Robinson, H R, 1975 *The Armour of imperial Rome*. London

Rodwell, W, Rowley, T, (ed) 1975 *The 'small towns' of Roman Britain*, BAR Brit Ser **15**. Oxford

Rodwell, W, (ed) 1980 *Temples, churches and religion in Roman Britain*, BAR Brit Ser **77(i)**. Oxford

Rogers, G B, 1974 *Poteries sigillées de la Gaule centrale, I: les motifs non figurés*, Gallia suppl **28**. Paris

Rogerson, A, 1977 *Excavations at Scole 1973*, East Anglian Archaeol Rep **5**. Dereham, Norfolk, 97–224

Saunders, C, & Havercroft, A, 1977 A kiln of the potter Oastrius and related excavations at Little Munden, Bricket Wood, *Hertfordshire Archaeol*, **5**, 109–56

Saville, G E, (ed) 1986 *Alcester – a history*. Studley: Alcester and District Local History Society

Seaby, W A, 1945 A Roman building at Alcester, *Trans Birmingham Warwickshire Archaeol Soc*, 66, 1945–6 (1950), 35–48

Sherlock, R J, 1957 Excavations at Deritend, *Trans Birmingham Warwickshire Archaeol Soc*, **73**, 1955, 109–14

Silver, I A, 1969 The ageing of domestic animals, in D Brothwell & E S Higgs (eds) *Science in archaeology*. London, 283–302

Simpson, G, & Rogers, G, 1969 Cinnamus de Lezoux et quelques potiers contemporains, *Gallia*, **27**, 3–14

Slater, T R, 1982 Urban genesis and medieval town

plans in Warwickshire and Worcestershire, in Slater & Jarvis (eds) 1982, 173–202

Slater, T R, & Jarvis, P J, (eds) 1982 *Field and forest: an historical geography of Warwickshire and Worcestershire*. Norwich

Stanfield, J A, 1929 Unusual forms of *terra sigillata*, *Archaeol J*, **86**, 113–51

Stanfield, J A, & Simpson, G, 1958 *Central Gaulish potters*. London

Stanley, M, & Stanley, B, 1964 The Romano-British potters field at Wappenbury, Warwickshire, *Trans Birmingham Warwickshire Archaeol Soc*, **79**, 1960–61, 93–108

Stead, I M, 1976 *Excavations at Winterton Roman villa and other Roman sites in north Lincolnshire 1958–1967* DOE Archaeol Rep **9**. London: HMSO

Stead, I M, & Rigby, V, 1986 *Baldock. The excavation of a Roman and pre-Roman settlement 1968–72*, Britannia Monogr Ser **7**. London

Strong, D E, 1966 *Greek and Roman gold and silver plate*. London

Swan, V G 1984 *The pottery kilns of Roman Britain*, RCHM Suppl Ser **5**. London

Taylor, S J, 1969 Alcester, Warks, nos 27–33 Bleachfield Street, *W Midlands Archaeol News Sheet*, **12**, 21–2

Taylor, S J, 1972 Birch Abbey, Alcester, Warks, *W Midlands Archaeol News Sheet*, **15**, 14

Terrisse, J-R, 1968 *Les céramiques sigillées Gallo-Romaines des Martres-de-Veyre (Puy de Dôme)*, Gallia Supplement **19**. Paris

Thompson, F H, 1958 A Romano-British pottery kiln at North Hykeham, Lincolnshire: with an appendix on the typology, dating and distribution of rustic ware, in Great Britain, *Antiq J*, **38**, 15–51

Thompson, F H, 1976 The excavation of the Roman amphitheatre at Chester, *Archaeologia*, **105**, 127–239

Thompson, I, 1982 *Grog-tempered 'Belgic' pottery of south-eastern England*, BAR Brit Ser **108**. Oxford

Todd, M, 1975 Margidunum and Ancaster, in Rodwell & Rowley 1975, 211–23

Trow, S D, 1990 By the northern shores of Ocean: some observations on acculturation process at the edge of the Roman world, in T Blagg & M Millett (eds) *The early Roman empire in the west*. Oxford, 103–18

Tyers P, 1978 The poppyhead beakers of Britain and their relationship to the barbotine decorated vessels of the Rhineland and Switzerland, in Arthur & Marsh 1978, 61–108

Tyers P, 1983 *Verulamium region white ware*, Early Roman pottery from the City of London **4**. London: privately published

Van Arsdell, R D, 1989 *Celtic coinage in Britain*. London

van Lith, S M E, 1977 Römisches Glas aus Velsen, *Oudheidkundig Mededelingen uit het Rijksmuseum van Oudheden te Leiden*, **58**, 1–62

Vanderhoefen, M, 1976 *Funde aus Asciburgium Heft VI. Terra sigillata aus Südgallien: die reliefverzierten Gefässe II*. Duisburg

VCH, 1945 *The Victoria history of the county of Warwick. Vol III, Barlichway Hundred*. London

Vince, A, 1977 The medieval and post-medieval ceramic industry of the Malvern region, in Peacock (ed) 1977, 257–306

Vollenweider, M L, 1972 *Die Porträtgemmen der römischen Republik*, Plate Volume. Mainz

Vollenweider, M L, 1974 *Die Porträtgemmen der römischen Republik*, Text Volume. Mainz

Wacher, J 1975 *The towns of Roman Britain*

Wacher, J, & McWhirr, A, 1982 *Cirencester excavations I; early Roman occupation at Cirencester*. Cirencester: Cirencester Excavation Committee

Ward, M, forthcoming The samian ware, in S Large and P R Scott, *Excavations at Piercebridge*

Waters, P L, 1976 Romano-British pottery site at Great Buckmans Farm, *Trans Worcestershire Archaeol Soc*, 3 ser, **15**, 63–72

Webster, G, 1958 The Roman military advance under Ostorius Scapula, *Archaeol J*, **115**, 49–98

Webster, G, 1965 The Roman forts at Greensforge, *Trans Birmingham and Warwickshire Archaeol Soc*, **80** (for 1962), 82–3

Webster, G, 1980 *The Roman invasion of Britain*. London

Webster, G, 1981 *Rome against Caratacus*. London

Webster, G, & Booth, N, 1966 A Romano-British kiln at Swanpool, near Lincoln, *Antiq J*, **27**, 61–79

Webster, P V, 1976 Severn Valley ware: a preliminary study, *Trans Bristol Gloucestershire Archaeol Soc*, **94**, 1977, 18–46

Webster, P V, 1977 The samian pottery, in A Gentry, J Ivens, and H McClean, Excavations at Lincoln Road, London borough of Enfield, November 1974–March 1976, *Trans London Middlesex Archaeol Soc*, **28**, 128–34

Wedlake, W J, 1982 *The excavation of the shrine of Apollo at Nettleton, Wiltshire 1956–1971* Rep Res Comm Soc Antiq London **40**. London

Wheeler, R E M, 1923 *Segontium and the Roman occupation of Wales*, Y Cymmrodor **33**, London

Wheeler, R E M, 1930 *London in Roman times*, London Museum Catalogues **3**. London

Wheeler, R E M, & Wheeler, T V, 1928 The Roman amphitheatre at Caerleon, Monmouthshire, *Archaeologia*, **78**, 111–218

Wheeler, R E M, & Wheeler, T V, 1932 *Report on the excavation of the prehistoric, Roman and post-Roman site in Lydney Park, Gloucestershire*, Rep Res Comm Soc Antiq London **9**. London

Whiting, W H, & May, T, 1931 *Report on the excavations of the Roman cemetery at Ospringe, Kent*, Rep Res Comm Soc Antiq London **8**. London

Wild, F, 1975 Samian ware, in Robertson (ed) 1975, 141–77

Wild, F, 1979 Watercrook: samian ware, in T W Potter, *Romans in north-west England*, Cumberland Westmoreland Antiq Archaeol Soc Res Ser **1**. Kendal, 269–91

Williams, B J, & Whittaker, A, 1974 *Geology of the country around Stratford-upon-Avon and Evesham*, Institute of Geological Sciences Memoirs of the Geological Survey of Great Britain. London: HMSO

Williams, D F, 1977 The Romano-British black-burnished industry: an essay on characterisation by heavy mineral analysis, in Peacock (ed) 1977, 163–220

Williams, J H, 1979 *St Peter's Street Northampton excavations 1973–6*, Northampton Development Corporation Archaeol Monogr **2**. Northampton

Wilson, B, Grigson, C, & Payne, S, (eds) 1982 *Ageing and sexing animal bones from archaeological sites*, BAR Brit Ser **109**. Oxford

Wishart, D, 1978 *Clustan user manual* (3rd edn). Edinburgh

Woods, P J, & Hastings, B C, 1984 *Rushden: the early fine wares*. Rushden

Young, C J, 1977 *Oxfordshire Roman pottery*, BAR Brit Ser **43**. Oxford

Zadoks-Josephus, J A N, Peters, W J T, & Witteveen, A W, 1973 *Description of the collections in the Rijksmuseum G M Kam at Nijmegen VII: the figural bronzes*. Nijmegen

Zazoff, P, 1975 *Antike Gemmen in Deutschen Sammlungen IV Kestner-Museum, Hanover*. Wiesbaden

Zeepvat, R, 1987 Tiles, in Mynard (ed) 1987, 118–25

Zienkiewicz, J D, 1986 *The legionary fortress baths at Caerleon. Vol II, the finds*. Cardiff

Index *Peter Gunn*

Notes

1. Main page references are in **bold**. Page references in *italics* indicate pages where illustrations/tables/plates can be found. There may also be textual references on these pages.
2. Bibliographical references are not indexed, and there are no separate entries for Roman or Romano-British references.

Actium, Battle of 122
aerial photography 301
AES 76–7 *see* Explosion site excavations (AES 76–7)
agricultural tools *240*, 242, *243*, 299
agriculture 3
Agrippa 122
air raid shelter, Explosion site (AES 76–7) 165
AL 28 *see* Baromix excavations 1988 (AL 28)
ALB 75 *see* Lloyd's Bank excavations (ALB 75)
ALC 69 *see* Baromix excavations 1969 (ALC 69)
ALC 72/2 *see* Baromix excavations 1972 (ALC 72/2)
animal husbandry 280, 281, 284, 285, 288, 299
animals
   prints in tiles 264
   in symbol gems 121–2
   see also bones, animal
antler fragments 289, 299
Arles, mint 27, 176
Arrow, River 1, 125
Arrow valley 306
badger bones 289

Baetica, *amphorae* 48
Bagendon, Glos 116
Baginton, Warwicks 302
Baldock, Herts 246
Baromix excavations 1969 (ALC 69) xviii, 6, 7, **7–17**, *8*, *11*, *26*, 301, 303, 304, 305
   finds **27–8**, **67–91**
   Phase A 1, 7–9, *10*, 25
   Phase B 1, 9, *10*, 25
   Phase C 1, 9, *12*, 13, 25
   Phase D 1, *12*, 13, 25
   Phase E 1, 13, *14*, *15*, 25–6
   Phase F 1–3, 13, *14*, 15, 26
   Phase G 3, 15, *16*, *17*, 26
   Phase H 3, 15, *16*, *17*, 26
   see also pottery
Baromix excavations 1972 (ALC 72/2) xviii, 6, 7, **18–25**, *26*, 301, 304, 305
   finds **27–8**, **67–91**
   Phase A *18*, *19*, 25
   Phase B 1, 18–19, *19*, *20*, 25
   Phase C 1, 18, *19*, *20*, *21*, 24
   Phase D 1, 19–21, *21*, 25
   Phase E 1, 21–3, *22*, 25
   Phase F 1, 3, 21, *22*, 23–4, 26

Phase G 3, 24–5, *24*, 26
Phase H 3, 25, 26
see also pottery
Baromix excavations 1988 (AL 28) xviii, 1, 3, 7, **92–103**, 301, 304, 305
basket work, possible 165
beads
   glass 68, *69*, *70*, 255, *256*, 258–9, 300
   jet *248*, 249, 299
beakers *see* glassware; pottery
beam slots
   Baromix (AL 28) 93
   Baromix (ALC 69)
     structure 1 Phase A 7
     timber aisled structure 1
   Baromix (ALC 72/2) Phase A 18
   Explosion site (AES 76–7) building V 141, 143, *144*
   Lloyd's Bank (ALB 75) 105, 110, 111, 114, 116, 119
bell, copper alloy 70, 71, *72*
Bidford Grange 306
Binton, Alcester 260
Birch Abbey 1, 114, 294
   No. 6 3, 30, 90, 302, 303
bird bones 265, 267, 289, 299
blades, iron *240*, 242, *243*
Bleachfield Street 1, 104, 114, 115, 121, 124, 298, 302, 303, 305
   No. 33 *see* Baromix excavations 1969 (ALC 69); Baromix excavations 1972 (ALC 72/2)
   Nos 1–5 1, 47, *125*, *126*, 298
   see also Explosion site excavations (AES 76–7)
bodkins, bone 83
bone, worked
   Baromix (AL 28) *102*, 103
   Baromix (ALC 69/ALC 72/2) **83–6**, *84–5*
   Explosion site (AES 76–7) 232, **249–54**, *250*, *252–3*, *254*, 299
bones, animal **265–90**, 297, 299
   ageing 275, 279, 283–4, 287
   butchery evidence 165, 275, 290, 297
     cattle 3, 267, 271, 275, 282–3, 284, 299, 305
     domestic fowl 289
     pigs 274, 288
     sheep/goats 286–7
   epiphyseal fusion data 278–9, 285–6, 288
   exploitation evidence 280, 281, 283–4, 287

bones, animal (*cont.*)
  fragment numbers 265, *266–70*, 271, *272–4*, 275, *276–8*
  metrical analysis 281–2, *282*, *286*, 287, 288
  pathology 283, 287
  sexual dimorphism 279–81, *280–1*
  tooth eruption data 275, 278, *279*, 284–5, 287–8
bones, human
  Lloyd's Bank (ALB 75) 122–3
  see also burials; cremation burials
bottles *see* glassware
Boudiccan rebellion 303
boundary ditches, Lloyd's Bank (ALB 75) 3, 114
bowls *see* glassware; pottery
bracelets
  bone 249, 253, *254*, 299
  copper alloy 232, 233–4, *235*, 299
  iron *240*, 241, 299
  shale 86, *87*, 88, 232, 247, *248*, 249, 299
  silver 115
Bricket Wood, Herts, pottery kiln 48
Brockley Hill pottery kilns 179
brooches 301
  copper alloy 70, 71, *72*, 232
Brunehaut Liberchies, Belgium 259
buckle pin, possible *240*, 241
building materials 264–5
  daub 264–5, 294
  opus signinum 265
  plaster 146, 265
  see also mortar
building stone 260, *261*, 262
buildings *see* structures
Burden, Mr David 124
burgage tenure 297–8
burials
  with glassware 255, 257, 258, 259
  Lloyd's Bank (ALB 75)
    infant inhumations Phase III 3, *107*, 110, *111*, *112*, 114, 123, 305
    age 123
    Burial B 123
    Burial C xviii, 123
    Burial D 123
    Burial F 110, *111*
    Burial H 110, *111*
    Burial J *107*, 110, 114, 123
    Burial K 123
    Burial M 123
    pathology 123
    sex 123
  Thornborough, Bucks 68
  see also cremation burials
butchery evidence 165, 275, 290, 297
  of cattle 3, 267, 271, 275, 282–3, 284, 299, 305
  of domestic fowl 289
  of pigs 274, 288
  of sheep/goats 286–7
Butt Road Cemetery, Colchester 241

Caerleon, Gwent, legionary baths: finds 68, 122
Caistor-by-Norwich, pottery 179

Camelon, Stirlingshire 33
Campania, *amphorae* 179
Camulodunum 255
candlestick, tripod, iron 242, *243*
Carausius, Emperor, coins 26, 27, 90
cat bones 266, 289
cattle bones 265, 266, 267, 297
  ageing 275, 279, 283–4
  butchery evidence 3, 267, 271, 275, 282–3, 284, 299, 305
  epiphyseal fusion data 278–9
  exploitation evidence 280, 281, 283–4
  fragment numbers 267, *268–70*, 271, 274
  other metrical analysis 281–2, *282*
  pathology 283
  sexual dimorphism 279–81, *280–1*
  tooth eruption data 275, 278, *279*
cemeteries
  Butt Road Cemetery, Colchester 241
  see also burials; cremation burials
cesspits, Explosion site (AES 76–7) 165, 166
charcoal, Explosion site (AES 76–7) 141, 293
Chase Wood, Kenilworth 264
Chesterton, Warwicks, pottery 184, 299
Chichester, W Sussex 53, 90
chisels, iron 80, 81, *82*, *240*, 242
Cirencester, Glos 192
  fort 302–3
clay
  burnt
    Baromix (ALC 69) 9
    Baromix (ALC 72/2) 19
  floors 169, 294
coal *293*
cobbling/cobbled surfaces
  Baromix 1969 (ALC 69) 8, 13
  Baromix 1972 (ALC 72/2)
    Phase C 18, 19, 24
    Phase E 22
    Phase F 23
    Phase G 24–5, 80
  Explosion site (AES 76–7) 3
coins *27–8*, 90, 116, *117*, 125, 156, 160, *173–6*, 301
  of Carausius 26, 27, 90
  of Constantine, House of 27, 158
  of Crispus 166
  of Domitian 135
  of Faustina Junior 144
  of Licinius I 156
  of Nero 144
  pre-Roman 116
  of Salonina 166
  of Vespasian 25, 27, 95–6, 103
Colchester, Essex 83, 116, 258, 259, 303
  Butt Road Cemetery 241
coleopteran remains 290
colonia 303
comb fragment, bone 83, *84*
Constantine, House of, coins 158
Constantine I, Emperor, coins 27
Constantine II, Emperor, coin 27

Index

copper alloy objects
   Baromix (AL 28) 3, *102*, 103
   Baromix (ALC 69/ALC 72/2) 1, 25, **70–6**, 71, *72–6*, 86, 302
   (bronze) tap, Baromix (ALC 72/2) 3, 70, *75*, 76, 90
   Explosion site (AES 76–7) 158, **232–9**, *235–6*, *238–9*, 259, 260, 299
   Lloyd's Bank (ALB 75) *122*
copper alloy working 299
counters
   ceramic 40, 47, 189
   glass *256*, 258, 259, 300
Coventry, sandstone 262
craft tools, iron 81
cremation burials
   Lloyd's Bank (ALB 75) 3
     age 123
     Burial A 110, 120, 122, 123
     sex 123
Crewe Farm, pottery 184
Crispus, coin 166
crucibles, Explosion site (AES 76–7) 158, *256*, 259–60
cups *see* glassware; pottery

dating
   Baromix 1969/1972 phases 25–6
   Explosion site (AES 76–7) 124–5, 127, 140–1, 152, 158, 166
   see also pottery
decapitation, child burial (Lloyd's Bank (ALB 75)) 110, 114
deer bones 289
dishes *see* pottery
ditches, Lloyd's Bank (ALB 75) 3, 105, 110–11, 114, 119, 120
Dobunni 51, 54, 116, 303
Dodderhill, Droitwich: fort 302, 303
dog bones 266–7, 288–9
Dog and Partridge public house 127
dolphins, in symbol gems 120, *121*
domestic fowl bones 267, 289, 299
domestic implements, iron 241, 242, *243*, 246
Domitian, Emperor, coin 135
drains
   ?stone, Baromix (ALC 69) Phase B 9
   possible, Explosion site (AES 76–7) period 7 *149*, *152*
   stone-lined, Baromix (ALC 72/2) Phase F 3, *23*
dress fittings
   iron *240*, 241, *246*
   see also bracelets
Droitwich, Worcs 51, 181, 183, 302, 306
Durben Collection 241
Durotriges 51, 181, 192

Ebrington Hill, nr Stratford-upon-Avon 262
evaluation trenches, Baromix (AL 28)
   trench 1 3, *92*, *93*
   trench 2 3, *92*, *93*, *94*, *95*
   trench 3 3, *92*, *94*, 304
   trench 4 3, *92*, *94*, *95*

Exeter
   animal bone comparison 274, 278, 279, 281, *282*, 283, 284, 285, *286*, 287, 288, 289
   'Belgic' pottery tradition 50
   glassware 68
Explosion site excavations (AES 76–7) xviii, 1, 3, 6, 22, 30, 49, 90, *104*, **124–72**, 301, 302, 303, 305
   dating/chronology 124–5, 127, 294–8
   finds **173–5**, **232–93**
   site I 124, 125, *126*, 127, *134*
     period 1 127, *128*, *129*, 294
     period 2 128, *129–30*, 131, 294, 301
     period 3 *129*, *130*, 131, 135, 294
     period 4 124, 127, *129*, *130*, 135, *136*
     period 5 127, *129*, 135–7, *136–9*, 140, 143, 145, 294–5
     period 6 *129*, 131, 137, *139*, 140, 141, *142–4*, 145
     period 7 124, 135, *139*, 143, 145–6, *147*, *149*, 150–1, *152*, 153, 158
     period 8 *139*, 152–3, *154*, 159
     period 9 127, *139*, 156, *157*, 158, *159*, 160
     period 10 *159*, 160–6, *161*, *162*, 168, 297
     period 10A 166, *167*, 168
     period 11 *162*, 168–9, *168*, 170
     period 12 *162*, 168, *169*, *171*, *172*
     period 13 169
     period 14 169
   site II 124, 125, *126*, 127, *132–3*, 146, 294, 298
     period 2 127, 131, *172*, 294
     period 3 127, 135, *172*, 294
     period 4 135, *172*
     period 5 140–1, 151, *172*
     period 6 145, 151, *172*
     period 7 145, *148*, 149, *150*, 151–2, *151*, 156, *172*
     period 8 153, *155*, 156, *172*
     period 9 *155*, 160, *172*
     period 10 *155*, *163*, 164, *172*, 297
     period 11 *155*, 168, *172*
     period 12 *155*, 169, *172*
     period 13 *155*, 169
     period 14 *155*, 169
   see also pottery; structures

Faustina Junior, coins 144
Felixstowe, Suffolk 257
ferrules, iron 77, *78*, 79, 81, 242, *243*
fish bones 265, 267, 289–90, 299
fish hooks, copper alloy 233, *236*, 237
Fishbourne 258, 289
floors
   Baromix 1972 (ALC 72/2)
     Phase D: 'burnt clay' 20, 41
     Phase H: tessellated 90
   Explosion site (AES 76–7) 163
     building V *137*, 143, *144*, 146, 153, 156, 202, 203
     clay 294
        building I 169
     limestone: of building III 166
food and diet 267, 275, 289, 299

320

Forest of Dean 260
fort, origins 301–5, *304*
Fosse Way 302
Fulford Report 6
gaming pieces
   ceramic 189
  glass 255, *256*, 258, 259

Gas House Lane site 53, 115, 120–1, 301, 305, 306, 307, 308
Gateway Supermarket site 51, 120, 307
geology, Explosion site (AES 76–7) 125–6
Germany, symbol gems 121
glassware
   Baromix (AL 28) *102*
   Baromix (ALC 69/ALC 72/2) **67–70**, *68–70*, 90 1, *90*
   Explosion site (AES 76–7) *254*, **254–9**, *256*, 300
   beads 68, *69*, *70*, 255, *256*, 258–9
   bottle glass 68, *69*, 255, *256*, 257–8
   bowls/beakers/cups 68, *69*, *70*, *254*, 255–7, 258
   jars *254*, 255, 257
   jugs/flasks 255, *256*, 257, 258
   vessel types (uncertain) *256*, 258
   window glass 68, 90, 255, 259, 299
Gloucester 302, 303
   butchery evidence 283
   pottery 47–8, 50, 54, 180, 181, 192
gold, in coins 116
gravel surfaces
   Baromix 1988 (AL 28) 3, 93, 94
   Explosion site (AES 76–7) 140, 299
     period 3 131, 135, 294
     period 4 124, 127, 131, *136*
     period 7 143, 144, 145–6, 150, 153, 159, 295
Great Buckman's Farm, Malvern 181, 307
Greensforge: fort 302
gullies
   Baromix 1972 (ALC 72/2)
     Phase E 23
     Phase F 23
   Lloyd's Bank (ALB 75) 105, 110, 116
gullies/slots
   Baromix 1969 (ALC 69) Phase B 9
   Baromix 1972 (ALC 72/2) Phase E 21

handles, iron 242, *243*
hare bones 289
Harrold, Beds 308
hearths
   Baromix 1969 (ALC 69) structure 1 Phase A 8
   Explosion site (AES 76–7) 298
     building V 141, 156, 295, 298
     metalworking slag 83, 259
Hengistbury, Hants 116
Henry I, King 297–8
Hereford, pottery 99
High Street structures 298
hobnails, iron 77, 80, 81, 241
Hockley Chemical site 303
horn cores 284
horse bones 266, 288

Horsfall, R J 127
Housesteads, Northumberland 80
Hughes, H V 127

Icklingham, Suffolk 242
inhumations *see* burials
insect remains 290
intaglio, Lloyd's Bank (ALB 75) 121–2, *121*
Iron Age
   building tradition 294
   see also pottery
iron objects
   Baromix (ALC 69/ALC 72/2) **77–83**, *78–9*, *80*, *82*, *83*
   Explosion site (AES 76–7) *240*, **241–7**, *242–6*, 299
iron smithing slag, Explosion site (AES 76–7) 158, 259, 293, 299

jars *see* glassware; pottery
jet objects, Explosion site (AES 76–7) 232, **247–9**, *248*, 299
joiner's dogs, iron 77, 81, *244*, 246

keys, iron 77, 80, 81, *82*, 299
Kingsholm, Gloucester, pottery 50, 54, 192
knife blades, iron 80, 81, *82*, 242, *243*
Krefeld Gellep, glass counters 259

lamps, ceramic
   Baromix (ALC 69) 88
   Negro's head lamp, Explosion site (AES 76–7) 158, 187, *188*
Lankhills, Winchester 259
Lapworth, Warwicks 182, 264
lead objects
   Baromix (ALC 69/ALC 72/2) **77**, **79–80**, *80*, *81*, *82*
   Explosion site (AES 76–7) **239–41**, *240*
lead waste slag, Baromix (ALC 69/ALC 72/2) 80
leather fragments (for footwear) 80, 81
Les Martres-de-Veyre: samian ware 25, 34, 35, 36, 41, 97, 119, 140, 177, 199
Lezoux potters 33, 40, 41, 46, 178
Licinius I, coin 156
lime (*Tilia*) 246
Lloyd's Bank excavations (ALB 75) xviii, 1, 3, 90, *104*, **104–15**, *105*, 126, 301, 302, 303, 305, 306
   area II *107*, 110
   finds **116–23**
   Phase I 3, 105, *106*
   Phase II 3, 105, 108, *109*, *110*
   Phase III 3, 110–11, *112*
   Phase IV 3, 111, *112*
   Phase V 3, 111, *112*
   Phase VI 111
   Phase VII 111, *113*, *114*
   see also pottery
lock fittings, iron 241, *244*, 246, 299
London 306
   coinage 27
   glassware 259
   iron finds 241
Long Melford, Suffolk, glassware 68
loom weights, clay 90

Index

Lower Oversley Lodge fort 301, 302, 303
Lower Runhams, Lenham, Kent 257
Lullingstone Villa 258, 259
'Lunt, The', Warwicks: Roman fort 50, 302, 303
Lyons 27, 176

Magistrates Court site 301
Mahany, C M: excavations 294
    site D 304
    Site E 303
    Site G 302, 303
    Site L 302
    Site M 301
malting kilns, possible
    Baromix (ALC 69/ALC 72/2) 3, 15, *17*, 25
    Explosion site (AES 76–7) 298
Malton, N Yorks, infant burials 114
Malvern, Worcs, pottery 49, 181, 189, 307
Mancetter, Warwicks 259, 302
Mancetter-Hartshill, Warwicks, pottery kilns 179, 189, 202, 300
medical equipment 86
medieval period 3
    Baromix excavations 3, 15, 77
    Explosion site (AES 76–7) 3, 124, 125, 126, 141, 145, 156, 160, 163, *168*, 265, 297–8
    Lloyd's Bank (ALB 75) 111, *113*, *114*, 115
    see also pottery
Meeting Lane, Alcester 189, 298
metalwork
    Explosion site (AES 76–7) 3
    see also copper alloy objects; iron objects; lead objects; military metalwork
metalworking slag
    Baromix (ALC 69/ALC 72/2) 80, 83
    Explosion site (AES 76–7) 158, 259, 293, 299
Metchley: forts 302, 303
militaria 192
    Baromix (ALC 69/ALC 72/2) 89–90
military metalwork 192
    Baromix (AL 28) 3, 94, *102*, 103, 301
    Baromix (ALC 69/ALC 72/2) 1, 25, 70–1, 301, 302
    Explosion site (AES 76–7) 3, 294
Millstone Grit 260
Milton Keynes, Bucks 51, 264
mirror fragments, copper alloy 233, *235*, 237, 299
Molyneux, Mr N A D 124
mortar
    Baromix 1972 (ALC 72/2) Phase F 23–4
    Explosion site (AES 76–7) building V 136, 140, 141, 143, 144, 145, 146, 153, 156

nail cleaners, copper alloy 232
nails, iron 77, 79, 80, 81, 241, *244*, 245, 247
Nazeingbury, Essex 274
Neatham, Hants 53, 90, 91
needles, bone 83, *85*, 86
Nero, Emperor, coins 144

oak remains 293
Octavian 122
oppida 116

Ostorius Scapula 302
ovens
    Baromix 1972 (ALC 72/2) Phase C 19
    Baromix 1988 (AL 28) 3, *93*, 94
    possible, Explosion site (AES 76–7) 3, 298
    see also malting kilns
oyster shells *290*

palettes, stone 86
Pas de Calais, *mortaria* 48, 54, 306
pathology
    animal bone 283, 287
    human bone 123
pendants, copper alloy 3, *102*, 103, 233
pig bones 265, 266, 267
    butchery evidence 274, 288
    epiphyseal fusion data 288
    fragment numbers *268*, 274, 275, *276–8*
    metrical analysis 288
    tooth eruption evidence 287–8
pins
    bone 83, *84*, *85*, *250*, 251, *252*, *253*, 299
    copper alloy 71, *73*, *75*, 76
    jet 247, *248*
pits
    Baromix 1969 (ALC 69)
        Phase B 9
        Phase D 13
        Phase G 15
    Baromix 1972 (ALC 72/2) Phase C 19
    Baromix 1988 (AL 28) 93, 94
    Explosion site (AES 76–7) 3, 141, *144*, 149, 156, 158–9, *159*, 160, 214–15, 219, 227, 294
        medieval 145
        period 1 127, 143
        period 10 164–6
    Lloyd's Bank (ALB 75), Pit 5 105, 119
plant remains, Explosion site period 2 well 131, 290, *291–2*, 293, 298
plasterwork, Explosion site (AES 76–7) building V 146, 265
pollen, Explosion site well 131, 290, *291*, 293
Pompey, Sextus 122
Portchester Castle, animal bone comparison 275, 278, *279*, 281–2, 284, 285–6, *285*, 287, 288
post pipes, Baromix 1988 (AL 28) 93
posthole structures *see* structures
postholes
    Baromix 1969 (ALC 69)
        Phase A 8
        Phase B 9
        Phase G 15
        Phase H 15
    Baromix 1972 (ALC 72/2) 19
        Phase B 18
        Phase E 22
        Phase G 24, 25
    Baromix 1988 (AL 28) 3, 93, 94
    Explosion site (AES 76–7) 135, 140, 141, 143, 144, 145, 146, *149*, 150–1, *152*, 153, 159, 163–4
    Lloyd's Bank (ALB 75) 105, 116

pottery
  Baromix (AL 28) 98–102, 306
    see also individual pottery types
  Baromix (ALC 69/ALC 72/2) 28–31, *29*, *30*, 99–100, 306, 307
    see also individual pottery types
  Explosion site (AES 76–7) 53, 54, 177, 306, 307–8, *307*
    graffito 189, 232
    period 1 189–92, *191*, *193–4*, *195*
    period 2 189–99, *191*, *194*, *196*, *197–8*
    period 3 189–92, *191*, *198*, 199, *200*
    period 4 189–92, *191*, 199, *200–2*
    period 5 *191*, *201*, 202–3, *204*, *205*
    period 6 *191*, 202–6, *205*, *207–10*
    period 7 *191*, 202–3, 206, *208*, 210, *211*
    period 8 *191*, 202–3, 210, *211*, *212*, 213
    period 9 *191*, *212*, 213–15, *216–18*, 219, *220–5*, 226
    period 10 *191*, 213, *225*, 226–7, *228–31*
    period 10A 227, 232
    periods 11–14 (post-Roman) *231*, 232
    see also individual pottery types
  Lloyd's Bank (ALB 75) *118*, *120*, 306
    see also individual pottery types
  functional analysis
    Baromix (AL 28) *100*
    Baromix (ALC 69/ALC 72/2) *52*, 53
  graffito, Explosion site (AES 76–7) 189, 232
  amphorae 189, 306, 307
    Baromix (AL 28) 99
    Baromix (ALC 69/ALC 72/2) 48, 54
    Explosion site (AES 76–7) 178–9, 184, 185, 192, 199, 202, 203, 206, 210, 213, 214, 215, 226, 227, 299
    Dressel 20 types 48, 99, 192, 199, 306
    Gaulish fabrics 178, 210, 213, 226, 306
    globular Dressel 20 179
    Rhodian fabrics 178, 179, 203, 226, 227
    Spanish fabrics 48, 54, 178, 202, 206, 210, 213, 214, 226, 306
    trade in 189, 192
  bag beaker 47
  beakers 100, 184–5, 214, 306
    barbotine decorated 178, 232
    Black-Burnished ware 183
    Central Gaulish 178
    'cut-glass' decoration 37, 40
    local reduced fabric 50
    Mancetter-Hartshill (*mortaria*) 48
    Nene Valley 178, 185, 204, 206
    Oxfordshire colour-coated 153, 213
    Oxfordshire fabrics 47, 178, 185, 227
    Rhenish wares 178, 185, 215
    roughcast 178
    Severn Valley ware 49, 181
    white ware 199
  'Belgic' forms 50, 51, 181, 189
    Baromix (ALC 69/ALC 72/2) 50, 53
    Explosion site (AES 76–7) 182, 184, 192
    Black-Burnished ware 26, 30, 49, 51, 53, 181, 189, 202, 203, 306, 307, 308

  Baromix (ALC 69/ALC 72/2) 20, 21, 25, 26, 50–1
  Explosion site (AES 76–7) 50, 145, 146, 158, 165, 182–3, 184, 185, 189, 195, 199, 204, 206, 213, 214, 215, 226, 227, 232, 307
    for dating 128
  Lloyd's Bank (ALB 75) 119, 120
  bowls 53, 100, 180, 184, 195, 202, 203, 213, 215, 308
    beaded and flanged 26
    Black-Burnished ware 26, 120, 158, 159, 183, 184, 214, 215, 227
    carinated 184, 185, 199
      reduced fabric 182
      Severn Valley ware 181
    decorated samian ware 33
    early local fabric 51
    flanged
      Black-Burnished ware 158, 199
      Severn Valley ware 181
    grey ware 184, 185
    local reduced fabric 50
    Nene Valley colour-coated ware 184
    Nene Valley ware 120
    Oxfordshire red colour-coated 120
    samian ware 33, 34, 36, 41, 100, 140, 184
    Severn Valley ware 26, 49, 181, 184, 199, 210, 215
    white ware 184
  butt beakers 116, 121, 185, 199, 306
  Castor boxes 178
    Nene Valley ware 185
  Central Gaulish fabrics, Explosion site (AES 76–7) 178, 215
  coarse sand-tempered rustic ware, Baromix (AL 28) 99
  coarse wares
    Baromix (AL 28) 100, *101*, 102
    Baromix (ALC 69/ALC 72/2) **48–53**, 54, *55–65*, 66–7
    Explosion site (AES 76–7) 125, 131, 140, 177, 184, *188*, 203, 226, 300
  coarse-gritted fabrics, Explosion site (AES 76–7) 183, 184
  colour-coated fabrics, Explosion site (AES 76–7) 177–8
  colour-coated fabrics (imported), Baromix (ALC 69/ALC 72/2) 47
  cooking pots 184, 215
    Black-Burnished ware 145, 165, 182, 183, 184, 199, 202, 203, 213, 214, 215, 227, 232
    Malvernian 182, 199
    Malvernian metamorphic 51
    shell-gritted 183
  cups 100, 184
    Central Gaulish 178
    imported colour-coated 47
    Rhenish ware 185
    samian ware 33, 34, 41, 46, 47, 185
  dishes 53, 184, 202, 214, 215
    Black-Burnished ware 51, 120, 183, 184, 206, 215
    samian ware 33, 35, 37
    Severn Valley ware 181, 202

Index

pottery (*cont.*)
   early local & oxidised fabrics, Baromix (ALC 69/ALC 72/2) 51
   Fabric G11, Baromix (ALC 69/ALC 72/2) 51, 53
   fine wares 30
      Explosion site (AES 76–7) 125, 177, 213, 214, 215, 299–300, 307–8
      see also colour-coated fabrics; mica-dusted fabrics
   flagons 53, 54, 184
      colour-coated 178
      mica-dusted 48
      mortaria 48, 192, 306
      Nene Valley colour-coated ware 185
      Oxfordshire colour-coated ware 185
      oxidised coarse ware 185
      samian ware 44, 47
      Severn Valley ware 181, 232
      trade in 48
      white ware 180, 185, 213
      white-slipped 185
         Baromix (AL 28) 99
         Baromix (ALC 69/ALC 72/2) 47
         Explosion site (AES 76–7) 180, 199, 202, 213, 214, 215, 226
      white-slipped oxidised, Lloyd's Bank (ALB 75) 116, 119
   goblets, samian 37, 40
   grey wares 53, 306, 307, 308
      Baromix (AL 28) 99, 306
      Explosion site (AES 76–7) 181, 182, 183, 184, 185, 189, 192, 195, 199, 202, 203, 206, 210, 213, 214, 215, 226, 227, 232, 300, 307
      Lloyd's Bank (ALB 75) 116, 119
   grog-tempered fabrics, Baromix (AL 28) 99, 306
   handmade fabrics, Explosion site (AES 76–7) 180, 184, 192
   Iron Age 189, 301
   Iron Age-style handmade
      Baromix (ALC 69/ALC 72/2) 51
      Explosion site (AES 76–7) 180, 184, 192
   'jar-beakers' 184–5
      Black-Burnished ware 185
      samian ware 185
   jars 53, 90, 184, 195, 199, 202, 203, 204, 213, 214
      Black-Burnished ware 26, 204
      globular 182
      grey ware 182, 184, 189, 192, 199, 210, 215
      handmade 180
      lattice-decorated, BB1 26
      Nene Valley fabrics 178
      Oxfordshire fabrics 178, 180
      pyriform 50, 181, 184
         grey ware 182, 189
      Saxon 111
      Severn Valley ware 49, 181, 184, 203, 213, 214, 215
      shell-gritted 51, 215, 227
      storage 131, 182, 306
         fabric G11 51, 53
         Oolitic limestone-tempered 116
         organically tempered 99
      pink-grogged ware 183
      white ware 180
   jugs, Severn Valley ware 181
   lamps, ceramic *88*, 158, 187, *188*
   Lezoux Ware
      Baromix (ALC 69/ALC 72/2) 47
      Explosion site (AES 76–7) 213
   lids 53, 54, 184, 199, 203, 213
      grey ware 185
      Severn Valley ware 181, 199
   local reduced fabrics, Baromix (ALC 69/ALC 72/2) 49–50, 51
   Lyons ware, Baromix (AL 28) 99, 100, 306
   Malvern ware, Explosion site (AES 76–7) 184, 195, 199, 202, 213, 300
   Malvernian metamorphic fabrics 30, 54
      Baromix (ALC 69/ALC 72/2) 51
      Explosion site (AES 76–7) 183
   Malvernian metamorphic-tempered ware 49, 306, 307
      Baromix (AL 28) 99
   Malvernian Paleozoic Limestone-tempered ware 99, 306
   Mancetter-Hartshill products 30, 48, 203
      Explosion site (AES 76–7) 179
   Mancetter-Hartshill white ware
      Baromix (AL 28) 99
      Explosion site (AES 76–7) 180, 199, 213, 214, 215, 227
   medieval 30
      Baromix (ALC 69/ALC 72/2) 26
      Explosion site (AES 76–7) 160, 164, 168, 169, 232, *233–4*, 297
   mica-dusted fabrics
      Baromix (AL 28) 99
      Baromix (ALC 69/ALC 72/2) 47–8
      Explosion site (AES 76–7) 177, 192, 215, 299, 300
   mortaria 47, 179, 180, 189, 195, 306, 307
      Baromix (ALC 69/ALC 72/2) 36–7, 46, 48, 53, 54
      Explosion site (AES 76–7) 127, 179, 184, 185, 187, *188*, 189, 192, 199, 202–3, 204, 206, 214, 215, 226, 227, 300
      Oxfordshire colour-coated ware 179, 232
      Oxfordshire white ware 48
      stamps 48, 127, 187, *188*, 189
         Braruco 179
         Quintus Valerius Veranius 179, 180, 192
      trade in 48, 189, 192
      Verulamium region 48, 54, 192, 195, 206, 215, 306
      white slip 48, 204, 206, 232
      white-coated ware 179
      see also Oxfordshire *mortaria*
   Moselkeramik, Baromix (ALC 69/ALC 72/2) 47
   Nene Valley black colour-coated ware, Lloyd's Bank (ALB 75) 119
   Nene Valley colour-coated wares 202
      Baromix (ALC 69/ALC 72/2) 26, 47
      Explosion site (AES 76–7) 177, 178, 184, 185, 199, 206, 213, 214, 215, 226, 227, 232

324

pottery (*cont.*)
  Nene Valley ware 30, 47, 204, 206, 300, 308
  Nene Valley white ware, Explosion site (AES 76–7) 180, 300
  New Forest ware, Explosion site (AES 76–7) 178, 213, 214, 215, 226, 300
  Oxfordshire Burnt white ware, Explosion site (AES 76–7) 180, 232
  Oxfordshire colour-coated wares
    Baromix (ALC 69/ALC 72/2) 26, 47
    Explosion site (AES 76–7) 153, 177, 178, 185, 206, 213, 214, 215, 226, 227, 232, 308
  Oxfordshire *mortaria* 179
    Baromix (ALC 69/ALC 72/2) 26, 47
    Explosion site (AES 76–7) 204, 206, 213, 215, 227
  Oxfordshire parchment ware
    Baromix (ALC 69/ALC 72/2) 48
    Explosion site (AES 76–7) 180, 214, 226, 227
  Oxfordshire products 30, 204, 307
    Baromix 1972 (ALC 72/2) 24
  Oxfordshire red colour-coated, Lloyd's Bank (ALB 75) 120
  Oxfordshire white ware *mortaria* 48
  Oxfordshire white wares, Explosion site (AES 76–7) 180, 204, 213, 214, 215, 226, 227
  oxidised coarse wares, Explosion site (AES 76–7) 185
  oxidised wares
    Baromix (AL 28) 99, 100
    Explosion site (AES 76–7) 180–2, 183, 185, 192, 199, 203, 226
  oxidised white-slipped fabrics, Explosion site (AES 76–7) 195
  Pink-grogged ware
    Baromix 1972 (ALC 72/2) 26
    Explosion site (AES 76–7) 183, 213, 214, 226, 232, 300
  reduced wares
    Explosion site (AES 76–7) 182, 183, 192, 226, 227
    see also grey wares; local reduced fabrics
  Rhenish wares, Explosion site (AES 76–7) 178, 185, 213, 214, 215, 226
  rustic ware 9, 100, 304, 306
  rusticated grey ware 116
  rusticated ware 145
  rusticated/coarse wares, Explosion site (AES 76–7) 140
  samian ware **31–47**, 54, 68, 305, 306, 307
    Baromix (AL 28) *96–8*, 99, 100, 103
    Baromix (ALC 69/ALC 72/2) xviii, 19, 23, 25, 26, 31, *32–6*, 37, *38–40*, 41, *42–6*, 47, 53, 89–90, 90–1, *90*
    Explosion site (AES 76–7) 91, 177, 184, 185, *186*, 187, *188*, 189, 192, 195, *195–6*, *199*, *202*, 203, *204*, *209–10*, 213, 214, 215, 294
    for dating 125, 127, 128, 131, 135, 140
    Lloyd's Bank (ALB 75), xviii, 116, 119, 121
    of Cinnamus 25, 36, 40, 47, 98
    imitation 47
    of Secundus 36

stamps 38, 40, 46–7, 97, 127, 177, 185, *186*, 187
sandy black ware 99
sandy grey ware 119
Savernake ware 116, 121, 306
Saxon 111, 115, *120*, 121
Severn Valley wares 30, 49, 51, 53, 306–7, 308
  Baromix (AL 28) 99, 100
  Baromix (ALC 69/ALC 72/2) 26, 49, 50, 51
  Explosion site (AES 76–7) 49, 177, 180, 181–2, 183–4, 185, 192, 195, 199–202, 203, 206, 210, 213, 214, 215, 226, 227, 232, 300
  Lloyd's Bank (ALB 75) 110, 116, 119
shell-gritted wares 30, 53, 213
  Baromix (ALC 69/ALC 72/2) 51
  Explosion site (AES 76–7) 158, 183, 214, 215, 226, 227, 232
shell-tempered ware
  Baromix (ALC 69/ALC 72/2) 26
  Explosion site (AES 76–7) 184, 215, 232, 300, 307, 308
  Lloyd's Bank (ALB 75) 120
St Neots type ware, Explosion site (AES 76–7) 168
Stamford ware, Explosion site (AES 76–7) 168
strainers, Severn Valley ware 181, 206
tankards 53, 182, 184, 213, 214, 215
  grey ware 185, 202
  Severn Valley ware 49, 181, 185, 192, 206, 213, 215
trade 48, 189, 192, 202, 213, 299, 300, 306, 307, 308
Verulamium region
  mortaria 48, 54, 192, 195, 206, 215, 306
  white ware
    Baromix (AL 28) 99
    Explosion site (AES 76–7) 179, 180, 199, 213, 215
Warwickshire Museum fabrics, Lloyd's Bank (ALB 75) 116, 119
wheelmade shell-tempered ware
  Baromix 1969 (ALC 69) 26
  Lloyd's Bank (ALB 75) 120
white ware
  Explosion site (AES 76–7) 179–80, 184, 185, 199, 213, 300
  Lloyd's Bank (ALB 75) 116
white-slipped flagon fabrics *see* flagons
Primrose Hill, Alcester, building stone 260
Priory Road 301
probe, copper alloy *76*, 86

querns *87*, 88, 260, *261*

raven bones 289
Rheinzabern potters 37, 38, 44
Richborough, Kent, glassware 68, 257, 259
ring, iron 247
roads/trackways
  Baromix 1969 (ALC 69) 1, 294, 304
    Phase A 8
    Phase B 9

Index

roads/trackways, Baromix 1969 (ALC 69) (*cont.*)
    Phase C 9
    Phase D 9, 13
    Phase F 13
    Phase G 15, *17*
    see also cobbling/cobbled surfaces
Roman Army 302
    14th Legion 302
    Legio II Augusta 121–2
    see also militaria; military metalwork
roofing slates, Explosion site (AES 76–7) 160, 164, 165, 166, 260, *261*, 262, 298–9
rubbish, Explosion site (AES 76–7)
    building V 146, 295
    pits 158, 165
Ryknild Street 302, 304

Salonina, coin 166
salt supply 302
Salt Way 114, 301
Saxon period 3, 111, 114–15, 305–6
seeds 290, *292*
Seggs Lane 104, 301, 304
Segontium, Gwynedd 89, 91
Seine-Rhine region, glassware 68, 255
Shakenoak Farm, Oxon, animal bone comparison 280, 281, *286*, 288
shale bracelets 86, *87*, 88, 232, 247, *248*, *249*, 299
shale vessel fragment 247, *248*, 249, 299
sheep/goat bones 265, 266, 267, 297, 299
    butchery practices 286–7
    epiphyseal fusion data 285–6
    exploitation evidence 287
    fragment numbers *268*, 271, *272–4*, 275
    metrical analysis *286*, 287
    pathology 287
    tooth eruption evidence 284–5
Silchester, Hants 116, 257
silver
    bracelet fragment 115
    in coins 116
Siscia, coin from 176
Skeleton Green, Herts, 2nd-century grave 257
slates, roofing, Explosion site (AES 76–7) 160, 164, 165, 166, 260, *261*, 262, 298–9
slots
    Baromix (AL 28) 3
    Baromix (ALC 69) 3
        Phase B 9
        Phase C 9, 13
        Phase D 13
        structure 1 7–8
    Baromix (ALC 72/2) 3
        Phase B/C 18, 19, 20
        Phase E slot/gully 21
    Explosion site (AES 76–7)
        building V 137, 140, *143*, 146
        building VI *150*, 151, 295
smithing slag 83, 158, 259, 293, 299
smithing tools, iron 81
soils, Explosion site (AES 76–7) 126
South Shields, Durham 259

spadeshoes, iron 77, *78*, *79*, 81
spindle-whorls 40, 189
St Albans, Herts 116
stakeholes
    Baromix (ALC 69) Phase A 8
    Baromix (ALC 72/2)
        Phase F drain 23
        Phases B/C 18–19
stokehole, Baromix (ALC 69) Phase H 15, *17*
stone, building 260, *261*, 262
    roofing slates 160, 164, 165, 166, 260, *261*, 262, 298–9
stone objects
    Baromix 1969 (ALC 69) *86–8*
    Explosion site (AES 76–7) 260, *261*, 262
    tessera, limestone 90, 260
stone structures *see* stone, building; structures
stone-built ovens *see* malting kilns
stone-lined drains *see* drains
Strageath, Perthshire 33
Stratford Road 304
Stratford-upon-Avon 298, 306
streets
    street A 1, 301, 302, 303, 304–5
    street B 303
    street C 3, 303, 305
    street D 1, 92, 94, 114, 115, 302, 303, 305
    street E 104, 114, 115, 303–4
    street F 304
Stretton-on-Fosse, Glos 184
structural fittings, iron 81, 241, *244*, 246–7
structures
    Baromix (AL 28)
        post-built 3, 305
        stone-founded 3, 94, 95
    Baromix (ALC 69)
        bath building demolition phase E 90
        structure 1 phase A 7–8
        structure 2 phase B 9
        structure 3 phases B/C 9, 13
        structure 4 9
        structure 6 (posthole) phase C 13
        structure 7 (aisled?) phase D 1, 13, 90
        structure 8 (post-built hut) phase E 1, 13, *15*
        timber rectilinear 1, 25, 294, 301
    Baromix (ALC 72/2) 18, 20–1
        rectilinear 18, 19, 25
        stone 7
            phase G 3, 25, 90
        timber rectilinear 1, 25, 294, 301
    Explosion site (AES 76–7)
        17th-century house 298
        building I 156, *169*, 298
        building II (timber) 160, 164, 165, 166, *167*, *168*, 227, 232, 297
        building III (timber) 146, 160, 164, 165, 166, 227, 297
        building IV
            period 8 153, 164, 213, 297
            period 9 158, 214
            period 10 163

Index

structures, Explosion site (AES 76–7) (*cont.*)
    building V 124, 128, 131, 135, 176, 202, 203, 265, 298, 305
        clay floor *137*, 156
        period 5 127, 135, *136–7*, 140, 143, 145, 294–5, *296*
        period 6 expansion 131, 137, 140, 141, *142–4*, 145, 146, 204–6, 264, 295, *296*
        period 7 145, 146, *149*, 151, 156, 210, 295, *296*
        period 8 153, 213, 297
        period 9 156, 158, 160, 214, 297
        period 10 demolition 160, 164, 165, 166, 226, 297
        portico/veranda, possible 140, 145, 146, 295
        room 1 *136*, *137*, *141*, 146, 156, 160, 210, 295, 297, 298
        room 2 136, 137, 140, 141, 143, 146, 160, 166, 295, 297, 298
            2a 141, 145, 146, 153
            2b 141, *144*, *149*, 153
        room 3 137, 140, 141, *143*, 145, 146, 153, 295
        room 4 137, 141, *143*, 144, 145, 146, 151, 153, 295
        timber building at right angles to 153
        timber/stonework 136, 137, 140, 141, 143, 144, 146, 156, 166, 260, 298
        walls 136, *137*, 141, *143*, 146, 156, 160, 204
    building VI 124, 176, 265, 295, 298, 299, 305
        period 7 135, 145, 146, *149*, *150*, *151*, *152*, 206, 295, *296*
        period 8 153, 213, 297
        period 9 159–60, 214, 297
        period 10 160, 163, 164, 165, 226–7, 297
        stonework 150, 160, 260, 298
        timber lean-to *149*, 150, 151, *152*, 153, 159, 295, 297, 299
        timber structure 145, 149, 150, 298
        walls 149, *150*, 160, 164
    building VIA 160, *163*, 164, 166, 226–7, 297
    building VII, period 3 131, 135, 294
    medieval 298
    stone 90
    stone/timber 3
    stonework 3, 163, 166
    timber 3, 293
        periods 2/3 128, 131, 294
        periods 9/10/10A 158, 160, 163, 164, 165, 166
  Gas House Lane site 305
  Lloyd's Bank, posthole structure 3
  see also wells
styli, iron 77, *78*, 79, 81, *240*, 241, 299
surfaces
  pebbled, Explosion site (AES 76–7) 135, 145
  'yard' area, Explosion site (AES 76–7) 151, 156, 295, 297
  see also cobbling/cobbled surfaces; gravel surfaces
Swan Street 104, 126, 304
symbol gem, Lloyd's Bank (ALB 75) 121–2, *121*

tankards *see* pottery
tanks
  Explosion site (AES 76–7) *150*, *151*
  stone-flagged, Lloyd's Bank 3, *107*, 111, *114*, 115
    Tank 2 *107*, 111, *114*
Theodosius, House of, coins 176
Thornborough, Bucks, Flavian burial 68
Tibbet's Close 301
Tiddington, Warwicks
  glassware 300
  metalwork 70
  pottery 99, 177, 184, 199, 299, 306
    amphorae 48, 178
    'Belgic' forms 50, 189
    colour-coats 47
    early local/oxidised fabrics 51, 100, 306
    Iron Age 180
    local reduced fabrics 50
    mortaria 179
    Oxfordshire fabrics 47
    samian ware 177
    Severn Valley ware 181
    shell-gritted wares 183
    white-slipped flagons 47, 180
  pottery kilns 54, 182
tiles
  Explosion site (AES 76–7) 127, 128, 144, 146, 260, *261*, *262*, *263*, *264*, 294, 298
  imbrices 127, *261*, *262*, *264*
  tegulae 127, *261*, *262*, *264*
timber lining of well, Lloyd's Bank 3, 105, 108, *110*
timber slots
  Baromix 1969 (ALC 69) Phases B/C 9
  Baromix 1972 (ALC 72/2)
    Phase E gully 21
    Phases B/C 18, 19, 20
timber structures *see* structures
toilet items, copper alloy 232
tools, iron 81, *240*, 241, 242, *243*, 246, 299
topography
  Explosion site (AES 76–7) 125–6
  urban 303–5
Towcester, Northants, Park Street 257
trade, in pottery 48, 189, 192, 202, 213, 299, 300, 306, 307, 308
trenches
  trial trenching, Explosion site (AES 76–7) 124
  see also evaluation trenches
Trier
  glassware 255
  mint 176
  potters 37, 38, 44, 47, 178, 300
Tripontium, Warwicks, pottery 184, 299
tweezers, copper alloy 232

Usk, S Wales 54

Verulamium
  glassware 257, 258
  ironwork 242
  pottery 53, 90, 189, 202, 214, 215, 226, 300
    mortaria 48, 54, 192, 195, 206, 215, 306

Index

Vespasian, Emperor, coins 25, 27, 95–6, 103
vessels
   copper alloy handles 70–1, 73, *74*
   shale fragment 247, *248*, 249, 299
   see also glassware; pottery
vexillation fortresses 302
vicus 302, 303
Vindolanda, Northumberland 246

Waddon Hill, Dorset, intaglio 121
Wall, Staffs 50, 302, 303
walls
   Wall 1, Lloyd's Bank (ALB 75) 105, 110, 119
   Wall 2, Lloyd's Bank (ALB 75) 110, 111, 120
   see also structures
Wanborough, Wilts, metalwork 70
Wappenbury, Warwicks, pottery kilns 50, 215, 226, 227
Warwick 306
Warwickshire Museum 124
Wasperton, Warwicks, pottery 177, 179, 180, 184, 299
Watling Street 302

wattle 23, 265, 294
weight/plumbob, lead 239, *240*
wells
   Explosion site (AES 76–7)
     building II period 10A 166, 297
     period 2 128, 131, 199, 290, *291–2*, 293, 298
   Lloyd's Bank (ALB 75) 3
     Well 1 105, *108*, 116
     Well 2 105, 108, *110*, 111, 114, 119, 120
whetstone 260, *261*
wic settlement 115, 306
Wilmcote, Alcester 260
window glass *see* glassware
window grille fragment, iron 241, *244*, 246
wood, preserved 246
Woodcuts 259
Worcester 306
writing equipment, iron 77, *78*, 79, 81, *240*, 241, *246*, 299
Wroxeter, Shrops, pottery 48, 54, 180, 181

York 306
   glassware 257, 258